Fodor's

CARIBBEAN CRUISE PORTS OF CALL

Welcome to the Top Caribbean Ports

Cruising in the Caribbean doesn't mean staying on a ship the entire time. Because of the proximity of the islands to each other, most cruise ships hop from island to island, usually visiting a different port every day. While your time on shore may be short in some ports, every island offers something fun, either a lovely beach or a unique activity, or perhaps just a busy duty-fee shopping strip.

TOP REASONS TO GO

★ **Beaches:** Almost all islands have lovely beaches, many easily reached with just a day in port.

★ **History:** French, British, Dutch, and Spanish colonial remnants can be found throughout the Caribbean.

★ **Private Islands:** Every cruise line offers their own island or cove where guests come ashore for activities and beach time.

★ **Activities:** Horseback rides, zip lines, whale-watching trips, sailing excursions, scuba dives and other activities can be enjoyed on a day ashore.

★ **Food:** For those interested in Caribbean cuisine, opportunities abound to enjoy meat patties, curries, and even beach barbecues.

★ **Shopping:** Shopping for jewelry, watches, and duty-free liquor is a mainstay for cruise passengers. Some islands also offer unique crafts and fine art.

Contents

Fodor's Features

Flavors of the Caribbean 32

MAPS

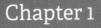

EXPERIENCE A CARIBBEAN CRUISE

20 ULTIMATE EXPERIENCES

Caribbean Cruise Ports of Call offers terrific experiences that should be on every traveler's list. Here are Fodor's top picks for a memorable trip.

1 Relaxing on a Blushing Beach in Bermuda

With a gently-curving crescent of pink sand lapped by turquoise waters and backed by uncluttered South Shore Park, Horseshoe Bay Beach is the perfect spot to swim, play, and soak up the sun.

2 Cave Tubing in Belize

Overland journeys and undersea adventures are just part of the Belize experience. Subterranean rivers provide thrilling passage through spooky caves.

3 Snorkeling in the Cayman Islands

There are plenty of snorkel sites in the Cayman Islands to spot colorful reefs and tropical fish, including Grand Cayman's popular Stingray City.

4 Whale-Watching in the Dominican Republic

The DR boasts the Caribbean's largest whale-watching industry, and December through March more than 200 humpback whales migrate from Iceland and North America to reproduce in Samaná Bay.

5 Hiking in Guadeloupe

Nearly 200 miles of trails twist through Guadeloupe National Park's practically untouched terrain past waterfalls and forests, and the tallest peak in the Lesser Antilles, Soufrière volcano.

6 French Fare in Martinique

Cuisine in Martinique mixes the island's French heritage with Caribbean creole. In capital Fort-de-France, find local flavors at Grand Marché, the island's largest market.

7 Sea Turtles in Costa Rica

Tortuguero, Costa Rica's most famous spot to take in the amazing spectacle of turtle nesting, where a mother turtle buries her eggs on shore and dozens of hatchlings scurry across the sand to reach the ocean.

8 History in St. Kitts and Nevis

Known as the "Gibraltar of the West Indies," St. Kitts's Brimstone Hill Fortress is worth a stop. And Nevis's biggest claim to fame is it's the birthplace of Alexander Hamilton.

9 Sunsets in Antigua

The 490-foot-high Shirley Heights Lookout point hosts a weekly Sunday sundowner party from its perch, which shows off one of the most scenic shots of the bays below.

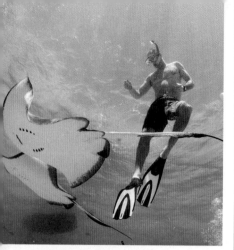

10 Stingray City, Grand Cayman

You can interact with gracefully balletic, silken stingrays, so "tame" you can feed them as they beg for handouts on this shallow sandbar in the North Sound.

11 Kayaking in Bonaire

Lac Bay's mangrove forest is one of the best-preserved in the Caribbean.

12 Tasting Rum in Barbados

Established in 1703, Mount Gay Rum is the world's oldest rum company. They take great pride in their history, offering fascinating tours with plenty of samples.

13 Reggae in Jamaica

Reggae was born in Jamaica in the 1960s and is the "heartbeat" of its people. Its rhythms can be heard everywhere from jerk shacks to the island's infamous summer reggae festival.

14 Off-Roading in Aruba

Cruise on the back of an ATV through abandoned gold mines and past twisted divi-divi trees and cacti in Aruba's desert-like Arikok National Park, which covers 20 percent of the island.

15 Sailing in the British Virgin Islands

The B.V.I. holds the reputation as the "Sailing Capital of the Caribbean," with the Sir Francis Drake Channel ensuring plenty of safe anchorages. There's also untouched islands and secluded cays to explore.

16 Window Shopping in St. Barth

Even if you can't splurge on a new bag at Dolce & Gabbana or timepiece at Rolex, you can still indulge in fantastic window shopping at the island's 200-plus (duty-free) luxurious boutiques.

17 The Pitons in St. Lucia

These distinctive peaks are the symbol of St. Lucia. Stay right between them at Viceroy's Sugar Beach resort, climb them with a guide, or simply marvel at their beauty.

18 History in Puerto Rico

In the second oldest city in the "New World," San Juan's historic district is a maze of cobblestone streets crowned by two 500-year-old forts, El Morro and San Cristóbal.

19 Exploring Mayan Ruins in Mexico

There are over three dozen Mayan ruins in the Yucatán Peninsula, including Chichén Itzá's iconic pyramids.

20 Shopping and Sailing in the U.S.V.I

Sailing is a popular pastime around St. John, but if shopping is more your thing, head to Charlotte Amalie (St. Thomas) and Christiansted (St. Croix) for art and duty-free finds.

WHAT'S WHERE: PORTS OF EMBARKATION

Ports are listed in alphabetical order.

1 Baltimore, Maryland. Two ships are now based in Baltimore, offering year-round cruising opportunities.

2 Charleston, South Carolina. Carnival typically bases one ship in Charleston year-round, but others call here.

3 Fort Lauderdale, Florida. One of the busiest cruise ports sees a wide variety of ships of every shape and size going to all Caribbean destinations.

4 Galveston, Texas. Several ships sail from Galveston, primarily to the Western Caribbean and the Bahamas, both seasonally and year-round.

5 Jacksonville, Florida. Carnival bases one ship in Jacksonville, offering 4- and 5-day cruises to the Bahamas year-round.

6 Miami, Florida. Florida's most popular cruise port offers the widest variety of cruises to the largest number of destinations in the Caribbean.

7 Mobile, Alabama. Carnival bases a ship in Mobile and offers weekly cruises year-round.

8 New Orleans, Louisiana. As many as three ships sail from New Orleans year-round, with others offering seasonal service or port calls.

9 New York, New York. Ships sail from three different ports—in Manhattan, Brooklyn, or New Jersey—to the Caribbean, Bermuda, and the Bahamas.

10 Norfolk, Virginia. Carnival offers regularly scheduled seasonal service out of Norfolk, and other lines call here throughout the year.

11 Port Canaveral, Florida. With its proximity to Orlando, Disney has made Port Canaveral one of its primary ports, but the number of ships that embark here is growing.

12 San Juan, Puerto Rico. A few southern Caribbean cruises depart from San Juan, which puts them within easy reach of even Aruba on a week-long cruise.

13 Tampa, Florida. Tampa's port sees mostly western Caribbean cruises.

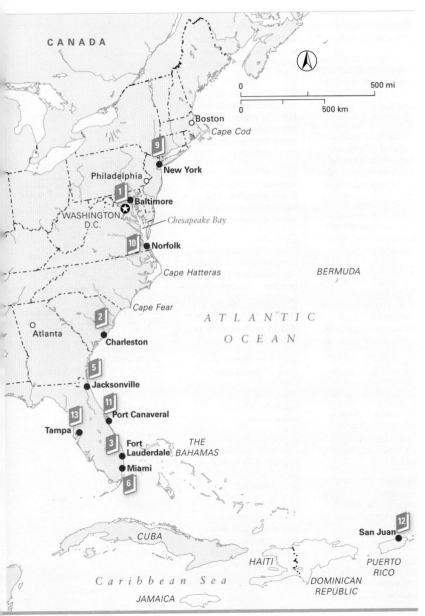

WHAT'S WHERE: WESTERN CARIBBEAN

Ports are listed in alphabetical order.

1 Belize City, Belize. The capital of Belize is a gateway to the cayes as well as the country's interior.

2 Calica (Playa del Carmen), Mexico. Just south of Playa del Carmen, this cruise port offers easy access to the area's sights.

3 Cartagena, Colombia. On Colombia's Caribbean coast, Cartagena is steeped in history.

4 Colón, Panama. At the mouth of the Panama Canal, Colón gives you access to all the country's best sights along the Canal.

5 Costa Maya (Mahahual), Mexico. A purpose-built cruise port is closer to less-visited Maya sights.

6 Cozumel, Mexico. Across the channel from Playa del Carmen, it's famed for its reefs and diving.

7 Falmouth, Jamaica. This small town hosts some of the world's biggest cruise ships.

8 Grand Cayman, Cayman Islands. Georgetown gives access to Stingray City and gorgeous Seven Mile Beach.

9 Harvest Caye, Belize. Built as a private-island experience by Norwegian, this port opened in 2017.

10 Key West, Florida. The southernmost point in the U.S. is known for Ernest Hemingway, its many bars, and its laid-back attitude.

11 Montego Bay, Jamaica. Jamaica's second-biggest city is surrounded by beautiful beaches and historic plantations.

12 Ocho Rios, Jamaica. Near the famous Dunn's River Falls, Ocho Rios is surrounded by beautiful beaches.

13 Progreso, Mexico. On Mexico's Yucatán Peninsula, Progreso is close to Chichén Itzá.

14 Puerto Limón, Costa Rica. This port is near the country's famous Tortuguero Canals, zip lines, and other natural attractions.

15 Roatán, Honduras. This tranquil island is popular with Americans for its beautiful beaches and Garífuna culture.

16 Santo Tomás de Castilla, Guatemala. A stop at this port gives passengers access to the remote Quiriguá and Copán archaeological sites.

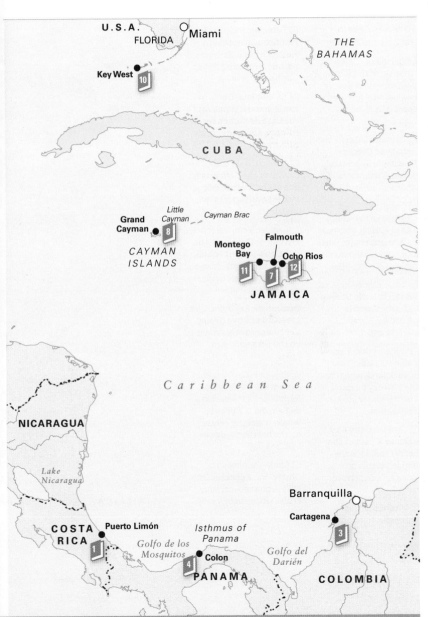

WHAT'S WHERE: EASTERN CARIBBEAN

Ports are listed in alphabetical order.

1 Bermuda. This Atlantic island is a popular cruise port in the summer months, especially from the East Coast.

2 Castaway Cay, Bahamas. Disney Cruise Line's private island is near Great Abaco.

3 Catalina Island, Dominican Republic. The beautiful islet near La Romana is also used as a private island stop for some cruise lines.

4 CoCo Cay, Bahamas. Formerly Little Stirrup Cay, this island is owned by Royal Caribbean.

5 Grand Turk, Turks & Caicos Islands. This small island, which is the country's capital, is also a popular cruise destination.

6 Great Stirrup Cay, Bahamas. Part of the Berry Islands in the Bahamas, this is now Norwegian's private island.

7 Half Moon Cay, Bahamas. Holland America operates its private-island experience on Little San Salvador Island.

8 Labadee, Haiti. This peninsula in northern Haiti is a popular cruise port developed by Royal Caribbean.

9 La Romana, Dominican Republic. Home to the Casa de Campo resort, this town is in the southeastern DR.

10 Nassau, Bahamas. The capital of the Bahamas is one of the Caribbean's busiest cruise ports.

11 Princess Cays, Bahamas. Near the southern end of Eleuthera, the Bahamas' longest island, this is the private-island stop for Princess Cruises.

12 Puerto Plata, Dominican Republic. The new Amber Cove Cruise Center is near this town on the DR's northern coast.

13 Samaná (Cayo Levantado), Dominican Republic. Santa Bárbara de Samaná is a popular whale-watching center on the northern edge of Samaná Bay.

14 Santo Domingo, Dominican Republic. The DR's capital hosts many cruise ships every year.

WHAT'S WHERE: SOUTHERN CARIBBEAN

Ports are listed in alphabetical order.

1 Antigua. St. John's is a major cruise destination.

2 Aruba. Oranjestad is the gateway to the island's beaches.

3 Barbados. Bridgetown is on the island's south coast.

4 Bequia, Grenadines. Feel transported back to the Caribbean of the 1950s.

5 Bonaire. The island's reefs are a big hit with divers.

6 Curaçao. Historic Willemstad is a beautiful cruise-ship stop.

7 Dominica. Explore an undisturbed natural environment.

8 Grenada. Grand Anse is one of the most beautiful beaches.

9 Guadeloupe. Pointe-à-Pitre is also Guadeloupe's biggest city.

10 Martinique. Cosmopolitan Fort-de-France offers myriad opportunities to explore.

11 Nevis. Alexander Hamilton's birthplace is up-and-coming.

12 San Juan, Puerto Rico. The island's capital has a wealth of history and culture.

13 St. Barthélemy. Gustavia's shopping area will transport you to the French Riviera.

14 St. Croix. Frederiksted is once again hosting cruise ships.

15 St. John. Cruz Bay is visited directly by some smaller ships.

16 St. Kitts. Extensive rainforests and looming mountains.

17 St. Lucia. Castries was home to Nobel laureate Derek Walcott.

18 St. Maarten. The Dutch capital, Phillipsburg, hosts many cruise ships.

19 St. Thomas. Charlotte Amalie is a gateway for shopping and Magens Bay Beach.

20 St. Vincent. This less-visited port offers tall mountains and clear water for sailing.

21 Tobago. Less developed, this island is paired with Trinidad.

22 Tortola. Tortola has rebuilt its port after Hurricane Irma in 2017.

23 Trinidad. Port of Spain is an occasional cruise stop.

24 Virgin Gorda. The Baths is one of the Caribbean's most unique beaches.

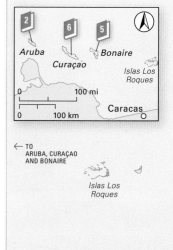

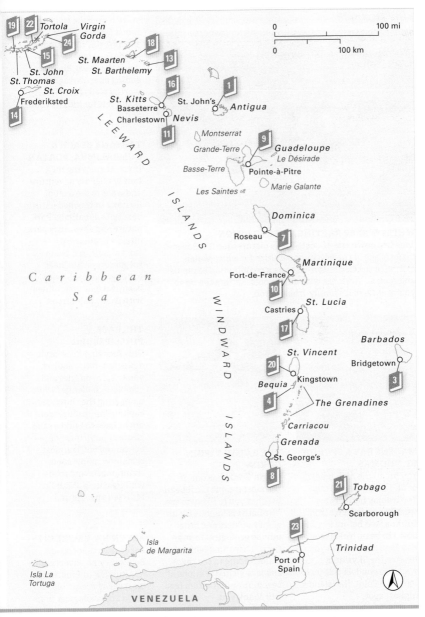

Tortola Virgin Gorda

St. Maarten
St. Barthelemy

St. John
St. Thomas
St. Croix
Frederiksted

St. Kitts
Basseterre
Charlestown Nevis

St. John's
Antigua

L E E W A R D

Montserrat
Grande-Terre
Guadeloupe
Le Désirade
Basse-Terre
Pointe-à-Pitre
Marie Galante
Les Saintes

I S L A N D S

Dominica
Roseau

Martinique
Fort-de-France

St. Lucia
Castries

Barbados
Bridgetown

St. Vincent
Kingstown
Bequia
The Grenadines

C a r i b b e a n
S e a

W I N D W A R D

Carriacou
Grenada
St. George's

I S L A N D S

Tobago
Scarborough

Isla
de Margarita

Trinidad

Port of
Spain

Isla La
Tortuga

VENEZUELA

0   100 mi
0   100 km

Best Caribbean Shore Excursions

WHITE-WATER RAFTING, PUERTO LIMÓN

This trip down one of Costa Rica's picturesque Río Reventazón is one of the best opportunities for white-water rafting in the Caribbean, offering a combination of rapids and relaxed stretches with quiet pools. Rafters can be as young as 12, so it's family-friendly, too.

MAGENS BAY & SKYRIDE, ST. THOMAS

You hit all the high points of St. Thomas in one trip. You'll enjoy Instagram-worthy scenic views from Drake's Seat before heading down to beautiful Magens Bay for 2 hours. Then you head to the Skyride, a 7-minute gondola ride up to Paradise Point, the island's highest spot.

THE BATHS, VIRGIN GORDA

Virgin Gorda has one of the most unique Caribbean beaches you're likely to see. The Baths is famous for its giant boulders and other unique geological formations. There are plenty of trails leading to sea caves and less-visited sections of beach. Your Instagram feed will thank you.

ZIP-LINING & RIVER TUBING, MONTEGO BAY

Combine something exciting with something relaxing. After a thrilling, multistage zip line, which ends with a 1,100-foot stretch over the river and forest (and speeds of up to 35 mph), you commandeer a tube for a low-key trip down the Great River, ending at an Instagram-worthy waterfall. The trip is suitable for kids as young as 6.

TABYANA BEACH & GUMBALIMBA, ROATÁN

If you are looking for a family-friendly adventure and want to see a bit of Roatán's untouched natural beauty, Gumbalimba Park, a nature and adventure park, offers a popular zip line, fun animals, and beautiful gardens. After, head to Tabyana Beach, with beautiful blue water lined with shady palm trees.

THE RACE, PHILLIPSBURG

This *Amazing Race*–style adventure tour requires you to solve puzzles and complete challenges while navigating the Dutch-side capital, Phillipsburg. You might have to build a sand castle or jump into the ocean, and you'll almost certainly sample some traditional island foods while learning about St. Maarten's people and history.

ALTUN HA, BELIZE CITY

For cruises that call at Belize City, an excursion to Altun Ha, the country's most easily accessible Maya archaeological site,

Rafting on the Martha Brae

is reachable in a two-hour guided cruise along the Belize River. You can climb the 60-foot Temple of the Sun God for outstanding views of the 13 remaining structures surrounding two plazas.

CAVE AND MANGROVES BY KAYAK, SAMANÁ

Proximity to remarkable Los Haitises National Park is one of the best things about a port call in Santa Bárbara de Samaná (it's just a 45-minute boat ride from the cruise pier). You'll see the peninsula's beautiful limestone formations, Bird Cay, San Gabriel Cave, and the Caribbean's largest surviving mangrove forest.

MARTHA BRAE RAFTING, FALMOUTH

A tranquil three-mile journey on a bamboo river raft is one of the most relaxing and enjoyable excursions you can have in Jamaica. The Martha Brae River is easily reachable from Falmouth or Montego Bay, and the affable guides have a reputation for keeping you entertained.

RUM & BANANAS TOUR, FORT-DE-FRANCE

Martinique is famous for its aged *rhum argricole*, distilled from sugar cane juice. This boozy half-day tour takes you on a tram ride through L'Habitation Belfort, a lush banana plantation, and then on to Habitation Clément for a tour and rum tasting.

Best Under-the-Radar Cruise Ports in the Caribbean

FORT-DE-FRANCE, MARTINIQUE
Martinique sees almost no cruise ships between April and October. An overseas *département* of France, the mountainous island is also known for its white-sand beaches and for Mount Pelée, its dormant volcano.

HARVEST CAYE, BELIZE
This purpose-built development is currently used only by Norwegian Cruise Line and its sister companies. Offshore from Placencia, it features a docking pier, beach, pool, restaurants, and activities, or you can take shore excursions to the mainland, including the nearby Nim Li Punit Maya site.

BEQUIA, ST. VINCENT & THE GRENADINES
Beautiful Bequia is itself an under-the-radar island. At only 7 square miles, it has little tourism infrastructure and is visited exclusively by small ships. Port Elizabeth, its only town, has a few restaurants and shops that sell mostly handmade souvenirs (model boats are a specialty of the island).

WILLEMSTAD, CURAÇAO
Curaçao gets a cruise-ship call almost every day from November through March, but ships are fewer and farther at other times. The capital, Willemstad, has an urban character absent from many Caribbean destinations—a delight of winding streets, shops, and sidewalk cafés—with a famous floating market.

ROSEAU, DOMINICA
Although Dominica sees a fair number of cruise-ships in November and December, there are few for the rest of the year. The island's 290 square miles are sparsely populated, and the capital Roseau serves as the gateway to the island's lush flora and fauna, protected by an extensive national park system. It also has the oldest continually operating synagogue in the Americas.

ST. GEORGE'S, GRENADA
A major source of nutmeg, cloves, ginger, cinnamon, and cocoa, as well as exotic flowers and rare fruits, Grenada, is far enough south in the Caribbean that it doesn't get as many ships. The island is known for Grand Anse, in the capital St. George's, one of Caribbean's best and longest beaches, as well as its waterfalls.

ST. JOHN'S, ANTIGUA
Ships dock in Antigua's capital, which is also the island's shopping and dining hub. Nearby English Harbour is where you'll find Nelson's Dockyard, a UNESCO World Heritage Site, which is still a working

St. George's Grenada

marina for yachts and ships. Nearby is Shirley Heights, a military lookout with sweeping views of English Harbour, and stunning Dickenson Bay.

PUERTO PLATA, DOMINI-CAN REPUBLIC

Puerto Plata is busier with the opening of Amber Cove, a massive, purpose-built cruise-ship port complex between the city and Playa Grande. The port offers easy access to the city and its malecón, amber museum, cable car (to the summit of 2,601-foot Mount Isabel de Torres), and aquarium. It has its own bars, restaurants, shops, pool, and zip line.

SCARBOROUGH, TOBAGO

Trinidad's smaller sister island is renowned for its natural beauty and lush, mountainous terrain, and occasionally receives cruise ships. A short taxi ride from the island's capital, Scarborough, Pigeon Point is Tobago's most beautiful beach—a long expanse of white sand and blue water. Beyond, deep fertile valleys run north and south of the mountainous center to the island's southern tip.

CHARLESTOWN, NEVIS

Nevis sees only a few smaller cruise ships, since most others cannot dock. With its tiny capital, Charlestown, the birthplace of Alexander Hamilton is covered by lush hills and dominated by 3,232-foot Mount Nevis as well as long stretches of isolated beachfront.

Avoid the Crowds in the Top Cruise Ports

NASSAU, BAHAMAS
Multiple ships call at Nassau almost every day, and passengers flood the downtown area to shop for souvenirs and duty-free liquor. Those who stray from the beaten path will be rewarded by distinctive, locally made objects, a short ride away at Craft Cottage Bahamas on the grounds of Doongalik Studios.

GRAND CAYMAN, CAYMAN ISLANDS
You can avoid the crowds in George Town and popular Stingray City by heading instead to the less-visited North Side. Consider Queen Elizabeth II Botanic Park's Blue Iguana Nature Reserve, a rare place to see these endangered creatures.

COZUMEL, MEXICO
Blazing-white cruise ships parade in and out of Cozumel, the most popular port in the western Caribbean, which can see six ships on a busy day. San Miguel's waterfront can be overwhelmed, but if you walk five minutes away or go to Playa Palancar or Playa Uvas, you can avoid the worst of the crowds.

ST. THOMAS, U.S. VIRGIN ISLANDS
St. Thomas hosts up to six ships a day. While the crowds head to Magens Bay beach or Charlotte Amalie to shop, you can go instead to 14 Dronningens Gade, just off the downtown shopping strip, to visit the boyhood home of impressionist artist Camille Pissarro, now a quiet, second-floor gallery.

SAN JUAN, PUERTO RICO

One of the Caribbean's busiest cruise ports often hosts three or four ships every day. Large groups board buses for an expensive city tour of Casa Bacardí, but you can do it almost as easily on your own by taking a cheap local ferry and a taxi from the ferry dock (you can even book the tour in advance online).

BASSETERRE, ST. KITTS

St. Kitts sees one to three ships almost every day. Many passengers get no further than the Port Zante mall, which is steps from the dock, but you can take a relaxed island tour on the St. Kitts Scenic Railway; you'll still be with your fellow cruise passengers, but it's a relaxing trip.

BRIDGETOWN, BARBADOS

Escape the bustling capital (and up to four cruise ships) to an unusual attraction. Bushy Park offers visitors a novel and unexpected Caribbean adventure focused on motorsports, where you can drive everything from a go-kart to a high-performance race car.

GRAND TURK, TURKS & CAICOS ISLANDS

Grand Turk is small enough that you notice when 4,500 passengers descend en masse from a giant ship. The Grand Turk Cruise Center and its neighboring beaches and bars are mobbed on ship days, but Pillory Beach, a short ride away, is just as beautiful and not nearly as crowded.

ORANJESTAD, ARUBA

Aruba stays busy year-round, with as many as three ships a day. Its attractive, candy-color capital Oranjestad can accommodate a lot of passengers but can feel crowded. The vast Arikok National Park offers many activities and tours to places where you won't see other people.

PHILLIPSBURG, ST. MAARTEN

St. Maarten can see as many as five ships a day. While most of these passengers head into Phillipsburg or to one of the nearby beaches, you should go to Simpson Bay. Just a 15-minute drive beyond the cruise pier is the Carousel gelateria, popular for its excellent ice cream and historic merry-go-round.

The Caribbean's Best Outdoor Activities

WATER SPORTS

The Caribbean is *the* place for water sports—kayaking, paddleboarding, windsurfing, kitesurfing, snorkeling—and rates at beachfront lodgings usually include free use of nonmotorized equipment.

HORSEBACK RIDING

Horseback riding on the beach while the sun sets is a quintessential Caribbean dream that can be made reality in Anguilla, Aruba, the Dominican Republic, Guadeloupe, Jamaica, Martinique, Puerto Rico, St. Kitts & Nevis, Saint Lucia, St. Maarten/St. Martin, Turks & Caicos Islands, and the U.S. Virgin Islands.

ZIP-LINING

Fly with the birds above the rain forest canopy, passing occasional waterfalls and wildlife as you zip from platform to platform tethered to a zip line in Antigua, the Dominican Republic, Jamaica, Puerto Rico, St. Kitts, St. Lucia, St. Maarten/St. Martin, and Trinidad—with more coming aboard all the time.

BOATING AND SAILING

Whether you charter a boat or captain a vessel yourself, the Caribbean's many secluded bays and inlets are ideal for boating and sailing. From either the USVI or the BVI, for example, more than 100 islands and cays can be explored within a 50-nautical-mile radius—cruising to a different beach or yacht harbor every day is a truly unique way to experience the Caribbean. Antigua and St. Lucia host major sailing regattas each year, which attract sailors from around the world.

DIVING AND SNORKELING

The best conditions for diving and snorkeling—clear water, lots of marine life, and numerous wreck sites—can be found throughout the Caribbean's crystalline blue waters. Some of the best spots are in the Cayman Islands, as well as in Curaçao, St. Lucia, and the Virgin Islands (both U.S. and British).

WHALE-WATCHING

Samaná, in the northeastern Dominican Republic, is revered for its shimmering water, champagne-hue strands, and superior sportfishing. But its signature aquatic activity is world-class whale-watching in season (January through March), as pods of humpbacks mate and calve. Other opportunities for a whale-watching trip include Guadeloupe, Jamaica, Martinique, Puerto Rico, St. Lucia, and the Turks & Caicos Islands.

There are trails for every level of hiker in Antigua.

FISHING

Fish—barracuda, bonefish, billfish, dolphin, kingfish, marlin, sailfish, swordfish, tarpon, wahoo, yellowfin tuna, or the ravenous lionfish (a threat to local species, but delicious)—are biting year-round in the Caribbean, and half- and full-day deep-sea, reef, and coastal fishing charters are available on almost every island. Many billfish are catch-and-release; sometimes, you can take your catch back to your resort, where you can have it prepared for dinner.

HIKING

Hiking in the Caribbean is often associated with lush rain forests. That wouldn't be wrong, but on mountainous islands—like Antigua, Guadeloupe, Jamaica, Martinique, St. Kitts, St. Lucia, and Nevis—an often-challenging hike to a mountain summit or caldera can also provide spellbinding views.

BIKES, SCOOTERS, AND ATVS

Many hotels have cruising bikes available for guests to take out for a leisurely spin, but serious mountain bikers will find worthwhile tracks in Barbados, the Dominican Republic, Nevis, St. Lucia, and the Turks & Caicos Islands. Scooters are available to rent on almost every island in the Caribbean, and they are a great way to see the sights. Daredevils might want to join an ATV excursion in the Dominican Republic, Jamaica, or St. Lucia.

BIRDWATCHING

The watching part isn't so active, but hiking through rain forests, up mountain trails, and across savannas will give you the opportunity to see more species of bird than you can count—including nine different parrot species that make their nests in the Caribbean.

FLAVORS OF THE
CARIBBEAN

As a key entry point to the New World, the Caribbean region has a rich culinary tradition that reflects the diversity of its immigrants. This melting pot of Spanish, African, French, English, and Dutch influences has resulted in dishes packed with fresh ingredients and bold, spicy flavors and seasonings.

Local produce is varied and includes lima beans, black-eyed peas, corn, yams, sweet potatoes, cassava, taro, and endless varieties of fruit. Rice and beans are ever-present staples, commonly seasoned with ingredients like curry, cilantro, soy sauce, and ginger. The spice-forward "jerk" style of marinated and rubbed meat, fish, and fowl is prevalent. Jamaica, Haiti, Guadeloupe, and other French Caribbean islands savor goat meat in dishes like goat water, a tomato-based stew, which is the official national dish of Montserrat and a speciality on St. Kitts and Nevis. Fresh-caught seafood from local waters also figures prominently in the cuisine.

Modern menus don't stray too far from tradition, opting instead for clever twists rather than reinvention, like flavoring black beans with tequila and olive oil, or serving rice spiked with coconut and ginger. No matter where your culinary curiosities take you in these islands, plan on a well-seasoned eating adventure.

(opposite) Dasheene Restaurant at Ladera Resort, St. Lucia, (top) Jerk pork, a signature Jamaican dish, (bottom) scotch bonnet peppers.

THE ISLANDS' GLOBAL FLAVORS

Island cuisine developed through waves of wars, immigration, and native innovations from the 15th century through the mid-19th century. Early Amerindian native peoples, the Arawaks and the Caribs, are said to have introduced the concept of spicing food with chili peppers, a preparation that remains a hallmark of Caribbean cuisine. Pepper pot stew was a staple for the Caribs, who would make the dish with *cassareep*, a savory sauce made from cassava. The stew featured wild meats (possum, wild pig, or armadillo), squash, beans, and peanuts, which were added to the cassareep and simmered in a clay pot. The dish was traditionally served to guests as a gesture of hospitality. Today's recipes substitute meats like pig trotters, cow heel, or oxtail.

Caribbean-style curried goat

As European colonization took place, traders and settlers brought new fruits, vegetables, and meats. Their arrival coincided with that of African slaves, many en route to the Americas. Every explorer, settler, trader, and slave culturally expanded the palette of flavors. Although Caribbean cooking varies from island to island, trademark techniques and spices unite the cuisine.

SPANISH INFLUENCES

Christopher Columbus sailed to the Caribbean in 1492, at the behest of the Spanish crown. When he returned to colonize the islands a year later, he brought ships laden with coconut, chickpeas, cilantro, eggplant, onions, and garlic. The Bahamas, Hispaniola, and Cuba were among Columbus' first findings, and as a result, Cuba and nearby Puerto Rico have distinctly Spanish-accented cuisine, including *paella* (a seafood- or meat-studded rice dish), *arroz con pollo* or *pilau* (chicken cooked with yellow rice), and white-bean Spanish stews.

Arroz con Pollo

FRENCH TECHNIQUE

As tobacco and sugar crops flourished and the Caribbean became a center of European trade and colonization, the French settled Martinique and Guadeloupe in 1635 and later expanded to St. Barthélemy, St. Martin, Dominica, Grenada, St. Lucia, and western Hispaniola. French culinary technique meets the natural resources of the islands to create dishes like whelk (sea snail) grilled in garlic butter, fish cooked *en papillote* (baked in parchment paper), and *crabs farcis* (land crab meat that is steamed, mixed with butter, breadcrumbs, ham, chilis, and garlic, then stuffed back into the crab shells and grilled).

DUTCH INGENUITY

Beginning in the 1620s, traders from the Dutch East India Company brought Southeast Asian ingredients like soy sauce to the islands of Curaçao and St. Maarten. Dutch influence is also evident throughout Aruba and Bonaire (all have been under Dutch rule since the early 19th century), where dishes like *keshi yeni,* or "stuffed cheese," evolved from stuffing discarded rinds of Edam cheese with minced meat, olives, and capers. Another Dutch-influenced dish is *boka dushi* (Indonesian-style chicken satay), which translates to "sweet mouth" in the islands' Papiamento dialect.

Paella

Boka dushi

Roti

Jerk meat

Whelk

ENGLISH IMPORTS

British settlers brought pickles, preserves, and chutneys to the Caribbean, and current-day chefs take advantage of the islands' indigenous fruits to prepare these items. British influence also is evidenced by the Indian and Chinese contributions to Caribbean cuisine. British (and Dutch) colonists brought over indentured laborers from India and China to work on sugar plantations, resulting in the introduction of popular dishes like curry goat and *roti,* an Indian flatbread stuffed with vegetables or chicken curry.

AFRICAN INGREDIENTS

The African slave trade that began in the early 1600s contributed foods from West Africa, including yams, okra, plantains, breadfruit, pigeon peas, and oxtail. Slave cooks often had to make do with plantation leftovers and scraps, yielding dishes like cow heel soup and pig-foot souse (a cool soup with pickled cucumber and meat), both of which are still popular today. One of the most significant African contributions to the Caribbean table is "jerking," the process of dry-rubbing meat with allspice, Scotch bonnet peppers, and other spices. Although the cooking technique originated with native Amerindians, it was the

Jamaican Maroons, a population of runaway African slaves living in the island's mountains during the years of slavery, who developed and perfected it, resulting in the style of jerk meat familiar in restaurants today.

CARIBBEAN'S NATURAL BOUNTY

Soursop

Despite its spicy reputation, Caribbean food isn't always fiery; rather the focus is on enhancing and intensifying flavors with herbs and spices. Food plays a major role in island culture, family life, and traditions, and no holiday would be complete without traditional dishes prepared from the island's natural products.

TANTALIZING TROPICAL FRUIT

Breadfruit, a versatile starch with potato-like flavor, can be served solo—baked or grilled—or added to soups and stews.

Rich **coconut** milk frequently appears in soups, stews, sauces, and drinks to help temper hot, spicy flavors.

The bright pink flesh of the tropical fruit **guava** tastes somewhat like a pear and strawberry combination that is pleasantly sweet when mature. It is used in compotes, pastes, jellies, and (especially) as juice.

The pungent smell of **jackfruit** may be off-putting for some, but its sweet fleshy meat is popular in milkshakes.

Papaya is sweet and floral tasting when ripe; unripe, it can be shredded and mixed with spices and citrus for a refreshing salad. It's often used in fruit salsas that are served with seafood.

The brightly flavored **passion fruit** is commonly puréed and used in sauces, drinks, and desserts.

The dark-green skinned, creamy fleshed **soursop** is known for its sweet-tart juice used in drinks, sorbets, and ice creams.

The fibrous stalks of **sugarcane**, a giant grass native to India, can be consumed in several forms, including freshly extracted juice and processed sugar.

Tamarind is the fruit of a large tree. The sticky pulp of its pod is used in chutneys, curries, and candy to impart a slightly sweet, refreshingly sour flavor.

FARM-FRESH VEGETABLES

Cassava (also called yucca) is used much like a potato in purées, dumplings, soups, and stews. Cassava root flour is made into tapioca.

Chayote is a versatile member of the squash and melon family, often used raw in salads or stuffed with cheese and tomatoes and baked.

Dasheen (taro) is much like a potato, but creamier. It can be added to stews or sliced thinly and fried like a potato chip.

Jackfruit

Fitweed (or French thistle) is a tropical herb related to coriander (cilantro), and is popular in Caribbean seasonings.

Pod-like **okra** is commonly used in *callaloo*, the national dish of Trinidad and Tobago. The creamy, spicy stew is made of leafy dasheen leaves, okra, and crabmeat.

Plantain is a cooking staple across the Caribbean, often sliced, pounded, dipped in a seasoned batter, and deep-fried.

The bright red **sorrel** is boiled, sweetened, and chilled for a traditional Christmas beverage.

Tamarind

Chayote

Curry powder

Conch salad

SWEET AND SAVORY SPICES

Native **allspice**, also called Jamaican pepper, is the dried unripe berry of the evergreen pimento tree. Native Jamaicans once used it to preserve meats, but today it's an essential ingredient in jerk preparations and Caribbean curries.

Curries are intensely seasoned gravy-based dishes originating from India—they are most prevalent on the islands of Jamaica, Trinidad, and Tobago.

Native Carib people pioneered the use of **chili peppers** in the islands for hot, spicy flavoring, using primarily habaneros and Scotch bonnet peppers.

Ginger is used raw or dried and ground into a powder that adds flavor and heat to ginger beer, sweet potatoes, or coconut milk-based sauces.

The mix of spices in **jerk** seasoning vary, but typically include scallions, thyme, allspice, onions, and garlic.

The tiny island of Grenada is the second largest exporter of **nutmeg** in the world. Nutmeg often accents sauces, vegetables, drinks, and ice cream.

ISLAND FISH AND SEAFOOD

Bonito is a medium-sized fish in the mackerel family. Atlantic bonito is moderately fatty, with a firm texture and darker color. It's served blackened, grilled (sometimes with fruit-based salsas), or Jamaican jerk style.

On many islands, especially the Bahamas, **conch**—large shellfish—are made into conch fritters, a mix of conch meat, corn meal, and spices that are deep fried and make an excellent snack.

Cascadura fish is a small fish found in the freshwater swamps of Trinidad and Tobago. The fish is typically served in curry with a side of rice or dumplings.

Flying fish are named for the wing-like fins that enable them to glide or "fly" over water. Firm in texture, this fish is typically served

steamed or fried. Flying fish is a staple in Bajan cuisine and is found in abundance off the coast of Barbados.

Kingfish is another word for wahoo, a delicate white fish commonly fished off the coasts of St. Croix and Barbados. Wahoo is served *escabeche* style, marinated in a vinegar mixture, then fried or poached.

Land crab is found throughout the islands. Delicate in flavor, common preparations include curried crab stewed in coconut milk, stuffed crab, and crab soup.

Mahi mahi is fished off the coast of St. Croix. With a subtle, sweet flavor, the firm, dark flesh lends itself to soy sauce glazes and Asian preparations.

Salt fish is a dish made from dried cod, often seasoned with tomatoes, onions, and thyme. Stir-fried ackee (a tropical fruit with nutty-flavored flesh) and saltfish is Jamaica's national dish.

Allspice

Salt fish

THE RISE OF RUM

The Caribbean is the world center for rum production, with many islands having their own brands and styles of rum. Dozens of rum companies operate throughout the islands. Although larger, mainstream brands like Bacardi, Captain Morgan, and Mount Gay are available on every island, you may have to look locally for the smaller brands. The best-quality rums are dark, aged rums meant for sipping, priced from $30 to $700 a bottle. For excellent sipping rum at the lower end of the spectrum, try Appleton or Rhum Barbancourt. For mixed drinks, use clear or golden-color rums that are less expensive and pair well with fruit juices or cola. Spiced and flavored rums are also popular in cocktails. Here are some of the best rums you'll encounter at an island bar:

Appleton Estate (Jamaica) The Estate VX is an amber-color rum with subtle brown sugar aromas and a smooth, toasted honey finish. Excellent mixer for classic cocktails.

Bacardi (Bermuda, PR) Superior is a clear, mild rum with subtle hints of vanilla and fresh fruits. It is smooth and light on the palate. Best in mixed drinks.

Captain Morgan (PR) Its Black Label Jamaica Rum is dark, rich, and smooth, with strong notes of vanilla. Sip it iced or with a splash of water.

Clarke's Court (Grenada) The Original White is clear with a touch of sweetness

Ron Barceló

and a hint of heat, best used as a mixer.

Cruzan (VI) Less strong and sweet than most rums, the White Rum is smooth, and best suited for mixing.

Havana Club (Cuba) The Añejo 3 Años is deceiving—light in color and body and delicate in flavor. It is a nice rum to sip neat.

Mount Gay Rum (Barbados) Eclipse, the brand's flagship rum, has a golden color with a butterscotch caramel nose and sweet taste on the palate with mouth-warming flavor.

Pusser's (BVI) Self-described as "the single malt of rum," the aged 15-year variety boasts notes of cinnamon, woody spice, and citrus. A good sipping rum.

Rhum Barbancourt (Haiti) Aged 15 years, this premium dark rum is distilled twice in copper pot stills and often called the "Cognac of Rum." Sip it neat.

Ron Barceló (DR) The Añejo is dark copper in color, with a rich flavor, while the aged Imperial boasts notes of toffee on the nose, and a buttery smooth finish.

Shillingford Estates (Dominica) Its most popular product, Macoucherie Spiced, is a blend of rum, the bark of the Bois Bande tree, and spices.

Mount Gay Rum

(left) Pusser's Rum, (right) Havana Club

ISLANDS' BEST BREWS

Beer in the Caribbean was largely homemade for centuries, a tradition inherited from British colonial rulers. The first commercial brewery in the islands was founded in Trinidad and Tobago in 1947.

In the islands, do what the locals do: drink local beer. Whatever brand is brewed on-island is the one you'll find at every restaurant and bar. And no matter where you go in the Caribbean, there's a local island brew worth trying. Another plus: local brands are almost always cheaper than imports like Corona or Heineken. Most island beers are pale lagers, though you'll find a smattering of Dutch-style pilsners and English-style pale ales. The beers listed below are our top picks for beachside sipping:

Kalik

Banks Beer (Banks Breweries, Barbados) A straw-colored lager that is light tasting with a touch of maltiness on the nose and tongue.

Blackbeard Ale (Virgin Islands Brewing Co., Virgin Islands) This English pale ale–style beer is bright amber in color with a creamy white head. Well-crafted beer with a nice hoppy bite at the finish.

Balashi Beer (Brouwerij Nacional Balashi N.V., Aruba) Refreshingly light, this Dutch pilsner boasts mild flavor, slight sweetness, and subtle hop bitterness.

Legends Premium Lager (Banks Breweries, Barbados) One of the Caribbean's best brews, this golden yellow lager offers crisp hops and a clean finish. Distinctive toasty, malt character.

Carib Lager Beer (Carib Brewery, Trinidad and Tobago) This great beach refresher is a pale yellow color with a foamy head. Fruity and sweet malty corn aromas, it is sometimes referred to as the "Corona of the Caribbean."

Kalik Gold (Commonwealth Brewery LTD., New Providence, Bahamas) Clear straw color with gentle hoppy, herbal notes, this is an easy drinking, warm weather lager.

Medalla Light (Puerto Rico) This bright gold lager is substantial for a light beer. It's a local favorite.

Red Stripe (Jamaica) The Jamaican lager pours golden yellow in color with lots of

Banks Beer

Carib Lager Beer

carbonation. Light bodied, crisp, and smooth.

Piton (St. Lucia) Light and sparkly with subtle sweetness, this pale yellow lager is pleasant enough, but barely flavored.

Presidente (Domincan Republic) Slight citrus aroma, light body, and fizziness, plus a clean finish make for easy drinking. Perfect pairing for barbecued meats.

Wadadli (Antigua Brewery Ltd., Antigua and Barbuda) A crisp, light-bodied American-style lager. Toasty malt on the nose.

(left) Red Stripe, (right) Presidente

Best Caribbean Souvenirs

Liquor is undoubtedly cheaper in the Caribbean than almost anywhere else, but perfume and cosmetics may be just as cheap in your local mall. You *may* find good buys on watches and jewelry, but before buying any big-ticket item, know what it costs in your local stores.

COFFEE

The Caribbean is a major coffee-growing region. One of the most famous varieties is Blue Mountain coffee from Jamaica (as well as less expensive High Mountain coffee), but you'll also find excellent coffee from the Dominican Republic, Puerto Rico, Honduras, and Costa Rica.

HAITIAN PAINTINGS

If you find yourself in Haiti, you'll see that the island has a long tradition of painting. Galleries all over the Caribbean sell the works of Haitian artists, some of them prominent and some not.

HOT SAUCE

Almost every island has its own brand of locally made pepper sauce, some hotter than others. Better sauces include Pickapeppa (some slightly sweet) from Jamaica, Brimstone Flavors (made from scotch bonnet peppers) from St. Kitts, Bee Sting from Costa Rica, PeppaJoy from the Turks & Caicos Islands, and Lottie's (a yellow, mustard-based sauce) from Barbados. You can get these in almost any gift shop or grocery store.

JEWELRY

Jewelry shopping is one of the top activities for tourists. But if you are looking for something that's actually made in and native to the Caribbean, two gems stand out. Larimar is found only in the Dominican Republic. Colombian emeralds are also beautiful. Amber from the Dominican Republic and Colombia is also widely famous. Whatever your fancy, make sure you are buying from a reputable dealer who can guarantee the stone's authenticity (amber in particular).

RUM

You can find some great Caribbean-made rums on a number of islands—Appleton Estate in Jamaica, Mount Gay in Barbados, Cruzan in the U.S. Virgin Islands, and John Watling's in Nassau. In many cases, you'll be able to both taste and buy bottles at the source. Whether you get one for yourself or an aged bottle for a gift, this locally made souvenir will hit the spot, and while many of these rums are found virtually everywhere, a few are only available locally.

SPICES

Although Grenada is world-renowned for its nutmeg, spices are grown all over the Caribbean and make for lightweight, easy-to-carry souvenirs. Nutmeg likely originated in East Asia, but allspice is native to the region. Vanilla is native to Mexico, and you'll find reasonably priced (and often locally made) extracts in most markets. And various pepper blends, especially scotch bonnet, are native to the Caribbean and ground for seasoning, as well as made into hot sauces. Look for any number of jerk seasoning mixes in Jamaica.

WOOD CARVINGS

Whether from lignum vitae, cedar, mahogany, or mango wood, almost every island has a wood-carving tradition. You'll find a lot of carved fish and nautical-themed items, as well as masks. Some of the most accomplished work is done in Jamaica. But the *vejigante* masks of Puerto Rico are world-famous, as are other Taíno-influenced designs. Much of this work is done for the mass-market tourist trade, so examine the workmanship before buying, and even if they cost more, look for hand-carved items over machined ones.

Chapter 2

PLANNING YOUR CARIBBEAN CRUISE

Updated by
Brian Major

If you're considering a cruise but can't decide whether it's really for you, it's tempting to ask, "What's so special about a cruise vacation?" It's a good question. Until the age of the airplane, ocean travel was simply a means to get to your far-flung destination—often the only way. But even in the early decades of the 20th century, venerable ocean liners such as the *Normandie* offered the occasional round-trip cruise to an exotic locale.

Passengers on those earliest cruises didn't have a fun-in-the-sun mind-set as they sailed to faraway ports. They sailed to broaden their horizons and learn about ports of call that couldn't be reached by overland travel. Perhaps they booked a cruise to Panama to observe the construction of the canal or, like the *Normandie's* passengers, were bound for Brazil and the bold excitement of Carnaval.

Regardless of why they went, early cruisers steamed toward the unfamiliar with far fewer comforts than contemporary passengers enjoy. On the *Normandie,* air-conditioned comfort was available only in the ship's first-class dining room, although passengers could at least find relief from Rio's heat by taking a dip in one of the era's few outdoor swimming pools at sea. In those days, if an ocean liner had a permanent swimming pool, it was often indoors and deep in the hull.

Carnival Cruise Lines executives like to reminisce about the tiny "gyms" on their early ships, which were converted ocean liners, and then point to how far ship design has evolved. It was even difficult to find the casino on Carnival's first "Fun Ship," *Mardi Gras,* let alone locate the indoor swimming pool. That's hardly the case today. Designed for contemporary travelers and tastes, modern cruise ships carry passengers amid conveniences unheard of in the heyday of the North Atlantic ocean liner (the first decades of the 20th century, before air travel to Europe was practical or even possible) or in the earliest vessels permanently dedicated to cruises (which started in the early 1970s). As more than 28 million passengers discovered when they went to sea in 2018, there's a lot to like on ships these days.

The allure of a modern sea cruise is its ability to appeal to a wide range of vacationers as a safe and convenient way to travel. Today's cruise ships are lively and luxurious floating resorts that offer something to satisfy the expectations of almost everyone. The first thing you'll find is that, although cruise ships differ dramatically in the details and how they craft and deliver the cruise experience, most ships have the same basic features. And although the decisions and considerations in booking one cruise over another can be complex, the more you know about cruise travel in general, the better prepared you'll be when it comes to making your choices.

Choosing Your Cruise

Just as Caribbean islands have distinct histories and cultures, cruise ships also have individual personalities, which vary by size, the year they were built, and their style. On one hand, they can be bold, brassy, and exciting—totally unlike home, but a great place to visit. Big ships offer stability and a huge variety of activities and facilities. On the other hand, small ships feel intimate—like private clubs or, more appropriately, personal yachts. For every big-ship fan there is someone who would never set foot aboard a "floating resort." Examine your lifestyle, and you're sure to find a cruise ship to match.

After giving some thought to your itinerary and where in the Caribbean you might wish to go, the ship you select is the most vital factor in your Caribbean cruise vacation, since it will determine not only which islands you will visit, but also how you will see them. Big ships visit major ports of call, such as St. Thomas, St. Maarten/St. Martin, Nassau, and San Juan. When they call at smaller islands with shallower ports (including popular Grand Cayman), passengers must disembark aboard shore tenders (small boats that ferry dozens of passengers to shore at a time)—or they may skip these smaller ports entirely. Small and midsize ships can visit smaller islands such as St. Barths, St. Kitts, or St. John more easily; passengers are sometimes able to disembark directly onto the pier without having to wait for tenders to bring them ashore.

Itineraries

You'll want to give some consideration to your ship's Caribbean itinerary when you are choosing your cruise. The length of the cruise will determine the variety and number of ports you visit, but so will the type of itinerary and the point of departure. **Round-trip** cruises start and end at the same point and usually explore ports close to one another; **one-way** cruises start at one point and end at another and range farther afield.

Almost all cruises in the Caribbean are round-trip cruises. On Caribbean itineraries you have the option of departing from several U.S. mainland departure points. Ships sailing out of San Juan can visit up to five ports in seven days, while cruises out of Florida or Galveston, Texas, can reach up to four ports in the same length of time. Cruise lines are also offering eight- and nine-day Caribbean cruises from New York City, calling at up to five ports. The Panama Canal can also be combined with a Caribbean cruise: the 50-mile (83-km) canal is a series of locks, which make up for the height difference between the Caribbean and the Pacific. Increasingly popular are partial transit cruises that enter the Panama Canal, anchor in Gatún Lake for a short time, and depart through the same set of locks.

EASTERN CARIBBEAN ITINERARIES

Eastern Caribbean itineraries consist of two or three days at sea as well as stops at some of the Caribbean's busiest cruise ports. A typical cruise will usually take in three or four ports of call, such as St. Thomas in the U.S. Virgin Islands, Antigua, the Dominican Republic, San Juan, or St. Maarten/St. Martin, along with a visit to the cruise line's "private" island for beach time. Every major cruise line has at least two of those popular islands on its itineraries. Some longer itineraries might also include others, such as

Tortola, Dominica, Barbados, St. Kitts, Martinique, or Grand Turk.

WESTERN CARIBBEAN ITINERARIES

Western Caribbean itineraries embarking from Galveston, Fort Lauderdale, Miami, Port Canaveral, New Orleans, or Tampa might include Belize, Cozumel, or the Costa Maya Cruise Port in Mexico, Key West, Grand Cayman, or Jamaica—all perfect for passengers who enjoy scuba diving, snorkeling, Caribbean culture and cuisine, and exploring Mayan ruins. Ships often alternate itineraries in the Western Caribbean with itineraries in the Eastern Caribbean on a weekly basis, offering the ability to schedule a 14-night back-to-back cruise on the same ship without repeating ports.

SOUTHERN CARIBBEAN ITINERARIES

Southern Caribbean cruises tend to be longer in duration, with more distant ports of call. They often originate in a port that is not on the U.S. mainland. Embarking in San Juan, for example, allows you to reach the lower Caribbean on a seven-day cruise with as many as four or five ports of call. Southern Caribbean itineraries might leave Puerto Rico for the Virgin Islands, Guadeloupe, Grenada, Curaçao, Barbados, Antigua, St. Lucia, Martinique, or Aruba. Smaller ships leave from embarkation ports as far south as Bridgetown, Barbados, and cruise through the Grenadines. Every major cruise line offers some Southern Caribbean itineraries, but these cruises aren't as popular as Western and Eastern Caribbean cruises.

OTHER ITINERARIES

In recent years shorter itineraries have grown in appeal to time-crunched and budget-constrained travelers. If you are planning your first cruise in the tropics, a short sailing to the Bahamas allows you to test your appetite for cruising before you take a chance on a longer and more expensive cruise. Embarking at Fort Lauderdale, Miami, Jacksonville, or Port Canaveral, you will cruise for three to five days, taking in at least one port of call (usually Nassau or Freeport in the Bahamas) and possibly a visit to a "private" island or Key West. Four- and five-night cruises may also include a day at sea. Cruises also depart from ports farther north on the East Coast; you might depart from Charleston, Baltimore, Norfolk, or New York City and cruise to Bermuda or the Bahamas.

When to Go

Average year-round temperatures throughout the Caribbean are 78°F–85°F, with a low of 65°F and a high of 95°F; downtown shopping areas always seem to be unbearably hot. Low season runs from approximately mid-September through mid-April (excluding the Thanksgiving and Christmas holidays). Many travelers, especially families with school-age children, make reservations months in advance for the most expensive and most crowded summer months and holiday periods; however, with the many new cruise ships that have entered the market, you can often book fairly close to your departure date and still find room, although you may not get exactly the kind of cabin you would prefer. A summer cruise offers certain advantages: temperatures are virtually the same as in winter (cooler on average than in parts of the U.S. mainland), island flora is at its most dramatic, the water is smoother and clearer, and although there is always a breeze, winds are rarely strong enough to rock a ship. Some Caribbean tourist facilities close down in summer, however, and many ships move to Europe, Alaska, or the northeastern United States.

Hurricane season runs a full six months of the year, from June 1 through November 30. Although cruise ships stay well out of the way of these storms, hurricanes and tropical storms (their less-powerful relatives) can affect the weather throughout the Caribbean for days, and damage to ports can force last-minute itinerary changes.

Cruise Costs

The average daily price for Caribbean itineraries varies dramatically depending on several circumstances. The cost of a cruise on a luxury line such as Silversea or Seabourn may be three to four times the cost of a cruise on a mainstream line such as Carnival or even premium lines like Princess. *When* you sail will also affect your costs: published brochure rates are usually highest during the peak summer season and holidays. When snow blankets the ground and temperatures are in single digits, a Caribbean cruise can be a welcome respite and less expensive than land resorts, which often command top dollar in winter months.

Solo travelers should be aware that single cabins have virtually disappeared from cruise ships, with the exception of Norwegian Cruise Line's *Norwegian Epic, Breakaway,* and *Getaway* and some single cabins on Cunard Line, Royal Caribbean and Holland America Line ships. Taking a double cabin can cost twice the advertised per-person rates (which are based on double occupancy). Some cruise lines will find same-sex roommates for singles; each then pays the per-person, double-occupancy rate.

TIPS
One of the most delicate—yet frequently debated—topics of conversation among cruise passengers involves the matter of tipping. Whom do you tip? How much? What's "customary" and "recommended"? Should parents tip the full amount for children, or is just half adequate? Why do you have to tip at all?

When transfers to and from your ship are a part of your air-and-sea program, gratuities are generally included for luggage

handling. In that case, do not worry about the interim tipping. However, if you take a taxi to the pier and hand over your bags to a stevedore, be sure to tip him. Treat him with respect and pass along at least $5.

During your cruise, room-service waiters generally receive a cash tip of $1 to $3 per delivery. A 15% to 18% gratuity will automatically be added to each bar bill during the cruise. If you use salon and spa services, a similar percentage might be added to the bills there as well. If you dine in a specialty restaurant, you may be asked to provide a one-time gratuity for the service staff.

Nowadays, tips for cruise staff generally add up to about $12 to $22 per person per day, depending on the category of your accommodations. You tip the same amount for each person who shares the cabin, including children, unless otherwise indicated. Most cruise lines now either automatically add gratuities to passengers' onboard charge accounts or offer the option.

EXTRAS
Cruise fares typically include accommodations, onboard meals and snacks, and most onboard activities. Not normally included are airfare, shore excursions, tips, soft drinks, alcoholic drinks, or spa treatments. Some lines now add a room service fee; for instance Norwegian Cruise Line charges $7.95 for all room service, with the exception of suites, and Royal Caribbean adds a $3.95 fee for late-night orders. Port fees, fuel surcharges, and sales taxes are generally added to your fare at booking but are often included in quoted rates.

Cabins

In years gone by, cabins were almost an afterthought. The general attitude of both passengers and the cruise lines used to be that a cabin is a cabin—used only for

Recommended Gratuities by Cruise Line

Each cruise line has a different tipping policy. Some allow you to add tips to your shipboard account, and others expect you to dole out the dollars in cash on the last night of the cruise. Here are the suggested tipping amounts for each line covered in this book. Gratuity recommendations are often higher if you're staying in a suite with extra services, such as a butler.

Azamara Club Cruises: No tipping expected

Carnival Cruise Lines: $12.95–$13.95 per person per day

Celebrity Cruises: $14.50–$18 per person per day

Costa Cruises: $13.50–$16.50 per person per day

Crystal Cruises: No tipping expected

Cunard Line: $11.50–$13.50 per person per day

Disney Cruise Line: $12 per person per day

Holland America Line: $13.50–$15 per person per day

MSC Cruises: $12.50 per person per day

Norwegian Cruise Line: $14.50–$17.50 per person per day

Oceania Cruises: $16–$23 per person per day

Ponant: No tipping expected

Princess Cruises: $13.50–$15.50 per person per day

Regent Seven Seas Cruises: No tipping expected

Royal Caribbean International: $14.50–$17.50 per person per day

Seabourn Cruise Line: No tipping expected

Seadream Yacht Club: No tipping expected

Silversea Cruises: No tipping expected

Star Clippers: $8 per person per day

Viking Ocean Cruises: $15 per person per day

Windstar Cruises: $13.50 per person per day

---

changing clothes and sleeping. That's why the cabins on most older cruise ships are skimpy in size and short on amenities.

Most cabin layouts on a ship are identical or nearly so. Commanding views fetch higher fares, but you should know that cabins on the highest decks are also more susceptible to side-to-side movement; in rough seas you could find yourself tossed right out of bed. On lower decks, you'll pay less and find more stability, particularly in the middle of the ship—even upper-level cabins in the middle of the ship are steadier.

Some forward cabins have a tendency to be oddly shaped, as they follow the contour of the bow. They are also likely to be noisy; when the ship's anchor drops, you won't need a wake-up call. In rough seas you can feel the ship's pitch (its upward and downward motion) more in the front. Should you go for the stern location instead? You may feel the pitch there, too, and possibly some vibration. You're also more likely to hear engine and machinery noise, and depending on the ship, you might find soot on your balcony railings. However, many passengers feel the view of the ship's wake (the ripples it leaves behind as its massive engines move it forward) is worth any noise or vibration they might encounter there.

Above all, don't be confused by all the categories listed in cruise-line brochures; price levels are more likely to reflect cabin location than any physical differences in the cabins themselves. Shipboard accommodations fall into four basic configurations: inside cabins, outside cabins, balcony cabins, and suites.

INSIDE CABINS

An inside cabin has no window or porthole. These are always the least expensive cabins and are ideal for passengers who would rather spend their vacation funds on excursions or other incidentals than on upgraded accommodations. Inside cabins are generally just as spacious as the lowest category of outside cabins, and decor and amenities are similar. Parents sometimes book an inside cabin for their older children and teens, while they stay across the hall in an outside cabin with a window or balcony. On some newer ships, inside cabins have "virtual" windows that show a picture of the outside of the ship, giving the illusion you aren't completely inside.

OUTSIDE CABINS

A standard outside cabin has either a picture window or porthole. To give the illusion of more space, these cabins might also rely on the generous use of mirrors for an even airier feeling. Two twin beds can be joined together to create one large bed. Going one step further, standard and larger outside staterooms on modern ships are often outfitted with a small sofa or loveseat with a cocktail table or small side table. Some larger cabins may have a combination bathtub-shower instead of just a shower.

BALCONY CABINS

A balcony (or verandah) cabin is an outside cabin with floor-to-ceiling glass doors that open onto a private deck. Although the cabin may have large expanses of glass, the balcony is sometimes cut out of the cabin's square footage (depending on the ship). Balconies are usually furnished with two chairs and a table for lounging and casual dining outdoors. However, you should be aware that balconies are not always completely private; sometimes your balcony is visible from those next door and from above. The furnishings and amenities of balcony cabins are otherwise much like those in standard outside cabins.

SUITES

Suites are the most lavish accommodations afloat, and although they are always larger than regular cabins, suites do not always have separate rooms for sleeping. They almost always have amenities that standard cabins do not have. Depending on the cruise line, you may find a small refrigerator or minibar stocked with complimentary soft drinks, bottled water, and the alcoholic beverages of your choice. Top suites on some ships include complimentary laundry service and complex entertainment centers with large flat-screen TVs, in-cabin espresso or cappucino makers, and iphone docks. An added bonus to the suite life is the extra level of services many ships offer—for exmaple, afternoon tea and evening canapés delivered to your suite and served by a white-gloved butler.

Although "minisuites" on most contemporary ships have separate sitting areas with a sofa, chair, and cocktail table, don't let the marketing skill of the cruise lines fool you: so-called minisuites are usually little more than slightly larger versions of standard balcony cabins and seldom include the extra services and elaborate amenities you can get in regular suites. They're still generally a good value for the price, if space matters.

ACCESSIBILITY ISSUES

All major cruise lines offer a limited number of staterooms designed to be wheelchair- and scooter-accessible. Booking a newer vessel will generally assure more

DECIPHER YOUR DECK PLAN

LIDO DECK

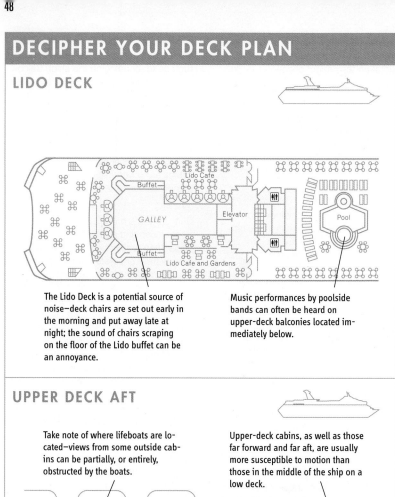

The Lido Deck is a potential source of noise—deck chairs are set out early in the morning and put away late at night; the sound of chairs scraping on the floor of the Lido buffet can be an annoyance.

Music performances by poolside bands can often be heard on upper-deck balconies located immediately below.

UPPER DECK AFT

Take note of where lifeboats are located—views from some outside cabins can be partially, or entirely, obstructed by the boats.

Upper-deck cabins, as well as those far forward and far aft, are usually more susceptible to motion than those in the middle of the ship on a low deck.

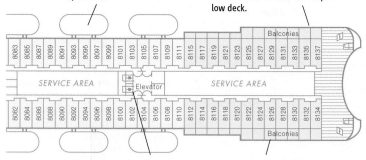

Cabins near elevators or stairs are a double-edged sword. Being close by is a convenience; however, although the elevators aren't necessarily noisy, the traffic they attract can be.

Balcony cabins are indicated by a rectangle split into two sections. The small box is the balcony.

MAIN PUBLIC DECK

Cabins immediately below restaurants and dining rooms can be noisy. Late sleepers might be bothered by early breakfast noise, early sleepers by late diners.

Theaters and dining rooms are often located on middle or lower decks.

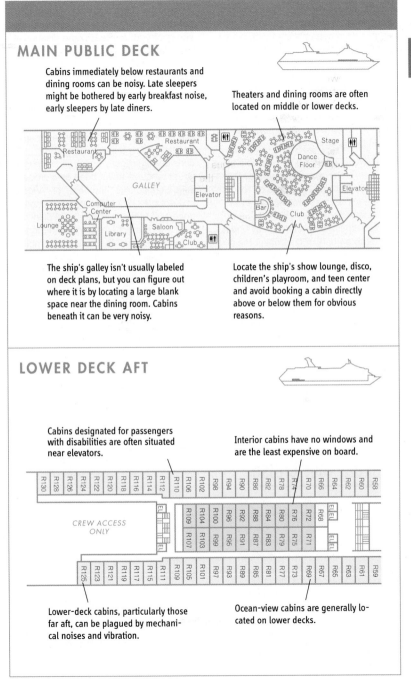

The ship's galley isn't usually labeled on deck plans, but you can figure out where it is by locating a large blank space near the dining room. Cabins beneath it can be very noisy.

Locate the ship's show lounge, disco, children's playroom, and teen center and avoid booking a cabin directly above or below them for obvious reasons.

LOWER DECK AFT

Cabins designated for passengers with disabilities are often situated near elevators.

Interior cabins have no windows and are the least expensive on board.

Lower-deck cabins, particularly those far aft, can be plagued by mechanical noises and vibration.

Ocean-view cabins are generally located on lower decks.

choices. On newer ships, public rooms are generally more accessible, and more facilities have been planned with wheelchair-users in mind. Auxiliary aids, such as flashers for the hearing impaired and buzzers for visually impaired passengers, as well as lifts for swimming pools and hot tubs, are sometimes available. However, more than the usual amount of planning is necessary for smooth sailing if you have special needs.

For example, when a ship is unable to dock—as is the case in Grand Cayman—passengers are taken ashore on tenders that are sometimes problematic even for the able-bodied to negotiate. Some people with limited mobility may find it difficult to embark or disembark the ship when docked because of the steep angle of the gangways during high or low tide. In some situations, crew members may offer assistance that involves carrying guests, but if the sea is choppy when tendering is a necessity, that might not be an option.

Passengers who require continuous oxygen or have service animals will have further hurdles to overcome. You can bring both aboard a cruise ship, but you should be prepared to present up-to-date records for your service animal if requested.

Booking Your Cruise

As a rule, the majority of cruisers still plan their trips nine to twelve months ahead of time, though the booking window has narrowed over time. It follows, then, that a longer booking window should give you the pick of sailing dates, ships, itineraries, cabins, and flights to the port city. If you're looking for a standard itinerary and aren't choosy about the vessel or dates, you could wait for a last-minute discount, but they are more difficult to find than in the past.

If particular shore excursions are important to you, consider booking them when you book your cruise to avoid disappointment later.

Using a Travel Agent

Whether it is your first or 50th sailing, your best friend when booking a cruise is a knowledgeable, experienced travel agent. The last thing you want when considering a costly cruise vacation is an agent who has never been on a cruise, calls a cruise ship "the boat," or—worse still—quotes brochure rates. The most important steps in cruise-travel planning are research, research, and more research. Booking a cruise is a complex process, and it's seldom wise to try to go it alone, particularly the first time. But how do you find a cruise travel agent you can trust?

The most experienced and reliable agent will be certified as an Accredited Cruise Counselor (ACC), Master Cruise Counselor (MCC), or Elite Cruise Counselor (ECC) by the Cruise Lines International Association (CLIA). These agents have completed demanding training programs, including touring or sailing on a specific number of ships. Your agent should also belong to a professional trade organization. In North America, membership in the American Society of Travel Agents (ASTA) indicates that an agency has pledged to follow the code of ethics set forth by the world's largest association for travel professionals. In the best of all worlds, your travel agent is affiliated with both ASTA and CLIA.

Contrary to what conventional wisdom might suggest, cutting out the travel agent and booking directly with a cruise line won't necessarily get you the lowest price. According to Cruise Lines International Association (CLIA), seven out of ten cruise bookings are still handled through travel agents. In fact, cruise-line

Before You Book

If you've decided to use a travel agent, ask yourself these 10 simple questions, and you'll be better prepared to help the agent do his or her job.

1. Who will be going on the cruise?

2. What can you afford to spend for the entire trip?

3. Where would you like to go?

4. How much vacation time do you have?

5. When can you get away?

6. What are your interests?

7. Do you prefer a casual or structured vacation?

8. What kind of accommodations do you want?

9. What are your dining preferences?

10. How will you get to the embarkation port?

reservation systems simply are not capable of dealing with tens of thousands of direct calls from potential passengers. Without an agent working on your behalf, you're on your own. Do not rely solely on Internet message boards for authoritative responses to your questions—that is a service more accurately provided by your travel agent.

TRAVEL AGENT PROFESSIONAL ORGANIZATION American Society of Travel Agents (*ASTA*) ⊕ *www.travelsense.org.*

CRUISE LINE ORGANIZATIONS Cruise Lines International Association (*CLIA*) ⊕ *www.cruising.org.*

Booking Your Cruise Online

In addition to local travel agencies, there are many hardworking, dedicated travel professionals working for websites. Both big-name travel sellers and mom-and-pop agencies compete for the attention of cyber-savvy clients; and it never hurts to compare prices from a variety of these sources. Some cruise lines even allow you to book directly with them through their websites or toll-free reservation call centers.

As a rule, Internet-based and toll-free brokers will do a decent job for you. They often offer discounted fares, though not always the lowest, so it pays to check around. If you know precisely what you want and how much you should pay to get a real bargain—and you don't mind dealing with an anonymous voice on the phone—make your reservations when the price is right. Just don't expect the personal service you get from an agent you know. Also, be prepared to spend a lot of time and effort on the phone if something goes wrong.

Before You Go

To expedite your preboarding paperwork, most cruise lines have convenient forms on their websites. As long as you have your reservation number, you can provide the required immigration information (usually your citizenship information and passport number), reserve shore excursions, and even indicate any special requests from the comfort of your home. A handful of less-wired cruise lines still mail preboarding paperwork to you or your travel agent for completion after you make your final payment, and they request that you return the forms before the cruise. No matter how you submit them, be sure to print out hard copies of any forms you fill out and bring them with you to the pier to smooth the embarkation process.

Documents

It is every passenger's responsibility to have proper identification. If you arrive at the embarkation port without it, you may not be allowed to board, *and the line will issue no fare refund.* Most travel agents know the requirements and can guide you to the proper agency to obtain what you need if you don't have it.

Everyone must have proof of citizenship and identity to travel abroad. All travelers (even young children) must present a passport or other approved document denoting citizenship and identity for all land and sea travel into the United States.

Like most rules, it has a confusing exception—U.S. citizens traveling within the Caribbean on closed-loop cruises (cruises that begin and end in the same port) are still permitted to depart from or enter the United States with proof of identity, which includes a government-issued photo ID, such as a driver's license, along with proof of citizenship, such as a certified birth certificate with seal issued by the state where you were born; a passport card or enhanced driver's licsense may also be sufficient for most cruises. However, you may still be required to present a full passport when you dock at a foreign port, depending on the islands or countries that your cruise ship is visiting. You also must have one to fly internationally—which will make it easier to fly from the United States to meet your ship at the first port should you miss the scheduled embarkation, or to leave the ship without significant delays and complications before the cruise ends if

you must fly back to the United States due to an emergency.

If your cruise begins in one U.S. port and ends in a different port, a passport is required; even for cruises that begin and end in the same port, cruise lines strongly recommend that all passengers travel with a valid passport, and some may very well require them. Check with your cruise line to ensure you have the appropriate documents for the stops you'll be making on your cruise.

Children under the age of 18, when they are not traveling with both parents, almost always require a letter of permission from the absent parent(s). Airlines, cruise lines, and immigration agents can deny minor children initial boarding or entry to foreign countries without proper proof of identification and citizenship and a notarized permission letter from absent or noncustodial parents. Your travel agent or cruise line can help with the wording of such a letter.

What to Pack

An absolute essential for women is a shawl or light sweater. Aggressive air-conditioning can make public rooms uncomfortable, particularly if you are sunburned from a day at the beach.

Put things you can't do without—such as prescription medication, spare eyeglasses, toiletries, a swimsuit, and change of clothes for the first day—in your carry-on. Most cruise ships provide soap, shampoo, and conditioner, so you probably won't need those.

And plan carefully. In fact, we'd strongly advise you to make a list so you don't forget anything.

What to Wear

In terms of your wardrobe, cruise wear falls into three categories: casual, informal, and formal. Cruise documents should include information indicating how many evenings fall into each category. You will know when to wear what by reading your ship's daily newsletter—each evening's dress code will be prominently stated.

For the day, you'll need casual wear. You'll typically need swimwear, a cover-up, and sandals for the pool or beach. Time spent ashore touring and shopping calls for shorts topped with T-shirts or polo shirts and comfy walking shoes. "Conservative" is a rule to live by in the Caribbean (most Caribbean islands are very socially conservative), and mix-and-match will save room in your suitcase. Forget denim, which is too hot, and concentrate on lighter fabrics that will breathe in the Caribbean heat. Although jeans are allowed in the dining rooms of most mainstream ships, at night casual generally means khaki-type slacks and nice polo or sport shirts for men. Ladies' outfits are sundresses, skirts and tops, or pants outfits. By sticking to two or three complementary colors and a few accessories, you can mix up tops and bottoms for a different look every night.

Informal dress—sometimes called "resort" or "smart" casual—is a little trickier. It applies only to evening wear, and can mean different things depending on the cruise line. Informal for women is a dressier dress or pants outfit; for men it almost always includes a dress shirt and slacks and maybe a sport coat. Check your documents carefully.

Formal night means dressing up, but these days even that is a relative notion and found primarily on high-end ships. You will see women in everything from simple cocktail dresses to glittering formal gowns. A tuxedo or dark suit is required for gentlemen. For children, Sunday best is entirely appropriate.

Insurance

It's a good idea to purchase travel insurance, which covers a variety of possible hazards and mishaps—including trip interruptions, lost or delayed baggage, medical emergencies, and other disruptions—when you book a cruise. Preexisting medical conditions are often covered only if you buy a policy at the time or within a few days of the initial booking. Any policy should insure you for travel and luggage delays. A travel policy will ensure that you can get to the next port of call should you miss your ship, or reimburse you for unexpected expenditures. Several travel insurance providers offer faster reimbursement for covered disruptions via mobile apps. Save your receipts for all out-of-pocket expenses to file your claim, and be sure to get an incident report from the airline at fault.

Insurance should also cover you for unexpected injuries and illnesses. The medical insurance program you depend on at home might not extend coverage beyond the borders of the United States. Medicare assuredly will not cover you if you are hurt or sick while abroad. It is worth noting that all ships of foreign registry are considered to be "outside the United States" by Medicare.

Nearly all cruise lines offer their own line of insurance. Compare the coverage and rates to determine which is best for you. Keep in mind that insurance purchased from an independent carrier is more likely to include coverage if the cruise line goes out of business before or during your cruise. Although it is a rare and unlikely occurrence, you do want to be insured in the event that it happens.

U.S. TRAVEL INSURERS Allianz Travel Insurance☎ *866/884–3556* ⊕ *www.allianztravelinsurance.com.* **Generali Global Assistance**☎ *800/874–2442* ⊕ *www.generalitravelinsurance.com.* **GeoBlue Travel Health Insurance**☎ *610/254–5850, 855/481–6647* ⊕ *www.geobluetravelinsurance.com.* **Travelex Insurance**☎ *800/228–9792* ⊕ *www.travelexinsurance.com.* **Travel Guard International**☎ *800/826–5248* ⊕ *www.travelguard.com.* **Travel Insured International**☎ *800/243–3174* ⊕ *www.travelinsured.com.*

Arriving and Embarking

Most cruise-ship passengers fly to the port of embarkation. If you book your cruise far enough in advance, you'll be given the opportunity to purchase an air-and-sea package, which may (or may not) save you money. You might actually get a lower fare by booking your flight independently, or you might find considerably more convenient flight times, so it's a good idea to shop around for the best fare and most convenient flights available. Independent air arrangements might save you enough to cover the cost of a hotel room in your embarkation port, so that you can arrive early—not a bad idea, in order to overcome jet lag and/or to avoid the possibility of a delayed flight.

Getting to the Port

If you buy an air-and-sea package from your cruise line, a uniformed cruise-line agent will meet you at baggage claim to smooth your way from airport to pier. You will need to claim your own bags and give them to the transfer driver so they can be loaded onto the bus. On arrival at the pier, luggage is automatically transferred to the ship for delivery to your cabin. The cruise-line ground transfer system can also be available to independent fliers. However, be sure to ask your

travel agent how much it costs; you may find that a taxi or shuttle service is less expensive and more convenient.

In addition to the busiest embarkation ports such as Miami, Fort Lauderdale, and New York City, cruises now leave from less-familiar port cities all around the East and Gulf coasts. Galveston (Texas), New Orleans (Louisiana), and Port Canaveral (Florida) have become major home ports in recent years and are considered now to be among the nation's top 10 cruise ports. Many people prefer to drive to these ports if they are close enough to home. Secure parking is always available, either within the port itself or nearby.

Boarding

After entering the cruise terminal, you'll usually go through airport-style security and then proceed to the check-in desk, where you'll present your cruise documents (as well as a credit card) and get your boarding card, which you'll use both to open your cabin and make any onboard charges. Then you wait to board until your group number is called. Procedures vary somewhat once you are greeted by staff members lined up just inside the ship's hull, but you'll have to produce your boarding card for the security officer. At some point—either at the check-in desk or when boarding the ship for the first time—you will be photographed for security purposes; your image will display when your boarding card is "swiped" into a computer as you leave and reboard the ship at ports of call. Depending on the cruise line, you will be directed to your cabin, or a steward will relieve you of your carry-on luggage and accompany you. Stewards on high-end cruise lines not only show you the way, but hand you a glass of champagne as a welcome-aboard gesture. However, if you board early, don't be surprised if you are told cabins are not "ready" for occupancy—passageways to accommodations may even be roped off. In that case you can explore the ship, have lunch, or simply relax until an announcement is made that you can go to your cabin.

On Board

Check out your cabin to make sure that everything is in order. Try the plumbing and set the thermostat to the temperature you prefer. Your cabin may feel warm while docked but will cool off when the ship is underway. You should find a copy of the ship's daily schedule in the cabin. Take a few moments to look it over—you will want to know what time the lifeboat (or muster) drill takes place (a placard on the back of your cabin door will indicate directions to your emergency station), as well as meal hours and the schedule for various activities and entertainment.

Bon voyage gifts sent by your friends or travel agent will be delivered sometime during the afternoon. Be patient if you are expecting deliveries, particularly on megaships. Cabin stewards participate in the ship's turnaround and are extremely busy, although yours will no doubt introduce themselves at the first available opportunity. It may also be a while before your checked luggage arrives (possibly not until late afternoon), so your initial order of business is usually the buffet, if you haven't already had lunch. Bring along the daily schedule to check over while you eat.

While making your way to the lido buffet, no doubt you'll notice bar waiters offering trays of colorful bon voyage drinks, often in souvenir glasses that you can keep. Beware—they are not complimentary! If you choose one, you will be asked to sign for it. Like the boarding photos, you are under no obligation to purchase.

Do your plans for the cruise include booking shore excursions and indulging in

spa treatments? The most popular tours sometimes sell out, and spas can be busy during sea days, so your next stops should be the Shore Excursion Desk to book tours and the spa to make appointments, if you didn't already book your spa visits and excursions in advance.

Dining room seating arrangements are another matter for consideration. If you aren't happy with your assigned dinner seating, speak to the maître d'. The daily schedule will indicate where and when to meet with him. If you plan to dine in the ship's specialty restaurant, make those reservations as soon as possible to avoid disappointment.

Paying for Things On Board

A cashless society prevails on cruise ships, and during check-in either an imprint is made of your credit card or you must make a cash deposit for use against onboard charges. Most expenditures are charged to your shipboard account (via a swipe of your key card) with your signature as verification, with the exception of some casino gaming.

You'll get an itemized bill listing your purchases at the end of the voyage, and any discrepancies can be discussed at the purser's desk. To save time, check the balance of your shipboard account before the last day by requesting an interim printout of your bill from the purser to ensure accuracy. On some ships you can even access your account on your stateroom television.

Dining

All food, all the time? Not quite, but it is possible to literally eat away the day and most of the night on a cruise. A popular cruise director joke is, "You came on as passengers, and you will be leaving as cargo." Although it is meant in fun, it does contain the ring of truth.

Fodor's Cruise Preparation Time Line ⊙

4–6 Months Before Sailing

■ Check with your travel agent or the State Department for the identification required for your cruise.

■ Gather the necessary identification you need. If you need to replace a lost birth certificate, apply for a new passport, or renew one that's about to expire, start the paperwork now. Doing it at the last minute is stressful and often costly.

60–75 Days Before Sailing

■ Make the final payment on your cruise fare. Though the dates vary, your travel agent should remind you when the payment date draws near. Failure to submit the balance on time can result in the cancellation of your reservation.

■ Make a packing list for each person you'll be packing for.

■ Begin your wardrobe planning now. Try things on to make sure they fit and are in good repair (it's amazing how stains can magically appear months after something has been dry cleaned). Set things aside.

■ If you need to shop, get started so you have time to find just the right thing (and perhaps to return or exchange just the right thing).

■ Make kennel reservations for your pets. (If you're traveling during a holiday period, you may need to do this even earlier.)

■ Arrange for a house sitter.

If you're cruising, but your kids are staying home:

■ Make childcare arrangements.

■ Go over children's schedules to make sure they'll have everything they need while you're gone (gift for a birthday party, supplies for a school project, permission slip for a field trip).

30 Days Before Sailing

■ If you purchased an air-and-sea package, call your travel agent for the details of your airline schedule. Request seat assignments.

■ If your children are sailing with you, check their wardrobes now (do it too early and the really little kids may actually grow out of garments).

■ Make appointments for any personal services you wish to have before your cruise (for example, a haircut or manicure).

■ Get out your luggage and check the locks and zippers. Check for anything that might have spilled inside on a previous trip.

■ If you need new luggage or want an extra piece to bring home souvenirs, purchase it now.

2–4 Weeks Before Sailing

■ Receive your cruise documents through the travel agent or print them from the cruise line's website.

■ Examine the documents for accuracy (correct cabin number, sailing date, and dining arrangements); make sure names are spelled correctly. If there's something you do not understand, ask now.

■ Read all the literature in your document package for suggestions specific to your cruise. Most cruise lines include helpful information.

■ Pay any routine bills that may be due while you're gone.

■ Go over your personalized packing list again. Finish shopping.

1 Week Before Sailing

■ Finalize your packing list and continue organizing everything in one area.

■ Buy film or digital media and

ensure your digital devices are in good working order; buy back-up chargers to be safe.

■ Refill prescription medications with an adequate supply.

■ Make two photocopies of your passport or ID and credit cards. Leave one copy with a friend and carry the other copy separately from the originals.

■ Get cash and/or traveler's checks at the bank. If you use traveler's checks, keep a separate record of the serial numbers. Get a supply of one-dollar bills for tipping baggage handlers (at the airport, hotel, pier, etc.).

■ You may also want to put valuables and jewelry that you won't be taking with you in the safety deposit box while you're at the bank.

■ Arrange to have your mail held at the post office or ask a neighbor to pick it up.

■ Stop newspaper delivery or ask a neighbor to bring it in for you.

■ Arrange for lawn and houseplant care or snow removal during your absence (if necessary).

■ Leave your itinerary, the ship's telephone number (plus the name of your ship and your stateroom number), and a house key with a relative or friend.

■ If traveling with young children, purchase small games or toys to keep them occupied while en route to your embarkation port.

3 Days Before Sailing

■ Confirm your airline flights; departure times are sometimes subject to change.

■ Put a card with your name, address, telephone number, and itinerary inside each suitcase.

■ Fill out the luggage tags that came with your document packet, and follow the instructions regarding when and how to attach them.

■ Complete any other paperwork that the cruise line included with your documents, either hard copy or online (foreign customs and immigration forms, onboard charge application, etc.). Do not wait until you're standing in the pier check-in line to fill them in!

■ Do last-minute laundry and tidy up the house.

■ Pull out the luggage and begin packing.

The Day Before Sailing

■ Take pets to the kennel.

■ Water houseplants and lawn (if necessary).

■ Dispose of any perishable food in the refrigerator.

■ Mail any last-minute bills.

■ Set timers for indoor lights.

■ Reorganize your wallet. Remove anything you will not need (local affinity cards, department store or gas credit cards, etc.), and put them in an envelope.

■ Finish packing and lock your suitcases.

Departure Day

■ Adjust the thermostat and double-check the door locks.

■ Turn off the water if there's danger of frozen pipes while you're away.

■ Arrange to be at the airport a minimum of two hours before your departure time (follow the airline's instructions).

■ Have government-issued photo ID and/or your passport ready for airport check-in.

■ Slip your car keys, parking claim checks, and airline tickets into your carry-on luggage. Never pack these items in checked luggage.

Onboard Extras

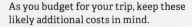

As you budget for your trip, keep these likely additional costs in mind.

Cocktails: $8–$15

Wine by the glass: $8–$15

Beer: $6–$8

Bottled water: $2.50–$5

Soft drinks: $2.50–$3

Specialty ice cream and coffee: $5–$7

Laundry: $2–$11 per piece (where self-launder facilities are unavailable)

Spa treatments: $145–$265

Salon services: $30–$149

Casino gambling: 1¢ to $10 for slot machines; $5 and up for table games

Bingo: $5–$15 per card for multiple games in each session

Food—tasty and plentiful—is available 24 hours a day on most cruise ships, and the dining experience at sea has reached almost mythic proportions. Perhaps it has something to do with legendary midnight buffets and the absence of menu prices, or maybe it's the vast selection and availability.

RESTAURANTS

Every ship has at least one main restaurant and a lido, or casual, buffet alternative. Increasingly important are specialty restaurants. Meals in the primary and buffet restaurants are included in the cruise fare; on most ships there's also 'round-the-clock room service (sometimes with a charge), midday tea and snacks, and late-night buffets. Most mainstream cruise lines levy a surcharge for dining in alternative restaurants that may also include a gratuity (fees are also not uncommon now for room service deliveries), although there generally is no additional charge on luxury cruise lines.

You may also find a pizzeria or a specialty coffee bar on your ship—increasingly popular favorites cropping up on ships old and new. Although pizza is usually complimentary (though on some ships it is not, when delivered by room service), expect an additional charge for specialty coffees at the coffee bar and, quite likely,

in the dining room as well. You will also likely be charged for sodas and drinks other than iced tea, regular coffee, tap water, and fruit juice during meals.

There is often a direct relationship between the cost of a cruise and the quality of its cuisine. The food is sophisticated on some (mostly expensive) lines, among them Regent Seven Seas and Silversea. In the more moderate price range, Celebrity Cruises has always been known for its fine cuisine, and Oceania Cruises scores high marks as well. The trend toward featuring specialty dishes and even entire menus designed by acclaimed chefs has spread throughout the cruise industry; however, on most mainstream cruise lines the food is of the quality that you would find in any good hotel banquet—perfectly acceptable but certainly not great.

SPECIALTY RESTAURANTS

A growing trend in shipboard dining is the emergence of sophisticated specialty restaurants that require reservations and frequently charge a fee. From as little as $29 per person for a complete steak dinner to $200 per person for an elaborate gourmet meal including fine wines paired with each course, specialty restaurants offer a refined dining option that cannot be duplicated in your ship's main

Drinking and Gambling Ages

Many underage passengers have learned to their chagrin that the rules that apply on land are also adhered to at sea. On most mainstream cruise ships you must be 21 to imbibe alcoholic beverages. There are exceptions—for instance, on cruises departing from countries where the legal drinking age is typically lower than 21. On some cruise lines, a parent who is sailing with his or her son(s) and/or daughter(s) who is between the ages of 18 and 20 may sign a waiver allowing the 18- to 20-year-old to consume

alcoholic beverages, generally limited to beer and wine. However, by and large, if you haven't achieved the magic age of 21, your shipboard charge card will be coded as booze-free, and bartenders won't risk their jobs to sell you alcohol.

Gambling is a bit looser, and 18-year-olds can try their luck on cruise lines such as Carnival, Celebrity, Holland America, Norwegian, Royal Caribbean, and Silversea; most other cruise lines adhere to the age-21 minimum.

restaurants. If you anticipate dining in your ship's intimate specialty restaurant, make reservations as soon as possible to avoid disappointment.

SPECIAL DIETS

Cruise lines make every possible attempt to ensure dining satisfaction. If you have special dietary considerations (for example, low-salt, kosher, or food allergies), be sure to indicate them well ahead of time and check to be certain your needs are known by your waiter once on board. In addition to the usual menu items, so-called spa, low-calorie, low-carbohydrate, or low-fat selections, as well as children's menus, are usually available. Requests for dishes not featured on the menu can often be granted if you ask in advance.

ALCOHOL

On all but the most upscale lines, you pay for alcohol aboard the ship, including wine with dinner. Wine typically costs about what you would expect to pay at a nice lounge or restaurant in a resort or in a major city. Wine by the bottle is a more economical choice at dinner than ordering it by the glass. Any wine you don't finish will be kept for you and

served the next night. Gifts of wine or champagne ordered from the cruise line (either by you, a friend, or your travel agent) can be taken to the dining room. Wine from any other source will incur a corkage fee of approximately $10 to $25 per bottle. Some (though not all) lines will allow you to carry wine aboard when you embark for the first time; most lines do not allow you to carry other alcohol on board (Viking Ocean Cruises being a notable exception).

Entertainment

Real treats are the folkloric shows or other entertainment arranged to take place while cruise ships are in port. Local performers come aboard, usually shortly before the ship sails, to present traditional songs and dances. It's an excellent way to get a glimpse of their performing arts.

Some ships also have a movie theater or offer in-cabin movies, or you may be able to rent or borrow movies to watch on your in-cabin DVD player, if you have one. The latest twist in video programming can be found on many cruise ships—huge outdoor LED screens where movies, music video concerts, news channels, sports events, and even the ship's activities are broadcast for passengers lounging poolside.

Enrichment programs have also become a popular pastime at sea. Port lecturers on many large contemporary cruise ships offer more information on ship-sponsored shore tours and shopping than insight into the ports of call themselves. If more cerebral presentations are important to you, consider a cruise on a line that features stimulating enrichment programs and seminars at sea. Speakers can include destination-oriented historians, popular authors, business leaders, political figures, radio or television personalities, and even movie stars.

LOUNGES AND NIGHTCLUBS

You'll often find live entertainment in the ship lounges after dinner (and even sometimes before dinner). If you want to unleash your inner American Idol, look for karaoke. Singing along in a lively piano bar is another shipboard favorite for would-be crooners.

Other lounges might feature easy-listening or jazz performances or live music for pre- and postdinner social dancing. Later in the evening, lounges pick up the pace with music from the 1950s, '60s, and '70s; clubs aimed at a younger crowd usually have more contemporary dance music during the late-night hours.

CASINOS

On most ships, lavish casinos pulsate with activity. On ships that feature them, the rationale for locating casinos where most passengers must pass either through or alongside them is obvious—the unspoken allure of winning. In addition to slot machines in a variety of denominations, cruise-ship casinos usually have table games. Casino hours vary based on the itinerary or location of the ship; most are required to close while in port, whereas others may be able to offer 24-hour slot machines while simply closing table games. Every casino has a cashier, and you may be able to charge a cash advance to your onboard account for a fee. And unlike most ship areas, smoking is still allowed in many cruise-ship casinos.

Sports and Fitness

Onboard sports facilities might include a court for basketball, volleyball, tennis—or all three—a jogging track, or even a ropes course high above the ship's top deck. Some ships are even offering innovative and unexpected features, such as rock-climbing walls, bungee trampolines, zip lines, a go-kart track on Norwegian Cruise Line's *Norwegian Bliss,* and surfing pools and bumper cars on some Royal Caribbean ships. For the less adventurous, there's always table tennis and shuffleboard.

Naturally, you will find at least one swimming pool, and possibly several. Cruise-ship pools are generally on the small side—more appropriate for cooling off than doing laps—and the majority contain filtered salt water. But some are elaborate affairs, with waterslides and interactive water play areas for family fun. Princess Grand–class ships have challenging, freshwater "swim against the current" pools for swimming enthusiasts who want to get their low-impact exercise while on board.

Shipboard fitness centers have become ever more elaborate, offering state-of-the-art exercise machines, treadmills, and stair steppers, not to mention free weights and weight machines. As a bonus, many fitness centers with floor-to-ceiling windows have the world's most inspiring sea views. Most ships offer some complimentary fitness classes, but you will also find classes in Pilates, spinning, or yoga (usually for a fee). Personal trainers are usually on board to get you off on the right foot (also for a fee).

Will I get Seasick?

Many first-time passengers are anxious about whether they'll be stricken by seasickness, but there is no way to tell until you actually sail. Modern vessels are equipped with stabilizers that eliminate much of the motion responsible for seasickness. On most Caribbean cruises, you will spend most of your time in reasonably calm, sheltered waters, but when your cruise includes time out in the open sea (say, between Miami and Puerto Rico), you may feel the ship's movement. However, today's modern cruise ships—particularly if your ship is a megaliner—provides a remarkably motion-free experience unless the seas are rough. You may feel slightly more movement on a small ship, but not by much, as these ships ply remote bays and coves that are even more sheltered than those traveled by regular cruise ships.

If you have a history of seasickness, don't book an inside cabin. For the terminally seasick, it will begin to resemble a movable coffin in short order. If you do become seasick, you can use common drugs such as Dramamine and Bonine (often handed out free at concierge desks when seas are rough). Some people find anti-seasickness wristbands helpful; these apply gentle pressure to the wrist in lieu of drugs. Worn behind the ear, the Transderm Scop patch dispenses a continuous metered dose of medication, which is absorbed into the skin and enters the bloodstream. Apply the patch four hours before sailing and it will continue to be effective for three days. It can be prescribed by the ship's physician, but it's usually cheaper and easier to get it from your own doctor.

Spas

With all the usual pampering and service in luxurious surroundings, simply being on a cruise can be a stress-reducing experience. Add to that the menu of spa and salon services at your fingertips and you have a recipe for total sensory pleasure. Spas have also become among the most popular of shipboard areas. While high-end Canyon Ranch has made inroads with the cruise industry by opening spas on an increasing number of ships, Steiner Leisure is still the largest spa and salon operator at sea (the company also operates the Mandara, Elemis, and Greenhouse spa brands), with facilities on more than 100 cruise ships worldwide.

In addition to facials, manicures, pedicures, massages, and sensual body treatments, other hallmarks of Steiner Leisure are salon services and products for hair and skin. Founded in 1901 by Henry Steiner of London, a single salon prospered when Steiner's son joined the business in 1926 and was granted a Royal Warrant as hairdresser to Her Majesty Queen Mary in 1937. In 1956 Steiner won its first cruise-ship contract to operate the salon on board the ships of the Cunard Line. By the mid-1990s Steiner Leisure began taking an active role in creating shipboard spas offering a wide variety of wellness therapies and beauty programs for both women and men.

Safety at Sea

Safety begins with you, the passenger. Once settled into your cabin, locate your life vests if they are stored there, and review the posted emergency instructions. Make sure the vests are in good condition, and learn how to secure them properly. Make certain the ship's purser knows if you have a physical infirmity that may hamper a speedy exit from your cabin, so that in an emergency he or she can quickly dispatch a crew member to assist you. If you're traveling with children, be sure that child-size life jackets are placed in your cabin.

Before your ship leaves the embarkation port, you'll be required to attend a mandatory lifeboat drill; you may or may not be required to bring your life vest and stand outside on deck near your assigned lifeboat. Do go and listen carefully (ship staff will take attendance and won't dismiss the passengers until everyone is accounted for). If you're unsure about how to use your vest, now is the time to ask. Some cruise lines no longer require you to bring your vest to the muster drill and instead store them near the muster station, but crew members are more than willing to assist if you have questions. Only in the most extreme circumstances will you need to abandon ship—but it has happened. The time you spend learning the procedure may serve you well in a mishap.

In actuality, the greatest danger facing cruise-ship passengers is fire. All cruise lines must meet international standards for fire safety, which require sprinkler systems, smoke detectors, and other safety features. Fires on cruise ships are not common, but they do happen, and these rules have made ships much safer. You can do your part by *not* using an iron in your cabin or leaving fabric items, such as towels, on your balcony, and by taking care to properly extinguish smoking materials. Never throw a lighted cigarette overboard—it could be blown back into an opening in the ship and start a fire (most ships don't allow smoking in cabins or on balconies any longer for this reason).

Other Shipboard Services

COMMUNICATIONS

Just because you are out to sea does not mean you have to be out of touch. However, ship-to-shore telephone calls can cost $2 to $15 a minute, so it makes more economic sense to use email to remain in contact with your home or office. Most ships have basic computer systems, and some newer vessels offer more high-tech connectivity—even in-cabin hookups or wireless connections for either your own laptop computer or tablet. Expect to pay an activation fee and subsequent charges in the $0.75- to $1-per-minute range for the use of these Internet services. Ships usually offer some kind of package so that you get a reduced per-minute price if you pay a fee up front.

The ability to use your own mobile phone for calls from the high seas is an alternative that is gaining in popularity. It's usually cheaper than using a cabin phone if your ship offers the service; however, it can still cost $2.50 to $5 a minute. A rather ingenious concept, the ship acts as a cell "tower" in international waters—you use your own cell phone and your own number when roaming at sea, and you can even send and receive

Crime on Ships

Crime aboard cruise ships has occasionally become headline news, thanks in large part to a few well-publicized cases. Most people never have any type of problem, but you should exercise the same precautions aboard a ship that you would at home. Keep your valuables out of sight—on big ships virtually every cabin has a small safe. Don't carry too much cash ashore, use your credit card whenever possible, and keep your money in a secure place, such as a front pocket that's harder to pick.

Single women traveling with friends should stick together, especially when returning to their cabins late at night. When assaults occur, it often comes to light that excessive drinking of alcohol is a factor. Be careful about whom you befriend, as you would anywhere, whether it's a fellow passenger or a member of the crew. Don't be paranoid, but do be prudent.

Your cruise is a wonderful opportunity to leave everyday responsibilities behind, but don't neglect to pack your common sense. After a few drinks it might seem like a good idea to sit on a railing or lean over the rail to get a better view of the ship's wake. Passengers have been known to fall. "Man overboard" is more likely to be the result of carelessness than criminal intent.

text messages and email with some smartphones (albeit with a surcharge in addition to any roaming fees). Before leaving home, ask your cellphone service provider to activate international roaming on your account. When in port, depending on the type of cell phone you own and the agreements your mobile service-provider has established, you may be able to connect to local networks ashore. Most GSM phones are also usable in Mexico and on Caribbean islands. Rates for using the maritime service, as well as any roaming charges, are established by your mobile service carrier and are worth checking into before your trip. To avoid excessive charges, it's a good idea to turn off your phone's data roaming option while at sea.

LAUNDRY AND DRY CLEANING

Most cruise ships offer valet laundry and pressing services (and some also offer dry cleaning). Expenses can add up fast, especially for laundry, since charges are per item and the rates are similar to those charged in hotels, unless your ship offers a fixed-price laundry deal (all you can stuff into a bag they provide for a single fee, which is common on longer cruises and even some weeklong cruises). If doing laundry is important to you and you do not want to send it out to be done, some cruise ships have a self-service laundry room (which usually features an iron and ironing board in addition to washers and dryers). If you book one of the top-dollar suites, laundry service may be included for no additional cost. Upscale ships such as those in the Regent Seven Seas, Viking Ocean, and Silversea fleets have complimentary self-service launderettes. On other cruise lines, such as Disney, Princess, Oceania, Carnival, and some Holland America ships, you can do your own laundry for about $4 or less per load. None of the vessels in the Norwegian, Royal Caribbean, or Celebrity fleets has self-service laundry facilities.

Disembarkation

All cruises come to an end eventually, and the disembarkation process actually begins the day before you arrive at your ship's final port. During that day your cabin steward delivers special luggage tags to your stateroom, along with customs forms and instructions on some itineraries.

The night before you disembark, you'll need to set aside clothing to wear the next morning when you leave the ship. Many people dress in whatever casual outfits they wear for the final dinner on board, or change into travel clothes after dinner. Also, do not forget to put your passport or other proof of citizenship, airline tickets, and medications in your hand luggage. The luggage tags go onto your larger bags, which are placed outside your stateroom door for pickup during the hours indicated. Your cruise line may offer self-assist disembarkation, and in that case, you do not have to put your luggage outside your stateroom the night before departure and may leave the ship early if you can take all your luggage with you.

A statement itemizing your onboard charges is delivered before you arise on disembarkation morning. Plan to get up early enough to check it over for accuracy, finish packing your personal belongings, and vacate your stateroom by the appointed hour. Any discrepancies in your onboard account should be taken care of before leaving the ship, usually at the reception desk. Breakfast is served in the main restaurant as well as the buffet on the last morning, but room service usually isn't available. Disembarkation procedures vary by cruise line, but you'll probably have to wait in a lounge or on deck for your tag color or number to be called.

Then you take a taxi, bus, or other transportation to your post-cruise hotel or to the airport for your flight home. If you are flying out the day your cruise ends, leave plenty of time to go through the usual check-in, passport control and customs, and security procedures at the airport.

Customs and Duties

U.S. CUSTOMS

Each individual or family must fill out a customs declaration form, which will be provided before your ship docks. Be sure to keep receipts for all purchases made outside the United States; you may also be asked to show officials the receipts along with what you've bought. After showing your passport to United States immigration officials upon disembarkation, you must collect your luggage from the dock.

You're always allowed to bring goods up to a certain value back home without having to pay any duty or import tax. There's also a limit on the amount of tobacco and liquor you can bring back duty-free, and some countries have separate limits for perfumes; for exact figures, check with your customs department. The values of so-called duty-free goods are included in these amounts. When you shop abroad—and in the Caribbean, this means all islands except for Puerto Rico, which is considered a part of the United States—if the total value of your goods is more than the duty-free limit, you'll have to pay a tax (most often a flat percentage) on the value of everything beyond that limit.

Individuals entering the United States from the Caribbean are allowed to bring in $800 worth of duty-free goods for personal use ($1,600 from the U.S. Virgin Islands), including 1 liter of alcohol (2 liters if one was produced in the Caribbean, and 5 liters from the USVI), one carton of cigarettes (or five if four were purchased in the U.S. Virgin Islands), and 100 non-Cuban cigars. Antiques and original artwork are also duty-free.

Chapter 3

PORTS OF EMBARKATION

3

Miami is the world's cruise capital, and more cruise ships are based here year-round than anywhere else. Caribbean cruises depart for their itineraries from several ports on both Florida coasts, as well as from cities on the Gulf Coast and East Coast of the United States.

Generally, if your cruise follows an Eastern Caribbean itinerary, you'll likely depart from Miami, Fort Lauderdale, Jacksonville, or Port Canaveral; short three- and four-day cruises to the Bahamas also depart from these ports. Most cruises on Western Caribbean itineraries depart from Tampa, New Orleans, Houston, or Galveston, although some depart from Miami as well. Cruises from farther up the East Coast of the United States, including such ports as Baltimore, Maryland; Charleston, South Carolina; and even New York City, usually go to the Bahamas or sometimes Key West and often include a private-island stop or a stop elsewhere in Florida. Cruises to the Southern Caribbean might depart from Miami if they are 10 days or longer, but more likely they will depart from San Juan, Puerto Rico, or some other port deeper in the Caribbean, often Barbados.

Regardless of which port you depart from, air connections may prevent you from leaving home on the morning of your cruise or going home the day you return to port. You may also wish to arrive early simply to give yourself a bit more peace of mind or to spend more time in one of these interesting port cities. Many people choose to depart from New Orleans or Galveston just to have an excuse to spend a couple of days in the city before or after their cruise.

Port Essentials

Car Rentals

MAJOR AGENCIES Alamo. ☏ *844/354–6962* ⊕ *www.alamo.com.* **Avis.** ☏ *800/230–4898* ⊕ *www.avis.com.* **Budget.** ☏ *800/218–7992* ⊕ *www. budget.com.* **Hertz.** ☏ *800/654–3131* ⊕ *www.hertz.com.* **National Car Rental.** ☏ *844/382–6875* ⊕ *www.nationalcar. com.*

SURCHARGES
To avoid a hefty refueling fee, fill the tank just before you turn in the car, but be aware that gas stations near rental outlets and airports may charge more than those farther away. This is a particular problem in Orlando, but it can be true in other Florida cities. If you plan to do a lot of driving (and if you can get a good price), it can sometimes be a better deal to buy a full tank of gas when you rent, so you can return the car with an empty tank. However, it's never a good deal to pay the huge surcharge for not returning a tank full, unless you simply have no other choice. Other surcharges may apply if you are under 25 or over 75, if you want to add an additional driver to the contract, or if you want to drive over state borders or out of a specific radius from your point

Security

All cruise lines have instituted stricter security procedures in recent years, and you may not be aware of all the changes.

Some are obvious—for example, only visitors who have been authorized well in advance are allowed onboard. Proper identification (government-issued photo ID) is required to board the ship, whether you are a visitor or passenger, and security personnel are stationed at points of entry. All carry-on items are searched by hand in every port (this applies to both crew and passengers).

Some of the changes are more behind-the-scenes. All luggage is scanned, whether you carry it aboard with you or not, for example, and all packages and provisions brought aboard are scanned.

In addition, every ship has added professionally trained security officers and taken many other measures to ensure the safety of passengers. Many cruise-line security personnel are former navy or marine officers with extensive maritime experience. Some cruise lines recruit shipboard security personnel from the ranks of former British Gurkha regiments. From Nepal, the Gurkhas are renowned as soldiers of the highest caliber.

of rental. You'll also pay extra for child seats, which are compulsory for children under 5, and for a GPS navigation system or electronic toll pass. You can sometimes avoid the charge for insurance if you have your own, either from your own policy or from a credit card; but know what you are covered for, and read the fine print before making this decision.

Hotels

Whether you are driving or flying into your port of embarkation, it is often more convenient to arrive the day before or to stay for a day after your cruise. For this reason we offer lodging suggestions near each port of embarkation.

Restaurants

For each port of embarkation, we offer some restaurant suggestions that are convenient to the cruise port and the other hotels we recommend. Unless otherwise noted, the restaurants we recommend accept major credit cards and are open for both lunch and dinner.

HOTEL AND RESTAURANT PRICES
Restaurant prices are based on the median main course price at dinner, excluding gratuity. Hotel prices are for two people in a standard double room in high season, excluding any taxes, service charges, and resort fees.

Baltimore, Maryland

Baltimore's charm lies in its neighborhoods. Although stellar downtown attractions such as the National Aquarium and Camden Yards draw torrents of tourists each year, much of the city's character can be found outside the Inner Harbor. Scores of Baltimore's trademark narrow redbrick row houses with white marble steps line the city's east and west sides. Some neighborhood streets are still made of cobblestone, and grand churches and museums and glassy towering high-rises fill out the growing skyline. Today, the city's blue-collar past mixes with present urban-professional revitalization. Industrial waterfront properties are giving way to high-end condos, and corner bars formerly dominated by National Bohemian beer—once made in the city—are adding microbrews to their beverage lists. And with more and more retail stores replacing old, run-down buildings and parking lots, Baltimore is one of the nation's up-and-coming cities.

ESSENTIALS
HOURS
During the summer tourist season, most of Baltimore's stores and attractions usually open around 9 am and close around 9 pm.

VISITOR INFORMATION
CONTACTS **Baltimore Visitor Center.** ✉ *401 Light St., Inner Harbor* ☎ *877/225–8466* ⊕ *baltimore.org.*

THE CRUISE PORT
Well marked and easily accessible by major highways, the South Locust Point Cruise Terminal is about a mile from center city. Several cruise lines offer seasonal cruises from the port; Grandeur of the Seas is based here year-round. Ships dock near the main cruise building, which itself is little more than a hub for arrivals and departures. There are few facilities for passengers in the immediate port area, which is out of walking distance to Baltimore's attractions.

AIRPORT
CONTACTS **Baltimore–Washington International Thurgood Marshall Airport.** (*BWI*) ✉ *Off Rte. 295 (Baltimore–Washington Pkwy.), 10 miles south of Baltimore, Hanover* ☎ *410/859–7111 airport information* ⊕ *www.bwiairport.com.*

AIRPORT TRANSFERS
During cruise season, taxis are the easiest transportation within the downtown area. They cost about $5 one-way and frequent the port. Taxis to Baltimore–Washington International Airport charge a flat rate of $35; private cars from companies like Carey Limousines can be more expensive. It could be cheaper to take a shared shuttle service, but do price shuttles before booking and understand that they can take extra time. Uber and Lyft also serve Baltimore. The MTA Light Rail is another option, but you'd still need to take a taxi from the light rail station. Rental cars are generally not necessary; if you fly into Baltimore, you can see the majority of Baltimore by taxi. Guided tours of the city range from $20 to $60.

CONTACTS **Airport Taxis.** ☎ *410/859–1100* ⊕ *www.bwiairporttaxi.com.* **BWI SuperShuttle.** ✉ *BWI Airport, Hanover* ☎ *800/258–3826* ⊕ *www.supershuttle.com.* **Carey Limousines.** ☎ *800/336–4646,* ⊕ *www.carey.com.*

PARKING
There's a secure parking lot next to the cruise terminal, where parking costs $15 per day. Drop off your luggage before parking.

CONTACTS **Baltimore Cruise Port Parking.** ⊕ *www.cruise.maryland.gov/content/parking-rates.*

Best Bets ⊙

■ **Camden Yards.** Tour the stadium or, better yet, see an Orioles game if the team is playing while you're in town.

■ **Fort McHenry.** This historic fort is where Francis Scott Key saw the Stars and Stripes flying during the War of 1812 and where he was inspired to write our National Anthem.

■ **The National Aquarium.** This excellent museum is a great destination for all.

Sights ▼

B&O Railroad Museum 5

Fort McHenry National Monument and Historic Shrine . 1

Maryland Science Center . 2

The National Aquarium 4

Oriole Park at Camden Yards .. 6

Port Discovery Children's Museum 3

Restaurants ▼

Azumi 1

Charleston 3

Cinghiale 4

Ouzo Bay 2

Hotels ▼

Four Seasons Baltimore 2

Hilton Baltimore 5

Kimpton Hotel Monaco Baltimore 4

Marriott Baltimore Waterfront 3

Sagamore Pendry Baltimore 1

Baltimore Inner Harbor

KEY

❶ Sights

❶ Restaurants

❶ Hotels

🚩 Tourist Information

Ports of Embarkation BALTIMORE, MARYLAND

Sights

B&O Railroad Museum

MUSEUM | The famous Baltimore & Ohio Railroad was founded on the site that now houses this museum, which contains more than 120 full-size locomotives and a great collection of railroad memorabilia, from dining-car china and artwork to lanterns and signals. The 1884 roundhouse (240 feet in diameter and 120 feet high) contains exhibits and historic objects. It adjoins one of the nation's first railroad stations. Train rides are available Wednesday through Sunday (weekends only in January). TraxSide Snax serves food and drinks. ⊠ *901 W. Pratt St., West Baltimore* ☎ *410/752–2490* ⊕ *www. borail.org* 🎫 *$20, $10 for train rides.*

★ Fort McHenry National Monument and Historic Shrine

MILITARY SITE | This star-shaped brick fort is forever associated with Francis Scott Key and "The Star-Spangled Banner," which Key penned while watching the British bombardment of Baltimore during the War of 1812. Through the next day and night, as the battle raged, Key strained to be sure, through the smoke and haze, that the flag still flew above Fort McHenry—indicating that Baltimore's defenders held firm. "By the dawn's early light" of September 14, 1814, he saw the 30- by 42-foot "Star-Spangled Banner" still aloft and was inspired to pen the words to a poem (set to the tune of an old English drinking song). A visit to the fort includes a 15-minute history film, guided tour, and frequent living-history displays on

Baltimore's National Aquarium is the most popular attraction in the city (and state).

summer weekends. To see how the formidable fortifications might have appeared to the bombarding British, catch a water taxi from the Inner Harbor to the fort instead of driving. ⊠ *E. Fort Ave., Locust Point* ✛ *From Light St., take Key Hwy. for 1½ miles and follow signs* ☎ *410/962–4290* ⊕ *www.nps.gov/fomc* ⊠ *$15.*

★ Maryland Science Center

MUSEUM | FAMILY | Originally known as the Maryland Academy of Sciences, this 200-year-old scientific institution is one of the oldest in the United States. Now housed in a contemporary building, the three floors of exhibits on the Chesapeake Bay, Earth science, physics, the body, dinosaurs, and outer space are an invitation to engage, experiment, and explore. The center has a planetarium, a simulated paleontological dinosaur dig, an IMAX movie theater with a screen five stories high, and a playroom especially designed for young children. ⊠ *601 Light St., Inner Harbor* ☎ *410/685–5225* ⊕ *www.mdsci.org* ⊠ *$25.95.*

★ The National Aquarium

ZOO | The most-visited attraction in Maryland has nearly 20,000 fish, sharks, dolphins, and amphibians dwelling in 2 million gallons of water. The Blacktip Reef exhibit mimics a coral reef in the Indo-Pacific waters, featuring pufferfish, stingrays, and more unusual creatures, such as the tasselled wobbegong, a carpet shark. In the Living Seashore exhibit, visitors can touch live stingrays. The aquarium also features reptiles, birds, plants, and mammals in its rain-forest environment, housed inside a glass pyramid 64 feet high. Atlantic bottlenose dolphins are part of several entertaining presentations that highlight their agility and intelligence. The aquarium's famed shark tank and Atlantic coral reef exhibits are spectacular. Arrive early to ensure admission, which is by timed intervals; by noon, the wait is often two to three hours, especially on weekends and holidays. ⊠ *501 E Pratt St., Pier 3, Inner Harbor* ☎ *410/576–3800* ⊕ *www.aqua.org* ⊠ *$39.95.*

★ Oriole Park at Camden Yards

SPORTS VENUE | FAMILY | Home of the Baltimore Orioles, Camden Yards and the nearby area bustle on game days. Since it opened in 1992, this nostalgically designed baseball stadium has inspired other cities to emulate its neotraditional architecture and amenities. The Eutaw Street promenade, between the warehouse and the field, has a view of the stadium; look for the brass baseballs embedded in the sidewalk that mark where home runs have cleared the fence, or visit the Orioles Hall of Fame display and the monuments to retired Orioles. Daily 90-minute tours take you to nearly every section of the ballpark, from the massive JumboTron scoreboard to the dugout to the state-of-the-art beer-delivery system. ✉ *333 W. Camden St., Downtown* ☎ *410/685–9800 general info, 410/547–6234 tour info, 888/848–2473 tickets to Orioles home games* ⊕ *www. theorioles.com* ✍ *Eutaw St. promenade free, tour $9.*

★ Port Discovery Children's Museum

MUSEUM | FAMILY | At this interactive museum, adults are encouraged to play every bit as much as children. A favorite attraction is the three-story KidWorks, a futuristic jungle gym on which the adventurous can climb, crawl, slide, and swing their way through stairs, slides, ropes, zip lines, and tunnels, and even across a narrow footbridge. Learn about the Earth's atmosphere as you splash around in Wonders of Water (rain slickers and shoes are provided). Cook food in Tiny's Diner, an interactive restaurant. A soccer field becomes a stage for dance-offs and virtual races. Changing exhibits allow for even more play. ✉ *35 Market Pl., Inner Harbor* ☎ *410/727–8120* ⊕ *www.portdiscovery.com* ✍ *$17.95.*

🍴 Restaurants

Baltimore loves crabs. Soft- or hardshell crabs, crab cakes, crab dip—the city's passion for clawed crustaceans seems to have no end. Flag down a Baltimore native and ask them where the best crab joint is, and you'll get a list of options. In addition to crabs and seafood, Baltimore's restaurant landscape also includes Italian, Afghan, Greek, American, Korean, Spanish, and other cuisines. The city's dining choices may not compare with those of New York, or even Washington, but it does have some real standouts. Note that places generally stop serving by 10 pm.

Azumi

$$$ | JAPANESE | In a town known for its local catch, Azumi's chef flies his fish in daily from Tokyo's famous fish market. Creative takes on Maryland specialties are sure to delight, such as the crab starter, made with tiny Sawagani crabs, which are fried whole and pop in your mouth like buttered popcorn. **Known for:** excellent sashimi, including fresh hamachi; extensive list of Japanese whiskeys; beautiful waterfront views in a luxury hotel setting. ⑤ *Average main: $31* ✉ *Four Seasons Hotel Baltimore, 725 Aliceanna St., Harbor East* ☎ *443/220–0477* ⊕ *www.azumirestaurant.com.*

★ Charleston

$$$$ | SOUTHERN | Chef-owner Cindy Wolf's cuisine has a South Carolina Low Country accent with French roots—and the results are unparalleled. Inside the glowingly lit dining room, classics like she-crab soup and shrimp and grits complement more elegant fare, such as a lobster bisque spiced with curry, and wild salmon with avocado. **Known for:** decadent desserts; excellent service; the city's most elegant dining room. ⑤ *Average main: $79* ✉ *1000 Lancaster St., Harbor East* ☎ *410/332–7373* ⊕ *www. charlestonrestaurant.com* ⊗ *Closed Sun.* 🏛 *Jacket and tie.*

Cinghiale

$$ | ITALIAN | The spotlight is on wine at Cinghiale (pronounced *ching-GYAH-lay*), an open, inviting space with tall, wide windows. Enjoy hand-cut pastas such as tagliatelle with tender chicken, greens, and walnuts, or lasagna with veal ragù. **Known for:** northern Italian fare; vast wine list of more than 600 bottles; sharp and unpretentious service. $ *Average main: $22* ✉ *822 Lancaster St., Harbor East* ☎ *410/547–8282* ⊕ *www.cgeno.com* ⊙ *No lunch.*

Ouzo Bay

$$$ | MEDITERRANEAN | Blink, and you may think you're in South Beach: this trendy restaurant has quickly become the city's most popular, where the suit-and-tie crowd sidles up to the elevated bar or takes a seat on the cushy outdoor terrace. Try the grilled octopus starter, tossed with lemon juice and capers, or the charcoal-grilled whole fish, be it wild sea bass, sole, or snapper. **Known for:** laid-back, sexy vibe; Mediterranean-style seafood; grilled lamp chops. $ *Average main: $35* ✉ *1000 Lancaster St., Harbor East* ☎ *443/708–5818* ⊕ *www.ouzobay.com.*

🛏 Hotels

When booking a hotel or bed-and-breakfast in Baltimore, focus on the Inner Harbor, where you're likely to spend a good deal of time. The downside to staying in hotels near the downtown area is the noise level, which can rise early in the morning and stay up late into the night—especially if there's a baseball or football game. For quieter options, head to neighborhoods like Fells Point and Canton.

For expanded reviews, visit Fodors.com.

★ Four Seasons Baltimore

$$$$ | HOTEL | The 18-story glass tower rises above the harbor, commanding prime views from each plush and comfortable (albeit minimalist) guest room. **Pros:** hands down, Baltimore's most luxurious hotel; impeccable service; within walking distance to the Inner Harbor and Fells Point. **Cons:** room rates are steep, even in the off-season; expensive valet parking;

ongoing construction around Harbor East can be noisy. $ *Rooms from: $499* ✉ *200 International Dr., Harbor East* ☎ *410/576–5800* ⊕ *www.fourseasons.com/baltimore* ⇌ *255 rooms* ⊙| *No meals.*

Hilton Baltimore

$ | HOTEL | The towering Hilton has an unparalleled view of Camden Yards and a skywalk that connects to the city's convention center. **Pros:** connected to the convention center; excellent ballpark views; on-site Coffee Bean & Tea Leaf. **Cons:** rooms are considerably smaller than those at similarly priced hotels in town; it's a chain hotel, albeit a nice one; busy convention hotel generates crowds. $ *Rooms from: $194* ✉ *401 W. Pratt St., Inner Harbor* ☎ *443/573–8700* ⊕ *www.hilton.com* ⇌ *757 rooms* ⊙| *No meals.*

Hotel Monaco Baltimore

$ | HOTEL | FAMILY | This boutique hotel is in the historic headquarters of the B&O Railroad—just 2½ blocks from the Inner Harbor and within easy walking distance of Oriole Park at Camden Yards. **Pros:** a posh downtown hotel at family-friendly prices; amenities include rooms with bunk beds, Xbox video-game systems; free bike-share program complete with a map of the best downtown routes. **Cons:** the reception area is on the building's second floor; ongoing construction project across the street (former Mechanic Theater); expensive valet parking. $ *Rooms from: $179* ✉ *2 N. Charles St., Downtown* ☎ *410/692–6170* ⊕ *www.monaco-baltimore.com* ⇌ *202 rooms* ⊙| *No meals.*

Marriott Baltimore Waterfront

$$ | HOTEL | The city's tallest hotel and one of a handful directly on the Inner Harbor, this 31-story Marriott has a neoclassical interior that uses multihued marble, rich jewel-tone walls, and photographs of Baltimore architectural landmarks. **Pros:** nice amenities; great location and view; water taxi stop right out front. **Cons:** pricey compared to nearby hotels in the same category; expensive valet parking;

room renovation still has yet to happen. $ *Rooms from: $239* ✉ *700 Aliceanna St., Harbor East* ☎ *410/385–3000* ⊕ *www.marriott.com* ⤴ *751 rooms* ⊖| *No meals.*

Sagamore Pendry Baltimore

$$$ | **HOTEL** | **FAMILY** | The cornerstone of Fells Point has long been the Rec Pier building, once an immigration hub, then later the setting for the TV series *Homicide: Life on the Street*, and now a 128-room boutique gem that has inspired a neighborhood-wide renaissance. **Pros:** stunning infinity pool overlooking the harbor and Domino Sugar Factory; gorgeous circa-1914 ballroom with original windows and state-of-the-art technology; free Wi-Fi throughout. **Cons:** expensive valet parking; no spa; service can be pretentious. $ *Rooms from: $319* ✉ *1715 Thames St., Fells Point* ☎ *443/552–1400* ⊕ *www.pendryhotels.com* ⤴ *128 rooms* ⊖| *No meals.*

ⓨ Nightlife

Fells Point (just east of the Inner Harbor), Federal Hill (due south), and Canton (due east) have hosts of bars, restaurants, and clubs that draw a rowdy, largely collegiate crowd. If you're seeking quieter surroundings, head for the upscale comforts of downtown or Mount Vernon clubs and watering holes.

BARS AND LOUNGES

The Brewer's Art

BARS/PUBS | Housed in a turn-of-the-century brownstone that belonged to an investment banker, the Brewer's Art has a well-deserved reputation for great beer. At any given time, the on-site brew house produces a half dozen Belgian-style beers—one fine example of which is their Resurrection, an abbey brown ale. Upstairs is an elegant bar and lounge with ornate woodwork, marble pillars, and chandeliers, plus a dining room with terrific food; downstairs, the dimly lit subterranean bar makes a

great spot for sharing secrets. ✉ *1106 N. Charles St., Mount Vernon* ☎ *410/547–6925* ⊕ *www.thebrewersart.com.*

Club Charles

BARS/PUBS | With its stylized art deco surroundings, the funky Club Charles is a favorite hangout for an artsy crowd, moviegoers coming from the Charles Theater across the street, and, reputation has it, John Waters. Above the bar is a large mural of the zodiac, painted in 1941, which was reclaimed from a theater in New York. For a bar, the food is surprisingly good. ✉ *1724 N. Charles St., Station North Arts District* ☎ *410/727–8815* ⊕ *www.clubcharles.us.*

Grand Central

BARS/PUBS | This gay hot spot just might have the best dance floor in Baltimore. It features a fog machine, intelligent lighting, and video screens that can help you get your groove on. Strategically located bars make it easy to secure refreshment. For more relaxed entertainment, the upstairs loft has couches and pool tables. Or, you can view Charles Street's twinkling lights from the second-floor outdoor deck. ✉ *1003 N. Charles St., Mount Vernon* ☎ *410/752–7133* ⊕ *www. grandcentralclub.com.*

Max's Taphouse

BARS/PUBS | The enormous bar at Max's Taphouse is heaven for beer lovers—it boasts an artillery range of taps, with more than 140 draft brews and about 1,200 more in bottles. Think of it as an educational experience, as you'll want to sample a frosty pint you've never heard of before. Max's is located in the center of Fells Point, where tourists mix with locals, who often stop in to catch an Orioles or Ravens game. A tasty menu of bar favorites, such as tater tots served in a bowl with pulled pork, cheese, and sour cream, adds depth to the experience. ✉ *737 S. Broadway, Fells Point* ☎ *410/675–6297.*

3

Ports of Embarkation | **BALTIMORE, MARYLAND**

Of Love and Regret

BARS/PUBS | Once a boarding house for the brewmasters of National Bohemian Brewery, which was located across the street, this is Stillwater Artisanal Ales' tasting room and restaurant. The award-winning craft brews are a far cry from Natty Boh's rather industrial taste. "Gypsy Brewer" Brian Strumke travels the world for inspiration, and the restaurant's seasonally aware menu (try the Bavarian hot pretzels with cheese in the colder months) reflects his latest interests. The decor is unpretentious, from the hand-built draft tower with custom, plain taps, to the poured concrete floor and tables sourced from a 120-year-old barn. ⊠ 1028 S. Conkling St., Baltimore ☎ 410/327–0760 ⊕ olarbmore.com.

The Owl Bar

BARS/PUBS | Not much has changed since this bar opened as a speakeasy in 1910. The signature owl statues flanking the bar served a useful purpose: During Prohibition, owner Colonel Consolvo kept barrels of whiskey in the basement, and if you saw the owls' eyes blinking, you knew it was safe to order a beverage. The thoughtful cocktail list includes an Owl Bar Manhattan and a Belvedere Martini. Belgian and German beers are served on tap, as well as a Heavy Seas Owl Bar lager. The vibe is casual, but the atmosphere, with stately Germanic influences like leaded glass windows, iron chandeliers, and herringbone brickwork, harken to days of finer quality craftsmanship. The kitchen serves comfort foods like crab cakes, pizza, burgers, and salads. It's in the former Belvedere Hotel. ⊠ 1 E. Chase St., Baltimore ☎ 410/347–0888 ⊕ www.theowlbar.com.

🛍 Shopping

Baltimore isn't the biggest shopping town, but it does have some malls and good stores here and there. Hampden (the "p" is silent), a neighborhood west of Johns Hopkins University, has funky shops selling everything from housewares to housedresses along its main drag, 36th Street (better known as "the Avenue"). Upscale boutiques and jewelry stores are located in the fashionable Harbor East district. Some interesting shops can be found along Charles Street in Mount Vernon and along Thames Street in Fells Point. Federal Hill has a few fun shops, particularly for furnishings and vintage items.

Harborplace and the Gallery

SHOPPING CENTERS/MALLS | At the Inner Harbor, the Pratt Street and Light Street pavilions of Harborplace and the Gallery contain almost 200 specialty shops that sell everything from business attire to children's toys. The Gallery has Forever 21, Urban Outfitters, and the Gap, among others. ⊠ 201 E. Pratt St., Baltimore ☎ 410/332–4191 ⊕ www.harborplace.com.

Charleston, South Carolina

Charleston looks like a movie set, an 18th-century etching brought to life. The spires and steeples of more than 180 churches punctuate her low skyline, and tourists ride in horse-drawn carriages that pass grandiose, centuries-old mansions and gardens brimming with heirloom plants. Preserved through the poverty following the Civil War and natural disasters like fires, earthquakes, and hurricanes, much of Charleston's earliest public and private architecture still stands. And thanks to a rigorous preservation movement and strict Board of Architectural Review, the city's new structures blend with the old ones. If you're boarding your cruise ship here, it's worth coming a few days early to explore the historic downtown and to eat in one of the many superb restaurants. In late spring, plan in advance for the Spoleto Festival USA. For more than 30 memorable years, arts patrons have gathered to enjoy the international dance, opera, theater, and other performances at venues citywide. Piccolo Spoleto showcases local and regional concerts, dance, theater, and comedy improv.

ESSENTIALS
HOURS
Most shops are open from 9 or 10 am to at least 6 pm, but some are open later. A new city ordinance requires bars to close by 2 am.

VISITOR INFORMATION
CONTACTS Charleston Visitor Center. ✉ *375 Meeting St., Upper King* ☎ *800/774–0006* ⊕ *www.charlestoncvb.com.*

THE CRUISE PORT
Cruise ships sailing from Charleston depart from the Union Pier Terminal, which is in Charleston's historic district. If you are driving, however, and need to leave your car for the duration of your cruise, take the East Bay Street exit off the majestic new Ravenel Bridge on I–17 and follow the "Cruise Ship" signs. On ship embarkation days police officers will direct you to the ship terminal from the intersection of East Bay and Chapel Streets. Cruise parking is located adjacent to Union Pier.

CONTACTS Port of Charleston. ✉ *Union Pier, 280 Concord St., Market* ☎ *843/958–8298 for cruise info* ⊕ *www.port-of-charleston.com.*

AIRPORT
CONTACTS Charleston International Airport (CHS). ✉ *5500 International Blvd., North Charleston* ☎ *843/767–7000* ⊕ *www.iflychs.com.*

AIRPORT TRANSFERS
Several cab companies service the airport; expect to pay between $25 and $35 for a trip downtown. Airport Ground Transportation arranges shuttles, which cost $12 to $15 per person to the downtown area, double for a return trip to the airport. CARTA's Bus No. 11, a

Best Bets

■ **Viewing Art.** The city is home to some 120 galleries, exhibiting art from Charleston, the South, and around the world. The Gibbes Museum of Art and a half dozen other museums add to the cultural mix.

■ **The Battery.** The views from the point, both natural and man-made, are the loveliest in the city. Look west to see the harbor; spot elegant Charleston mansions to the east.

■ **Historic Homes.** Charleston's preserved centuries-old stately homes, including the Nathaniel Russell House, are highlights.

public bus, now goes to the airport for a mere $3; it leaves downtown from the Meeting/Mary St. parking garage every 50 minutes, from 10 am until 10:30 pm, and makes a continuous loop around the airport.

CONTACTS Charleston International Airport Ground Transportation. ✉ *5500 International Blvd., North Charleston* ☎ *843/767–7000* ⊕ *www.chs-airport.com.*

PARKING
Parking costs $17 per day for regular vehicles, $50 per day for RVs or other vehicles more than 20 feet long. A free shuttle bus takes you to the cruise-passenger terminal. Be sure to drop your large luggage off at Union Pier before you park your car; only carry-on size luggage is allowed on the shuttle bus, so if you have any bags larger than 22 inches by 14 inches, they will have to be checked before you park. Also, you'll need your cruise tickets to board the shuttle bus.

👁 Sights

The heart of the city is on a peninsula, sometimes just called "downtown" by the nearly 60,000 residents who populate the area. Walking Charleston's peninsula is the best way to get to know the city. The main historic district is roughly bounded by Lockwood Boulevard to the west, Calhoun Street to the north, the Cooper River to the east, and the Battery to the south. Nearly 2,000 historic homes and buildings occupy this fairly compact area divided into South of Broad (Street) and North of Broad. King Street, the main shopping street in town, cuts through Broad Street, and the most trafficked tourist area ends a few blocks south of the Crosstown, where U.S. 17 cuts across Upper King. If you don't wish to walk, there are bikes, pedicabs, and trolleys. Street parking is irksome, as meter readers are among the city's most efficient public servants. Parking garages, both privately and publicly owned, charge around $1.50 an hour.

Charleston Museum

MUSEUM | FAMILY | Although housed in a modern-day brick complex, this institution was founded in 1773 and is the country's oldest museum. The collection is especially strong in South Carolina decorative arts, from silver to snuffboxes. There's also a large gallery devoted to natural history (don't miss the giant polar bear). Children love the permanent Civil War exhibition and the interactive "Kidstory" area, where they can try on reproduction clothing in a miniature historic house. The Historic Textiles Gallery features rotating displays that showcase everything from uniforms and flags to couture gowns, antique quilts, and needlework. Combination tickets that include the Joseph Manigault House and the Heyward-Washington House are a bargain at $28. ✉ 360 Meeting St., Upper King ☎ 843/722–2996 ⊕ www. charlestonmuseum.org 💲 $12; combination ticket with Heyward-Washington

House or Joseph Manigault House $18, combination ticket for all 3 sites $28.

Charleston Visitor Center

BUILDING | Exhibits about Lowcountry culture and a 36-minute film called Forever Charleston make a fine introduction to the city. ■ TIP→ The first 30 minutes are free at the center's parking lot, making it a real bargain. ✉ 375 Meeting St., Upper King ☎ 800/774–0006 ⊕ www.charleston-cvb.com 💲 Free.

Edmondston-Alston House

HISTORIC SITE | In 1825, Charles Edmondston built this house in the Federal style on Charleston's High Battery. About 13 years later, second owner Charles Alston began transforming it into the Greek revival structure seen today. The home is furnished with family antiques, portraits, silver, and fine china. ✉ 21 E. Battery, South of Broad ☎ 843/722–7171 ⊕ www. edmondstonalston.com 💲 $12.

★ Fort Sumter National Monument

ARCHAEOLOGICAL SITE | FAMILY | Set on a man-made island in Charleston's harbor, this is the hallowed spot where the Civil War began. On April 12, 1861, the first shot of the war was fired at the fort from Fort Johnson across the way. After a 34-hour battle, Union forces surrendered and Confederate troops occupied Fort Sumter, which became a symbol of Southern resistance. The Confederacy managed to hold it, despite almost continual bombardment, from August 1863 to February 1865. When it was finally evacuated, the fort was a heap of rubble. Today, the National Park Service oversees it, and rangers give interpretive talks. To reach the fort, take a private boat or one of the ferries that depart from Patriots Point in Mount Pleasant and downtown's Fort Sumter Visitor Education Center, which includes exhibitions on the antebellum period and the Civil War. There are seven trips daily to the fort between mid-March and mid-August, fewer the rest of the year. ✉ Charleston ☎ 843/883–3123 ⊕ www. nps.gov/fosu 💲 Fort free, ferry $23.

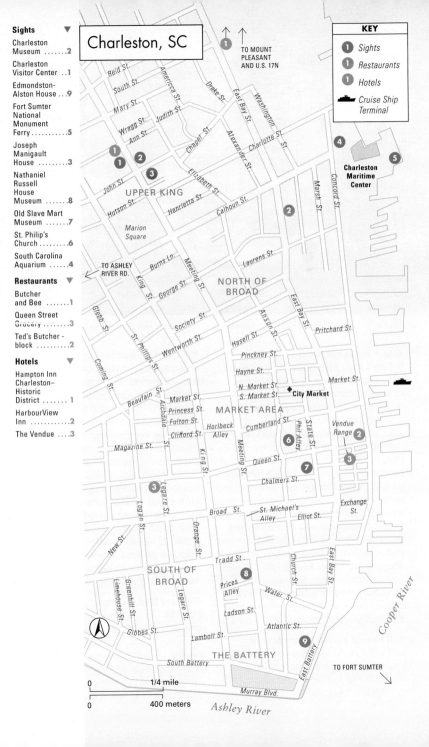

The Nathaniel Russell House Museum preserves one of Charleston's best 19th-century Federal-style homes.

Joseph Manigault House

HISTORIC SITE | An extraordinary example of Federal architecture, this 1803 residence and National Historic Landmark reflects the urban lifestyle of a well-to-do rice-planting family and the Africans they enslaved. Engaging guided tours reveal a stunning spiral staircase, rooms that have been preserved in period style, and American, English, and French furniture from the early 19th century. Outside, stroll through the artfully maintained period garden; unfortunately, most of the historic out buildings were torn down long ago, now replaced with interpretive signs that note their former locations. ⊠ *350 Meeting St., Upper King* ☎ *843/723–2926* ⊕ *www.charlestonmuseum.org* ✎ *$12; combination ticket with Heyward-Washington House or Charleston Museum $18, combination ticket for all 3 sites $28.*

★ Nathaniel Russell House Museum

HISTORIC SITE | One of the nation's finest examples of Federal-style architecture, the Nathaniel Russell House was built in 1808 and has been restored to a 19th-century aesthetic. Its grand beauty is proof of the immense wealth Russell accumulated as one of the city's leading merchants. In addition to the famous "free-flying" staircase that spirals up three stories with no visible support, the ornate interior is distinguished by Charleston-made furniture as well as paintings and works on paper by well-known American and European artists, including Henry Benbridge, Samuel F. B. Morse, and George Romney. The extensive formal garden is worth a leisurely stroll. ⊠ *51 Meeting St., South of Broad* ☎ *843/724–8481* ⊕ *www.historiccharleston.org/house-museums* ✎ *$12, combination ticket with Aiken-Rhett House Museum $18.*

Old Slave Mart Museum

BUILDING | This is thought to be the state's only extant building that was used for slave auctioning, a practice that ended here in 1863. It was once part of a complex called Ryan's Mart, which also contained a slave jail, kitchen, and morgue. The structure is now a museum that shares the history of Charleston's role in the slave trade, a horrific part of the city's history, but one that is important to understand. Charleston was a commercial center for the South's plantation economy, and slaves were the primary source of labor both within the city as well as on the surrounding plantations. Galleries are outfitted with interactive exhibits, including push buttons that allow you to hear voices relating stories from the age of slavery. The museum sits on one of the few remaining cobblestone streets in town. ⊠ *6 Chalmers St., Market* ☎ *843/958–6467* ⊕ *www.charleston-sc.gov* ⊿ *$8* ⊘ *Closed Sun.*

St. Philip's Church

CEMETERY | Founded around 1680, St. Philip's didn't move to its current site until the 1720s, becoming one of the three churches that gave Church Street its name. The first building in this location (where George Washington worshipped in 1791) burned down in 1835 and was replaced with the Corinthian-style structure seen today. A shell that exploded in the churchyard while services were being held during the Civil War didn't deter the minister from finishing his sermon (the congregation gathered elsewhere for the remainder of the war). Amble through the churchyards, where notable South Carolinians such as John C. Calhoun are buried. If you want to tour the church, call ahead, as hours depend upon volunteer availability. ⊠ *142 Church St., Market* ☎ *843/722–7734* ⊕ *www. stphilipschurchsc.org.*

★ South Carolina Aquarium

ZOO | FAMILY | Get up close and personal with more than 5,000 creatures at this waterfront attraction, where exhibits invite you to journey through distinctive habitats. Step into the Mountain Forest and find water splashing over a rocky gorge as river otters play. Enter the open-air Saltmarsh Aviary to feed stingrays and view herons, diamondback terrapins, and puffer fish; gaze in awe at the two-story,

385,000-gallon Great Ocean Tank, home to sharks, jellyfish, and a loggerhead sea turtle. Kids love the touch tank, and the newly expanded *Sea Turtle Recovery* exhibition makes the celebrated sea turtle rehabilitation hospital accessible to all visitors. ⊠ *100 Aquarium Wharf, Ansonborough* ☎ *800/722–6455, 843/577–3474* ⊕ *www.scaquarium.org* ⊿ *$30.*

🍴 Restaurants

★ Butcher and Bee

$ | **MODERN AMERICAN** | Healthy and light but always satisfying, this local favorite has grown into new digs and expanded its lunch and dinner menus. The seasonal menu features creative salads, craft sandwiches, rice bowls, and a scrumptious breakfast menu that leaves patrons wanting to stick around for lunch. **Known for:** locally sourced, seasonal ingredients used in eclectic ways; drool-worthy sandwiches; big patio for outside dining. ⑤ *Average main: $12* ⊠ *1085 Morrison Dr., North Morrison* ☎ *843/619–0202* ⊕ *www.butcherandbee.com.*

Queen Street Grocery

$ | **FRENCH FUSION** | For crepes, breakfast sandwiches, and cold brew, locals turn to this venerable Charleston institution. Built in 1922, the corner building has served many purposes throughout the years: butcher shop, candy shop, and late-night convenience store, and now stays true to its roots as a neighborhood grocery store with much of its produce and other goods sourced locally. **Known for:** mouthwatering sweet and savory crepes; grab-and-go picnic items (including wine); dependable, old-school corner store. ⑤ *Average main: $10* ⊠ *133 Queen St., Broad Street* ☎ *843/723–4121* ⊕ *www.queenstreetgrocerycafe.com.*

★ Ted's Butcherblock

$ | **CAFÉ** | Land at Ted's on some lucky afternoon for a memorable greeting: the scent of smoked meat wafting from a grill perched near the entrance. Ted's operates as a one-stop butcher shop, supplying beef, game, seafood, and homemade sausages to complement its selection of artisanal cheeses, wine, and other specialty foods. **Known for:** Ultimate Burger Saturday, cooked on the Big Green Egg; Friday night dinner with wine pairing; daily sandwiches with memorable flavors. ⑤ *Average main: $10* ⊠ *334 E. Bay St., Ansonborough* ☎ *843/577–0094* ⊕ *www.tedsbutcherblock.com* ⊙ *Closed Sun.–Mon.*

🛏 Hotels

Hampton Inn Charleston–Historic District
$$ | HOTEL | Hardwood floors, a central fireplace, and leather furnishings in the lobby of what was once an 1860s railroad warehouse help elevate this chain hotel. **Pros:** hot breakfast; located near numerous restaurant and nightlife options; pleasant outdoor swimming pool area. **Cons:** lacks the charm of independent competitors; rooms are on the small side; no parking on-site (you have to use and pay for a city garage). ⑤ *Rooms from: $199* ⊠ *345 Meeting St., Upper King* ☎ *843/723–4000* ⊕ *www.hamptoninn.com* ⇄ *170 rooms* ¶◎¶ *Free Breakfast.*

HarbourView Inn
$$$$ | HOTEL | If you ask for a room with a view or even a private balcony here, you can gaze out on Charleston Harbor and on to the fountain at the center of Waterfront Park. **Pros:** continental breakfast can be delivered to your room or the rooftop; attractive rooftop terrace with soaring views; live music three nights a week, plus weekly beer and wine tastings. **Cons:** chain hotel feel in some parts; not as new and exciting as similarly priced options. ⑤ *Rooms from: $279* ⊠ *2 Vendue Range, Market* ☎ *843/853–8439* ⊕ *www.harbourviewcharleston.com* ⇄ *52 rooms* ¶◎¶ *Free Breakfast.*

★ The Vendue
$$ | B&B/INN | Thanks to its gorgeous art-filled space, the Vendue feels as much like a contemporary art museum as it does a boutique hotel. **Pros:** free bike rentals; soundproofing masks street noise; terrific on-site restaurant. **Cons:** no complimentary breakfast; some halls and spaces are small as in centuries past. ⑤ *Rooms from: $179* ⊠ *19 Vendue Range, Market* ☎ *843/577–7970* ⊕ *www. thevendue.com* ⇄ *84 rooms* ¶◎¶ *No meals.*

ⓨ Nightlife

The Cocktail Club
BARS/PUBS | This establishment characterizes the craft cocktail movement with its "farm-to-shaker" seasonal selection of creative concoctions. The bar showcases exposed brick walls and wooden beams inside its lounge areas, though warm evenings are best spent outside on the rooftop patio. Inside, some of Charleston's best bartenders muddle and shake clever mixtures like the Dad Bod (demerara rum, rye whiskey, Falernum, grenadine, and lime) and the Double Standard (a blend of serrano pepper–infused gin and cucumber vodka). ⊠ *479 King St., Suite 200, Upper King* ☎ *843/724–9411* ⊕ *www.thecocktailclubcharleston.com.*

The Griffon
BARS/PUBS | Dollar bills cover just about every square inch of the Griffon, helping the bar achieve nearly legendary status around the city. Its wood interior is dark, dusty, and well worn, yet charming. A rotating selection of draft beers comes from local breweries like Westbrook, Coast, and Holy City. It's a popular lunchtime and happy hour watering hole and hosts live music on weekend nights. ⊠ *18 Vendue Range, Market* ☎ *843/723–1700* ⊕ *www.griffoncharleston.com.*

🛍 Shopping

Charleston City Market
SHOPPING NEIGHBORHOODS | FAMILY | This cluster of shops, covered stands, and

restaurants fills Market Street between Meeting and East Bay Streets. Sweetgrass basket weavers work here amid trinket and souvenir booths, T-shirt shops, and upscale clothing boutiques. In the covered market, vendors have stalls selling everything from jewelry to purses to paintings of Rainbow Row. The middle section of the market is enclosed and air-conditioned. From April through December, there's a night market on Friday and Saturday from 6:30 until 10:30 pm, featuring local craftspeople and street musicians. ⊠ *E. Bay and Market Sts., Market* ⊕ *www.thecharlestoncitymarket.com.*

King Street

SHOPPING NEIGHBORHOODS | The city's main shopping strip is divided into informal districts: Lower King (from Broad Street to Market Street) is the Antiques District, lined with high-end dealers; Middle King (from Market to Calhoun Street) is the Fashion District, with a mix of national chains like Anthropologie and Pottery Barn and locally owned boutiques; and Upper King (from Calhoun to Spring Street) has been dubbed the Design District, known for both its restaurant scene and clothing and interior-design stores. Check out Second Sundays on King, when the street closes to cars all afternoon from Calhoun Street to Queen Street. Make sure to visit the Saturday farmers' market in Marion Square throughout the spring and summer months. ⊠ *Charleston.*

Fort Lauderdale, Florida

Collegians of the 1960s returning to Fort Lauderdale would be hard-pressed to recognize the onetime "Sun and Suds Spring Break Capital of the Universe" of the "Where the Boys Are" era. Today the beach is home to upscale shops, restaurants, and luxury resorts, while the downtown area has exploded with new office and luxury residential developments. The

Best Bets

- **The Beach.** With more than 20 miles of ocean shoreline, the scene at Greater Fort Lauderdale's best beaches, especially between Bahia Mar and Sunrise Boulevard, is not to be missed.

- **The Everglades.** Take in the wild reaches in or near the Everglades with an airboat ride. Mosquitoes are friendly, so arm yourself accordingly.

- **Las Olas Boulevard and the Riverwalk.** This is a great place to stroll before and after performances, dinner, libations, and other entertainment.

entertainment and shopping areas—Las Olas Boulevard, Riverfront, and Himmarshee Village—are thriving. And Port Everglades is giving Miami a run for its money in passenger cruising, with a dozen cruise-ship terminals, including the world's largest, hosting 34 cruise ships with some 3,000 departures annually. A captivating shoreline with wide ribbons of sand for beachcombing and sunbathing makes Fort Lauderdale and Broward County a major draw for visitors, and often tempts cruise-ship passengers to spend an extra day or two in the sun. Fort Lauderdale's 2-mile stretch of unobstructed beachfront has been further enhanced with a sparkling promenade designed more for the pleasure of pedestrians than vehicles.

ESSENTIALS
HOURS
Many museums close on Monday.

BOAT TOURS
A water taxi provides service along the intracoastal waterway in Fort Lauderdale between the 17th Street Causeway and Oakland Park Boulevard, and west into

downtown along New River and south to Hollywood, daily from 9 am until 11 pm. A day pass costs $28.

CONTACTS Water Taxi. ☎ *954/467–6677* ⊕ *watertaxi.com.*

VISITOR INFORMATION
CONTACTS Greater Fort Lauderdale Convention and Visitors Bureau. (*Hello Sunny*) ✉ *101 N.E. 3rd Ave., Suite 100, Fort Lauderdale* ☎ *954/765–4466* ⊕ *www. sunny.org.*

THE CRUISE PORT
Port Everglades, Fort Lauderdale's cruise port (nowhere near the Everglades, but happily near the beach and less than 2 miles [3 km] from the airport), is among the world's largest, busiest ports. It's also the straightest, deepest port in the southeastern United States, meaning you'll be out to sea in no time flat once your ship sets sail. In 2009, Cruise Terminal 18 was tripled in size to accommodate Royal Caribbean's Oasis-class ships, the 5,400-passenger *Oasis of the Seas* and sister *Allure of the Seas,* both of which relocated to Port Canaveral in 2016. This made room for the latest incarnation of the world's largest cruise ship, *Harmony of the Seas,* which debuted in November 2016. The terminal's mega size (240,000 square feet) accommodates the processing of arriving and departing passengers and their luggage simultaneously. The port is south of downtown Fort Lauderdale, spread out over a huge area extending into Dania Beach, Hollywood, and a patch of unincorporated Broward County. A few words of caution: Schedule plenty of time to navigate the short distance from the airport, your hotel, or wherever else you might be staying, especially if you like to be among the first to embark for your sailing. Increased security (sometimes you'll be asked for a driver's license and/or other identification—and occasionally for boarding documentation—upon entering the port, other times not) combined with increased traffic, larger parking facilities,

construction projects, roadway improvements, and other obstacles mean the old days of popping over to Port Everglades and running up a gangplank in the blink of an eye are history.

If you are driving, there are three entrances to the port. One is from 17th Street, west of the 17th Street Causeway Bridge, turning south at the traffic light onto Eisenhower Boulevard. Alternatively, to get to the main entrance, take the east–west State Road 84 to the intersection of Federal Highway (U.S. 1) and cross into the port. Or take I–595 east straight into the Port (I–595 becomes Eller Drive once inside the Port). I–595 runs east–west with connections to the Fort Lauderdale–Hollywood International Airport, Federal Highway (U.S. 1), I–95, State Road 7 (U.S. 441), Florida's Turnpike, Sawgrass Expressway, and I–75.

CONTACTS Port Everglades. ✉ *1850 Eller Dr., Fort Lauderdale* ☎ *954/523–3404* ⊕ *www.porteverglades.net/cruising/.*

AIRPORT
CONTACTS Fort Lauderdale–Hollywood International Airport. (*FLL*) ☎ *866/435–9355* ⊕ *www.broward.org.*

AIRPORT TRANSFERS
Fort Lauderdale–Hollywood International Airport is 4 miles (6 km) south of downtown and 2 miles (3 km, about 5 to 10 minutes) from the docks. If you haven't arranged an airport transfer with your cruise line, you can take an Uber or old-fashioned taxi to the cruise-ship terminals. The ride in a metered taxi costs about $17, depending on your departure terminal. Taxi fares for up to five passengers, regulated by the county, are $2.50 for the first 1/6 mile and $0.40 for each additional 1/6 mile, $0.40 per minute for waiting time, plus a $3 surcharge for cabs departing from the airport. Yellow Cab has a major presence, and Go Airport Shuttle provides limousine or shared-ride service to and from Port Everglades to all parts of Broward

County; fares to most Fort Lauderdale beach hotels are in the $25–$30 range.

CONTACTS Fort Lauderdale Shuttle.
☎ *954/525–7796, 866/ 386–7433* ⊕ *fort-lauderdaleshuttle.com.* **Go Airport Shuttle.** ☎ *954/561–8888, 800/244–8252* ⊕ *go-air-portshuttle.com.* **Yellow Cab Broward.** ☎ *954/777–7777* ⊕ *www.yellowcabbro-ward.com.*

PARKING
Two covered parking facilities close to the terminals are Northport (2,500 spaces) and Midport (2,000 spaces). Use the Northport garage if your cruise leaves from Terminal 1 or 2; use Midport if your cruise leaves from Terminal 19, 21, 22/24, 25, 26, 27, or 29. The Midport Surface Lot at Terminal 18 has its own 600 spaces and the Northport Surface Lot has 172 spaces for passengers leaving from Terminal 4. The cost is $15 per day for either garage or surface lot ($19 for oversize vehicles up to 20 feet); you pay by cash or credit card when you leave. To save a few bucks on your parking tab, two separate companies, Park 'N Fly ($12 per day) and Park 'N Go ($12 per day) provide remote parking just outside Port Everglades, at the exit off I–595, with shuttles to all cruise terminals. Book ahead online for even deeper discounts.

CONTACTS Park 'N Fly. ⊠ *2200 N.E. 7th Ave., at Port Everglades exit off I–595, Dania Beach* ☎ *954/779–1776* ⊕ *www.pnf.com.* **Park 'N Go.** ⊠ *1101 Eller Dr., at Port Everglades exit off I–595, Fort Lauderdale* ☎ *954/760–4525, 888/764–7275* ⊕ *www.bookparkngo.com.*

◉ Sights
Like its southeast Florida neighbors, Fort Lauderdale has been busily revitalizing for several years. In a state where gaudy tourist zones often stand aloof from workaday downtowns, Fort Lauderdale is unusual in that the city exhibits consistency at both ends of the 2-mile (3-km) Las Olas corridor. The sparkling look results from efforts to thoroughly improve both beachfront and downtown. Matching the downtown's innovative arts district, cafés, and boutiques is an equally inventive beach area with its own share of cafés and shops facing an undeveloped shoreline.

Billie Swamp Safari
NATURE PRESERVE | FAMILY | Four different ecosystems in the "River of Grass" are preserved by the Seminole Tribe of Florida, and Billie Swamp Safari's daily tours can introduce you to the elusive wildlife that resides in each area—by airboat or swamp buggy. Sightings of deer, turtles, raccoons, wild hogs, hawks, eagles, and alligators are likely but certainly not guaranteed. Animal exhibits, a petting zoo, and snake/critter shows provide a solid contingency plan. For the rugged adventurer, overnight camping in a native-style chickee hut (thatched-roof dwelling) is available. If a sleepover is too much, Twilight Expeditions offers a campfire with storytelling followed by a nighttime tour. Head to the Swamp Water Café to try Native American dishes like Seminole Indian Fry Bread with honey, Indian Tacos, and bison burgers. Check the website for showtimes and tour schedules. ⊠ *30000 Gator Tail Trail, Clewiston* ☎ *863/983–6101* ⊕ *www.billieswamp.com* ⊡ *Swamp Safari Day Package $50, Twilight Swamp Expedition $43.*

★ Bonnet House Museum and Gardens
BUILDING | FAMILY | This 35-acre subtropical estate endures as a tribute to Old South Florida. Prior to its "modern" history, the grounds had already seen 4,000 years of activity when settler Hugh Taylor Birch purchased the site in 1895. Birch gave it to his daughter Helen as a wedding gift when she married Frederic Bartlett, and the newlyweds built a charming home for a winter residence in 1920. Years after Helen died, Frederic married his second wife, Evelyn, and the artistically gifted couple embarked on a mission to embellish the property with

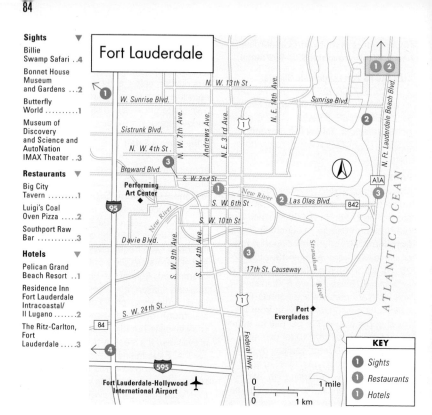

KEY

① Sights

① Restaurants

① Hotels

personal touches and surprises that are still evident today. This historic place is a must-see for its architecture, artwork, and horticulture. While admiring the fabulous gardens, look out for playful monkeys swinging from the trees. ⊠ *Bonnet House Museum and Gardens, 900 N. Birch Rd., Beachfront* ☎ *954/563–5393* ⊕ *www.bonnethouse.org* 🖼 *$20 house tour, $10 gardens only; $4 tram tour* ☉ *Closed Mon.*

★ Butterfly World

GARDEN | FAMILY | More than 80 native and international butterfly species live inside the first butterfly house in the U.S. and the largest in the world. The 3-acre site inside Coconut Creek's Tradewinds Park has aviaries, observation decks, waterfalls, ponds, and tunnels. There are lots of birds, too: kids love the lorikeet aviary, where birds alight on every limb.

⊠ *Butterfly World, 3600 W. Sample Rd., Coconut Creek* ☎ *954/977–4400* ⊕ *www.butterflyworld.com* 🖼 *$29.95* ☞ *Tradewinds Park gate fee $1.50 per person on weekends and holidays.*

Museum of Discovery and Science and AutoNation IMAX Theater

COLLEGE | FAMILY | There are dozens of interactive exhibits here to entertain children—and adults—through the wonders of science and Florida's delicate ecosystem. The state-of-the-art 7-D theater takes guests on a virtual tour of aviation technology, while the Ecodiscovery Center comes with an Everglades Airboat Adventure ride, resident otters, and an interactive Florida storm center. The 300-seat AutoNation IMAX theater is part of the complex and shows mainstream and educational films, some in 3-D, on the biggest screen in South Florida with a rare high-tech laser projection system. ⊠ *401 S.W. 2nd St., Downtown* ☎ *954/467–6637 Museum, 954/463–4629 IMAX* ⊕ *mods.org* 🏷 *Museum $19, IMAX tickets from $9.*

🔱 Beaches

Fort Lauderdale's beachfront offers the best of all possible worlds, with easy access not only to a wide band of beige sand but also to restaurants and shops. There are more than 20 miles of sparkling beaches, but the most popular stretch is 2 miles (3 km) south of Sunrise Boulevard along State Road A1A. Here you'll have clear views of the sea—typically across rows of colorful beach umbrellas—and of ships passing into and out of nearby Port Everglades. If you're on the beach, gaze back on the exceptionally graceful promenade.

Pedestrians rank above vehicles in Fort Lauderdale. Broad walkways line both sides of the beach road, and traffic has been trimmed to two gently curving northbound lanes, where in-line skaters skim past slow-moving cars. On the beach side, a low masonry wall doubles as an extended bench, separating sand from the promenade. At night the wall is accented with ribbons of fiber-optic color. The most crowded portion of beach is between Las Olas and Sunrise boulevards. The tackier aspects of this onetime strip—famous for the springtime madness spawned by the film *Where the Boys Are*—are now but a fading memory, with the possible exception of the iconic Elbo Room, an ever-popular bar at the corner of Las Olas and A1A.

North of the redesigned beachfront are another 2 miles (3 km) of open and natural coastal landscape. Much of the way parallels the Hugh Taylor Birch State Park, preserving a patch of primeval Florida.

Ship Names ⊙

Even as far back as ancient times, mariners have traditionally referred to their ships as "she." To a seaman, a ship is as beautiful and comforting as his mother or sweetheart. You could say a good ship holds a special place in his heart.

🍴 Restaurants

★ Big City Tavern
$$$ | MODERN AMERICAN | FAMILY | A must-visit Las Olas landmark, Big City Tavern mingles Asian entrées like shrimp pad Thai with Italian four-cheese ravioli and an American grilled-chicken Cobb salad. The crispy flatbread changes every day. **Known for:** eclectic menu; weekend brunch; fun bar scene. 💲 *Average main: $26* ⊠ *609 E. Las Olas Blvd., Downtown* ☎ *954/727–0307* ⊕ *www.bigcitylasolas.com.*

★ Luigi's Coal Oven Pizza
$$ | PIZZA | FAMILY | One of the best little pizza joints in South Florida, Luigi's Coal Oven Pizza has the full gamut of pizzas, phenomenal salads with fresh dressings, classics like eggplant parmigiana, and oven-baked chicken wings. For the Margherita Napoletana, the quality and flavors of the crust, cheese, and sauce are the result of Luigi's century-old recipe from Naples. **Known for:** traditional Neopolitan-style pizza; intimate dining room; coal-fired oven. 💲 *Average main: $19* ⊠ *1415 E. Las Olas Blvd., Downtown* ☎ *954/522–8888* ⊕ *www.luigiscoaloven-pizza.com.*

Southport Raw Bar
$$ | SEAFOOD | You can't go wrong at this unpretentious dive, where seafood reigns. Feast on raw or steamed clams, raw oysters, and peel-and-eat shrimp. **Known for:** affordable prices; fresh seafood; open late on weekends. 💲 *Average*

Did You Know?

More than 165 miles of canals and waterways earned Fort Lauderdale the nickname "the Venice of America."

main: $19 ✉ 1536 Cordova Rd., Intra-
coastal and Inland ☎ 954/525–2526
⊕ www.southportrawbar.com.

🛏 Hotels

Fort Lauderdale has a growing and varied
roster of accommodations, from beachfront luxury suites to intimate B&Bs to
chain hotels along the Intracoastal Waterway. If you want to be on the beach,
be sure to mention this when booking
your room, since many hotels advertise
"waterfront" lodging that is actually on
inland waterways, not the beach.

Pelican Grand Beach Resort
$$$ | RESORT | FAMILY | This bright yellow
Key West–style Noble House property
fuses a heritage seaside charm with
understated luxury. **Pros:** incredible spa;
directly on the beach; romantic restau-
rant. **Cons:** small fitness center; dated
room decor; small property. ⑤ *Rooms
from: $350 ✉ 2000 N. Ocean Blvd.,
Beachfront ☎ 954/568–9431 ⊕ www.
pelicanbeach.com ⤳ 159 rooms* ⑩ *No
meals.*

Residence Inn Fort Lauderdale Intracoastal/ Il Lugano
$ | HOTEL | This clean, modern hotel has
studios and suites with fully equipped
kitchens, private balconies with intra-
coastal views, plus amenities including
a pool and fitness center. **Pros:** docking
is available to guests; pet-friendly; bike
rentals available. **Cons:** lacks character
of other properties; "business traveler"
vibes; not on the beach. ⑤ *Rooms from:
$154 ✉ 3333 N.E. 32nd Ave., Intracoastal
and Inland ☎ 954/564–4400 ⊕ www.
marriott.com ⤳ 105 rooms* ⑩ *Free
Breakfast.*

★ The Ritz-Carlton, Fort Lauderdale
$$$$ | HOTEL | Twenty-four dramatically
tiered, glass-walled stories rise from
the sea, forming a resort that's helping
to revive a golden age of luxury travel.
Pros: prime beach location; exceptional
service; organic spa treatments. **Cons:**

expensive valet parking; cancel at least
14 days in advance or get hit with a
two-night penalty; extra-busy poolscape.
⑤ *Rooms from: $750 ✉ 1 N. Fort Lauder-
dale Beach Blvd., Beachfront ☎ 954/465–
2300 ⊕ www.ritzcarlton.com/FortLauder-
dale ⤳ 192 rooms* ⑩ *No meals.*

🍸 Nightlife

★ Seminole Hard Rock Hotel & Casino
CAFES—NIGHTLIFE | Seminole Hard Rock
Hotel & Casino is a Vegas-inspired
gaming and entertainment complex in
a fairly forlorn area of Hollywood. Once
inside the Hard Rock fortress, you'll feel
the excitement immediately. In addi-
tion to the AAA Four Diamond hotel,
there's a monster casino, a 5,500-seat
performance venue (Hard Rock Live),
plus dozens of restaurants, bars, and
nightclubs. ■TIP➔ **The Seminole Hard
Rock Hotel & Casino is not to be confused
with its neighbor, the Seminole Classic
Casino.** ✉ *1 Seminole Way, Hollywood
☎ 866/502–7529 ⊕ www.seminole-
hardrockhollywood.com.*

Stache, 1920's Drinking Den + Coffee Bar
BARS/PUBS | Inspired by the Roaring
Twenties, this speakeasy-style drinking
den and nightclub infuses party-hard
downtown Fort Lauderdale with some
class and pizzazz. Expect awesome craft
cocktails, inclusive of bespoke ice cubes
for old-school drinks like Manhattans
and Sidecars. Late night on Friday and
Saturday, anticipate great music and a
fun crowd. The 5,000-square-foot bar
opens at 7 am on the weekdays to serve
coffee. ✉ *109 S.W. 2nd Ave., Downtown
☎ 954/449–1025 ⊕ stacheftl.com.*

🛍 Shopping

The Galleria at Fort Lauderdale
SHOPPING CENTERS/MALLS | FAMILY | Fort
Lauderdale's most sophisticated mall is
just west of the Intracoastal Waterway.
The split-level emporium comprises Nei-
man Marcus, Apple, H&M, Macy's, and

dozens of specialty shops. You can chow down at the Capital Grille, Truluck's, P. F. Chang's China Bistro, or Seasons 52—or sip cocktails at Blue Martini. The mall itself is open Monday through Saturday 10–9, Sunday noon–6. The stand-alone restaurants and bars are open later. ✉ *2414 E. Sunrise Blvd., Intracoastal and Inland* ☎ *954/564–1015* ⊕ *www.galleria-mall-fl.com.*

★ Las Olas Boulevard

ANTIQUES/COLLECTIBLES | FAMILY | Las Olas Boulevard is the epicenter of Fort Lauderdale's lifestyle. Not only are 50 of the city's best boutiques, dozens of top restaurants, and eclectic art galleries found along this landscaped street, but Las Olas links the growing downtown area with Fort Lauderdale's beautiful beaches. ✉ *E. Las Olas Blvd., Downtown* ☎ *954/258–8382* ⊕ *lasolasboulevard.com.*

Galveston, Texas

A thin strip of an island in the Gulf of Mexico, Galveston is big sister Houston's beach playground—a year-round coastal destination just 50 miles away. Many of the first public buildings in Texas (including a post office, bank, and hotel) were built here, but most were destroyed in the Great Storm of 1900. Those that endured have been well preserved, and the Victorian character of the Historic Downtown Strand shopping district and the neighborhood surrounding Broadway is still evident. On the Galveston Bay side of the island (northeast), quaint shops and cafés in old buildings are near the Seaport Museum, harbor-front eateries, and the cruise-ship terminal. On the Gulf of Mexico side (southwest), resorts and restaurants line coastal Seawall Boulevard. The 17-foot-high seawall abuts a long ribbon of sand and provides a place for rollerblading, bicycling, and going on the occasional surrey ride. The city was

Best Bets ◉

■ **Historic Homes.** The island has some lovely historic homes to explore, particularly during early May, when the Historic Homes Tour lets you into many that aren't usually open to the public.

■ **Moody Gardens.** There are enough activities at this park to keep any kid happy.

■ **The Historic Downtown Strand District.** Galveston's historic district is a great place to stroll, shop, and eat.

badly damaged from flooding during Hurricane Ike in 2008, but businesses are now up and running, with few remnants of the storm.

Galveston is a port of embarkation for cruises on Western Caribbean itineraries. It's an especially popular port of embarkation for people living in the southeastern states who don't wish to fly to their cruise. Carnival and Royal Caribbean have ships based in Galveston, offering four-, five-, six-, and seven-day cruises along the Mexican coast and to Jamaica, Grand Cayman, Belize, Bahamas, Key West, and Honduras, plus a 14-night cruise to the Azores and Spain.

ESSENTIALS
HOURS
Shops in the historic district are usually open until at least 6 or 7. During peak season some stay open later. This is also the city's nightlife district, and is hopping until late.

VISITOR INFORMATION
CONTACTS Galveston Island Visitors Center. ✉ *2328 Broadway Blvd.* ⊕ *www.galveston.com/visitorscenter.*

THE CRUISE PORT

The relatively sheltered waters of Galveston Bay are home to the Texas Cruise Ship Terminal. It's only 30 minutes to open water from here. Driving south from Houston on I–45, you cross a long causeway before reaching the island. Take the first exit (Harborside Drive) left after you've crossed the causeway onto Galveston Island. Follow that for a few miles to the port. Turn left on 22nd Street (also called Kempner Street); there is a security checkpoint before you continue down a driveway. The drop-off point is set up much like an airport terminal, with pull-through lanes and curbside check-in.

CONTACTS Port of Galveston. ⊠ Harborside Dr. and 22nd St. ☎ 409/765–9321 ⊕ www.portofgalveston.com.

AIRPORT

CONTACTS George Bush Intercontinental Airport. ⊠ 2800 N. Terminal Rd., Houston ☎ 281/230–3100 ⊕ www.fly2houston. com. **William P. Hobby Airport.** ⊠ 7800 Airport Blvd., Houston ☎ 713/640–3000 ⊕ www.fly2houston.com.

AIRPORT TRANSFERS

The closest airports are in Houston, 50 miles from Galveston. Houston has two major airports: Hobby Airport, 9 miles (15 km) southeast of downtown, and George Bush Intercontinental, 15 miles (24 km) northeast of the city. Traffic into Galveston can be delayed because of ongoing construction.

Unless you have arranged airport transfers through your cruise line, you'll have to make arrangements to navigate the miles between the Houston airport at which you land and the cruise-ship terminal in Galveston. Galveston Limousine Service provides scheduled transportation (return reservations required) between either airport and Galveston hotels or the cruise-ship terminal. Hobby is a shorter ride (1 hour; $45 one-way, $80 round-trip), but Intercontinental (2 hours; $55 one-way, $100 round-trip) is served by more airlines, including international carriers. Taking a taxi allows you to set your own schedule, but can cost twice as much (it's also important to note that there aren't always enough taxis to handle the demands of disembarking passengers, so you might have to wait after you leave your ship). Negotiate the price before you get in.

CONTACTS Galveston Limousine Service. ☎ 800/640–4826 ⊕ www.galvestonlimo. com.

PARKING

Parking is coordinated by the Port Authority. After you drop off your checked luggage and passengers at the terminal, you receive a color-coded parking pass from the attendant, with directions to a parking lot for your cruise departure. The lots are approximately ½ mile (1 km) from the terminal. Check-in, parking, and boarding are generally allowed four hours prior to departure. A shuttle bus (carry-on luggage only) runs back and forth between the lots and the terminal every 7 to 12 minutes on cruise arrival and departure days (be sure to drop off your luggage before you park the car). The lot is closed other days. Port Authority security checks the well-lighted, fenced-in lots every two hours; there is also a limited amount of covered parking. Parking for a five-day cruise is $50, seven days is $70 ($80 covered). Cash, traveler's checks, and credit cards (Visa and MasterCard only) are accepted for payment.

◉ Sights

Historic Downtown Strand District

HISTORIC SITE | This shopping area is defined by the architecture of its 19th- and early-20th-century buildings, many of which survived the storm of 1900 and are on the National Register of Historic Places. When Galveston was still a powerful port city—before the Houston Ship Channel was dug, diverting most

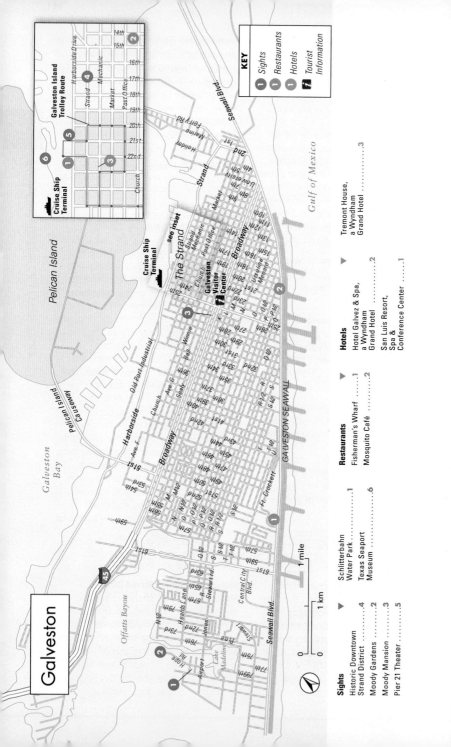

Galveston

KEY

- ● Sights
- ● Restaurants
- ● Hotels
- ℹ Tourist Information

Galveston Island Trolley Route

Cruise Ship Terminal

Cruise Ship Terminal

see inset

The Strand

Galveston Visitor Center

GALVESTON SEAWALL

Gulf of Mexico

Pelican Island

Galveston Bay

Pelican Island Causeway

Offatts Bayou

Lake Madeline

Central City Blvd

Seawall Blvd.

Harborside

Broadway

Strand

Broadway

Sights

- Historic Downtown Strand District 4
- Moody Gardens 2
- Moody Mansion 3
- Pier 21 Theater 5
- ▶ Schlitterbahn Water Park 1
- Texas Seaport Museum 6

Restaurants

- ▶ Fisherman's Wharf 1
- Mosquito Café 2

Hotels

- ▶ Hotel Galvez & Spa, a Wyndham Grand Hotel 2
- San Luis Resort, Spa & Conference Center 1
- ▶ Tremont House, a Wyndham Grand Hotel 3

boat traffic inland—this stretch, formerly the site of stores, offices, and warehouses, was known as the Wall Street of the South. As you stroll up the Strand, you'll pass dozens of shops and cafés. ☒ *2100 Strand Downtown, Galveston* ⊕ *www. galveston.com.*

Moody Gardens

GARDEN | FAMILY | Moody Gardens is a multifaceted entertainment and educational complex inside pastel-color glass pyramids. Attractions include the 13-story Discovery Pyramid, showcasing marine life from four oceans in tanks and touch pools; Rainforest Pyramid, a 40,000-square-foot tropical habitat for exotic flora and fauna; Discovery Pyramid, a joint venture with NASA featuring more than 40 interactive exhibits; and two theaters, one of which has a space adventure ride. Outside, Palm Beach has white-sand beach, landscaped grounds, man-made lagoons, a kid-size waterslide and games, and beach chairs. ☒ *1 Hope Blvd., Galveston* ☎ *800/582–4673* ⊕ *www.moodygardens.com.*

Moody Mansion

HOUSE | Moody Mansion, the residence of generations of one of Texas's most powerful families, was completed in 1895. Tour its interiors of exotic woods and gilded trim, filled with family heirlooms and personal effects. ☒ *2618 Broadway, Galveston* ☎ *409/762–7668* ⊕ *www. moodymansion.org* ☒ *$12.*

Pier 21 Theater

ARTS VENUE | At this Harborside Drive theater, watch the Great Storm of 1900 come back to life in a multimedia presentation that includes video clips of archival drawings, still photos, and narrated accounts from survivors' diaries. Also playing is a film about the exploits of pirate Jean Lafitte, who used the island as a base. ☒ *2100 Harborside Dr., Galveston* ☎ *409/763–8808* ⊕ *www.galveston-history.org* ☒ *$6.*

Schlitterbahn Water Park

AMUSEMENT PARK/WATER PARK | The entire family will have a fun time at this water park, located on the bay side of the island. Schlitterbahn features speed slides, lazy river rides, uphill water coasters, a wave pool (with surfing), and water playgrounds for the little ones. There's even a heated indoor water park for chilly winter months. During summer, less expensive afternoon-only rates are in effect, and ticket prices drop in the off-season. Closing times vary by the season, so outside of the busiest months of June through August, verify closing times on the park's website, or call for exact hours. ☒ *2026 Lockheed St., Galveston* ☎ *409/770–9283* ⊕ *www. schlitterbahn.com* ☒ *$52.99.*

Texas Seaport Museum

MUSEUM | Aboard the restored 1877 tall ship *Elissa*, detailed interpretive signs provide information about the shipping trade in the 1800s, including the routes and cargoes this ship carried into Galveston. Inside the museum building is a replica of the historic wharf and a one-of-a-kind computer database containing the names of more than 133,000 immigrants who entered the United States through Galveston after 1837. ☒ *2200 Harborside Dr., Galveston* ☎ *409/763–1877* ⊕ *www. galveston.com* ☒ *$12.*

⊕ Beaches

Galveston Island State Park

BEACHES | Galveston Island State Park, on the western, unpopulated end of the island, is a 2,000-acre natural beach habitat ideal for birding, walking, and renewing your spirit. It's open daily from 8 am to 10 pm. The Nature Center is open weekends from 10 to 2. ☒ *14901 FM 3005, 10 miles (16 km) southwest on Seawall Blvd., Galveston* ☎ *409/737–1222* ⊕ *www.galvestonislandstatepark. org* ☒ *$5.*

Seawall

BEACHES | The Seawall on the gulfside waterfront attracts runners, cyclists, and rollerbladers. Just below it is a long, free beach near many big hotels and resorts. ✉ *Seawall Blvd., Galveston* ☎ *409/797–5198* ⊕ *www.galveston.com.*

Stewart Beach Park

BEACHES | **FAMILY** | Stewart Beach Park has a bathhouse, amusement park, bumper boats, miniature-golf course, and a water coaster in addition to saltwater and sand. It's open weekdays 9 to 5, weekends 8 to 6, from March through May; weekdays 8 to 6 and weekends 8 to 7, from June through September; and weekends 9 to 5 during the first two weekends of October. ✉ *201 Seawall Blvd., Galveston* ☎ *409/797–5189* ⊕ *www.galveston.com.*

Restaurants

Fisherman's Wharf

$$$ | **SEAFOOD** | Even though Landry's has taken over this harborside institution, locals keep coming here for the reliably fresh seafood and reasonable prices. Dine indoors or watch the boat traffic (and waiting cruise ships) from the patio. **Known for:** big and busy; great views of the bay; shrimp po-boys. ⑤ *Average main: $24* ✉ *2200 Harborside Dr., Galveston* ☎ *409/765–5708* ⊕ *www.fishermanswharfgalveston.com.*

Mosquito Café

$$ | **AMERICAN** | This popular eatery in Galveston's historic East End serves fresh, contemporary food—including some vegetarian dishes—in a hip, high-ceilinged dining room and on an outdoor patio. Wake up with a fluffy egg frittata or a homemade scone topped with whipped cream, or try a large gourmet salad for lunch. **Known for:** bountiful breakfasts; no fried seafood; grilled seafood trio. ⑤ *Average main: $15* ✉ *628 14th St., Galveston* ☎ *409/763–1010* ⊕ *www.mosquitocafe.com* ⊙ *Closed Mon.*

Boarding Passes ◉

Modern ID cards and scanning equipment record passenger comings and goings on the majority of cruise ships these days. With a swipe through a machine (it looks much like a credit-card swipe at the supermarket), security personnel know who is on board the vessel at all times. On almost all ships, passengers' pictures are recorded digitally at check-in.

🛏 Hotels

Hotel Galvez & Spa, a Wyndham Grand Hotel

$$$$ | **HOTEL** | This renovated six-story Spanish colonial hotel, built in 1911, was once called "Queen of the Gulf." Teddy Roosevelt and Howard Hughes are just two of the many well-known guests who have stayed here. **Pros:** directly on beach; incredible pool area; beautiful grounds. **Cons:** rooms can be small (especially the bathrooms). ⑤ *Rooms from: $250* ✉ *2024 Seawall Blvd., Galveston* ☎ *409/765–7721* ⊕ *www.wyndham.com* ↪ *224 rooms* ⦿ *No meals.*

San Luis Resort, Spa & Conference Center

$$$$ | **RESORT** | A long marble staircase alongside a slender fountain with sculpted dolphins welcomes you to the beachfront elegance of this resort. **Pros:** great gulf views; nice pool area. **Cons:** no valet, and public parking is not convenient. ⑤ *Rooms from: $304* ✉ *5222 Seawall Blvd., Galveston* ☎ *409/744–1500* ⊕ *www.sanluisresort.com* ↪ *250 rooms* ⦿ *No meals.*

Tremont House, a Wyndham Grand Hotel

$$$$ | **HOTEL** | A four-story atrium lobby, with ironwork balconies and full-size palm trees, showcases an 1872 hand-carved rosewood bar in what was once a busy dry-goods warehouse. **Pros:** beautiful historical environment; free Wi-Fi; great location. **Cons:** not a fun scene for young single travelers. ⑤ *Rooms from: $214* ✉ *2300 Ship's Mechanic Row, Galveston* ☏ *409/763–0300* ⊕ *www.wyndham.com* ⤻ *119 rooms* ⦿ *No meals.*

ⓨ Nightlife

For a relaxing evening, choose any of the harborside restaurant–bars on Piers 21 and 22 to sip a glass of wine or a frozen Hurricane as you watch the boats go by.

The Grand 1894 Opera House

THEMED ENTERTAINMENT | The Grand 1894 Opera House stages musicals and hosts concerts year-round. It's worth visiting for the ornate architecture alone. Sarah Bernhardt and Anna Pavlova both performed on this storied stage. ✉ *2020 Postoffice St., Galveston* ☏ *800/821–1894* ⊕ *www. thegrand.com.*

⬤ Shopping

The Emporium at Eibands

ANTIQUES/COLLECTIBLES | More than 50 antiques dealers are represented at the Emporium at Eibands, an upscale showroom filled with custom uphol-stery, bedding and draperies, antique furniture, and interesting architectural finds. ✉ *2201 Postoffice St., Galveston* ☏ *409/750–9536* ⊕ *www.galveston.com.*

Old Strand Emporium

FOOD/CANDY | FAMILY | Old Strand Emporium is a charming deli and grocery reminiscent of an old-fashioned ice-cream parlor and sandwich shop, with candy bins, packaged nuts, and more. ✉ *2016 Strand, Galveston* ☏ *409/515–0715* ⊕ *www.galveston.com.*

Strand

SHOPPING NEIGHBORHOODS | The Strand is the best place to shop in Galveston. Old storefronts are filled with gift shops, antiques stores, and one-of-a-kind

Best Bets ⊙

■ **Budweiser Brewery Tour.** Behind the scenes on the making of one of the country's most popular beers.

■ **Jacksonville Zoo.** One of the best midsize zoos you'll visit.

■ **Museum of Contemporary Art Jacksonville.** Though small, this excellent museum is an unexpected treat in northeast Florida.

boutiques. ✉ *2100 Strand, Galveston* ⊕ *www.galveston.com.*

Jacksonville, Florida

One of Florida's oldest cities and at 758 square miles (1,926 square km) the largest city in the continental United States in terms of land area, Jacksonville is underrated and makes a worthwhile vacation spot for an extra day or two before or after your cruise. It offers appealing downtown riverside areas, handsome residential neighborhoods, the region's only skyscrapers, a thriving arts scene, and, for football fans, the NFL Jaguars and the NCAA Gator Bowl. Remnants of the Old South flavor the city, especially in the Riverside-Avondale historic district, where moss-draped oak trees frame prairie-style bungalows and Tudor Revival mansions, and palm trees, Spanish bayonets, and azaleas populate Jacksonville's landscape. Northeast of the city, Amelia Island and Fernandina Beach offer some of the nicest coastline in Florida.

ESSENTIALS
HOURS
Many museums close on Monday.

VISITOR INFORMATION
CONTACTS Visit Jacksonville. ☎ *800/733–2668* ⊕ *www.visitjacksonville.com.*

THE CRUISE PORT

Limited in the sizes of ship it can berth, Jaxport currently serves as home port to the *Carnival Ecstasy,* which departs weekly on four- and five-night cruises to Key West and the Bahamas during the fall and winter cruising seasons, with occasional weeklong sailings to Grand Turk, Half Moon Cay, and Nassau. The facility is fairly sparse, consisting basically of some vending machines and restrooms, but the embarkation staff receive high marks. The terminal itself was constructed as a temporary structure, but a permanent cruise terminal has yet to be erected.

CONTACTS Jacksonville Port Authority. ✉ *9810 August Dr., Jacksonville* ☎ *904/357–3302* ⊕ *www.jaxport.com.*

AIRPORT

Jaxport is about 15 minutes from Jacksonville International Airport. Take I–95 South to State Road 9A East. Follow 9A to Heckscher Drive (State Road 105) west until you reach August Drive. Head south on August Drive, and follow the signs to the cruise terminal.

CONTACTS Jacksonville International Airport. (*JAX*) ✉ *14201 Pecan Park Rd., Jacksonville* ☎ *904/741–4902* ⊕ *www.flyjacksonville.com.*

AIRPORT TRANSFERS

A taxi transfer from Jacksonville airport takes about 15 minutes and costs $30 for up to three passengers, not including tip. Uber and Lyft are also available, as is Super Shuttle. Any of these can get you to the cruise port.

CONTACTS Dana's Limousine & Transportation. ☎ *904/744–3333* ⊕ *www.danaslimo.com.*

PARKING

There is a fenced and guarded parking lot next to the cruise terminal, within walking distance. Parking costs $17 per day for regular vehicles, $34 for RVs. You can pay in advance on the Jaxport website, where you'll find more parking details, or you can pay with cash or a major credit card upon arrival.

◉ Sights

Because Jacksonville was settled along both sides of the twisting St. Johns River, a number of attractions are on or near a riverbank. Both sides of the river, which is spanned by myriad bridges, have downtown areas and waterfront complexes of shops, restaurants, parks, and museums; some attractions can be reached by water taxi or the Skyway Express monorail system—scenic alternatives to driving back and forth across the bridges—but a car is generally necessary.

★ Cummer Museum of Art & Gardens

GARDEN | The Wark Collection of early-18th-century Meissen porcelain is just one reason to visit this former St. Johns River estate, which includes 13 permanent galleries with more than 5,500 items spanning more than 4,000 years, and 3 acres of riverfront gardens that form a showcase for northeast Florida's seasonal blooms and indigenous fauna. Art Connections allows kids of all ages to experience art through interactive exhibits. The Thomas H. Jacobsen Gallery of American Art focuses on works by American artists, including Max Weber, N. C. Wyeth, and Paul Manship. Complimentary tour brochures at the front desk help visitors navigate the galleries, as do podcasts. ✉ *829 Riverside Ave., Riverside* ☎ *904/356–6857* ⊕ *www.cummermuseum.org* ⌨ *$10 (free Tues. 4–9)* ⊘ *Closed Mon.*

★ Jacksonville Zoo and Gardens

ZOO | **FAMILY** | The highly regarded zoo offers visitors the chance to hop on a train and explore different countries through the animals that live there, from the Land of the Tiger, a 2½-acre

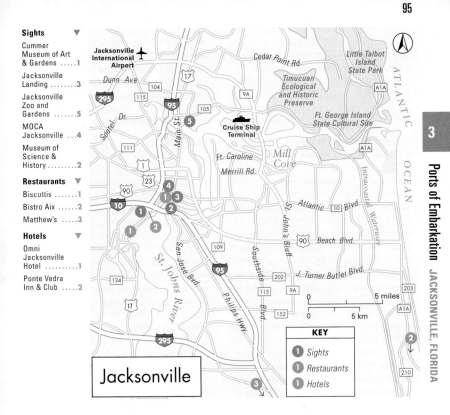

Sights ▼

Cummer
Museum of Art
& Gardens **1**

Jacksonville
Landing **3**

Jacksonville
Zoo and
Gardens **5**

MOCA
Jacksonville ...**4**

Museum of
Science &
History **2**

Restaurants ▼

Biscottis **1**

Bistro Aix **2**

Matthew's **3**

Hotels ▼

Omni
Jacksonville
Hotel **1**

Ponte Vedra
Inn & Club **2**

Jacksonville

KEY

1 *Sights*

1 *Restaurants*

1 *Hotels*

Asian attraction featuring Sumatran and Malayan tigers, to the African Plains area, which houses elephants, white rhinos, and two highly endangered leopards, in addition to other species of African birds and mammals. The Range of the Jaguar takes visitors to a 4-acre Central and South American exhibit, with exotic big cats as well as 20 other species native to the region. Among the other highlights are rare waterfowl and the Reptile House, which showcases some of the world's most dangerous venomous snakes. Wild Florida is a 2½-acre area with black bears, bald eagles, white-tailed deer, and other animals native to Florida, while RiverQuest reveals the ecology of the adjacent Trout River. Play Park contains a Splash Ground, a forest play area, two mazes, and a discovery building; Stingray Bay has a 17,000-gallon pool where visitors can pet and feed the mysterious creatures. The zoo opened a Manatee Critical Care Center in 2016. Parking is free. ⊠ *370 Zoo Pkwy., off Heckscher Dr. E, Jacksonville* ☎ *904/757–4463* ⊕ *www.jacksonvillezoo. org* ⊐ *$19.95.*

★ **MOCA Jacksonville**

MUSEUM | In this loftlike, five-story downtown building, the former headquarters of the Western Union Telegraph Company, a permanent collection of 20th-century art shares space with traveling exhibitions and a theater space. The museum, owned and managed by the University of North Florida, encompasses five galleries and ArtExplorium, a highly interactive educational exhibit for kids, as well as a funky gift shop and Nola MOCA, open for lunch on weekdays and for dinner on Thursday. MOCA Jacksonville also hosts film series, theater performances, and workshops throughout the year, and packs a big art-wallop into a relatively small 14,000 square feet. A once-a-month Art Walk is free to all. ⌗ *Hemming Plaza, 333 N. Laura St., Downtown* ☎ *904/366–6911* ⊕ *www.mocajacksonville.unf.edu* ⌗ *$8* ⊘ *Closed Mon.*

Museum of Science & History

MUSEUM | FAMILY | Known locally as MOSH, this museum is home to the Bryan-Gooding Planetarium. As a next-generation planetarium, it can project 3-D laser shows that accompany the ever-popular First Friday Cosmic Concerts. For those taking in the planetarium shows, the resolution is significantly sharper than that of the biggest HDTV on the market. Whether you're a kid taking in Sesame Street's *One World, One Sky,* or an adult star-gazing in the *Skies over Jacksonville* tour of the night sky, the experience is awesome. MOSH also has a wide variety of interactive exhibits and programs that include JEA PowerPlay: Understanding our Energy Choices; the Florida Naturalist's Center; and the Currents of Time, where you'll navigate 12,000 years of northeast Florida history. Nationally acclaimed traveling exhibits are featured along with signature exhibits on local history. ⌗ *1025 Museum Circle, Jacksonville* ☎ *904/396–6674* ⊕ *www.themosh.org* ⌗ *$15.*

🍴 Restaurants

Jaxport's location on Jacksonville's Westside means there aren't too many nearby restaurants. But by taking a 10- to 15-minute drive south, you'll find a wealth of restaurants for all tastes and price categories.

★ Biscottis

$$$ | AMERICAN | The local artwork on the redbrick walls is a mild distraction from the crowds jockeying for tables here for brunch, lunch, and dinner. The wide-ranging and locally sourced menus offer many unexpected delights, including a three-onion campanelle pasta and a bluefin tuna poke bowl. **Known for:** weekend brunch served until 3; decadent desserts from the bakery; ever-changing nightly entrée specials. ⑤ *Average main: $26* ⌗ *3556 St. Johns Ave., Jacksonville* ☎ *904/387–2060* ⊕ *www.biscottis.net.*

Bistro Aix

$$$ | FRENCH | Named after the French city (pronounced simply "X"), this sophisticated bistro-bar's leather booths, 1940s brickwork, and intricate marbled globes provide a perfect home for well-prepared French food. Regulars can't get enough of the classic bistro menu items, including creamy onion soup and escargot, entrées such as duck cassoulet, along with a variety of wood-fired pizzas and delectable desserts. **Known for:** steak frites au poivre; smaller options for some menu items; attentive service. ⑤ *Average main: $28* ⌗ *1440 San Marco Blvd., San Marco* ☎ *904/398–1949* ⊕ *www.bistrox.com* ⊘ *Closed Sun. No lunch Sat.*

★ Matthew's

$$$$ | ECLECTIC | No one can accuse chef Matthew Medure of resting on his laurels (of which there are many). Widely praised for culinary creativity and dazzling presentation at his signature San Marco restaurant, Medure's French- and Italian-inspired cuisine offers a wide range of choices, from caviar to sweets. **Known for:** create-your-own charcuterie platters; huge wine list; six-course Chef's Adventure Menu. ⑤ *Average main: $32* ⌗ *2107 Hendricks Ave., San Marco* ☎ *904/396–9922* ⊕ *www.matthewsrestaurant.com* ⊘ *Closed Sun. No lunch.*

🛏 Hotels

Hotels near the cruise terminals are few and far between, so most cruisers needing a room make the drive to Downtown (15 minutes) or to the Southbank or Riverside (20 minutes).

Omni Jacksonville Hotel

$ | HOTEL | FAMILY | Jacksonville's most luxurious and glamorous downtown hotel offers across-the-street convenience to the big theatrical or musical shows at the Times-Union Center. **Pros:** excellent on-site restaurant; pet-friendly; kids receive special backpack, milk, and cookies. **Cons:** fee for Wi-Fi and parking; pricey restaurant; can be chaotic when there's a show across the street. ⑤ *Rooms from: $180* ✉ *245 Water St., Jacksonville* ☎ *904/355–6664, 800/843–6664* ⊕ *www. omnijacksonville.com* ⤳ *354 rooms* ⭘ *No meals.*

★ Ponte Vedra Inn & Club

$$ | RESORT | FAMILY | Considered northeast Florida's premier resort for decades, this award-winning 1928 landmark continues to wow guests with its stellar service and large guest rooms housed in white-brick, red-tile-roof buildings lining the beach. **Pros:** accommodating, friendly staff; private beach; adults-only pool. **Cons:** charge for umbrellas and chaises on the beach; crowded pools at some times of year; remote location. ⑤ *Rooms from: $299* ✉ *200 Ponte Vedra Blvd., Ponte Vedra Beach* ☎ *904/285–1111, 800/234–7842* ⊕ *www.pontevedra.com* ⤳ *250 rooms, 33 suites* ⭘ *No meals.*

🛍 Shopping

San Marco Square

SHOPPING CENTERS/MALLS | More than a dozen interesting apparel, home, and jewelry stores and upscale restaurants surround the open square in 1920s Mediterranean Revival–style buildings. ✉ *San Marco Blvd. at Atlantic Blvd., San Marco* ⊕ *mysanmarco.com.*

The Shoppes of Avondale

SHOPPING CENTERS/MALLS | The highlights here include upscale clothing and accessories boutiques, art galleries, home-furnishings shops, a chocolatier, and trendy restaurants. ✉ *St. Johns Ave. between*

Best Bets 👁

■ **South Beach.** A 15-minute cab from the port, South Beach is great for people-watching, an art deco tour, or a bit of sun.

■ **Bayside Marketplace.** If you want to stay close to the port, grab some outdoor drinks and eclectic eats at super-touristy Bayside Marketplace.

■ **Bill Baggs Cape Florida State Park.** Unleash your outdoor enthusiasm at Key Biscayne's Bill Baggs Cape Florida State Park.

■ **Vizcaya Museum.** One of south Florida's largest historic homes is one of the city's best museums.

Talbot Ave. and Dancy St., Avondale ⊕ *www.shoppesofavondale.com.*

Miami, Florida

Miami is the busiest of Florida's very busy cruise ports. Because there's so much going on in Miami these days, you'll definitely want to schedule an extra day or two before and/or after your cruise to explore North America's most Latin city. Downtown is a convenient place to stay if you are meeting up with a cruise ship, but Miami Beach is still the crown jewel. The Art Deco District in South Beach—the square-mile section between 6th and 23rd Streets—remains the heart of Miami's vibrant nightlife and restaurant scene, but Mid-Beach and Downtown aren't too far behind. You may also want to explore beyond the beach, including the neighborhoods of Wynwood, the Design District, Little Havana, Coral Gables, and Coconut Grove.

ESSENTIALS
HOURS
Most of the area's attractions are open every day.

VISITOR INFORMATION
CONTACTS Greater Miami Convention & Visitors Bureau. ⊠ *701 Brickell Ave., Suite 2700, Miami* ☎ *305/539–3000, 800/933–8448 in U.S.* ⊕ *www.miamiandbeaches. com.* **Visit Miami Beach.** ⊠ *Visitor Center, 530 17th St., Miami Beach* ☎ *305/672–1270* ⊕ *www.miamibeachguest.com.*

THE CRUISE PORT
The Port of Miami, in downtown Miami near Bayside Marketplace and the MacArthur Causeway, justifiably bills itself as "the Cruise Capital of the World." Home to 18 cruise lines (including the global headquarters for Carnival, Norwegian, Royal Caribbean, and Oceania) and the largest year-round cruise fleet in the world, the port accommodates more than 4 million passengers a year for sailings from 3 to 14 days and sometimes longer duration. Seven air-conditioned terminals are decorated with dramatic public art installations reflecting sun-drenched waters off the Florida coastline and the Everglades ecosystems. There's duty-free shopping and limousine service. You can get taxis at all the terminals, and car-rental agencies offer shuttles to off-site lots.

If you are driving, take I–95 north or south to I–395. Follow the directional signs to the Biscayne Boulevard exit and then signs for Port Blvd. and N. America Way. After passing under the tunnel, follow the directional signs to your terminal.

CONTACTS PortMiami. ⊠ *1015 N. America Way, Miami* ☎ *305/347–5515* ⊕ *www. miamidade.gov/portmiami.*

AIRPORT
Subtropical, chaotic Miami International Airport (MIA), gateway to the Americas and a hub for American Airlines, is without doubt Florida's busiest airport on all counts. More than 100 international and domestic carriers are served, connecting to 150 destinations. For the travel-weary, there's the rather basic but soundproof 259-room Hotel MIA (smack in the middle of Concourse E). Besides Lost & Found in North Terminal D, amenities include doggie relief areas in Terminals D, E, and J, assorted ATMs (including a full-service Bank of America in Terminal D), plus food and shopping opportunities galore. Wi-Fi and charging stations are available at assorted locations. The MIA Mover, a 1¼-mile-long people mover, connects to the Miami Car Rental Center, with more than a dozen rental agencies from Hertz, Avis, and leisure-leader Alamo to Dollar, Payless, and Thrifty. From MIA, you also can access South Florida's Tri-Rail system connecting with Fort Lauderdale and Palm Beach airports.

CONTACTS Miami International Airport. (*MIA*) ⊠ *Miami International Airport, 2100 N.W. 42nd Ave., Miami* ☎ *305/876–7000, 800/825–5642 International* ⊕ *www. iflymia.com.*

AIRPORT TRANSFERS
If you have not arranged an airport transfer through your cruise line, you have a couple of options for getting to the cruise port. The first is a ride service like Uber or Lyft. Second is a taxi: fares are regulated by the county, with a flat fare of $27 from Miami International Airport (MIA); this fare is per trip, not per passenger, and includes tolls and a $1 airport surcharge but not a tip. SuperShuttle vans transport passengers between MIA and local hotels, as well as the PortMiami. At MIA the vans pick up at the ground level of each concourse (look for clerks with yellow shirts, who will flag one down). SuperShuttle service from MIA is available on demand; for the return it's best to make reservations 24 hours in advance. The cost from MIA to the cruise port is $27 per person, or $65 if you want a nonstop ride for yourselves.

CONTACTS SuperShuttle. ☎ *305/871–2000* ⊕ *miamisupershuttle.com.*

PARKING

Street-level lots are right in front of each of the cruise terminals. The port's three parking garages (each with an open-air top floor) accommodate 5,871 vehicles, with 56 spaces designated for guests with disabilities and another half-dozen or so for passengers with infants. The cost for all, payable in advance, is $22 per day ($44 for RVs, which can be parked in Lot 2, across from Terminal E) and $8 for short-term parking of less than four hours for drop-off or pick-up. You can pay by cash, credit card, or traveler's check, but not with a debit card. There is no valet parking, but a shuttle for cruise passengers (one is wheelchair-accessible) can pick you up at the parking garage/lot, take you to the appropriate terminal, and return you to your vehicle after your cruise.

◉ Sights

In the 1950s Miami was best known for alligator wrestlers and you-pick strawberry fields or citrus groves. Well, things have changed... big time! Miami on the mainland is South Florida's commercial hub, while its sultry sister Miami Beach (America's Riviera) encompasses 17 islands in Biscayne Bay. Seducing winter refugees with its sunshine, beaches, palm trees, and nightlife, this is what most people envision when planning a trip to Miami. If you want to do any exploring, you'll have to drive.

Art Deco Welcome Center and Museum

BUILDING | Run by the Miami Design Preservation League, the center provides information about the buildings in the district. An official Art Deco Museum opened within the center in October 2014, and a gift shop sells art deco memorabilia and posters from the 1930s through '50s, as well as books on Miami's history. Several tours also start here, including a self-guided audio tour and regular morning walking tours at 10:30 daily. On Thursday a second tour takes place at 6:30 pm. ✉ *1001 Ocean Dr., South Beach* ☎ *305/672–2014, 305/531–3484 for tours* ⊕ *www.mdpl.org* 🎟 *Tours $30.*

Bayside Marketplace

MARKET | FAMILY | Bayside Marketplace, a waterfront complex of entertainment, dining, and retail stores, was en vogue circa 1992 and remains popular due to its location near Port Miami. You'll find the area awash in cruise-ship-passenger chaos on most days (it's definitely *not* a draw for locals, more a place to kill time in between airport arrival and cruise embarkation), so expect plenty of souvenir shops, a Hard Rock Cafe, and stores like Gap and Sunglass Hut. Many boat tours leave from the marinas lining the festival marketplace. ✉ *401 Biscayne Blvd., Downtown* ☎ *305/577–3344* ⊕ *www.baysidemarketplace.com.*

Jungle Island

ZOO | FAMILY | This interactive zoological park is home to just about every unusual and endangered species you would want to see, including a rare albino alligator, a liger (lion and tiger mix), and myriad exotic birds. With an emphasis on the experiential versus mere observation, the park now offers several new attractions and activities, including private beaches, treetop zip-lining, aquatic activities, adventure trails, cultural activities, and enhanced VIP packages where you mingle with an array of furry and feathered friends. Jungle Island offers complimentary shuttle service to most Downtown Miami and South Beach hotels. ✉ *Watson Island, 1111 Parrot Jungle Trail, off MacArthur Causeway (I–395), Downtown* ☎ *305/400–7000* ⊕ *www.jungleisland. com* 🎟 *$44.99, plus $10 parking.*

★ Lincoln Road Mall

BUILDING | FAMILY | This open-air pedestrian mall boasts some of Miami's best people-watching. The eclectic interiors of myriad fabulous restaurants, colorful boutiques, art galleries, lounges, and cafés are often upstaged by the bustling

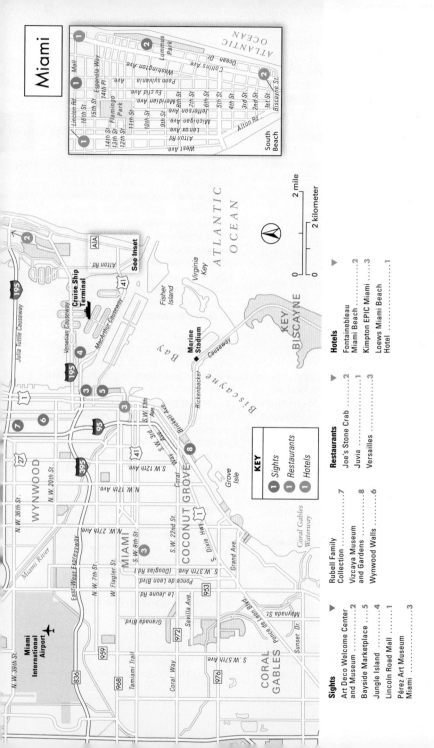

Miami

South Beach (Inset)

Lincoln Rd. Mall
16th St.
15th St.
Española Way
14th St.
14th Pl.
Washington Ave.
Pennsylvania Ave.
Euclid Ave.
Meridian Ave.
Jefferson Ave.
Michigan Ave.
Lenox Ave.
Alton Rd.
West Ave.
13th Ave.
12th Ave.
Flamingo Park
Lummus Park
Collins Ave.
Ocean Dr.
11th St.
10th St.
9th St.
8th St.
7th St.
6th St.
5th St.
4th St.
3rd St.
2nd St.
1st St.
Biscayne St.

ATLANTIC OCEAN

South Beach

Main Map

Miami International Airport

N.W. 39th St.
N.W. 36th St.
N.W. 20th St.
N.W. 17th Ave.
N.W. 27th Ave.

WYNWOOD
CORAL GABLES
MIAMI
CORAL GABLES
COCONUT GROVE

East-West Expressway
Miami River
N.W. 7th St.
W. Flagler St.
Tamiami Trail
Coral Way
Ponce de Leon Blvd. (Douglas Rd.)
S.W. 37th Ave.
S.W. 27th St.
S.W. 22nd St.
S.W. 24th St.
Sunset Dr.
Maynada St.
Sevilla Ave.
Granada Blvd.
Le Jeune Rd.
Ponce de Leon Blvd.
S.W. 57th Ave.
Grand Ave.
Dixie Hwy.
Coral Gables Waterway
Grove Isle

Julia Tuttle Causeway
Venetian Causeway
MacArthur Causeway
Alton Rd.
Cruise Ship Terminal
See inset

Birkerr Ave.
S.W. 13th Ave.
S.W. 3rd Ave.
S.W. 12th Ave.
N.W. 12th Ave.

Rickenbacker Causeway
Marine Stadium

Biscayne Bay
Fisher Island
Virginia Key
ATLANTIC OCEAN
KEY BISCAYNE

0   2 mile
0   2 kilometer

KEY
1 Sights
1 Restaurants
1 Hotels

Sights
Art Deco Welcome Center and Museum 2
Bayside Marketplace 5
Jungle Island 4
Lincoln Road Mall 1
Pérez Art Museum Miami 3
Rubell Family Collection 7
Vizcaya Museum and Gardens 8
Wynwood Walls 6

Restaurants
Joe's Stone Crab 2
Juvia 1
Versailles 3

Hotels
Fontainebleau Miami Beach 2
Kimpton EPIC Miami 3
Loews Miami Beach Hotel 1

outdoor scene. It's here among myriad alfresco dining enclaves that you can pass the hours easily beholding the beautiful people. Indeed, Lincoln Road is fun, lively, and friendly for everyone—old, young, gay, and straight—and their dogs. A few of the shops on Lincoln Road are owner-operated boutiques carrying a smart variety of clothing, furnishings, jewelry, and decorative elements, but more often you'll find typical upscale chain stores.

Two landmarks worth checking out at the eastern end of Lincoln Road are the massive 1940s keystone building at No. 420, which has a 1945 Leo Birchansky mural in the lobby, and the 1921 mission-style Miami Beach Community Church at Drexel Avenue. The Lincoln Theatre (541–545 Lincoln Rd. at Pennsylvania Avenue), is a classical four-story art deco gem with friezes, and now houses an H&M. ⊠ *Lincoln Rd. between Washington Ave. and Alton Rd., South Beach* ⊕ *www.lincolnroadmall.com.*

★ **Pérez Art Museum Miami** (*PAMM*)
MUSEUM | FAMILY | This über-high-design architectural masterpiece on Biscayne Bay is a sight to behold. Double-story, cylindrical hanging gardens sway from high atop the museum, anchored to stylish wood trusses that help create this gotta-see-it-to-believe-it indoor-outdoor museum. Large sculptures, Asian-inspired gardens, sexy white benches, and steel frames envelop the property. Inside, the 120,000-square-foot space houses multicultural art from the 20th and 21st centuries. Most of the interior space is devoted to temporary exhibitions, which have included the likes of *Ai Weiwei: According to What?* and *Grids: A Selection of Paintings by Lynne Golob Gelfman.* Even if you aren't a "museum type," come check out this magnum opus over lunch at Verde at PAMM, the museum's sensational waterfront restaurant and bar. ■TIP→ **Admission is free every first Thursday of the month and every**

second Saturday of the month. ⊠ *1103 Biscayne Blvd., Downtown* ☎ *305/375–3000* ⊕ *www.pamm.org* ⊠ *$16* ⊗ *Closed Wed.*

★ **Rubell Museum**
MUSEUM | Fans of edgy art will appreciate the Rubell Museum (formerly Rubell Family Collection). Mera and Don Rubell have accumulated work by artists from the 1970s to the present, including Jeff Koons, Cindy Sherman, Damien Hirst, and Keith Haring. New thematic and topical exhibitions debut annually, during Art Basel in December. (For example, a previous exhibition, *Still Human,* delved into the impact of the digital revolution on the human condition.) Admission always includes a complimentary audio tour; however, true art lovers should opt for a complimentary guided tour of the collection, offered Wednesday through Saturday at 3 pm. The collection moved to its new, larger home on the outskirts of Wynwood in 2019. ⊠ *95 N.W. 29th St., between N. Miami and N.W. 1st Aves., Wynwood* ☎ *305/573–6090* ⊕ *www.rfc.museum* ⊠ *$10* ⊗ *Closed Sept.–Nov.*

★ **Vizcaya Museum and Gardens**
HISTORIC SITE | FAMILY | Of the 10,000 people living in Miami between 1912 and 1916, about 1,000 of them were gainfully employed by Chicago industrialist James Deering to build this European-inspired residence. Once comprising 180 acres, this National Historic Landmark now occupies a 30-acre tract that includes a rockland hammock (native forest) and more than 10 acres of formal gardens with fountains overlooking Biscayne Bay. The house, open to the public, contains 70 rooms, 34 of which are filled with paintings, sculpture, antique furniture, and other fine and decorative arts. The collection spans 2,000 years and represents the Renaissance, baroque, rococo, and neoclassical periods. The 90-minute self-guided Discover Vizcaya Audio Tour is available in multiple languages for an additional $5. Moonlight tours, offered on evenings that are nearest the full moon,

Wynwood is famous for its walls covered by murals from famous contemporary artists, including these by Shepard Fairey.

provide a magical look at the gardens; call for reservations. ✉ *3251 S. Miami Ave., Coconut Grove* ☎ *305/250–9133* ⊕ *www.vizcaya.org* 🎫 *$22* 🕐 *Closed Tues.*

★ Wynwood Walls

LOCAL INTEREST | Between Northeast 25th and 26th Streets on Northwest 2nd Avenue, the Wynwood Walls are a cutting-edge enclave of modern urban murals, reflecting diversity in graffiti and street art. More than 50 well-known and lesser-known artists have transformed 80,000 square feet of warehouse walls into an outdoor museum of sorts (bring your camera). The popularity of the walls spawned the neighboring Wynwood Doors and Garden, an industrial space rife with metal roll-down gates also used as blank canvases, complemented by a garden with singular pieces of art and an eye-popping indoor gallery. ✉ *2520 N.W. 2nd Ave., Wynwood* ⊕ *www.thewynwoodwalls.com.*

🏖 Beaches

★ Bill Baggs Cape Florida State Park

BEACH—SIGHT | FAMILY | Thanks to inviting beaches, sunsets, and a tranquil lighthouse, this park at Key Biscayne's southern tip is worth the drive. In fact, the 1-mile stretch of pure beachfront has been named several times in Dr. Beach's revered America's Top 10 Beaches list. It has 18 picnic pavilions available as daily rentals, two cafés that serve light lunches that include several Cuban specialties, and plenty of space to enjoy the umbrella and chair rentals. Bill Baggs has bicycle rentals, a playground, fishing piers, and guided tours of the **Cape Florida Lighthouse,** South Florida's oldest structure. Free tours are offered at the restored cottage and lighthouse Thursday to Monday at 10 am and 1 pm. Be there a half hour beforehand. **Amenities:** food and drink; lifeguards; parking (no fee); showers; toilets. **Best for:** solitude; sunset; walking. ✉ *1200 S. Crandon Blvd., Key Biscayne* ☎ *305/361–5811* ⊕ *www.*

floridastateparks.org/park/Cape-Florida
🚗 $8 per vehicle, $2 per pedestrian.

★ South Beach

BEACH—SIGHT | A 10-block stretch of white sandy beach hugging the turquoise waters along Ocean Drive from 5th to 15th Streets is one of the most popular in America, known for drawing unabashedly model-like sunbathers and posers. With the influx of new luxe hotels and hot spots from 1st to 5th and 16th to 25th Streets, the South Beach stand-and-pose scene is now bigger than ever and stretches yet another dozen-plus blocks. The beaches crowd quickly on the weekends with a blend of European tourists, young hipsters, and sun-drenched locals. Separating the sand from the traffic of Ocean Drive is palm-fringed **Lummus Park,** with its volleyball nets and chickee huts (huts made of palmetto thatch over a cypress frame) for shade. The beach at **12th Street** is popular with gays, in a section often marked with rainbow flags. Locals hang out on 3rd Street beach, in an area called **SoFi** (South of Fifth). **Amenities:** food and drink; lifeguards; parking (fee); showers; toilets. **Best for:** partiers; sunrise; swimming; walking. ✉ Ocean Dr. from 5th to 15th Sts., then Collins Ave. to 25th St., South Beach.

🍴 Restaurants

At many of the hottest spots you'll need a reservation to avoid a long wait for a table. And when you get your check, note whether a gratuity is included; most restaurants add 15%–20% (ostensibly for the convenience of—and protection from—Latin-American and European tourists who are used to this practice in their homelands and would not normally tip), but you can reduce or supplement it depending on your opinion of the service.

★ Joe's Stone Crab

$$$$ | SEAFOOD | In South Beach's decidedly new-money scene, the stately Joe's Stone Crab is an old-school testament to good food and good service. Stone crabs, served with legendary mustard sauce, crispy hash browns, and creamed spinach, remain the staple at South Beach's most storied restaurant (which dates to 1913). **Known for:** best-of-the-best stone crab claws; key lime pie; no reservations (arrive very early). $ Average main: $46 ✉ 11 Washington Ave., South Beach ☎ 305/673–0365, 305/673–4611 for takeout ⊕ www.joesstonecrab.com ⏱ Closed mid-May–mid-Oct. No lunch Sun.–Mon.

★ Juvia

$$$$ | JAPANESE FUSION | High atop South Beach's design-driven 1111 Lincoln Road parking garage, rooftop Juvia commingles urban sophistication with South Beach seduction. Three renowned chefs unite to deliver an amazing eating experience that screams Japanese, Peruvian, and French all in the same breath, focusing largely on raw fish and seafood dishes. **Known for:** city and beach views; sunset cocktails on the terrace; bigeye tuna poke. $ Average main: $35 ✉ 1111 Lincoln Rd., South Beach ☎ 305/763–8272 ⊕ www.juviamiami.com ⏱ No lunch weekdays.

★ Versailles

$$ | CUBAN | FAMILY | Miami visitors looking for that "Cuban food on Calle Ocho" experience, look no further: the storied eatery, where old émigrés opine daily about all things Cuban, is a stop on every political candidate's campaign trail, and it should be a stop for you as well. Order a heaping platter of lechón asado (roasted pork loin), ropa vieja (shredded beef), or picadillo (spicy ground beef), all served with rice, beans, and fried plantains. **Known for:** gossipy locals at takeout window; old-school Little Havana setting; guava-filled pastelitos. $ Average main: $16 ✉ 3555 S.W. 8th St., Little Havana ☎ 305/444–0240 ⊕ www.versaillesrestaurant.com.

🛏 Hotels

Staying in downtown Miami will put you close to the cruise terminals and show you the pulse of this growing metropolis. But for fun in the sun, South Beach is still the center of the action in Miami Beach and just an Uber ride away from the port (although traffic can make for a long ride). Staying in the burgeoning Mid-Beach area, north of South Beach's Art Deco District, will still put you on the beach but nominally closer to the port.

★ Fontainebleau Miami Beach

$$$$ | **RESORT** | **FAMILY** | Vegas meets art deco at Miami's largest hotel, which has more than 1,500 rooms (in four separate towers, almost half of which are suites), 12 renowned restaurants and lounges, LIV nightclub, several pools with cabana islands, a state-of-the-art fitness center, and a 40,000-square-foot spa. **Pros:** expansive pool and beach areas; historic allure; great nightlife. **Cons:** lots of nonguests visiting grounds; massive size; loud, weekend parties outside. $ *Rooms from: $449* ✉ *4441 Collins Ave., Mid-Beach* ☎ *305/535–3283, 800/548–8886* ⊕ *www.fontainebleau.com* ⬐ *1504 rooms* ⦿ *No meals.*

★ Kimpton EPIC Miami

$$$ | **HOTEL** | In the heart of Downtown, Kimpton's pet-friendly, artful EPIC Hotel has 411 guest rooms with spacious balconies (many of them overlook Biscayne Bay) and fabulous modern amenities to match the sophistication of the common areas, which include a supersexy rooftop pool. **Pros:** sprawling rooftop pool deck; balcony in every room; complimentary wine hour, coffee, and Wi-Fi. **Cons:** some rooms have inferior views; congested valet area; sometimes windy around pool area. $ *Rooms from: $375* ✉ *270 Biscayne Blvd. Way, Downtown* ☎ *305/424–5226* ⊕ *www.epichotel.com* ⬐ *411 rooms* ⦿ *No meals.*

Loews Miami Beach Hotel

$$$$ | **HOTEL** | **FAMILY** | This two-tower megahotel has 790 rooms (all redesigned in 2018 with a soothing, sea-inspired motif), top-tier amenities, a massive spa, a great pool, and direct beachfront access, making it a great choice for families, businesspeople, groups, and pet lovers. **Pros:** excellent on-site seafood restaurant; resort atmosphere; pets welcome. **Cons:** insanely large; constantly crowded; pets desperate to go will need to wait several minutes to make it to the grass. $ *Rooms from: $459* ✉ *1601 Collins Ave., South Beach* ☎ *305/604–1601, 855/757–2061 for reservations* ⊕ *www.loewshotels.com/miami-beach* ⬐ *790 rooms* ⦿ *No meals.*

🍸 Nightlife

One of Greater Miami's most popular pursuits is barhopping. Options range from intimate enclaves to showy see-and-be-seen lounges to loud, raucous frat parties. There's a New York–style flair to some of the newer lounges, which are increasingly catering to a Manhattan party crowd who escape to Miami and Miami Beach for long weekends. No doubt, Miami's pulse pounds with nonstop nightlife that reflects the area's potent cultural mix. On sultry, humid nights with the huge full moon rising out of the ocean and fragrant night-blooming jasmine intoxicating the senses, who can resist Cuban salsa with some disco and hip-hop thrown in for good measure? When this place throws a party, hips shake, fingers snap, bodies touch. It's no wonder many clubs are still rocking at 5 am. If you're looking for a relatively nonfrenetic evening, your best bet is one of the chic hotel bars on Collins Avenue, or a lounge in Wynwood, the Design District, or Downtown.

Mobile's history is detailed in a historic building on Royal Street.

🛍 Shopping

Beyond its fun-in-the-sun offerings, Miami has evolved into a world-class shopping destination. People fly to Miami from all over the world just to shop. The city teems with sophisticated malls—from indoor, climate-controlled multistory temples of consumerism to sun-kissed, open-air retail enclaves—and bustling avenues and streets, lined at once with affordable chain stores, haute couture boutiques, and one-off "only in Miami"–type shops. Miami's shopping centers are record breakers. Several chain stores in the massive Aventura Mall rank as the best-selling outposts in the country, while Bal Harbour Shops flaunt the most lucrative square footage of any shopping arena in the country, with its sales reaching up to $2,555 per square foot. Following the incredible success of the Bal Harbour Shops in the highest of the high-end market (Chanel, Alexander McQueen, Etro, and Hermès), the Design District has followed suit. Beyond fabulous designer furniture showrooms, the district's tenants now include Dior Homme, Rolex, Prada, and an entire LVMH (Moët Hennessy Louis Vuitton) mall.

Mobile, Alabama

Fort Condé de la Mobille was the name given by the French in 1711 to the site known today as Mobile; around it blossomed the first white settlement in what is now Alabama. For eight years it was the capital of French Louisiana, and it remained under French control until 1763, long after the capital had moved to New Orleans. Mobile, known as "the Port City"—not to mention the birthplace of Mardi Gras—is noted for its tree-lined boulevards fanning westward from the riverfront. In the heart of busy downtown is Bienville Square, a park with an ornate cast-iron fountain and shaded by centuries-old live oaks. One of the city's main thoroughfares, Dauphin Street, has many thriving restaurants, bars, and shops.

ESSENTIALS

HOURS

Dauphin Street is dotted with eclectic boutiques offering clothing, art, and antiques—most of which close by 6 pm. Myriad restaurants, pubs, and bars (some offering live music) stay open later.

VISITOR INFORMATION

There's a Visit Mobile Welcome Center inside the Museum of Mobile at 111 S. Royal St.

THE CRUISE PORT

The cruise terminal is near the downtown area. *Carnival Fantasy* is based in Mobile year-round, offering mmostly4- and 5-day cruies, as well as a few longer ones, in the Western Caribbean. Free shuttles from Mobile's public transit system, Moda, run every 10 minutes from 7 am to 6 pm on weekends, and 9 to 5 on Saturday along a three-mile route that includes the cruise terminal. It's a good home port to consider if you want to drive, but it's less convenient by air, with just a few airlines flying to the Mobile Regional Airport; however, the Biloxi and Pensacola airports are a relatively short drive away.

CONTACTS Mobile, Alabama Cruise Terminal. ⊠ *201 S. Water St., Mobile* ☎ *251/338–7447* ⊕ *www.shipmobile. com.*

AIRPORT

American (via CLT and DFW), Delta (via ATL), and United (via IAH) offer flights into Mobile Regional Airport (MOB). Frontier offers two daily flights (from DEN and ORD) to Mobile Downtown Airport (BFM).

AIRPORT TRANSFERS

Taxis are available to the cruise terminal for about $30 each way (per trip, not per passenger). Both Uber and Lyft offer pickups at the airports.

Best Bets ◉

■ **Bellingrath Gardens.** One of the finest gardens in the South is just outside Mobile.

■ **Battleship Memorial Park.** Many people come to Mobile just to tour the USS *Alabama.*

■ **Oakleigh.** This well-preserved antebellum home is furnished with period antiques; it's a great experience if you like history.

PARKING

Parking is available in a garage immediately adjacent to the cruise terminal. A four-day parking pass is $72 for cars, $144 for RVs. You can pay by cash or credit card, and you can also pre-pay and reserve parking in advance of your cruise online.

CONTACTS Premium Parking. ⊠ *201 Water St., Mobile* ☎ *844/236–2011 toll-free, 24 hours* ⊕ *www.premiumparking.com.*

◉ Sights

Fort Condé

HISTORIC SITE | FAMILY | Experience colonial life at this former French outpost, where Mobile was born. Today, the city's French origins endure in its Creole cuisine and at this historic site. Roughly 150 years after the fort was destroyed, its remains were discovered during construction of the Interstate 10 interchange. A rebuilt portion houses the city's visitor center as well as a museum. Costumed guides conduct tours. ⊠ *150 S. Royal St., Mobile* ☎ *0251/802–3092* ⊕ *www.colonialmo-bile.com* ⊠ *$8.*

History Museum of Mobile

MUSEUM | FAMILY | Interactive exhibits and special collections of antique silver, weapons, and more tell the 300-year history of Mobile. The Southern Market/

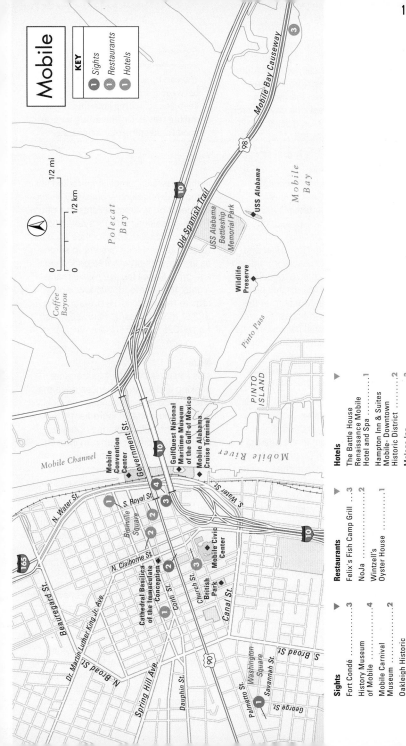

Sights ▶

Fort Condé 3

History Museum
of Mobile 4

Mobile Carnival
Museum 2

Oakleigh Historic
Complex 1

Restaurants ▶

Felix's Fish Camp Grill ...3

NoJa 2

Wintzell's
Oyster House 1

Hotels ▶

The Battle House
Renaissance Mobile
Hotel and Spa 1

Hampton Inn & Suites
Mobile- Downtown
Historic District 2

Malaga Inn 3

KEY

● Sights
● Restaurants
● Hotels

Mobile

Old City Hall, an 1857 National Historic Landmark Italianate building, houses the museum. A Civil War cannon, miniature houses, and souvenirs from Mobile's oldest mystic societies, the secretive social groups that stage the city's Mardi Gras celebrations, are on display. ⊠ *111 S. Royal St., Mobile* ☎ *0251/208–7569* ⊕ *www.museumofmobile.com* ✉ *$10*.

Mobile Carnival Museum

INFO CENTER | FAMILY | Mobile boasts America's oldest annual Carnival celebration, which started in 1703, 15 years before New Orleans was founded. Festivities, including parades and masquerade balls, begin in November and continue through Fat Tuesday in mid-February. Find the celebration schedule and learn about the city's Mardi Gras history at the Mobile Carnival Museum at the historic Bernstein-Bush house. Fourteen gallery rooms, a pictorial hallway, theater, den, and gift shop show off royal robes, crowns, scepters, and more. ⊠ *355 Government St., Mobile* ☎ *0251/432–3324* ⊕ *www.mobilecarnivalmuseum.com* ✉ *$8* ⊗ *Closed Tues. and Sun.*

Oakleigh Historic Complex

HISTORIC SITE | This antebellum Greek Revival–style mansion, in the heart of historic Oakleigh Garden District, is Mobile's official period house. Costumed guides give tours of the home, built between 1833 and 1838. See fine period furniture, portraits, silver, jewelry, kitchen implements, toys, and more. Tickets include a tour of the garden, the cook's house, and the neighboring Cox–Deasy House, an 1850s cottage furnished with simple 19th-century pieces. ⊠ *350 Oakleigh Pl., Mobile* ☎ *0251/432–1281* ⊕ *www.historicoakleigh.com* ✉ *$10* ⊗ *Closed Tues.–Thur.*

Restaurants

Felix's Fish Camp Grill

$$ | SEAFOOD | FAMILY | Gulf seafood, grilled steaks, and seasonal specials are served

in this massive, camplike tin-roofed shack complex overlooking Mobile Bay, including views of downtown lights at night. The huge selection offers everything from traditional regional dishes such as turtle soup and fried oysters to surprises like crayfish-smothered pork chops and grits. **Known for:** live music many nights; fried seafood; window tables require reservations. ⑤ *Average main: $22* ⊠ *1530 Battleship Pkwy., Spanish Fort* ☎ *0251/626–6710* ⊕ *www.felixsfish-camp.com*.

NoJa

$$$$ | MEDITERRANEAN | Mediterranean cooking and Asian influences drive the creative menu that changes seasonally and taps sustainable ingredients. Selections might include orange-honey-lacquered duck breast with rum-infused Jasmine rice, seared sea scallops with Cajun seasoning and sweet marsala, and, for dessert, ginger doughnuts with vanilla bean or popcorn ice cream. **Known for:** wide-ranging international menu; popcorn icecream; outdoor patio seating. ⑤ *Average main: $40* ⊠ *6 N. Jackson St., Mobile* ☎ *0251/433–0377* ⊕ *www. nojamobile.com* ⊗ *Closed Sun.–Mon.*

Wintzell's Oyster House

$$ | SEAFOOD | Now a regional chain, this local favorite for seafood has been in business since 1938, serving a menu of mostly seafood (especially fresh and fried Gulf oysters) from its original location on Dauphin Street. A local favorite, the original location has a lot more home-spun charm than the newer branches, with bare wood tables and walls decorated

with hand-printed signs and slogans.
Known for: oysters, fresh on the half-shell and fried; other grilled and fried seafood; cold crab salad and fried Alabama blue crab claws. $ *Average main: $20* ⊠ *605 Dauphin St., Mobile* ☎ *251/432–4605* ⊕ *wintzellsoysterhouse.com.*

Hotels

Several local hotels offer cruise packages that include lodging, parking for the duration of your cruise, and a shuttle to the cruise terminal.

The Battle House Renaissance Mobile Hotel and Spa

$$$ | HOTEL | Celebrities, sports stars, a president, and a king have all stayed at this grand hotel that dates to 1852. **Pros:** historic-district packages; government and military discount. **Cons:** buffet breakfast fee; valet parking fee. $ *Rooms from: $195* ⊠ *26 N. Royal St., Mobile* ☎ *0251/338–2000* ⊕ *www.marriott.com* ⇨ *238 rooms* ⎸❍⎸ *No meals.*

Hampton Inn & Suites Mobile - Downtown Historic District

$$ | HOTEL | Located on Mobile's Mardi Gras parade route, the hotel is lined with balcony rooms. **Pros:** close to the airport; most area attractions within a 10- to 15-minute drive. **Cons:** smoking allowed in outdoor areas; late-checkout fee; no pets. $ *Rooms from: $169* ⊠ *62 S. Royal St., Mobile* ☎ *0251/436–8787* ⊕ *hamptoninn3.hilton.com* ⇨ *150 rooms* ⎸❍⎸ *Free Breakfast.*

Malaga Inn

$$ | B&B/INN | A lush courtyard with a fountain anchors this delightful, historic inn built as twin town houses in 1862. **Pros:** historic location with tours available; complimentary off-street parking. **Cons:** courtyard may be occupied by special events. $ *Rooms from: $118* ⊠ *359 Church St., Mobile* ☎ *251/438–4701, 800/235–1586 toll-free* ⊕ *malagainn.com* ⇨ *39 rooms* ⎸❍⎸ *Free Breakfast.*

Nightlife

Most of Mobile's nightlife centers around downtown's former commercial district, Dauphin Street, which today has a number of restaurants and nightspots spread out over several blocks. Mobilians have taken to calling the area "LoDa," short for Lower Dauphin.

Shopping

Most shopping in Mobile is in malls and shopping centers in the suburbs. Stores are generally open Monday to Saturday 10–9, Sunday noon–6. Antiques buffs may be interested in Mobile's many antiques stores that are in the Loop area of midtown (where Government Street, Airport Boulevard, and Dauphin Island Parkway converge); several shops are within walking distance of each other.

New Orleans, Louisiana

The spiritual and cultural heart of New Orleans is the French Quarter, where the city was settled by the French in 1718. You could easily spend several days visiting museums, shops, and eateries in this area, but you can also quickly get a feel for the place. If you have time, the rest of the city's neighborhoods, radiating out from this focal point, also make for a rewarding ramble. The mansion-lined streets of the Garden District and Uptown, the aboveground cemeteries that dot the city, and the open air along Lake Pontchartrain provide a nice balance to the commercialization of the Quarter. Despite its sprawling size, New Orleans has a small-town vibe, perhaps due to locals' shared cultural habits and history.

ESSENTIALS
HOURS

Shops in the French Quarter tend to be open late, but stores in most malls close by 9. Restaurants tend to be open late as well, and many bars never close their doors.

TOURS

Several local tour companies give two- to four-hour city tours by bus that include the French Quarter, the Garden District, uptown New Orleans, and the lakefront. Prices range from $25 to $125 per person, depending on the kind of experience. Both Gray Line and New Orleans Tours offer a longer itinerary that combines a two-hour city tour by bus with a two-hour steamboat ride on the Mississippi River. Gray Line and Tours by Isabelle both offer tours of Hurricane Katrina devastation as well.

CONTACTS New Orleans Tours.
☎ *504/592–1991* ⊕ *www.notours.com.*

VISITOR INFORMATION
CONTACTS New Orleans & Company.
✉ *2020 St. Charles Ave., New Orleans*
☎ *800/672–6124, 504/566–5011* ⊕ *www.neworleans.com.*

THE CRUISE PORT

The Julia Street Cruise Terminal is at the end of Julia Street on the Mississippi River; the Erato Street Cruise Terminal is just to the north. Both terminals are behind the Ernest N. Morial Convention Center. You can walk to the French Quarter from here in about 10 minutes; it's a short taxi ride to the Quarter or nearby hotels. Carnival and Norwegian both base ships here year round.

If you are driving, you'll probably approach New Orleans on I-10. Take the exit for Business 90 West/Westbank (locally known as the Pontchartrain Expressway), and proceed to the Tchoupitoulas Street/South Peters Street exit. Continue to Convention Center Boulevard, where you will take a right turn. Continue to Henderson Street, where you will turn left, and then continue to Port of New Orleans Place. Take a left on Port of New Orleans Place to Julia Street Terminals 1 and 2, or take a right to get to the Robin Street Wharf.

CONTACTS Port of New Orleans. ✉ *Port of New Orleans Pl., New Orleans* ☎ *504/522–2551* ⊕ *www.portnola.com.*

AIRPORT
CONTACTS Louis Armstrong New Orleans International Airport. (*MSY*) ✉ *900 Airline Dr.* ☎ *504/303–7500* ⊕ *www.flymsy.com.*

AIRPORT TRANSFERS

Shuttle-bus service to and from the airport and the cruise port is available through Airport Shuttle New Orleans. Buses leave regularly from the ground level near the baggage claim. Return trips to the airport need to be booked in advance. A one-way ticket is $20 per person and a round-trip ticket $38. The trip takes about 30 minutes.

A cab ride to or from the airport from uptown or downtown New Orleans costs a flat $33 for the first two passengers and $14 for each additional passenger. At the airport, pick-up is on the lower level, outside the baggage claim area. There may be an additional charge for extra baggage.

CONTACTS Airport Shuttle New Orleans. ✉ *4220 Howard Ave., New Orleans* ☎ *504/522–3500, 866/596–2699* ⊕ *www.airportshuttleneworleans.com.*

PARKING

If you are spending some time in the city before or after your cruise, finding a parking space is fairly easy in most of the city except for the French Quarter, where meter maids are plentiful and tow trucks eager. If in doubt about a space, pass it up and pay to use a parking lot. Avoid parking spaces at corners and curbs: less than 15 feet between your car and the corner will result in a ticket. Watch for temporary "No Parking" signs, which pop up along parade routes and film shoots. Long-term and overnight parking are extremely expensive at hotels and garages. Parking for the duration of your cruise is available for $16 per night and can be found on Erato Street; if you want, SeaCaps will take your bags directly to the ship so you just have to deal with your hand luggage. RVs can park in a lot on Poydras Street next to Terminal 2 at the Julia Street dock for $32 per night.

◎ Sights

The French Quarter, the oldest part of the city, lives up to all you've heard: it's alive with the sights, sounds, odors, and experiences of a major entertainment hub. At some point, ignore your better judgment and take a stroll down Bourbon Street, past the bars, restaurants, music clubs, and novelty shops that have given this strip its reputation as the playground of the South. Be sure to find time to stop at Café Du Monde for chicory-laced coffee and beignets. With its beautifully landscaped gardens surrounding elegant antebellum homes, the Garden District is mostly residential, but most home-owners do not mind your enjoying the sights from outside the cast-iron fences surrounding their magnificent properties.

Garden District. Jackson Avenue divides the Garden District into two sections. Upriver from Jackson is the wealthy Upper Garden District, where the homes are meticulously kept. Below Jackson, the Lower Garden District is considerably rougher. Although the homes here are often just as structurally beautiful, most of them lack the recent restorations of those of the Upper Garden District. The streets are also less well patrolled—wander cautiously. Magazine Street, lined with antiques shops and coffeehouses (ritzier along the Upper Garden District, hipper along the Lower Garden District), serves as a southern border to the Garden District; and St. Charles Avenue forms the northern border.

★ **Audubon Aquarium of the Americas**
ZOO | FAMILY | This giant aquatic show-place perched on the Mississippi riverfront has four major exhibit areas: the Amazon Rain Forest, the Mississippi River, the Gulf of Mexico, and the new

Best Bets ◉

■ **Audubon Aquarium of the Americas.** Especially good for families is this fantastic aquarium on the edge of French Quarter.

■ **Eating Well.** One highlight of New Orleans is dining. If you ever wanted to splurge on a great restaurant meal, this is the place to do it. At the very least, have a beignet at Café Du Monde.

■ **Live Music** Few cities love to party as much as New Orleans, where you can find excellent locally and nationally known bands every night of the week.

Great Maya Reef gallery, all of which have fish and animals native to their respective environments. The aquarium's spectacular design allows you to feel like you're part of these watery worlds by providing close-up encounters with the inhabitants. One special treat is Parakeet Pointe, where you can spend time amid hundreds of parakeets and feed them by hand. A gift shop and café are on the premises. Woldenberg Riverfront Park, which surrounds the aquarium, is a tranquil spot with a view of the Mississippi. You can combine tickets for the aquarium and the **Entergy IMAX Theater** ($29.95), but the best deal is the Audubon Experience, which includes the aquarium, IMAX Theater, **Audubon Insectarium**, and **Audubon Zoo** for $44.95 (tickets are good for 30 days). ⊠ *1 Canal St., French Quarter* ☎ *504/861–2537, 800/774–7394* ⊕ *www. audubonnatureinstitute.org* ☜ *$29.95.*

Beauregard-Keyes House and Garden Museum
MUSEUM | This stately 19th-century mansion was briefly home to Confederate general and Louisiana native P.G.T. Beauregard, but a longer-term resident was the novelist Frances Parkinson Keyes,

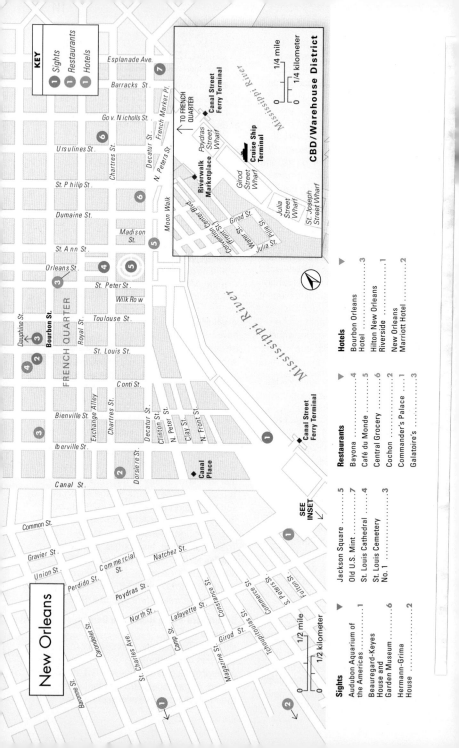

New Orleans

0   1/2 mile
0   1/2 kilometer

FRENCH QUARTER

Bourbon St.

KEY
- ① Sights
- ① Restaurants
- ① Hotels

Mississippi River

SEE INSET

CBD/Warehouse District

0   1/4 mile
0   1/4 kilometer

Mississippi River

TO FRENCH QUARTER

Canal Street Ferry Terminal

Riverwalk Marketplace

Cruise Ship Terminal

Poydras Street Wharf

Girod Street Wharf

Julia Street Wharf

St. Joseph Street Wharf

Moon Walk

Canal Place

Canal Street Ferry Terminal

Sights ▶
Audubon Aquarium of the Americas	1
Beauregard-Keyes House and Garden Museum	6
Hermann-Grima House	2
Jackson Square	5
Old U.S. Mint	7
St. Louis Cathedral	4
St. Louis Cemetery No. 1	3

Restaurants ▶
Bayona	4
Café du Monde	5
Central Grocery	6
Cochon	2
Commander's Palace	1
Galatoire's	3

Hotels ▶
Bourbon Orleans Hotel	3
Hilton New Orleans Riverside	1
New Orleans Marriott Hotel	2

who found the place in a sad state when she arrived in the 1940s. Keyes restored the home—today filled with period furnishings—and her studio at the back of the large courtyard remains intact, complete with family photos, original manuscripts, and her doll, fan, and teapot collections. Keyes wrote 40 novels there, all in longhand, among them local favorite *Dinner at Antoine's*. Even if you don't have time for a tour, take a peek at the beautiful walled garden through the gates at the corner of Chartres and Ursulines Streets. Landscaped in the same sun pattern as Jackson Square, it blooms year-round. ⊠ *1113 Chartres St., French Quarter* ☎ *504/523–7257* ⊕ *www. bkhouse.org* ⊠ *$10* ⊗ *Closed Sun.*

Hermann-Grima House

MUSEUM | Noted architect William Brand built this Georgian-style house in 1831, and it's one of the largest and best-preserved examples of American architecture in the Vieux Carré. Cooking demonstrations on the open hearth of the Creole kitchen are held most Thursdays from November through April. You'll want to check out the gift shop, which has many local crafts and books. ⊠ *820 St. Louis St., French Quarter* ☎ *504/274– 0750* ⊕ *www.hgghh.org* ⊠ *$15* ⊗ *Closed Wed.*

★ Jackson Square

MUSEUM | FAMILY | Surrounded by historic buildings and atmospheric street life, this beautifully landscaped park is the heart of the French Quarter. **St. Louis Cathedral** sits at the top of the square, while the **Cabildo** and **Presbytère,** two Spanish colonial buildings, flank the church. The handsome brick apartments on each side of the square are the **Pontalba Buildings.** During the day, dozens of artists hang their paintings on the park fence and set up outdoor studios where they work on canvases or offer to draw portraits of passersby. Musicians, mimes, tarot-card readers, and magicians perform on the

flagstone pedestrian mall, many of them day and night.

A **statue of Andrew Jackson,** victorious leader in the Battle of New Orleans in the War of 1812, commands the center of the square; the park was renamed for him in the 1850s. The words carved in the base on the cathedral side of the statue ("The Union must and shall be preserved") are a lasting reminder of the Federal troops who occupied New Orleans during the Civil War and who inscribed them. ⊠ *701 Decatur St., French Quarter* ⊕ *www.experiencene- worleans.com.*

St. Louis Cemetery No. 1

CEMETERY | The oldest and most famous of New Orleans's cities of the dead, founded in the late 1700s, is just one block from the French Quarter. Stately rows of crypts are home to many of the city's most legendary figures, including Homer Plessy of the *Plessy v. Ferguson* 1896 U.S. Supreme Court decision establishing the "Jim Crow" laws ("separate but equal"), and voodoo queen Marie Laveau, whose grave is still a popular pilgrimage among the spiritual, the superstitious, and the curious. Visitors are required to be part of a tour group in order to enter the cemetery, so join one of the many groups that come through each day. The nonprofit group **Save Our Cemeteries** (*504/525–3377)* gives guided tours daily leaving from the Basin Street Station Visitors Center at 501 Basin Street. ⊠ *499 Basin St., bounded by Basin, Conti, Tremé, and St. Louis Sts., Tremé* ⊠ *Save Our Cemeteries tours $20.*

Old U.S. Mint

MUSEUM | Minting began in 1838 in this ambitious Ionic structure, a project of President Andrew Jackson's. The New Orleans mint was to provide currency for the South and the West, which it did until Louisiana seceded from the Union in 1861. Both the short-lived Republic of Louisiana and the Confederacy

A statue of General Andrew Jackson presides over his namesake park, Jackson Square.

minted coins here. When Confederate supplies ran out, the building served as a barracks—and then a prison—for Confederate soldiers. The production of U.S. coins recommenced only in 1879; it stopped again, for good, in 1909. After years of neglect, the federal government handed the Old Mint over to Louisiana in 1966. The state now uses the building for exhibitions of the Louisiana State Museum collection, and the New Orleans Jazz National Historical Park has events here. After repairs from damage by Hurricane Katrina, the museum reopened to the public in 2007.

The first-floor exhibit recounts the history of the mint. The principal draw, however, is the second floor, dedicated to items from the **New Orleans Jazz Collection**. At the end of the exhibit, displayed in its own room like the Crown Jewels, you'll find Louis Armstrong's first cornet.

The **Louisiana Historical Center,** which holds the French and Spanish Louisiana archives, is open to researchers by appointment. At the foot of Esplanade Avenue, notice the memorial to the French rebels against early Spanish rule. The rebel leaders were executed on this spot and gave nearby Frenchmen Street its name. ⊠ *400 Esplanade Ave., French Quarter* ☎ *504/568–6993* ⊕ *louisianas-tatemuseum.org* 🎟 *$9.*

St. Louis Cathedral

RELIGIOUS SITE | The oldest active Catholic cathedral in the United States, this beautiful church and basilica at the heart of the Old City is named for the 13th-century French king who led two crusades. The current building, which replaced two structures destroyed by fire, dates from 1794 (although it was remodeled and enlarged in 1851). The austere interior is brightened by murals covering the ceiling and stained-glass windows along the first floor. Pope John Paul II held a prayer service for clergy here during his New Orleans visit in 1987; to honor the occasion, the pedestrian mall in front of the cathedral was renamed Place Jean Paul Deux. Of special interest is his portrait in a Jackson Square setting, which hangs on the cathedral's inner side wall. Docents often give free tours. You can also pick up a brochure ($1) for a self-guided tour. Books about the cathedral are available in the gift shop.

■TIP→ **Nearly every evening in December there's a free concert at the cathedral, in addition to the free concert series throughout the year.**

The statue of the Sacred Heart of Jesus dominates **St. Anthony's Garden,** which extends behind the cathedral to Royal Street. The garden is also the site of a monument to 30 crew members of a French ship, who died in a yellow fever epidemic in 1857. The garden has been redesigned by famed French landscape architect Louis Benech, who also redesigned the Tuileries gardens in Paris. ✉ *615 Père Antoine Alley, French Quarter* ☎ *504/525–9585* ⊕ *www.stlouiscathedral.org* ◿ *Free* ☞ *Mass daily at 7:30 am.*

🍴 Restaurants

Regardless of where you decide to eat, don't miss the beignets at Café Du Monde.

★ Bayona

$$$ | MODERN AMERICAN | "New World" is the label Louisiana native Susan Spicer applies to her cooking style, the delicious hallmarks of which include goat cheese croutons with mushrooms in madeira cream, a Bayona specialty, and delightfully flavorful vegetable soups, like Caribbean pumpkin or cream of garlic. A legendary favorite at lunch is the sandwich of smoked duck, cashew butter, and pepper jelly. **Known for:** chef Susan Spicer; smoked duck sandwich; global flavors. ⑤ *Average main: $30* ✉ *430 Dauphine St., French Quarter* ☎ *504/525–4455* ⊕ *www.bayona.com* ⊗ *Closed Sun. No lunch Mon.–Tues.*

★ Café Du Monde

$ | CAFÉ | FAMILY | No visit to New Orleans is complete without a chicory-laced café au lait paired with the addictive, sugar-dusted beignets at this venerable institution. The tables under the green-and-white-stripe awning are jammed with locals and tourists at almost every hour. **Known for:** beignets; café au lait; local landmark. ⑤ *Average main: $3* ✉ *800 Decatur St., French Quarter* ☎ *504/525–4544* ⊕ *www.cafedumonde.com.*

Central Grocery

$ | DELI | FAMILY | This old-fashioned grocery store creates authentic muffulettas, a gastronomic gift from the city's Italian immigrants. Made by filling nearly 10-inch round loaves of seeded bread with ham, salami, provolone and Emmentaler cheeses, and olive salad, the muffuletta is nearly as popular locally as the po'boy. (Central Grocery also sells a vegetarian version.) The sandwiches are available in wholes and halves (they're huge—unless you're starving, you'll do fine with a half). **Known for:** muffulettas; lively setting; central location. ⑤ *Average main: $8* ✉ *923 Decatur St., French Quarter* ☎ *504/523–1620* ⊕ *www.centralgrocery. com* ⊗ *No dinner.*

★ Cochon

$$$ | CAJUN | Chef-owned restaurants are common in New Orleans, but this one builds on owner Donald Link's family heritage as he, working with co-owner Stephen Stryjewski (who received a James Beard Award for his work here), prepares Cajun dishes he learned to cook at his grandfather's knee. The interior may be a bit too hip and noisy for some patrons, but the food makes up for it. **Known for:** cochon de lait; rabbit and dumplings; fried boudin. ⑤ *Average main: $26* ✉ *930 Tchoupitoulas St., Warehouse District* ☎ *504/588–2123* ⊕ *www.cochonrestaurant.com.*

★ Commander's Palace

$$$ | CREOLE | No restaurant captures New Orleans's gastronomic heritage and celebratory spirit as well as this grande dame of New Orleans fine dining. Upstairs, the Garden Room's glass walls have marvelous views of the giant oak trees on the patio below. **Known for:** turtle soup; jazz brunch; historic gem. ⑤ *Average main: $35* ✉ *1403 Washington Ave., Garden District* ☎ *504/899–8221* ⊕ *www. commanderspalace.com.*

★ **Galatoire's**

$$$ | CREOLE | With many of its recipes dating to 1905, Galatoire's epitomizes the old-style French Creole bistro. Fried oysters and bacon en brochette are worth every calorie, and the brick-red rémoulade sauce sets a high standard. **Known for:** rémoulade sauce; formal dress; old-school vibes. ⑤ *Average main: $30* ✉ *209 Bourbon St., French Quarter* ☎ *504/525–2021* ⊕ *www.galatoires.com* ◷ *Closed Mon.* ⌂ *Jacket required.*

🛏 Hotels

You can stay in a large hotel near the cruise-ship terminal or in more intimate places in the French Quarter. Hotel rates in New Orleans tend to be on the high end, though deals abound.

Bourbon Orleans Hotel

$$$ | HOTEL | This hotel's location is about as central as it gets, though the beautiful courtyard and pool provide welcome sanctuary from the loud, 24-hour Bourbon Street action just outside the door. **Pros:** welcome cocktail, complimentary coffee and tea in the lobby, and a free bottle of artesian water in the room; fitness center; Roux restaurant on-site; live entertainment in the on-site bar. **Cons:** lobby level is often crowded; street-facing rooms can be noisy. ⑤ *Rooms from: $400* ✉ *717 Orleans St., French Quarter* ☎ *504/523–2222* ⊕ *www. bourbonorleans.com* ⤴ *218 rooms, 28 suites* ⦿ *No meals.*

Hilton New Orleans Riverside

$$$ | HOTEL | FAMILY | The superb river and city views are hard to beat, and the guest rooms come with all the modern amenities, in close proximity to shops and the casino. **Pros:** well-maintained facilities; hotel runs like a well-oiled machine; great security; two heated outdoor swimming pools. **Cons:** the city's biggest hotel; typical chain service and surroundings. ⑤ *Rooms from: $232* ✉ *2 Poydras St., Central Business District* ☎ *504/561–0500, 855/760–0870* ⊕ *www. hiltonneworleansriverside.com* ⤴ *1,622 rooms, 74 suites* ⦿ *No meals.*

New Orleans Marriott Hotel

$$$ | HOTEL | FAMILY | This centrally located 41-story skyscraper boasts fabulous views of the Quarter, downtown, and the Mississippi River. **Pros:** centrally located; stunning city and river views. **Cons:** typical chain hotel; lacks charm; charge for Wi-Fi in the rooms (access is free from the lobby). ⑤ *Rooms from: $329* ✉ *555 Canal St., French Quarter* ☎ *504/581–1000, 800/228–9290* ⊕ *www. neworleansmarriott.com* ⤴ *1,329 rooms* ⦿ *No meals.*

🍸 Nightlife

No American city places such a premium on pleasure as New Orleans. From swank hotel lounges to sweaty dance clubs, refined jazz clubs, and raucous Bourbon Street bars, this city is serious about frivolity. And famous for it: Partying is more than an occasional indulgence in this city—it's a lifestyle. Bars tend to open in the early afternoon and stay open into the morning hours; live music, though, follows a more restrained schedule. Some jazz spots and clubs in the French Quarter stage evening sets around 6 or 9 pm; at a few clubs, such as the Palm Court, the bands actually finish by 11 pm. But this is the exception. For the most part, gigs begin between 10 and 11 pm, and locals rarely emerge for an evening out before 10. Keep in mind that the lack of legal closing time means that shows advertised for 11 may not start until after midnight.

Mulate's

MUSIC CLUBS | Across the street from the Convention Center, this large venue seats 400, and the dance floor quickly fills with couples twirling and two-stepping to authentic Cajun bands from the countryside. Regulars love to drag first-timers to the floor for impromptu lessons. The home-style Cajun cuisine is acceptable, but what matters is the nightly music. ⌨ *201 Julia St., Warehouse District* ☎ *504/522–1492* ⊕ *www.mulates.com.*

Pat O'Brien's

BARS/PUBS | Sure, it's touristy, but there are reasons Pat O's has been a must-stop on the New Orleans drinking trail since Prohibition. Friendly staff, an easy camaraderie among patrons, and a signature drink—the pink, fruity, and extremely potent Hurricane, which comes with a souvenir glass—all make this French Quarter stalwart a pleasant afternoon diversion. There's plenty of room to spread out, from the elegant side bar and piano bar that flank the carriageway entrance to the lush (and in winter, heated) patio. Expect a line on weekend nights, and if you don't want your glass, return it for the deposit. ⌨ *718 St. Peter St., French Quarter* ☎ *504/525–4823* ⊕ *www.patobriens.com.*

★ Preservation Hall

MUSIC CLUBS | **FAMILY** | At this cultural landmark founded in 1961, a cadre of distinguished New Orleans musicians, most of whom were schooled by an ever-dwindling group of elder statesmen, nurture the jazz tradition that flowered in the 1920s. There is limited seating on benches—many patrons end up squatting on the floor or standing in back—and no beverages are served, although you can bring your own drink in a plastic cup. Nonetheless, legions of satisfied music lovers regard an evening at this all-ages venue as an essential New Orleans experience. Cover charge is $20 (cash only) for nightly performances, a bit higher for special appearances. A limited number of advanced "Big Shot" tickets ($35–$50) guarantee you a seat and let you skip the line. ⌨ *726 St. Peter St., French Quarter* ☎ *504/522–2841* ⊕ *www.preservation-hall.com.*

★ The Spotted Cat

MUSIC CLUBS | Jazz, old-time, and swing bands perform nightly at this rustic club right in the thick of the Frenchmen Street action. Sets start at 4 pm on weekdays and 2 pm on weekends. Drinks cost a little more at this cash-only destination, but there's never a cover charge and the entertainment is great—from the popular bands to the cadres of young, rock-step swing dancers. ⌨ *623 Frenchmen St., Faubourg Marigny* ⊕ *www.spottedcatmusicclub.com.*

★ Tipitina's

MUSIC CLUBS | Rub the bust of legendary New Orleans pianist Professor Longhair (or "Fess") inside this Uptown landmark named for one of the late musician's popular songs. The old concert posters on the walls read like an honor roll of musical legends, both local and national. The midsize venue boasts an eclectic and well-curated calendar, particularly during the weeks of Jazz Fest. The long-running Sunday afternoon Cajun dance party still packs the floor. Although the neighborhood isn't dangerous, it's far enough out of the way to require a cab trip. ⌨ *501 Napoleon Ave., Uptown* ☎ *504/895–8477* ⊕ *www.tipitinas.com.*

⬤ Shopping

The fun of shopping in New Orleans is in the regional items available throughout the city, in the smallest shops or the biggest department stores. You can take home some of the flavor of the city: its pralines (pecan candies), seafood (packaged to go), Louisiana red beans and rice, coffee (pure or with chicory), and creole and Cajun spices (cayenne pepper, chili, and garlic). There are even packaged mixes of such local favorites as jambalaya, gumbo, beignets, and the sweet red local cocktail called the Hurricane. Cookbooks also share the secrets of preparing distinctive New Orleans dishes. The French Quarter is well known for its fine antiques shops, located mainly on Royal and Chartres Streets. The main shopping areas in the city are the French Quarter, with narrow, picturesque streets lined with specialty, gift, fashion, and antiques shops and art galleries; the Central Business District (CBD), populated mostly with jewelry, specialty, and department stores; the Warehouse District, best known for contemporary arts galleries and cultural museums; Magazine Street, home to antiques shops, art galleries, home-furnishing stores, dining venues, fashion boutiques, and specialty shops; and the Riverbend/Maple Street area, filled with clothing stores and some specialty shops.

Jax Brewery

SHOPPING CENTERS/MALLS | A historic factory building that once produced Jax beer now holds a mall filled with local shops and a few national chain stores, like Chico's, along with a food court and balcony overlooking the Mississippi River. Shops carry souvenirs, clothing, books, artwork, and more, with an emphasis on New Orleans–themed items. The mall is open daily. On hot summer days, it's an air-conditioned refuge. ⊠ *600 Decatur St., French Quarter* ☎ *504/566–7245* ⊕ *thejaxbrewery.com.*

The Shops at Canal Place

SHOPPING CENTERS/MALLS | This high-end shopping center focuses on national chains, including Saks Fifth Avenue, Michael Kors, Anthropologie, Banana Republic, J.Crew, Lululemon, and BCBG Max Azria. But the mall also includes quality local shops. A highlight is the Mignon Faget jewelry store, which carries the renowned local designer's full line of upscale, Louisiana-inspired creations. ⊠ *333 Canal St., Central Business*

Bring a Mug 🍽

Take along an insulated mug with a lid that you can fill at the beverage station in the buffet area. Your drinks will stay hot or cold, and you won't have to worry about spills. Most bartenders will fill the mug with ice and water or a soft drink. With a straw, your ice will not melt instantly while you lounge at the pool.

District ☎ *504/522–9200* ⊕ *www.canalplacestyle.com.*

New York, New York

A few cruise lines now base Caribbean-bound ships in New York City year-round; other ships do seasonal cruises to New England and Bermuda or trans-Atlantic crossings. If you're coming to the city from outside the immediate area, you can easily arrive the day before and do a bit of sightseeing and perhaps take in a Broadway show. The cruise port in Manhattan is fairly close to Times Square and Midtown hotels and theaters. But the New York City region now has three major cruise ports. Besides Manhattan, you can also leave from Cape Liberty Terminal in Bayonne, New Jersey, on Celebrity and Royal Caribbean ships, or from a cruise terminal in Red Hook, Brooklyn, which serves Princess ships as well as Cunard's *Queen Mary 2*.

ESSENTIALS
HOURS

They say that New York never sleeps, and that's particularly true around Times Square, where some stores are open until 11 pm or later, even during the week. Most stores outside of the immediate Times Square area are open from 9 or 10 until 6 or 7. Many museums close on Monday.

TOURS

You can take a hop-on, hop-off bus tour of Manhattan, either uptown or downtown, but the time you waste standing still in traffic minimizes what you can see.

VISITOR INFORMATION

CONTACTS NYC & Company. ⊕ *www. nycgo.com.* **Times Square Alliance.** ⊠ *Midtown West* ☎ *212/768–1560* ⊕ *www. timessquarenyc.org.*

THE CRUISE PORT

If your cruise is leaving from "New York City" it may be leaving from any one of three cruise piers, only two of which are actually in New York City.

The **Manhattan Cruise Terminal** is on the far west side of Manhattan, five very long blocks from the Times Square area, between 48th and 52nd Streets; the vehicle entrance is at 55th Street. Traffic can be backed up in the area on days that cruise ships arrive and depart, so allow yourself enough time to check in and go through security. There are no nearby subway stops, though city buses do cross Midtown at 50th and 42nd Streets. If you don't have too much luggage, it is usually faster and more convenient to have a taxi drop you off at the intersection of 50th Street and the West Side Highway, directly across the street from the entrance to the lower level of Pier 88 (Pier 90, also used by many ships, is next door); then you can walk right in and take the escalator or elevator up to the embarkation level.

Cape Liberty Terminal in Bayonne is off Route 440. From the New Jersey Turnpike, take Exit 14A, then follow the signs for 440 South, and make a left turn into the Cape Liberty Terminal area (on Port Terminal Boulevard). If you are coming from Long Island, you cross Staten Island, and after crossing the Bayonne Bridge take Route 440 North, making a right into the terminal area. If you are

coming from Manhattan, you can also reach the terminal by public transportation. Take the New Jersey Transit light-rail line from the PATH trains in Hoboken; get off at the 34th Street stop in Bayonne, and from there you can call for a taxi to the terminal (about 2 miles [3 km] away); there may be a free shuttle bus on cruise sailing dates, but confirm that with your cruise line.

The **Brooklyn Cruise Terminal** at Pier 12 in Red Hook, which opened in April 2006, is not convenient to public transportation, so you should plan to take a taxi, drive, or take the bus transfers offered by the cruise lines (about $45 per person from either LaGuardia or JFK). There is a secure, 500-car outdoor parking lot on-site. To reach the terminal from LaGuardia Airport, take I–278 West (the Brooklyn-Queens Expressway) to Exit 26, Hamilton Avenue; the terminal entrance is actually off Bowne Street. From JFK, take I–278 East (again, the Brooklyn-Queens Expressway), and then the same exit. If you arrive early, there's not much in the neighborhood, but there are a few delis and restaurants about 15 minutes away on foot; the area is a safe place to walk around during daylight hours, though it's very industrial. Red Hook is the home of ships from the Princess and Cunard cruise lines.

CONTACTS Brooklyn Cruise Terminal. ⊠ *72 Bowne St., Red Hook* ☎ *718/855–5590* ⊕ *www.nycruise.com.* **Cape Liberty Cruise Port.** ⊠ *14 Port Terminal Blvd., Bayonne* ☎ *201/436–2080* ⊕ *www.cruiseliberty. com.* **Manhattan Cruise Terminal.** ⊠ *711 12th Ave., at 55th St., Midtown West* ⊹ *Taxi/car entrance is at 55th St.; passenger entrances at 48th and 50th Sts.* ☎ *212/641–4440* ⊕ *www.nycruise.com.*

AIRPORT

CONTACTS LaGuardia Airport. (*LGA*) ⊠ *Flushing* ☎ *718/533–3400* ⊕ *www. laguardiaairport.com.* **JFK International Airport.** (*JFK*) ☎ *718/244–4444* ⊕ *www. jfkairport.com.* **Newark Liberty International**

Airport. *(EWR)* ☎ *973/961–6000* ⊕ *www. newarkairport.com.*

AIRPORT TRANSFERS

A cab to or from JFK airport to the Manhattan Cruise Terminal will cost $52 (a flat fare) plus tolls and tip; expect to pay at least $35 on the meter if you are coming from LaGuardia and at least $60 or $70 (not including tolls of about $10 and the tip) from Newark in a car service. For the latter, it's usually more cost-effective to call a car service to pick you up; regular taxis can be prohibitively expensive. If possible, reserve a car in advance, and call when you pick up your bags to find out where to meet it.

The Cape Liberty Cruise Terminal costs approximately $30 from Newark airport, $90 from JFK (plus tolls and tip, so count on at least $120 and be aware that taxis are not obligated to take this route from JFK), and $90 from LaGuardia (plus tolls and tip; count on paying more than $110). Royal Caribbean offers bus service from several Mid-Atlantic and Northeast cities on sailing dates, but confirm with the cruise line.

If your cruise is leaving from Brooklyn, the taxi fare will be much cheaper if you fly into either La Guardia (about $35) or JFK (about $45); you'll pay at least $80 for a car service from Newark Airport (not including tolls and tip, and perhaps more in a regular taxi). Cruise lines provide bus transfers from all three of the area's airports, but it may be cheaper to take a taxi if you are traveling with more than one other person. Note that all these taxi fares do not include tolls and tips. From Newark, the tolls to Brooklyn can be substantial, adding almost $20 to the fare.

Both Carmel (☎ *866/666–6666* ⊕ *www. carmellimo.com*) and Dial 7 (☎ *212/777– 7777* ⊕ *www.dial7.com*) car services serve all three of the area's airports, as do Uber and Lyft. Regular taxis are plentiful; just don't take a New Jersey taxi to a New York City cruise port, either in

Best Bets ◉

■ **An Art Museum.** Take your pick: the Met, MoMA, or Frick, but museumgoing is a true highlight of New York.

■ **A Broadway Show.** The theater experience in New York is arguably the best in the world.

■ **Central Park.** Even if you have time for just a stroll, come if the weather is good; it's about 30 minutes from the cruise terminal by foot.

Manhattan or Brooklyn, unless you want to pay through the nose.

PARKING

You can park at the Manhattan Cruise Terminal for a staggering $40 per day; the fee is payable in advance by cash or credit card (no Amex).

Parking at Cape Liberty Terminal in Bayonne is $22 per day, payable by cash or major credit card.

Parking at Red Hook, Brooklyn, costs $25 per night, payable in cash or with Visa, Mastercard, or Amex.

◉ Sights

There's no way to do justice to even the most popular tourist stops in New York. Below is information about several top attractions. If you have only one day in the city, choose one or two attractions and buy a Metro card to facilitate easy transfers between the subway and bus (put on as much money as you think you'll use in a day, but no less than $5.50, which is good for two rides at $2.75 each + $1 for the card, which can be shared). Times Square is approximately 20 minutes by foot from the cruise terminal; just walk straight out of the gate and east along 48th Street. There's a moving series of panels about the World Trade Center at the Ground Zero site across from the Millennium Hotel (take the 1 train to Chambers Street or the E to World Trade Center); there's another series of memorial panels underneath at the World Trade Center PATH station, which is accessible from the main street-side memorial area.

★ American Museum of Natural History

MUSEUM | FAMILY | With 45 exhibition halls and more than 34 million artifacts and specimens, the world's largest and most important museum of natural history can easily occupy you for a day. The dioramas might seem dated but are still fun. The dinosaur fossils and exhibits, including a massive T. rex, are probably the highlight for many people. A 94-foot model of a blue whale, another museum icon, is suspended from the ceiling in the **Milstein Hall of Ocean Life.** Attached to the museum is the **Rose Center for Earth and Space,** with various exhibits and housing the **Hayden Planetarium** and an **IMAX Theater.** The museum has plans for an expansion, which is due to open by 2021. The actual entry fee is a donation; you must pay something, but it can be as little as you wish; just be aware that many of the wonderful features (not to mention special exhibits) cost extra and must be paid for in full. Check the website for special programs, including sleepovers for kids. ⊠ *Central Park W, at 79th St., Upper West Side* ☎ *212/769–5100* ⊕ *www.amnh.org* 🖙 *$23 suggested donation, includes admission to Rose Center for Earth and Space; $28 includes an IMAX or space show* Ⓜ *B, C to 81st St.–Museum of Natural History.*

★ Brooklyn Bridge (Manhattan Entrance)

BRIDGE/TUNNEL | "A drive-through cathedral" is how the journalist James Wolcott once described the Brooklyn Bridge, one of New York's noblest and most recognizable landmarks, perhaps rivaling Walt Whitman's comment that it was "the best, most effective medicine

my soul has yet partaken." The bridge stretches over the East River, connecting Manhattan and Brooklyn. A walk across its promenade—a boardwalk elevated above the roadway, shared by pedestrians and (sometimes aggressive) cyclists—is a quintessential New York experience, and the roughly 40-minute stroll delivers exhilarating views. If you start from Lower Manhattan (enter from the east side of City Hall), you'll end up in the heart of Brooklyn Heights, but you can also take the subway to the Brooklyn side and walk back to Manhattan. It's worth noting that, from late morning through early evening, the narrow path gets very congested, especially when the weather is nice. Head there early in the morning to find the magical quiet hours. ⊠ *East River Dr., Financial District* Ⓜ *4, 5, 6 to Brooklyn Bridge–City Hall; J, Z to Chambers St.*

★ Central Park

CITY PARK | FAMILY | Central Park's creators had a simple goal: to design a place where city dwellers could go to forget the city. Without Central Park's 843 acres of meandering paths, tranquil lakes, ponds, and open meadows, New Yorkers might be a lot less sane. The busy southern section of Central Park, from 59th to 72nd Street, is where most visitors get their first impression. You can drop by the zoo (near 64th Street, on the east side) or the famous Bethesda Fountain (midpark, at around 72nd Street), but the main draw is just to wander the lanes. North of the reservoir and up to 110th Street, Central Park is less crowded and feels more rugged.

Central Park has one of the lowest crime rates in the city. Still, use common sense and stay within sight of other park visitors, and in general, avoid the park after dark. Directions, park maps, and events calendars can be obtained at two 5th Avenue information booths, at East 60th Street and East 72nd Street. You can also download the Central Park Conservancy's

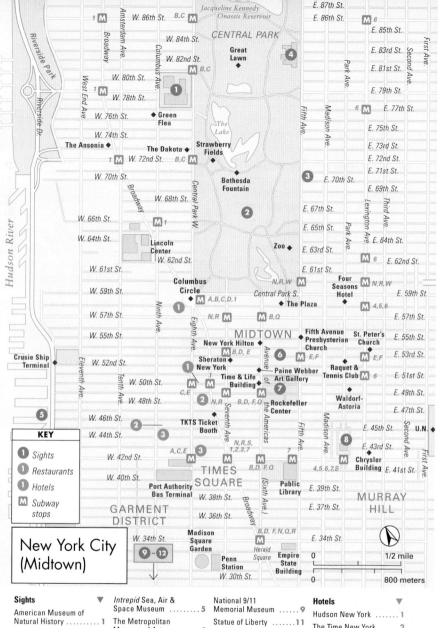

New York City (Midtown)

KEY
- ❶ Sights
- ❶ Restaurants
- ❶ Hotels
- Ⓜ Subway stops

Sights ▼			
American Museum of Natural History 1	Intrepid Sea, Air & Space Museum 5	National 9/11 Memorial Museum 9	**Hotels** ▼
Brooklyn Bridge 12	The Metropolitan Museum of Art 4	Statue of Liberty 11	Hudson New York 1
Central Park 2	Museum of Jewish Heritage—A Living Memorial to the Holocaust 10	Top of the Rock 7	The Time New York 2
Frick Collection 3		**Restaurants** ▼	Westin New York at Times Square 3
Grand Central Terminal 8	The Museum of Modern Art (MoMA) 6	5 Napkin Burger 2	
		Marseille 3	
		Toloache 1	

free app for a GPS-enabled map to help you navigate the park.

If you want food, there are often specialty food carts, mostly in the southern half of the park. Other reliable options include the café next to the Boathouse Restaurant (midpark at 74th Street), or the park's branch of Le Pain Quotidien (midpark at 69th Street). For something a little more iconic, you can stop for brunch, lunch, or dinner at the Tavern on the Green. ⊠ *Central Park* ☎ *212/794–6564 for Dairy Visitor Center, 212/360–2726 for custom walking tours, 212/310–6600 for Central Park Conservancy* ⊕ *www.centralparknyc. org* Ⓜ *1, A, B, C, D to 59th St.–Columbus Circle; N, R, W to 5th Ave./59th St.*

★ Frick Collection

MUSEUM | Henry Clay Frick (1849–1919) made his fortune amid the soot and smoke of Pittsburgh, where he was a coke (a coal fuel derivative) and steel baron, but this lovely art museum, once Frick's private New York residence, is decidedly removed from soot. With an exceptional collection of works from the Renaissance through the late 19th century that includes Édouard Manet's *The Bullfight* (1864), a Chinard portrait bust (1809), three Vermeers, three Rembrandts, works by El Greco, Goya, Van Dyck, Hogarth, Degas, and Turner, as well as sculpture, decorative arts, and 18th-century French furniture, everything here is a highlight.

The Portico Gallery, an enclosed portico along the building's 5th Avenue garden, houses the museum's growing collection of sculpture, and the tranquil indoor garden court is a magical spot for a rest. An audio guide, available in six languages, is included with admission, as are the year-round temporary exhibits. Children under 10 are not admitted. ⊠ *1 E. 70th St., at 5th Ave., Upper East Side* ☎ *212/288–0700* ⊕ *www.frick.org* ⊠ *$22; pay-what-you-wish Wed. 2–6; free 1st Fri. of the month (except Sept., Jan.)*

⊘ *Closed Mon.* Ⓜ *6 to 68th St.–Hunter College.*

★ Grand Central Terminal

BUILDING | Grand Central is not only the world's largest (48 acres and 44 platforms) and the nation's busiest railway station, but also one of the world's most magnificent public spaces. The **main concourse** stands roughly 12 stories high and is modeled after an ancient Roman public bath. Overhead, a twinkling fiber-optic map of the constellations covers the ceiling. Of course, Grand Central still functions primarily as a railroad station, its majesty preserved in part by Jacqueline Kennedy Onassis's 1975 campaign to save it as a landmark. Underground, trains travel upstate and to Connecticut via the Metro-North commuter rail; the subway connects here as well.

To best admire Grand Central's exquisite Beaux Arts architecture, try to avoid rush hour and head up one of the staircases at either end, where upscale restaurants occupy the balcony spaces. There you can survey the concourse and feel the terminal's dynamism. Then, if you can find it, head to the southwest corner to reach the **The Campbell** cocktail lounge. Located around and below the main concourse are fantastic shops and eateries— including the Grand Central Oyster Bar.

The **Municipal Art Society** (☎ *212/935– 3960* ⊕ *www.mas.org/tours*) leads an official daily walking tour for $30 beginning in the main concourse at 12:30 (⊕ *www.docentour.com/gct*). Alternatively, rent a headset ($9) at GCT Tour windows and take a self-guided audio tour at your own pace (⊕ *www.grandcentralterminal.com/tours*). ⊠ *Main entrance, 42nd St. and Park Ave., Midtown East* ☎ *212/935–3960* ⊕ *www.grandcentralterminal.com* Ⓜ *4, 5, 6, 7, S to Grand Central–42nd St.*

Intrepid Sea, Air & Space Museum

MUSEUM | FAMILY | The museum is centered on the 900-foot-long WWII-era

Did You Know?

The statue on top of Bethesda Fountain was designed by Emma Stebbins, the first woman to be commissioned for a major work of art in New York City, in 1868.

aircraft carrier *Intrepid*, Manhattan's only floating museum. A Lockheed A-12 spy plane, a British Airways Concorde, helicopters, seaplanes, and more than two dozen other aircraft are part of the museum's unparalleled collection. Visitors can also explore the submarine *Growler*, the only American guided-missile submarine open to the public. The space shuttle *Enterprise*, NASA's original prototype orbiter, is a visitor favorite. Through exhibitions, educational programming, and the foremost collection of technologically groundbreaking aircraft and vessels, visitors of all ages are taken on an interactive journey through history to learn about American innovation and bravery. This museum is within easy walking distance of the main cruise piers in Manhattan. ⊠ *Pier 86, 12th Ave. at 46th St., Midtown West* ☎ *212/245–0072, 877/957–7447* ⊕ *www.intrepidmuseum.org* ⊠ *$33 (free for U.S. military/veterans)* Ⓜ *A, C, E to 42nd St.–Port Authority.*

★ The Metropolitan Museum of Art

MUSEUM | If Manhattan held no other museum than the colossal Metropolitan Museum of Art, you could still occupy yourself for days roaming its labyrinthine corridors. The Metropolitan Museum has more than 2 million works of art representing 5,000 years of history, so it's a good idea to plan ahead; looking at everything here could take a week. The famous **Egyptian collection** (including the Temple of Dendur) is reason enough to visit. Other don't-miss sections include the magnificent **Islamic Galleries,** the collections of impressionist paintings, the **American Wing,** and the **Anna Wintour Costume Center.** Keep in mind that the **British Galleries** are closed for renovations (reopening winter 2020), and the **European Paintings Galleries** will be partially closed in two phases as gallery skylights are replaced between 2018 and 2022. In fall 2018, the Met announced the complete overhaul of the Africa, Oceania, and Americas collections, with work scheduled to begin in 2020. Check the

website for updates. Admission includes three-day entry to the museum's modern-art outpost, the Met Breuer (Madison Avenue and 75th Street), as well as the Cloisters Museum and Gardens in northern Manhattan. ⊠ *1000 5th Ave., at 82nd St., Upper East Side* ☎ *212/535–7710* ⊕ *www.metmuseum.org* ⊠ *$25 for 3-day ticket (includes Met Breuer and Met Cloisters); $25 suggested donation for New York State residents (full donation includes 3-day ticket to Met Breuer and Met Cloisters); $7 for audio guide* Ⓜ *4, 5, 6 to 86th St.*

Museum of Jewish Heritage—A Living Memorial to the Holocaust

MUSEUM | In a granite hexagon rising 85 feet above Robert F. Wagner Jr. Park at the southern end of Battery Park City, this museum pays tribute to the 6 million Jews who perished in the Holocaust. The third-floor exhibits cover postwar Jewish life. It's one of the best such museums in the country. The museum's east wing has a theater, memorial garden, library, galleries, and café. A free audio guide, with narration by Meryl Streep and Itzhak Perlman, is available at the admissions desk. ⊠ *36 Battery Pl., Battery Park City, Financial District* ☎ *646/437–4202* ⊕ *www.mjhnyc.org* ⊠ *$16 (free Wed. and Thurs. 4–8)* ⊘ *Closed Sat. and some Jewish holidays* Ⓜ *4, 5 to Bowling Green; 1, R, W to Rector St.*

★ The Museum of Modern Art (MoMA)

MUSEUM | The masterpieces—Monet's *Water Lilies,* Picasso's *Les Demoiselles d'Avignon,* Van Gogh's *Starry Night*—are still here, but for now the main draw at the MoMA is, well, the MoMA. A "modernist dream world" is how critics have described the museum, known for its brilliant special exhibitions. Unfortunately, the museum has become a victim of its own success, which means lines are sometimes down the block. For the shortest wait, get here before the museum opens; you can avoid some of the crowding by entering through the 54th Street side. ⊠ *11 W. 53rd St., between 5th and 6th Aves., Midtown West* ☎ *212/708–9400* ⊕ *www.moma. org* 🎫 *$25* Ⓜ *E, M to 5th Ave./53rd St.; F to 57th St.; B, D, E to 7th Ave.*

National 9/11 Memorial Museum

MUSEUM | Beside the reflecting pools on the 9/11 Memorial Plaza is the glass pavilion of the Memorial Museum. The museum descends some seven stories down to the bedrock the Twin Towers were built on, and the vast space displays a poignant, powerful collection of artifacts, memorabilia, photographs, and multimedia exhibits, as well as a gallery that takes visitors through the history of events surrounding both the 1993 and 2001 attacks. You may appreciate the tissue boxes around the museum when experiencing the memorial wall with portraits and personal stories of those who perished. There's also a panoramic media installation about the site's "rebirth," as well as World Trade Center–related art and history exhibits that change throughout the year. Giant pieces of the towers' structural steel and foundations are displayed, along with the partially destroyed Ladder Company 3 fire truck. You can also see the remnants of the Survivors Stairs, which allowed hundreds of people to escape the buildings that fateful September day. ⊠ *180 Greenwich St., between Fulton St. and Liberty St. Walkway, Financial District* ☎ *212/266–5211* ⊕ *www.911memorial.org/museum* 🎫 *$26 (free Tues. 5–8 pm)* Ⓜ *1, R, W to Cortlandt St.; 2, 3, 4, 5, A, C, J, Z to Fulton Center; E to World Trade Center.*

★ Statue of Liberty

MEMORIAL | Though you must endure a long wait and onerous security, it's worth the trouble to see one of the iconic images of New York. Access to the crown is strictly limited, and tickets must be booked months in advance; otherwise, it's possible to view the museum in the pedestal, but even those tickets often sell out. Much more interesting—and

well worth exploring—is the Ellis Island museum, which traces the story of immigration in New York City with moving exhibits throughout the restored processing building. Go early if you want to see everything, and allow plenty of time for security and lines. The ferry stops first at the statue and then continues to Ellis Island. ⊠ *Liberty Island, Financial District* ☎ *212/363–3200, 877/523–9849 ticket reservations* ⊕ *www.libertyellisfoundation.org* 🎫 *Free; ferry $18.50 round-trip (includes Ellis Island), crown tickets additional $3* Ⓜ *4, 5 to Bowling Green; 1 to South Ferry; R, W to Whitehall St.*

★ Top of the Rock

VIEWPOINT | Rockefeller Center's multi-floor observation deck, the Top of the Rock, provides views that rival those from the Empire State Building. Arriving pre-sunset affords a view of the city that morphs into a dazzling wash of colors, with a bird's-eye view of the Empire State Building and the Chrysler Building, and sweeping views northward to Central Park and south to the Statue of Liberty. Timed-entry ticketing eliminates long lines. Indoor exhibits include films of Rockefeller Center's history and a model of the building.

Rapid elevators lift you to the 67th-floor interior viewing area, and then an escalator leads to the outdoor deck on the 69th floor for sightseeing through nonreflective glass safety panels. Then, take another elevator or stairs to the 70th floor for a 360-degree outdoor panorama of New York City on a deck that is only 20 feet wide and nearly 200 feet long. Especially interesting is a Plexiglas screen on the floor with footage showing Rock Center construction workers dangling on beams high above the streets. A Sun & Stars ticket ($54) allows you to visit twice and see the city as it rises and sets in the same day. ⊠ *30 Rockefeller Plaza, 50th St. entrance, between 5th and 6th Aves., Midtown West* ☎ *212/698–2000* ⊕ *www. topoftherocknyc.com* 🎫 *$38* Ⓜ *B, D, F, M*

Lower Manhattan's iconic sights include the Statue of Liberty.

to 47th–50th Sts./Rockefeller Center; E, M to 5th Ave./53rd St.

🍴 Restaurants

The restaurants we recommend below are all in Midtown West, near Broadway theaters and hotels. Make reservations at all but the most casual places or face a mind-numbing wait.

5 Napkin Burger

$$ | **BURGER** | This perennially packed Hell's Kitchen burger place and brasserie has been a magnet for burger lovers since day one. Though there are many menu distractions—including matzo ball soup, shrimp tempura, and salad bowls—the main attractions are the juicy burgers, like the original 10-ounce chuck with a tangle of onions, Gruyère cheese, and rosemary aioli. **Known for:** messy, delicious burgers of all kinds; deep-fried delights; wildly indulgent desserts. $ *Average main: $17* ✉ *630 9th Ave., at 45th St., Midtown West* ☎ *212/757-2277* ⊕ *www.5napkinburger.com* Ⓜ *A, C, E to 42nd St.–Port Authority.*

Marseille

$$$ | **MEDITERRANEAN** | With great food and a convenient location near several Broadway theaters, Marseille is perpetually packed. The Mediterranean creations are continually impressive, including the bouillabaisse, the signature dish of the region for which the restaurant is named—a mélange of mussels, shrimp, and whitefish in a fragrant broth, topped with a garlicky crouton and served with rouille on the side. **Known for:** three-course dinner; bouillabaisse and steak frites; delicious desserts. $ *Average main: $25* ✉ *630 9th Ave., at 44th St., Midtown West* ☎ *212/333-2323* ⊕ *www.marseillenyc.com* Ⓜ *A, C, E to 42nd St.–Port Authority.*

Toloache

$$ | **MEXICAN** | The bilevel eatery at this bustling Mexican cantina just off Broadway has a festive vibe, with several seating options: bar, balcony, main dining room, and ceviche bar. Foodies

flock here for three types of guacamole (traditional, fruited, and spicy), well-executed ceviches, Mexico City–style tacos with Negra Modelo–braised brisket, and quesadillas with black truffle and *huitlacoche* (a corn fungus known as "the Mexican truffle"). **Known for:** quesadilla with huitlacoche; good Latin flavors; broad tequila selection. $ *Average main: $21* ⊠ *251 W. 50th St., near 8th Ave., Midtown West* ☎ *212/581–1818* ⊕ *www. toloachenyc.com* Ⓜ *1, C, E to 50th St.; N, R, W to 49th St.*

🛏 Hotels

There are no real bargains in the Manhattan hotel world, and you'll find it difficult to get a decent room for under $200 during much of the year. Occasional weekend deals can be found, however. All the hotels we recommend for cruise passengers are in Manhattan on the West Side, in relatively easy proximity to the Manhattan cruise ship terminal. If you are flying in the day before a cruise departing from Bayonne, you may want to stay at a Newark Airport hotel that offers free transportation to and from the airport. You can take a taxi to Cape Liberty Terminal on your day of departure.

Hudson New York

$ | HOTEL | Fashionistas and other modish folks who mind their budgets are drawn to this stylish, affordable hotel with its fabulous lobby (resembling a set from *A Midsummer Night's Dream*), multiple bars and lounges perfect for people-watching, and contemporary art that's an escape from the usual hotel design. **Pros:** fabulous, elegant bar; gorgeous Francesco Clemente fresco in lobby; breathtaking Sky Terrace. **Cons:** staff can be cold; tiny rooms; overpriced cocktails. $ *Rooms from: $250* ⊠ *356 W. 58th St., between 8th and 9th Aves., Midtown West* ☎ *212/554–6000* ⊕ *www. hudsonhotel.com* ⊃ *878 rooms* ⊙ *No meals* Ⓜ *1, A, B, C, D to 59th St.–Columbus Circle.*

The Time New York

$$$ | HOTEL | One of the neighborhood's first boutique hotels, this spot near the din of Times Square is a contemporary retreat with a futuristic glass elevator that transports guests to the second-floor lobby and beyond. **Pros:** popular Serafina restaurant downstairs; surprisingly quiet for Times Square location; good turndown service. **Cons:** service is inconsistent; location isn't for everyone; a bit pricey for the area. $ *Rooms from: $459* ⊠ *224 W. 49th St., between Broadway and 8th Ave., Midtown West* ☎ *212/246–5252, 877/846–3692* ⊕ *www.thetimeny.com* ⊃ *167 rooms* ⊙ *No meals* Ⓜ *1, C, E to 50th St.; N, R, W to 49th St.*

Westin New York at Times Square

$$ | HOTEL | This giant Midtown hotel has all the amenities and service you expect from a reliable brand, at fairly reasonable prices, including comfortable rooms with coffeemakers, iPhone docks, 24-hour room service, and a spacious work desk. **Pros:** central for Midtown attractions; big rooms; great gym. **Cons:** congested area near the Port Authority; not the best location for prime dining and nightlife; rooms are a bit nondescript. $ *Rooms from: $329* ⊠ *270 W. 43rd St., at 8th Ave., Midtown West* ☎ *212/201–2700* ⊕ *www. westinny.com* ⊃ *873 rooms* ⊙ *No meals* Ⓜ *A, C, E to 42nd St.–Port Authority.*

🎭 Performing Arts

Scoring tickets to Broadway shows is fairly easy except for the very top draws. For the most part, the top ticket price for Broadway musicals is now around $145; the best seats for Broadway plays can run as high as $130.

Telecharge

TICKETS | ⊠ *New York* ☎ *212/239–6200, 800/447–7400* ⊕ *www.telecharge.com.*

Ticketmaster

TICKETS | ⊠ *New York* ☎ *866/448–7849 for automated service, 800/745–3000* ⊕ *www.ticketmaster.com.*

TKTS Times Square

THEATER | ✉ *Duffy Sq., 47th St. and Broadway, Midtown West* ☎ *212/912–9770* ⊕ *www.tdf.org/tkts* Ⓜ *1, 2, 3, 7, N, Q, R, S to Times Sq.–42nd St.*

🛍 Shopping

You can find a major store from virtually any designer or chain in Manhattan. High-end designers tend to be along Madison Avenue, between 55th and 86th Streets. Some are along 57th Street, between Madison and 7th Avenues. Fifth Avenue, starting at Saks Fifth Avenue (at 50th Street) and going up to 59th Street, is a hodgepodge of high-end shopping, including the Bergdorf Goodman department store at 58th Street, and more accessible options. More interesting, independently owned boutiques can be found in SoHo (between Houston and Canal, West Broadway and Lafayette) and the East Village (between 14th Street and Houston, Broadway and Avenue A). Chinatown is chock-full of designer knockoffs, crowded streets, and dim sum palaces; though frenetic during the day, it's still a fun stop. The newest group of stores in Manhattan is at the Time Warner Center, at Columbus Circle (8th Avenue and 59th Street). This high-rise mall has upscale stores and some of the city's best-reviewed and most expensive new restaurants.

Norfolk, Virginia

Founded in 1680, Norfolk is no newcomer to the cruise business. One famous passenger, Thomas Jefferson, arrived here in November 1789 after a two-month crossing of the Atlantic. More than 200 years later, this historic seaport welcomes cruise passengers in the summer for departures to the Bahamas and Bermuda. Situated at the heart of nautical Hampton Roads, Norfolk is home to the largest naval base in the world and

is also a major commercial port. Stroll through Waterside, with shops close to the water; walk to the excellent Nauticus Museum, and make sure to stop at MacArthur's burial site.

ESSENTIALS

HOURS

Most stores are open weekdays from 10 to 9. Some museums close on Monday and/or Tuesday.

VISITOR INFORMATION

CONTACTS Norfolk Convention and Visitors Bureau. ✉ *232 E. Main St., Norfolk* ☎ *757/664–6620, 800/368–3097* ⊕ *www.visitnorfolktoday.com.*

THE CRUISE PORT

The Half Moone Cruise and Celebration Center, as Norfolk calls its cruise terminal, is in the center of the attractive, downtown waterfront. It's within walking distance of numerous attractions and amenities. From I-264, take the City Hall exit (Exit 10). At the light, turn right on St. Paul's Boulevard, and follow the signs to the Cedar Grove parking lot.

CONTACTS Half Moone Cruise and Celebration Center. ✉ *1 Waterside Dr., Norfolk* ⊕ *www.cruisenorfolk.org.*

AIRPORT TRANSFERS

Norfolk International Airport (ORF) is 9 miles (15 km; 20 minutes) from the cruise terminal. A shared shuttle costs $7.50 to $22 per person one-way, and a taxi costs about $18 to $25.

CONTACTS Black and White Cabs. ✉ *6304 Sewells Point Rd., Norfolk* ☎ *757/853–0411* ⊕ *www.norfolkblackandwhite-cabs.com.* **James River Transportation.** ☎ *866/823–4626* ⊕ *http://jamesrivertrans.com/.* **Yellow Cab.** ✉ *6304 Sewells Point Rd., Norfolk* ☎ *757/727–7777* ⊕ *www.yellowcabofnorfolk.com.*

PARKING

Cedar Grove Parking is the designated facility for cruise passengers. The parking fee ($15 daily) is paid upon entering the lot; Visa, MasterCard, American Express,

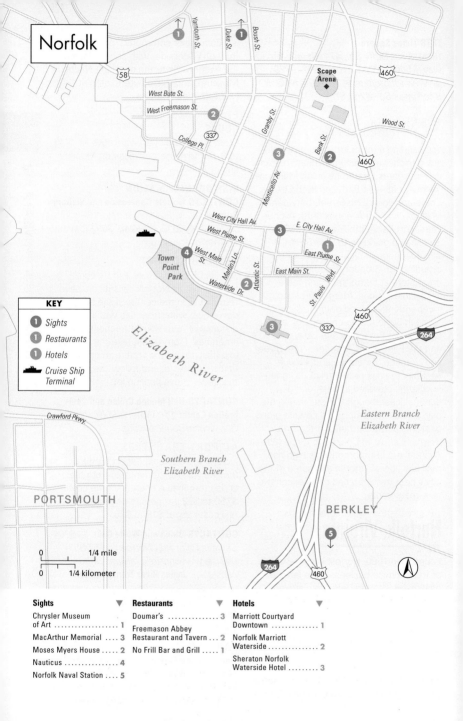

Norfolk

Scope Arena

Yarmouth St.
Duke St.
Boush St.

58

West Bute St.
West Freemason St. ②

Granby St.
Bank St. ②
Wood St.
460

College Pl.
337

Monticello Av.

460

West City Hall Av.
West Plume St.
E. City Hall Av.
③

Town Point Park
④
West Main St.
Martin's Ln.
Atlantic St.
East Plume St. ①
East Main St.
St. Paul's Blvd.
Waterside Dr.

③
337
460
264

KEY
① Sights
① Restaurants
① Hotels
⚓ Cruise Ship Terminal

Elizabeth River

Eastern Branch Elizabeth River

Crawford Pkwy.

Southern Branch Elizabeth River

PORTSMOUTH

BERKLEY

⑤

0   1/4 mile
0   1/4 kilometer

264
460

cash, and traveler's checks are accepted. Less than 1 mile (1½ km) from I–264, this lot is located on Monticello Avenue between Virginia Beach Boulevard and Princess Anne Road in Downtown Norfolk. Shuttles run regularly to the cruise terminal.

◉ Sights

History meets high-tech in this waterfront city. From 18th-century historic homes and a major art museum to 20th-century battleships and nuclear-powered aircraft carriers, Norfolk has many interesting sites to explore, several of them free and most within walking distance of the cruise terminal.

Chrysler Museum of Art

MUSEUM | By any standard, the Chrysler Museum of Art downtown qualifies as one of America's major art museums. The permanent collection includes works by Rubens, Gainsborough, Renoir, Picasso, Cézanne, Matisse, Warhol, and Pollock—a list that suggests the breadth available here. Classical and pre-Columbian civilizations are also represented. The decorative-arts collection includes exquisite English porcelain and art nouveau furnishings. The Chrysler is home to one of the most important glass collections in America, with objects from the 6th century BC to the present and particularly strong holdings in Tiffany, French art glass, and English cameo, as well as artifacts from ancient Rome and the Near and Far East. ⊠ 1 Memorial Pl., Norfolk ☎ 757/664–6200 ⊕ www.chrysler.org ◱ Free ⊗ Closed Mon.

MacArthur Memorial

MEMORIAL | The MacArthur Memorial is the burial place of one of America's most distinguished military officers. General Douglas MacArthur (1880–1964) agreed to this navy town as the site for his monument because it was his mother's birthplace. In the rotunda of the old City Hall, converted according to MacArthur's

Best Bets ◉

■ **Chrysler Museum of Art.** Though far from New York, Chicago, or Los Angeles, this is one of the major art museums in the United States.

■ **Nauticus.** The National Maritime Center is one of the region's most popular attractions, and especially good for families.

■ **Norfolk Naval Station.** This giant naval base, the home of the Atlantic Fleet, is an impressive site in itself.

design, is the mausoleum; 11 adjoining galleries house mementos of MacArthur's career, including his signature corncob pipe and the Japanese instruments of surrender that concluded World War II. However, this is a monument not only to General MacArthur but to all those who served in wars from the Civil to the Korean War. Its Historical Center holds 2½ million documents and more than 100,000 photographs, and assists scholars, students, and researchers from around the world. The general's staff car is on display in the gift shop, where a 24-minute biography is shown. ⊠ Bank St. at City Hall Ave., MacArthur Sq., Norfolk ☎ 757/441–2965 ⊕ www. macarthurmemorial.org ◱ Free (donations accepted) ⊗ Closed Mon.

Moses Myers House

MUSEUM | The Federal redbrick Moses Myers House, built by its namesake between 1792 and 1796, is exceptional, and not just for its elegance. The furnishings, 70 precent of them original, include family portraits by Gilbert Stuart and Thomas Sully. A transplanted New Yorker as well as Norfolk's first Jewish resident, Myers made his fortune in Norfolk in shipping, then served as a diplomat and a customhouse officer.

Norfolk's Chrysler Museum of Art houses an important collection of historic glass in addition to many great paintings.

His grandson married James Madison's grandniece; his great-grandson served as mayor; and the family kept the house for five generations. In 2005 the home had extensive repairs to bring it back to the 19th century. Exhibits throughout the house feature letters and other artifacts from several generations of the Myers family. ⊠ *323 E. Freemason St., Norfolk* 🕾 *757/333–1087* ⊕ *www.chrysler.org/ about-the-museum/historic-houses/the-moses-myers-house* 🖼 *Free* 🕑 *Closed Mon.–Tues.*

Nauticus

LIGHTHOUSE | FAMILY | A popular attraction on Norfolk's redeveloped downtown waterfront, Nauticus is a maritime science museum featuring hands-on exhibits, interactive theaters, and high-definition films that celebrate the local connection to the seaport. Visitors can touch a shark, learn about weather and underwater archaeology, and explore the mysteries of the Elizabeth River. A NOAA Environmental Resource Center is an invaluable stop for educational materials. Temporary exhibits in both the Changing Gallery and Forecastle Gallery keep things fresh. The Hampton Roads Naval Museum on the second floor and the battleship *Wisconsin* adjacent to the building are also popular attractions operated by the U.S. Navy, and are included in the Nauticus admission. ⊠ *1 Waterside Dr., Norfolk* 🕾 *757/664–1000* ⊕ *www. nauticus.org* 🖼 *$15.95* 🕑 *Closed Mon. Labor Day–Memorial Day.*

Norfolk Naval Station

LIGHTHOUSE | On the northern edge of the city, the Norfolk Naval Station is an impressive sight, home to more than 100 ships of the Atlantic Fleet. The base was built on the site of the Jamestown Exposition of 1907; many of the original buildings survive and are still in use. Several large aircraft carriers, built at nearby Newport News, call Norfolk home port and can be seen from miles away, especially at the bridge-tunnel end of the base. You may see two, each with a crew of up to 6,300, beside slightly smaller amphibious carriers that discharge marines in both helicopters and amphibious assault craft. The submarine piers, floating dry docks, supply center, and air station are all worth seeing. The *Victory Rover* and *Carrie B.* provide boat tours from downtown Norfolk to the naval station; Hampton Roads Transit operates tour trolleys most of the year, departing from the naval-base tour office. Visitor access is by tour only, and photo ID is required to enter the base. (Note: You will be required to present additional ID with state ID from Illinois, Minnesota, Missouri, New Mexico, Washington, and American Samoa). ✉ *9079 Hampton Blvd., Norfolk* ☎ *757/444–7955* ⊕ *www. cnic.navy.mil* 🎫 *Tour $10 (cash only; there is no ATM on premises).*

 Restaurants

Downtown Norfolk has many fine-dining restaurants as well as casual eateries in Waterside Festival Marketplace, where there's a versatile food court, and in the MacArthur Center Mall, including Johnny Rockets—good food values for the price.

Doumar's

$ | DINER | FAMILY | After he introduced the world to its first ice cream cone at the 1904 World's Fair in St. Louis, Abe Doumar founded this drive-in institution in 1934. It's still operated by his family. **Known for:** barbecue sandwiches; ice cream cones; curb-side service. 💲 *Average main: $3* ✉ *20th St. at Monticello Ave., Norfolk* ☎ *757/627–4163* ⊕ *www. doumars.com* 🕓 *Closed Sun.*

★ Freemason Abbey Restaurant and Tavern

$$ | AMERICAN | This former church near the historic business district has been drawing customers for a long time, and not without reason. It has 40-foot-high cathedral ceilings and large windows, making for an airy and dramatic dining experience. **Known for:** dining in a former church; Sunday brunch; gluten-free. 💲 *Average main: $22* ✉ *209 W.*

Freemason St., Norfolk ☎ *757/622–3966* ⊕ *www.freemasonabbey.com.*

No Frill Bar and Grill

$ | AMERICAN | This expansive café is in an antique building in the heart of Ghent. Beneath a tin ceiling and exposed ductwork, a central bar is surrounded by several dining spaces with cream-and-mustard walls and wooden tables. **Known for:** salads and sandwiches; Sunday brunch; comfort food Tuesdays with meatloaf. 💲 *Average main: $14* ✉ *806 Spotswood Ave., at Colley Ave., Norfolk* ☎ *757/627–4262* ⊕ *www.nofrillgrill.com.*

🛏 Hotels

There are hotels within walking distance of the cruise port, or if you have a car, you can save a little money by staying at one of the numerous chain motels on the outskirts of town.

Marriott Courtyard Downtown

$ | HOTEL | This eight-story hotel is near everything visitors want to see and where business travelers need to be. **Pros:** convenient downtown location; walking distance to many attractions; attached shopping mall is really nice. **Cons:** parking is quite costly and shared with the mall. 💲 *Rooms from: $149* ✉ *520 Plume St., Norfolk* ☎ *757/963–6000, 800/321–2211* ⊕ *www.marriott. com* 🛏 *140 rooms* 🍽 *No meals.*

Norfolk Marriott Waterside

$$ | HOTEL | Located in the redeveloped downtown area, this hotel is connected to the Waterside Festival Marketplace shopping area by a ramp, and it's close to Town Point Park, site of many festivals. **Pros:** great central location; two blocks from the Waterside Festival Marketplace. **Cons:** parking is pricey, and a walk with luggage. 💲 *Rooms from: $199* ✉ *235 E. Main St., Norfolk* ☎ *757/627–4200, 800/228–9290* ⊕ *www.marriott.com* 🛏 *414 rooms* 🍽 *No meals.*

Sheraton Norfolk Waterside Hotel

$$ | **HOTEL** | "Modern" is the word for this hotel's furnishings, from the bright, spacious lobby to the ample rooms and large suites. **Pros:** the only hotel that is truly on the waterfront; nice touches such as snacks and cold water served all day; restaurant has a terrific view of Portsmouth. **Cons:** parking is pricey (for Norfolk); smallish rooms have too much furniture. $ *Rooms from: $180* ✉ *777 Waterside Dr., Norfolk* ☎ *757/622–6664* ⊕ *www.sheratonnorfolkwaterside.com* ⤸ *446 rooms* ⍟ *No meals.*

🛍 Shopping

d'Art Center

ART GALLERIES | You can meet painters, sculptors, glassworkers, jewelers, photographers, and other artists at work in their studios at the d'Art Center. The art is for sale. ✉ *Selden Arcade, 740 Duke St., Norfolk* ☎ *757/625–4211* ⊕ *www.d-art-center.org* ⊘ *Closed Sun.–Mon.*

Ghent

SHOPPING NEIGHBORHOODS | An eclectic mix of chic shops, including antique stores, bars, and eateries, lines the streets of Ghent, a turn-of-the-20th-century neighborhood that runs from the Elizabeth River to York Street, to West Olney Road and Llewellyn Avenue. The intersection of Colley Avenue and 21st Street is the hub. ✉ *Norfolk.*

Palace Shops

SHOPPING CENTERS/MALLS | In Ghent, the upscale clothing and shoe boutiques at the Palace Shops are a good place to search out some finery. ✉ *21st St. at Llewellyn Ave., Norfolk* ☎ *757/622–9999* ⊕ *www.palaceshopsghent.com.*

Port Canaveral, Florida

This once-bustling commercial fishing area is still home to a small shrimping fleet, charter boats, and party fishing

Best Bets 👁

■ **Kennedy Space Center.** Kennedy Space Center in Titusville is the region's biggest attraction.

■ **Merritt Island.** If you want to get out and commune with nature, this is the place, especially for bird-watchers.

■ **Orlando Theme Parks.** With Orlando just an hour away, many cruisers combine a theme-park visit with their cruise.

boats, but its main business these days is as a cruise-ship port. Although Cocoa Beach isn't the spiffiest place around, the north end of the port is becoming quite clean and neat. That's where Carnival, Disney, Norweigan, and Royal Caribbean set sail, as well as Sun Cruz and Sterling casino boats. Port Canaveral is now Florida's second-busiest cruise port and home to two of the world's largest cruise ships, Royal Caribbean's *Oasis of the Seas* and her sister ship, *Allure of the Seas.* Because of Port Canaveral's proximity to Orlando theme parks (about an hour away), many cruisers combine a short cruise with a stay in the area. The port is also convenient to popular Space Coast attractions such as the Kennedy Space Center and United States Astronaut Hall of Fame in Titusville.

ESSENTIALS
HOURS
Most of the area's attractions are open every day.

VISITOR INFORMATION
CONTACTS Space Coast Office of Tourism. ☎ *877/572–3224, 321/433–4470* ⊕ *www.visitspacecoast.com.*

THE CRUISE PORT
Port Canaveral sees more than 4 million passengers passing through its terminals annually, almost equal to Miami.

The port has six modern cruise terminals. A new version of Terminal 5, serving Carnival Cruise Lines, debuted in June 2016 after a $48 million makeover. The port is also home to ships from Disney, Norweigan, and Royal Caribbean. Other lines operate seasonally. The port serves as the embarkation point for three- to nine-day cruises to the Bahamas, as well as Southern, Western, and Eastern Caribbean itineraries.

In Brevard County, Port Canaveral is on State Road 528 (also known as the Beeline Expressway), which runs straight to Orlando, where you'll find the nearest airport. To drive to Port Canaveral from there, take the north exit out of the airport, staying to the right, to S.R. 528 (Beeline Expressway) East. Take S.R. 528 directly to Port Canaveral; it's about a 45-minute drive.

CONTACTS Canaveral Port Authority.
☎ 321/783–7831 ⊕ www.portcanaveral. com.

AIRPORT TRANSFERS
If you are flying into the area, the Orlando airport is 45 minutes west from the docks. If you have not arranged airport transfers with your cruise line, you will need to make your own arrangements. Taxis and Uber are expensive, but many companies offer shared minivan and bus shuttles to Port Canaveral. You can explore options on the Orlando Airports website. Some shuttles charge for the entire van, which is a good deal for groups but not for individuals or couples; some will charge a per-person rate. Expect to pay at least $40 to $60 per person round-trip, and check the Internet for coupons and special offers. You will need to make a reservation in advance regardless of which service you use.

Some cruisers who want to do some exploring before the cruise rent a car at the airport and drop it off at the port, which houses several major rental-car agencies.

PARKING
Outdoor gated lots and a six-story parking garage are near the terminals and cost $17 per day (for either a car or RV), paid by major credit card (Discover, Master-Card, and Visa only).

◉ Sights

With the Kennedy Space Center just 20 minutes away, there is plenty to do in and around Cape Canaveral, though many folks opt to travel the extra hour into Orlando to visit the popular theme parks.

Brevard Museum of History & Natural Science
MUSEUM | FAMILY | This is the place to come to get the lay of the land in other eras. Not to be missed are Ice Age–era creatures such as a fully articulated mastodon, giant ground sloth, and saber-tooth cat, all of which lived in the area. The Windover Archaeological Exhibit features 7,000-year-old artifacts indigenous to the region. In 1984, a shallow pond revealed the burial ground of more than 200 native people who lived in the area about 7,000 years ago. Preserved in the muck were bones and, to the archae-ologists' surprise, the brains of these ancient people. Hands-on activities draw in children, who love the Imagination Center, where they can act out history or reenact a rocket flight. Nature lovers appreciate the museum's butterfly gar-den and the nature center, with 22 acres of trails encompassing three distinct ecosystems—sand pine hills, lake lands, and marshlands. ✉ 2201 Michigan Ave., Cocoa ☎ 321/632–1830 ⊕ www.myflor-idahistory.org ☜ $9 ☉ Closed Sun.–Wed.

★ Brevard Zoo
ZOO | FAMILY | At this Association of Zoo and Aquariums–accredited zoo you can stroll along the shaded boardwalks and get a close-up look at rhinos, giraffes, cheetahs, alligators, crocodiles, lemurs, jaguars, eagles, river otters, kangaroos,

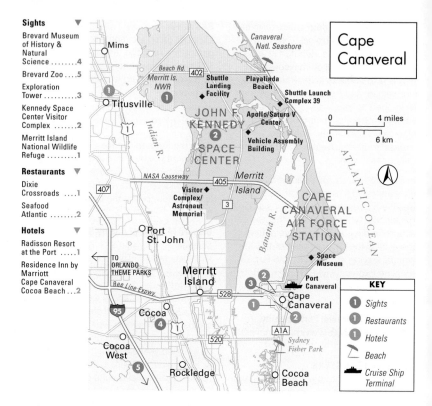

KEY

❶ Sights

❶ Restaurants

❶ Hotels

⌇ Beach

⛴ Cruise Ship Terminal

and exotic birds. Keeper chats are held throughout the day in which zookeepers feed and highlight various animals. Stop by Paws-On, an interactive learning playground with a petting zone, wildlife detective training academy, and the Indian River Play Lagoon. Hand-feed a giraffe in Expedition Africa or a lorikeet in the aviary; and step up to the Wetlands Outpost, an elevated pavilion that's a gateway to 22 acres of wetlands through which you can paddle kayaks and keep an eye open for the 4,000 species of wildlife that live in these waters and woods. Adventurers seeking a chimp's-eye view can zip-line through the zoo on Treetop Trek. ⊠ *8225 N. Wickham Rd., Melbourne* ☎ *321/254–9453* ⊕ *www.brevardzoo.org* 🎫 *$19.95.*

Exploration Tower

LOCAL INTEREST | FAMILY | The best view at Port Canaveral is no longer from the top of a cruise ship. In fact, the view from atop this towering seven-story structure makes the cruise ships look—well, not so massive after all. The tower, a short walk from the cruise port, is equal parts museum and scenic overlook. The seventh-floor observation deck offers impressive views of the cruise port, the Atlantic Ocean, the Banana River, and even the Vehicle Assembly Building at Kennedy Space Center. Other floors house exhibits highlighting the cultural history of the area, from space flight to surfing, bird and sea life to the rich maritime history. Kids will enjoy interactive exhibits, including a virtual ship's bridge that allows you to pilot a boat through the Canaveral Channel and into the

Atlantic. A theater shows a 20-minute film dedicated to the history of Brevard County, and a small café sells refreshments and baked goods. The ground floor houses a visitor information center. ⊠ *670 Dave Nisbet Dr., Cape Canaveral* ☎ *321/394–3408* ⊕ *www.explorationtower.com* 🔗 *$6.50.*

★ **Kennedy Space Center Visitor Complex**
HISTORIC SITE | FAMILY | This must-see attraction, just southeast of Titusville, is one of Central Florida's most popular sights. Located on a 140,000-acre island 45 minutes outside Orlando, Kennedy Space Center is NASA's launch headquarters. The visitor complex gives guests a unique opportunity to learn about—and experience—the past, present, and future of America's space program. Interactive programs include the Heroes & Legends attraction, which chronicles the men and women who've journeyed to space, and features the U.S. Astronaut Hall of Fame. If you want a low-key overview of the facility take the bus tour, included with admission. Buses depart every 15 minutes. Stops include the Apollo/Saturn V Center, where the launch of America's first lunar mission, 1968's Apollo VIII, is re-created with a ground-shaking, window-rattling liftoff. The Apollo/Saturn V Center also features one of three remaining Saturn V moon rockets. Astronaut Encounter Theater has two daily programs where retired NASA astronauts share their adventures in space travel and show a short film. The most moving exhibit is the Astronaut Memorial, a 70,400-pound black-granite tribute to astronauts who lost their lives in the name of space exploration.

More befitting Walt Disney World or Universal Studios, the Shuttle Launch Experience is the center's most spectacular attraction. Designed by a team of astronauts and NASA experts, the 44,000-square-foot structure simulates the sensations experienced in an actual space-shuttle launch. The journey culminates with a breathtaking view of Earth from space. The only back-to-back twin IMAX theater in the world is in the complex, too. ⊠ *Kennedy Space Center Visitor Complex, S.R. 405, Titusville* ☎ *877/313–2610* ⊕ *www.kennedyspacecenter.com* 🔗 *$57 (includes bus tour, IMAX movies, visitor complex shows and exhibits); specialty tours $25; Lunch with an Astronaut $29.99.*

★ **Merritt Island National Wildlife Refuge**
HIKING/WALKING | Owned by NASA but part of the National Wildlife Refuge System, this 140,000-acre refuge, which adjoins the Canaveral National Seashore, acts as a buffer around Kennedy Space Center while protecting 1,000 species of plants and 500 species of wildlife, 15 of which are considered threatened or endangered by the federal government. It's an immense area dotted by brackish estuaries and marshes, coastal dunes, hardwood hammocks, and pine forests. You can borrow field guides and binoculars at the visitor center (5 miles east of U.S. 1 in Titusville on State Road 402) to track down falcons, ospreys, eagles, turkeys, doves, cuckoos, owls, and woodpeckers, as well as loggerhead turtles, alligators, wild boar, and otters. A 20-minute video about refuge wildlife and accessibility—only 10,000 acres are developed—can help orient you. This is a wild, natural area, not a zoo or theme park. Visitors should use appropriate caution, as this is home to snakes, alligators, and stinging insects.

You might take a self-guided driving tour along the 7-mile Black Point Wildlife Drive. Several roads and trails are vulnerable to hurricane damage, and may be closed if there has been a strong storm. Check the website or call ☎ *321/861–2352* for updates on closures. If you exit the north end of the refuge, look for the Manatee Observation Deck, just north of the Haulover Canal (maps are at the visitor center). They usually show up in spring and fall. There are also fishing

Did You Know?

Known as the Moon Rockets, the Saturn Vs stood over 363 feet high. NASA sent more than a dozen of these expendable rockets skyward between 1967 and 1973. See one at the Apollo/Saturn V Center.

camps, fishing boat ramps, and six hiking trails scattered throughout the area. If you do want to fish, a free downloadable permit is required. The refuge does not close when there is a rocket launch. ⊠ Visitor Center, S.R. 402, 5 miles east of U.S. 1 across Titusville Causeway, Titusville ☎ 321/861–0667, 321/861–0669 visitor center ⊕ www.fws.gov/refuge/ merritt_island ⊡ Black Point Wildlife Dr. $10 per vehicle per day.

ORLANDO THEME PARKS
SeaWorld Orlando
AMUSEMENT PARK/WATER PARK | FAMILY |
In the world's largest marine adventure park, every attraction is devoted to demonstrating the ways that humans can protect the mammals, birds, fish, and reptiles that live in the ocean and its tributaries. The presentations are gentle reminders of our responsibility to safeguard the environment, and you'll find that SeaWorld's use of humor plays a major role in this education. The park is small enough that, armed with a map that lists showtimes, you can plan a chronological approach that flows easily from one attraction to the next. Near the intersection of Interstate 4 and the Beeline Expressway; take I–4 to Exit 71 or 72 and follow signs. ⊠ 7007 Sea Harbor Dr., International Drive ☎ 888/800–5447 ⊕ www.seaworld.com ⊡ From $104.99 for a 1-day ticket ($20 cheaper if bought online in advance).

Universal Orlando
AMUSEMENT PARK/WATER PARK | FAMILY |
The resort consists of **Universal Studios** (the original movie theme park, which includes The Wizarding World of Harry Potter–Diagon Alley), **Islands of Adventure** (the second theme park, which includes The Wizarding World of Harry Potter–Hogsmeade), **Volcano Bay** (an extensive water park), and **CityWalk** (the dining-shopping-nightclub complex). Although it's bordered by residential neighborhoods and the thickly trafficked International Drive, Universal Orlando is surprisingly expansive yet intimate and accessible, with two massive parking complexes, easy walks to all attractions, and a motor launch that cruises to most of the resort-owned hotels. With two full theme parks, two days are almost required to see the major attractions, but you may find yourself wanting to spend more time, especially if you want to devote a day to the water park. ⊠ 1000 Universal Studios Plaza, Orlando ☎ 407/363–8000 ⊕ www. universalorlando.com ⊡ 1-day, 1-park ticket from $115.

★ Walt Disney World
AMUSEMENT PARK/WATER PARK | FAMILY |
Walt Disney World is a huge complex of theme parks and attractions, each of which is worth a visit. Parks include the **Magic Kingdom**, a family favorite and the original here; **Epcot**, Disney's international, educational park; **Disney Hollywood Studios**, a movie-oriented theme park; and **Disney's Animal Kingdom**, which is much more than a zoo. Beyond these, there are water parks, elaborate minigolf courses, a sports center, resorts, restaurants, and nightlife. If you have only one day, you'll have to concentrate on a single park; Disney Hollywood Studios or Animal Kingdom are easiest to do in a day. Arrive early and expect to stay until park closing, which might be as early as 5 pm for Animal Kingdom or as late as 11 pm during busy seasons at the Magic Kingdom. The most direct route to the Disney Parks from Port Canaveral is State Road 528 (the Beeline Expressway) to Interstate 4; when you get through Orlando, follow the signs to Disney and expect traffic. ⊠ Lake Buena Vista ☎ 407/824–4321 ⊕ disneyworld.disney. go.com ⊡ 1-day, 1-park ticket from $109 (park-hopper option extra).

🌀 Beaches

Playalinda Beach
BEACH—SIGHT | The southern access for the Canaveral National Seashore, remote Playalinda Beach has pristine sands and

is the longest stretch of undeveloped coast on Florida's Atlantic seaboard. You can, however, see the launch pads at Cape Kennedy from the beach. Hundreds of giant sea turtles come ashore here from May through August to lay their eggs. Fourteen parking lots anchor the beach at 1-mile intervals. From Interstate 95, take Exit 249 and head east. Bring bug repellent in case of horseflies, and note that you may see some unauthorized clothing-optional activity. **Amenities:** lifeguards (seasonal); parking (fee); toilets. **Best for:** solitude; swimming; walking. ⊠ *S.R. 402, at the northern end of Beach Rd., Titusville* ☎ *321/267–1110* ⊕ *www.nps.gov/cana* ⊠ *$10 per vehicle for national seashore.*

Jetty Park

BEACH—SIGHT | A wonderful taste of the real Florida, this 4½-acre beach and oceanfront campground has picnic pavilions, bike paths, and a 1,200-foot-long fishing pier that doubles as a perfect vantage point from which to watch a liftoff from Cape Canaveral or to glimpse the gigantic cruise ships as they depart the port for the Bahamas. Lifeguards are on duty year-round, and all manner of equipment from beach chairs and umbrellas to bodyboards to beach wheelchairs is available for rent. A jetty constructed of giant boulders adds to the landscape, and a walkway that crosses it provides access to a less-populated stretch of beach. Real and rustic, this is Florida without the theme-park varnish. **Amenities:** food and drink; lifeguards; parking (fee); showers; toilets; water sports. **Best for:** sunrise; surfing; swimming; walking. ⊠ *400 Jetty Rd., Cape Canaveral* ☎ *321/783–7111* ⊕ *www.jettyparkbeachandcampground. com* ⊠ *$15 cars, $20 RVs. Cash only.*

🍴 Restaurants

The Cove at Port Canaveral has several restaurants if you are looking for a place to eat right at the port.

Dixie Crossroads

$$$ | SEAFOOD | FAMILY | This sprawling restaurant is always crowded and festive, but it's not just the rustic setting that draws throngs of people—it's the seafood. The specialty is rock shrimp, which are served fried, broiled, or steamed. **Known for:** locally caught rock shrimp; corn fritters dusted with powdered sugar; long waits for tables at peak hours. ⑤ *Average main: $24* ⊠ *1475 Garden St., 2 miles east of I–95 Exit 220, Titusville* ☎ *321/268–5000* ⊕ *www.dixiecrossroads.com.*

Seafood Atlantic

$$ | SEAFOOD | Locals think of this casual waterfront seafood market/eatery as a well-kept secret, but more and more cruise patrons are making their way here for a pre- or postcruise treat. The market is connected to the restaurant, guaranteeing not only freshness but an array of choices. **Known for:** variety of shrimp; crab cakes; views of departing and arriving cruise ships. ⑤ *Average main: $19* ⊠ *520 Glen Cheek Dr., Cape Canaveral* ☎ *321/784–1963* ⊕ *www.seafoodatlantic. org* ⊗ *Closed Mon.–Tues.*

🛏 Hotels

Many area hotels offer cruise packages that include one night's lodging, parking for the duration of your cruise, and transportation to the cruise port.

Radisson Resort at the Port

$ | HOTEL | For cruise-ship passengers who can't wait to get under way, this splashy resort, done up in pink and turquoise, already feels like the Caribbean. **Pros:** tropical landscaping in pool area; on-site eateries; free Wi-Fi. **Cons:** rooms around the pool can be noisy; loud air-conditioning in some rooms; no complimentary breakfast. ⑤ *Rooms from: $124* ⊠ *8701 Astronaut Blvd., Cape Canaveral* ☎ *321/784–0000, 888/201–1718* ⊕ *www.radisson.com/capecanaveralfl* ⬞ *356 rooms* ⊙*l No meals.*

Residence Inn by Marriott Cape Canaveral Cocoa Beach

$$ | HOTEL | Billing itself as the closest all-suites hotel to the Kennedy Space Center is this four-story Residence Inn, painted a cheery yellow. **Pros:** helpful staff; free breakfast buffet; free Wi-Fi. **Cons:** less than picturesque views; street noise in some rooms; fee for parking. ⑤ *Rooms from: $279* ⊠ *8959 Astronaut Blvd., Cape Canaveral* ☎ *321/323–1100, 800/331–3131* ⊕ *www.marriott.com* ➥ *150 suites* ⏐⊙⏐ *Free Breakfast.*

🛍 Shopping

Cocoa Beach Surf Company

SURFING | This huge surf complex sits inside the Four Points by Sheraton resort, and has three floors of boards, apparel, sunglasses, and anything else a surfer, wannabe-surfer, or souvenir-seeker could need. Also on-site are a 5,600-gallon fish and shark tank and the Shark Pit Bar and Grill. You can rent surfboards, bodyboards, and wet suits, as well as umbrellas, chairs, and bikes. And staffers teach wannabes, from kids to seniors, how to surf. There are group, semiprivate, and private lessons available in one-, two-, and three-hour sessions. All gear is provided. ⊠ *Four Points by Sheraton, 4001 N. Atlantic Ave., Cocoa Beach* ☎ *321/799–9930* ⊕ *www.cocoabeach-surf.com* ➲ *From $40.*

★ Ron Jon Surf Shop

SPORTING GOODS | It's impossible to miss the flagship and original Ron Jon: It takes up nearly two blocks along Route A1A and has a giant surfboard and an art-deco facade painted orange, blue, yellow, and turquoise. What started in 1963 as a small T-shirt and bathing-suit shop has evolved into a 52,000-square-foot superstore that's open every day 'round the clock. The shop rents water-sports gear as well as chairs and umbrellas, and it sells every kind of beachwear, surf wax, plus the requisite T-shirts and flip-flops.

⊠ *4151 N. Atlantic Ave., S.R. A1A, Cocoa Beach* ☎ *321/799–8888* ⊕ *www.ronjon-surfshop.com.*

San Juan, Puerto Rico

In addition to being a major port of call, San Juan is also a common port of embarkation for cruises on Southern Caribbean itineraries.

For information on dining, shopping, nightlife, and sightseeing see San Juan, Puerto Rico in Chapter 4.

THE CRUISE PORT

Most cruise ships dock within a couple of blocks of Old San Juan; however, there is a second cruise pier across the bay, and if your ship docks there you'll need to take a taxi to get anywhere on the island. The Paseo de la Princesa, a tree-lined promenade beneath the city wall, is a nice place for a stroll; you can admire the local crafts and stop at the refreshment kiosks. Major sights in the Old San Juan area are mere blocks from the piers, but be aware that the streets are narrow and steeply inclined in places.

AIRPORT

CONTACTS Aeropuerto Internacional Luis Muñoz Marín. ☎ *787/289–7240* ⊕ *www.aeropuertosju.com.*

AIRPORT TRANSFERS

If you are embarking or disembarking in San Juan, the ride to or from the Luis Muñoz Marín International Airport, east of downtown San Juan, to the docks in Old San Juan takes about 20 minutes, depending on traffic. White "Taxi Turístico" cabs, marked by a logo on the door, have a fixed rate of $19 to and from the cruise-ship piers; there is a $1 charge for each piece of luggage. Other taxi companies charge by the mile, which can cost a little more. Be sure the driver starts the meter, or agree on a fare beforehand.

VISITOR INFORMATION
CONTACTS Puerto Rico Tourism Company.
☎ 787/522–5960 ⊕ www.discoverpuertorico.com.

🛏 Hotels

If you are planning to spend one night in San Juan before your cruise departs, you'll probably find it easier to stay in Old San Juan, where the cruise-ship terminals are. But if you want to spend a few extra days in the city, there are other possibilities near good beaches a bit farther out. We make some nightlife suggestions in the San Juan port of call section.

The Gallery Inn
$$ | B&B/INN | No two rooms in this 200-year-old mansion are alike, but all have four-poster beds, handwoven tapestries, and quirky antiques in every nook and cranny. **Pros:** one-of-a-kind lodging; ocean views; wonderful classical music concerts. **Cons:** several narrow, winding staircases; an uphill walk from the rest of Old San Juan; sometimes-raucous pet macaws and cockatoos. ⑤ *Rooms from: $160* ✉ *204–206 Calle Norzagaray, Old San Juan* ☎ *787/722–1808* ⊕ *www.thegalleryinn.com* 🛏 *25 rooms* ⏐⊙⏐ *Free Breakfast.*

★ Hotel El Convento
$$$ | HOTEL | There's no longer anything austere about this 350-year-old former convent. **Pros:** lovely historic building; atmosphere to spare; plenty of nearby dining options. **Cons:** near some noisy bars; small pool; small bathrooms. ⑤ *Rooms from: $285* ✉ *100 Calle Cristo, Old San Juan* ☎ *787/723–9020* ⊕ *www.elconvento.com* 🛏 *58 rooms* ⏐⊙⏐ *No meals.*

Sheraton Old San Juan Hotel
$$$ | HOTEL | FAMILY | Rooms facing the water at this triangular hotel have spectacular views of the mammoth cruise ships that sail in and out of the nearby harbor. **Pros:** harbor views; near many dining options; great precruise option.

Best Bets ◉

■ **Busch Gardens.** The area's best theme park is a good family destination.

■ **Florida Aquarium.** The aquarium is next to the cruise port, so you can easily walk there, making it a good option if you have only a couple of hours to kill before boarding (they'll even store your luggage if you want to visit after disembarking).

■ **The Dalí Museum.** One of the finest and most interesting museums in the United States.

■ **Ybor City.** For nightlife and restaurants, this historic district is Tampa's hot spot.

Cons: chain-hotel feel to guest rooms; uphill walk to the rest of Old San Juan; casino has closed. ⑤ *Rooms from: $259* ✉ *100 Calle Brumbaugh, Old San Juan* ☎ *787/289–1914* ⊕ *www.sheratonoldsanjuan.com* 🛏 *240 rooms* ⏐⊙⏐ *No meals.*

Tampa, Florida

It may not have the glitz of Miami or the "magic" of Orlando, but the Tampa Bay area has that elusive quality that many attribute to the "real" Florida; here you'll find some of the state's best and most unspoiled beaches and lots of history. Tampa Bay is also the state's second-largest metro area and it showcases broad cultural diversity, as well as Florida's third-busiest airport, a vibrant business community, world-class beaches, and superior hotels and resorts—many of them historic. This all adds up to an excellent place to spend a week or even a lifetime. Several ships are based here year-round and seasonally, most for Western Caribbean itineraries.

ESSENTIALS
HOURS
Some museums are closed on Monday.

VISITOR INFORMATION
CONTACTS Visit Tampa Bay. ✉ *201 N. Franklin St., Tampa* ☎ *800/448–2672, 813/223–1111* ⊕ *www.visittampabay.com.* **Ybor City Chamber Visitor Information Center.** ✉ *1800 E. 9th Ave., Ybor City* ☎ *813/241–8838* ⊕ *www.ybor.org.*

THE CRUISE PORT
Tampa is the largest shipping port in the state of Florida, and it's becoming ever more important to the cruise industry, now with three passenger terminals. In Tampa's downtown area, the port is linked to nearby Ybor City and the rest of the Tampa Bay Area by the TECO streetcar line.

CONTACTS Port Tampa Bay. ✉ *1101 Channelside Dr., Tampa* ☎ *813/905–7678, 800/741–2297* ⊕ *www.tampaport.com/cruise.*

AIRPORT
CONTACTS Tampa International Airport. ☎ *813/870–8700* ⊕ *www.tampaairport.com.*

AIRPORT TRANSFERS
SuperShuttle provides shared van service to and from the airport and the cruise terminal. Expect to pay about $25 per person.

CONTACTS Blue One Transportation. ☎ *813/282–7351* ⊕ *www.blueonetransportation.com.* **SuperShuttle.** ☎ *727/571–4220* ⊕ *www.supershuttle.com.*

PARKING
Parking is available at the port directly across from the terminals. For Terminal 2 (Carnival), parking is in a garage across the street. For Terminal 3 (Royal Caribbean and Norwegian), parking is also in a garage across the street. For Terminal 6 (Holland America), parking is outdoors in a guarded, enclosed lot. The cost is generally charged by the cruise line (from $105 per week), payable by credit card (MasterCard or Visa) or by cash in advance; valet parking is available for the same rate but with the addition of a $20 "convenience fee."

◉ Sights

Florida's west-coast crown jewel as well as its business and commercial hub, Tampa has high-rises and heavy traffic. Amid the bustle is the region's greatest concentration of restaurants, nightlife, stores, and cultural events.

Adventure Island
AMUSEMENT PARK/WATER PARK | FAMILY |
From spring until fall, Busch Gardens' water park promises heat relief with rides like Everglides, Aruba Tuba, and Key West Rapids. Tampa's most popular "wet" park features waterslides and artificial wave pools, along with tranquil "beaches" in a 30-acre package. Try Colossal Curl, a massive thrill ride that's the tallest waterslide in the park. Another of the attraction's headliners, Riptide, challenges you to race three other riders on a sliding mat through twisting tubes and hairpin turns. Planners of this park also took the younger kids into account, with offerings such as Fabian's Funport, which has a scaled-down pool and interactive water gym. Along with a volleyball complex and a rambling river, there are cafés, snack bars, picnic and sunbathing areas, changing rooms, and private cabanas. Good discounts are offered on the park's website. ✉ *10001 N. McKinley Dr., Central Tampa* ✛ *Less than 1 mile north of Busch Gardens* ☎ *888/800–5447* ⊕ *www.adventureisland.com* 🎫 *From $59.99 (online $25.99); parking $25* ☉ *Closed Nov.–Feb.*

★ Busch Gardens
AMUSEMENT PARK/WATER PARK | FAMILY |
Drawing some 4½ million visitors each year, Busch Gardens Tampa is a major theme park, with seven popular roller coasters being the biggest lure. But this is also a world-class zoo, with more than

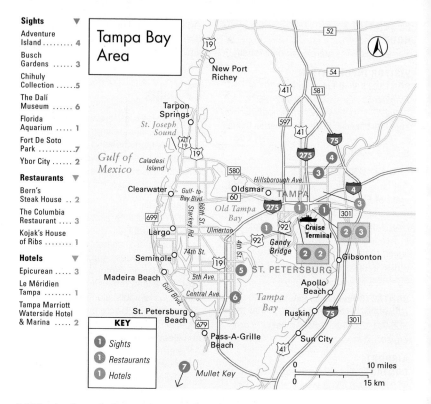

Tampa Bay Area

KEY

❶ Sights

❶ Restaurants

❶ Hotels

2,000 animals, and a live entertainment venue that provides a full day (or more) of fun for the whole family. If you want to beat the crowds, start in the back of the park and work your way around clockwise. The 335-acre adventure park's habitats offer views of some of the world's most endangered and exotic animals. For the best animal sightings, go to their habitats early, when it's cooler. Catering to the shorter set, the Sesame Street Safari of Fun is a 5-acre kids' playground with Sesame-themed rides, shows, and water adventures. The Air Grover Rollercoaster takes kids (and parents) on minidives and twisty turns over the Sahara, while Jungle Flyers gets them swinging and screeching. If you're looking to cool off, your best bets are Congo River Rapids, Stanleyville Falls (a flume ride), or Bert and Ernie's Water Hole—complete

with bubblers, geysers, water jets, and dumping buckets. Character lunches are available (but you might want to wait until after your rides). ✉ 10165 N. McKinley Dr., Central Tampa ☎ 813/884–4386, 888/800–5447 ⊕ www.buschgardens. com ☎ From $109.99 ($84.99 advance); parking $25.

★ **Chihuly Collection**

MUSEUM | An electrifying 10,000-square-foot Albert Alfonso–designed building is home to world-renowned glass sculptor Dale Chihuly's work. Here, impossibly vibrant, larger-than-life pieces such as Float Boat and Ruby Red Icicle sit next to some of the famed sculptor's smaller and more under-the-radar works. You can tour the museum independently or with one of its volunteer docents (no added cost; tours are given hourly on the half hour during the week). Each display is perfectly lighted against a shade of gray paint handpicked by Chihuly himself, which adds to the drama of the designs. Don't miss *Mille Fiori* (*Thousand Flowers*), a spectacular, whimsical glass montage mimicking a wildflower patch, critters and all. Check out the gift shop at the end if you'd like to take some of the magic home with you. Your admission includes access to Morean Arts Center's glassblowing studio, where you can watch resident artists create a unique glass piece before your eyes. ⌧ *720 Central Ave., Downtown* ☎ *727/896–4527* ⊕ *www.moreanartscenter.org/chihuly* ⌧ *$19.95.*

★ The Dalí Museum

MUSEUM | Inside and out, the waterfront Dalí Museum, which opened on 1/11/11 (Dalí is said to have been into numerology), is almost as remarkable as the Spanish surrealist's work. The state-of-the-art building incorporates a surreal geodesic glass structure called the Enigma, as well as an outdoor labyrinth and a DNA-inspired spiral staircase leading up to the collection. And all this even before you've seen the collection, which is one of the most comprehensive of its kind—courtesy of Ohio magnate A. Reynolds Morse, a friend of Dalí's.

Here you can scope out his early impressionistic works and see how the painter evolved into the visionary he's now seen to be. The mind-expanding paintings in this downtown headliner include *Eggs on the Plate without the Plate*, *The Hallucinogenic Toreador*, and more than 90 other oils. You'll also discover more than 2,000 additional works including watercolors, drawings, sculptures, photographs, and objets d'art. The museum also hosts temporary collections from the likes of Pablo Picasso and Andy Warhol. Free hour-long tours are led by well-informed docents. ⌧ *1 Dalí Blvd., St. Petersburg* ☎ *727/823–3767* ⊕ *www. thedali.org* ⌧ *$25, parking $10.*

Florida Aquarium

ZOO | FAMILY | Although eels, sharks, and stingrays are the headliners, the Florida Aquarium is much more than a giant fishbowl. This architectural landmark features an 83-foot-high, multi-tier glass dome; 250,000 square feet of air-conditioned exhibit space; and more than 20,000 aquatic plants and animals representing species native to Florida and the rest of the world—from black-tip sharks to leafy sea dragons.

Floor-to-ceiling interactive displays, behind-the-scenes tours, and in-water adventures allow kids to really get hands-on—and even get their feet wet.

But you don't have to get wet to have an interactive experience: the *Ocean Commotion* exhibit offers virtual dolphins and whales and multimedia displays. The Coral Reef Gallery is a 500,000-gallon tank with viewing windows, an awesome 43-foot-wide panoramic opening, and a walk-through tunnel. The *Journey to Madagascar* exhibit features ring-tailed lemurs, hissing cockroaches, and an Indian Ocean coral reef to showcase the nation's vast diversity of creatures and ecosystems.

If you have an extra 90 minutes, try the Wild Dolphin Adventure Cruise, which takes up to 130 passengers onto Tampa Bay in a 72-foot catamaran for an up-close look at bottlenose dolphins and other wildlife. ⌧ *701 Channelside Dr., Downtown* ☎ *813/273–4000* ⊕ *www. flaquarium.org* ⌧ *Aquarium from $24.95; combination ticket with Dolphin Cruise $49.90; combination ticket with Penguins: Backstage Pass $70; Dive with the Sharks $160; Shark Swim $110; parking $6.*

★ Fort De Soto Park

BEACH—SIGHT | FAMILY | Spread over five small islands, 1,136-acre Fort De Soto Park lies at the mouth of Tampa Bay. It has 7 miles of waterfront (much of it beach), two fishing piers, a 4-mile

Busch Gardens is the most popular theme park in Tampa.

hiking, cycling, and skating trail, picnic-and-camping grounds, and a historic fort that kids of any age can explore. For those traveling with their canine family members, there is a long and popular dog beach just north of the main fishing pier. Its namesake fort was built on the southern end of Mullet Key to protect sea lanes in the Gulf during the Spanish-American War. Roam the fort or wander the beaches of any of the islands within the park. Kayaks and beach cruisers are available for rental, and mementos can be found at a souvenir shop/grill on the park's north side. ⊠ *3500 Pinellas Bayway S, Tierra Verde* ☎ *727/582–2267* ⊕ *www.pinellascounty.org/park/05_ft_desoto.htm* 🖃 *$5.*

Ybor City
NEIGHBORHOOD | Tampa's Latin quarter is one of only a few National Historic Landmark districts in Florida. Bordered by Interstate 4 to the north, 22nd Street to the east, Adamo Drive to the south, and Nebraska Avenue to the west, it has brick-paved streets and wrought-iron balconies. Cubans brought their cigar-making industry to Ybor (pronounced *EE-bore*) City in 1886, and the smell of cigars—hand-rolled by Cuban immigrants—still wafts through the heart of this east Tampa area, along with the strong aroma of roasting coffee. These days the neighborhood makes for an interesting visit, as empty cigar factories and historic social clubs have been transformed into boutiques, art galleries, restaurants, and nightclubs. Nevertheless, it can also be seedy and rowdy at times. ⊠ *Ybor City.*

🌊 Beaches

★ Caladesi Island State Park
BEACH—SIGHT | Quiet, secluded, and still wild, this 3½-mile-long barrier island is one of the best shelling beaches on the Gulf Coast, second only to Sanibel. The park also has plenty of sights for birders—from common sandpipers to majestic blue herons to rare black skimmers—and miles of trails through scrub oaks, saw palmettos, and cacti (with

tenants such as armadillos, rabbits, and raccoons). The landscape also features mangroves and dunes, and the gradual slope of the sea bottom makes this a good spot for novice swimmers and kids. You have to get to Caladesi Island by private boat (there's a 108-slip marina) or through its sister park, the Honeymoon Island State Recreation Area, where you take the hourly ferry ride across to Caladesi ($14 per person). You can also paddle yourself over in a kayak. **Amenities:** food and drink; showers; toilets. **Best for:** solitude; swimming. ⊠ *Dunedin Causeway, Dunedin* ☎ *727/469–5918* ⊕ *floridastateparks.org/parks-and-trails/ caladesi-island-state-park* ⊠ *$6 per boat, $2 per kayaker.*

★ Pass-a-Grille Beach

BEACH—SIGHT | FAMILY | At the southern tip of St. Pete Beach (past the Don Cesar), this is the epitome of Old Florida. One of the most popular beaches in the area, it skirts the west end of charming, historic Pass-a-Grille, a neighborhood that draws tourists and locals alike with its stylish yet low-key mom-and-pop motels and restaurants. There's a sunset celebration each night at a pavilion/snack shop on the stretch of beach between the ends of 9th and 10th Avenues. On weekends check out the Art Mart, an open-air market showcasing the work of local artists. **Amenities:** food and drink; parking; showers; toilets. **Best for:** sunset; windsurfing. ⊠ *1000 Pass-a-Grille Way, St. Pete Beach.*

🍴 Restaurants

★ Bern's Steak House

$$$$ | STEAKHOUSE | With the air of an exclusive club, this is one of the finest steak houses—if not *the* finest—in Florida. Rich mahogany paneling and ornate chandeliers define the legendary circa-1956 Bern's, where the chef himself ages the beef, grows much of the produce, and roasts the coffee. **Known for:** colossal wine list; exclusive

atmosphere; after dinner, a trip upstairs to the famous dessert room. $ *Average main: $36* ⊠ *1208 S. Howard Ave., Hyde Park* ☎ *813/251–2421* ⊕ *www.berns-steakhouse.com* 🎩 *Jacket and tie.*

★ The Columbia Restaurant

$$$ | SPANISH | Make a date for some of the best Latin cuisine in Tampa. A fixture since 1905, this magnificent structure with an old-world air and spacious dining rooms takes up an entire city block and seems to feed the entire city—locals as well as visitors—throughout the week, but especially on weekends. **Known for:** paella a la Valenciana (with seafood, chicken, and pork); 1905 salad (with ham, olives, cheese, and garlic); delicious sangria. $ *Average main: $28* ⊠ *2117 E. 7th Ave., Ybor City* ☎ *813/248–4961* ⊕ *www. columbiarestaurant.com.*

Kojak's House of Ribs

$ | SOUTHERN | Few barbecue joints can boast the staying power of this family-owned and -operated pit stop. Located along a shaded stretch in South Tampa, it debuted in 1978 and has since earned a following of sticky-fingered regulars who have turned it into one of the most popular barbecue stops in central Florida. **Known for:** barbecue meat dishes (especially spareribs); great sangria; serene setting. $ *Average main: $13* ⊠ *2808 W. Gandy Blvd., South Tampa* ☎ *813/837–3774* ⊕ *kojaksbbq.net* ☉ *Closed Mon.*

🛏 Hotels

If you want to be close to the cruise-ship terminal, then you'll have to stay in Tampa; but if you want to spend more time in the area and perhaps stay on the beach, St. Petersburg and the beaches are close by.

★ Epicurean

$$$ | HOTEL | Brought to you in part by the people at Bern's Steak House (which happens to be across the street), this vibrant, cuisine-centric installment of Marriott's Autograph Collection is an

absolute must for foodies, but it doesn't make nonfoodies feel left out. **Pros:** excellent service; great location; tons of amenities. **Cons:** can get pricey; exclusive vibe; not the best option for families. $ *Rooms from: $329 ⊠ 1207 S. Howard Ave., SoHo ☎ 813/999–8700, 855/829–2536 ⊕ epicureanhotel.com ⇆ 137 rooms ❌ No meals.*

Le Méridien Tampa

$$ | HOTEL | A meticulous renovation transformed this historic, marble-lined former federal courthouse into Tampa's most talked-about boutique hotel. **Pros:** close to downtown attractions; fascinating for history buffs; lots of amenities. **Cons:** traffic in surrounding area can be a nightmare; all that marble makes for loud echoes in the hallways. $ *Rooms from: $269 ⊠ 601 N. Florida Ave., Downtown ☎ 813/221–9555, 877/782–0116 for reservations ⊕ lemeridientampa.com ⇆ 130 rooms ❌ No meals.*

Tampa Marriott Waterside Hotel & Marina

$$ | HOTEL | Located across from the Tampa Convention Center, this downtown hotel was built for conventioneers but is also convenient to tourist spots such as the Florida Aquarium and the Ybor City and Hyde Park shopping and nightlife districts. **Pros:** great downtown location; near sights, dining, nightlife; direct access to Riverwalk. **Cons:** gridlock during rush hour; streets tough to maneuver; half the rooms overlook concrete-walled channel to Tampa Bay. $ *Rooms from: $234 ⊠ 700 S. Florida Ave., Downtown ☎ 888/268–1616 for reservations, 813/221–4900 ⊕ www.marriott.com ⇆ 719 rooms ❌ No meals.*

🅨 Nightlife

Although there are plenty of boarded-up storefronts in Ybor City, it has the biggest concentration of nightclubs (as well as the widest variety), most of which are found along 7th Avenue. It becomes a little like Bourbon Street in New Orleans on weekend evenings.

Gaspar's Grotto

BARS/PUBS | Spanish pirate Jose Gaspar was known for swashbuckling up and down Florida's west coast in the late 18th and early 19th century. His legend has inspired a massive, raucous street festival each winter. This Ybor City drinkery has adopted his name, and rightly so. Decked out in tons of pirate memorabilia, it's the cornerstone to any night spent barhopping on the Ybor strip. The sangria is a good choice, but the aged rums may be a better fit here. You'll also find a food menu that goes well beyond standard bar fare. ⊠ *1805 E. 7th Ave., Ybor City ☎ 813/248–5900 ⊕ www.gasparsgrotto. com.*

The Hub Bar

BARS/PUBS | Considered something of a dive—but a lovable one—by a loyal and young local following that ranges from esteemed jurists to nose-ring-wearing night owls. The Hub, which dates back to 1946, is known for strong drinks and a jukebox that goes well beyond the usual. ⊠ *719 N. Franklin St., Downtown ☎ 813/229–1553.*

🅢 Shopping

International Plaza

SHOPPING CENTERS/MALLS | If you want to grab something at Neiman Marcus or Nordstrom, this is the place. You'll also find Gucci, Tory Burch, Burberry, Tiffany & Co., Louis Vuitton, and many other upscale shops. Stick around after hours, when watering holes in the mall's courtyard become a high-end club scene. ⊠ *2223 N. West Shore Blvd., Airport Area ⊕ www.shopinternationalplaza.com.*

Old Hyde Park Village

SHOPPING CENTERS/MALLS | It's a typical upscale shopping district in a quiet, shaded neighborhood near the water. Boutiques and upscale chains like Suitsupply, Lululemon, and Anthropologie are mixed in with popular bistros and sidewalk cafés. ⊠ *1602 W. Swann Ave., Hyde Park ⊕ www.hydeparkvillage.com.*

Chapter 4

PORTS OF CALL

4

Nowhere in the world are conditions better suited to cruising than in the Caribbean Sea. Tiny island nations, within easy sailing distance of one another, form a chain of tropical enchantment that curves from Cuba in the north all the way down to the coast of Venezuela.

There's far more to life in the Caribbean than sand and coconuts, however. The islands are vastly different, with a variety of cultures, topographies, and languages represented. Colonialism has left its mark, and the presence of the Spanish, French, Dutch, Danish, and British is still felt. Slavery, too, has left its cultural legacy, adding African traditions, music, and cuisine into the West Indian colonial amalgam. The one constant, however, is the weather. Despite the islands' southerly latitude, the climate is surprisingly gentle, due in large part to the cooling influence of trade winds.

The Caribbean is made up of the Greater Antilles and the Lesser Antilles. The former consist of those islands closest to the United States: Cuba, Jamaica, Hispaniola (Haiti and the Dominican Republic), and Puerto Rico. (The Cayman Islands lie south of Cuba.) The Lesser Antilles, including the Virgin, Windward, and Leeward islands (among others), are greater in number but smaller in size, and constitute the southern half of the Caribbean chain.

Going Ashore

Traveling by cruise ship presents an opportunity to visit many places in a short time. The flip side is that your stay in each port of call will be brief. For this reason cruise lines offer shore excursions, which maximize passengers' time. There are a number of advantages to shore excursions arranged by your ship: In some destinations, transportation may be unreliable, and a ship-packaged tour is the best way to see distant sights. Also, you don't have to worry about missing the ship. The disadvantage of a shore excursion is the cost: you usually pay more for the convenience of having the ship do the legwork for you, but it's not always a lot more. Of course, you can always book a tour independently, hire a taxi, or use foot power to explore on your own. For each port of call included in this guide we've provided some suggestions for the best ship-sponsored excursions—in terms of both quality of experience and price—as well as some suggestions for what to do if you want to explore on your own.

Arriving in Port

When your ship arrives in a port, it will tie up alongside a dock or anchor out in a harbor. If the ship is docked, passengers walk down the gangway to go ashore. Docking makes it easy to move between the shore and the ship.

CLEARING THE SHIP

Before anyone is allowed to walk down the gangway or board a tender, the ship must be cleared for landing. Immigration and customs officials board the vessel to examine the ship's manifest or possibly passports and sort through red tape. It may be more than an hour before you're allowed ashore. You will be issued a boarding pass, which you'll need to get back on board.

TENDERING

If your ship anchors in the harbor, you will have to take a smaller boat (called a launch or tender) to get ashore. Tendering is a nuisance, but participants in ship-sponsored shore excursions are given priority. Passengers wishing to disembark independently may be required to gather in a public room, get sequenced tendering passes, and wait until their numbers are called. The ride to shore may take as long as 20 minutes. If you don't like waiting, plan to go ashore an hour or so after the ship drops its anchor. On a very large ship, the wait for a tender can be quite long and frustrating.

Because tenders can be difficult to board, passengers with mobility problems may not be able to visit certain ports. Larger ships are more likely to use tenders. It is usually possible to learn before booking a cruise whether the ship will dock or anchor at its ports of call.

Returning to the Ship

Cruise lines are strict about sailing times, which are posted at the gangway and elsewhere and announced in the daily

Buying Liquor and Perfume 💼

If you buy duty-free liquor or perfume while in a Caribbean port, don't forget that you may not bring it aboard your flight home. You will have to put it in your checked bags. Many liquor stores will pack your bottles in bubble wrap and pack them in a good cardboard box. Take advantage of this service.

schedule of activities. Be sure to be back on board (not on the dock waiting to get a tender back to the ship) at least an hour before the announced sailing time or you may be stranded. If you are on a shore excursion that was sold by the cruise line, however, the captain will wait for your group before casting off. That is one reason many passengers prefer ship-packaged tours.

If you're not on one of the ship's tours and the ship sails without you, immediately contact the cruise line's port representative, whose phone number is often listed on the daily schedule of activities. You may be able to hitch a ride on a pilot boat, although that is unlikely. Passengers who miss the boat must pay their own way to the next port.

Caribbean Essentials

Currency

The U.S. dollar is the official currency on Puerto Rico, the U.S. Virgin Islands, the Turks & Caicos, Bonaire, and the British Virgin Islands. On Grand Cayman you will usually have a choice of Cayman or U.S. dollars when you take money out of an ATM, and you may even be able to get change in U.S. dollars. In Cozumel,

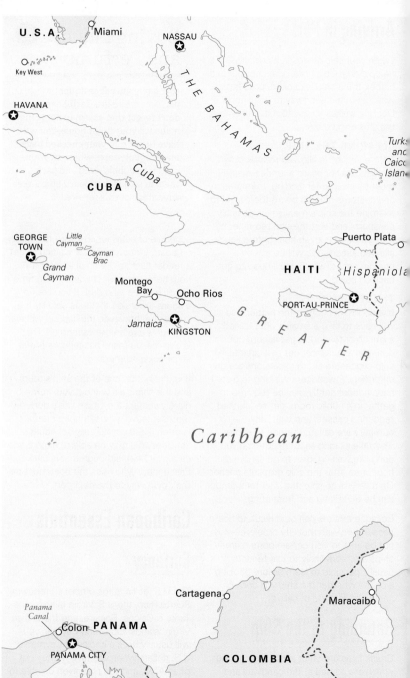

Caribbean

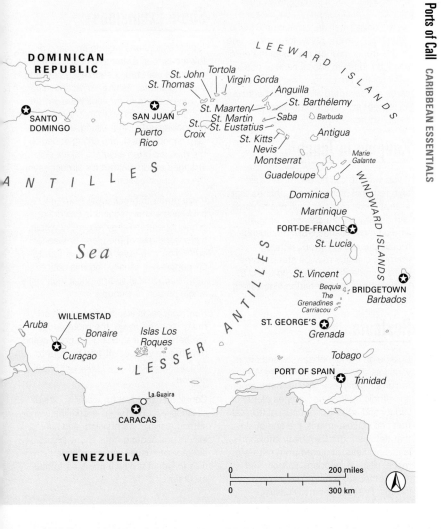

ATLANTIC OCEAN

DOMINICAN
REPUBLIC

LEEWARD ISLANDS

St. John Tortola
St. Thomas Virgin Gorda
Anguilla
St. Barthélemy
SANTO
DOMINGO
SAN JUAN
St. Maarten/
St. Martin Saba
St. Eustatius
St. Kitts
Nevis
Montserrat
Guadeloupe
Barbuda
Antigua
Marie
Galante

Puerto
Rico
St.
Croix

A N T I L L E S

WINDWARD ISLANDS

Dominica
Martinique
FORT-DE-FRANCE
St. Lucia

Sea

St. Vincent
Bequia
The
Grenadines
Carriacou
BRIDGETOWN
Barbados

L E S S E R   A N T I L L E S

ST. GEORGE'S
Grenada

Aruba
WILLEMSTAD
Bonaire
Islas Los
Roques
Curaçao

Tobago

PORT OF SPAIN
Trinidad

La Guaira
CARACAS

VENEZUELA

| 0 | | 200 miles |
| 0 | | 300 km |

Calica, Costa Maya, and Progreso, the Mexican peso is the official currency. The euro is used in a handful of French islands (St. Barth, St. Martin, Martinique, Guadeloupe). Most other Caribbean destinations use the Eastern Caribbean dollar, which is pegged to the U.S. dollar. Other countries (Bahamas, Curaçao, Aruba, Belize, Honduras, Barbados), have their own currencies, but in most Caribbean ports U.S. paper currency (not coins) is accepted readily. When you pay in dollars you'll almost always get change in local currency, so it's best to carry bills in small denominations. If you need local currency (say, for a trip to one of the French islands that uses the euro), change money at a local bank or use an ATM for the best rate. Most major credit cards are accepted all over the Caribbean, except at local market stalls and small establishments.

Keeping in Touch

If you want to call home, most cruise-ship terminal facilities have phones that accept credit cards or local phone cards (almost always the cheapest option). And on most islands GSM multiband mobile phones will work, although roaming charges may be steep (some plans include Puerto Rico and the U.S. Virgin Islands in their nationwide calling regions).

Restaurants

Cuisine on the Caribbean's islands is as varied as the islands themselves. The region's history as a colonial battleground and ethnic melting pot creates plenty of variety and adds lots of unusual tropical fruit and spices. In fact, the one quality that defines most Caribbean cooking is its spiciness, acquired from nutmeg, mace, allspice, peppers, saffron, and many other seasonings grown on the islands. Dress is generally casual, although throughout the islands beachwear is inappropriate most anywhere except on the beach. Unless otherwise noted, prices are given in U.S. dollars.

WHAT IT COSTS in Dollars			
$	$$	$$$	$$$$
RESTAURANTS			
under $20	$20–$30	$31–$40	over $40

Shore Excursions

Typical excursions include an island or town bus tour, a visit to a beach or rum factory, a boat trip, a snorkeling or diving trip, and charter fishing. In recent years, however, shore excursions have gotten more adventurous, with mild river-rafting, parasailing, jet-skiing, hiking, zip-lining (and canopy tours), and biking added to the mix. It's often easier to take a ship-arranged excursion, but it's almost never the cheapest option.

If you prefer to break away from the pack, find a knowledgeable taxi driver or tour operator—they're usually within a stone's throw of the pier—or wander around on your own. A group of four to six people will usually find this option more economical and practical than will a single person or a couple.

Renting a car is also a good option on many islands—again, the more people, the better the deal. But get a good island map before you set off, and be sure to find out how long it will take you to get around.

Conditions are ideal for water sports of all kinds—scuba diving, snorkeling, windsurfing, sailing, waterskiing, and fishing excursions abound. Your shore-excursion director can usually arrange these activities for you if the ship offers no formal excursion.

Private Islands

When evaluating the "best" Caribbean ports of call, many repeat cruise passengers often add the cruise lines' own private islands to their lists of preferred destinations.

The cruise lines established "private" islands to provide a beach break on an island (or part of one) reserved for their exclusive use. While most passengers don't select an itinerary based solely upon calling at a private island, they usually consider them a highlight of their cruise vacation. The very least you can expect of your private island is lush foliage and a wide swath of beach surrounded by azure water. Facilities vary, but a beach barbecue, water-sports equipment rental, lounge chairs, hammocks, and restrooms are standard. Youth counselors come ashore to conduct sand-castle building competitions and lead junior pirates on swashbuckling island treasure hunts.

The use of strollers and wheelchairs equipped with all-terrain wheels may be offered on a complimentary first-come, first-served basis. However, with the exception of some participation sports on the beach, plan to pay for most water toys and activities. Costs associated with private-island fun and recreation can range from $10 to $15 for a float to $30 to $35 for rental of an entire snorkeling outfit for the day (mask, fins, snorkel vest, a mesh bag, fish identification card, and fish food). You will also have to pay to reserve a beach umbrella or personal covered beach lounger (up to $45 per day). Shore excursions are also offered at most private islands, including kayaking ($60 to $70), parasailing (usually over $100 for 10 minutes or less), or a trip on a a zip line for $95. Private cabanas are among the most expensive facilities (starting at $300 per day), and Perfect Day at Coco Cay even has an elaborate water park that starts at $39 for a half-day visit. You might also find open-air massage cabanas with pricing comparable to the spa charges onboard.

There is generally no charge for food or basic beverages such as those served aboard ship. Soft drinks and tropical cocktails can usually be charged to your shipboard account, as can paid activities like motorized water sports, stingray encounters, private cabanas, and other options that vary by cruise line. With the introduction of more resort-style amenities on private islands, there are more opportunities to spend money on things like dining in restaurants that carry an extra charge.

You might want to bring a small amount of cash ashore for souvenir shopping, which is almost always possible from vendors set up on or near the beach.

Even if you do nothing more than lie in a shaded hammock and sip fruity tropical concoctions, the day can be one of the most fun and relaxing of your entire cruise.

4

Ports of Call CARIBBEAN ESSENTIALS

Antigua (St. John's)

Some say Antigua has so many beaches that you could visit a different one every day for a year. Most have snow-white sand, and many are backed by lavish resorts that offer sailing, diving, windsurfing, and snorkeling. The largest of the British Leeward Islands, Antigua was the headquarters from which Lord Horatio Nelson (then a mere captain) made his forays against the French and pirates in the late 18th century. You may wish to explore English Harbour and its carefully restored Nelson's Dockyard, as well as tour old forts, historic churches, and tiny villages. Appealing aspects of the island's interior include a small tropical rain forest ideal for hiking and zip-lining, ancient Native American archaeological digs, and restored sugar mills. Due to time constraints, it's best to make trips this far from port with an experienced tour operator, but you can easily take a taxi to any number of fine beaches on your own and escape from the hordes descending from the ship.

ESSENTIALS
CURRENCY
Eastern Caribbean (EC) dollar. U.S. dollars are generally accepted.

TELEPHONE
GSM tri-band mobile phones (850, 900 and1900 bands) from the United States and United Kingdom usually work on Antigua. Mobile companies include Digicel, LIME, INET.

COMING ASHORE
Although some ships dock at the deep-water harbor in downtown St. John's, most use Heritage Quay, a multimillion-dollar complex with shops, condominiums, a casino, and restaurants. Most St. John's attractions are an easy walk from Heritage Quay; the older part of the city is eight blocks away. A tourist information booth is in the main docking building.

Best Bets

- **Dickenson Bay Beach.** This is one of Antigua's best beaches.

- **Ecotourism.** Explore the island's forested interior on foot or its surrounding coves by kayak.

- **Jolly Harbour.** A cheap day pass at the Jolly Harbour Resort is a great day at the beach.

- **Nelson's Dockyard.** This is one of the Caribbean's best historic sights, with many stores, restaurants, and bars.

- **St. John's.** There's excellent duty-free shopping, especially in Heritage Quay and Redcliffe Quay.

If you intend to explore beyond St. John's, consider hiring a taxi-driver guide. Taxis meet every cruise ship. They're unmetered; fares are fixed, and drivers are required to carry a rate card. Agree on the fare before setting off (make sure you know whether the price quoted is one-way or round-trip), and plan to tip drivers 10%. Some cabbies may take you from St. John's to English Harbour and wait for a "reasonable" amount of time (about a half hour) while you look around, for about $50; you can usually arrange an island tour for around $25 per hour. Renting your own car usually isn't practical, since you must purchase a $20 temporary driving permit in addition to the car-rental fee, which is usually about $50 per day in the high season.

Sights

ST. JOHN'S
Antigua's capital, with some 45,000 inhabitants (approximately half the island's population), lies at sea level at the inland end of a sheltered northwestern bay. Although it has seen better days,

Antigua

ATLANTIC OCEAN

0 ———— 2 miles
0 ———— 2 kilometers

Boon Pt. · Hodges Bay · Prickly Pear Island · Beggar's Pt. · Long Island
Dickenson Bay · Cedar Grove · Bird Island · Guiana Island
Runaway Beach · Deepwater Harbour · Cruise Ship Terminal · V.C. Bird Int'l. Airport · North Sound · Crump Island
Andes · Five Islands · Potters · Parham · Long Bay · **Devil's Bridge**
Hawksbill's Beaches · St. John's see inset map · Parham Rd. · Willikies · Nonsuch Bay
Fullerton Pt. · Jennings · Pares · Green Island
Pearns Pt. · Jolly Harbour · All Saints · Freetown
Darkwood Beach · Bolans · Boggy Peak · Fig Tree Dr. · Ft. George · Willoughby Bay · Half Moon Bay
Johnson's Pt. · Urlings · Falmouth · Falmouth Bay · English Harbour · Mamora Bay
Johnson's Point/ Crabbe Hill · Old Road · Nelson's Dockyard
Cades Reef · Carlisle Bay · Pigeon Point · Rendezvous Bay · Shirley Heights

Caribbean Sea

Guadeloupe Passage

St. John's inset map:
Newgate St. · Church St. · Museum of Antigua and Barbuda · Long St. · High St. · Cathedral of St. John the Divine · St. Marys St. · Heritage Quay · Redcliffe St. · Redcliffe Quay · Nevis St. · Temple St. · Cross St. · Market St. · St. John's Harbour · St. John's

KEY

☂ Beaches
◥ Dive Sites

---

a couple of notable historic sights and some good waterfront shopping areas make it worth a visit.

At the far south end of town, where Market Street forks into Valley and All Saints Roads, haggling goes on every Friday and Saturday, when locals jam the **Public Market** to buy and sell fruits, vegetables, fish, and spices. (Ask before you aim a camera; your subject may expect a tip.) This is old-time Caribbean shopping: a jambalaya of sights, sounds, and smells.

Cathedral of St. John the Divine

HISTORIC SITE | At the south gate of the Anglican Cathedral of St. John the Divine are figures of St. John the Baptist and St. John the Divine, said to have been taken from one of Napoléon's ships and brought to Antigua. The original church was built in 1681, replaced by a stone building in 1745, and destroyed by an earthquake in 1843. The present neo-baroque building dates from 1845; the parishioners had the interior completely encased in pitch pine, hoping to forestall future earthquake damage. Tombstones bear eerily eloquent testament to the colonial days. ⊠ *Between Long and Newgate Sts., St. John's* ☎ *268/462–0820* ⊕ *www.thestjohnscathedral.com.*

Heritage Quay

COMMERCIAL CENTER | Shopaholics head directly for Heritage Quay, an ugly multimillion-dollar complex. The two-story buildings contain stores that sell duty-free goods, sportswear, down-island imports (paintings, T-shirts, straw baskets), and local crafts. There are also restaurants, a bandstand, and a casino. Cruise-ship passengers disembark here from the 500-foot-long pier. Expect heavy shilling. ⊠ *High and Thames Sts., St. John's* ⊕ *www.heritagequayantigua.com.*

Museum of Antigua and Barbuda

MUSEUM | Signs at the Museum of Antigua and Barbuda say "Please touch," encouraging you to explore Antigua's past. Try your hand at the educational video games or squeeze a cassava through a *matapi* (grass sieve). Exhibits interpret the nation's history, from its geological birth to its political independence in 1981. There are fossil and coral remains from some 34 million years ago; models of a sugar plantation and a wattle-and-daub house; an Arawak canoe; and a wildly eclectic assortment of objects from cannonballs to 1920s telephone exchanges. The museum occupies the former courthouse, which dates from 1750. The superlative museum gift shop carries such unusual items as calabash purses, seed earrings, warri boards (warri being an African game brought to the Caribbean), and lignum vitae pipes, as well as historic maps and local books (including engrossing monographs on various subjects by the late Desmond Nicholson, a longtime resident). ⊠ *Long and Market Sts., St. John's* ☎ *268/462–1469, 268/462–4930* ⊕ *www.antiguamuseums. net* 🎫 *$3* 🕑 *Closed Sun.*

★ Redcliffe Quay

COMMERCIAL CENTER | Redcliffe Quay, at the water's edge just south of Heritage Quay, is the most appealing part of St. John's. Attractively restored (and superbly re-created) 19th-century buildings in a riot of cotton-candy colors house shops, restaurants, galleries, and boutiques are linked by courtyards and landscaped walkways. ⊠ *Redcliffe St., St. John's* ⊕ *www.historicredcliffequay.com.*

ELSEWHERE ON ANTIGUA

Devil's Bridge

NATURE SITE | Located in the Indian Town Point National Park, this natural wonder was formed by the thrashing waves of the Atlantic Ocean against the delicate limestone of the coastline over hundreds of years. Visitors are tempted to cross the bridge for the thrill, but do so at their own risk. If visiting during Easter, the skies over the bridge are home to hundreds of kites during the annual **Kite Festival.** ⊠ *Dockyard Dr., Long Bay* ⊕ *www.nationalparksantigua.com.*

Falmouth

TOWN | This coastal town with grand views of Falmouth Harbour is said to be one of the first towns in Antigua and Saint Paul's Anglican Church, within, is believed to be the first church erected in the nation; this uncertain history does not deflect from the township's sleepy beauty. There is also a vendor's mall quizzically placed on a busy, meandering road, where visitors stop to pick up tchotchkes and witness a breathtaking view of Falmouth and English harbors.

Ft. George

TOWN | East of Liberta—one of the first settlements founded by freed slaves—on Monk's Hill, this fort was built between 1689 and 1720. Among the ruins are the sites for 32 cannons, water cisterns, the base of the old flagstaff, and some of the original buildings. ⊠ *Great Fort George Monk's Hill Trail, St. Paul.*

★ Nelson's Dockyard

HISTORIC SITE | Now a UNESCO World Heritage Site, Antigua's most famous attraction is the world's only Georgian-era dockyard still in use, a treasure trove for history buffs and nautical nuts alike. When the Royal Navy abandoned the station at English Harbour in 1889, it fell into a state of decay, though adventuresome yachties still lived there in near-primitive conditions. The Society of the Friends of English Harbour began restoring it in 1951; it reopened with great fanfare as Nelson's Dockyard on November 14, 1961. Within the compound are crafts shops, restaurants, and two splendidly restored 18th-century hotels. The Dockyard National Park also includes serene nature trails accessing beaches, rock pools, and crumbling plantation ruins

Nelson's Dockyard at English Harbour is a UNESCO World Heritage Site.

and hilltop forts. The **Dockyard Museum,** in the original Naval Officer's House, presents ship models, mock-ups of English Harbour, displays on the people who worked there and typical ships that docked. ✉ *Dockyard Dr., English Harbour Town* ☎ *268/481–5041 for National Parks Authority, visitor's services, 268/460–1379 main office,* ⊕ *www.nationalparksantigua.com* ✉ *$2 suggested donation.*

Shirley Heights

VIEWPOINT | This bluff affords a spectacular view of English Harbour and Falmouth Harbour. The heights are named for Sir Thomas Shirley, the governor who fortified the harbor in 1781. At the top is Shirley Heights Lookout, a restaurant built into the remnants of the 18th-century fortifications. Most notable for its boisterous Sunday barbecues that continue into the night with live music and dancing, it serves dependable burgers, pumpkin soup, grilled meats, and rum punches.

Not far from Shirley Heights is the **Dow's Hill Interpretation Centre,** where observation platforms provide still more sensational vistas of the English Harbour area. A multimedia sound-and-light presentation on island history and culture, spotlighting lifelike figures and colorful tableaux accompanied by running commentary and music, results in a cheery, if bland, portrait of Antiguan life from Amerindian times to the present. ✉ *Dockyard Dr., Shirley Heights* ☎ *268/481–5021, 268/481–5022* ⊕ *www.nationalparksantigua.com* ✉ *$8.*

🏖 Beaches

Crabbe Hill/Johnson's Point

BEACH—SIGHT | This series of connected, deserted beaches on the southwest coast looks out toward Montserrat, Guadeloupe, and St. Kitts. Notable beach bar–restaurants include OJ's, Jacqui O's BeachHouse, and Turner's. The water is generally placid, though not good for snorkeling. **Amenities:** food and drink. **Best for:** sunset; swimming; walking. ⊹ *3 miles (5 km) south of Jolly Harbour complex, on main west-coast road.*

Dickenson Bay

BEACH—SIGHT | Along a lengthy stretch of well-kept powder-soft white sand and exceptionally calm water, you can find small and large hotels (including Siboney Beach Club, Sandals, and Rex Halcyon Cove), water sports, concessions, and beachfront restaurants (Coconut Grove and Ana's on the Beach are recommended). There's decent snorkeling at either point. **Amenities:** food and drink; water sports. **Best for:** partiers; snorkeling; swimming; walking. ✛ *2 miles (3 km) northeast of St. John's, along main coast road.*

Pigeon Point

BEACH—SIGHT | Near Falmouth Harbour lie two fine white-sand beaches reasonably free of seaweed and driftwood. The leeward side is calmer, the windward side is rockier, and there are sensational views and snorkeling around the point. Several restaurants and bars are nearby, though Bumpkin's (and its potent banana coladas) and the more upscale bustling Catherine's Cafe Plage satisfy most on-site needs. **Amenities:** food and drink. **Best for:** snorkeling; swimming; walking. ✉ *Off main south-coast road, southwest of Falmouth.*

🍴 Restaurants

Big Banana—Pizzas in Paradise

$$ | PIZZA | FAMILY | Renovated in 2019, Big Banana has modern rustic decor befitting its past as an 18th-century rum house, and it's fortunately retained its former charm and distinction as one of the most popular casual dining eateries on island. The menu includes pizza, burgers, wraps, and scrumptious down-home local food—try the catch of the day, which, when paired with flavorsome fruit crushes (the coconut is divine), is a great way to end a day of window-shopping in the quays. **Known for:** wide selection of pizzas; lively atmosphere; family-friendly dining. ⑤ *Average main: $18* ✉ *Redcliffe Quay, Redcliffe St., St. John's*

☏ *268/480–6985* ⊕ *www.bigbanana-anti-gua.com* ⊙ *Closed Sun.*

Coconut Grove

$$$ | ECLECTIC | Coconut palms grow through the roof of this open-air thatched restaurant, flickering candlelight illuminates colorful local murals, waves lap the white sand, and the waitstaff provide just the right level of service. Jean-François Bellanger's dishes artfully fuse French culinary preparations with island ingredients. Top choices include pan-seared mahimahi served with a vegetable medley and garlic butter sauce, and sautéed shrimp with roasted plantain finished with a garlic basil white wine sauce. **Known for:** breakfast, lunch, and dinner service; on the beach; steamed cockles. ⑤ *Average main: $30* ✉ *Siboney Beach Club, Marina Bay Rd., Dickenson Bay* ☏ *268/462–1538* ⊕ *www.coconut-groveantigua.com.*

🛍 Shopping

Heritage Quay, in St. John's, has 35 shops (many are duty-free) that cater to the cruise-ship crowd, which docks almost at its doorstep. Outlets here include Benetton, the Body Shop, Sunglass Hut, Dolce & Gabbana, and Oshkosh B'Gosh. There are also shops along **St. John's, St. Mary's, High,** and **Long Streets.** The tangerine-and-lilac-hue four-story **Vendor's Mall** at the intersection of Redcliffe and Thames Streets gathers the pushy, pesky vendors who once clogged the narrow streets. It's jammed with stalls; air-conditioned indoor shops sell some higher-price, if not higher-quality, merchandise. On the west coast the Mediterranean-style, arcaded **Jolly Harbour Marina** holds some interesting galleries and shops, as do the marinas and the main road snaking around English and Falmouth harbors.

Redcliffe Quay, on the waterfront at the south edge of St. John's, is by far the most appealing shopping area. Several restaurants and more than 30 boutiques, many with one-of-a-kind wares, are set around landscaped courtyards shaded by colorful trees.

⚡ Activities

ADVENTURE TOURS

Adventure Antigua

TOUR—SPORTS | The enthusiastic Eli Fuller, who is knowledgeable not only about the ecosystem and geography of Antigua but also about its history and politics (his grandfather was the American consul), runs Adventure Antigua. His thorough seven-hour excursion (Eli dubs it "re-creating my childhood explorations") includes stops at Guiana Island (for lunch and guided snorkeling; turtles, barracuda, and stingrays are common sightings), Pelican Island (more snorkeling), Bird Island (hiking to vantage points to admire the soaring ospreys and frigate and red-billed tropic birds), and Hell's Gate (a striking limestone rock formation where the more intrepid may hike and swim through sunken caves and tide pools painted with pink and maroon algae). The company also offers a fun "Xtreme Circumnavigation" variation on a racing boat catering to adrenaline junkies who "feel the need for speed." It also visits Stingray City and Nelson's Dockyard, and offers a more sedate Antigua Classic Yacht sail-and-snorkel experience that explains the rich Caribbean history of boatbuilding. ☎ *268/726–6355* ⊕ *www. adventureantigua.com.*

Stingray City Antigua

TOUR—SPORTS | FAMILY | Stingray City Antigua is a carefully reproduced "natural" environment nicknamed by staffers "the retirement home," although the 30-plus stingrays (ranging from infants to seniors) are frisky. You can stroke, feed, even hold the striking gliders—"They're like puppy dogs," one guide swears—as well as snorkel in deeper protected waters. The tour guides do a marvelous job of explaining the animals' habits, from feeding to

breeding, and their predators (including man). ⊠ *Seaton's Village* ☎ *268/562–7297* ⊕ *www.stingraycityantigua.com.*

DIVING

Antigua is an unsung diving destination, with plentiful undersea sights to explore, from coral canyons to sea caves. Barbuda alone features roughly 200 wrecks on its treacherous reefs. The most accessible wreck is the 1890s bark *Andes*, not far out in Deep Bay, off Five Islands Peninsula. Among the favorite sites are **Green Island, Cades Reef,** and **Bird Island** (a national park). Memorable sightings include turtles, stingrays, and barracudas darting amid basalt walls, hulking boulders, and stray 17th-century anchors and cannon. One advantage is accessibility in many spots for shore divers and snorkelers. Double-tank dives run about $90.

Dockyard Divers

SCUBA DIVING | With over 40 years of diving experience and nearly half of those off the coasts and around the reefs of the Caribbean, ex-merchant seaman Captain Tony Fincham and Dockyard Divers offer diving and snorkeling trips and private scuba instruction in some of the most sought-after dive sites on the southern coast (including Pillars of Hercules and Stingray Alley), which are suitable for both novice and experienced divers. For certified divers, two tanks will run you $99 and a five-day, two-tank dive package is a steal at $445. ⊠ *Nelson's Dockyard, English Harbour Town* ☎ *268/729–3040* ⊕ *www.dockyard-divers.com.*

KAYAKING

"Paddles" Kayak Eco Adventure

TOUR—SPORTS | Paddles takes you on a 3½-hour tour of serene mangroves and inlets with informative narrative about the fragile ecosystem of the swamp and reefs and the rich diversity of flora and fauna. The tour ends with a hike to sunken caves and snorkeling in the North Sound Marine Park, capped by a rum punch at the fun Creole-style clubhouse nestled amid botanic gardens.

Experienced guides double as kayaking and snorkeling instructors, making this an excellent opportunity for novices. Conrad and Jennie's brainchild is one of Antigua's better bargains. Guests must be able to swim. ⊠ *Seaton's Village* ☎ *268/463–1944, 268/720–4322* ⊕ *www. antiguapaddles.com.*

ZIP-LINING

Antigua Rainforest Canopy Tours

TOUR—SPORTS | Zip above the canopies of Antigua's rain forest at Antigua Rainforest Canopy Tours, a one-of-a-kind experience where young, energetic "rangers" ensure a safe and raucous time 200 to 300 feet above the ground. There's even a café for post-ride relaxation. Tours kick off on the hour between 9 am and 1 pm, but during the off-season be sure to call for their pared-down schedule. ⊠ *Fig Tree Dr., Wallings* ☎ *268/562–6363* ⊕ *www. antiguarainforest.com* ✆ *From $85.*

Aruba (Oranjestad)

Few islands can boast the overt dedication to tourism and the quality of service that Aruba offers. The arid landscape is full of attractions to keep visitors occupied, and the island offers some of the most dazzling beaches in the Caribbean. Casinos and novelty nightclubs abound in Oranjestad, giving the capital an almost Las Vegas appeal. To keep tourists coming back year after year, the island boasts a tremendous variety of restaurants ranging from upscale French eateries to toes-in-the-sand casual dining. Aruba may not be an unexplored paradise, but hundreds of thousands of tourists make it a point to beat a path here every year. Because it's not a very large island, cruise-ship visitors can expect to see a large part of the island on their day ashore. Or they can simply see several of the beautiful beaches. Whether you're planning to be active or to simply relax, this is an ideal cruise port.

Best Bets ◉

■ **Oranjestad.** Aruba's capital is pretty and easy to explore on foot, and it's impossible to get lost.

■ **Eagle Beach.** One of the most beautiful beaches in the Caribbean, with miles of white sand.

■ **Nightlife.** If your ship stays in port late, take advantage of the island's great bar scene and its many casinos.

■ **Snorkeling.** Though you can't dive here, you can snorkel to get a glimpse of what's under the sea.

■ **Windsurfing.** Constant wind allows this adrenaline sport to thrive in Aruba.

ESSENTIALS
CURRENCY

The Aruban florin. The florin is pegged to the U.S. dollar, and Arubans accept U.S. dollars readily. Be aware that the Netherlands Antilles florin used on Curaçao is not accepted on Aruba.

TELEPHONE

SETAR, Digicel, and MIO are the major cell phone companies. GSM (900, 1800, and 1900 bands) will generally work in Aruba.

COMING ASHORE

The Port of Oranjestad is a busy place and is generally full of eager tourists looking for souvenirs or a bite to eat. The Renaissance Marketplace is right on the port, as are a number of souvenir shops and some decent and inexpensive restaurants. The main shopping areas of Oranjestad are all within 10 minutes' walk of the port, but there is a free old-fashioned trolley that starts at the new cruise welcome center. It loops around the main shopping areas of Oranjestad and allows hop-on, hop-off rides.

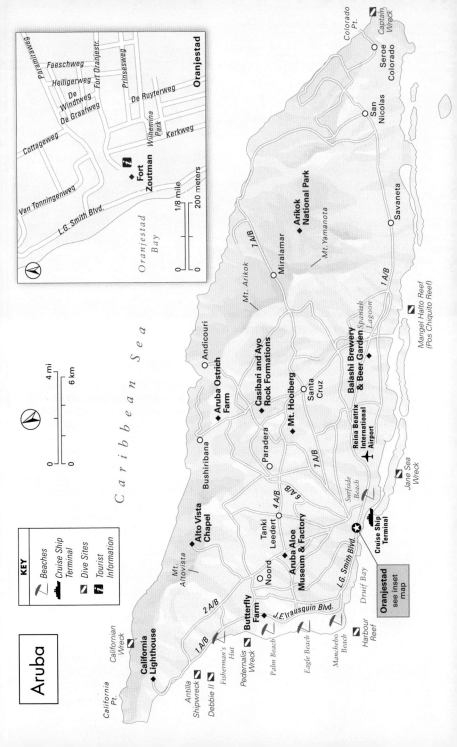

A view of the colorful buildings in Aruba's capital, Oranjestad.

Taxis can be flagged down on the street that runs alongside the port (look for license plates with a "TX" tag), but it's best to ask a doorman at resorts like the Renaissance Marina to hail one. Rates are fixed (i.e., there are no meters; the rates are set by the government and displayed on a chart), though you and the driver should agree on the fare before your ride begins. An hour-long island tour should cost about $45 with up to four people. If you want to rent a car, you can do so for a reasonable price. Driving is on the right (just as in the United States) and it's pretty easy to get around, though a four-wheel-drive vehicle does help in reaching some of the more out-of-the-way places. The downtown bus terminal is within walking distance of the pier as well, and buses stop all along the most popular beaches.

◉ Sights

ORANJESTAD AND ENVIRONS
Aruba's capital is best explored by the free ecotrolley—a hop-on, hop-off affair—and on foot. Major improvements downtown have opened up the back roads of Main Street and have created many resting spaces and pedestrian-only lanes. New small malls, restaurants, attractions, and museums can be explored there. Also worth exploring is the new linear park and boardwalk and the new outdoor art spaces along the waterfront.

Aruba Aloe Museum & Factory
FARM/RANCH | Aruba has the ideal conditions to grow the aloe vera plant. It's an important export, and there are aloe stores all over the island. The museum and factory tour reveal the process of extracting the serum to make many products used for beauty, health, and healing. Guided or self-guided tours are available in English, Dutch, Spanish, and Papiamento. There's a store to purchase their products on-site, and they are

also available online. ✉ *Pitastraat 115, Oranjestad* ☎ *800/952–7822* ⊕ *www. arubaaloe.com* 🎫 *Free.*

Balashi Brewery & Beer Garden

RESTAURANT—SIGHT | Aruba is the only nation in the world to make beer out of desalinated seawater, and it's really good beer! They also make a version called Chill with added lemon flavor and new upscale brews called Hopi Bon ("very good" in Papiamento) and Hopi Stout (good stout). See how it's all done at the factory just outside of Oranjestad proper and sample some of the beers afterward. There is also a lovely outdoor beer garden for lunch and drinks that's open until 3 pm weekdays. Closed-toe shoes are required for the factory tour, which is offered Monday through Thursday from 9 am to noon. ✉ *Balashi 62, Balashi* ☎ *297/585–8700* ⊕ *www.balashibrewery.com* 🎫 *$10, includes one free beer* ⊗ *Closed weekends. No tours Fri.*

Fort Zoutman

MILITARY SITE | One of the island's oldest edifices, Aruba's historic fort was built in 1796 and played an important role in skirmishes between British and Curaçao troops in 1803. The Willem III Tower, named for the Dutch monarch of that time, was added in 1868 to serve as a lighthouse. Over time the fort has been a government office building, a police station, and a prison; now its historical museum displays Aruban artifacts in an 18th-century house. This is also the site of the weekly Tuesday-night welcome party called the Bon Bini festival, with local music, food, and dance. If you visit with Aruba Walking Tours you can climb to the roof for great views. ✉ *Zoutmanstraat, Oranjestad* ☎ *297/588–5199* 🎫 *$5* ⊗ *Closed Sun.*

PALM BEACH AND NOORD

★ Butterfly Farm

FARM/RANCH | **FAMILY** | Hundreds of butterflies and moths from around the world flutter about this spectacular garden. Guided tours (included in the price of admission) provide an entertaining look into the life cycle of these insects, from egg to caterpillar to chrysalis to butterfly or moth. After your initial visit, you can return as often as you like for free during your vacation. ■**TIP**➔ **Go early in the morning when the butterflies are most active; wear bright colors if you want them to land on you.** Early morning is also when you are most likely to see the caterpillars emerge from their cocoons and transform into butterflies or moths. A small café out front serves healthy light drinks and snacks. ✉ *J. E. Irausquin Blvd., across from Divi Phoenix Aruba Beach Resort, Palm Beach* ☎ *297/586–3656* ⊕ *www.thebutterflyfarm.com* 🎫 *$15 (good for return visits).*

WESTERN TIP (CALIFORNIA DUNES)

★ Alto Vista Chapel

BUILDING | Meaning "high view," Alto Vista was built in 1750 as the island's first Roman Catholic Church. The simple yellow and orange structure stands out in bright contrast to its stark desertlike surroundings, and its elevated location affords a wonderful panoramic view of the northwest coast. Restored in 1953, it still holds regular services today and also serves as the culmination point of the annual walk of the cross at Easter. You will see small signposts guiding the faithful to the Stations of the Cross all along the winding road to its entrance. This landmark is a typical stop on most island tours. ■**TIP**➔ **Make sure to buy coconut water from the famous coconut man out front.** ✉ *Alto Vista Rd., Noord* ⊕ *Follow the rough, winding dirt road that loops around the island's northern tip, or from the hotel strip, take Palm Beach Rd. through three intersections and watch for the asphalt road to the left.*

★ California Lighthouse

LIGHTHOUSE | **FAMILY** | Built in 1910, the landmark lighthouse on the island's eastern tip is open to the public, and visitors can climb the spiral stairs to discover a fabulous panoramic view. Declared a national monument in 2015, the lighthouse was named after the merchant ship *Californian*, which sunk nearby, the tragedy that inspired its construction. ⊠ *2 Hudishibana, Westpunt* ☎ *297/699–0995* 🖃 *$5.*

SANTA CRUZ
Mt. Hooiberg
NATURE SITE | Named for its shape (*hooiberg* means "haystack" in Dutch), this 541-foot peak lies inland just past the airport. If you have the energy, you can climb the some 562 steps to the top for an impressive view of Oranjestad (and Venezuela on clear days). It is the island's second-highest peak; Mt. Jamanota at 617 feet is the tallest. ■**TIP→ It's a very hot climb with no shade, so wear a hat, apply plenty of sunscreen, and bring water.** ⊠ *Hooiberg 11, near Santa Cruz, Paradera.*

ARIKOK NATIONAL PARK AND ENVIRONS
★ Arikok National Park
HIKING/WALKING | **FAMILY** | There are more than 20 miles of trails concentrated in the island's eastern interior and along its northeastern coast. Arikok Park is crowned by Aruba's second-highest mountain, the 577-foot Mt. Arikok, so you can also go climbing there. Hiking in the park, whether alone or in a group led by guides, is generally not too strenuous, but it is hot. You'll need sturdy shoes to grip the granular surfaces and climb the occasionally steep terrain. You should also exercise caution with the strong sun—bring along plenty of water and wear sunscreen and a hat. At the park's main entrance, the Arikok Visitor Center houses exhibits, restrooms, and food concessions, and provides maps and marked trail information, park rules, and features. Free guided minitours are the best way to get oriented at the park entrance. Tour operators also offer four-wheeling and horseback tours across the rugged Arikok landscape. You can

also download hiking maps from their website for self-guided tours. ⊠ *Santa Cruz* ☎ *297/585–1234* ⊕ *www.arubanationalpark.org* 🖃 *$11 park entrance, $28 year pass* ⊙ *Park closes at 4 pm.*

Aruba Ostrich Farm
FARM/RANCH | **FAMILY** | Everything you ever wanted to know about the world's largest living birds can be found at this farm and ranch. There are emus, too. A large *palapa* (palm-thatched roof) houses a gift shop and restaurant that draws large bus tours, and tours of the farm are available every half hour starting at 9 am until 4 pm, seven days a week. Feeding the ostriches is fun, and you can also hold an egg in your hands. There is a full-service restaurant on-site. ⊠ *Matividiri 57, Paradera* ☎ *297/585–9630* ⊕ *www.arubaostrichfarm.com* 🖃 *$14.*

Casibari and Ayo Rock Formations
ARCHAEOLOGICAL SITE | The odd-looking massive boulders at Ayo and Casibari are a mystery as they don't match the island's geological makeup in any other spot. They seem to have just cropped up out of nowhere, but they're cool to see and Casibari is fun to climb with man-made steps and handrails and tunnels set within the weird rock formation. Kids will love this all-natural jungle gym. You are not permitted to climb Ayo, but it's still worth a visit to see the ancient pictographs in a small cave (the entrance has iron bars to protect the drawings from vandalism). At the base of Casibari there's a café-bar-restaurant open for lunch and dinner, and the rocks around the outdoor dining area are lit up at night in neon colors. ⊠ *Paradera* ⊕ *www.aruba.com.*

🏖 Beaches

Virtually every popular Aruba beach has resorts attached, but because nearly all beaches are public, there is never a problem with access. However, lounges, showers, and shade palapas are reserved for hotel guests.

★ Eagle Beach

BEACH—SIGHT | Aruba's most photographed stretch of sand, Eagle Beach is not only a favorite with visitors and locals, but also of sea turtles. More sea turtles nest here than anywhere else on the island. This pristine stretch of blinding white sand and aqua surf is ranked among the best beaches in the world. Many of the hotels have facilities on or near the beach, and refreshments are never far away, but chairs and shade palapas are reserved for resort guests only. **Amenities:** food and drink; toilets; parking (no fee). **Best for:** sunsets; swimming; water sports. ⊠ *J. E. Irausquin Blvd., north of Manchebo Beach, Druif.*

★ Manchebo Beach (*Punta Brabo*)

BEACH—SIGHT | Impressively wide, the white-sand shoreline in front of the Manchebo Beach Resort (technically where Eagle Beach begins) is the backdrop for the numerous yoga classes now taking place under the giant palapa since the resort began offering health and wellness retreats. This sandy stretch is the broadest on the island; in fact you can even get a workout just getting to the water! Waves can be rough and wild at certain times of the year, though, so mind the current and undertow when swimming. ■TIP➔ **The Bucuti beach bar no longer serves walk-ins and is now reserved exclusively for guests. Amenities:** food and drink; toilets. **Best for:** swimming; sunsets; walking. ⊠ *J. E. Irausquin Blvd., Druif* ✛ *At Manchebo Beach Resort.*

★ Palm Beach

BEACH—SIGHT | This is the island's most populated and popular beach running along the high-rise resorts, and it's crammed with every kind of water-sports activity and food-and-drink emporium imaginable. It's always crowded no matter the season, but it's a great place for people-watching, sunbathing, swimming, and partying; and there are always activities happening like paddleboarding, and even paddleboard yoga. The water is pond-calm; the sand, powder-fine. **Amenities:** food and drink; showers; toilets; water sports. **Best for:** partiers; swimming. ⊠ *J. E. Irausquin Blvd. between Divi Phoenix Resort and Ritz-Carlton Aruba, Palm Beach.*

🍴 Restaurants

★ Cuba's Cookin'

$$$ | CUBAN | This red-hot landmark establishment in the heart of Renaissance Marketplace specializes in traditional Havana specialties and is the only spot on Aruba where you can enjoy Cuban breakfast and an authentic Cuban sandwich for lunch. Their boast of having the best mojitos in town is a fair claim, and there's even a surprisingly good selection of gluten-free, vegetarian, and vegan fare on offer. **Known for:** melt-in-your-mouth ropa vieja (Cuba's national skirt steak dish); hot live music and alfresco dancing seven nights a week; an impressive selection of original Cuban art. ⑤ *Average main: $28* ⊠ *Renaissance Marketplace, L. G. Smith Blvd. 82, Oranjestad* ☎ *297/588–0627* ⊕ *www.cubascookin. com.*

Gostoso Restaurante

$$$ | CARIBBEAN | FAMILY | Locals adore the magical mixture of Portuguese, Aruban, and international dishes on offer at this consistently excellent establishment. The decor walks a fine line between kitschy and cozy, but the atmosphere is relaxed and informal and outdoor seating is available. **Known for:** hearty Venezuelan-style mixed grill; large choice of authentic Aruba stobas (stews); popular local hangout. ⑤ *Average main: $28* ⊠ *Caya Ing. Roland H. Lacle 12, Oranjestad* ☎ *297/588–0053* ☉ *Closed Mon.*

🛍 Shopping

The only real duty-free shopping is in the departures hall of the airport. (Passengers bound for the United States should be sure to shop before proceeding through U.S. customs in Aruba.) Downtown stores do have very low sales tax though and some excellent bargains on high-end luxury items like gold, silver, and jewelry. Major credit cards are welcome everywhere, as are U.S. dollars. Aruba's souvenir and crafts stores are full of Dutch porcelains and figurines, as befits the island's heritage. Dutch cheese is a good buy, as are hand-embroidered linens and any products made from the native aloe vera plant. Local arts and crafts run toward wood carvings and earthenware emblazoned with "Aruba: One Happy Island" and the like, but there are many shops with unique Aruban items like designer wear and artwork. Don't try to bargain unless you are at a flea market; Arubans consider it rude to haggle.

★ Renaissance Mall

CLOTHING | Upscale, name-brand fashion and luxury brands of perfume, cosmetics, and leather goods are what you'll find in the array of 60 stores spanning two floors in this mall located within and underneath the Renaissance Marina Resort. You'll also find specialty items like cigars and designer shoes plus high-end gold, silver, diamonds, and quality jewelry at low- or no-duty prices. Cafés and high-end dining, plus a casino and spa, round out the offerings. Shopping until 8 pm daily. ⊠ *Renaissance Marina Resort, L. G. Smith Blvd. 82, Oranjestad* ☎ *297/582–4622* ⊕ *www.shoprenaissancearuba.com.*

★ Renaissance Marketplace

SHOPPING CENTERS/MALLS | FAMILY | The Renaissance Marketplace is more of a dining and gathering spot along the marina than a market. It's a lively spot with a few souvenir shops and specialty stores. There is also a modern cinema. But mostly it's full of eclectic dining emporiums and trendy cafés, and they have live music some weekends in their alfresco square. The Wind Creek Seaport casino is also there, and it's steps from the cruise terminal on the marina. It also is the place for the big annual Christmas Fair. ⊠ *L. G. Smith Blvd. 82, Oranjestad* ☎ *297/582–4622* ⊕ *www.renaissancearubaresortandcasino.com.*

Royal Plaza Mall

SHOPPING CENTERS/MALLS | It's impossible to miss this gorgeous colonial-style, cotton-candy-colored building with the big gold dome gracing the front street along the marina. It's one of the most photographed in Oranjestad. Three levels of shops (both indoors and out) make up this artsy arcade full of small boutiques, cigar shops, designer clothing outlets, gift and jewelry stores, and souvenir kiosks. Great dining and bars are found within as well. ⊠ *L. G. Smith Blvd. 94, Oranjestad* ☎ *297/588–0351* ⊕ *www. aruba.com.*

🏃 Activities

DIVING AND SNORKELING

With visibility of up to 90 feet, the waters around Aruba are excellent for snorkeling and diving. Advanced and novice divers alike will find plenty to occupy their time, as many of the most popular sites—including some interesting shipwrecks—are found in shallow waters ranging from 30 to 60 feet. Coral reefs covered with sensuously waving sea fans and eerie giant sponge tubes attract a colorful menagerie of sea life, including gliding manta rays, curious sea turtles, shy octopuses, and grunts, groupers, and other fish. Marine preservation is a priority on Aruba: regulations by the Conference on International Trade in Endangered Species make it unlawful to remove coral, conch, and other marine life from the water, and the new Marine

Park Foundation is ensuring the protection of the reefs.

There are many snorkeling trips for all ages with large operators, and DePalm Island also has excellent snorkeling. Scuba diving operator prices vary depending on the trip. If you want to go all the way, complete open-water certification takes at least four days worth of instruction.

★ DePalm Pleasure Sail & Snorkeling

SNORKELING | FAMILY | The luxury catamaran *DePalm Pleasure* offers three-stop snorkel trips to the island's most popular fish-filled spots daily including the *Antilla* shipwreck. They also offer the option to try SNUBA. The romantic sunset sails are popular excursions. Buffet and open bar are included. Hotel pickup and drop-off are also included (unless within easy walking distance of their pier on Palm Beach). ⊠ *Palm Beach, DePalm Pier, between the Hilton and the Riu resorts, Noord* ☎ *297/522–4400* ⊕ *www.depalm-tours.com.*

GOLF
★ Tierra del Sol

GOLF | Stretching out to 6,811 yards, this stunning course is situated on the northwest coast near the California Lighthouse and is Aruba's only 18-hole course. Designed by Robert Trent Jones Jr., Tierra del Sol combines Aruba's native beauty (cacti and rock formations, stunning views) with good greens and beautiful landscaping. Wind can also be a factor here on the rolling terrain, as are the abundant bunkers and water hazards. Greens fees include a golf cart equipped with GPS and a communications system that allows you to order drinks for your return to the clubhouse. The fully stocked golf shop is one of the Caribbean's most elegant, with an extremely attentive staff. This course hosts numerous events including the annual Aruba International Pro-Am Golf Tournament every August. ⊠ *Tierra del Sol Resort, Caya di Solo 10, Malmokweg* ☎ *297/586–7800* ⊕ *www.*

tierradelsol.com/golf ⊠ *From $79 for 9 holes* 🏌 *18 holes, 6811 yards, par 71.*

KAYAKING
★ Clear Kayak Aruba

KAYAKING | FAMILY | This is the only Aruba outfitter that offers clear-bottom sea kayaks, and the only one offering night tours as well. By day, groups paddle through the natural mangroves at Mangel Halto with a guide who can tell you how the roots create a natural nursery for juvenile marine life; the route also passes over lots of big, healthy coral full of colorful tropical fish. A second tour begins at Arashi Beach at dusk; then, after dark, the kayaks are lit up with LED lights that attract marine life to their clear bottoms. You must be age 12 or older to participate. ⊠ *Savaneta 402, Savaneta* ☎ *297/566–2205* ⊕ *www.clearkayakaruba.com* ⊠ *From $60.*

WINDSURFING

The southwestern coast's tranquil waters at Fisherman's Huts make windsurfing conditions ideal for both beginners and intermediates alike, and expert instruction and modern equipment rental will have you up on the waves in no time. Aruba has some of the best windsurfers in the world, and the annual Hi-Winds Competition also attracts the world's best each year, bringing out big crowds to party on the beach.

★ Aruba Active Vacations

TOUR—SPORTS | This major outdoor activity center includes kiteboarding, windsurfing, mountain bike tours and rentals, stand-up paddleboarding, and landsailing. The outfit offers instructions and rentals for all. They're located on one of Aruba's most ideal beaches for windsurfing and kiteboarding, at Fisherman's Huts. ⊠ *Near Fisherman's Huts beside Ritz-Carlton Aruba, Malmokweg* ☎ *297/586–0989* ⊕ *www.aruba-active-vacations.com.*

Barbados (Bridgetown)

Barbadians (Bajans) are a warm, friendly, and hospitable people, who are genuinely proud of their country and culture. Although tourism is the island's number one industry, the island has a sophisticated business community and stable government, so life here doesn't skip a beat after passengers return to the ship. Barbados is the most "British" island in the Caribbean. Afternoon tea is a ritual, and cricket is the national sport. The atmosphere, though, is hardly stuffy. This is still the Caribbean, after all. Beaches along the island's south and west coasts are picture-perfect, and all are available to cruise passengers. On the rugged east coast, the Atlantic Ocean attracts world-class surfers. The northeast is dominated by rolling hills and valleys, while the interior of the island is covered with acres of sugarcane and dotted with small villages. Historic plantations, a stalactite-studded cave, a wildlife preserve, rum distilleries, and tropical gardens are among the island's attractions. Bridgetown is the capital city, and its downtown shops and historic sites are a short walk or taxi ride from the pier.

ESSENTIALS
CURRENCY
The Barbados dollar (BDS$) is pegged to the U.S. dollar at the rate of BDS$1.98 to US$1. U.S. dollars (but not coins) are accepted universally across the island.

TELEPHONE
Digicel and Flow are the primary mobile phone service providers. GSM (900, 1800 and 1900 MHz frequency bands) and UMTS (B1 2100) both work on the island.

COMING ASHORE
Up to eight ships at a time can dock at Bridgetown's Deep Water Harbour, on the northwest side of Carlisle Bay near Bridgetown. The cruise-ship terminal has duty-free shops, handicraft vendors, a

Best Bets

- **The East Coast.** The island's windward coast, with its crashing surf, is a "don't-miss" sight.
- **Harrison's Cave.** This extensive limestone cave system is deep beneath Barbados.
- **Mount Gay Rum Visitors Centre.** Stop by for a tour and a tasting.
- **Flower Gardens.** Andromeda Botanic Gardens and the Flower Forest are both scenic and fragrant.
- **St. Nicholas Abbey.** Not an abbey at all, this is one of the oldest Jacobean-style houses in the Western Hemisphere.

post office, a telephone station, a tourist information desk, and a taxi stand. To get downtown, follow the shoreline to the Careenage. It's a 15-minute walk or a $5 taxi ride.

Taxis await ships at the pier. Drivers accept U.S. dollars and appreciate a 10% tip. Taxis are unmetered. From Bridgetown, one-way fares are $22 to Holetown, $30 to Speightstown, $18 to St. Lawrence Gap, and $38 to Bathsheba. Drivers can also be hired for an hourly rate of about $40 for up to three people. You can rent a car, but rates are steep ($70 to $80 per day during the high season) and some agencies require a two-day rental. You'll also need a temporary driving permit (BDS$10), so it may not make sense. Driving is on the left, British-style.

Sights

BRIDGETOWN
This bustling capital city—inscribed in 2011, along with its Garrison, into the UNESCO World Heritage List—is a duty-free port with a compact shopping

area. The principal thoroughfare is Broad Street, which leads west from National Heroes Square. A shuttle service (☎ 246/227–2200) operates between hotels and downtown during business hours.

Mount Gay Rum Visitors Centre

WINERY/DISTILLERY | On this popular tour, you learn the colorful story behind the world's oldest rum—made in Barbados since 1703. Although the modern distillery is in St. Lucy Parish, in the far north, tour guides here explain the rum-making process. Equipment, both historic and modern, is on display, and rows and rows of barrels are stored in this location. Tours conclude with a tasting and the opportunity to buy duty-free rum and gifts—and even have lunch or cocktails (no children on cocktail tour), depending on the day. The lunch or cocktail tour includes transportation. ⊠ Exmouth Gap, Brandons, Spring Garden Hwy., Bridgetown ☎ 246/227–8864 ⊕ www.mountgayrum.com ☑ $20, $70 with cocktails, $75 with lunch ⊗ Closed Sun.

Synagogue Historic District

MUSEUM | Providing for the spiritual needs of one of the oldest Jewish congregations in the western hemisphere, the Nidhe Israel Synagogue was formed by Sephardic Jews who arrived in 1628 from Brazil and introduced sugarcane to Barbados. The adjoining cemetery has tombstones dating from the 1630s. The original house of worship, built in 1654, was destroyed in an 1831 hurricane, rebuilt in 1833, and restored in 1986 with the assistance of the Barbados National Trust. The adjacent museum, opened in 2009 in a restored coral-stone building from 1750, documents the story of the Barbados Jewish community. A significant project in 2017 improved the grounds and restored artisans' workshops and other buildings on the newly designated Synagogue Historic Site. Friday-night services are held during the

winter months, but the building is open to the public year-round. Shorts are not acceptable during services but may be worn at other times. ⊠ Synagogue La., Bridgetown ☎ 246/436–6869 ⊕ synagoguehistoricdistrict.com ☑ Synagogue free, museum $12.50 ⊗ Closed weekends.

SOUTH COAST

Bushy Park Barbados

TRANSPORTATION SITE (AIRPORT/BUS/FERRY/ TRAIN) | Bushy Park in Saint Philip parish is a 2.2 kilometer, FIA Grade Three motorsports course that hosts professional auto racing events, including the annual Global Rally Cross Championship. Visitors can test their skills in a variety of race cars, from go-karts to Suzuki Swift Sport race cars. The track is open to the public on days when races are not scheduled. ⊠ Gaskin ☎ 246/537–1360 ⊕ www.bushyparkbarbados.com ☑ From $35 for go-karts, from $180 for driving experiences.

★ Sunbury Plantation House and Museum

HISTORIC SITE | Lovingly rebuilt after a 1995 fire destroyed everything but the thick flint-and-stone walls of this 350-year-old greathouse, Sunbury offers an elegant glimpse of the 18th and 19th centuries on a Barbadian sugar estate. Period furniture, old prints, and a collection of horse-drawn carriages lend an air of authenticity. A buffet luncheon ($24 per person, $35 on Sunday) and high tea ($17.50) are served daily in the Courtyard Restaurant; you can also order à la carte. A five-course candlelight dinner ($125 per person, including drinks, minimum 12 people, reservations required) is served at the 200-year-old mahogany table in the dining room. ⊠ Six Cross Rds., Sunbury ⊹ Off Hwy. 5; look for the sign at the roundabout ☎ 246/423–6270 ☑ $10.

CENTRAL BARBADOS

★ Andromeda Botanic Gardens

GARDEN | More than 600 beautiful and unusual plant specimens from around the world are cultivated in 6 acres of

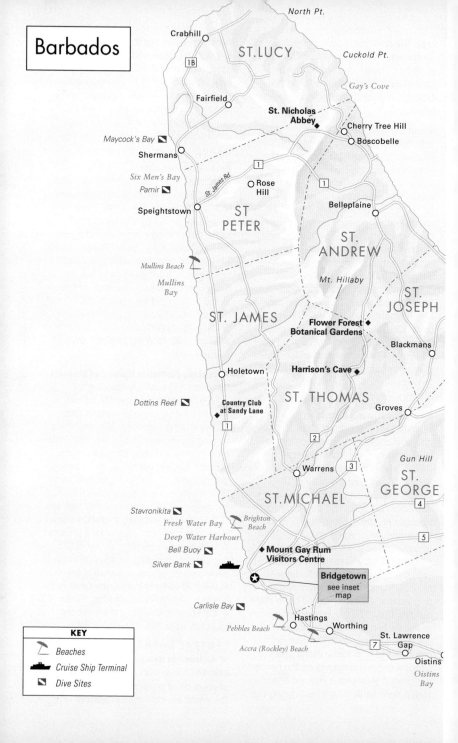

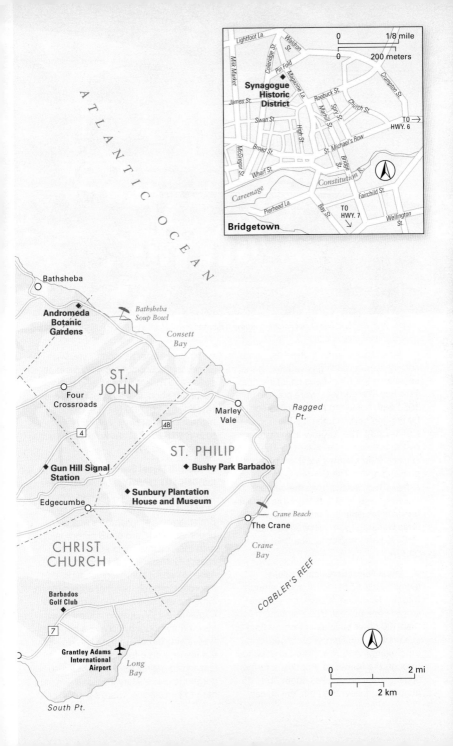

ATLANTIC OCEAN

Bridgetown

Lightfoot La.
Waldron St.
Coleridge St.
Pin Fold
Magazine La.
Milk Market
Synagogue Historic District
Crumpton St.
Roebuck St.
James St.
Church St.
Spry St.
Marhill St.
Swan St.
High St.
St. Michael's Row
McGregor St.
Broad St.
Bridge St.
Wharf St.
Constitution R.
Fairchild St.
Careenage
Pierhead La.
Bay St.
Wellington St.
TO HWY. 6
TO HWY. 7

0   1/8 mile
0   200 meters

Bathsheba

Andromeda Botanic Gardens

Bathsheba Soup Bowl

Consett Bay

ST. JOHN

Four Crossroads

Marley Vale

Ragged Pt.

4   4B

ST. PHILIP

Gun Hill Signal Station

Bushy Park Barbados

Sunbury Plantation House and Museum

Edgecumbe

Crane Beach
The Crane

CHRIST CHURCH

Crane Bay

COBBLER'S REEF

Barbados Golf Club

7

Grantley Adams International Airport

Long Bay

South Pt.

0   2 mi
0   2 km

Visitors to St. Nicholas Abbey can purchase artisanal rum and traditional Barbadian.

gardens nestled among streams, ponds, and rocky outcroppings overlooking the sea above the Bathsheba coastline near Tent Bay. The gardens were created in 1954 with flowering plants collected by the late horticulturist Iris Bannochie (1914–1988). They're now administered by the Barbados National Trust. The Gallery Shop features local art, photography, and crafts. The Garden Café serves sandwiches, salads from the gardens, desserts, and drinks. ■TIP➔ **The entrance fee includes unlimited return visits within three weeks.** ✉ *Bathsheba* ☎ *246/433–9384* ⊕ *www.andromedabarbados.com* ✉ *$15.*

★ Flower Forest Botanical Gardens

GARDEN | It's a treat to meander among fragrant flowering bushes, canna and ginger lilies, puffball trees, and more than 100 other species of tropical flora in a cool, tranquil forest of flowers and other plants. A ½-mile (1-km) path winds through the 53.6-acre grounds, a former sugar plantation; it takes about 30 to 45 minutes to follow the path, or you can wander freely for as long as you wish. Benches throughout provide places to pause and reflect. There's also a snack bar, a gift shop, and a beautiful view of Mt. Hillaby, at 1,100 feet the island's highest point. ✉ *Hwy. 2, Richmond* ☎ *246/433–8152* ⊕ *www.flowerforestbarbados.com* ✉ *$15.*

★ Gun Hill Signal Station

HISTORIC SITE | FAMILY | The 360-degree view from Gun Hill, at 700 feet, was of strategic importance to the 18th-century British army. Using lanterns and semaphore, soldiers here could communicate with their counterparts at the south coast's Garrison and the north's Grenade Hill about approaching ships, civil disorders, storms, or other emergencies. Time moved slowly in those days, and Captain Henry Wilkinson whiled away his off-duty hours by carving a huge lion from a single rock—on the hillside below the tower. Come for a short history lesson but mainly for the view; it's so gorgeous that military invalids were sent here to convalesce. There's a small café for refreshments. ✉ *Fusilier Rd., Gun Hill* ☎ *246/429–1358* ⊕ *www.barbadosnationaltrust.org* ⊠ *$6* ⊗ *Closed Sun.*

★ Harrison's Cave

CAVE | FAMILY | This limestone cavern, complete with stalactites, stalagmites, subterranean streams, and a 40-foot underground waterfall, is a rare find in the Caribbean—and one of Barbados's most popular attractions. Tours include a nine-minute video and an hour-long underground journey via electric tram. The visitor center has interactive displays, life-size models and sculptures, a souvenir shop, a restaurant, and elevator access to the tram for people with disabilities. Tram tours fill up fast, so book ahead. More intrepid visitors may like the 1½-hour walk-in tour or 4-hour eco-adventure tour, exploring nature trails and some of the cave's natural passages. ✉ *Allen View, Welchman Hall* ⊹ *Off Hwy. 2* ☎ *246/417–3700* ⊕ *www.harrisonscave.com* ⊠ *Tram tour $30, walk-in $20, eco-adventure $100.*

NORTHERN BARBADOS

★ St. Nicholas Abbey

HOUSE | The island's oldest greathouse (circa 1650) was named after the original British owner's hometown, St. Nicholas Parish near Bristol, and Bath Abbey nearby. Its stone-and-wood architecture makes it one of only three original Jacobean-style houses still standing in the western hemisphere. It has Dutch gables, finials of coral stone, and beautiful grounds that include formal gardens, an old sugar mill, an avenue of mahogany trees, and a gully filled with tropical trees and plantings. The first floor, fully furnished with period furniture and portraits of family members, is open to the public. A fascinating home movie, shot by a previous owner's father, records Bajan life in the 1930s. Behind the greathouse is a rum distillery with a 19th-century steam press. Visitors can purchase artisanal plantation rum, browse the gift shop's traditional Barbadian products, and

enjoy light refreshments at the Terrace Café. ✉ *Cherry Tree Hill Rd., Moore Hill* ☎ *246/422–5357* ⊕ *www.stnicholasabbey.com* ⊠ *$23* ⊗ *Closed Sat.*

⊗ Beaches

Geologically, Barbados is a coral-and-limestone island (not volcanic) with few rivers and, as a result, beautiful beaches, particularly along the island's southern and southeastern coastlines.

The west coast has some lovely beaches as well, but they're more susceptible to erosion after major autumn storms, if any, have taken their toll.

Accra Beach (*Rockley Beach*)

BEACH—SIGHT | FAMILY | This popular beach, adjacent to the Accra Beach Hotel, has a broad swath of white sand with gentle surf and a lifeguard, plenty of nearby restaurants for refreshments, a playground, and beach stalls for renting chairs and equipment for snorkeling and other water sports. The South Coast Boardwalk, great for walking or running, begins here and follows the waterfront west—past private homes, restaurants, and bars—for about a mile (1½ km) to Needham's Point. **Amenities:** food and drink; lifeguards; parking (no fee); water sports. **Best for:** snorkeling; swimming; walking. ✉ *Hwy. 7, Rockley.*

Mullins Beach

BEACH—SIGHT | FAMILY | At this popular beach just south of Speightstown, the water is safe for swimming and snorkeling. There's easy parking on the main road, and refreshments are available nearby at Shakka's Beach Spa. A beach vendor rents chairs and umbrellas. **Amenities:** food and drink. **Best for:** sunset; swimming; walking. ✉ *Hwy. 1B, Mullins.*

★ Pebbles Beach

BEACH—SIGHT | FAMILY | On the southern side of Carlisle Bay, just south of Bridgetown, this broad half circle of white sand is one of the island's best family-friendly beaches—and it can become crowded on weekends and holidays. The southern end of the beach wraps around the Hilton Barbados; the northern end is adjacent to the Radisson Aquatica Resort Barbados and a block away from Island Inn. Park at Harbour Lights or at the Boatyard Bar and Bayshore Complex, both on Bay Street, where you can also rent umbrellas and beach chairs and buy refreshments. Arrive early in the morning (before 7 am) to watch race horses from Garrison Savannah taking a swim. **Amenities:** food and drink. **Best for:** snorkeling; swimming; walking. ⊠ *Off Bay St., Garrison* ✛ *South of Bridgetown.*

 Restaurants

Shaker's Bar & Grill

$$ | **CARIBBEAN** | Locals and visitors alike gather at this no-frills hangout for drinks—perhaps a Banks beer or two, a margarita, a pitcher of sangria, or whatever wets their whistle—and delicious local food. Simple dishes like beer-battered flying fish, grilled catch of the day, barbecued chicken, grilled steak, or a solid cheeseburger deliver the goods, but the barbecued ribs are the main event. **Known for:** finger-lickin' barbecued ribs; small, busy, convivial "rum shop" on a quiet side street; cash only. ⑤ *Average main: $17* ⊠ *Browne's Gap, Rockley* ☎ *246/228–8855* ⊕ *www.shakersbarbados.com/visit.html* ▭ *No credit cards* ⊗ *Closed Sun.–Mon. and mid-Aug.–mid-Sept. No lunch.*

★ Waterfront Café

$$$ | **CARIBBEAN** | **FAMILY** | This busy bistro on the walkway facing the south side of the Careenage is the perfect place to enjoy a drink, snack, or meal—and to people-watch. Locals and tourists alike gather for alfresco, all-day dining on sandwiches, salads, fish, pasta, pepperpot stew, and tasty Bajan snacks such as buljol, fish cakes, or plantation pork (plantains stuffed with spicy minced pork). **Known for:** casual waterfront dining; flying fish and cou-cou; live jazz at dinnertime. ⑤ *Average main: $30* ⊠ *The Careenage, Bridgetown* ☎ *246/427–0093* ⊕ *www.waterfrontcafe.com.bb* ⊗ *No dinner Sun.–Wed.*

🛍 Shopping

Duty-free luxury goods—china, crystal, cameras, porcelain, leather items, electronics, jewelry, perfume, and clothing—are found at Bridgetown's Broad Street department stores and their branches, shops in the high-end Limegrove Lifestyle Centre in Holetown, the Bridgetown Cruise Terminal (for passengers only), and the departure lounge at Grantley Adams International Airport. Prices are often 30% to 40% less than full retail. To buy goods at duty-free prices, you must produce your passport, immigration form, or driver's license, along with departure information (such as flight number and date or cruise ship name) at the time of purchase—or you can have your purchases delivered free to the airport or harbor for pickup; duty-free alcohol, tobacco products, and some electronic equipment *must* be delivered to you at the airport or harbor.

Bridgetown's **Broad Street** is the primary downtown shopping area. **DaCosta Manning Mall,** in the historic Colonnade Building on Broad Street, has more than 25 shops that sell everything from Piaget watches to postcards; across the street, **Mall 34** has 22 shops where you can buy duty-free goods, souvenirs, and snacks. At the **cruise-ship terminal** shopping arcade, passengers can buy both duty-free goods and Barbadian-made crafts at more than 30 boutiques and a dozen vendor carts and stalls. And the **airport departure lounge** is a veritable shopping mall.

Best of Barbados

CRAFTS | Best of Barbados showcases the works of artist Jill Walker, who founded the shops (along with her architect husband) in 1975. Their daughter is now in charge. Products range from her framable prints, housewares, and textiles to arts and crafts in both native style and modern designs. Everything is made or designed on Barbados. Branch shops are at Chattel House Village in Holetown, at Southern Palms Resort in St. Lawrence Gap, at the cruise-ship terminal, and in the airport departure lounge. ⊠ *Quayside Centre, Main Rd., Rockley* ☎ *246/622–1761* ⊕ *www.best-of-barbados.com.*

🏃 Activities

FISHING
Billfisher Deepsea Fishing

FISHING | *Billfisher III*, a 40-foot Viking Sport Fisherman, accommodates up to six passengers with three fishing chairs and five rods. Captain Ralphie White's full-day charters include a full lunch; all trips include drinks and transportation to and from the boat. ⊠ *Bridge House Wharf, Cavans La., The Careenage, Bridgetown* ☎ *246/431–0741* ⊕ *www.greatadventuresbarbados.com.*

GOLF
Barbados Golf Club

GOLF | The first public golf course on Barbados, an 18-hole championship course (two returning 9s), was redesigned in 2000 by golf course architect Ron Kirby. The course has hosted numerous competitions, including the European Senior tour in 2003. Several hotels offer preferential tee-time reservations and reduced rates. Cart, trolley, club, and shoe rentals are all available. ⊠ *Hwy. 7, Durants* ☎ *246/538–4653* ⊕ *www.barbadosgolfclub.com* 🏷 *$105 for 18 holes; $65 for 9 holes; 3-, 5-, and 7-day passes $255, $400, $525, respectively* ⚑ *18 holes (2 returning 9s), 6805 yds, par 72.*

★ Country Club at Sandy Lane

GOLF | At this prestigious club, golfers can play the Old Nine or either of two 18-hole championship courses: the Tom Fazio–designed Country Club Course and the spectacular Green Monkey Course, which is reserved for hotel guests and club members. The layouts offer a limestone-quarry setting (Green Monkey), a modern style with lakes (Country Club), and traditional small greens and narrow fairways (Old Nine). Golfers can use the driving range for free. The Country Club Restaurant and Bar, overlooking the 18th hole, is open to the public. Caddies, trolleys, clubs, and shoes are available for rent, as are GPS-equipped carts that alert you to upcoming hazards, give tips on how to play holes, and let you order refreshments. ⊠ *Sandy Lane Hotel, Hwy. 1* ☎ *246/444–2000, 866/444–4080 in U.S.* ⊕ *www.sandylane.com/golf* 🏷 *Country Club: $240 for 18 holes ($200 hotel guests); $150 for 9 holes ($130 guests); 7-day pass $1,350 ($1,250 guests). Green Monkey: $390 for 18 holes (guests only). Old Nine: $90 for 9 holes ($75 guests); 7-day pass $560 ($450 guests)* ⚑ *Green Monkey: 18 holes, 7343 yds, par 72; Country Club: 18 holes, 7060 yds, par 72; Old Nine: 9 holes, 3345 yds, par 36.*

Belize City, Belize

Central America's only English-speaking nation probably has the greatest variety of flora and fauna of any country of its size in the world. Here you'll often find more iguanas or howler monkeys than humans. A few miles off the mainland is the Belize Barrier Reef, a great wall of coral stretching the entire 200-mile (333-km) length of the coast, and a sector of the Mesoamerican Barrier Reef System, which stretches from Cancún to the Honduras Bay Islands. Over 200 cayes (pronounced *keys*) dot the reef like punctuation marks, and three coral atolls lie farther out to sea. All are superb for diving and snorkeling. Many, like Ambergris Caye (pronounced *AM-bur-griss key*) and Caye Caulker, are cheery resort islands with ample bars and restaurants, easily reachable on day trips from Belize City. The main choice you'll have to make is whether to stay in Belize City for a little stroll and shopping, and perhaps a dram at one of the Fort George hotels or restaurants, or alternatively to head out by boat, rental car, taxi, or tour on a more active adventure.

ESSENTIALS
CURRENCY
Since U.S. currency is universally accepted, there's no need to acquire the Belize dollar (BZ$2 to US$1).

FLIGHTS
Especially if you are going to Ambergris Caye, you may prefer to fly, or you can water-taxi over and fly back to maximize your time. There are nearly hourly flights on two local airlines. The flight to Caulker (CUK) takes about 10 minutes and to San Pedro (SPR), on Ambergris, about 25 minutes. The cost is about BZ$190 round-trip to either island. Belize City's Sir Barry Bowen Municipal Airport (TZA) offers a much better selection of flights (and is much closer) than Philip S. W. Goldson International Airport (BZE) northwest of the city.

CONTACTS Maya Island Air. ✉ *Belize City Municipal Airstrip, Marine Parade Harbor Front* ☎ *223–1403 reservations* ⊕ *www.mayaislandair.com.* **Tropic Air.** ✉ *San Pedro Airstrip, San Pedro Town* ☎ *226–2626 reservations in Belize, 800/422–3435 toll-free reservations in U.S. and Canada* ⊕ *www.tropicair.com.*

TELEPHONE
Calling locally or internationally is easy, but rates are high; around BZ$1.30 a minute for calls to the United States. To call the United States, dial 00 + 1 + the area code and number. Pay phones, which are located in the Belize Tourism Village, where you are tendered, and elsewhere downtown, accept only prepaid Digitel phone cards, available in shops in denominations from BZ$5 to BZ$50. Your U.S.-based GSM phone will probably

Best Bets ◉

■ **Belize Zoo.** Though small, this collection of native Belize wildlife is excellent.

■ **Cave Tubing.** If you are not claustrophobic, this is an unforgettable excursion.

■ **Diving.** Belize is known as one of the world's best dive destinations. For the certified, this is a must.

■ **Snorkeling in Hol Chan.** The water is teeming with fish, and you don't need to be certified to enjoy the underwater world here.

work on Belize's GSM 1900 system, but you will pay a high surcharge to use it abroad. Data charges can be frightfully high; look for a Wi-Fi connection or make your online time very quick. Foreign calling cards are generally blocked in Belize. Call ☎ *113* for local directory assistance, ☎ *115* for an in-country operator, and ☎ *114* for an international operator. Belize's nationwide emergency number is ☎ *911.*

VISITOR INFORMATION
CONTACTS Belize Tourism Board. (*BTB*) ✉ *64 Regent St., Commercial District* ☎ *227–2420, 800/624–0686 in U.S.* ⊕ *www.travelbelize.org.*

COMING ASHORE
Because Belize City's harbor is shallow, passengers are tendered in. If you're going the independent route, try to get in line early for the tenders, as it sometimes takes 90 minutes or more for all the passengers to be brought ashore.
■ TIP→ **Pay attention also to when the last tender is scheduled back to your ship at the end of the day.** You will land at the Belize Tourism Village complex on Fort Street—alternatively called the Fort Street Tourism Village. It has a collection of gift shops, restaurants, and tour operators

Belize

MEXICO

Buena Vista

Shipstern Wildlife Reserve

Orange Walk

COROZAL DISTRICT

Bahía de Chetumal

Ambergris Caye

August Pine Ridge

Shipyard

San Pedro

Blue Creek Village

San Felipe

Crooked Tree Wildlife Sanctuary

Hol Chan Marine Reserve

Crooked Tree

Altun Ha

Caye Caulker

ORANGE WALK DISTRICT

New River

Northern Hwy.

Belize City see inset map

Caye Chapel

Community Baboon Sanctuary

Burrell Boom

Ladyville

St. George's Caye

Belize Zoo

BELIZE DISTRICT

Belize City

Turneffe Islands

Guanacaste Park

Hattieville

Spanish Lookout

Western Hwy.

Rio Belize

Northern Lagoon

BELMOPAN

Roaring Creek

Southern Lagoon

Manatee Road

Gales Point

St. Herman's Blue Hole National Park

Hummingbird Hwy.

0   15 miles
0   15 km

Hummingbird Highway

Dangriga

Museum of Belize

Orange St.

Albert St.

Swing Bridge

Fort George Lighthouse and Bliss Memorial

Cathedral of St. John the Baptist

Belize Harbour

Government House/ House of Culture

Belize City

nicely situated along the harbor. Bathrooms are spick-and-span, too. Taxis, tour guides, and car-rental desks are readily available. Cabs cost BZ$7 to BZ$10 for one person between any two points in the city, plus BZ$1 for each additional person. (Negotiate a price in advance; the driver may not have a meter.) Taxi fares at night are slightly higher. Outside the city, and from downtown to the suburbs, you're charged by the distance you travel. Hourly rates are negotiable, but expect to pay around $30, or $150 for the day. Drivers are required to display a Taxi Federation rate card. There's no need to tip cab drivers. You can also rent a car at the Tourism Village, but rates can be high (at least $75 per day), gas is expensive, and roads are in bad shape. Green directional signs point you to nearby destinations such as the Belize Zoo. The Wet Lizard,

next to the Tourism Village, also organizes tours for cruise-ship passengers.

At this writing, Belize City is constructing an $82 million cruise terminal on an island just off the coast. Opening of the new Stake Bank terminal is scheduled for 2021.

Norwegian owns and operates Harvest Caye, an island with a docking facility off Belize's southern coast near Placencia, 175 km (105 miles) south of Belize City. Although it's designed to be a self-contained center for cruise visitors, you'll also find excursions to the mainland from Harvest Caye.

◉ Sights

Many Belizeans will tell you that the best way to see Belize City is through a rearview window. But, with an open

Easily accessible from Belize City, Altun Ha Mayan site was first excavated in the 1960s.

mind to its peculiarities and with a little caution (the city has a crime problem, but the tourist police keep a close watch on cruise-ship passengers), you may decide Belize City has a raffish, atmospheric charm rarely found in other Caribbean ports of call. The city lost out on its role as the country's capital some five decades ago, its coastal setting presenting particular vulnerability to hurricanes, but it remains the vibrant economic and cultural heart of Belize.

BELIZE CITY

A 5- to 10-minute stroll from the colorful Belize Tourism Village brings you into the other worlds of Belize City. On the north side of Haulover Creek is the colonial-style Fort George district, where large old homes, stately but sometimes down at the heels, take the breezes off the sea and share their space with hotels and restaurants. On the south side is bustling Albert Street, the main commercial thoroughfare. But don't stroll too far, since parts of Belize City are unsafe. During the daylight hours, as long as you stay within

the main commercial district and the Fort George area—and ignore the street hustlers—you should have no problem.

Cathedral of St. John the Baptist

RELIGIOUS SITE | On Albert Street's south end is the oldest Anglican church in Central America and the only one outside England where kings were invested. From 1815 to 1845, four kings of the Mosquito Kingdom (a British protectorate along the coast of Honduras and Nicaragua) were crowned here. The cathedral, built of brick brought here to what once was British Honduras as ballast on English ships, is thought to be the oldest surviving building in Belize from the colonial era. Its foundation stone was laid in 1812. Inside, it has whitewashed walls and mahogany pews. The roof is constructed of local sapodilla wood, with mahogany beams. Residents of the city usually refer to the cathedral as simply "St. John's." ■ TIP→ You can combine a visit to the cathedral with a visit to the House of Culture, as they are just across the street from each other. The street is safe to visit during day; as dusk approaches, take a taxi. ⊠ *Albert St. at Regent St., opposite House of Culture, Commercial District* ☎ *227/3029* ⊕ *www.anglicandioceseof-belize.com* ⊠ *Free.*

Fort George Lighthouse and Bliss Memorial

LIGHTHOUSE | Towering 15 meters (49 feet) over the entrance to Belize Harbor, the lighthouse stands guard on the tip of Fort George Point. It was designed and funded by one of the country's greatest benefactors, Baron Henry Edward Ernest Victor Bliss. The English nobleman never actually set foot on the Belizean mainland, though in his yacht he visited the waters offshore. In his will he bequeathed most of his fortune to the people of Belize, and the date of his death, March 9, is celebrated as a national holiday, now officially called National Heroes and Benefactors Day. Bliss is buried here, in a small, low mausoleum perched on the seawall, up a short run of limestone steps. The lighthouse and mausoleum are for photo ops only—you can't enter. ⊠ *Marine Parade, near the Radisson Fort George Hotel, Fort George* ☎ *222/5665 Belize Port Authority* ⊕ *www.portauthority.bz* ⊠ *Free.*

★ Government House/House of Culture

HOUSE | FAMILY | The city's finest colonial structure is said to have a design inspired by the illustrious British architect Sir Christopher Wren. Built in 1814, it was once the residence of the governor-general, the British monarchy's representative in Belize. Following Hurricane Hattie in 1961, the decision was made to move the capital inland to Belmopan, and the house became a venue for social functions and a guesthouse for visiting VIPs. (Queen Elizabeth stayed here in 1985, Prince Philip in 1988.) Now it's open to the public. You can peruse its archival records, and art and artifacts from the colonial era, or mingle with the tropical birds that frequent the gardens. Renovations are in the works for the building and gardens. ⚠ **If going here after dark, take a**

cab, because it's close to some of the city's most crime-ridden areas. ⊠ *Regent St. at Southern Foreshore, opposite Cathedral of St. John the Baptist, Commercial District* ☎ *227/0518* ⊕ *www.nichbelize. org* ⊠ *BZ$10* ☉ *Closed Sun.*

★ Museum of Belize

MUSEUM | FAMILY | This small but fascinating museum, under the aegis of the National Institute of Culture and History (NICH), was the Belize City jail from 1857 to 1993. Permanent displays include ancient jade and other Mayan artifacts; medicinal, ink, and alcoholic-beverage bottles dating from the 17th century; Belize and British Honduran coins and colorful postage stamps; and an actual prison cell. Temporary exhibitions change periodically. ⊠ *8 Gabourel La., Belize Central Bank Compound, Fort George* ☎ *227/0518 NICH office at House of Culture* ⊕ *www.nichbelize.org* ⊠ *BZ$10* ☉ *Closed Sun.*

Swing Bridge

BRIDGE/TUNNEL | As its name suggests, the bridge spanning Haulover Creek in the middle of Belize City actually swings. When needed to allow a boat through or by special request of visiting dignitaries, four men hand-winch the bridge a quarter-revolution so waiting boats can continue upstream (when it was the only bridge in town, this snarled traffic for blocks). The bridge, made in England, opened in 1923; it was renovated and upgraded in 1999. Outsiders' recommendations to automate the swing mechanics or—heaven forbid—rebuild the bridge entirely are always immediately rejected. No one wants to eliminate the city's most unusual landmark. Before the Swing Bridge arrived, cattle were "hauled over" the creek in a barge. The bridge appears in a scene of the 1980 movie, *The Dogs of War,* set in a fictitious African country but mostly filmed in Belize. ⊠ *Haulover Creek, Queen and Albert Sts., Commercial District.*

INLAND FROM BELIZE CITY

Altun Ha

ARCHAEOLOGICAL SITE | FAMILY | A team from the Royal Ontario Museum first excavated the site in the early 1960s and found 250 structures spread over more than 1,000 square yards. At Plaza B, in the Temple of the Masonry Altars, archaeologists unearthed the grandest and most valuable piece of Mayan art ever discovered—the head of the sun god Kinich Ahau. Weighing nearly 10 pounds, it was carved from a solid block of green jade. The head is kept in a solid steel vault in the Central Bank of Belize, though it is occasionally displayed at the Museum of Belize. The jade head appears on all denominations of Belize currency. If the Masonry Altars temple looks familiar to you, it's because an illustration of the Masonry Altars structure appears on Belikin beer bottles. Because the Altun Ha site is small, it's not necessary to have a tour guide, but licensed guides may offer their services when you arrive.

Tours from Belize City, Orange Walk, and Crooked Tree also are options. Altun Ha is a regular stop on cruise ship excursions, and on days when several ships are in port in Belize City (typically midweek) Altun Ha may be crowded. Several tour operators in San Pedro and Caye Caulker also offer day trips to Altun Ha, often combined with lunch at the nearby Maruba Resort Jungle Spa. Most of these tours from the cayes are by boat, landing at Bomba Village. From here, a van makes the short ride to Altun Ha. If traveling independently or on a tour that includes it, you can stop at Maruba Resort Jungle Spa for a drink, lunch, or a spa treatment. ⊠ *Rockstone Pond Rd., off Old Northern Hwy., Maskall Village* ✛ *From Belize City, take Northern Hwy. north to Mile 18.9. Turn right (east) on Old Northern Hwy., which is only partly paved, and go 14 miles (23 km) to signed entrance road at Rockstone Pond Rd. to Altun Ha on left. Follow this paved road 2* miles (3 km) to visitor center ☎ *822–2106 NICH/Belize Institute of Archeology* ⊕ *www.nichbelize.org* 🎫 *BZ$10.*

★ Belize Zoo

NATURE PRESERVE | FAMILY | Turn a sharp corner on the jungle trail, and suddenly you're face-to-face with a jaguar, the largest cat in the Western Hemisphere. The big cat growls a deep rumbling threat. You jump back, thankful that a strong but inconspicuous fence separates you and the jaguar. Along with jaguars, the zoo's nearly 50 species of native Belize mammals include the country's four other wild cats: the puma, margay, ocelot, and jaguarundi. The zoo also has a tapir, a relative of the horse and rhino known to locals as the mountain cow; it is Belize's national animal. You'll also see jabiru storks, a harpy eagle, scarlet macaws, howler monkeys, crocodiles, and many snakes, including the fer-de-lance. The zoo has an excellent gift shop. ■ **TIP➔ Plan to stay for at least two hours.** ⊠ *Mile 29, George Price Hwy., Belize City* ☎ *822/8000* ⊕ *www.belizezoo.org* 🎫 *BZ$30 adults.*

Community Baboon Sanctuary

NATURE PRESERVE | FAMILY | Spanning a 20-mile (32-km) stretch of the Belize River, the reserve was established in 1985 by a group of local farmers. The black howler monkey (*Alouatta pigra*)—an agile bundle of black fur with a disturbing roar—was then zealously hunted throughout Central America and was facing extinction. (Belizeans refer to the black howler as a "baboon," but baboons are not found in the wild in the Americas.) Today the sanctuary is home, on some 200 private properties, to some 2,000 black howler monkeys, as well as numerous species of birds and mammals. Thanks to ongoing conservation efforts countrywide, you can see the howler monkeys in many other areas of Belize, including at Lamanai in northern Belize, along the Macal, Mopan, and Belize rivers in western Belize, near

Monkey River and around Punta Gorda in southern Belize. You will also see howlers, along with spider monkeys, at Tikal. Exploring the Community Baboon Sanctuary is easy, thanks to about 3 miles (5 km) of trails that start near a small museum and visitor center. The admission fee includes a 45-minute guided nature tour during which you definitely will see howlers. Some guides may ask you to pay extra to hold or pet the howlers—this isn't appropriate, and don't encourage it. Other themed tours—birding, canoeing, crocodiles—are priced à la carte, although the admission per couple is little more than the per-person rate. ✉ *Bermudian Landing, 31 miles (50 km) northwest of Belize City, Bermudian Landing* ⊕ *If heading north on Northern Hwy., turn west at Mile 13.2 onto Burrell Boom Rd. Go 3 miles (5 km) and turn right just beyond new bridge over Belize River. Signs to Bermudian Landing mark the turn. Stay on this road approximately 12 miles (20 km) to Bermudian Landing. If going west on Western Hwy., turn north on Burrell Boom Rd. at round-about at Mile 15.5 of Western Hwy., and go 9 miles (15 km) to new bridge over Belize River. Just before bridge, turn left. Signs to Bermudian Landing mark the turn. Stay on this road approximately 12 miles (20 km) to Bermudian Landing* ☎ *245/2007* 💲 *BZ$14; tours from BZ$24.*

★ Crooked Tree Wildlife Sanctuary

BODY OF WATER | The sanctuary's visitor center is at the end of the causeway. Stop here to pay your admission or arrange a guided tour of the sanctuary or rent a canoe for a do-it-yourself trip. The sanctuary, one of the country's top bird-watching spots, is managed by the Belize Audubon Society. You can also walk through the village and hike birding trails around the area. If you'd prefer to go by horseback, you pay by the hour. The visitor center has a free village and trail map. If you're staying overnight, your hotel can arrange canoe or bike rentals and set up tours and trips. Although

tours can run at any time, the best time is early in the morning, when birds are most active. ✉ *Crooked Tree Village* ☎ *223–5004 Belize Audubon Society in Belize City* ⊕ *www.belizeaudubon.org* 💲 *BZ$8.*

★ Hummingbird Highway

NATIONAL/STATE PARK | One of the most scenic roadways in Belize, the Hummingbird Highway, a paved two-lane road, runs 54.5 miles (91 km) from the junction of the George Price Highway (formerly Western Highway) at Belmopan to Dangriga. Technically, only the first 32 miles (53 km) is the Hummingbird—the rest is the Stann Creek District Highway, but most people ignore that distinction and call it all the Hummingbird. As measured from Belmopan at the junction of the George Price Highway, the Hummingbird first winds through limestone hill country, passing St. Herman's Cave (Mile 12.2) and the inland Blue Hole (Mile 13.1). It then starts rising steeply, with the Maya Mountains on the west or right side, past St. Margaret's village and Five Blues Lake (Mile 23). The views, of green mountains studded with cohune palms and tropical hardwoods, are incredible. At the Hummingbird Gap (Mile 26, elevation near 1,000 feet, with mountains nearby over 3,000 feet), you're at the crest of the highway and now begin to drop down toward the Caribbean Sea. At Middlesex village (Mile 32), technically the road becomes the Stann Creek District Highway and you're in Stann Creek District. Now you're in citrus country, with groves of grapefruit and Valencia oranges. Near Steadfast village (watch for signs around Mile 37) there's the 1,600-acre Billy Barquedier National Park, where you can hike to waterfalls. At Mile 48.7 you pass the turn-off to the Southern Highway and at Mile 54.5 you enter Dangriga, with the sea just ahead. ■**TIP**➜ **If driving, keep a watch for "sleeping policemen," speed bumps to slow traffic near villages. Most are signed, but a few are not. Also, gas up in Belmopan, as there are few service stations**

until you approach Dangriga. ✉ *Belmopan to Dangriga, Hummingbird Hwy., Belmopan.*

St. Herman's Blue Hole National Park

BODY OF WATER | FAMILY | Less than a half hour south of Belmopan, the 575-acre St. Herman's Blue Hole National Park has a natural turquoise pool surrounded by mosses and lush vegetation, wonderful for a cool dip. The "inland Blue Hole" is actually part of an underground river system. On the other side of the hill is St. Herman's Cave, once inhabited by the Maya. There's a separate entrance to St. Herman's. A path leads up from the highway, but it's quite steep and difficult to climb unless the ground is dry. To explore St. Herman's cave beyond the first 300 yards or so, you must be accompanied by a guide (available at the park), and no more than five people can enter the cave at one time. With a guide, you also can explore part of another cave system here, the Crystal Cave (sometimes called the Crystalline Cave), which stretches for miles; the additional cost is BZ$20 per person for a two-hour guided tour. The main park visitor center is 12.5 miles (20.5 km) from Belmopan. The park is managed by the Belize Audubon Society, which administers a network of seven protected areas around the country. ✉ *Mile 42.5, Hummingbird Hwy., Belmopan* ☎ *223–5004 Belize Audubon Society in Belize City* ⊕ *www.belizeaudubon.org* 🎫 *BZ$8.*

THE CAYES
AMBERGRIS CAYE

Friendly, prosperous, and tidy, Ambergris is the queen of the cayes. It has one of the highest literacy rates in the country and an admirable level of awareness about the fragility of the reef. The large number of substantial private homes being built on the edges of town is proof of how much tourism has enriched San Pedro, the island's only town. A water taxi from the Marine Terminal takes about 75 minutes and costs BZ$40 each way. You can also fly.

★ Hol Chan Marine Reserve

SCUBA DIVING | The reef's focal point for diving and snorkeling near Ambergris Caye and Caye Caulker is the spectacular Hol Chan Marine Reserve. It's a 20-minute boat ride from San Pedro, and about 30 minutes from Caye Caulker. Hol Chan (Maya for "little channel") is a break in the reef about 100 feet wide and 20 to 35 feet deep, through which tremendous volumes of water pass with the tides. Shark-Ray Alley, now a part of Hol Chan, is famous as a place to swim, snorkel, and dive with sharks (nearly all nurse sharks) and Southern stingrays. The expanded 21-square-mile (55-square-km) park has a miniature "Blue Hole" and a 12-foot-deep cave whose entrance often attracts the fairy basslet, an iridescent purple-and-yellow fish frequently seen here. The reserve is also home to a large moray eel population.

Varying in depth from 50 feet to 100 feet, Hol Chan's canyons lie between buttresses of coral running perpendicular to the reef, separated by white, sandy channels. You may find tunnel-like passageways from one canyon to the next. It's exciting to explore, because as you come over each hill you don't know what you'll see in the "valley." Because fishing generally is off-limits here, divers and snorkelers can see abundant marine life. There are throngs of squirrelfish, butterfly fish, parrotfish, and queen angelfish, as well as Nassau groupers, barracuda, and large shoals of yellowtail snappers. Unfortunately, also here are lionfish, an invasive Indo-Pacific species that is eating its way—destroying small native fish populations—from Venezuela to the North Carolina coast. Altogether, more than 160 species of fish have been identified in the marine reserve, along with 40 species of coral, and five kinds of sponges. Hawksbill, loggerhead, and green turtles have also been found here, along with spotted and common dolphins, West Indian manatees, stingrays and several species of sharks.

⚠ **The currents through the reef can be strong here at times, so tell your guide if you're not a strong swimmer, and ask for a snorkel vest or float. Also, although nurse sharks are normally docile and very used to humans, they are wild creatures that on rare occasions have bitten snorkelers or divers who disturbed them.** ✉ *Off southern tip of Ambergris Caye, Ambergris Caye* ☎ *526–2247 in San Pedro* ⊕ *www. holchanbelize.org* ✐ *BZ$25 (normally included in snorkel or dive tour price).*

CAYE CAULKER

On Caye Caulker, where the one village is home to around 2,000 people, brightly painted houses on stilts line the coral-sand streets. Although the island is being developed more each year, flowers still outnumber cars 10 to 1. (Golf carts, bicycles, and bare feet are the preferred means of transportation.) The living is easy, as you might guess from all the "no shirt, no shoes, no problem" signs at the bars. This is the kind of place where most of the listings in the telephone directory give addresses like "near football field." A water taxi from the Marine Terminal costs about BZ$55 each way and takes 45 minutes to an hour.

🏖 Beaches

Although the barrier reef limits the wave action and brings seagrass to the shore floor, the wide sandy beaches of Ambergris Caye are among the best in Belize. All beaches in Belize are public. **Mar de Tumbo,** 1½ miles (3 km) south of town near the Tropica Hotel, is the best beach on the south end of the island. **North Ambergris,** accessible by water taxi from San Pedro or by golf cart over the bridge to the north, has miles of narrow beaches and fewer people. The beach at **Ramon's Village,** across from the airstrip, is the best in the town area. The beaches

on Caulker are not as good as those on Ambergris. Along the front side of the island is a narrow strip of sand, but the water is shallow and swimming conditions are poor. **The Split,** on the north end of the village (turn to your right from the main public pier), is the best place on Caye Caulker for swimming.

🍴 Restaurants

Nerie's

$ | **LATIN AMERICAN** | Often packed, Nerie's is the *vox populi* of dining in Belize City. The many traditional dishes on the menu include fry jacks for breakfast and cowfoot soup for lunch. Ⓢ *Average main: BZ$14* ✉ *Queen and Daly Sts., Commercial District* ☎ *223/4028* ▭ *No credit cards* ⊘ *Closed Sun.*

★ Riverside Tavern

$$ | **AMERICAN** | One of the city's most popular and agreeable restaurants serves up dependably good food, with friendly service and safe parking. The signature hamburgers, which come in several sizes from 6 oz. to enormous, are arguably the best in Belize. Ⓢ *Average main: BZ$28* ✉ *2 Mapp St., off Freetown Rd., Commercial District* ☎ *223/5640* ⊘ *No dinner Sun.*

🛍 Shopping

Belize does not have the crafts tradition of neighboring Guatemala and Mexico, and imported goods are expensive thanks to high duties, but hand-carved items of ziricote or other local woods make good souvenirs. Near the Swing Bridge at Market Square is the **Commercial Center,** which has some food and craft vendors on the first floor and a restaurant and shops on the second. The **Belize Tourism Village,** where the ship tenders come in, is a collection of bright and clean gift shops selling T-shirts and Belizean and Guatemalan crafts. Beside the Tourism Village is an informal **Street Vendor Market,** with funkier goods and performances by a "Brukdown" band or a group of Garifuna drummers.

Belizean Handicraft Market Place

CRAFTS | This handicraft-market complex has Belizean souvenir items, including hand-carved figurines, handmade furniture, pottery, and woven baskets. The prices are about as good as you'll find anywhere in Belize, and the sales clerks are friendly. It is just a short stroll from the harbor front, the Belize Tourism Village, and many of the hotels in the Fort George area, including the Radisson Fort George and The Great House. ⊠ *2 S. Park St., across from Memorial Park, Fort George* ☎ *223/3637* ☉ *Closed Sun.*

🏃 Activities

CANOPY TOURS

You may feel a little like Tarzan as you dangle 80 feet above the jungle floor, suspended by a harness, moving from one treetop platform to another. Cruise passengers can do combo trips through Butts Up that include both zip-lining and cave tubing.

CAVE TUBING

Very popular with cruise passengers are river-tubing trips that go through a cave, where you'll turn off your headlamp for a minute of absolute darkness, but these are not for the claustrophobic or those afraid of the dark.

Butts Up

ADVENTURE TOURS | Despite the risqué name, the folks here get top marks from cruise passengers for their cave-tubing tours. You can choose from a basic cave-tubing outing (BZ$100 per person) or add a zip-line or ATV tour for a total of BZ$150. A separate zipline tour with a visit to the ruins at Altun Ha is also available. Although most of the company's business is with cruise ship passengers, overnight visitors also can do the tours. ⊠ *Near Terminal 1, Tourism Village, Fort George* ☎ *605/1575, 888/637–3351* ⊕ *www.cave-tubing.com* 🖃 *From BZ$100.*

DIVING AND SNORKELING

Most companies on Ambergris Caye offer morning and afternoon single-tank dives; snorkel trips begin midmorning or early afternoon. Dive and snorkeling trips that originate in Caye Caulker are a bit cheaper.

Amigos del Mar

FISHING | Established in 1987, Amigos del Mar is perhaps the island's most consistently recommended dive operation. The SSI/SDI facility has a dozen dive boats, 16 contracted divemasters, and a range of local dives as well as trips to Turneffe Atoll and Lighthouse Reef in a fast 56-foot dive boat. You can choose from a local two-tank dive or a 12-hour trip to the Blue Hole, including the park entry fee and lunch. In addition to various tours, Amigos del Mar offers an open-water certification course, as well as snorkel and fishing trips. ⊠ *On pier off Barrier Reef Dr., near Mayan Princess Hotel, San Pedro Town* ☎ *226–2706, 800/882–6159 in U.S.* ⊕ *www.amigosdivebelize.com.*

INDEPENDENT TOURS

Several Belize City–based tour guides and operators offer custom trips for ship passengers; companies will usually meet you at the Belize Tourism Village.

Ecological Tours & Services

ADVENTURE TOURS | Ecological Tours specializes in shore excursions and can take you on snorkeling trips to Caye Caulker, Goff's Caye, or Ambergris Caye. The latter includes a short flyover tour of the reef and islands. These folks also arrange a variety of cave-tubing excursions, with or without a zip-line tour. ⊠ *Belize Tourism Village, Fort St., Belize City* ☎ *625–1636* ⊕ *www.ecotoursbelize.com* 🖃 *From BZ$90.*

Bequia, St. Vincent & the Grenadines

Bequia (pronounced *BECK-way*) is the Carib word for "island of the cloud." Nine miles (14½ km) south of St. Vincent's southwestern shore, hilly and green Bequia is and the largest and most populous of the 32 islands and cays that make up St. Vincent & the Grenadines. The capital of Bequia is Port Elizabeth, a tiny town with waterfront bars, restaurants, and shops where you can buy handmade souvenirs, including the exquisitely detailed model sailboats for which Bequia is famous. Although boatbuilding, whaling, and fishing have been the predominant industries here for generations, Bequia has now become almost synonymous with sailing. Its picturesque Admiralty Bay is one of the prettiest in the Caribbean and a favorite anchorage for both privately owned and chartered yachts. With superb views, snorkeling, hiking, and swimming at several golden-sand beaches, the island has much to offer the international mix of visitors who frequent its shores.

ESSENTIALS
CURRENCY
Eastern Caribbean (EC) dollar, but U.S. dollars are widely accepted.

TELEPHONE
The country code for St. Vincent & the Grenadines is 1 784. Digicel and Flow are the major mobile providers, using GSM (850, 900, and 1800 bands).

COMING ASHORE
Cruise ships that call on Bequia anchor offshore in Admiralty Bay and tender passengers to the jetty in Port Elizabeth or to nearby beaches. Although it's the capital of Bequia, Port Elizabeth is a tiny waterfront town that is only a few blocks long and one block deep. A tourist information booth is on the jetty, shops and restaurants face the bay, and taxis are always lined up under the almond trees to meet passengers arriving via either cruise ship or the St. Vincent–Bequia ferry, which docks alongside the jetty. Water taxis are available for transportation between the jetty and nearby beaches for about $6 (EC$15) per person each way, but keep in mind that most of these operators are not regulated; ride at your own risk.

To see the views, villages, beaches, and other places of interest in Bequia, the best bet is to hire a taxi. Most taxis are pickup trucks, with a covered bed that is fitted with seating for four or six people. The driver will show you the sights in a couple of hours, point out a place for lunch, and (if you wish) drop you at a beach for swimming and snorkeling and pick you up later on. Negotiate the fare in advance, but expect to pay about $30 per hour for the tour. A rental car will cost about $55 per day and, unless you already have an international driver's license, requires a temporary local permit ($38 at the Revenue Office in Port Elizabeth).

◉ Sights

To see the views, villages, beaches, and boatbuilding sites around Bequia, hire a taxi at the jetty in Port Elizabeth. Several usually line up under the almond trees to meet each ferry from St. Vincent. The driver will show you the sights in a couple of hours, point out a place for lunch, and (if you wish) drop you at a beach for swimming and snorkeling and pick you up later on. Negotiate the fare in advance, but expect to pay about $30 per hour for the tour. Water taxis are available for transportation between the jetty in Port Elizabeth and the beaches. The cost is about $6 (EC$15) per person each way, but keep in mind that most of these operators are not regulated; ride at your own risk.

Port Elizabeth is the main town on tiny Bequia.

Admiralty Bay
BODY OF WATER | This huge sheltered bay on the leeward side of Bequia is a favorite yacht anchorage. Year-round it's filled with boats; in season, they're moored transom to bowsprit. It's the perfect spot for watching the sun dip over the horizon each evening—either from your boat or from the terrace bar at one of Port Elizabeth's waterfront hotels or restaurants. ⊠ *Port Elizabeth.*

Hamilton Battery/Ft. Hamilton
VIEWPOINT | Just north of Port Elizabeth, 300 feet above Admiralty Bay, a British fort constructed in the late 1700s protected the harbor from American privateers and French marauders. The fort was named for Alexander Hamilton, who was born on Nevis in 1755. His father James, who never married Alexander's mother, apparently lived on Bequia between 1774 and 1794. Today, the fort is gone; the spot is simply a breezy place to enjoy a magnificent view. Hike or take a taxi from the center of town (fair warning: the road is very steep and winding). ⊠ *Belmont Rd., Hamilton, Port Elizabeth.*

Old Hegg Turtle Sanctuary
NATURE PRESERVE | **FAMILY** | In the far northeast of the island, Orton "Brother" King, a retired skin-diving fisherman, tends to more than 200 endangered hawksbill turtles until they can be released back into the sea. Call ahead, and he'll be glad to show you around and tell you how his project has increased the turtle population in the waters surrounding Bequia. ⊠ *Park Beach, Union Vale, Industry Bay* ☏ *784/458–3245* ⊕ *www.turtles.bequia. net* ✉ *$5 donation requested.*

Port Elizabeth
COMMERCIAL CENTER | Bequia's capital and only town, locally referred to as "the Harbour," is on the northeastern side of Admiralty Bay. The ferry from St. Vincent docks at the jetty in the center of the tiny town, which is only a few blocks long and a couple of blocks deep. Walk north along Front Street (which faces the water) to the open-air market, where you can buy local fruits and vegetables and

some handicrafts; farther along, you will find some of Bequia's famous model-boat shops. Walking south from the jetty, Belmont Walkway meanders along the bay past shops, cafés, restaurants, bars, and small hotels. ■TIP➔ An "official" tourist information booth is located on the jetty. ⊠ *Port Elizabeth.*

Beaches

Bequia has clean, uncrowded white-sand beaches. Some can be reached via a short water-taxi ride from the jetty at Port Elizabeth; others require land transportation.

★ Friendship Bay Beach
BEACH—SIGHT | FAMILY | This spectacular horseshoe-shape, mile-long (1½-km-long) beach on Bequia's mid-southern coast can be reached by land taxi or by boat. Refreshments are available at Bequia Beach Hotel's Bagatelle grill. **Amenities:** food and drink. **Best for:** snorkeling; swimming; walking. ⊠ *Friendship.*

★ Lower Bay Beach
BEACH—SIGHT | FAMILY | This broad, palm-fringed beach on the southern shore of Admiralty Bay, south of Port Elizabeth and Princess Margaret Beach, is reachable by land or water taxi or a healthy hike from town. It's an excellent beach for swimming and snorkeling. Refreshments are available at La Plage or De Reef Bar & Restaurant, both right on the beach. **Amenities:** food and drink; toilets; water sports. **Best for:** snorkeling; swimming. ⊠ *Lower Bay.*

★ Princess Margaret Beach
BEACH—SIGHT | FAMILY | Quiet and wide with a natural stone arch at one end, the beach is not far from Port Elizabeth's Belmont Walkway—but you still need to take a water or land taxi to get here. When you tire of the water, snoozing under the palm and seagrapes is always an option. Plan to have lunch at Jack's Beach Bar. **Amenities:** food and drink; toilets. **Best for:** snorkeling; swimming;

Best Bets

■ **Explore Port Elizabeth.** Walk along the Port Elizabeth waterfront. Don't miss the model-boat builders' studios.

■ **Island Tour.** Taxi drivers are always available at the jetty in Port Elizabeth to take you on an island tour (two hours, about $60). If you wish, the driver will drop you off for lunch or for a swim at the beach and pick you up later.

■ **Lay on the Beach.** Enjoy one of the island's quiet beaches for a day of relaxation.

walking. ⊠ *Between Port Elizabeth and Lower Bay, Port Elizabeth.*

Restaurants

Gingerbread Café
$$$ | CAFÉ | FAMILY | Perhaps the best spot to enjoy an alfresco breakfast, lunch, or snack is sitting at a table under an enormous almond tree at the edge of Admiralty Bay. French toast and pancakes—and warm cinnamon buns—are always available at breakfast, while lunch-goers might have a roti (turnover filled with chicken or conch), a tuna wrap, or a burger and fries. **Known for:** perfect view of the harbor activity; friendly gathering place; freshly baked sweets. $ *Average main: $22* ⊠ *Gingerbread Hotel, Belmont Walkway, Port Elizabeth* ☎ *784/458–3800* ⊕ *www.gingerbreadhotel.com.*

Jack's Beach Bar
$$$ | CARIBBEAN | FAMILY | Jack's is a perfect spot for lunch when you're enjoying a day at Princess Margaret Beach … or any day when you're on Bequia. The sandwiches, salads, burgers and fries, or the grilled catch of the day along with a refreshing cold drink will certainly satisfy.

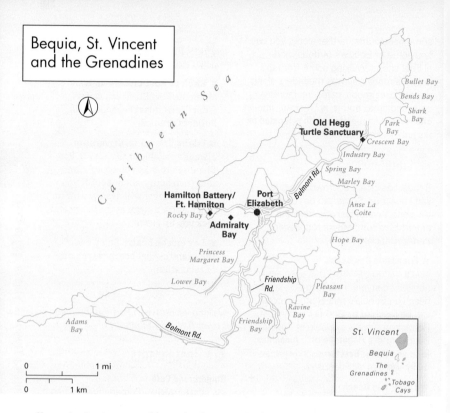

Bequia, St. Vincent and the Grenadines

Caribbean Sea

Bullet Bay
Bends Bay
Shark Bay
Park Bay
Crescent Bay
Industry Bay
Spring Bay
Marley Bay

Old Hegg Turtle Sanctuary

Hamilton Battery/ Ft. Hamilton

Port Elizabeth

Belmont Rd.

Rocky Bay

Admiralty Bay

Anse La Coite

Princess Margaret Bay

Hope Bay

Lower Bay

Friendship Rd.

Pleasant Bay

Ravine Bay

Adams Bay

Belmont Rd.

Friendship Bay

St. Vincent
Bequia
The Grenadines
Tobago Cays

0 — 1 mi
0 — 1 km

Known for: fresh sea-to-table seafood; great casual, beachy, yet stylish vibe; Sunday brunch. $ *Average main: $30* ✉ *Princess Margaret Beach, between Port Elizabeth and Lower Bay, Port Elizabeth* ☎ *784/458–3809.*

🛍 Shopping

Long renowned for their boatbuilding skills, Bequians have translated that craftsmanship to building model boats. In their Port Elizabeth workshops, you can watch as hair-thin lines are attached to delicate sails or individual strips of wood are glued together for decking. Other Bequian artisans scrimshaw, carve wood, throw pottery, crochet, or work with fabric (designing or hand-painting it first, then creating clothing and gift items for sale). Bequia's shops are mostly on **Front Street,** just steps from the jetty where

the ferry arrives in Port Elizabeth, and on **Belmont Walkway,** its waterfront extension south of the jetty, where shops and studios showcase gifts and handmade articles. North of the jetty there's an open-air market; farther along that road, you'll find the model-boat workshops. Opposite the jetty, at **Bayshore Mall,** shops sell ice cream, baked goods, stationery, gifts, and clothing; there's also a grocery, liquor store, pharmacy, travel agent, and bank. Shops are open weekdays from 8 to 5, Saturday from 8 to noon.

Bequia Bookshop

BOOKS/STATIONERY | Head here for Caribbean literature, cruising guides and charts, Caribbean flags, beach novels, souvenir maps, and exquisite scrimshaw and one-of-a-kind whalebone knives carved by Bequian scrimshander Sam

McDowell. ✉ *Belmont Walkway, Port Elizabeth* ☎ *784/458–3905.*

Local Color

JEWELRY/ACCESSORIES | This shop stocks an excellent selection of unusual hand-made jewelry, wood carvings, scrimshaw, and resort clothing. It's above the Port-hole restaurant, near the jetty. ✉ *Belmont Walkway, Port Elizabeth* ☎ *784/458–3202* ⊘ *Closed Oct.*

★ Mauvin's Model Boat Shop

CRAFTS | At Mauvin Hutchins' workshop, you can purchase the ultimate Bequia souvenir—a handmade model "Bequia boat"—or special-order a replica of your own yacht. The models are incredibly detailed and quite expensive, priced from a few hundred to several thousand dollars. The simplest models take about a week to make; a few are always available for immediate sale. ✉ *Front St., Port Elizabeth* ☎ *784/458–3669* ⊘ *Closed Sun.*

★ Sargeant Brothers Model Boat Shop

CRAFTS | In addition to the handcrafted, expertly rigged, and authentically detailed model boats on display—everything from traditional Bequia whaling boats and clas-sic schooners to modern-day cruisers—the Sargeant brothers (Timothy, Winston, and Lawson) build custom models on commission. ✉ *Front St., Port Elizabeth* ☎ *758/458–3344.*

🜨 Activities

BOATING AND SAILING

With regular trade winds, visibility for 30 miles (48 km), and generally calm seas, Bequia is a big draw for those sailing the Grenadines—which easily rates among the best blue-water sailing anywhere in the world. At Port Elizabeth, you'll find all kinds of options: day sails or weekly char-ters, bareboat or fully crewed, monohulls or catamarans. Prices for day trips start at about $140 per person.

★ *Friendship Rose*

BOATING | FAMILY | This 80-foot schooner spent its first 25 years ferrying both passengers and mail between Bequia and neighboring islands. In the late 1960s it was refitted, and the *Friendship Rose* now takes passengers on day trips from Bequia to Mustique and the Tobago Cays. Breakfast, lunch, snacks, drinks, and snorkeling gear are included in the price ($125 for Mustique, $150 for the Tobago Cays). ■TIP→ One child under 12 per adult sails free. ✉ *Waterfront, Port Eliza-beth* ☎ *784/457–3888, 784/457–3739, 784/529–8046* ⊕ *www.friendshiprose. com.*

Sail Grenadines

BOATING | The experienced team at this family-owned outfit has been sailing the Grenadines for more than 15 years and now operates out of Bequia. The fleet of well-maintained yachts includes mono-hulls, catamarans, and a 113-foot Benetti power boat. Vessels can be chartered for a week or more, either skippered or bareboat. ✉ *Bequia Marina, Belmont Rd., Port Elizabeth* ☎ *473/533–2909, 855/533–5035 in U.S.* ⊕ *www.sailgrenadines.com.*

DIVING AND SNORKELING

About 35 dive sites around Bequia and nearby islands are accessible within 15 minutes by boat. The leeward side of the 7-mile (11-km) reef that fringes Bequia has been designated a marine park. **The Bullet,** off Bequia's northeast point, has limited access because of rough seas, but it's good for spotting rays, barracuda, and the occasional nurse shark. **Devil's Table** is a shallow dive at the northern end of Admiralty Bay that's rich in fish and coral and has a sailboat wreck nearby at 90 feet. **The Wall** is a 90-foot drop off West Cay. Expect to pay dive operators $70 for a one-tank dive and $120 for a two-tank dive, including equipment. Dive boats welcome snorkelers for about $20 per person, but for the best snorkeling in Bequia, take a water taxi to the bay at Moonhole and arrange a pickup time.

Bequia Dive Adventures

SCUBA DIVING | This company offers PADI instruction courses and takes small groups on three dives daily. Rates include all equipment; harbor pickup and return is included for customers staying on yachts. Courses range from "Discover Scuba Diving" to "Divemaster," plus 11 specialty courses. ⊠ *Belmont Walkway, Port Elizabeth* ☎ *784/458–3826* ⊕ *www. bequiadiveadventures.com.*

Dive Bequia

SCUBA DIVING | Dive and snorkel tours, night dives, and full equipment rental is available from Dive Bequia. The company's two 30-foot custom-built dive boats leave the dock on three trips each day. PADI instructors provide resort and certification courses, including several interactive e-learning courses. ⊠ *Gingerbread Hotel, Belmont Walkway, Port Elizabeth* ☎ *784/458–3504* ⊕ *www. divebequia.com.*

Bermuda

Basking in the Atlantic, 508 miles (817 km) due east of Cape Hatteras, North Carolina, restrained and polite Bermuda is a departure from other sunny, beach-strewn isles. You won't find laid-back locals wandering around barefoot proffering piña coladas. Although Bermuda is still somewhat formal—and despite the gorgeous weather—it is still common to see residents wearing heels or jackets, ties, Bermuda shorts, and knee socks, whether on the street by day or in restaurants at night. On Bermuda's 22 square miles (57 square km) you will discover that pastel cottages, quaint shops, and manicured gardens betray a more staid, suburban way of life. A self-governing British colony since 1968, Bermuda has maintained some of its English character even as it is increasingly influenced by American culture. Most cruise ships make seven-night loops from U.S. embarkation ports, with four nights at sea and

Best Bets ◉

■ **Gibbs Hill Lighthouse.** Make the climb to the top, where the reward is an expansive view of the inlets and harbors.

■ **National Museum of Bermuda.** Absorb Bermuda's nautical and military history in this Royal Navy Dockyard museum.

■ **St. George's.** Attend the pierside show hosted by the town crier, where gossips and nagging wives are plunged into the water in a ducking stool.

three tied up in port. Increasingly popular are round-trip itineraries originating in northeastern embarkation ports that include a single day or overnight port call in Bermuda before continuing south to the Bahamas or the Caribbean.

ESSENTIALS
CURRENCY

The Bermuda dollar (BMD$) is on par with the U.S. dollar. You can use American money anywhere.

TELEPHONE

To make a local call, simply dial the seven-digit number; Bermuda's country code is 441. International calling cards are widely available for purchase and can be used at one of Bermuda's many public telephones.

COMING ASHORE

Three Bermuda harbors serve cruise ships: Hamilton (the capital), St. George's, and King's Wharf.

King's Wharf, in the Royal Naval Dockyard at the westernmost end of the island, is the busiest of the three cruise-ship berthing areas, and it is where most vessels dock. Although the Dockyard appears isolated on a map, it is well connected to the rest of the island by taxi, bus, and ferry. The visitor information center can be found along the pier and adjacent to the ferry dock.

In Hamilton, smaller cruise ships tie up right on the city's main drag, Front Street. A brand-new visitor information center is next to the ferry terminal, also on Front Street and nearby; maps and brochures are displayed in the cruise terminal itself.

St. George's accommodates a handful of smaller cruise ships every year at Penno's Wharf, located just minutes from the heart of the city. A visitor information center is located at 25 York Street, within walking distance of the pier.

Taxis are the fastest and easiest way to get around the island, but they are also quite expensive. Four-seater taxis charge $7.90 for the first mile and $2.75 for each subsequent mile. A personalized taxi tour of the island costs $50 per hour for one to four people and $70 per hour for five to seven, excluding tip. If you can round up a group of people, this is often cheaper than an island tour offered by your ship. Tip drivers 15%. Rental cars are prohibited, but visitors can now rent electric two-seat vehicles, which are a much safer option than scooters, which are only recommended for experienced riders. There are electrical outlets set up to plug in these vehicles found across the island, so you'll never have to worry about running out of charge. The island has a good bus and ferry system.

◉ Sights

HAMILTON

Bermuda's capital since 1815, the city of Hamilton is a small, bustling harbor town. It's the economic and social center of Bermuda, with busy streets lined with shops and offices. International influences, from both business and tourism, have brought a degree of sophistication unusual in so small a city. There are several museums and galleries to explore, but the favorite pastimes are shopping

in Hamilton's numerous boutiques and dining in its many upscale restaurants.

★ Bermuda Underwater Exploration Institute (BUEI)

MUSEUM | FAMILY | The 40,000-square-foot Ocean Discovery Centre at the institute showcases local contributions to oceanographic research and undersea discovery. Highlights include the world-class shell collection amassed by resident Jack Lightbourn (three of the 1,000 species were identified by and named for Lightbourn himself) and a gallery honoring native-born archaeologist Teddy Tucker featuring booty from Bermudian shipwrecks. The equipment that made such discoveries possible is displayed, including a replica of the bathysphere William Beebe and Otis Barton used in their record-smashing 1934 dive. (Forget the Bermuda Triangle: the real mystery is how they descended a half mile in a metal ball less than 5 feet in diameter!) A more modern "submersible," Nautilus-X2, lets wannabe explorers take a simulated seven-minute trip to the ocean floor. Special events, like lectures, glowworm cruises, and whale-watching trips, are available for an added fee. The on-site Harbourfront restaurant is a lovely choice for lunch. ■TIP→ **Pedestrians may access the facility by following the sidewalk on the water side of Front Street. Motorists must drive out of town on Front Street, round the traffic circle, and exit at the lane signposted for the BUEI.** ✉ 40 Crow La., Hamilton ✛ Off E. Broadway ☎ 441/292–7219 ⊕ www.buei.bm ✎ $15.

City Hall & Arts Centre

GOVERNMENT BUILDING | Set back from the street, City Hall contains Hamilton's administrative offices as well as two art galleries and a performance hall. Instead of a clock, its tower is topped with a bronze wind vane—a prudent choice in a land where the weather is as important as the time. The building itself was designed in 1960 by Bermudian architect Wilfred Onions, a champion of balanced

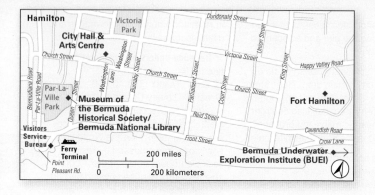

Hamilton

City Hall & Arts Centre

Victoria Park

Dundonald Street

Washington Street
Washington Lane
Burnaby Street

Church Street

Victoria Street

Union Street

King Street

Happy Valley Road

Bermudiana Road
Par-La-Ville Road

Par-La-Ville Park

Queen Street

Parliament Street

Court Street

Church Street

Fort Hamilton

Museum of the Bermuda Historical Society/ Bermuda National Library

Reid Street

Cavendish Road

Crow Lane

Visitors Service Bureau

Ferry Terminal

Point Pleasant Rd.

Front Street

0   200 miles

0   200 kilometers

Bermuda Underwater Exploration Institute (BUEI) →

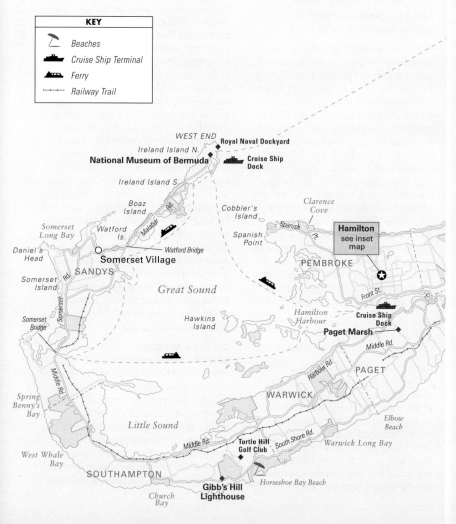

KEY

- Beaches
- Cruise Ship Terminal
- Ferry
- Railway Trail

WEST END
Ireland Island N.
Royal Naval Dockyard
National Museum of Bermuda
Cruise Ship Dock

Ireland Island S.

Boaz Island

Malabar Rd.

Cobbler's Island

Clarence Cove

Spanish Pt.

Hamilton
see inset map

Watford Is.

Watford Bridge

Somerset Village

Spanish Point

PEMBROKE

Somerset Long Bay

Daniel's Head

SANDYS

Somerset Island

Great Sound

Front St.

Somerset Rd.

Hawkins Island

Hamilton Harbour

Cruise Ship Dock

Paget Marsh

Somerset Bridge

Middle Rd.

PAGET

Spring Benny's Bay

Little Sound

Harbour Rd.

WARWICK

Elbow Beach

West Whale Bay

Middle Rd.

Turtle Hill Golf Club

South Shore Rd.

Warwick Long Bay

SOUTHAMPTON

Church Bay

Gibb's Hill Lighthouse

Horseshoe Bay Beach

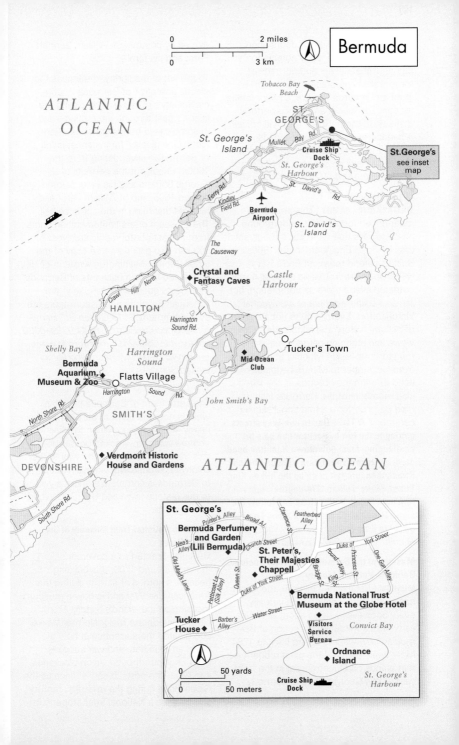

simplicity. Massive cedar doors open onto an impressive lobby notable for its beautiful chandeliers and portraits of mayors past and present. To the left is The Earl Cameron Theatre, a major venue for concerts, plays, and dance performances. To the right are the civic offices. A handsome cedar staircase leads upstairs to two upper-floor art galleries, or you can take an elevator. ⊠ *17 Church St., Hamilton* ☎ *441/292–1234* 🖅 *Free.*

★ Fort Hamilton

MILITARY SITE | **FAMILY** | This imposing, moat-ringed fortress has underground passageways that were cut through solid rock by Royal Engineers in the 1860s. Built to defend the West End's Royal Naval Dockyard from land attacks, it was outdated even before its completion, but remains a fine example of a polygonal Victorian fort. Even if you're not a big fan of military history, the hilltop site's stellar views and stunning gardens make the trip worthwhile. On Monday at noon, from November to March, bagpipes echo through the grounds as the kilt-clad members of the Bermuda Islands Pipe Band perform a traditional skirling ceremony. ■ **TIP**➔ **Due to one-way streets, getting to the fort by scooter can be a bit challenging. From downtown Hamilton head north on Queen Street, turn right on Church Street, then turn left to go up the hill on King Street. Make a sharp (270-degree) right turn onto Happy Valley Road and follow the signs. Pedestrians may walk along Front Street to King Street.** ⊠ *Happy Valley Rd., Hamilton* ☎ *441/292–1234* 🖅 *Free.*

Museum of the Bermuda Historical Society/Bermuda National Library

MUSEUM | Established in 1839, the library has a reference section with virtually every book ever written about Bermuda, as well as a microfilm collection of Bermudian newspapers dating back to 1784. Mark Twain admired the giant rubber tree that stands on Queen Street in the front yard of this Georgian house, formerly owned by postmaster William Bennett Perot and his family.

To the left of the library entrance is the electic collection of Bermuda Historical Society's museum, chronicling the island's past through interesting—and in some cases downright quirky—artifacts. One display, for instance, is full of Bermudian silver dating from the 1600s. Check out the portraits of Sir George Somers and his wife, painted around 1605, and of William Perot and his wife that hang in the entrance hall. The museum offers limited-edition prints from its vast photographic archives. You can also pick up a free copy of the letter George Washington wrote in 1775; addressed to the inhabitants of Bermuda, it requests gunpowder for use in the American Revolution. Museum tours are by appointment. ⊠ *13 Queen St., Hamilton* ✛ *Opposite Reid St.* ☎ *441/299–0029 library, 441/295–2487 museum* ⊕ *www.bnl.bm* 🖅 *Free* ☉ *Museum and library closed Sun.*

ST. GEORGE'S

The settlement of Bermuda began in what is now the town of St. George's nearly 400 years ago, when the *Sea Venture* was shipwrecked on Bermuda's treacherous reefs on its way to the colony of Jamestown, Virginia. No trip to Bermuda is complete without a visit to this historic town and UNESCO World Heritage Site.

Bermuda National Trust Museum at the Globe Hotel

MUSEUM | Erected as a governor's mansion around 1700, this building became a hotbed of activity during the American Civil War and is now a museum focusing on the island's history. From here, Confederate Major Norman Walker coordinated the surreptitious flow of guns, ammunition, and war supplies from England, through Union blockades, into American ports. It saw service as the Globe Hotel during the mid-19th century and became a National Trust property in

Hamilton's Front Street is the top shopping spot in Bermuda.

1951. A short video, *Bermuda, Centre of the Atlantic,* recounts the history of Bermuda, and a memorabilia-filled exhibit entitled "Rogues & Runners: Bermuda and the American Civil War" describes St. George's when it was a port for Confederate blockade runners. This is also the location of the Trustworthy Gift Shop. ⌧ *32 Duke of York St., St. George's* ☎ *441/297–1423* ⊕ *www.bnt.bm* ⌧ *$5; $10 combination ticket includes admission to Tucker House and Verdmont (Smith's Parish)* ⊗ *Closed Sun.*

★ Bermuda Perfumery and Garden (Lili Bermuda)

MUSEUM | Originally in Hamilton Parish but in historic Stewart Hall since 2005, this perfumery founded in 1928 allows you to visit to learn about the process of making the scents. Although the location changed, the techniques did not: the perfumery still manufactures and bottles all its island-inspired scents on-site using more than 3,000 essential oils extracted from frangipani, jasmine, oleander, and passionflower. Guides are available to explain the entire process, and there's a small museum that outlines the company's history. You can also wander around the gardens and stock up on your favorite fragrances in the showroom. ⌧ *Stewart Hall, 5 Queen St., St. George's* ☎ *441/293–0627* ⊕ *www.lilibermuda.com* ⌧ *Free* ⊗ *Closed Sun.*

Ordnance Island

ISLAND | The island, directly across from King's Square, is dominated by a splendid bronze statue of Sir George Somers, commander of the *Sea Venture.* Somers looks surprised that he made it safely to shore—and you may be surprised that he ever chose to set sail again when you spy the nearby *Deliverance.* It's a full-scale replica of one of two ships—the other was the *Patience*—built under Somers's supervision to carry survivors from the 1609 wreck onward to Jamestown. But considering the ship's size (just 57 feet from bow to stern), *Deliverance* hardly seems seaworthy by modern standards. In complete contrast, Ordnance Island is often host to some of the world's most spectacular motor and sailing yachts, who use Bermuda as a mid-Atlantic stopover. ⊠ *Across from King's Sq., St. George's.*

★ St. Peter's, Their Majesties Chappell

RELIGIOUS SITE | Because parts of this whitewashed stone church date back to 1620, it holds the distinction of being the oldest continuously operating Anglican church in the Western Hemisphere. Befitting its age, St. Peter's has many treasures. The red cedar altar, carved in 1615 under the supervision of Richard Moore (a shipwright and the colony's first governor) is the oldest piece of wood-work in Bermuda. The late 18th-century bishop's throne is believed to have been salvaged from a shipwreck, and the bap-tismal font, brought to the island by early settlers, is an estimated 900 years old. There's also a fine collection of Commun-ion silver from the 1600s in the vestry. Nevertheless, it's the building itself that leaves the most lasting impression. With rough-hewn pillars, exposed cedar beams, and candlelit chandeliers, the church is stunning in its simplicity.

After viewing the interior, walk into the churchyard to see where prominent Ber-mudians, including Governor Sir Richard Sharples who was assassinated in 1973, are buried. A separate graveyard for slaves and free blacks (to the west of the church, behind the wall) is a reminder of Bermuda's segregated past. ⊠ *33 Duke of York St., St. George's* ☎ *441/297–2459* ⊕ *www.stpeters.bm* ✉ *$2 donation* ⊗ *Closed Sun., except for worship.*

Tucker House

MUSEUM | Owned and lovingly maintained as a museum by the Bermuda National Trust, Tucker House was built in the 1750s for a merchant who stored his wares in the cellar (a space that now holds an archaeological exhibit). But it's been associated with the Tucker family ever since Henry Tucker purchased it in 1775. The house is essentially a tribute to this well-connected clan whose

members included a Bermudian gover-nor, a U.S. treasurer, a Confederate navy captain, and an Episcopal bishop.

The kitchen, however, is dedicated to another notable—Joseph Hayne Rainey—who is thought to have operated a barber's shop in it during the Civil War. (Barber's Alley, around the corner, is also named in his honor.) As a freed slave from South Carolina, Rainey fled to Bermuda at the outbreak of the war. Afterward he returned to the United States and, in 1870, became the first black man to be elected to the House of Representatives. A short flight of stairs leads down to the kitchen, originally a separate building, and to an enclosed kitchen garden. ⊠ *5 Water St., St. George's* ☎ *441/297–0545* ⊕ *www. bnt.bm* ✉ *$5; $10 combination ticket includes admission to Bermuda National Trust Museum at the Globe Hotel and Verdmont (in Smith's Parish)* ⊗ *Closed Sun.–Tues.*

ELSEWHERE ON THE ISLAND

★ Bermuda Aquarium, Museum & Zoo (BAMZ)

ZOO | FAMILY | Established in 1926, the Bermuda Aquarium, Museum & Zoo (BAMZ for short) is one of Bermuda's top attractions, with harbor seals, flocks of flamingos, exhibits on local animals and marine life, and a coastal walkway with stunning water views. In the aquarium the big draw is the North Rock Exhibit, a 140,000-gallon tank that gives you a diver's-eye view of the area's living coral reefs (one of the largest living coral collections in the world) and the colorful marine life it sustains. The museum section has multimedia and interactive displays focusing on native habitats and the impact humans have on them. The island-themed zoo displays more than 300 birds, reptiles, and mammals. Don't miss the Islands of Australasia exhibit with its lemurs, wallabies, and tree kangaroos, or Islands of the Caribbean, a walk-through enclosure that gets you within arm's length of ibises and golden lion tamarins (a type of monkey). Other popular areas include an outdoor seal pool, tidal touch tank, and cool kid-friendly Discovery Room. Take a break at Beastro (part of the popular Buzz café chain), on the zoo grounds, for good food and great views. ⊠ *40 North Shore Rd., Flatt's Village* ☎ *441/293–2727* ⊕ *www. bamz.org* ☞ *$10.*

★ Crystal and Fantasy Caves

NATURE SITE | As far back as 1623, Captain John Smith (of Pocahontas fame) commented on the "vary strange, darke, and cumbersome" caverns that today are a popular attraction. Nevertheless, it came as a surprise when two boys, attempting to retrieve a lost ball, discovered Crystal Cave in 1907. The hole through which the boys descended is still visible. Inside, tour guides will lead you across a pontoon bridge that spans a 55-foot-deep subterranean lake. Look up to see stalactites dripping from the ceiling or down through the perfectly clear water to see stalagmites rising from the cave floor. Amateur spelunkers can also journey through geologic time at Crystal's smaller sister cave, Fantasy. Set aside 30 minutes to see one cave; 75 minutes if you plan to take in both. ■ **TIP**→ **More than a few people have lost important items to the depths of the caves by accidentally dropping them over the edge. Keep items tucked away safely.** ⊠ *8 Crystal Caves Rd.* ⊹ *Off Wilkinson Ave.* ☎ *441/293–0640* ⊕ *www. caves.bm* ☞ *One cave $24; combination ticket $35* Ⓜ *Bus 1, 3, 10, or 11.*

Gibbs Hill Lighthouse

LIGHTHOUSE | **FAMILY** | Designed in London and opened in 1846, this cast-iron lighthouse soars above Southampton Parish, stands 117 feet high and 362 feet above the sea, and offers a 185-step climb to the top for panoramic island views. The light was originally produced by a concentrated burner of four large, circular wicks. Today the beam from the 1,000-watt bulb can be seen by ships 40 miles out to sea and by planes 120 miles away at 10,000 feet. The haul up the spiral stairs is an arduous one—particularly if you dislike heights or tight spaces. But en route to the top you can stop to catch your breath on eight landings, where photographs and drawings of the lighthouse help divert attention from your aching appendages. Once you take in the views up top and return to solid ground, stop in at the Dining Room for refreshments. ⊠ *68 St. Anne's Rd.* ☎ *441/238–8069* ⊕ *www.bermudalighthouse.com* ☞ *$2.50* ⊘ *Closed Feb.*

★ National Museum of Bermuda

MUSEUM | **FAMILY** | Ensconced in Bermuda's largest fort, the museum displays its collections of maritime and historical artifacts in old munitions warehouses that surround the parade grounds and Keep Pond at the Dockyard. Insulated from the rest of the Dockyard by a moat and massive stone ramparts, it is entered by way of a drawbridge. At the Shifting House, right inside the entrance, rooms hold relics from some of the 350-odd ships wrecked on the island's reefs. Other buildings are devoted to seafaring pursuits such as whaling, shipbuilding, and yacht racing.

More displays are in the 19th-century Commissioner's House, on the museum's upper grounds. Built as both home and headquarters for the Dockyard commissioner, the house served as a World War I barracks and was used for military intelligence during World War II. Today it contains exhibits on Bermuda's social and military history. A must-see is the Hall of History, a mural of Bermuda's history covering 1,000 square feet. Painting it took local artist Graham Foster more than 3½ years. You'll also want to photograph the sheep that graze outside the building, mowing the grass. Mind your feet! They're very good at their work. ⊠ *The Keep, Maritime La., Dockyard* ☎ *441/234–1418* ⊕ *www.nmb.*

4

Ports of Call **BERMUDA**

bm 🎫 *$15; includes admission to Dolphin Quest Bermuda.*

Paget Marsh Nature Reserve

NATURE PRESERVE | Along with some of the last remaining stands of native Bermuda palmetto and cedar, this 25-acre reserve—virtually untouched since presettlement times and jointly owned and preserved by the Bermuda National Trust and the Bermuda Audubon Society—contains a mangrove forest and grassy savanna. These unspoiled habitats can be explored via a boardwalk with interpretive signs describing the endemic flora and fauna. When lost in the cries of the native and migratory birds that frequent this natural wetland, you can quickly forget that bustling Hamilton is just minutes away. ✉ *Lovers La., off South Rd.* ☎ *441/236–6483* ⊕ *www.bnt. bm* 🎫 *Free* Ⓜ *Bus 2, 7, or 8.*

Verdmont Historic House and Gardens

HOUSE | **FAMILY** | Opened as a museum in 1956, this National Trust property is notable for its Georgian architecture, but what really sets this place apart is its pristine condition. Though the house was used as a residence until the mid-20th century, virtually no structural changes were made to Verdmont since it was erected around 1710. Former owners never even added electricity or plumbing (so the "powder room" was strictly used for powdering wigs).

The house is also known for its enviable collection of antiques. Some pieces—such as the early-19th-century piano—were imported from England. Most are 18th-century cedar, however, crafted by Bermudian cabinetmakers. Among the most interesting artifacts are the pint-size furnishings and period toys that fill Verdmont's upstairs nursery. A china coffee service, said to have been a gift from Napoléon to U.S. President James Madison, is also on display. The president never received it, though, since the ship bearing it was seized by a privateer and brought to Bermuda. Verdmont also

has its share of resident ghosts: among them, an adolescent girl who died of typhoid there in 1844. ✉ *6 Verdmont La.* ⊹ *Off Collector's Hill* ☎ *441/236–7369* ⊕ *www.bnt.bm* 🎫 *$5; $10 combination ticket with Bermuda National Trust Museum in Globe Hotel and Tucker House* ☉ *Closed Thurs. and Sat.–Tues.*

🏖 Beaches

Elbow Beach

BEACH—SIGHT | **FAMILY** | Swimming and bodysurfing are great at this beach, which is bordered by the prime strand of sand reserved for guests of the Elbow Beach hotel on the left, and the ultraexclusive Coral Beach Club beach area on the right. It's a pleasant setting for a late-evening stroll, with the lights from nearby hotels dancing on the water. If you're planning a daytime visit during summer months, arrive early to claim your spot as this popular beach is often crowded. In addition to sunbathers and joggers, groups of locals gather here to play football and volleyball. Protective coral reefs make the waters some of the safest on the island and a good choice for families. It's possible to rent chairs, umbrellas, and other gear from the hotel-owned beach facility, but it can be quite expensive. A lunch wagon sometimes sells fast food and cold drinks during the day, and Mickey's Beach Bar (part of the Elbow Beach hotel) is open for lunch and dinner, though reservations are useful. **Amenities:** parking (free); water sports. **Best for:** snorkeling; swimming; walking. ✉ *Elbow Beach, Off South Shore Rd.* 🎫 *Free* Ⓜ *Bus 2 or 7 from Hamilton.*

★ Horseshoe Bay

BEACH—SIGHT | **FAMILY** | When locals say they're going to "the beach," they're generally referring to Horseshoe Bay, the island's most popular. With clear water, a 0.3-mile (0.5-km) crescent of pink sand, a vibrant social scene, and the uncluttered backdrop of South Shore Park, Horseshoe Bay has everything you could ask of a Bermudian beach. An on-site bar and restaurant, changing rooms, beach-rental facilities, and lifeguards add to its appeal. The Annual Bermuda Sand Castle Competition also takes place here.

The undertow can be strong, especially on the main beach. A better place for children is **Horseshoe Baby Beach,** at the western end of Horseshoe Bay. Sheltered from the ocean by a ring of rocks, this cove is shallow and almost perfectly calm. In summer, toddlers can find lots of playmates. **Amenities:** food and drink; lifeguards; parking (free); showers; toilets. **Best for:** partiers; swimming; walking. ✉ Off South Shore Rd. ⧉ Free Ⓜ Bus 7 from Hamilton.

Tobacco Bay

BEACH—SIGHT | The most popular beach near St. George's, this small north-shore strand with ample parking is huddled in a coral cove surrounded by rock formations. Its beach house serves burgers and salads as well as specialty cocktails. Equipment rentals including umbrellas, chairs, floaties, and snorkel sets. It's a 10-minute hike from the bus stop in the town of St. George's, or you can flag down a taxi. In high season the beach is busy, especially midweek, when the cruise ships are docked; check the website for information on Friday-night events, bonfires, and live music. **Amenities:** food and drink; parking (free); toilets; water sports. **Best for:** snorkeling; swimming. ✉ 9 Coot's Pond Rd., St. George's ⧉ Off Barry Rd. ☎ 441/297–2756 main ⊕ www.tobaccobay.bm ⧉ Free Ⓜ Bus 10 or 11 from Hamilton.

 **Restaurants**

The Docksider Pub & Restaurant

$ | **BRITISH** | Whether it's high noon, happy hour, or late Saturday night, locals love to mingle at this sprawling Front Street sports bar. Classic pub fare with a Bermudian twist—think nachos with homemade chili, barbecue chicken leg with peas 'n' rice, and fish-and-chips—pairs perfectly with the impressive variety of beers, ciders, and spirits. Join the English Premier League Football fans that gather en masse to watch their favorite teams or sip your dessert—a Dark 'n' Stormy—out on the porch as you watch Bermuda stroll by. **Known for:** passionate sports fans; crowded nightlife drinking scene; weekend brunch. ⑤ Average main: $19 ✉ 121 Front St., Hamilton ☎ 441/296–3333 ⊕ www.docksider.bm.

Frog & Onion Pub

$$ | **BRITISH** | **FAMILY** | Housed in the former Royal Naval Dockyard warehouse, this nautical-themed restaurant is loved locally for its good, satisfying food, craft beers, and lively atmosphere. The menu caters to every palate and includes juicy burgers, hearty house-made pub pies, and a selection of fresh local fish plates. **Known for:** lively spot with games area in back; flights of local Bermuda beers; music in summer. ⑤ Average main: $21 ✉ The Cooperage, 4 Freeport Rd., Dockyard ☎ 441/234–2900 ⊕ www.irg.bm/frog-and-onion.

🛍 Shopping

Hamilton has the greatest concentration of shops in Bermuda, and Front Street is its pièce de résistance. Lined with small pastel-color buildings, this most fashionable of Bermuda's streets houses sedate department stores and snazzy boutiques, with several small arcades and shopping alleys leading off it. A smart canopy shades the entrance to the 55 Front Street Group, which houses Crisson Jewelers. Modern Butterfield Place has galleries and boutiques selling, among other things, Longchamp leather goods. The Emporium, a renovated building with an atrium, has a range of shops, from antiques to souvenirs.

St. George's Water Street, Duke of York Street, Hunters Wharf, Penno's Wharf, and Somers Wharf are the sites of numerous renovated buildings that house branches of Front Street stores, as well as artisans' studios. Historic King's Square offers little more than a couple of T-shirt and souvenir shops.

In the West End, **Somerset Village** has a few shops, but they hardly merit a special shopping trip. However, the **Clocktower Mall,** in a historic building at the Royal Naval Dockyard, has a few more shopping opportunities, including branches of Front Street shops and specialty boutiques. The Dockyard is also home to the Craft Market, the Bermuda Arts Centre, and Bermuda Clayworks.

 Activities

BICYCLING
The best and sometimes only way to explore Bermuda's nooks and crannies— its little hidden coves and 18th-century tribe roads—is by bicycle or motor scooter. A popular option for biking in Bermuda is the **Railway Trail,** a dedicated cycle path blissfully free of cars. Running intermittently the length of the old Bermuda Railway ("old Rattle 'n' Shake"), this trail is scenic and restricted to pedestrian and bicycle traffic. You can ask the staff at any bike-rental shop for advice on where to access the trail.

Oleander Cycles
BICYCLING | The agency is known primarily for its selection of motorbikes and scooters for rent and sale, although bicycles, as well as electric powered two-seaters, are also available to rent. Single and double bikes are available, and a damage waiver is charged. Oleander Cycles' main store is in Paget, but its Southampton location is convenient for The Reefs Resort & Club guests since it's right across the street. ⊠ *6 Valley Rd.* ⊹ *Off Middle Rd.* ☎ *441/236–5235* ⊕ *www.oleandercycles. bm* ✉ *From $41 for 2 hours.*

GOLF
Golf courses make up nearly 17% of the island's 21.6 square miles. The scenery on the courses is usually spectacular, with flowering trees and shrubs decked out in multicolor blossoms against a backdrop of brilliant blue sea and sky. The layouts are remarkably challenging, thanks to capricious ocean breezes, daunting natural terrain, and the clever work of world-class golf architects.

Mid Ocean Club
GOLF | The elite Mid Ocean Club is a 1921 Charles Blair Macdonald design revamped in 1953 by Robert Trent Jones Sr. *Golf Digest* ranks it among the top 100 courses outside the United States. The club has a genteel air and a great sense of history. Even though it's expensive, a round of play is worthwhile, as you walk with a caddy to savor the traditional golf experience and the scenery. There are many holes near ocean cliffs, but you'll want to linger on the back tee of the last hole, where the view up the coast is spectacular. Overlooking the 18th hole and the south shore, the Mid Ocean's pink clubhouse is classically Bermudian down to the interior cedar trim. The pro shop offers a range of golfing goodies. The Clubhouse is open to visitors for breakfast, lunch, dinner, or drinks before or after their round of golf. Nonmembers can play midweek; be sure to reserve your tee time early as the calendar books up months in advance. Caddies, club rentals, and shoe rentals are all available. ⊠ *1 Mid Ocean Dr., Tucker's Town* ⊹ *Off South Shore Rd.* ☎ *441/293–1215* ⊕ *www.themidocean-club.com* ✉ *$275 for nonmembers ($32 for cart); $65 for caddy* ⅃ *18 holes, 6548 yards, par 71.*

Turtle Hill Golf Club
GOLF | Spreading across the hillside below the high-rise Fairmont Southampton, this executive golf course is known for its steep terrain, giving players who opt to walk (for sunset tee times only) an

excellent workout. The Ted Robinson design is a good warm-up for Bermuda's full-length courses, offering a legitimate test of wind and bunker play. The front nine has almost constant views of the ocean and is more difficult than the back nine, with tight holes calling for careful club selection. Club rentals and lessons are also available. Because the hotel and its restaurants are so close, there's no golf clubhouse per se, just a 10th-hole Golf Hut for snacks and drinks. ⊠ *Fairmont Southampton , 101 South Shore Rd.* ☎ *441/239–6952* ⊕ *www.fairmont. com/southampton-bermuda* 🖃 *$99 before noon (with cart), $69 after 12 pm (with cart), $45 sunset (walking)* 🏌 *18 holes, 2684 yards, par 54.*

SNORKELING

Snorkeling cruises are generally offered from April through September. Smaller boats, which limit capacity to 10 to 16 passengers, offer more personal attention and focus more on the beautiful snorkeling areas themselves. Guides on such tours often relate interesting historical and ecological information about the island. Some larger boats take up to 40 passengers.

★ Captain Kirk's Coral Reef Adventures

SNORKELING | Pick your adventure with Captain Kirk's Coral Reef Adventures, but regardless of which option you want, prepare for memorable hours with a wide option of boats and tours. Depending on the weather, you can choose to stop at two of three exciting locations: a shipwreck, a secluded island beach, or one of Bermuda's beautiful coral reefs. Or book a day out fishing on the *Jolly Roger*. Snorkeling equipment, masks, and vests are provided; plus you can peer into the turquoise waters right through the glass bottom of some of the boats. The 31-foot *Pisces* holds up to 20 people and departs from Dockyard. ⊠ *Royal Naval Dockyard, North Arm, Dockyard* ☎ *441/236–1300* ⊕ *www.kirksadventures.com* 🖃 *From $50.*

Bonaire (Kralendijk)

Starkly beautiful Bonaire is the consummate desert island. Surrounded by pristine waters, it is a haven for divers and snorkelers, who flock here from around the world to take advantage of the excellent visibility, easily accessed reefs, and bountiful marine life. Bonaire is the most rustic of the three "ABC islands" (along with Aruba and Curaçao), and despite its dependence on tourism, it manages to maintain its identity and simple way of life. There are many good restaurants, most of which are within walking distance of the port. Most of the island's 14,000-some inhabitants live in and around Kralendijk, which must certainly qualify as one of the cutest and most compact capitals in the Caribbean. The best shopping is to be found along the very short stretch of road that constitutes "downtown." Bonaire's beaches tend to be small and rocky, but there is a nice stretch of sandy beach at Lac Bay. It is entirely possible to see almost all of the sights and sounds of the island in one day by taking one of the island tours on offer.

ESSENTIALS
CURRENCY
U.S. dollar.

TELEPHONE
The country code for Bonaire is 599; 717 is the exchange for every four-digit number on the island. Digicel and CHIPPIE are the service providers. GSM (900, 1800 and 1900 bands) phones work in Bonaire.

COMING ASHORE
One of the great benefits of Bonaire to cruise passengers is that the port is right in downtown Kralendijk. A four-minute walk takes you to most of the best shopping and restaurants on the island.

Bonaire lives for tourism; upon the arrival of a cruise ship, the locals are ready, and an impromptu crafts market springs up in

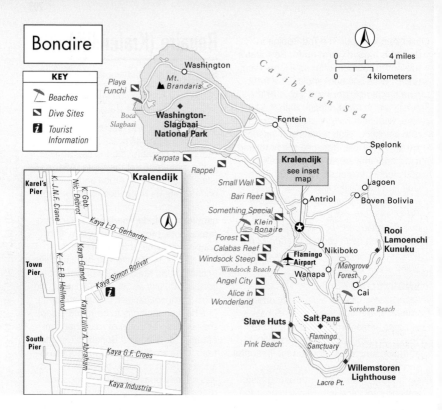

Bonaire

KEY

- Beaches
- Dive Sites
- Tourist Information

Washington

Playa Funchi

Mt. Brandaris

Boca Slagbaai

Washington-Slagbaai National Park

Fontein

Karpata

Rappel

Kralendijk see inset map

Spelonk

Caribbean Sea

0 — 4 miles
0 — 4 kilometers

Small Wall

Bari Reef

Antriol

Lagoen

Boven Bolivia

Something Special

Klein Bonaire

Forest

Calabas Reef

Windsock Steep

Windsock Beach

Angel City

Alice in Wonderland

Nikiboko

Flamingo Airport

Wanapa

Mangrove Forest

Rooi Lamoenchi Kunuku

Cai

Sorobon Beach

Slave Huts

Pink Beach

Salt Pans

Flamingo Sanctuary

Willemstoren Lighthouse

Lacre Pt.

Kralendijk

Karel's Pier

K. J.N.F. Crane

Nic. Debrot

K. Gob.

Kaya L.D. Gerhardts

Town Pier

Kaya Grandi

K. C.E.B. Hellmund

Kaya Lullio A. Abraham

Kaya Simon Bolivar

South Pier

Kaya G.F. Croes

Kaya Industria

the park across from the port entrance. Taxis wait right at the port and operate on fixed government rates. All the sights of Kralendijk are within easy walking distance, and a taxi ride to one of the larger resorts on the island will run between $10 and $17. Drivers will conduct half-day tours; they charge about $28 per hour for up to four passengers. Fares increase by 50% between midnight and 6 am, but few cruise ships stay overnight.

Sights

Two routes—one north and one south from Kralendijk, the island's small capital—are possible on the 24-mile-long (39-km-long) island; either route will take from a few hours to a full day, depending on whether you stop to snorkel, swim, dive, or lounge. Those pressed for time will find that it's easy to explore the entire island in a day if stops are kept to a minimum.

KRALENDIJK

Bonaire's small, tidy capital city (population 3,000) is five minutes from the airport. The main drag, J. A. Abraham Boulevard, turns into **Kaya Grandi** in the center of town. Along it are most of the island's major stores, boutiques, and restaurants. Across Kaya Grandi, opposite Littman's jewelry store, is Kaya L. D. Gerharts, with several small supermarkets, a handful of snack shops, and some of the better restaurants. Walk down the narrow waterfront avenue called Kaya C.E.B. Hellmund, which leads straight to the **North and South piers.** In the center of town, the Harbourside Mall has chic boutiques. Along this route is **Ft. Oranje,** with its cannons. From December through April, cruise ships dock in the harbor once or twice a week. The diminutive ocher-and-white structure that looks like a tiny Greek temple is the produce market, where one can find plenty of fresh produce brought over from Venezuela. Pick up the brochure *Walking and Shopping in Kralendijk* from the tourist office to get a map and complete list of all the monuments and sights in the town.

SOUTH BONAIRE

The trail south from Kralendijk is chock-full of icons, both natural and man-made, that reveal part of Bonaire's history. Rent a vehicle and head out along the Southern Scenic Route. The roads wind through dramatic desert terrain, full of organ-pipe cacti and spiny-trunk mangroves—huge stumps of saltwater trees that rise from the marshes like witches. Watch for wild goats, wild donkeys, and lizards of all sizes.

★ Rooi Lamoenchi Kunuku

MUSEUM VILLAGE | FAMILY | Owner Ellen Herrera restored her family's homestead north of Lac Bay, in the Bonairean *kadushi* (cactus) wilderness, to educate tourists and residents about the history and tradition of authentic kunuku living and to show unspoiled terrain in two daily tours. Although the site is open daily from 3:30 to 6:30, you must make an appointment in advance. Expect visits to take a couple of hours. ⊠ *Kaya Suiza 23* ☎ *599/717–8489* 💲 *$21.*

Salt Pans

FACTORY | Rising like mountains of snow, the salt pans are hard to miss. Harvested once a year, the "ponds" are owned by Cargill, Inc., which has reactivated the 19th-century salt industry with great success (one reason for that success is that the ocean on this part of the island is higher than the land, which makes irrigation a snap). Keep a lookout for the three 30-foot obelisks (white, blue, and red) that were used to guide the trade boats coming to pick up the salt. Look also in the distance across the pans to the abandoned solar saltworks that's now a

Best Bets 👁

- **Diving.** Bonaire is one of the world's top diving destinations. Shore diving is especially good.

- **Snorkeling.** With reefs close to shore, there's good snorkeling right off the beach.

- **Flamingo spotting.** These shy, graceful birds are one of Bonaire's scenic delights.

- **Kralendijk.** The accessible town has a nice assortment of restaurants and stores.

- **Washington Slagbaai National Park.** Bonaire's best land-based sight is this well-preserved national park.

designated flamingo sanctuary. With the naked eye you might be able to make out a pink-orange haze just on the horizon; with binoculars you will see a sea of bobbing pink bodies. The sanctuary is completely protected, and no entrance is allowed (flamingos are extremely sensitive to disturbances of any kind). ⊠ *South Bonaire.*

Slave Huts

ARCHAEOLOGICAL SITE | The salt industry's history is revealed in Rode Pan, the site of two groups of tiny slave huts. The white huts are on the right side of the road, opposite the salt flats; the second grouping, called the red slave huts, stretches across the road toward the island's southern tip. During the 19th century, slaves worked the salt pans by day and slept in the cramped huts. Each Friday afternoon they walked many hours to Rincon to weekend with their families, returning each Sunday. The Red Slave area is a popular dive spot during low wind and calm seas. When the wind is strong and waves prevail, the local

Washington Sagbaai National Park was once a working plantation.

windsurf posse heads to Red Slave to catch the swell. ⊠ *South Bonaire.*

Willemstoren Lighthouse

LIGHTHOUSE | Bonaire's first lighthouse was built in 1837 and is now automated (but closed to visitors). Take some time to explore the beach and notice how the waves, driven by the trade winds, play a crashing symphony against the rocks. Locals stop here to collect pieces of driftwood in spectacular shapes and to build fanciful pyramids from objects that have washed ashore. ⊠ *South Bonaire.*

NORTH BONAIRE

The Northern Scenic Route takes you into the heart of Bonaire's natural wonders—desert gardens of towering cacti (*kadushi*, used to prepare soup, and the thornier *yatu*, used to build cactus fencing), tiny coastal coves, and plenty of fantastic panoramas. The road also weaves between eroded pink-and-black limestone walls and eerie rock formations with fanciful names such as the Devil's Mouth and Iguana Head (you'll need a vivid imagination and sharp eye

to recognize them). Brazil trees growing along the route were used by Indians to make dye (pressed from a red ring in the trunk). Inscriptions still visible in several island caves were made with this dye.

A snappy excursion with the requisite photo stops will take about 2½ hours, but if you pack your swimsuit and a hefty picnic basket (forget about finding fast food), you could spend the entire day exploring this northern sector. Head out from Kralendijk on Kaya Gobernador N. Debrot until it turns into the Northern Scenic Route. Once you pass the Radio Nederland towers, you cannot turn back to Kralendijk. The narrow road becomes one-way until you get to Landhuis Karpata, and you have to follow the cross-island road to Rincon and return via the main road through the center of the island.

★ Washington Slagbaai National Park

NATIONAL/STATE PARK | **FAMILY** | Once a plantation producing divi-divi trees (the pods were used for tanning animal skins), aloe (used for medicinal lotions), charcoal, and goats, the park is now a model of conservation. It's easy to tour the 13,500-acre tropical desert terrain on the dirt roads with a jeep, but think twice about coming here if it has rained recently—the mud you may encounter will be more than inconvenient. If you're planning to hike, bring everything you may need. Goats and donkeys may dart across the road, and if you keep your eyes peeled, you may catch sight of large iguanas camouflaged in the shrubbery. Right inside the park's gate, flamingos roost on the salt pad known as Salina Mathijs, and exotic parakeets congregate at the base of 784-foot Mt. Brandaris, Bonaire's highest peak. Some 130 species of birds fly in and out of the shrubbery in the park. Swimming, snorkeling, and scuba diving are permitted, but you're asked not to frighten the animals or remove anything from the grounds. To enter, you'll need a photo ID and proof that you've paid the Bonaire National Parks Foundation's annual Nature Fee. ✉ *Washington Slagbaai National Park* ☎ *599/ 717–8444* ⊕ *stinapabonaire.org/ washington-slagbaai* ✉ *Annual Nature Fee proof of purchase ($25 nondivers, $45 divers).*

☺ Beaches

Although most of Bonaire's charms are underwater, there are a few beautiful beaches. Don't expect long strands of white sand, but many dive and snorkel sites have suitable entries for swimmers. Bonaire's pristine water and protected reefs offer stunning settings for sunrise or sunset viewing. Several hotels have lovely beaches that are accessible for nonguests for a nominal entrance fee. Before heading to the beach and entering the waters, be sure to pay the Bonaire National Parks Foundation's requisite Nature Fee ($25 nondivers, $45 divers). It's good for a year and can be paid at dive shops, hotels, tour operators, and the tourism office; save the receipt,

which will also allow access to Washington–Slagbaai National Park.

Klein Bonaire

BEACH—SIGHT | FAMILY | Just a water-taxi hop across from Kralendijk, this little island offers picture-perfect white-sand beaches. Klein Bonaire is one of Bonaire's most popular snorkel spots. Local boat tours frequent the island in hopes of spotting turtles. The area is protected, so absolutely no development has been allowed. Make sure to pack everything before heading to the island, including water and an umbrella to hide under because there are no refreshment stands or changing facilities, and there's almost no shade to be found. Boats leave from the Pier, across from It Rains Fishes, and the round-trip water-taxi ride costs roughly $15 per person. **Amenities:** none. **Best for:** snorkeling; solitude; swimming. ⊕ *www.watertaxikleinbonaire.com.*

Sorobon Beach

BEACH—SIGHT | FAMILY | One of Bonaire's most beautiful beaches is also *the* place to windsurf. The sand is powdery white, and the gin-clear water is shallow, allowing swimmers to walk up to the reef on a calm-breeze day. You can also rent a stand-up paddleboard (SUP) and cruise the shallows looking for turtles; the snorkeling here is amazing, too. Keep in mind, though, that all sea life is protected, so no touching or removing shells or creatures. On-site windsurf shops offer equipment and lessons. Two restaurants offer diverse menus, including tropical drinks. The public beach area near the marina has restrooms and huts for shade. **Amenities:** food and drink; parking; showers; toilets; water sports. **Best for:** snorkeling; paddleboarding; windsurfing. ✉ *Kaya IR. Randolph Statius van Eps, Sorobon Beach, Sorobon* ✛ *Take E.E.G. Blvd. south from Kralendijk to Kaya IR. Randolph Statius van Eps, and then follow this route straight on to Sorobon Beach.*

Windsock Beach

BEACH—SIGHT | Near the airport (just off E.E.G. Boulevard), this pretty little spot looks out toward the north side of the island and has about 200 yards of white sand along a rocky shoreline. It's a popular dive and snorkel site, and swimming conditions are good. ■**TIP→** **There is often a food truck parked next door at Te Amo Beach, another great snorkeling beach.** **Amenities:** none. **Best for:** snorkeling; swimming. ⊠ *Off E.E.G. Blvd., near Flamingo Airport* ☞ *Kite City Food Truck is on-site serving delectable culinary delights.*

 ## Restaurants

Boudoir

$ | **ECLECTIC** | An excellent patio eatery at the Royal Palm Mall offers a range of soups, salads, sandwiches, and burgers that should please even the most discerning diners. **Known for:** great sandwiches; casual eatery with good quality fare; avocado specialties. ⑤ *Average main: $9* ⊠ *Royal Palm Mall, Kaya Grandi 26 F/G, Kralendijk* ☎ *599/717–4321* ⊕ *www.bonaireboudoir.com.*

★ Hang Out Beach Bar

$ | **CARIBBEAN | FAMILY** | Overlooking Lac Bay, the training ground for the famous Bonaire Windsurf Team, Hang Out Beach Bar offers libations and tasty delights including fresh homemade smoothies and healthy and delicious salads and sandwiches. There's also always a daily special—usually fresh-caught fish. **Known for:** great sangria and signature cocktails; Thursday-night barbecue and Friday-night tapas; special live music evenings with local and international talent. ⑤ *Average main: $10* ⊠ *Kaminda Sorobon 12, Kralendijk* ☎ *599/717–5064* ⊕ *www.hangoutbeachbar.com.*

🛍 Shopping

You can get to know all the shops in Kralendijk in an hour or so. Almost all the shops are on Kaya Grandi and adjacent streets and in tiny malls. Harbourside Mall is a pleasant, open-air mall with several fine air-conditioned shops. ■**TIP→** **Don't take home items made from tortoiseshell; they aren't allowed into the United States. Remember, too, that it's forbidden to take sea fans, coral, conch shells, and all other forms of marine life off the island.**

JanArt Gallery

ART GALLERIES | On the main drag in town, JanArt Gallery sells unique paintings, prints, and art supplies; artist-owner Janice Huckaby has been on the island for more than two decades and has painted more than 1,000 original paintings of Bonaire. She also conducts art classes. ⊠ *Kaya Grandi 14, Kralendijk* ☎ *599/717–0955* ⊕ *www.janartbonaire.com.*

★ Littman's

JEWELRY/ACCESSORIES | Owner Steven Littman handpicks many of the items available in this upscale jewelry and gift shop, in business since 1981, during his regular trips to Europe. Look for Rolex, Omega, Cartier, and Tag Heuer watches; fine gold jewelry; antique coins; nautical sculptures; resort clothing; and accessories. Typical savings are about 15% off U.S. prices. There's a second location in the Harbourside Mall. ⊠ *Kaya Grandi 33, Kralendijk* ☎ *599/717–7750* ⊕ *www.littmanjewelers.com.*

🚴 Activities

BIKING

Bonaire is generally flat, so bicycles are an easy way to get around if you are physically fit. Because of the heat, it's essential to carry water if you're planning to cycle for any distance and especially if your plans involve exploring the deserted interior. There are more than 180 miles

(290 km) of unpaved routes (as well as the many paved roads) on the island.

Tropical Travel

BICYCLING | This tour operator offers bikes for $11 per day or $55 per week (a $300 deposit is required). ⊠ *Plaza Resort Bonaire, J. A. Abraham Blvd. 80, Kralendijk* ☎ *599/701–1232* ⊕ *www.tropicaltravel-bonaire.com.*

DIVING AND SNORKELING

Bonaire has some of the best reef diving this side of Australia's Great Barrier Reef. It takes only 5 to 25 minutes to reach many sites; the current is usually mild; and although some reefs have sudden, steep drops, most begin just offshore and slope gently downward at a 45-degree angle. General visibility runs 60 to 100 feet. You can see several varieties of coral: knobby-brain, giant-brain, elkhorn, staghorn, mountainous star, gorgonian, and black. You can also encounter schools of parrot fish, surgeonfish, angelfish, eel, snapper, and grouper. Shore diving is excellent just about everywhere on the leeward side. There are sites suitable for every skill level; they're clearly marked by yellow stones on the roadside.

The best snorkeling spots are on the island's leeward side, where you have shore access to the reefs, and along the west side of Klein Bonaire, where the reef is better developed. All snorkelers and swimmers must pay a $25 Nature Fee, which allows access to the waters around the island and Washington Slagbaai National Park for one calendar year. The fee can be paid at most dive shops.

DIVE OPERATORS

Many of the dive shops listed *below* offer PADI and NAUI certification courses and SSI, as well as underwater photography and videography courses. Some shops are also qualified to certify dive instructors. Full certification courses cost approximately $385; open-water refresher courses run about $240; a one-tank

boat dive with unlimited shore diving costs about $40; a two-tank boat dive with unlimited shore diving is about $65. As for equipment, renting a mask, fin, and snorkel costs about $12 altogether; for a buoyancy compensator (BC) and regulator, expect to pay about $20.

Most dive shops on Bonaire offer a complete range of snorkel gear for rent and will provide beginner training; some dive operations also offer guided snorkeling and night snorkeling. The cost for a guided snorkel session is about $50 and includes slide presentations, transportation to the site, and a tour. Gear rental is approximately $10 per 24-hour period.

Wannadive

SCUBA DIVING | Wannadive is a casual, efficient dive company with two island locations. In addition to working with divers of all skill levels and interests—beginner to professional, recreational to technical—they have a large inventory of rental dive and snorkel equipment, offer repair services, and run daily boat-dive trips to Klein Bonaire. ⊠ *Kaya Gobernador N. Debrot 73, Kralendijk* ☎ *599/717–8884* ⊕ *www.wannadive.com.*

Calica (Playa del Carmen), Mexico

Just minutes away from Calica, Playa del Carmen has become one of Mexico's fastest-growing communities, with a pace almost as hectic as Cancún's. Hotels, restaurants, and shops multiply here faster than you can say "Kukulcán." Some are branches of Cancún establishments whose owners have taken up permanent residence in Playa, while others are owned by American and European expats (predominately Italians) who came here years ago. It makes for a varied, international community. Avenida 5, the first street in town parallel to the beach, is a long pedestrian walkway with shops, cafés, and street performers; small hotels and stores stretch north from this avenue. Avenida Juárez, running east–west from the highway to the beach, is the main commercial zone for the Riviera Maya corridor. Here locals visit the food shops, pharmacies, hardware stores, and banks that line the curbs. People traveling the coast by car usually stop here to stock up on supplies—its banks, grocery stores, and gas stations are the last ones until Tulum.

ESSENTIALS
CURRENCY
The Mexican peso. U.S. dollars and credit cards are widely accepted in the area, from the port to Playa del Carmen, but it's best to have pesos (and small bills) when you visit ruins, where cashiers often run out of change.

TELEPHONE
Most pay phones accept prepaid Ladatel cards, sold in 30-, 50-, or 100-peso denominations. To use the card, insert it in the pay phone's slot, dial 001 (for calls to the United States) or 01 (for calls within Mexico), followed by the area code and number. Credit is deleted from the card as you use it, and the balance is displayed on the small screen on the phone. Most triband mobile phones from the U.S. work in Mexico, though you must pay roaming charges.

COMING ASHORE
The port at Calica, about 3 miles south of the town of Playa del Carmen (between Playa del Carmen and the Xcaret theme park), is small. Sometimes ships actually dock, and other times passengers are tendered to shore. There is a makeshift market at the port, where locals sell crafts. Beyond that, there is not much to do, and you'll need to head into Playa del Carmen proper to find restaurants and even tour operators. If you really want to shop, skip the vendors at the port and head to Playa del Carmen's Avenida 5, where you can easily spend an afternoon browsing shops and enjoying restaurants.

Best Bets

- **A Day at Xcaret.** Particularly for families, this ecological theme park is a great way to spend the day.

- **Beaches.** The beaches in the Riviera Maya are stellar.

- **Diving.** From Playa del Carmen it's only a short hop to some of the Yucatán's best dive sites.

- **Shopping.** Playa del Carmen's Avenida 5 can easily keep you occupied for your day in port if you are a shopaholic.

Taxis and tour buses are available at the port to take you to Playa del Carmen and other destinations, but lines often form as passengers wait for taxis, so plan accordingly if you really want to pack a lot of activity into your day. Your taxi will have you in Playa del Carmen or in Xcaret in under 10 minutes, but you'll pay a whopping $10 for the short trip.

Sights

PLAYA DEL CARMEN
3 miles (5 km) north of Calica

Once upon a time, Playa del Carmen was a fishing village with a ravishing deserted beach. The villagers fished and raised coconut palms to produce copra, and the only foreigners who ventured here were beach bums and travelers catching ferries to Cozumel. That was a long time ago, however. These days the beach is far from deserted, although it is still delightful, with alabaster-white sand and turquoise-blue waters. In fact Playa has become one of Latin America's fastest-growing communities, with a population of more than 135,000 and a pace almost as hectic as Cancún's. The ferry pier, where the hourly boats arrive from and depart for Cozumel, is another

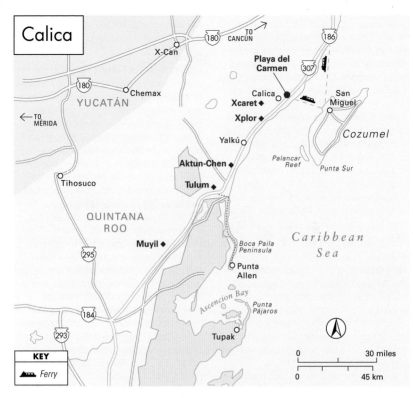

Calica

TO CANCÚN

X-Can

Playa del Carmen

YUCATÁN

Chemax

Calica
Xcaret ◆
Xplor ◆

San
Miguel

TO
MÉRIDA

Yalkú

Cozumel

Aktun-Chen ◆

Palancar
Reef

Punta Sur

Tihosuco

Tulum ◆

QUINTANA
ROO

Muyil ◆

Caribbean
Sea

Boca Paila
Peninsula

Punta
Allen

Ascencion Bay

Punta
Pájaros

Tupak

KEY

Ferry

0   30 miles
0   45 km

busy part of town. The streets leading from the dock have shops, restaurants, cafés, a hotel, and food stands. If you take a stroll north from the pier along the beach, you'll find the serious sun worshippers. On the pier's south side is the sprawling Playacar complex. The development is a labyrinth of residences and all-inclusive resorts bordered by an 18-hole championship golf course.

SOUTH OF CALICA

★ Aktun-Chen (*Indiana Joe's*)

CAVE | FAMILY | The name is Mayan for "the cave with cenotes inside," and these amazing underground caverns— estimated to be about 5 million years old—are the area's largest. You walk through the underground passages, past stalactites and stalagmites, until you reach the cenote with its various shades of deep green. There's also an on-site

canopy tour and one cenote where you can take a swim. ■ **TIP→ This top family attraction isn't as crowded or touristy as Xplor, Xel-Há, and Xcaret.** ✉ *Carretera 307, Km 107, opposite Bahia Principe resort, between Akumal and Xel-Ha, Akumal* ☎ *998/806–4962* ⊕ *www.aktun-chen. com* ✆ *Cave tour MX$500; cenote tour MX$500; canopy tour MX$650.*

Muyil (*Chunyaxché*)

ARCHAEOLOGICAL SITE | This photogenic archaeological site just 15 km (9 miles) down the 307 from Tulum, at the northern end of the Sian Ka'an biosphere reserve, is underrated. Once known as Chunyaxché, it's now called by its ancient name, Muyil (pronounced *moo-HILL*). It dates from the late preclassic era, when it was connected by road to the sea and served as a port between Cobá and the Mayan centers in Belize and Guatemala. The most notable site at Muyil today is the remains of the 56-foot **Castillo**—one of the tallest on the Quintana Roo coast—at the center of a large acropolis. During excavations of the Castillo, jade figurines representing the moon and fertility goddess Ixchel were found. Recent excavations at Muyil have uncovered some smaller structures. The ruins stand near the edge of a deep-blue lagoon and are surrounded by almost impenetrable jungle, so be sure to bring insect repellent. You can drive down a dirt road on the side of the ruins to swim or fish in the lagoon. ⊠ *Carretera 307, 16 km (10 miles) south of Tulum, Sian Ka'an* ⊕ *www.inah.gob.mx* ☎ *MX$40.*

★ Tulum

ARCHAEOLOGICAL SITE | Tulum is one of the few Mayan cities known to have been inhabited when the conquistadores arrived in 1518. In the 16th century it was a trade center, a safe harbor for trade goods from rival Mayan factions who considered the city neutral territory. The city reached its height when its merchants, made wealthy through trading, for the first time outranked Maya priests in authority and power. Although you can see the ruins thoroughly in two hours, you might want to allow extra time for a swim or a stroll on the beach. The largest and most photographed structure, the Castillo (Castle), looms at the edge of a 40-foot limestone cliff just past the Temple of the Frescoes. The front wall of the Castillo has faint carvings of the Descending God and columns depicting the plumed serpent god, Kukulcán, who was introduced to the Maya by the Toltecs. A few small altars sit atop a hill at the north side of the cove, with a good view of the Castillo and the sea.

■**TIP**→ **To avoid the longest lines, be sure to arrive before 11 am. Outside the entrance are dozens of vendors selling Mexican crafts, so bring some extra cash for souvenirs.** ⊠ *Carretera 307, Km 133, Tulum* ☎ *983/837–2411* ☎ *MX$65 entrance;*

MX$54 parking; MX$67 video fee; MX$27 shuttle from parking to ruins.

Xcaret

NATURE PRESERVE | **FAMILY** | Among the most popular attractions are the Paradise River raft tour that takes you on a winding, watery journey through the jungle; the Butterfly Pavilion, where thousands of butterflies float dreamily through a botanical garden while New Age music plays in the background; and an ocean-fed aquarium, where you can see local sea life drifting through coral heads and sea fans. The entrance fee covers only access to the grounds and the exhibits; all other activities and equipment—from sea treks and dolphin tours to lockers and swim gear—are extra. The expensive Plus Pass includes park entrance, lockers, snorkel equipment, food, and drinks. You can buy tickets from any travel agency or major hotel along the coast. ⊠ *Carretera 307, Km 282, Xcaret* ☎ *984/206–0038, 855/326–0682 in U.S.* ⊕ *www.xcaret.com* ☎ *Basic Pass MX$1,780; Plus Pass MX$2,320; Night Pass MX$1,420.*

Xplor

AMUSEMENT PARK/WATER PARK | **FAMILY** | Designed for thrill seekers, this 125-acre park features underground rafting in stalactite-studded water caves and cenotes. Swim in a stalactite river, ride in an amphibious vehicle, or soar across the park on 13 of the longest ziplines in Mexico. Daytime admission (valid 9 am to 5 pm) includes all food, drink, and equipment. A separate evening admission from 5:30 to 10:30 pm includes "Xplor Fuego" activities, which includes similar things but with a nighttime theme. Mix-and-match packages can be purchased online to include both day and evening admission and entry to Xcaret next door. ⊠ *Carretera 307, Km 282* ☎ *984/147–6560, 888/922–7381* ⊕ *www. xplor.travel* ☎ *Xplor MX$2,500; Xplor Fuego MX$1,790* ☉ *Closed Sun.*

Playa del Carmen's main beach begins near the ferry docks.

Beaches

Playa del Carmen Main Beach

BEACH—SIGHT | The community's most central section of beach stretches from the ferry docks up to Calle 14 at Panama Jack Grand Porto Playa, a swath of deep white sand licked by turquoise water. The beach and water are clean, but there is some boat traffic that makes swimming less idyllic. Snorkelers aren't likely to see much here, but you can't beat the beach for convenience: countless bars and restaurants are a short walk away on 5th Avenue, masseurs compete (discreetly) to knead out your kinks, and it's easy to find a dive shop ready to take you out to sea. The closer you get to the docks, the more people you'll find. If you're looking for seclusion, head farther north outside Playa del Carmen. **Amenities:** food and drink; water sports. **Best for:** swimming; walking. ⊠ *Between ferry docks and Calle 14, Playa del Carmen.*

 Restaurants

Babe's Noodles & Bar

$$ | **THAI** | Photos and paintings of old Hollywood pinup models share decor space with a large stone Buddha at this Swedish-owned restaurant that serves up a surprising, tasty mix of Asian and European food. It's known for local, interesting fare cooked to order and made with only the freshest ingredients (including sauces handmade every day by the owners). **Known for:** Thai curries; pad Thai; Swedish meatballs with lingonberries imported from Sweden. ⑤ *Average main: 200 MP* ⊠ *Calle 10 between Avs. 5 and 10, Playa del Carmen* ☎ *984/879–3569* ⊕ *www. babesnoodlesandbar.com* ۩ *Closed Mon. No lunch in low season.*

Hot Casual Food

$$ | **CAFÉ** | This cheap streetside breakfast café with the utilitarian name opens at 7 am, and it's one of the few places where you can get breakfast before early-morning sightseeing. Known for Mexican egg dishes like the chile-and-cheese omelet, which will get your day off to a spicy start, Hot also serves more pedestrian packaged muffins and pastries. **Known for:** open from early morning to night; good sandwiches and salads for lunch; fresh juices. $ *Average main: 110 MP* ⊠ *Av. 5 between Calles 38 and 40, Playa del Carmen* ☎ *984/803–4268* ⊕ *www. hotcasualfood.com.*

Shopping

Playa del Carmen's Avenida 5 between Calles 4 and 10 is the best place to shop along the coast. Boutiques sell folk art and textiles from around Mexico, and clothing stores carry lots of sarongs and beachwear made from Indonesian batiks. A shopping area called Calle Corazón, between Calles 12 and 14, has a pedestrian street, art galleries, restaurants, and boutiques.

La Hierbabuena Artesanía

CRAFTS | Owner Melinda Burns offers a collection of fine Mexican clothing and crafts at Hierbabuena. ⊠ *Av. 5 between Calles 8 and 10, Playa del Carmen* ☎ *984/873–1741.*

Activities

DIVING
The Abyss
SCUBA DIVING | PADI and SSI affiliated, the Abyss offers introductory courses and dive trips. It also runs dives in Tulum through the cenotes. ⊠ *Av. 1 between Calles 10 and 12, Playa del Carmen* ☎ *984/876–3285* ⊕ *www.abyssdivecenter.com* ⊠ *From MX$920.*

Tank-Ha Dive Center
SCUBA DIVING | Playa's original dive outfit has PADI-certified teachers and runs diving and snorkeling excursions to the reefs and caverns. Dive packages and Cozumel trips are available, too. ⊠ *Av. 1 between Calles 20 and 22, Playa del Carmen* ☎ *984/873–0302* ⊕ *www.tankha. com* ⊠ *From MX$700.*

GOLF
Grand Coral Golf Riviera Maya
GOLF | This 18-hole championship course was designed by Nick Price. Not as busy (or expensive) as neighboring courses at Mayakoba or Playacar, Grand Coral is challenging without being overly intimidating. You'll face a good amount of bunkers and water on the holes. The greens are slow, but the course is well maintained. If you can swing it, opt for the all-inclusive package that covers food and drink. Otherwise greens fees cover only the cart, bottled water, and golf tees. ⊠ *Grand Coral Riviera Maya, Carretera 307, Km 294, Playa del Carmen* ☎ *984/109–6025, 888/212–3209 in U.S.* ⊕ *www.grandcoralgolf.com* ⊠ *$175 for 18 holes* ⅃. *18 holes. 7043 yards. Par 71.*

Cartagena, Colombia

Ever wondered what the "Spanish Main" refers to? This is it. Colombia's Caribbean coast invokes ghosts of conquistadores, pirates, and missionaries journeying to the New World in search of wealth, whether material or spiritual. Anchoring this shore is the magnificent colonial city of Cartagena (officially Cartagena de Indias, or Cartagena of the Indies), founded in 1533. Gold and silver passed through here en route to Spain, making the city an obvious target for pirates (including Sir Francis Drake), hence the construction of Cartagena's trademark walls and fortresses. The Ciudad Amurallada (walled city) is a near-perfect historic destination—emanating history from the cobblestones, the ancient trees presiding over cool patches of respite in Plaza Bolivar, and the houses of traders, nuns, or generals that have been turned into fine boutique hotels. Cruise passengers will find that security is quite visible (without being oppressive) here in the country's top tourist destination. Take the same precautions you would visiting any city of one million people, and you should have a grand time.

ESSENTIALS
CURRENCY
The Colombian peso (US$1 = 3,300 pesos). Peso prices are denoted with the "$" sign too. If they carry a lot of zeros, they likely are not dollar prices, but always ask.

SAFETY
Security is tighter in Cartagena than elsewhere in Colombia, so you certainly can navigate the city on your own. (Knowing some Spanish helps.) However, beware of pickpockets in the tourist areas and avoid going out at odd hours or being too isolated on Playa Blanca; since the completion of the bridge linking it to the mainland, muggings have become more frequent. The nationwide emergency number is ☎ 123.

TELEPHONE
The Terminal de Cruceros has ample phones for your use. Local numbers in Cartagena have seven digits. For international calls, dial 009 followed by country and area codes and local number. Most stateside providers have roaming options in this region of Colombia for calls back to the United States; if you have a triband GSM phone, it should work.

COMING ASHORE
Cruise ships dock at the modern Terminal de Cruceros (cruise terminal) on Isla de Manga, an island connected by a bridge to the historic city center, about 2 miles (3 km) northwest of the walled city. You'll find telephones, Internet cafés, and a duty-free shop in the terminal.

A small army of taxis waits in front of the terminal. Expect to pay 15,000 pesos for the 10-minute drive to the walled city; the same fare will get you to the nearby beaches at Bocagrande. Drivers are all too happy to take you on a do-it-yourself guided tour. Most charge around 20,000 pesos for an hour of waiting time. Once you are in the walled city, Cartagena is

Best Bets ◉

- **Cruise the Harbor.** Admire the city's formidable walls and fortresses from the sea.

- **Islas del Rosario.** The beaches are an hour away by boat.

- **Aviario Nacional de Colombia.** One of the world's best aviaries.

- **Walk Las Murallas.** Walk the city's massive stone walls.

- **Visit Palacio de la Inquisición.** Cartagena's most-visited sight.

so compact that walking the labyrinth of cobblestone streets is the most enjoyable way to get around, but you need to take a taxi if you visit the Cerro de la Popa.

◉ Sights

Cartagena's walled city is small enough to be easily walkable. A ride in a horse-drawn carriage (or *coche,* as it is known locally) has always been a time-honored—and controversial—way to see the city as a tourist. There are questions about the conditions under which these animals are kept, and we do not recommend their use.

★ **Aviario Nacional de Colombia** (*National Aviary of Colombia*)
NATURE PRESERVE | FAMILY | This impressive bird sanctuary is the country's best and South America's largest. In a nation famed for avian biodiversity it's an opportunity not to be missed. Colombians are justifiably proud of the Andean condor, their not-so-colorful national bird, and the condor gets ample coverage here, but scarlet macaws, blue-winged tanagers, and cocks on the rock will give your camera a workout. There are three distinct biomes (tropical jungle, coastal, and desert) as well as 21 areas

Cartagena

Caribbean Sea

TO AIRPORT

Laguna del Cabrero

CHAMBACÚ

Puente Chambacú

SAN DIEGO

Castillo de San Felipe de Barajas

Av. L. C. López

Cerro de la Popa

LA MATUNA

Concolón

CENTRO

Avda. Santander

Parque del Centenario

Laguna de San Lazaro

PL. DE LA INDEPENCIA

Plaza de Santo Domingo

Las Murallas

Getsemaní

Calle Larga

Playa de Barahona

Playa del Arsenal

Avda. Santander

Convento y Iglesia de San Pedro Claver

Museo Histórico Cartagena de Indias

TO BOCAGRANDE

Aviario Nacional de Colombia

0 ___ 1 mile
0 ___ 1 km

to explore that are home to 190 species of birds. If you wish to take everything in, a self-guided walk should last around 2½ hours. A guided tour speeds things up a bit. All exhibit signs are in Spanish and English. Plan on about a 45-minute drive to get out here from the city. You can easily combine the aviary with beach time at Playa Blanca. ⊠ *Barú Island, Km 14.5, Vía Barú, just past Barú Bridge, Cartagena* ☎ *5/673–4045* ⊕ *www.aviarionacional.co* 💲 *40,000 pesos.*

★ Castillo de San Felipe de Barajas

LOCAL INTEREST | What began in 1657 as a small fort designed to protect the overland entrance to Cartagena grew over the following century into a sprawling stone behemoth covering the entire hill. The largest of its kind on the continent, it's a fascinating example of asymmetrical military construction unseen in Europe.

The unique layout allowed for devastatingly efficient lines of coverage for some 63 cannons lining the walls, and the fort would never fall. Another ingenious device was a maze of tunnels—minimally lit today to allow for spooky exploration—that connects vital points of the fort. If you don't speak Spanish, an English audio guide makes the visit infinitely richer. The fort is an easy enough walk from Getsemaní with great views of the city; the best time to go is in the afternoon. A taxi shouldn't cost more than the standard minimum 6,000 pesos, although most drivers will want to charge you 8,000. ⊠ *Av. Pedro de Heredia at Carrera 17, Cartagena* ☎ *5/656–6803* 💲 *25,000 pesos.*

★ Cerro de la Popa

BUILDING | Make this one of your first stops on any visit to get the best possible grasp of the city's geography and its role as a fortified protector of a crucial headland, as well as a more modern context for the historic center that is now surrounded by a sprawling city. Because of its strategic location, the white-walled 17th-century monastery here intermittently served as a fortress during the colonial era. It now houses a museum and a chapel dedicated to the Virgen de la Candelaria, Cartagena's patron saint, with a stunning gilded altar and religious relics up to 500 years old. Taxis charge around 10,000 pesos one way to bring you here (plus the wait and return trip, expect to pay between 40,000 and 50,000 pesos) and the sight can be included on one of Cartagena's popular *chiva* (horsedrawn carriage) tours. Under no circumstances should you walk between the city center and the hill; occasional muggings of tourists have been reported along the route. For spectacular views of Cartagena, ascend the hill around sunset. ⊠ *Barrio Pie de la Popa Cra. 29, Cartagena* ✛ *3 km (2 miles) southeast of Ciudad Amurallada* 🕾 ▦ *8,000 pesos* ☉ *Closed Mon.–Tues.*

Convento y Iglesia de San Pedro Claver

LOCAL INTEREST | Cartagena's most impressive religious building, the church's yellow dome is an icon of the city skyline, and the carved stone facade dominates the small plaza below that is surrounded by restaurants and often filled with street vendors and musicians. Constructed at the beginning of the 17th century, the cool, peaceful interior centers around the lush green courtyard of the cloister, most of which is open to visitors, including a small museum that displays African and Haitian art and a variety of religious relics. To the right is the rather austere church, dominated by an ornate altar, which also holds the bones of San Pedro Claver, for whom the building and plaza are named. Claver was a Spanish Jesuit monk who spent 40 years in Cartagena—visitors can also enter the cell where he lived—dedicated

to healing and ministering to the tens of thousands of slaves who passed through the port annually. Known as the "Slave of the Slaves," he was canonized in 1888, the first in the new world to receive this honor. There is some information in English, but we recommend hiring an English-speaking guide at the ticket office. ⊠ *Carrera 4 No. 31–00, Centro* 🕾 *5/664-4741* ▦ *9,000 pesos.*

★ Getsemaní

NEIGHBORHOOD | Once run-down and troubled, the Getsemaní neighborhood just beyond the posher parts of the historic walled city now exudes fresh but still bohemian energy, thanks to an infusion of new restaurants and bars, as well as boutique hotels. Locals hang out and chat on the narrow streets like Callejón Angosto and gather at Plaza de la Santísima Trinidad, the heart of the neighborhood. In the plaza, look for the statue of Pedro Romero, who fought for independence from Spain. Abundant street art along Calle de la Sierpe (and other avenues) and gritty edges keep the scene real and down to earth, at least for now. You can stroll Getsemaní day or night to check things out; weekend evenings are very lively. ⊠ *Bordered by Calle del Arsenal, Av. Daniel Lemaitre, and Av. Luis Carlos López, Cartagena.*

Las Murallas

BUILDING | Cartagena survived only because of its walls, and its *murallas* remain today the city's most distinctive feature, part of a UNESCO World Heritage Site that draws visitors to the historic and well-preserved city center full of plazas, shops, and diversions. Repeated sacking by pirates and foreign invaders convinced the Spaniards of the need to enclose the region's most important port. Construction began in 1600 and finished in 1796. The Puerta del Reloj is the principal gate to the innermost sector of the walled city. Its four-sided clock tower was a relatively late addition (1888), and has become the symbol of the city. Walking along the thick walls (you can enter at many points, and there are overpriced bars in some parts) is one of Cartagena's time-honored pastimes, especially late in the afternoon when you can watch the setting sun redden the Caribbean. (Depending on time of year, the sun sets here between 5:30 and 6:30 pm.) ⊠ *Area bounded by Bahía de las Ánimas, Laguna de San Lázaro, and Caribbean Sea, Centro.*

★ **Museo Histórico de Cartagena de Indias** (*Palacio de la Inquisición*)

MUSEUM | One of Cartagena's most visited tourist sites documents the darkest period in the city's history. A baroque limestone doorway off Plaza de Bolívar marks the entrance to the 1770 Palace of the Inquisition, the headquarters of the repressive arbiters of political and spiritual orthodoxy who once exercised jurisdiction over Colombia, Ecuador, and Venezuela. Although the museum displays benign colonial and pre-Columbian artifacts and also has a brief overview of the city's history with maps and models, most people congregate on the ground floor to "Eeewww!" over the implements of torture (racks and thumbscrews, to name but two) and the displays on how to judge a witch. We recommend you hire an English-speaking guide since many displays need explanations and all signs are in Spanish. ⊠ *Plaza de Bolívar, Centro* ☎ *5/664–4570* ⊕ *www.muhca.gov.co* ⊡ *21,000 pesos.*

Plaza de Santo Domingo

PLAZA | The eponymous church looming over the plaza is the oldest in the city and a contrast to the plaza's generally festive and bustling atmosphere. At night the area is particularly attractive as it fills up with tables from surrounding bars and restaurants. A popular, eye-catching landmark since 2000 is Colombian artist Fernando Botero's large bronze *Gertrudis,* a sculpture of a plump, naked woman. Don't pass by the Iglesia de Santo Domingo: built in 1539, the church has a simple whitewashed interior, bare limestone pillars, a raised choir, and an adjacent cloistered seminary. Local lore says the bell tower's twisted profile is the work of the Devil, who, dispirited at having failed to destroy it, threw himself into the plaza's well. For a fee you can take an audio tour. ⊠ *Calle Santo Domingo and Carrera Santo Domingo, Centro.*

🏖 Beaches

Cartagena—a city almost totally surrounded by water, with the Caribbean once forming its very walls—is quite simply not a beach destination. Time and money is much better spent here getting lost wandering cobbled streets between shady plazas and every now and then dipping into the city's ever-growing gastronomic scene. The most popular nearby beaches options have lost much of their appeal as tourism has boomed, although a great beach day can be had if you head into it with reasonable expectations.

Bocagrande, although a cheap taxi ride away, will disappoint most beach lovers. It offers only a strip of gray-tinged sand tucked up against a busy road lined by towering apartment buildings and hotels that look more like a Miami skyline than a South American one. Beachgoers will be constantly hassled by traders and insistent masseurs.

Though much more attractive, with white sands and clear waters, the much loved **Playa Blanca** has suffered from the bridge connecting Barú Island to the mainland, and the beach fills up with vendors, particularly on the arrival of tour boats from the harbor. Relaxation is often ruined by constant sales pitches for massages, beach chairs, and Jet Ski rides. Easy access has also led to an increase in petty crime, so keep an eye on your valuables at all times, and avoid the beach at odd hours or by yourself.

The best bet to get your feet wet is a tour to the coral archipelago, **Las Islas del**

Historic Cartagena's most impressive sight may be Covento y Iglesia de San Pedro Claver's yellow dome.

Rosario. Although the coral reefs around the islands have suffered bleaching from recent high temperatures and have lost much of their previous splendor, a day out snorkeling or diving will be a pleasure for all but the most hardened scuba enthusiasts. Visibility is usually good, and there is still plenty of coral and sea life to be found. Day trips to the islands can be arranged from the harbor, but the hassle and risk of scams is not worth it. Instead, you will get a much better tour—and quite possibly a better price—if you join a tour organized by your cruise ship.

🍴 Restaurants

Caffé Lunático
$$$ | TAPAS | Set on a lovely and generally calm Getsemaní street, this funky café dominated by a graffitti mural serves the tastiest breakfast in town. Try the *arepita lunática* for one of the best examples of the local breakfast classic. **Known for:** evening tapas menu; brunch with 2 hours of free mimosas; great value. ⓢ *Average*

main: 27,000 pesos ✉ Calle Espiritu Santo 29–184, Cartagena ☎ 5/660–1735 ⊕ www.caffelunatico.com.

★ Cocina de Pepina
$$$ | CARIBBEAN | One of the most recommended local favorites is a no-frills bastion of Cartagena cuisine built on the impressive research and skill of chef and culinary historian María "Pepina" Yances. Although Doña Pepina passed away in 2014, her energy and recipe book have been carried forward by her family, and the restaurant remains a must-visit for those keen to sample local classics. **Known for:** recipes from a local celebrity chef; mote de queso (yam, coconut, and cheese soup); peppers stuffed with ground beef. ⓢ *Average main: 35,000 pesos* ✉ *Callejón Vargas 9A–06, Cartagena* ☎ *5/664–2944* ⊙ *No dinner Sun.–Mon.*

🛍 Shopping

Think "Juan Valdez" if you're looking for something to take the folks back home. Small bags of fine Colombian coffee, the country's signature souvenir, are available in most tourist-oriented shops. Colombia also means emeralds, and you'll find plenty in the jewelry shops on or near Calle Pantaleón, beside the cathedral. Don't forget the duty-free shop in the Terminal de Cruceros for those last-minute purchases.

Las Bóvedas, a series of arched store-rooms in the Ciudad Amurallada's northern corner now houses about two dozen shops with the best selection of local and national crafts. If you're looking for emeralds, visit the jewelry shops on or near Calle Pantaleón, beside the cathedral.

 Activities

DIVING

Coral reefs line the coast south of Cartagena, although warm-water currents have begun to erode them in recent years. There is still good diving to be had in the Islas del Rosario, an archipelago of 27 coral islands about 21 miles (35 km) southwest of the city.

★ **Diving Planet**

DIVING/SNORKELING | The best, friendliest, and most professional diving outfit in the city offers a good variety of dives and snorkeling expeditions. Quality gear and dive instructors make this a great choice for beginners looking to get started or experienced divers looking for the best the nearby oceans have to offer. ⊠ *Calle Estanco del Aguardiente (Calle 38) 5–09, Centro* ☎ *5/660–0450* ⊕ *www.divingplanet.org.*

Castaway Cay, Bahamas

Disney's Castaway Cay has a dock, so passengers simply step ashore (rather than tendering, as is required to reach some cruise lines' private islands). Like everything associated with Disney, the line's private island is almost too good to be true. Located in the Abacos, a chain in the Bahamas, only 10% of Castaway Cay is developed, leaving plenty of unspoiled area to explore in Robinson Crusoe fashion. Trams are provided to reach three separate beaches designated for families with younger kids (Family Beach), active teens and adults (Sports Beach), and adults (Serenity Bay), and areas where Disney offers age-specific activities and extensive, well-planned children's activities; use of strollers is free. Biking and hiking are so popular that two nature trails—one of them with an observation tower—are mapped out. Passengers can swim to a water platform complete with two slides or cool off in a 2,400-square-foot water-play area equipped with water jets and a splash pad. A 1,200-square-foot soft wet deck area provides freshwater fun for children with an array of pop jets, geysers, and bubblers. There is no charge for the water-play facilities. Excursions range from as passive as a glass-bottom-boat tour to the soaring excitement of parasailing. An interactive experience with stingrays is educational and safe; the gentle creatures' barbs are blunted for safety. In addition to beach games, island-style music, a shaded game pavilion, and barbecue fare served in two buffet areas with covered seating and several beverage stations (plus one extra-charge restaurant at Serenity Bay), there are shops, massage cabanas by the sea, and even a post office. Shopping can be done with your ship's keycard (Castaway Cay souvenirs are sold only on the island, not on the ship). Popular with couples as well as families, private rental cabanas provide the luxury of a deluxe beach retreat with an option to add the personalized service of a cabana host. Teens have their own private retreat just steps from the beach. And when parents need a break, there's free childcare at Scuttle's Cove. **Available Activities:** basketball, bicycles, billiards, fishing, hiking, jet-skiing, kayaking, paddleboats, parasailing, Ping-Pong, sailing, shuffleboard, snorkeling, soccer, volleyball, water cycles.

Catalina Island, Dominican Republic

An unspoiled island paradise, Catalina Island is just off the coast of the Dominican Republic, about a half-hour by boat from Bayahibe, and is used as a private-island experience by Costa Cruises. Guests can also opt for boating excursions along the Chavón River or a visit to Altos de Chavón, a re-creation of a Mediterranean-style European village. However, the island's white-sand beach is idyllic, so many passengers will be content just having some food and lounging in the warm, clear water. Otherwise water-toy rentals, banana-boat rides, and sailing tours are available from independent concessionaires. Local vendors set up souvenir shops offering crafts and T-shirts. The ship provides the food for a lunch barbecue and tropical beverages at the beach bar. **Available activities:** hiking, jet-skiing, massages, organized games, sailing, shopping, snorkeling, volleyball, waterskiing.

CoCo Cay, Bahamas

Originally known as Little Stirrup Cay, CoCo Cay is within view of Great Stirrup Cay (Norwegian Cruise Line's private island) with snorkeling that is just as good, especially around a sunken airplane and a replica of Blackbeard's flagship, *Queen Anne's Revenge*. In 2019, Royal Caribbean launched "Perfect Day at CoCo Cay," a $250 million upgrade and expansion of the 140-acre island in the Berry chain between Nassau and Freeport. The island now features Thrill Waterpark, billed as the first full-scale waterpark on a cruise-line private island, for which you'll pay $39 to $99 for a half or full day of fun. Bars, cabanas (high extra fee), shaded walkways, and thousands of beach umbrellas and umbrella-shaded loungers (most rented out for the day) dot the third of the island that is currently developed. There are also three restaurants (Captain Jack's has extra charges), five beaches, a three-station zip line (from $79), a helium balloon attraction (from $39), shopping options, and extensive new landscaping. **Activities:** hiking, jet-skiing, kayaking, organized games, scuba diving, shopping, snorkeling, volleyball.

Colón, Panama

When you consider the decades it took to build the canal, not to mention the lives lost and government failures and triumphs involved during its construction, it's no surprise that the Panama Canal is often called the Eighth Wonder of the Modern World. Best described as an aquatic bridge, the Panama Canal connects the Caribbean Sea with the Pacific Ocean by raising ships up and over Central America, through artificially created Gatún Lake, the highest point at 85 feet above sea level, and then lowering them back to sea level by using a series of locks, or water steps. A masterful engineering feat, three pairs of locks—Gatún, Pedro Miguel, and Miraflores—utilize gravity to fill and drain as ships pass through chambers 1,000 feet long by 110 feet wide that are "locked" by doors weighing 80 tons apiece, yet actually float into position. It took engineers more than 100 additional years to expand the canal to accommodate today's largest ships (called "post-Panamax" because they exceed the canal's original dimensions). Most cruise ships pass through the canal's original locks seasonally, when repositioning from one coast to the other; however, partial transits have become an increasingly popular "destination" on regularly scheduled 10- and 11-night Caribbean itineraries. These loop cruises enter the canal from the Caribbean Sea and sail into Gatún Lake, where they remain for a few hours as passengers are tendered ashore for excursions. Ships then pass back through the locks, returning to the Caribbean and stopping at either Cristóbal Pier or Colón 2000 Pier to retrieve passengers at the conclusion of their tours.

A day transiting the canal's Gatún Locks begins before dawn, as your passenger ship passes through Bahía Limón and lines up with dozens of other vessels to await its turn to enter. Before your ship can proceed, two pilots and a narrator will board. The sight of a massive cruise ship being raised dozens of feet into the air by water is so mesmerizing that passengers eagerly crowd to all forward decks at the first lock. If you don't find a good viewing spot, head for the rear decks, where there is usually more room and the view is just as intriguing. If you remain aboard, as many passengers do, you'll find plenty of room up front later in the day, as your ship retraces its path down to the sea. Due to the tight scheduling of the day's activities—it takes at least 90 minutes for a ship to pass through the Gatún locks—passengers who wish to go ashore early in the day are advised to sign up for one of the many available shore excursions.

ESSENTIALS
CURRENCY
The U.S. dollar. Panama calls the dollar the *balboa* and designates prices with a *B/.* sign in front of the number. Panama mints its own coins, which they circulate along with U.S. coins.

TELEPHONE
You'll find telephones inside Colón's cruise terminal, where you can purchase phone cards, a handy and inexpensive way to make calls.

COMING ASHORE
Colón, Panama's second-largest city, has little to offer of historic interest, and is simply a jumping-off point to the rain forest and a wide variety of organized tours. You'll dock at either the Colón 2000 or Cristóbal port, about 20 blocks from each

Best Bets ◉

■ **See the new Panama Canal.** The Agua Clara Visitor Center offers the best view of the expanded canal.

■ **Kayak on Gatún Lake.** Paddle among the islands and mangrove forests.

■ **Panama Railway.** Take a train trip to Panama City.

■ **Portobelo.** Visit historic Panamanian forts.

■ **Rain Forest Aerial Tram.** See the rain forest canopy from above.

other on opposite sides of downtown. Both terminals have phones and shopping. Organized excursions focus on the Panama Canal or the pleasant north coast village of Portobelo, 70 km (42 miles) northeast. Infrequent cruise itineraries may include a day docked in Colón, rather than a partial canal transit. However, no matter how much time your ship spends in Colón, it is always easier (and safer) to take an organized shore excursion. ⚠ **The city itself can be quite dangerous, even during the day; under no circumstances should you wander on your own.**

Although entry time into the canal is always approximate, passenger ships have priority, and most pass through the Gatún locks early in the morning. Passengers booked on shore excursions begin the tendering process soon after the ship sets anchor, which can be as early as 8:30 am. Alternatives to excursions offered by your cruise ship are available from independent tour operators and can be arranged in advance through websites or travel agents. You will likely be informed that Panamanian regulations restrict passengers going ashore in Gatún Lake to only those who have booked the cruise line's excursions; however, anyone who has a shore-excursion

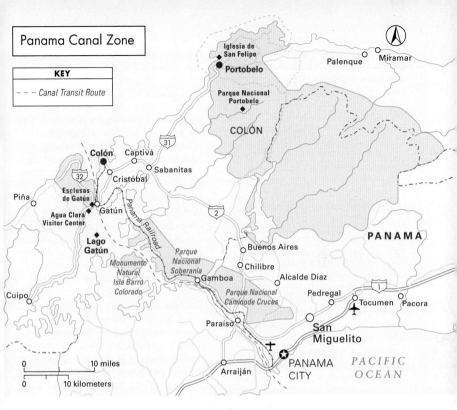

Panama Canal Zone

KEY

– – – Canal Transit Route

reservation with a local company should be able to leave the vessel. Before making independent tour arrangements, confirm with your cruise line that you will be allowed to go ashore after presenting your private tour confirmation to the shore-excursion staff on board the ship.

Colón 2000

Two blocks from the Zona Libre is the city's cruise-ship port, Colón 2000, which is basically a two-story strip mall next to the dock where ships tie up and passengers load onto buses for day trips. It has a supermarket, restaurants, and shops. A second terminal is the home port for Royal Caribbean's *Enchantment of the Seas*, with the Panamanian government aggressively courting other cruise companies to set up shop here, too. ⊠ *Paseo Gorgas, Colón* ☎ *447–3197.*

👁 Sights

COLÓN

The provincial capital of Colón, beside the canal's Atlantic entrance, has clearly seen better days, as the architecture of its older buildings attests. Its predominantly Afro-Caribbean population has long had a vibrant musical scene, and in the late 19th and early 20th centuries Colón was a relatively prosperous town. But it spent the second half of the 20th century in steady decay, and things have only gotten worse in the 21st century. ⚠ **Travelers who explore Colón on foot are simply asking to be mugged. We strongly recommend you stick with the safety of organized shore excursion here.**

Agua Clara Visitor Center

LOCAL INTEREST | Not far from the Gatún locks, this visitor center offers the best view of the newly completed Panama Canal expansion, which allows a new generation of larger, so-called post-Panamax ships to traverse the canal. A video presentation provides an introduction to the canal's history and expansion, but the open-air observation area is the most interesting part, since it offers hilltop views of the project. The facility has a playground and gift shop, as well as a pleasant open-air restaurant operated by Panama City's El Panamá hotel. The restaurant, which is open for lunch daily noon–4 (call *507/215–9927* for reservations) offers great views of Gatún Lake. ✛ *5 km (3 miles) south of Colón; turn right just before railroad tracks and make 1st right* ☎ *276–8325* ⊕ *www.visitcanaldepanama.com* ☞ *$10.*

Esclusas de Gatún (*Gatún Locks*)
MARINA | Twelve kilometers (7 miles) south of Colón are the Esclusas de Gatún, a triple-lock complex that's nearly a mile long and raises and lowers ships the 85 feet between sea level and Gatún Lake. There's a small visitor center with a viewing platform and information about the boats passing through is broadcast over speakers. The visitor center doesn't compare to the one at the Miraflores locks close to Panama City, but given the sheer magnitude of the Gatún locks (three sets of locks, as opposed to two at Miraflores) it is an impressive sight, especially when packed with ships. You have to cross the locks on a swinging bridge to get to San Lorenzo and the Represa de Gatún (Gatún Dam), which holds the water in Gatún Lake. At 2½ km (1½ miles) long, it was the largest dam in the world when it was built, a title it held for several decades. Get there by taking the first left after crossing the locks. ✉ *12 km (7 miles) south of Colón, Colón* ⊕ *www.visitcanaldepanama.com* ☞ *$5.*

LAGO GATÚN (GATÚN LAKE)

Covering about 163 square miles, an area about the size of the island nation Barbados, Gatún Lake extends northwest from the Parque Nacional Soberanía to the locks of Gatún, just south of Colón. The lake was created when the U.S. government dammed the Chagres River, between 1907 and 1910, so that boats could cross the isthmus at 85 feet above sea level. By creating the lake, the United States saved decades of digging that a sea-level canal would have required. It took several years for the rain to fill the convoluted valleys, turning hilltops into islands and killing much forest (some trunks still tower over the water nearly a century later). When it was completed, Gatún Lake was the largest man-made lake in the world. The canal route winds through its northern half, past several forest-covered islands (the largest is Barro Colorado, one of the world's first biological reserves). To the north of Barro Colorado are the Islas Brujas and Tigres, which together hold a primate refuge (visitors aren't allowed). The lake itself is home to crocodiles—forego swimming here—manatees, and peacock bass, a species introduced from South America and popular with fishermen.

PORTOBELO

Portobelo is an odd mix of colonial fortresses, clear waters, lushly forested hills, and a town of cement-block houses crowded amid the ancient walls. It holds some of Panama's most interesting colonial ruins, with rusty cannons still lying in wait for an enemy assault, and is a UNESCO World Heritage Site, together with San Lorenzo.

Iglesia de San Felipe

RELIGIOUS SITE | One block east of Real Aduana is the Iglesia de San Felipe, a large white church dating from 1814 that's home to the country's most venerated religious figure: the Cristo Negro (Black Christ). According to legend, that statue of a dark-skinned Jesus carrying a cross arrived in Portobelo in the 17th century on a Spanish ship bound for Cartagena, Colombia. Each time the ship tried to leave, it encountered storms and had to return to port, convincing the captain to leave the statue in Portobelo. Another legend has it that in the midst of a cholera epidemic in 1821 parishioners prayed to the Cristo Negro, and the community was spared. The statue spends most of the year to the left of the church's altar, but once a year it's paraded through town in the Festival del Cristo Negro. Each year the Cristo Negro is clothed in a new purple robe, donated by somebody who's earned the honor. Behind San Felipe are the ruins of the Iglesia de San Juan de Dios, which date from 1589. ⊠ *Calle Principal, Portobelo* ☎ *448–2055.*

Parque Nacional Portobelo (*Portobelo National Park*)
NATIONAL/STATE PARK | Parque Nacional Portobelo is a vast marine and rain-forest reserve contiguous with Chagres National Park that protects both natural and cultural treasures. It extends from the cloud forest atop 3,212-foot Cerro Brujo down to offshore islands and coral reefs, and comprises the bay and fortresses of Portobelo.

You can't miss the remains of the three Spanish fortresses that once guarded Portobelo Bay. The first is **Fuerte Santiago de la Gloria,** with about a dozen cannons and sturdy battlements built out of blocks of coral. Portobelo's largest and most impressive fort is **Fuerte San Jerónimo,** at the end of the bay. Surrounded by the "modern" town, it was originally built in the 1600s and rebuilt to its current state in 1758. Its large interior courtyard was once a parade ground, but it's now the venue for annual celebrations. **Fuerte San Fernando,** across the bay from Fuerte Santiago, consists of two battlements—one near the water and one on the hill above. The upper fortress affords a great view of the bay and is a good place to see birds because of the surrounding forest. Local boatmen who dock their boats next to Fuerte Santiago or Fuerte San Jerónimo can take you across the bay to explore Fuerte San Fernando for a few dollars.

⊠ *Surrounding Portobelo, Portobelo* ☎ *442–8348 park office* ⊕ *www.miambiente.gob.pa* 🖃 *$5.*

Real Aduana (*Royal Customs House*)
BUILDING | Near the entrance to Fuerte San Jerónimo is the Real Aduana, where servants of the Spanish crown made sure that the king and queen got their cut from every ingot that rolled through town. Built in 1630, the Real Aduana was damaged during pirate attacks and then destroyed by an earthquake in 1882, only to be rebuilt in 1998. It is an interesting example of colonial architecture—note the carved coral columns on the ground floor—and it houses a simple museum with some old coins, cannonballs, and displays on Panamanian folklore. ⊠ *Calle de la Aduana, Portobelo* ☎ *448–2024* ⊕ *www.inac.gob.pa* 🖃 *$5.*

🍴 Restaurants

PORTOBELO

Restaurante Los Cañones
$$ | SEAFOOD | This rambling restaurant with tables among palm trees and Caribbean views is one of Panama's most attractive lunch spots. The food and service fall a little short of the setting, but not so far that you'd want to scratch it from your list. **Known for:** whole fried snapper (pescado entero); king crab in ginger sauce (centolla al jengibre); outdoor dining area. 💲 *Average main: $13* ⊠ *2 km (1 mile) before Portobelo on left, Portobelo* ☎ *448–2980* ▭ *No credit cards* ⊗ *Closed Mon.*

🛍 Shopping

COLÓN

Both Cristóbal and Colón 2000 have large shopping malls, where you will find Internet access, telephones, refreshments, and duty-free souvenir shops in relatively secure environments. Stores in both locations feature local crafts such as baskets, wood carvings, and toys, as well as liquor, jewelry, and the ubiquitous souvenir T-shirts. In addition to shops and cafés, Cristóbal Pier features an open-air arts and craft market; Colón 2000 Pier has a well-stocked supermarket. Portobelo has a wide-ranging artisan market next to Iglesia de San Felipe.

The most unique locally made souvenirs are colorful appliquéd *molas,* the whimsical textile artwork created by native Kuna women, who come from the San Blas Islands; they are likely to be hand-stitching new designs while they sell the ones they just completed. If you take an excursion to Portobelo, the best selection can be found in the artisan market next to Iglesia de San Felipe, where there are other locally made souvenirs that are well worth bargaining for.

Costa Maya (Mahahual), Mexico

Puerto Costa Maya is an anomaly. Unlike other tourist attractions in the area (the island of Cozumel being the primary Yucatán cruise port), this port of call near Mahahual has been created exclusively for cruise-ship passengers. The complex, sometimes referred to as "New Mahahual," comprises theme restaurants like Hard Rock Cafe and Señor Frog's, as well as boutique shops and chain stores such as Lapis Jewelry.

Prior to a devastating 2007 hurricane, there was no real reason to go into the small nearby fishing village of Mahahual (pronounced *ma-ah-WAL*). Although there are still about 300 residents, post-hurricane renovations have put the village on the map; it now has its own pier as well as a smattering of hotels, restaurants, and shops. Be sure to venture beyond "New Mahahual," which lacks the charm of the nearby beachfront area. Its cement boardwalk along the beach has made Mahahual an ideal spot for a sunset stroll. The crystal-clear waters

Best Bets

■ **Chacchoben.** This archaeological site is near the Belize border.

■ **Kohunlich.** A Maya city now in ruins, Kohunlich is best known for its great temples with sculpted masks.

■ **Mahahual.** Plenty of fine sand and glassy waters make for a cushy afternoon in the sun at this small fishing village near the cruise pier.

■ **Xcalak.** Discover excellent saltwater fly-fishing and deserted beaches at this national reserve.

and unspoiled beaches are delightful for snorkeling, diving, and fishing.

ESSENTIALS
CURRENCY
The Mexican peso. U.S. dollars and credit cards are widely accepted in the area.

TELEPHONE
Most pay phones accept prepaid Ladatel cards, sold in 30-, 50-, or 100-peso denominations. To use the card, insert it in the pay phone's slot, dial 001 (for calls to the United States) or 01 (for calls within Mexico), followed by the area code and number. Credit is deleted from the card as you use it, and the balance is displayed on the small screen on the phone. Most triband mobile phones from the U.S. work in Mexico, though you must pay roaming charges.

COMING ASHORE
At first glance, the port complex itself may seem to be little more than an outdoor mall. You disembark at a docking pier (which can accommodate three ships at once) and head to a 70,000-square-foot bazaar-type compound where shops selling local crafts—jewelry, pottery, woven straw hats and bags, and embroidered dresses—are

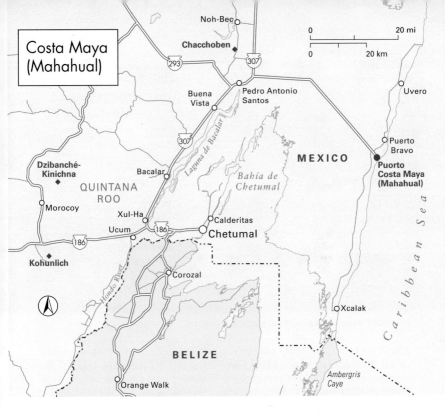

interspersed with duty-free stores and souvenir shops. There are two alfresco restaurants that serve seafood, American-friendly Mexican dishes like tacos and quesadillas, and cocktails at shaded tables. An outdoor amphitheater stages daily performances of traditional music and dance. Taxis wait at the port entrance to take you to Mahahual itself, a ride of about 5 to 10 minutes.

◉ Sights

MAHAHUAL
Tiny Mahahual (also spelled Majahual) has something of a split personality. With a population of only 600, it's a quiet beachfront outpost with clear, calm waters, good snorkeling and diving, and not a whole lot to do. That's just the way its Mexican and expat U.S. and Canadian residents like it. When the cruise ships are in port, however, this sleepy spot wakes up. Passengers flood its waterside palapa restaurants, beach clubs, and the boardwalk fronting the town's few blocks—it's lively but can be overwhelming.

FURTHER AFIELD
Chacchoben
ARCHAEOLOGICAL SITE | Excavated in 2005, Chacchoben (pronounced *CHA-cho-ben*) is an ancient city that was a contemporary of Kohunlich and the most important trading partner with Guatemala north of the Bacalar Lagoon area. Several newly unearthed buildings are still in good condition. The lofty **Templo Uno,** the site's main temple, was dedicated to the Mayan sun god, Itzamná, and once held a royal tomb. (When archaeologists found it, though, it had already been looted.) Most of the site was built around AD

Kohunlich is mostly visited by cruise-ship passengers who call in Mahahual.

200, in the Petén style of the early classic period, although the city could have been inhabited as early as 200 BC. It's thought that inhabitants made their living growing cotton and extracting chewing gum and copal resin from the trees. ⊠ *Felipe Carrillo Puerto* ✛ *From Carretera 307, turn right on Carretera 293 south of Cafetal, continue 9 km (5½ miles) passing Lázaro Cardenas town* ⊕ *www.inah.gob.mx* ✉ *MX$55.*

Dzibanché-Kinichná

ARCHAEOLOGICAL SITE | The alliance between sister cities Dzibanché and Kinichná was thought to have made them the most powerful cities in southern Quintana Roo during the Mayan classic period (AD 100–1000).

At Dzibanché ("place where they write on wood," pronounced *zee-ban-CHE*), several carved wooden lintels have been found; the most perfectly preserved sample is in a supporting arch at the **Plaza de Xibalba**. Also at the plaza is the **Templo del Búho** (Temple of the Owl), atop which a recessed tomb was discovered—only

the second of its kind in Mexico (the first was at Palenque in Chiapas). More buildings and three plazas have been restored as excavation continues. The carved stone steps at **Edificio 13** and **Edificio 2** (Buildings 13 and 2) still bear traces of stone masks. A copy of the famed lintel of **Templo IV** (Temple IV), with eight glyphs dating from AD 618, is housed in the Museo de la Cultura Maya in Chetumal. Four more tombs were discovered at **Templo I** (Temple I). ⊠ *Carretera 186 (Chetumal–Escárcega), 80 km (50 miles) west of Chetumal, Chetumal* ✛ *Following Carretera 186 (Chetumal–Escárcega), turn north at Km 58 and pass through town of Morocoy; continue 2 km (1 mile) farther, and turn right at sign for Dzibanché. The entrance is 7 km (4½ miles) away* ☎ ⊕ *www.inah.gob.mx* ✉ *MX$55.*

Kohunlich

ARCHAEOLOGICAL SITE | Kohunlich (pronounced *KO-hoon-lich*) is renowned for the giant stucco masks on its principal pyramid, the **Edificio de los Mascarones** (Mask Building), among others. It also has one of Quintana Roo's oldest ball courts and the remains of a great drainage system at the **Plaza de las Estelas** (Plaza of the Stelae). Kohunlich was built and occupied during the classic period by various Maya groups. This explains the eclectic architecture, which includes the Petén and Río Bec styles. Although there are 14 buildings to visit, it's thought that there are at least 500 mounds on the site waiting to be excavated. This site doesn't have a great deal of tourist traffic, so it's surrounded by thriving flora and fauna. ⊠ *Off Carretera 186 (Chetumal–Escárcega), 65 km (46 miles) west of Chetumal, Chetumal ✛ Follow Carretera 186 west of Chetumal for 65 km (40 miles); continue another 9 km (5½ miles) south on side road to ruins* ⊕ *www.inah.gob.mx* ✆ *MX$65.*

☺ Beaches

The cruise ships that stop here daily have made Mahahual's beach the liveliest place in town. Seaside restaurants dish out cerveza and ceviche, and several vendors offer boat tours and rental equipment like glass-bottom kayaks. The strip of beach edging the cruise complex has been outfitted with colorful lounge chairs and *hamacas* (hammocks), and may tempt you to linger and sunbathe. The main beach in the center of town has fine sand and calm waters, great for swimming and snorkeling. Some hotel owners have opened beach clubs to cater to cruise passengers looking for a day (and a drink) in the sun.

Nacional Beach Club

RESORT—SIGHT | This colorful beach club, exclusively for overnight guests and cruise-ship passengers who purchase a VIP beach club package, is the only one on the Mahahual strip with a pool. Bungalows start at $65 a night and VIP Beach Breaks for cruise passengers are $110 per adult. Both will get you access to the club's pool, restaurant, beach chairs, umbrellas, showers, and changing facilities; VIP guests can also expect a free 20-minute massage (upgrade to an hour for $25), all-you-can-drink cocktails, all-you-can-eat food, and transportation from the port. Margaritas can be delivered to you beachside, or you can escape the heat by grabbing a bite in the enclosed patio. Free Wi-Fi is also included. There's decent snorkeling right out front, and equipment is available next door at Gypsea Divers. Even if you don't get in the water, the four shades of turquoise are breathtaking. Cash only. **Amenities:** food and drink; showers; toilets. **Best for:** partiers; snorkeling; swimming. ⊠ *Av. Mahahual, Mahahual* ☏ *983/834–5719* ⊕ *www.nacionalbeachclub.com.*

Playa Xcalak

BEACH—SIGHT | Snorkelers and divers love this stretch of coastline, but beachgoers might be a little disappointed. The beach alongside Xcalak town is narrow—eaten away by past hurricanes—and often covered in seaweed and piles of garbage washed in on the tide. The hotels and B&Bs north of town do their best to keep their beaches clean and comfortable, making them the area's best spots for swimming or kayaking. Sections of the beach connect to a network of protected mangroves frequented by manatees. Moreover, the offshore reef of nearby Banco Chinchorro is great for snorkeling, diving, and fishing. **Amenities:** none. **Best for:** snorkeling; swimming. ⊠ *Xcalak.*

♨ Restaurants

There are seven outlets in the port complex serving food and drink. If you want to explore the village, you'll find other options.

Fernando's 100% Agave

$$ | **MEXICAN** | Fernando's friendly, homey restaurant—which serves as a sort of visitors bureau—seems to change locations often but remains a Mahahual institution. The affordable menu features

Mexican and Yucatecan specialties with a generous splash of gringo. **Known for:** homemade tequila; Yucatecan specialties; good margaritas. $ *Average main: 190 MP* ⊠ *Plaza Martillo between Calles Coronado and Martillo, Mahahual* ⊹ *North of soccer field* ☎ *983/834–5609* ⊘ *Closed Mon.*

⬤ Shopping

While most cruise passengers choose to shop in the mall at the cruise pier, in the town of Mahahual itself, vendors line the *malecón* (beach walkway) and sell crafts on days when cruise ships are in town.

🏃 Activities

If you want to have a truly authentic Mexican experience, take advantage of the day tours offered to outlying areas. They give you a chance to see some of the really spectacular sights in this part of Mexico, many of which are rarely visited. This is one port where the shore excursion is the point, and there are no options except to purchase what your ship offers.

Among the best tours are those that let you explore the gorgeous (and usually deserted) Maya ruins of Kohunlich, Dzibanché-Kinichná, and Chacchoben. The ancient pyramids and temples at these sites, surrounded by jungle that's protected them for centuries, are still dazzling to behold. Because the sites are some distance from the port complex—and require some road travel in one of the port's air-conditioned vans—these tours are all-day affairs. One of the most popular activities with cruise passengers is the three-hour ATV excursion along jungle roads and the Mahahual coastline. Although an adventure, ATVs tend to be a nuisance to residents and business owners, not to mention wildlife.

Cozumel, Mexico

Cozumel, with its sun-drenched ivory beaches fringed with coral reefs, fulfills the tourist's vision of a tropical Caribbean island. It's a heady mix of the natural and the commercial. Despite a miniconstruction boom in the island's sole city, San Miguel, there are still wild pockets scattered throughout the island where flora and fauna flourish. Smaller than Cancún, Cozumel surpasses its fancier neighbor in many ways. It has more history and ruins, superior diving and snorkeling, more authentic cuisine, and a greater diversity of handicrafts at better prices. The numerous coral reefs, particularly the world-renowned Palancar Reef, attract divers from around the world. On a busy cruise-ship day the island can seem completely overrun, but it's still possible to get away, and some good Maya sights are within reach on long (and expensive) shore excursions.

ESSENTIALS

CURRENCY

The Mexican peso, but U.S. dollars and credit cards are widely accepted in the area.

TELEPHONE

Most pay phones accept prepaid Ladatel cards, sold in 30-, 50-, or 100-peso denominations. To use the card, insert it in the pay phone's slot, dial 001 (for calls to the United States) or 01 (for calls within Mexico), followed by the area code and number. Credit is deleted from the card as you use it, and the balance is displayed on the small screen on the phone. Most triband mobile phones from the U.S. work in Mexico, though you must pay roaming charges.

COMING ASHORE

As many as six ships call at Cozumel on a busy day, disembarking passengers at the downtown Punta Langosta pier in the center of San Miguel or docking at the two piers, the International and Puerto

Maya piers, 4 miles (6 km) south. (Ships will occasionally tender their passengers into the downtown pier.)

From Punta Langosta you can walk into town or catch the ferry to Playa del Carmen. Taxi tours are also available. A four-hour island tour (4 people maximum), including the ruins and other sights, costs about $70 to $100, but negotiate the price before you get in the cab. The international pier is close to many beaches, but you'll need a taxi to get into town. There's rarely a wait for a taxi, but prices are high and drivers are often aggressive, asking double or triple the reasonable fare. When in doubt, ask to see the rate card required of all taxi drivers. Expect to pay $10 for the ride into San Miguel from the pier. Tipping is not necessary.

Passenger ferries to Playa del Carmen leave Cozumel's main pier approximately every other hour from 5 am to 10 pm. They also leave Playa del Carmen's dock about every other hour on the hour, from 6 am to 11 pm (but note that service sometimes varies according to demand). The trip takes 45 minutes. Verify the times: bad weather and changing schedules can prompt cancellations.

◉ Sights

San Miguel is not tiny, but you can easily explore the waterfront and plaza area on foot. The main attractions are the small eateries and shops that line the streets and the main square, where the locals congregate in the evening.

Chankanaab Beach Adventure Park

AMUSEMENT PARK/WATER PARK | FAMILY | Chankanaab, translated as "small sea," consists of a saltwater lagoon, an archaeological park, and a botanical garden, with reproductions of a Maya village and Olmec, Toltec, Aztec, and Maya stone carvings scattered throughout. You can swim at the beach, and there's plenty for snorkelers and divers to see beneath the surface—picture underwater caverns,

Best Bets ◉

■ **Diving and Snorkeling.** Excellent reefs close to shore make either diving or snorkeling a must-do activity.

■ **Maya Ruins.** Some of the most famous and dazzling ruins are reachable from Cozumel, and if you have never seen a Maya pyramid, this is your chance.

■ **People-Watching.** You can spend hours just sitting in the main plaza (or at a sidewalk café) watching island life pass by.

a sunken ship, crusty old cannons and anchors, and a sculpture of the Virgen del Mar (Virgin of the Sea), all populated by parrotfish and sergeant majors galore. The seal show is included in your admission. To preserve the ecosystem, rules forbid touching the reef or feeding the fish. You'll find dive shops, restaurants, gift shops, a snack stand, and dressing rooms with lockers and showers right on the sand. Chankanaab also has a Dolphin Discovery facility where visitors can swim with the much-loved marine mammals (⊕ www.dolphindiscovery. com). ✉ Carretera Sur, Km 9, Cozumel ☎ 987/872–0833 ⊕ www.cozumelparks. com ✆ MX$399 ⊙ Closed Sun. except holidays.

Museo de la Isla

MUSEUM | FAMILY | Filling two floors of a former hotel, Cozumel's museum has displays on natural history—the island's origins, endangered species, topography, and coral-reef ecology—as well as human history during the pre-Columbian and colonial periods. The photos of the island's transformation over the 20th and 21st centuries are especially fascinating, as is the exhibit of a typical Maya home. Guided tours are available. ✉ Av. Rafael E. Melgar, between Calles 4 and 6 Norte,

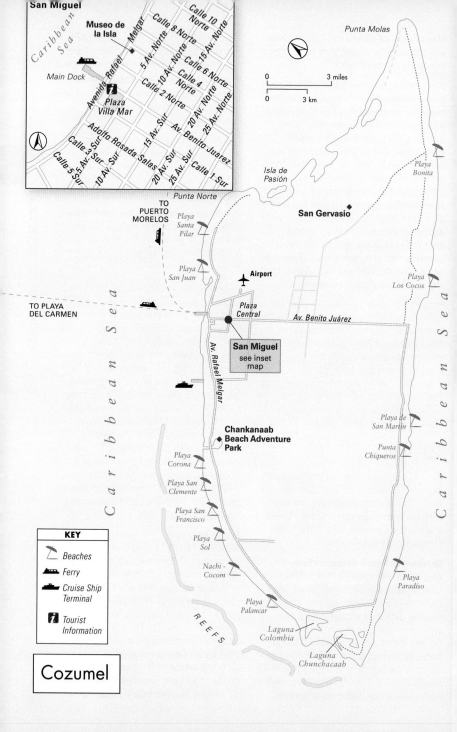

San Miguel

Caribbean Sea

Museo de la Isla

Main Dock

Plaza Villa Mar

Avenida Rafael Melgar

Calle 10 Norte
Calle 8 Norte
15 Av. Norte
5 Av. Norte
Calle 6 Norte
10 Av. Norte
Calle 4 Norte
Calle 2 Norte
15 Av. Norte
20 Av. Norte
25 Av. Norte

Adolfo Rosada Salas
Calle 3 Sur
5 Av. Sur
10 Av. Sur
15 Av. Sur
20 Av. Sur
25 Av. Sur
Av. Benito Juárez
Calle 1 Sur

Calle 5 Sur

Punta Molas

0   3 miles
0   3 km

Isla de Pasión

San Gervasio

Playa Bonita

Punta Norte

TO PUERTO MORELOS

Playa Santa Pilar

Playa San Juan

Airport

Plaza Central

Av. Benito Juárez

Playa Los Cocos

TO PLAYA DEL CARMEN

Av. Rafael Melgar

San Miguel
see inset map

Caribbean Sea

Chankanaab Beach Adventure Park

Playa Corona

Playa San Clemente

Playa San Francisco

Playa Sol

Nachi-Cocom

Playa de San Martín

Punta Chiqueros

Playa Paradíso

Caribbean Sea

KEY

Beaches
Ferry
Cruise Ship Terminal
Tourist Information

Playa Palancar

R E E F S

Laguna Colombia

Laguna Chunchacaab

Cozumel

Cozumel ☎ *987/872–1475* ⊕ *www.cozu-melparks.com* ✉ *MX$80* ⊘ *Closed Sun.*

San Gervasio

ARCHAEOLOGICAL SITE | Rising from the jungle, these temples make up Cozumel's largest remaining Maya and Toltec site. San Gervasio was the island's capital and ceremonial center, dedicated to the fertility goddess Ixchel. The classic- and postclassic-style buildings and temples were continuously occupied from AD 300 to 1500. Typical architectural features include limestone plazas and arches atop stepped platforms, as well as stelae and bas-reliefs. Don't miss the temple **Las Manitas,** with red handprints all over its altar. Water and light snacks are available to purchase, and bug spray is recommended—and be sure to wear your walking shoes for this adventure. ■**TIP→ Plaques in Maya, Spanish, and English clearly describe each structure, but it's worth hiring a guide to fully appreciate the site.** ⊠ *Benito Juárez Transversal Rd., Km 7.5, Cozumel* ✛ *From San Miguel, take cross-island road east to San Gervasio access road; turn left and follow road 7 km (4½ miles)* ☎ *987/872–0833* ⊕ *www.cozumelparks.com* ✉ *MX$100* ⊘ *Closed Sun.*

⦿ Beaches

Cozumel's beaches vary from sandy, treeless stretches to isolated coves to rocky shores. Most of the development is on the leeward (western) side. Beach clubs have sprung up on the southwest coast; admission, however, is usually free, as long as you buy food and drinks. Clubs offer typical tourist fare: souvenir shops, palapa restaurants, kayaks, and cold beer. A cab ride from San Miguel to most clubs costs about $15 each way. Reaching beaches on the windward (eastern) side is more difficult, but the solitude is worth it.

Playa Las Casitas

BEACH—SIGHT | FAMILY | Hugely popular with locals, Playa Las Casitas has several large palapa-style restaurant-bars, small palapas and palm trees for shade, calm waters, and a long stretch of beach. Swim out 150 yards from the north end to enjoy the fish-filled artificial reefs. Windsurfers and stand-up paddleboards are also available for rent. The beach is fairly deserted on weekdays but completely packed on Sunday, the traditional day for family outings. **Amenities:** food and drink; parking (no fee); toilets; water sports. **Best for:** snorkeling; sunsets; swimming. ⊠ *Carretera Norte at Blvd. Aeropuerto, Cozumel* ✉ *Free.*

Playa Palancar

BEACH—SIGHT | South of the resorts, down a dirt road and way off the beaten path, lies serene Playa Palancar—a long, walkable beach with hammocks hanging under coconut palms. The on-site dive shop can outfit scuba enthusiasts for trips to the famous Palancar and Columbia reefs, just offshore; boats will take snorkelers out every two hours from 9 to 5. There's also a nice open-air restaurant-bar here if you'd rather just relax. **Amenities:** food and drink; parking (no fee); showers; toilets; water sports. **Best for:** snorkeling; swimming; walking. ⊠ *Carretera Sur, Km 19.5, Cozumel* ⊕ *www.facebook.com/palancarczm/]* ✉ *Free.*

Punta Chiqueros

BEACH—SIGHT | FAMILY | Sheltered by an offshore reef, this half-moon cove is the first popular swimming area as you drive north on the coastal road. Part of a longer beach that some locals call "Playa Bonita," it has fine sand, clear water, turtle nests, and moderate waves. At lunchtime, you can linger over fried fish at a casual eatery that's also named **Playa Bonita. Amenities:** food and drink; parking (no fee); toilets. **Best for:** sunsets; surfing; swimming; walking. ⊠ *Carretera C-1, Km 38, Cozumel* ✉ *Free.*

🍴 Restaurants

★ Guido's Restaurant

$$$ | ITALIAN | Chef Yvonne Villiger works wonders with fresh fish—if the wahoo with capers and black olives is on the menu, don't miss it. But Guido's is best known for pizzas that are baked in a wood-fired oven and served by an incredibly attentive staff. **Known for:** fresh seafood; sangria; puffy garlic bread. ⑤ *Average main: 320 MP* ⊠ *Av. Rafael E. Melgar 23, between Calles 6 and 8 Norte, San Miguel* ☎ *987/869–2589* ⊕ *www. guidoscozumel.com* ☉ *No lunch Sun.*

Pancho's Backyard

$$$ | MEXICAN | FAMILY | Marimbas play beside a bubbling fountain in the charming courtyard behind one of Cozumel's best folk-art shops. The English menu is geared toward tourists and priced in pesos, but regional ingredients like smoky chipotle chile make even the standard steak stand out for a true Mexican-inspired meal. **Known for:** open-air courtyard dining; strong margaritas; seared tuna steaks. ⑤ *Average main: 220 MP* ⊠ *Av. Rafael E. Melgar 27, between Calles 8 and 10 Norte, San Miguel* ☎ *987/872–2141.*

🛍 Shopping

Cozumel's main souvenir-shopping area is downtown on or near the waterfront; tourist-trap malls at the cruise-ship piers sell jewelry, perfume, sportswear, and low-end souvenirs at high-end prices.

Most downtown shops accept U.S. greenbacks, and many goods are priced in dollars. But to get better prices, pay with pesos and stick to cash—some shops tack a hefty surcharge on credit-card purchases. Shops, restaurants, and streets are always crowded between 10 am and 2 pm, but slow down in the evening. Traditionally, stores are open from 9 to 9, although most do close on Sunday morning.

■**TIP**→ When you shop for souvenirs, be sure you don't buy anything made with black coral. It's an endangered species, and you'll be barred from bringing it to the United States (and other countries).

🏃 Activities

DIVING AND SNORKELING

Cozumel is famous for its reefs. In addition to Chankanaab Nature Park, a great dive site is La Ceiba Reef, in the waters off La Ceiba and Sol Caribe hotels. Here lies the wreckage of a sunken airplane blown up for a Mexican disaster movie. Cozumel has plenty of dive shops to choose from.

Blue Angel Scuba and Scuba School

SCUBA DIVING | FAMILY | The combo dive-and-snorkel excursions arranged by Blue Angel allow family members to have fun together, even if not all are scuba enthusiasts. Dedicated dive trips to local reefs and PADI courses are also offered. Inquire about the snorkel trip to the crystal-blue waters called El Cielo. Dive-and-hotel packages are available at its hotel of the same name. ⊠ *Blue Angel Resort, Carretera Costera Sur, Km 2.2, Cozumel* ☎ *987/872–0819* ⊕ *www. blueangelresort.com* ✉ *Snorkel trips from MX$1,200; 2-tank dives from MX$1,805.*

Eagle Ray Divers

SCUBA DIVING | Snorkeling trips and dive instruction are available through Eagle Ray Divers. (The three-reef snorkel trip lets nondivers explore beyond the shore.) As befits its name, the company keeps track of the eagle rays that appear off Cozumel from December to February and runs trips for advanced divers to walls where the rays congregate. Beginners can also see rays around some of the reefs. ⊠ *La Caleta Marina, near Presidente InterContinental, Cozumel* ☎ *987/872– 5735, 866/465–1616 in U.S.* ⊕ *www. eagleraydivers.com* ✉ *2-tank dives from MX$1,425.*

FISHING

The waters off Cozumel teem with more than 230 species of fish, making this one of the world's best deep-sea fishing destinations. During billfish migration season from late April through June, blue marlin, white marlin, and sailfish are plentiful, and world-record catches aren't uncommon.

The larger sportfishing boats are located in the Puerto Abrigo marina just north of San Miguel. Fishing boats are also located at **Marina Fonatur,** the marina on the south side, near the Presidente Inter-Continental resort. Some sportfishing companies are affiliated with dive shops and offer a full range of water activities. Hotels can help arrange daily charters—some offer special deals, with boats leaving from their own docks.

Albatros Charters

FISHING | FAMILY | Half- and full-day outings that include boat and crew, tackle and bait, plus libations and lunch (quesadillas or your own fresh catch) are organized by Albatros Charters. Customized dive trips are also available. ⊠ *Marina Puerto de Abrigo, Av. Rafael E. Melgar Norte, Puerto Abrigo* ☎ *987/872–7904, 888/333–4643 in U.S.* ⊕ *www.albatroscharters.com* ✉ *From MX$9,300 for 6 people fishing.*

Tres Hermanos

DIVING/SNORKELING | FAMILY | This outfit specializes in deep-sea and fly-fishing trips. It also offers scuba-diving excursions and snorkel trips. Boats are available for group charters, allowing you to move at your own pace. ⊠ *Marina Puerto de Abrigo, Av. Rafael E. Melgar Norte, Puerto Abrigo* ☎ *987/107–2030* ⊕ *www.3HCozumelAdventures.com* ✉ *From MX$7,125 for 4 people.*

Curaçao (Willemstad)

Try to be on deck as your ship sails into Curaçao. The tiny Queen Emma floating bridge swings aside to allow ships to pass through the narrow channel. Pastel gingerbread buildings on shore look like dollhouses, especially from a large cruise ship. Although the gabled roofs and red tiles show a Dutch influence, the gleeful colors of the facades are particular to Curaçao. It's said that an early governor of the island suffered from migraines that were aggravated by the color white, so all the houses were painted in hues from magenta to mauve. Thirty-five miles (56 km) north of Venezuela and 42 miles (68 km) east of Aruba, Curaçao is—at 38 miles (61 km) long and 3 to 7½ miles (5 to 12 km) wide—the largest of the three neighboring islands. Though always sunny, it's never stiflingly hot here because of the constant trade winds. Water sports attract enthusiasts from all over the world, and the reef diving is excellent.

ESSENTIALS
CURRENCY

Currency in Curaçao is the florin (also called the guilder) and is indicated by *fl* or *NAf* on price tags, but U.S. dollars are accepted almost everywhere.

TELEPHONE

Digicel and CHIPPIE are the two main mobile service providers; GSM (900, 1800 and 1900 bands) service is supported on the island.

COMING ASHORE

Ships dock at the terminal just beyond the Queen Emma Bridge, which leads to the floating market, cafés, and the shopping district. The walk to downtown takes less than 10 minutes. Easy-to-read maps are posted dockside and in the shopping area. The terminal has a duty-free shop, telephones, and a taxi stand.

Taxi rates are fixed. The government-approved rates, which do not include waiting time, can be found in a brochure called "Taxi Tariff Guide," available at the airport, hotels, cruise-ship terminals, and the tourist board. Rates are for up to four passengers. There's a 25% surcharge after 11 pm. It's easy to see the sights on Curaçao without going on an organized shore excursion. Downtown can be done on foot, and a taxi for up to four people will cost about $45 per hour. Taxi fares to places in and around the city range from $10 to $30. Car rentals are available but not cheap.

◉ Sights

WILLEMSTAD

Dutch settlers came here in the 1630s, about the same time they sailed through the Narrows to Manhattan, bringing with them original red-tile roofs, first used on the trade ships as ballast and later incorporated into the architecture of Willemstad. Much of the original colonial structures remain, but this historic city is constantly reinventing itself and the government monument foundation is always busy restoring buildings in one urban neighborhood or another. The salty air causes what is called "wall cancer," resulting in the ancient abodes continually crumbling over time. The city is cut in two by Santa Anna Bay. On one side is Punda (the Point)—crammed with shops, restaurants, monuments, and markets and a new museum retracing its colorful history—and on the other side is Otrobanda (literally, "the Other Side"), with lots of narrow, winding streets and alleyways (*steekjes* in Dutch), full of private homes notable for their picturesque gables and Dutch-influenced designs. In recent years the ongoing regeneration of Otrobanda has been apparent, marked by a surge in development of new hotels, restaurants, and shops; the rebirth, concentrated near the waterfront, was spearheaded by the creation of the elaborate Kura Hulanda complex. The old districts of Pietermaai and Scharloo are also being revitalized with restored

Best Bets ◉

- **Diving.** After Bonaire, Curaçao has probably the best diving in the region.

- **Punda.** Willemstad's chic and beautiful shopping area is a joy to explore on foot.

- **Curaçao Sea Aquarium.** Explore the wonders of the ocean without getting wet.

- **Floating Market.** This unique market is a fun destination, even though it's mostly fruits and vegetables.

- **Kura Hulanda Museum.** This is the island's best historical museum.

mansions and new dining, lodging, and entertainment options.

There are three ways to cross the bay: by car over the Juliana Bridge; by foot over the Queen Emma pontoon bridge (locally called "the Swinging Old Lady"); or by free ferry, which runs when the pontoon bridge is swung open for passing ships. All major hotels outside town offer free shuttle service to town once or twice daily. Shuttles coming from the Otrobanda side leave you at Riffort. From there it's a short walk north to the foot of the pontoon bridge. Shuttles coming from the Punda side leave you near the main entrance to Ft. Amsterdam.

Floating Market

MARKET | Curaçao is such an arid island that most of the fruit and vegetables need to be imported. The floating market consists of dozens of Venezuelan schooners laden with tropical fruits and vegetables that dock to sell their wares on the Punda side of the city. Mangoes, papayas, and exotic vegetables vie for space with freshly caught fish and herbs and spices. The buying is best at 6:30 am

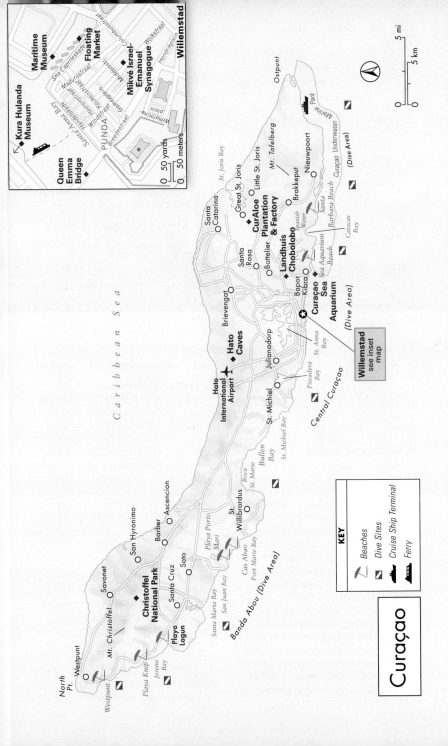

Curaçao

KEY

	Beaches
	Dive Sites
	Cruise Ship Terminal
	Ferry

Willemstad (inset map)

PUNDA

- Kura Hulanda Museum
- Maritime Museum
- Floating Market
- Mikvé Israel-Emanuel Synagogue
- Queen Emma Bridge

Santa Anna Bay

Sha Caprileskade
Madurostraat
Heerenstraat
Breedestraat
Hendrikplein
Wilhelminaplein
Columbusstraat
Gomezplein
Windstraat
Kuiperstraat
Waaigat
Wolksstraat

Willemstad

Main island

- North Pt.
- Westpunt
- Playa Knip
- Jeremi Bay
- Mt. Christoffel
- Christoffel National Park
- Savonet
- San Hyronimo
- Barber
- Ascencion
- Santa Cruz
- Soto
- Playa Lagun
- Santa Marta Bay
- San Juan Bay
- Cas Abao
- Port Marie Bay
- Boca St. Marie
- Playa Porto Mari
- St. Willibrordus
- St. Marie Bay
- Bullen Bay
- St. Michiel Bay
- St. Michiel
- Piscadera Bay
- Julianadorp
- Hato International Airport
- Hato Caves
- Brievengat
- Santa Catarina
- Santa Rosa
- Botelier
- Great St. Joris
- Little St. Joris
- St. Joris Bay
- CurAloe Plantation & Factory
- Landhuis Chobolobo
- Bapor Kibra
- Curaçao Sea Aquarium
- Sea Aquarium Beach
- Spanish Water
- Caracas Bay
- Brakkeput
- Mt. Tafelberg
- Nieuwpoort
- Santa Barbara Beach
- Curaçao Underwater Marine Park
- Ostpunt

Banda Abou (Dive Area)

Central Curaçao

St. Anna Bay

Willemstad see inset map

Curaçao Underwater (Dive Area)

Caribbean Sea

5 mi
5 km

A daring, mast-eye view of the Handelskade in Punda.

(too early for many people on vacation), but there's plenty of action throughout the afternoon. Vendors will stay on island for months away from their families—forming their own little community—awaiting fresh supplies each day. ✉ *Sha Caprileskade, Punda.*

★ Kura Hulanda Museum

MUSEUM | Pet project of Dutch billionaire philanthropist Jacob Gelt-Dekker, who brought the Otrobanda neighborhood back to life in the 1990s, this fascinating anthropological museum in a restored 18th-century village reveals the island's diverse roots. It's built around the former mercantile square (Kura Hulanda means "Holland Courtyard") where the Dutch once housed slaves before they were sold and exported. Somber exhibits of the transatlantic slave trade are tempered by sections that highlight the origins of the diaspora, including relics from West African empires, examples of pre-Columbian gold, and Antillean art. Call ahead for guided tours or rent an audio guide. ✉ *Klipstraat 9, Otrobanda*

☎ *5999/434–7700* ⊕ *www.kurahulanda. com/en/museumx* ✉ *$10* ⊗ *Closed Sun.*

★ Landhuis Chobolobo

HISTORIC SITE | The famed blue Curaçao liqueur, which is made from the peels of bitter laraha oranges, originated at this distillery. The family-run operation, located on a heritage estate that dates from the 1800s, offers a choice of guided tours that include tastings, cocktails, and even mixology lessons. Free self-guided tours also include samples. ✉ *Landhuis Chobolobo, Saliña* ☎ *5999/461–3526* ⊕ *www.chobolobo.com* ✉ *From $12.50* ⊗ *Closed weekends.*

★ Maritime Museum

MUSEUM | Model ships, historic maps, nautical charts, navigational equipment, audiovisual displays, and more convey more than 500 years of maritime and island history at this museum designed to resemble the interior of a ship. Topics include the development of Willemstad as a trading city, Curaçao's role as a contraband hub, *De Alphen* (a Dutch freighter that exploded and sank in St. Anna Bay in 1778 and was excavated in 1984), the slave trade, the development of steam navigation, and the role of the Dutch navy on the island. The museum also offers themed guided tours, including a popular ferry excursion through Curaçao's harbor. ⊠ *Van der Brandhofstraat 7, Punda* ☎ *5999/465–2327* ⊕ *www.curacaomaritime.com* 🎫 *Museum $7* 🕙 *Closed Sun.–Mon. in low season.*

Mikvé Israel-Emanuel Synagogue
RELIGIOUS SITE | The Western Hemisphere's oldest temple in continuous use is one of Curaçao's most important sights and draws thousands of visitors per year. The synagogue was dedicated in 1732 by a Jewish community that had grown from the original 12 families who came from Amsterdam in 1651 and included Jews who fled persecution by the Inquisition in Portugal and Spain. White sand covers the synagogue floor for two symbolic reasons: a remembrance of the 40 years Jews spent wandering the desert, and a re-creation of the sand used by secret Jews, or *conversos,* to muffle sounds from their houses of worship during the Inquisition. The Jewish Cultural Museum, in the back of the temple, displays antiques and artifacts from around the world. Many of the objects are used in the synagogue, making it a "living" museum. ⊠ *Hanchi Snoa 29, Punda* ☎ *5999/461–1067* ⊕ *www.snoa.com* 🎫 *$10; donations also accepted.*

★ Queen Emma Bridge
BRIDGE/TUNNEL | Affectionately called "the Swinging Old Lady," this bridge, which is beautifully lit at night, crosses Santa Anna Bay, connecting the two sides of Willemstad (Punda and Otrobanda). The bridge swings open at least 30 times a day to allow passage of ships to and from the sea. The original bridge, built in 1888, was the brainchild of the American consul Leonard Burlington Smith, who made a mint off the tolls he charged for using it: $0.02 per person for those wearing shoes, free to those crossing

barefoot. (Although he meant to help the poor, the rich often saved money by crossing barefoot, and the poor would often borrow shoes to cross because they were too proud to admit they could not afford the toll!) Today it's free to everyone. The bridge was dismantled and completely repaired and restored in 2005 and also restored further in 2015. ⊠ *Willemstad* ⊕ *www.curacao.com.*

ELSEWHERE ON CURAÇAO
★ Christoffel National Park
MUSEUM | The 1,239-foot Mt. Christoffel, Curaçao's highest peak, is at the center of this 4,450-acre garden and wildlife preserve. The preserve offers guided hikes, jeep safaris, mountain biking, deer-watching (the island's elusive white-tailed deer are very shy), animal presentations, cave explorations, and special activities like full-moon nature walks. Visitors can also hike the mountain on their own. The exhilarating climb takes about two hours for a reasonably fit person. Throughout the park are eight hiking trails and a 20-mile (32-km) network of driving trails; the old Savonet plantation house there (one of the island's first plantations) has been restored and now serves as a modern museum with exhibits retracing the region's history as far back as the original Indian inhabitants. ■ **TIP**→ **There's a separate entrance fee to the museum but you can also get a combination pass that includes the park and museum for less.** ⊠ *Christoffel Park, Savonet* ☎ *5999/462–4242 for info and tour reservations* ⊕ *www.christoffelpark.org* 🎫 *$14.*

CurAloe Plantation & Factory
TOUR—SIGHT | The island's successful CurAloe line of products is sold in shops throughout Curaçao. On a visit to the company's plantation (admission is free), you can see more than 100,000 plant specimens, learn about aloe's myriad cosmetic and medicinal applications, and sample and purchase products. Informative videos tell the story; a helpful staff answer questions. ⊠ *Kaminda Mitologia,*

Groot St. Joris, Willemstad ☎ *5999/767–5577* ⊕ *www.ecocityprojects.com.*

★ Curaçao Sea Aquarium

ZOO | FAMILY | Located in Sea Aquarium Park—along with the independently operated Animal Encounters, Dolphin Academy, and Substation Curaçao—the island's original and largest marine attraction is entertaining and educational for all ages. Admission allows access to more than 40 saltwater tanks full of sea life; dolphin and sea lion shows; shark-feeding sessions; and opportunities to interact with stingrays, sea turtles, and flamingoes. For extra fees, you can also swim and snorkel with dolphins or get up close to sea lions under the supervision of a trainer as part of the Sea Lion Encounter program. Don't miss the cool new Ocean Lens underwater observatory. A snack bar and souvenir shop are also on-site. ⊠ *Seaquarium Beach, Bapor Kibra* ☎ *5999/461–6666* ⊕ *www.csapark. com* ☜ *$21.*

Hato Caves

CAVE | Stalactites and stalagmites form striking shapes in these 200,000-year-old caves. Hidden lighting adds to the dramatic effect. Indians who used the caves for shelter left petroglyphs about 1,500 years ago. More recently, slaves who escaped from nearby plantations used the caves as a hideaway. Hour-long guided tours wind down to the pools in various chambers. Keep in mind that there are 49 steps to climb up to the entrance and the occasional bat might not be to everyone's taste. A new Indian Trail walking path and cactus garden enlighten visitors about local vegetation. The space is also available for special events. Located just two minutes from Hato International Airport. ⊠ *Rooseveltweg z/n, Hato* ☎ *5999/868–0379* ⊕ *curacaohatocaves.com* ☜ *$9.*

🏖 Beaches

Cas Abao

BEACH—SIGHT | FAMILY | This white-sand gem has the brightest blue water in Curaçao, a treat for swimmers, snorkelers, and sunbathers alike. Full services include a beach bar and restaurant, lockers, changing rooms on-site, and even full massages surfside are available. It can become crowded on weekends, especially Sunday, when local families descend in droves. You can rent beach chairs, paddle boats, and snorkeling and diving gear. The entry fee is $5 to $6 per car, more on weekends, and the beach is open from 8 am to 6 pm. **Amenities:** food and drink; lifeguards; parking; showers; toilets; water sports. **Best for:** partiers; snorkeling; swimming. ⊠ *West of St. Willibrordus, about 3 miles (5 km) off Weg Naar Santa Cruz* ✛ *Turn off Westpunt Hwy. at the junction onto Weg Naar Santa Cruz; follow until the turnoff for Cas Abao, and then drive along the winding country road for about 10 mins to the beach.*

Playa Knip

BEACH—SIGHT | FAMILY | Two protected coves offer crystal-clear turquoise waters. Big (Groot) Knip, also known as Playa Kenepa, is an expanse of alluring white sand, perfect for swimming and snorkeling. You can rent beach chairs and hang out under the *palapas* (thatch-roof shelters) or cool off with ice cream at the snack bar. This spot is also famous for cliff jumping by locals and adventurous visitors. There are restrooms here but no showers. It's particularly crowded on Sunday and school holidays. Just up the road, also in a protected cove, sister beach Little (Klein) Knip is a charmer, too, with picnic tables and palapas. There's no fee for these beaches. **Amenities:** food and drink; lifeguards; parking; toilets; water sports. **Best for:** snorkeling; sunrise; sunset; swimming. ⊠ *Just east of Westpunt, Banda Abou.*

★ Playa PortoMari

BEACH—SIGHT | FAMILY | Set beneath an historic plantation site, you'll find calm, clear water and a long stretch of white sand and full facilities on this beach. A decent bar and restaurant, well-kept showers, changing facilities, and restrooms are all on-site; a nature trail is nearby. The double coral reef (explore one, swim past it, explore another) is a special feature that makes this spot popular with snorkelers and divers. The entrance fee is $3. **Amenities:** food and drink; lifeguards; parking; showers; toilets. **Best for:** partiers; snorkeling; swimming; walking. ✉ *Off Willibrordus Rd.* ⊹ *From Willemstad, drive west on Westpunt Hwy. for 4 miles (7 km); turn left onto Willibrordus Rd. at the PortoMari billboard, and then drive 3 miles (5 km) until you see a large church; follow signs on the winding dirt road to the beach* ☎ *5999/864–7558* ⊕ *www.playaportom-ari.com* ⊗ *Closes at 6:30 pm.*

🍴 Restaurants

★ Gouverneur de Rouville Restaurant & Café

$$$ | ECLECTIC | Dine on the verandah of a restored 19th-century Dutch mansion overlooking Santa Anna Bay. Consistently good local and international fish, chicken, and beef dishes attract locals and visitors alike (reserve ahead if you want a table with a harbor view); be sure to stick around after dinner for live music at the bar, which stays open late. **Known for:** "green egg" barbecue specials; authentic stobas (stews) and keshi yena (cheese stuffed with meat); legendary Cuban banana soup (lunch only). ⑤ *Average main: $25* ✉ *De Rouvilleweg 9, Otrobanda* ☎ *5999/462–5999* ⊕ *www. de-gouverneur.com.*

Scampi's Restaurant

$$$ | SEAFOOD | Part of the Waterfort Terrace, this open-air dining spot serves an interesting selection of steak and seafood dishes, including some with Asian twists or Latin American heat (there's also a children's menu). The setting can be very romantic in the evening thanks to stellar views of the sun setting over the port and a roster of signature cocktails like Coastal Kiss and Fancy Scampis. **Known for:** Thursday-night happy hour with live music; great harbor views; fresh catch of the day and lobster. ⑤ *Average main: $22* ✉ *Waterfort Terrace, Water-fortstraat 41-42, Punda* ☎ *5999/465–0769* ⊕ *www.scampiscuracao.com* ⊗ *No lunch.*

🛍 Shopping

From Dutch classics like embroidered linens, Delft earthenware, and cheeses to local artwork and handicrafts, shopping in Willemstad can turn up some fun finds. But don't expect major bargains on watches, jewelry, or electronics; Willemstad is not a duty-free port (the few "duty-free" establishments are simply absorbing the cost of some or all of the tax rather than passing it on to consumers). However, if you come prepared with some comparison prices, you might still dig up some good deals. But there are new complexes out of downtown now for ultimate retail therapy—Mambo Beach Boulevard has an eclectic collection of trendy shops at the Sea Aquarium Park and the Sambil megamall is a massive multilevel shopping and entertainment complex in Veeris Commercial Park with hundreds of modern stores and trendy boutiques.

★ Boolchand's

CAMERAS/ELECTRONICS | The Caribbean's best-known brand for electronics, Boolchand's is a legendary family-run chain, with a Punda flagship store and many other branches around Curaçao. They have a reputation for offering fair prices on high-quality electronics, tech, cameras, watches, jewelry, crystal, and more. ✉ *Breedstraat 50, Punda* ☎ *5999/461–6233* ⊕ *www.boolchand.com.*

Cigar Emporium

TOBACCO | A sweet aroma permeates the Cigar Emporium, where you can find the largest selection of Cuban cigars on the island, including H. Upmann, Romeo y Julieta, and Montecristo. Visit the climate-controlled cedar cigar room. ⊠ *Gomezplein 4, Punda* ☏ *5999/465–3955.*

★ Serena's Art Factory

ART GALLERIES | You might have noticed brightly painted sculptures of colorful Caribbean women in many public places around the island, not to mention miniature versions of them for sale as souvenirs. These are Chichis®—created by the artist Serena Janet Israel and unique to Curaçao. *Chichi* means "big sister" in the local lingo, and the figures are meant to exude the warmth of matronly Caribbean women; new characters, including a man and a child, have also been created. Serena has trained many local female artists to paint them, and you're also welcome to paint your own for a one-of-a-kind souvenir at Serena's Art Factory near the Ostrich Farm. Two-hour walk-in workshops are offered regularly. A stand-alone shop in Willemstad's Punda district also sells Chichi items and offers some workshops. ⊠ *Jan Louis 87a* ☏ *5999/738–0648* ⊕ *www.chichi-curacao. com* ▣ *Free tour of factory.*

🏃 Activities

BIKING

Wanna Bike Curaçao

BICYCLING | FAMILY | The island's premier biking outfit, Wanna Bike offers mountain bike tours all over Curaçao with professional guides and top equipment. They are also the founders of the Mountain Bike Kids Club and organize many mountain bike clinics throughout the year. Their sister company "Wanna Go Outdoors" organizes corporate retreats and team-building events centered around biking and eco-adventures. Note, though, that cash is king; credit cards

aren't accepted. ⊠ *Jan Thiel Beach z/n, Jan Thiel, Willemstad* ☏ *5999/527–3720* ⊕ *www.wannabike.com.*

DIVING AND SNORKELING

The **Curaçao Underwater Marine Park** includes almost a third of the island's southern diving waters. Scuba divers and snorkelers can enjoy more than 12½ miles (20 km) of protected reefs and shores, with normal visibility from 60 to 150 feet. With water temperatures ranging from 75°F to 82°F (24°C to 28°C), wet suits are generally unnecessary. No coral collecting, spearfishing, or littering is allowed. Some of the most popular dive sites are the Mushroom Forest, the wreck of the *Superior Producer,* and the Blue Room secret cave at Westpunt. Snorkelers and divers also enjoy the little sunken tugboat at Spanish Water. Wall diving is good around the Sea Aquarium Park and they also offer open-water dives with dolphins. The north coast—where conditions are dangerously rough—is not recommended for diving.

Introductory scuba resort courses are often done in resort pools and prices vary. To become fully PADI certified, carve out at least four or five days of your holiday for instruction and practice and at least one open-water dive. Prices vary depending on operation.

★ Ocean Encounters

SCUBA DIVING | Curaçao's largest dive operator offers a vast roster of scheduled shore and boat dives, packages, certified PADI instruction, and snorkeling opportunities. They cover the island's most popular dive sites, including the wreck of the adorable little *Superior Producer* tugboat—where barracudas hang out— and the renowned Mushroom Forest. In addition, Ocean Encounters runs the unique Animal Encounters experience at the Sea Aquarium, with whom they also partner to sponsor a children's sea camp each July. Be sure to inquire about the outfit's Sleep & Dive packages at Lion's Dive, Sunscape Resort, Floris

Suites, Dolphin Suites, and Avila Beach Hotel. ✉ *Sea Aquarium Park, Bapor Kibra* ☎ *5999/461–8131* ⊕ *www.oceanencounters.com/en.*

Dominica (Roseau)

In the center of the Caribbean archipelago, wedged between the two French islands of Guadeloupe to the north and Martinique to the south, Dominica is a wild place. So unyielding is the terrain that colonists surrendered efforts at colonization, but the last survivors of the Caribbean's original people, the Carib Indians, call its rugged northeast section home. Dominica (29 miles (47 km) long and 16 miles (26 km) wide) is an English-speaking island, though family and place names are a mélange of French, English, and Carib. The capital is Roseau (pronounced *rose-OH*). If you've had enough of casinos, crowds, and swim-up bars and want to take leave of everyday life—to hike, bike, trek, spot birds and butterflies in the rain forest; explore waterfalls; discover a boiling lake; kayak, dive, snorkel, or sail in marine reserves; or go out in search of the many resident whale and dolphin species—this is the place to do it.

ESSENTIALS
CURRENCY
The Eastern Caribbean dollar (EC$), but U.S. dollars are widely accepted.

TELEPHONE
LIME and Digicel are the primary cell phone providers using GSM (850, 900, and 1900 bands). The country code is 1 767.

COMING ASHORE
Most ships dock along Roseau's bayfront. A visitor center sits across the street from the pier in the old post office. Taxis, minibuses, and tour operators are available at the berths. Choose one that is certified and don't be afraid to ask questions. Be explicit when discussing

Best Bets

■ **Kalinago Barana Autê.** This reserve is a great place to learn about the "fierce" Caribs.

■ **Rain Forest Trips.** Hiking in Dominica's rain forest is the best way to experience its natural beauty.

■ **Snorkeling in Champagne.** A bubbling volcanic vent makes you feel as if you are snorkeling in Champagne.

■ **Whale-Watching.** November through February offers the best whale-watching in the Caribbean.

■ **Indian River.** A rowboat ride on the river is relaxing and peaceful.

where you want to go and how much you will pay. The drivers should quote a fixed fare based on distance, which is regulated by the Division of Tourism and the Transportation Board. Drivers should also offer their services for tours anywhere on the island beginning at US$30 per hour for up to four people; a four- to five-hour island tour for up to four people will cost approximately US$200. You can rent a car in Roseau for about $55 to $100 per day, not including the $12 driving permit. Be aware that navigating the island is difficult, so you may want to opt for a guided tour.

◉ Sights

Despite the small size of this island, it can take a couple of hours to travel between the popular destinations. Many sights are isolated and difficult to find; you may be better off taking an organized excursion. If you do go it alone, drive carefully; roads can be narrow, winding, and unmarked. Plan at least eight hours to see the highlights. To fully experience

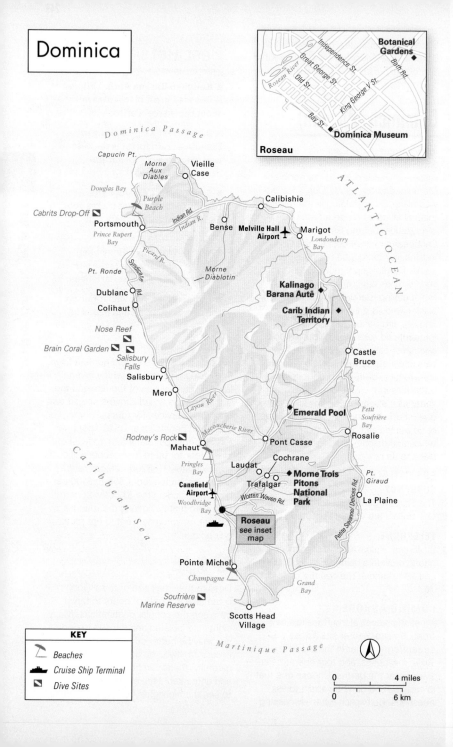

Dominica

Roseau

Botanical Gardens
Barth Rd.
Independence St.
Great George St.
Roseau River
Old St.
King George V St.
Bay St.
Dominica Museum

Dominica Passage

Capucin Pt.

Morne Aux Diables

Vieille Case

Douglas Bay

Calibishie

Cabrits Drop-Off

Purple Beach

Indian Rd.

Indian R.

Bense

Melville Hall Airport

Marigot

Londonderry Bay

Portsmouth

Prince Rupert Bay

Picard R.

Syndicate Rd.

Pt. Ronde

Morne Diàblotin

Kalinago Barana Autê

Dublanc

Colihaut

Carib Indian Territory

Nose Reef

Brain Coral Garden

Salisbury Falls

Salisbury

Castle Bruce

Mero

Layou River

Emerald Pool

Petit Soufrière Bay

Rodney's Rock

Macoucherie River

Rosalie

Mahaut

Pont Casse

Pringles Bay

Laudat

Cochrane

Morne Trois Pitons National Park

Pt. Giraud

Canefield Airport

Trafalgar

Woodbridge Bay

Watten Waven Rd.

Petite Savanne Delices Rd.

La Plaine

Roseau
see inset map

Caribbean Sea

Pointe Michel

Champagne

Grand Bay

Soufrière Marine Reserve

Scotts Head Village

Martinique Passage

ATLANTIC OCEAN

KEY

- Beaches
- Cruise Ship Terminal
- Dive Sites

0   4 miles

0   6 km

the island, set aside about five days so you can enjoy the water and take some hikes.

ROSEAU

Although it's one of the smallest capitals in the Caribbean, Roseau has the highest concentration of inhabitants of any town in the eastern part of the region. The vernacular architecture and a bustling marketplace transport visitors back in time. Although you can walk the entire town in about an hour, you'll get a much better feel for the place on a leisurely stroll.

For some years now, the Society for Historical Architectural Preservation and Enhancement (SHAPE) has organized programs and projects to preserve the city's architectural heritage. Several interesting buildings have already been restored. **Lilac House,** on Kennedy Avenue, has three types of gingerbread fretwork, latticed verandah railings, and heavy hurricane shutters. The **J. W. Edwards Building,** at the corner of Old and King George V Streets, has a stone base and a wooden second-floor gallery. The **Old Market Plaza** is the center of Roseau's historic district, which was laid out by the French on a radial plan rather than a grid, so that Hanover, King George V, and Old Streets radiate outward from this area. South of the marketplace is the Fort Young Hotel, built as a British fort in the 18th century; the nearby statehouse, public library, and Anglican cathedral are also worth a visit. New developments at the bayfront on Dame M. E. Charles Boulevard have brightened up the waterfront.

Botanical Gardens

GARDEN | FAMILY | The 40-acre Botanical Gardens, founded in 1891 as an annex of London's Kew Gardens, is a great place to relax, stroll, or watch a cricket match. In addition to the extensive collection of tropical plants and trees, there's also a parrot aviary. At the Forestry Division office, which is also on the garden grounds, you can find numerous publications on the island's flora, fauna, and national parks. The forestry officers are particularly knowledgeable on these subjects and can also recommend good hiking guides. ⊠ *Valley Rd., Roseau* ☎ *767/266–3807, 767/266–3812* ⊕ *www. dominicagardens.com* ⛵ *Free.*

Dominica Museum

MUSEUM | The old post office now houses the Dominica Museum. This labor of love by local writer and historian Dr. Lennox Honychurch contains furnishings, documents, prints, and maps that date back hundreds of years; you can also find an entire Carib hut as well as Carib canoes, baskets, and other artifacts. ⊠ *Dame M. E. Charles Blvd., opposite cruise-ship berth* ☎ *767/615–5096* ⛵ *$3* ⊙ *Closed weekends (unless a cruise ship is in port).*

ELSEWHERE ON DOMINICA
Carib Indian Territory

ARCHAEOLOGICAL SITE | FAMILY | In 1903, after centuries of conflict, the Caribbean's first settlers, the Kalinago (more popularly known as the Caribs), were granted approximately 3,700 acres of land on the island's remote, mountainous, northeast coast. Here a hardened lava formation, **L'Escalier Tête Chien** (Snake's Staircase), runs down into the Atlantic. The name is derived from a snake whose head resembles that of a dog. The ocean alongside Carib Territory is particularly fierce, and the shore is full of countless coves and inlets. Approximately 3,000 natives reside here. Craftspeople have retained their knowledge of basket weaving, wood carving, and canoe building through generations. They fashion long, elegant canoes from the trunk of a single *gommier* tree. ⊕ *www.caribterritory.com.*

Emerald Pool

NATURE PRESERVE | FAMILY | Quite possibly the most visited nature attraction on the island, this emerald-green pool fed by a 50-foot waterfall is an easy trip to make. To reach this spot in the vast Morne Trois Pitons National Park, you follow a trail that starts at the side of the road near the reception center (an easy 20-minute walk). Along the way, there are lookout points with views of the windward (Atlantic) coast and the forested interior. This spot is popular with cruise-ship tour groups. ⊠ *Morne Trois Pitons National Park* ⌚ *$3 for preorganized tours; $5 for private and stay-over visitors; $12 weekly pass for all national parks.*

Kalinago Barana Autê

MUSEUM VILLAGE | **FAMILY** | You might catch canoe builders at work at Kalinago Barana Autê, the Carib Territory's place to learn about Kalinago customs, history, and culture. A guided, 45-minute tour explores the village, stopping along the way to see some traditional dances and to learn about plants, dugout canoes, basket weaving, and cassava bread making. The path offers wonderful viewpoints of the Atlantic and a chance to glimpse Isukulati Falls. There's also a good souvenir shop. ⊠ *Crayfish River, Salibia* ☎ *767/245–4660* ⊕ *kalinagoterritory.com/attractions/the-kalinago-barana-aute* ⌚ *$10.*

★ Morne Trois Pitons National Park

HOT SPRINGS | A UNESCO World Heritage Site, this 17,000-acre swath of lush, mountainous land in the south-central interior (covering 9% of Dominica) is the island's crown jewel. Named after one of the highest mountains on the island (at 4,600 feet), it contains the island's famous "boiling lake," majestic waterfalls, and cool mountain lakes. A system of trails has been developed in the park, and access to the park is possible from most points on the island, though the easiest approaches are via the small mountaintop villages of Laudat (pronounced *lau-DAH*) and Cochrane.

At the base of Morne Micotrin you can find two crater lakes: the first, at 2,500 feet above sea level, is **Freshwater Lake.** According to a local legend, it's haunted by a vindictive mermaid and a monstrous serpent. Farther on is **Boeri Lake,** fringed

with greenery and purple hyacinths floating on its surface.

On your way to Boiling Lake you pass through the **Valley of Desolation,** where harsh sulfuric fumes have destroyed virtually all the vegetation in what must once have been a lush forested area. At the beginning of the Valley of Desolation trail is the **TiTou Gorge,** where you can swim in the pool or relax in the hot-water springs along one side.

The national park contains some of the island's most spectacular waterfalls, including **Sari Sari Falls,** accessible through the east-coast village of La Plaine. The 45-minute hike to them can be hair-raising, but the sight of water cascading some 150 feet into a large pool is awesome. Just beyond the village of Trafalgar and up a short hill is the reception facility, where you can purchase passes to the national park and find guides to take you on a rain-forest trek to the twin **Trafalgar Falls**; the 125-foot-high waterfall is called the Father, and the wider, 95-foot-high one, the Mother. You need a guide for the arduous 75-minute hike to **Middleham Falls.** Guides for all these hikes are available at the trailheads; still, it's best to arrange a tour before setting out. ⊕ *www.natureisland.com/MTPNatPark.html* ⌚ *$3 for preorganized tours; $5 per site for private and stay-over visitors; $12 weekly pass for all national parks.*

🏖 Beaches

★ Champagne

BEACH—SIGHT | **FAMILY** | On the southwest coast, just south of the village of Pointe Michel, this stony beach is hailed as one of the best spots for swimming, diving, and (especially) snorkeling. Forget the sunning, though, because the beach is strewn with rocks. Champagne gets its name from volcanic vents that constantly puff steam into the sea, which makes you feel as if you are swimming in warm

Emerald Pool is one of Dominica's most popular natural attractions.

Champagne. A boardwalk leads to the beach from Soufrière/Scotts Head Marine Reserve. **Amenities:** none. **Best for:** snorkeling; swimming. ⊠ *Soufrière ✛ 1 mile (1½ km) south of Pointe Michel.*

🍴 Restaurants

★ The Palisades Restaurant

$$$ | ECLECTIC | FAMILY | Dine in the air-conditioned interior or on the wrap-around balcony of this elegant, romantic, recently refurbished restaurant at the southern end of Roseau's bay front. The changing menu regularly features traditional international and local dishes as well as seafood creations such as lionfish *bon femme,* char-grilled lobster, or jerk octopus. **Known for:** local dishes like callalou and "Fort Nut" soup ; soothing seaside location; spinach ice cream. $ *Average main: US$25* ⊠ *Fort Young Hotel & Dive Resort, Victoria St., Roseau* ☎ *767/285–6377, 767/448–5000* ⊕ *www.fortyounghotel.com/palisades-restaurant* ⊘ *No lunch Sat. No dinner Mon. and Tues. Closed Sept.*

Guiyave

$$ | CARIBBEAN | This popular restaurant in a quaint Caribbean town house also has a shop downstairs serving a scrumptious selection of sweet and savory pastries, tarts, and cakes, which can also be ordered upstairs, along with breakfast and a Caribbean buffet for lunch. Choose to dine either in the airy dining room or on the sunny, narrow balcony perched above Roseau's colorful streets. **Known for:** authentically local setting; great people-watching; freshly squeezed tropical juices. $ *Average main: US$16* ⊠ *15 Cork St., Roseau* ☎ *767/448–2930, 767/448–1723* ⊘ *Closed Sun. No dinner.*

👜 Shopping

Dominicans produce distinctive handicrafts, with various communities specializing in their specific products. The crafts of the Carib Indians include traditional baskets made of dyed *larouma* reeds and waterproofed with tightly woven *balizier* leaves. These are sold in the Carib Indian Territory and Kalinago Barana Autê as well as in Roseau's shops. Vertivert straw rugs, screw-pine tableware, *fwije* (the trunk of the forest tree fern), and wood carvings are just some examples. Also notable are local herbs, spices, condiments, and herb teas. Café Dominique, the local equivalent of Jamaican Blue Mountain coffee, is an excellent buy, as are the Dominican rums Macoucherie and Soca. Proof that the old ways live on in Dominica can be found in the number of herbal remedies available. One stimulating memento of your visit is rum steeped with *bois bandé* (scientific name *Richeria grandis*), a tree whose bark is reputed to have aphrodisiacal properties. It's sold at shops, vendors' stalls, and supermarkets.

One of the easiest places to pick up a souvenir is the Old Market Plaza, just behind the Dominica Museum, in Roseau. Slaves were once sold here, but today handcrafted jewelry, T-shirts, spices, souvenirs, batik, and trays, plus lacquered and woven bamboo boxes are available from a group of vendors in open-air booths set up on the cobblestones. They are usually busiest when there's a cruise ship berthed across the street. On these days you can also find a vast number of vendors along the bayfront.

Kalinago Barana Autê

CRAFTS | Kalinago Barana Autê sells carvings, pottery, and lovely handwoven baskets, which you can watch the women weave. ⊠ *Salybia, Carib Territory* 🕾 *767/445–7979* ⊕ *kalinagoterritory.com/ attractions/the-kalinago-barana-aute.*

🏃 Activities

ADVENTURE SPORTS
★ Wacky Rollers

TOUR—SPORTS | FAMILY | For Jeep safaris, river-tubing experiences, sea-kayaking excursions, and other soft-adventure tours Wacky Rollers is your outfitter. Its newest activity, Wacky RIB Adventure,

features snorkeling, whale- and dolphin-watching, and coastal cruises on a 35-foot, rigid, inflatable boat. Although the office is in Roseau, the park where most outings take place is in Hillsborough Estate, 20 to 25 minutes north of town. ⊠ *Front St., Roseau* 🕾 *767/616– 8276* ⊕ *www.wackyrollers.com* 🖻 *From $80.*

DIVING AND WHALE-WATCHING

Not only is Dominica considered one of the top 10 dive destinations in the world by *Skin Diver* and *Rodale's Scuba Diving* magazines, but it has won many other awards for its underwater sites. They are truly memorable. The west coast of the island has awesome sites, but the best are those in the southwest—within and around **Soufrière/Scotts Head Marine Reserve.** This bay is a submerged volcanic crater. The Dominica Watersports Association has worked along with the Fisheries Division for years to establish this reserve and has set stringent regulations to prevent the degradation of the ecosystem. Within ½ mile (¾ km) of the shore there are vertical drops from 800 feet to more than 1,500 feet, with visibility frequently extending to 100 feet. Shoals of boga fish, creole wrasse, and blue cromis are common, and you might even see a spotted moray eel or a honeycomb cowfish. Crinoids (rare elsewhere) are also abundant here, as are giant barrel sponges. There is a $2 fee per person to dive, snorkel, or kayak in the reserve. Other noteworthy dive sites include **Salisbury Falls, Nose Reef, Brain Coral Garden,** and—even farther north—**Cabrits Drop-Off** and **Toucari Reef.** The conditions for underwater photography, particularly macrophotography, are unparalleled. Rates start at about $55 for a single-tank dive and about $90 for a two-tank dive, or from about $75 for a resort course with one open-water dive. All scuba-diving operators also offer snorkeling. Equipment rents for $10 to $25 per day; trips with gear range from $15 to $35 per day. Tax (10%) is not included.

Dominica records the highest species counts of resident cetaceans in the southern Caribbean region, so it's not surprising that tour companies claim 90% sighting success for their excursions. Humpback whales, false killer whales, minke whales, and orcas are all occasionally seen, as are several species of dolphin. But the resident sperm whales (they calve in Dominica's 3,000-foot-deep waters) are truly the stars of the show. During your 3½-hour expedition, which costs about $55 plus tax, you may be asked to assist in recording sightings, data that can be shared with local and international organizations. Although there are resident whale and dolphin populations, more species can be observed from November through February. Turtle-watching trips are also popular.

Dive Dominica

SCUBA DIVING | Dive Dominica, one of the island's dive pioneers, has four boats and is now the in-house operator at the Fort Young Hotel. In addition to conducting PADI and Nitrox-certification courses, this four-boat operation offers diving, snorkeling, and whale-watching trips and packages. ⊠ Fort Young Hotel, Victoria St., Roseau ☎ 767/448–2188, 646/502–6800 in U.S. ⊕ www.fortyounghotel.com.

HIKING

Dominica's majestic mountains, clear rivers, and lush vegetation conspire to create adventurous hiking trails. The island is crisscrossed by ancient footpaths of the Arawak and Carib Indians and of the Nègres Maroons, escaped slaves who established camps in the mountains. Existing trails range from easygoing to arduous. To make the most of your excursion, you'll need sturdy hiking boots, insect repellent, a change of clothes (kept dry), and a guide. Hikes and tours run $25 to $80 per person, depending on destinations and duration. A poncho or light raincoat is recommended. Some of the natural attractions within the island's

national parks require visitors to purchase a site pass, sold for varying numbers of visits. A single-entry site pass costs $5, and a week pass $12. The Discover Dominica Authority's information offices at the Bayfront (Dame Charles Boulevard) can recommend guides.

Bertrand Jno Baptiste

HIKING/WALKING | Local bird and forestry expert Bertrand Jno Baptiste leads hikes up Morne Diablotin and along the Syndicate Nature Trail; if he's not available, ask him to recommend another guide. ☎ 767/245–4768.

Falmouth, Jamaica

Falmouth, which was founded in 1769, prospered from Jamaica's status as the world's leading sugar producer. Midway between Ocho Rios and Montego Bay—and with more than 80 sugar estates nearby—the town was meticulously mapped out in the colonial tradition, with streets named after British royalty and heroes. The richness of the town's historic Georgian structures, many of which are still occupied and maintained, is reflected in its heritage. The city has long been heralded for its forward-thinking hygiene policies (the first piped water supply system in the Western Hemisphere, established here in 1799, continues to be a source of pride) and progressive politics (Falmouth was the birthplace of Jamaica's abolitionist movement in the early 19th century). The site of many slave revolts, Falmouth's residents turned scores of the town's buildings into safe houses for escaped slaves until the practice of slavery was outlawed in Jamaica in 1838.

In 1966 the Jamaican government declared Falmouth a national monument. The city has been seeing a revival since the opening of a purpose-built cruise port in 2011, and although some buildings may seem unimpressive as they undergo restoration, they are still rich in history.

ESSENTIALS
CURRENCY
The Jamaican dollar, but the U.S. dollar is accepted virtually everywhere.

TELEPHONE
The country code for Jamaica is 1 876. Digicel and Flow are the major mobile phone providers, using GSM (850, 900, 1800, and 1900 bands).

COMING ASHORE
Cruise ships, including the world's largest, are able to dock at the Falmouth Cruise Port's two berths. A visitor information facility is in the pier area. The town is right outside the port gates, and places of interest are easily within walking distance. Currency-exchange booths are in the pier area as well as just outside the entrance gate on Seaboard Street. The cruise-port area has Wi-Fi service (for a fee) for passengers with laptops. The Falmouth tourist trolley offers a half-hour tour of the town with regular departures from the Port Transportation Center. Tickets and trolley schedules are available in the trolley kiosk at the Taxi Shelter building.

For travel out of town, taxis are available. Taxis are priced by the hour at $35 for up to four people for either a guided tour or transportation to a specific destination. You can also take a chartered bus to the beach for $20 round-trip. Falmouth's location, about 30 minutes from Montego Bay and about an hour from Ocho Rios, means most tours offered at those ports available from Falmouth as well. Many of the most popular and adventurous tours are operated by Chukka Caribbean and can only be booked by passengers directly with their cruise lines, as space is presold to ships for their arrival dates. Coaches for prebooked tours pick up passengers inside the port, but authorized independent tour operators are also available to arrange tours on the spot.

Best Bets ◉

■ **Good Hope Plantation.** The expansive view of the plantation grounds and surrounding countryside from the front garden includes the Martha Brae River.

■ **Historic Falmouth Walking Tour.** Absorb Falmouth's Colonial-era history and discover the town's landmarks and Georgian architectural treasures.

■ **Tharp House.** Located within the Falmouth Cruise Port, the town home of sugar planter John Tharp is one of Falmouth's most historic buildings. Once a tax collector's office, it is now expected to become a maritime museum.

Car rental isn't recommended off the main highways in Jamaica because of the narrow roads and aggressive drivers.

◉ Sights

Falmouth's streets, which were laid out in a grid plan in the mid-1700s, are easily explored on your own. However, even with a map, finding your way around can be confusing due to a lack of street signs. If you become disoriented or require directions, look for a member of the Falmouth Tourism Courtesy Corps, wearing an official white shirt and hat—they are on hand to assist visitors. The one-hour trolley tour, which leaves from inside the cruise port, is an excellent way to see the historic sites and buildings and help you avoid getting lost.

Points of interest include the Falmouth Courthouse and the adjacent Cenotaph War Memorial; Water Square, where Falmouth residents got running water before New York City; Fort Balcarres, built to guard Falmouth Harbour; and Barrett House ruins, the remains of the town

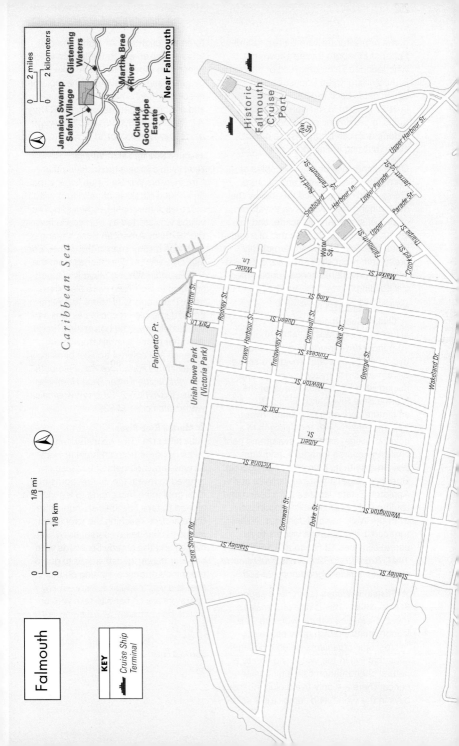

home of planter Edward Barrett (grandfather of Elizabeth Barrett Browning), who founded Falmouth. Also of interest is the William Knibb Baptist Church, which dates back to 1832 and was rebuilt in 1837 by Baptist missionary William Knibb, a pro-emancipation activist. St. Peter's Anglican Church is the oldest public building in Falmouth still in use.

Other sights include fine examples of Falmouth's Georgian-era architecture. These buildings are recognizable by their double-hung sash windows, keystones, columns, symmetry of facade, and full-length verandahs. Constructed of a native limestone over brick, and remarkably preserved, most structures are occupied as either private residences or commercial buildings.

NEAR FALMOUTH

★ Chukka Good Hope Estate

AMUSEMENT PARK/WATER PARK | About a 20-minute drive inland from Falmouth, this 2,000-acre estate provides a sense of Jamaica's rich history as a sugar-producing island, incredible views of the Martha Brae River, and loads of fun. An adventure park offers zip-lining, river tubing, a greathouse tour, access to a colonial village, an aviary, swimming pool, challenge course for adults, and kids' play area (with its own challenge course). Guests may get a taste of Jamaica at the Appleton Estate Jamaica Rum Tavern and Jablum Cafe or enjoy spicy goodness from the Walkerswood Jerk Hut. Adventure park passes entitle visitors to all estate activities. ⌧ Falmouth ☎ 876/619–1441, 876/619–1382 ⊕ www.chukka.com/destination-gallery/good-hope ☜ $69.

★ Glistening Waters (Luminous Lagoon)

BEACH—SIGHT | This is one of Jamaica's most fascinating natural wonders. The lagoon emits a bluish glow caused by microscopic organisms called dinoflagellates that live in the water and create a natural phenomenon called bioluminescence. There are only five bioluminescent bays in the world, and Jamaica's is said

to be the brightest. At night, one-hour tours are taken out to the lagoon where guests are allowed to touch, take pictures, and even swim in the bioluminescent waters. There is also a marina and a restaurant at the location. ⌧ Hwy. A1, Trelawny ☎ 876/954–3229 ⊕ www.glisteningwaters.com ☜ $25.

Jamaica Swamp Safari Village

ZOO | With a large sign declaring that "Trespassers Will Be Eaten," this attraction on the outskirts of Falmouth will most fascinate reptile enthusiasts. The village was started as a crocodile farm in the 1970s by American Ross Kananga, who was a stunt man in the James Bond film Live and Let Die. Scenes from the film Papillon, starring Steve McQueen and Dustin Hoffman, were also shot here. The property is home to a number of Jamaican crocodiles as well as the Jamaican yellow boa snake. There are other exotic animals from South America and colorful tropical birds in the aviary. ⌧ Foreshore Rd., Falmouth ⊹ Right beside Better Price Hardware Store ☎ 876/617–2798 ⊕ www.jamaicaswampsafari.com ☜ $25.

★ Martha Brae River

BODY OF WATER | This gentle waterway takes its name from an Arawak woman who drowned herself because she refused to reveal the whereabouts of a local gold mine. According to legend, she agreed to take her Spanish inquisitors there and, on reaching the river, used magic to change its course, drowning herself and the greedy Spaniards with her. Her duppy (ghost) is said to guard the mine's entrance. Rafting on this river is a very popular activity—many operators are on hand to take you for a glide downstream. ⌧ Trelawny ⊹ 4½ miles (7 km) southeast of Falmouth ☎ 876/952–0889 ⊕ www.jamaicarafting.com ☜ From $65.

🍴 Restaurants

Falmouth has a large Margaritaville restaurant and bar, which is a destination for some passengers not going on organized tours. Those planning a shopping trip to the Half Moon shopping village can eat at one of the restaurants there. Good Hope Great House also offers afternoon tea to visitors who choose to do a tour there.

Club Nazz and Restaurant

$ | JAMAICAN | This restaurant is in a restored, brightly painted Georgian-style building that once served as a courthouse. Locals and visitors alike dig into Jamaican cuisine, such as curried goat, oxtail, jerk meat, and of course seafood; for the less adventurous, there are burgers and fries. **Known for:** affordable local seafood dishes; live music; nightclub atmosphere. $ *Average main: $10 ⊠ 23 Market St., 100 yards west of Water Sq., Falmouth* ☎ *876/615–1571.*

Pepper's Jerk Center

$$$ | JAMAICAN | Set in a former slave quarters, Pepper's Jerk Center is where locals and tourists in Falmouth go to get authentic Jamaican meals, seafood dishes, and delicious jerk (marked with the restaurant's very own special jerk sauce). The restaurant is located in the town's center and is just a short walk away from the Falmouth Port. **Known for:** jerk chicken; curry chicken; rum punch. $ *Average main: $26 ⊠ 22 Duke St., Trelawny* ☎ *876/617–3472* ⊕ *www.peppersjerkcenter.com.*

🛍 Shopping

Coming ashore, you will find more than four dozen shops along the cruise port's pedestrian thoroughfares housing well-known international and established Jamaican merchants. Also in the port is a covered open-air craft market, where many vendors offer their wares, including hand-carvings, and items such as T-shirts, caps, and local seasonings.

In town, souvenir vendors set up on Seaboard Street near the Courthouse. Water Square is the location of the Albert George market, where artisans offer local craftwork that showcases the history and culture of the area. The upscale Shops at Rose Hall and Half Moon shopping village are within easy reach by taxi between Falmouth and Montego Bay.

🏃 Activities

Most adventure activities offered to cruise-ship passengers in Montego Bay and Ocho Rios, including water sports, trips to nearby beaches, golf, river-rafting, scuba diving, and sightseeing, are also available to cruise passengers in Falmouth. See both Montego Bay and Ocho Rios for more information. Chukka at Good Hope offers the majority of activities aimed at cruise passengers out of Good Hope Plantation.

ADVENTURE ACTIVITIES
Chukka at Good Hope

ZIP LINING | This thrilling zip-line experience starts in the heart of the jungle and then flies through the rain forest and over rivers while providing spectacular mountain views. The 2½-hour tour is for ages six and older. In addition, the property offers an ATV safari, river tubing, dune buggies, bird aviary, and Appleton Rum tasting. Tours of the old sugar estate, highlighting a waterwheel and trading house, are also available. ⊠ *Chukka Good Hope, Falmouth* ☎ *876/619–1441, 876/619–1382, 877/424–8552 in U.S.* ⊕ *chukka.com* ⊠ *$129.99.*

FISHING
Glistening Waters Marina

FISHING | Offering deep-sea fishing and other charter trips from Glistening Waters (20 minutes east of Montego Bay), this marina also runs night tours of the lagoon, which is iridescent due to microscopic dinoflagellates that glow when they move. ⊠ *North Coast Hwy.,*

Falmouth ☎ *876/954–3229* ⊕ *www.
glisteningwaters.com.*

GUIDED TOURS
Falmouth Heritage Walks
WALKING TOURS | This leisurely paced walk
takes you through Falmouth's commercial
and residential streets while your guide
shares the little-known history of the
town and what made it a rich and significant port in the late 18th and early 19th
centuries. Your guide will also explain
how the movement to abolish slavery
was essentially founded in Falmouth
when you visit the former home and
grave of the famous abolitionist William
Knibb. The full tour takes about 2 hours
15 minutes. ⊠ *Falmouth* ☎ *876/407–2245*
✆ *From $30.*

Falmouth Tours by Trolley
GUIDED TOURS | The easiest way to see
the historic sites of Falmouth is on this
covered trolley with a guide who offers
a lively commentary about the town and
its many historical buildings. The majority
of these are Georgian in style and date
to the 18th century. The one-hour tours
are conducted on cruise ship days, which
are normally Tuesday through Thursday,
and the tours make two stops: one by
the sea and the other by St. Peter's
Anglican Church. ⊠ *Falmouth Cruise
Port, Falmouth* ☎ *876/509–0454* ⊕ *www.
falmouthtoursbytrolley.com* ✆ *From $25.*

Grand Cayman,
Cayman Islands

The largest and most populous of the
Cayman Islands, Grand Cayman is
also one of the most popular cruise
destinations in the Western Caribbean,
largely because it doesn't suffer from the
ailments afflicting many larger ports: pan-
handlers, hasslers, and crime. Instead,
the Cayman economy is a study in stability, and the environment is healthy and
prosperous. Although the island is rather

Best Bets 👁

■ **Diving.** If you're a diver, you'll
find several good sites close to
shore.

■ **Queen Elizabeth II Botanic
Garden.** This beautiful garden has
native plants and rare blue iguanas.

■ **Seven Mile Beach.** One of the
Caribbean's best beaches is a short
ride from the cruise-ship pier.

■ **Shopping.** George Town has a
wide range of shops near the pier.

■ **Stingray City.** This is some of the
most fun you can have on a Caribbean adventure.

featureless, Grand Cayman is a diver's
paradise, with pristine waters and a
colorful variety of marine life. Compared
with other Caribbean ports, there are
fewer things to see on land here; instead,
the island's most impressive sights are
underwater. Snorkeling, diving, and
glass-bottom-boat and submarine rides
top every ship's shore-excursion list, and
can also be arranged at major aquatics
shops if you don't go on a ship-sponsored
excursion. Cayman is also famous for its
nearly 600 offshore banks; not surprisingly, the standard of living is high and
nothing is cheap.

ESSENTIALS
CURRENCY
The Cayman Island dollar (CI$1 to
US$1.25). The U.S. dollar is accepted
everywhere, and most ATMs dispense
cash in either currency.

TELEPHONE
The country code for the Cayman Islands
is 1 345. Digicel and LIME are the major
cell phone providers, which use GSM
(850, 900, 1800 and 1900 bands).

COMING ASHORE

Ships anchor in George Town Harbour and tender passengers onto Harbour Drive, the center of the shopping district. If you just want to walk around town and shop or visit Seven Mile Beach, you're probably better off on your own, but the Stingray City Sandbar snorkeling trip is a highlight of many Caribbean vacations and fills up quickly on cruise-ship days, so it's often better to order that excursion from your ship, even though it will be more crowded and expensive than if you took an independent trip.

A tourist information booth is on the pier, and taxis queue for disembarking passengers. Although taxi fares may seem high, cabbies rarely try to rip off tourists. Fares are metered (and not cheap), but basic rates include as many as three passengers. Taxi drivers won't usually do hourly rates for small-group tours; you must arrange a sightseeing tour with a company. Car rentals range in price from $45 to $95 per day (plus a $20 driving permit), so they are a good option if you want to do some independent exploring. You can easily see the entire island and have time to stop at a beach in a single day. ■TIP→ Driving in the Cayman Islands is on the left (as in the United Kingdom), although the steering wheel may be on the left (as in the United States).

◉ Sights

GEORGE TOWN

Begin exploring the capital by strolling along the waterfront Harbour Drive to **Elmslie Memorial United Church,** named after the first Presbyterian missionary to serve in Cayman. Its vaulted ceiling, wooden arches, and sedate nave reflect the religious nature of island residents. In front of the court building, in the center of town, names of influential Caymanians are inscribed on the **Wall of History,** which commemorates the islands' quincentennial in 2003. Across the street is the **Cayman Islands Legislative Assembly**

Building, next door to the **1919 Peace Memorial Building.** In the middle of the financial district is the **General Post Office,** built in 1939. Let the kids pet the big blue iguana statues.

★ Cayman Islands National Museum

HISTORIC SITE | FAMILY | Built in 1833, the historically significant clapboard home of the national museum has had several different incarnations over the years, serving as courthouse, jail, post office, and dance hall. It features an ongoing archaeological excavation of the Old Gaol and excellent 3-D bathymetric displays, murals, dioramas, and videos that illustrate local geology, flora and fauna, and island history. There are also temporary exhibits focusing on aspects of Caymanian culture, a local art collection, and interactive displays for kids. ⊠ 3 Harbour Dr., George Town ☎ 345/949–8368 ⊕ www.museum.ky ⊠ $8 ⊗ Closed Sun.

Cayman Spirits/Seven Fathoms Rum

WINERY/DISTILLERY | Surprisingly, this growing company, established in 2008, is Cayman's first distillery. It's already garnered medals in prestigious international competitions for its artisanal small-batch rums (and is now making a splash with its smooth Gun Bay vodka as well). You can stop by for a tasting and self-guided tour (a more intensive, extensive guided tour costs $15) to learn how the rum is aged at 7 fathoms (42 feet) deep; supposedly the natural motion of the currents maximizes the rum's contact with the oak, extracting its rich flavors and enhancing complexity. ⊠ 68 Bronze Rd., George Town ☎ 345/925–5379, 345/926–8186 ⊕ www.caymanspirits.com.

ELSEWHERE ON THE ISLAND

Camana Bay Observation Tower

VIEWPOINT | FAMILY | This 75-foot structure provides striking 360-degree panoramas of otherwise flat Grand Cayman, sweeping from George Town and Seven Mile Beach to the North Sound. The double-helix staircase is impressive in its own right. Running alongside the steps

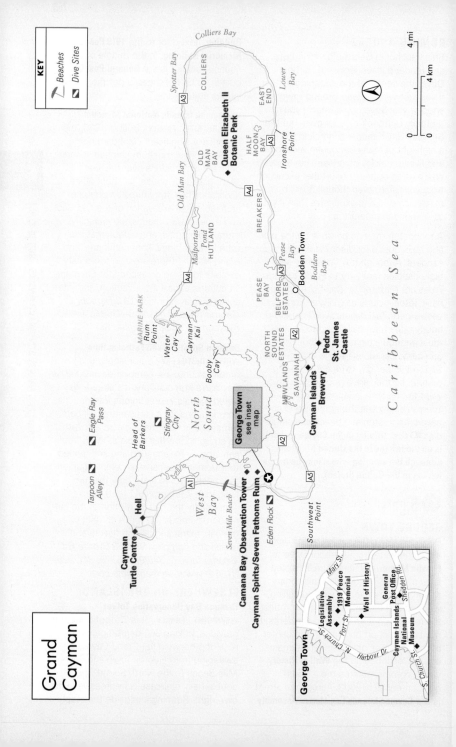

(an elevator is also available), a floor-to-ceiling mosaic replicates the look and feel of a dive from seabed to surface. Constructed of tiles in 114 different colors, it's one of the world's largest marine-themed mosaics. Benches and lookout points let you take in the views as you ascend. Afterward you can enjoy 500-acre Camana Bay's gardens, waterfront boardwalk, and pedestrian paths lined with shops and restaurants, or frequent live entertainment. ✉ *Between Seven Mile Beach and North Sound, Camana Bay ✛ 2 miles (3 km) north of George Town* ☎ *345/640–3500* ⊕ *www. camanabay.com* ✆ *Free.*

Cayman Islands Brewery

WINERY/DISTILLERY | In this brewery occupying the former Stingray facility, tour guides explain the iconic imagery of bottle and label as well as the nearly three-week brewing process: 7 days' fermentation, 10 days' lagering (storage), and 1 day in the bottling tank. The brewery's ecofriendly features are also championed: local farmers receive the spent grains to feed their cattle at no charge, while waste liquid is channeled into one of the Caribbean's most advanced water-treatment systems. Then, enjoy your complimentary tasting knowing that you're helping the local environment and economy. The little shop also offers cute merchandise and a happening happy hour that lures locals for liming (as a sign prominently chides: "No working during drinking hours"). ✉ *366 Shamrock Rd., Prospect* ☎ *345/947–6699* ⊕ *cib.ky* ✆ *$10.*

Cayman Turtle Centre

AMUSEMENT PARK/WATER PARK | **FAMILY** | Cayman's premier attraction has been transformed into a marine theme park with souvenir shops and restaurants. The turtles remain a central attraction, and you can tour ponds in the original breeding and research facility with thousands in various stages of growth, some up to 600 pounds and more than 70 years old.

The park helps promote conservation, encouraging interaction and observation. The freshwater **Breaker's Lagoon,** replete with cascades plunging over moss-carpeted rocks, evokes Cayman Brac. The saltwater **Boatswain's Lagoon,** replicating all the Cayman Islands and the Trench, teems with 14,000 denizens of the deep milling about a cannily designed synthetic reef. (You can snorkel here—lessons and guided tours are available.) Both lagoons have underwater 4-inch-thick acrylic panels that look directly into **Predator Reef,** home to six brown sharks, four nurse sharks, and other predatory fish such as tarpons, eels, and jacks. The free-flight **Aviary,** designed by consultants from Disney's Animal Kingdom, is a riot of color and noise with feathered friends representing the entire Caribbean basin. A winding interpretive nature trail culminates in the **Blue Hole,** a collapsed cave once filled with water. Audio tours are available with different focuses, from butterflies to bush medicine. ✉ *786 Northwest Point Rd., West Bay* ☎ *345/949–3894* ⊕ *www.turtle.ky* ✆ *$45 all-access, $18 Turtle Farm only.*

Hell

NATURE SITE | **FAMILY** | Quite literally the tourist trap from Hell, especially when overrun by cruise-ship passengers, this attraction does offer free admission, fun photo ops, and sublime surrealism. Its name refers to the quarter-acre of menacing shards of charred brimstone thrusting up like vengeful spirits (actually blackened and "sculpted" by acid-secreting algae and fungi over millennia). The eerie lunarscape is now cordoned off, but you can prove you had a helluva time by taking a photo from the observation deck. The attractions are the small post office and a gift shop where you can get cards and letters postmarked from Hell, not to mention wonderfully silly postcards titled "When Hell Freezes Over" (depicting bathing beauties on the beach), "The Devil Made Me Do It" bumper stickers, Scotch bonnet–based

Hell sauce, and "The coolest shop in Hell" T-shirts. Ivan Farrington, the owner of the Devil's Hang-Out store, cavorts in a devil's costume (horn, cape, and tails), regaling you with demonically bad jokes. ⊠ *Hell Rd., West Bay* ☎ *345/949–3358* 🖷 *Free.*

★ Pedro St. James Castle

HOUSE | Built in 1780, the greathouse is Cayman's oldest stone structure and the island's only remaining late-18th-century residence. In its capacity as courthouse and jail, it was the birthplace of Caymanian democracy, where in December 1831 the first elected parliament was organized and in 1835 the Slavery Abolition Act signed. The structure still has original or historically accurate replicas of sweeping verandahs, mahogany floors, rough-hewn wide-beam ceilings, outside louvers, stone and oxblood- or mustard-color limewashed walls, brass fixtures, and Georgian furnishings. The buildings are surrounded by 8 acres of natural parks and woodlands. There's also an impressive multimedia show, on the hour, complete with smoking pots, misting rains, and two screens. ⊠ *305 Pedro Castle Rd., Savannah* ☎ *345/947–3329* ⊕ *www.pedrostjames.ky* 🖷 *CI$10.*

★ Queen Elizabeth II Botanic Park

NATURE PRESERVE | **FAMILY** | This 65-acre wilderness preserve showcases a wide range of indigenous and nonindigenous tropical vegetation, approximately 2,000 species in total. Splendid sections include numerous water features and a Floral Colour Garden. A 2-acre lake and adjacent wetlands include three islets that provide a habitat and breeding ground for native birds just as showy as the floral displays. The nearly mile-long Woodland Trail encompasses every Cayman ecosystem from wetland to cactus thicket. You'll encounter birds, lizards, turtles, and agoutis, but the park's star residents are the protected endemic blue iguanas, the world's most endangered iguana, which are found only in Grand

Cayman. The Trust conducts 90-minute behind-the-scenes safaris Monday through Saturday at 11 am for $30. ⊠ *367 Botanic Rd., North Side* ☎ *345/947–9462* ⊕ *www.botanic-park.ky* 🖷 *CI$10.*

🏖 Beaches

★ Seven Mile Beach

BEACH—SIGHT | Grand Cayman's west coast is dominated by this famous beach—actually a 6½-mile (10-km) expanse of powdery white sand overseeing lapis water stippled with a rainbow of parasails and kayaks. Free of litter and pesky peddlers, it's an unspoiled (though often crowded) environment. Most of the island's resorts, restaurants, and shopping centers sit along this strip. The public beach toward the north end offers chairs for rent ($10 for the day, including a beverage), a playground, water toys aplenty, beach bars, restrooms, and showers. The best snorkeling is at either end, by the Marriott and Treasure Island or off Cemetery Beach, to the north. **Amenities:** food and drink; showers; toilets; water sports. **Best for:** partiers; snorkeling. ⊠ *West Bay Rd., Seven Mile Beach.*

🍴 Restaurants

Full of Beans Cafe

$ | **ECLECTIC** | On the surprisingly large, eclectic Asian-tinged menu using ultrafresh ingredients, standouts include homemade carrot cake, mango smoothies, cranberry-Brie-pecan salad, and rosemary-roasted portobello and pesto chicken panini. The espresso martini will perk up anyone wanting a pick-me-up. **Known for:** creative beverages (alcoholic and non); delectable sandwiches; colorful local art. ⑤ *Average main:* ⊠ *Pasadora Pl., Smith Rd., George Town* ☎ *345/943–2326, 345/814–0157* ⊕ *www.fullofbeans.ky.*

Grand Cayman's Seven Mile Beach is home to most of the island's restaurants, resorts, and shopping centers.

MacDonald's

$ | CARIBBEAN | One of the locals' favorite burger joints—not a fast-food outlet—MacDonald's does a brisk lunch business in stick-to-your ribs basics like rotisserie chicken and escoveitch fish. The decor features yellows and pinks, with appetizing posters of food and a large cartoon chicken mounted on the wall—all an afterthought, really, to the politicos, housewives in curlers, and gossipmongers. **Known for:** popular islander hangout; perennial local pick for best burger; juicy rotisserie chicken. $ *Average main: $11 ⊠ 99 Shedden Rd., George Town* ☎ *345/949–4640.*

🛍 Shopping

On Grand Cayman the good news is that there's no sales tax *and* there's plenty of duty-free merchandise. Locally made items to watch for include woven mats, baskets, jewelry made of a marblelike stone called Caymanite (from the cliffs of Cayman Brac), and authentic sunken treasure, though the latter is never

cheap. In addition, there are several noteworthy local artists, some of whose atelier-homes double as galleries, such as Al Ebanks, Horacio Esteban, and Luelan Bodden. Unique items include Cayman sea salt and luxury bath salts (solar harvested in an ecologically sensitive manner) and Tortuga rum and rum cakes. Seven Fathoms is the first working distillery actually in Cayman itself, its award-winning rums aged underwater (hence the name). Cigar lovers, take note: Some shops carry famed Cuban brands, but you must enjoy them on the island; bringing them back to the United States is illegal.

Although you can find black-coral products in Grand Cayman, they're controversial. Most of the coral sold here comes from Belize and Honduras; Cayman Islands' marine law prohibits the removal of live coral from its own sea, so most of it has been taken illegally. Black coral grows at a very slow rate (3 inches every 10 years) and is an endangered species. Buy other products instead.

★ Guy Harvey's Gallery and Shoppe

ART GALLERIES | World-renowned marine biologist, conservationist, and artist Guy Harvey showcases his aquatic-inspired, action-packed art in every conceivable medium, from tableware to sportswear (even logo soccer balls and Zippos). The soaring, two-story 4,000-square-foot space is almost more theme park than store, with monitors playing sport-fishing videos, wood floors inlaid with tile duplicating rippling water, dangling catboats "attacked" by shark models, and life-size murals honoring such classics as Hemingway's *The Old Man and the Sea*. Original paintings, sculpture, and drawings are expensive, but there's something (tile art, prints, lithographs, and photos) in most price ranges. ⊠ *49 S. Church St., George Town* ☎ *345/943–4891* ⊕ *www. guyharvey.com* ⊗ *Closed Sun.*

Tortuga Rum Company

FOOD/CANDY | This company bakes, then vacuum-seals more than 10,000 of its world-famous rum cakes daily, adhering to the original, "secret" century-old recipe. There are eight flavors, from banana to Blue Mountain coffee, as well as several varieties of candy, from taffy to truffles. The 12-year-old rum, blended from private stock though actually distilled in Guyana, is a connoisseur's delight for after-dinner sipping. You can buy a fresh rum cake at the airport on the way home at the same prices as at the factory store. ⊠ *Industrial Park, N. Sound Rd., George Town* ☎ *345/943–7663* ⊕ *www.tortugarumcakes.com.*

🏃 Activities

DIVING AND SNORKELING

One of the world's leading dive destinations, Grand Cayman's dramatic underwater topography features plunging walls, soaring skyscraper pinnacles, grottoes, arches, coral-encrusted caverns, swim-throughs adorned with vibrant sponges, and canyons patrolled by Lilliputian grunts to gargantuan groupers, hammerheads to hawksbill turtles.

Pristine clear water, breathtaking coral formations, and plentiful marine life mark the **North Wall,** a world-renowned dive area along the North Side of Grand Cayman. **Trinity Caves,** in West Bay, is a deep dive with numerous canyons starting at about 60 feet and sloping to the wall at 130 feet. The South Side is the deepest, its wall starting 80 feet deep before plummeting, though its shallows offer a lovely labyrinth of caverns and tunnels in such sites as Japanese Gardens. The less visited, virgin East End is less varied geographically beyond the magnificent Ironshore Caves and Babylon Hanging Gardens ("trees" of black coral plunging 100 feet) but teems with "Swiss cheese" swim-throughs and exotic life in such renowned gathering spots as the Maze.

Shore-entry snorkeling spots include **Cemetery Reef,** north of Seven Mile Beach, and the reef-protected shallows of the **north and south coasts.** Ask for directions to the shallow wreck of the *Cali* in the George Town harbor area; there are several places to enter the water, including a ladder at Rackam's Pub. Among the wreckage you'll find the winch and lots of friendly fish.

Stingray Sandbar is one of the best snorkeling spots in the Caribbean and is always filled with boats on cruise-ship days.

★ DiveTech

SCUBA DIVING | **FAMILY** | With comfortable boats and quick access to West Bay, DiveTech offers shore diving at its northwest-coast location, providing loads of interesting creatures, a miniwall, and the North Wall. Technical training (a specialty of owner Nancy Easterbrook) is unparalleled, and the company offers good, personable service as well as the latest gadgetry such as underwater DPV scooters and rebreathing equipment.

They even mix their own gases. Options include extended cross-training Ranger packages, Dive and Art workshop weeks, photography-video seminars with Courtney Platt, deep diving, free diving, search and recovery, stingray interaction, reef awareness, and underwater naturalist. Snorkel and diving programs are available for children eight and up, SASY (supplied-air snorkeling, with the unit on a personal flotation device) for five and up. Multiday discounts are a bonus. ✉ Lighthouse Point , 571 Northwest Point Rd., West Bay ✛ Near Boatswain's Beach ☎ 345/949–1700, 877/946–5658 Holiday Inn branch ⊕ www.divetech.com.

Red Sail Sports

SCUBA DIVING | FAMILY | Daily trips leave from most major hotels, and dives are often run as guided tours, good for beginners. If you're experienced and your air lasts long, ask the captain if you must come up with the group (when the first person runs low on air). Kids' options (ages 5 to 15) include SASY and Bubblemakers. The company also operates Stingray City tours, dinner and sunset sails, and water sports from Wave Runners to windsurfing. ☎ 345/949–8745, 345/623–5965, 877/506–6368 ⊕ www. redsailcayman.com.

FISHING

If you enjoy action fishing, Cayman waters have plenty to offer. Experienced, knowledgeable local captains charter boats with top-of-the-line equipment, bait, ice, and often lunch included in the price (usually $700 to $950 per half day, $1,200 to $1,600 for a full day). Options include deep-sea, reef, bone, tarpon, light-tackle, and fly-fishing. June and July are good all-around months for blue marlin, yellow- and blackfin tuna, dolphinfish, and bonefish. Bonefish have a second season in the winter months, along with wahoo and skipjack tuna.

R&M Fly Shop and Charters

FISHING | FAMILY | Captain Ronald Ebanks is arguably the island's most knowledgeable fly-fishing guide, with more than 10 years' experience in Cayman and Scotland. He also runs light-tackle trips on a 24-foot Robalo and 21-foot Sea Cat. Everyone from beginners—even children—to experienced casters enjoy and learn, whether wading or poling from a 17-foot Stratos Flats boat or his new sleek 17-foot Hobie Pro Angler kayaks. Free transfers are included. Captain Ronald even ties his own flies (he'll show you how). ☎ 345/947–3146, 345/916–5753 (mobile) ⊕ www.flyfishgrandcayman. com.

HIKING

Mastic Trail

HIKING/WALKING | This significant trail, used in the 1800s as the only direct path to the North Side, is a rugged 2-mile (3-km) slash through 776 dense acres of woodlands, black mangrove swamps, savanna, agricultural remnants, and ancient rock formations. It encompasses more than 700 species of flora and fauna, including Cayman's largest remaining contiguous ancient forest of mastic trees (one of the heavily deforested Caribbean's last examples). A comfortable walk depends on weather—winter is better because it's drier, though flowering plants such as the banana orchid blaze in summer. Call the National Trust to determine suitability and to book a guide ($30); tours run Tuesday through Friday mornings by appointment. Or walk on the wild side with a $5 guidebook covering the ecosystems, endemic wildlife, seasonal changes, poisonous plants, and folkloric uses of flora. The trip takes about three hours. ✉ Frank Sound Rd., East End ✛ Entrance by fire station at botanic park, Breakers ☎ 345/749–1121, 345/749–1124 for guide reservations ⊕ www.nationaltrust.org.ky.

Grand Turk, Turks & Caicos Islands

Just 7 miles (11 km) long and a little over 1 mile (1½ km) wide, Grand Turk, the political capital of the Turks & Caicos Islands, has been a longtime favorite destination for divers eager to explore the 7,000-foot coral-encrusted wall that drops down within yards of the shoreline. This tiny, quiet island is home to white-sand beaches, the National Museum, and a small population of wild horses and donkeys, which leisurely meander past the white-walled courtyards, pretty churches, and bougainvillea-covered colonial inns on their daily commute into town. The main settlement on the island is tranquil Cockburn Town, and that's where most of the small hotels, not to mention Pillory Beach, can be found. Although it has the second-largest number of inhabitants of all the Turks & Caicos Islands, Grand Turk's permanent population has still not reached 4,000.

ESSENTIALS
CURRENCY
The official currency on the islands is the U.S. dollar.

TELEPHONE
The area code is 1 649. All telephone service is provided by LIME and Digicel, and your U.S. cell phone may work on Grand Turk.

COMING ASHORE
Cruise ships dock at the southern end of Grand Turk, just south of the airport. The $40 million cruise center is about 3 miles (5 km) from tranquil Cockburn Town, Pillory Beach, and the Ridge, and far from most of the western shore dive sites. The center has many facilities: duty-free shopping, a free-form swimming pool, car-rental booths, tour operators, and even a dock from which many sea-bound excursions depart. The beautiful Governor's Beach is adjacent to the cruise-ship

Best Bets

- **Beaches.** The sand is powder-soft, the water azure.

- **Diving.** If you're certified, there are several world-class dive sites within easy reach.

- **Gibbs Cay.** To swim with stingrays, take a ship-sponsored trip here; the bonus is an excellent beach.

- **Front Street.** Colorful Front Street will give you the feeling you've stepped back in time.

- **Turks and Caicos National Museum.** Small but definitely worthy.

complex but others are right in and around Cockburn Town, as well as along the island's north shore.

If you want to visit Cockburn Town, it's reachable by taxi. Fares are per person and by zone; you'll find a rate card outside the cruise terminal. You can rent a car to explore the island independently or join an organized tour by bus, scooter, or ATV.

Grand Turk Cruise Terminal
Head to the website for cruise schedules, a list of the shops at the terminal, and options for excursions and transportation. ⊠ *South Base, Grand Turk Terminal* ⊕ *On the southern tip of the island, just south of the former U.S. Air Force Base* ☎ *649/946–1040* ⊕ *www.grandturkcc.com* ☉ *Closed when ships are not in port.*

◉ Sights

Pristine beaches with vistas of turquoise waters, small local settlements, historic ruins, and native flora and fauna are among the sights on Grand Turk. Fewer

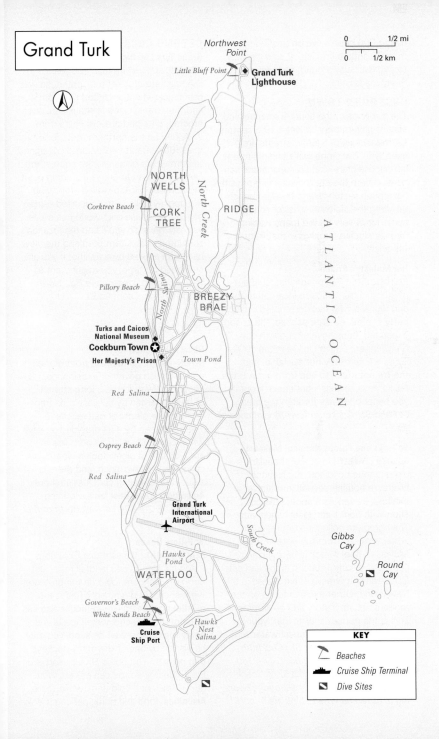

Grand Turk

Northwest Point

Little Bluff Point

Grand Turk Lighthouse

0   1/2 mi

0   1/2 km

NORTH WELLS

Corktree Beach

CORK-TREE

North Creek

RIDGE

Pillory Beach

North Salina

BREEZY BRAE

Turks and Caicos National Museum

Cockburn Town

Her Majesty's Prison

Town Pond

ATLANTIC OCEAN

Red Salina

Osprey Beach

Red Salina

Grand Turk International Airport

South Creek

Hawks Pond

WATERLOO

Gibbs Cay

Round Cay

Governor's Beach

White Sands Beach

Cruise Ship Port

Hawks Nest Salina

KEY	
⚓	Beaches
🚢	Cruise Ship Terminal
⬛	Dive Sites

than 4,000 people live on this 7½-square-mile (19-square-km) island, and it's easy to find your way around, as there aren't many roads.

COCKBURN TOWN

The buildings in the country's capital and seat of government reflect a 19th-century Bermudian style. Narrow streets are lined with low stone walls and old street lamps. The once-vital *salinas* (natural salt pans, where the sea leaves a film of salt) have been restored, and covered benches along the sluice ways offer shady spots for observing the many wading birds, including flamingos, that frequent the shallows.

Her Majesty's Prison

HISTORIC SITE | This prison was built out of stone in the 1830s to incarcerate men and women who had committed mostly petty crimes. As time passed, the prison expanded, housing even modern-day drug runners until it closed in the 1990s. Tours are currently not available, and there's not much to see from outside the tall limestone walls—but check it out if you happen to pass through the area. ⊠ *Pond St., Cockburn Town* ⊕ *visittci.com* 🖾 *$7.*

★ Turks and Caicos National Museum

GARDEN | **FAMILY** | In one of the island's oldest stone buildings, the National Museum houses several interactive exhibits, as well as a super little gift shop with books and local handicrafts. The complete collection of preserved artifacts raised from the noteworthy Molasses Reef Wreck is here. Dating back to the early 1500s, it is the earliest European shipwreck yet excavated in the New World. Other exhibits focus on the region's natural history and environment. This is the perfect spot to start your walking tour of the historical waterfront. ⊠ *Guinep House, Front St., Cockburn Town* ☎ *649/946–2160, 649/247–2160* ⊕ *www.tcmuseum.org* 🖾 *$7* ⊙ *Check sign outside for monthly schedule; opening is based on when ships are in port.*

BEYOND COCKBURN TOWN

Grand Turk Lighthouse

HISTORIC SITE | More than 150 years ago, the main structure of the lighthouse was prefabricated in the United Kingdom and then transported to the island; once erected, it helped prevent ships from wrecking on the northern reefs for more than 100 years. It was originally designed to burn whale oil as its light source. You can use this landmark as a starting point for a breezy cliff-top walk by following the donkey trails to the deserted eastern beach. The cruise-ship world has made its mark here, so you'll find the location's solitude can be interrupted and the view has been marred by a zip line. If you are stretched for time, you might want to take a pass. ⊠ *Lighthouse Rd., North Ridge* ⊕ *visittci.com* 🖾 *$3.*

Ⓢ Beaches

Governor's Beach

BEACH—SIGHT | Directly in front of the official British governor's residence, known as Waterloo, is a long stretch of beach framed by tall casuarina trees that provide plenty of natural shade. The beach can be a bit crowded on days when cruise ships are in port. There are a couple of picnic tables where you can enjoy a picnic lunch, and there is a decent snorkeling spot just offshore. **Amenities:** none. **Best for:** swimming; walking. ⊹ *20–30-min walk north of the Cruise Center.*

★ Pillory Beach

BEACH—SIGHT | It's said that Columbus made his New World landfall here, just north of Cockburn Town on the protected west shore. And why not? This is the prettiest beach on Grand Turk; it also has great off-the-beach snorkeling. As you enjoy the powdery white sand, you may be visited by one of the many donkeys that pass by. The Bohio Dive Resort is on Pillory Beach, so you can enjoy a wonderful lunch or a cold drink while there. **Amenities**: food and drink; parking (free);

Kids cooling off on a dock in Cockburn Town, Grand Turk.

toilets. **Best for**: snorkeling; swimming; walking. ✉ *Pillory Beach*.

🍴 Restaurants

★ Sand Bar

$$ | **CARIBBEAN** | Run by two Canadian sisters, this popular beachside bar is very good value and the perfect spot to enjoy island time—no shoes or shirt required. The menu includes fresh-caught fish, lobster, and conch, as well as typical North American fare—burgers, quesadillas, and chicken and ribs—served island-style with peas and rice. **Known for:** downhome island cooking; beachside dining; sunsets that will take your breath away. ⑤ *Average main: $20* ✉ *Duke St., Cockburn Town* ☎ *649/243–2666* ⊕ *www. grandturk-mantahouse.com* ▭ *No credit cards* ⊗ *Closed Sat.*

Secret Garden

$$ | **ECLECTIC** | This open-air spot is tucked away amid tall tamarind and neem trees in a courtyard garden behind the historical Salt Raker Inn. The Secret Garden serves simply prepared, local dishes such as grilled grouper and snapper, conch, and lobster. **Known for:** homemade desserts; great spot to mix with locals; best place on island for breakfast. ⑤ *Average main: $18* ✉ *Salt Raker Inn, Duke St., Cockburn Town* ☎ *649/946–2260, 649/243–5522* ⊕ *www.saltrakerinn.com*.

🛍 Shopping

Shopping in Grand Turk is hard to come by—choices are slim. Let's just say that no true shopaholic would want to come here for vacation. You can get the usual T-shirts and trinkets at all the dive shops, but there are only a few options for more interesting shopping opportunities: The Grand Turk Inn's boutique, the National Museum's gift shop, The Gallery-Grand Turk. However, there is a duty-free mall right at the cruise-ship center, where you'll find the usual array of upscale shops, including Ron Jon's Surf Shop, the largest Margaritaville in the world, and Piranha Joe's.

⚐ Activities

BICYCLING

Out of all the islands in Turks & Caicos, Grand Turk is the perfect island for biking: it's small enough that it is possible to tour it all that way. The island's mostly flat terrain isn't very taxing, and most roads have hard surfaces. Take water with you; there are few places to stop for refreshments. Most hotels have bicycles available, but you can also rent them for $20 per day from Grand Turk Diving across from the Osprey with a $200 deposit.

DIVING AND SNORKELING

With the wall just yards off shore, diving doesn't get any better than in Grand Turk. Divers may explore undersea cathedrals, coral gardens, and countless tunnels, or watch an octopus dance down a sandy slope. But take note: you must present your valid certification before you're allowed to dive. As its name suggests, the **Black Forest** offers staggering black-coral formations as well as the occasional black-tip shark. In the **Library** you can study fish galore, including large numbers of yellowtail snapper. The Columbus Passage separates South Caicos from Grand Turk, each side of the 22-mile-wide (35-km-wide) channel dropping 7,000 feet. From January through March, humpback whales migrate through en route to their winter breeding grounds. **Gibbs Cay,** a small cay a couple of miles off Grand Turk, is where you can swim with stingrays, and makes for a great excursion.

★ Blue Water Divers

SCUBA DIVING | In operation on Grand Turk since 1983, Blue Water Divers is the only PADI Green Star Award recipient-star dive center on the island, priding themselves on their personalized service and small group diving. There won't be more than eight of you headed out for a dive. In addition, Blue Water Divers offers Gibbs Cay snorkel and Salt Cay trips. ⊠ *Osprey Beach Hotel, The Atrium, 1 Duke St.,*

Cockburn Town ☎ *649/946–2432* ⊕ *www. grandturkscuba.com.*

Oasis Divers

FISHING | Oasis Divers provides excellent personalized service, with full gear handling and dive site briefing included. In addition, Oasis Divers offers a variety of other tours, including their land-based one on Segways, glass-bottom kayak tours, and whale-watching when the animals migrate past. It's a good spot to rent a kayak or paddleboard for some solo exploration, and if it's fishing you want to do, they offer deep-sea and reef fishing starting at $550 for a half-day charter. ⊠ *Duke St., Cockburn Town* ☎ *649/946–1128* ⊕ *www.oasisdivers. com.*

Great Stirrup Cay, Bahamas

Only 120 miles east of Fort Lauderdale in the Berry Island chain of the Bahamas, much of Great Stirrup Cay looks as it did when it was acquired by Norwegian Cruise Line in 1977, with bougainvilleas, seagrapes, and coconut palms as abundant as the colorful tropical fish that live in the reef. The first uninhabited island purchased to offer cruise-ship passengers a private beach day, Great Stirrup Cay's white-sand beaches are fringed by coral and ideal for swimming and snorkeling. Great Stirrup Cay was expanded in 2017, with new and revamped food and drink venues, rebuilt cabanas (from $445), and covered lounge chair sections, and new landscaping. A straw market, water-sports centers, bars, volleyball courts, beachside massage stations, a food pavilion, complimentary taco bar, à la carte Land Shark Bar & Grill, and a 40-feet-high and 175-feet-long Hippo inflatable waterslide round out the facilities. Complimentary sand wheelchairs are available on the island. For ease of access, an expansive boardwalk extends along the main beach and a paved pathway is located along the seawall. Extensive island improvements began in 2010 with the excavation of a new entrance channel for tenders and construction of tender docking facilities and a welcome pavilion that is now the site for landings. As a result, the beachfront has been expanded significantly to alleviate crowding. Private beachfront rental cabanas, two dining facilities, a kid's play area, wave runners, a floating Aqua Park with a variety of water toys, kayak tours through man-made rivers within the island, an ecocruise, and a stingray encounter experience are additional amenities. A resort-style lagoon retreat featuring a secluded beach, luxury beach villas, and exclusive dining options were added in the 2017 renovation. **Available Activities:** basketball, hiking, kayaking, massages, organized games, paddleboats, parasailing, Ping-Pong, sailing, shopping, snorkeling, volleyball.

Grenada (St. George's)

Nutmeg, cinnamon, cloves, cocoa ... those heady aromas fill the air in Grenada (pronounced *gruh-NAY-da*). Only 21 miles (33½ km) long and 12 miles (19½ km) wide, the Isle of Spice is a tropical gem of lush rain forests, white-sand beaches, secluded coves, exotic flowers, and enough locally grown spices to fill anyone's kitchen cabinet. St. George's is one of the most picturesque capital cities in the Caribbean; St. George's Harbour is one of the most picturesque harbors; and Grenada's Grand Anse Beach is one of the region's finest beaches. The island has friendly, hospitable people and enough good shopping, restaurants, historic sites, and natural wonders to make it a popular port of call. About one-third of Grenada's visitors arrive by cruise ship, and that number continues to grow each year.

Best Bets

- **The Beach.** Grand Anse Beach is one of the Caribbean's most beautiful.

- **Diving and Snorkeling.** Explore dozens of fish-filled sites off Grenada's southwest coast.

- **Market Square.** Market Square is a bustling produce and spice market.

- **Nutmeg.** Don't miss a visit to a nutmeg cooperative (and get a pocketful to take home).

- **Waterfalls.** Concord Falls, just south of Gouyave, and Annandale Falls are among the island's most spectacular.

4

Ports of Call   GRENADA (ST. GEORGE'S)

ESSENTIALS
CURRENCY
Eastern Caribbean (E.C.) dollar, but U.S. dollars are generally accepted.

TELEPHONE
The country code is 1 473. Digicel and Flow are the major mobile phone providers using GSM (850, 900, and 1800 bands).

COMING ASHORE
The Cruise Ship Terminal, located on the north side of St. George's, accommodates two large ships; up to four can anchor in the outer harbor. The terminal—which opens directly into the Esplanade Mall and the minibus terminus and is a block from Market Square—offers a full range of passenger facilities. You can easily tour the capital on foot, but be prepared to negotiate steep hills. If you don't want to walk up and down through town, you can find a taxi ($3 or $4 each way) or a water taxi ($4 each way) right at the terminal to take you around to the Carenage. To explore areas beyond St. George's, hiring a taxi or arranging a

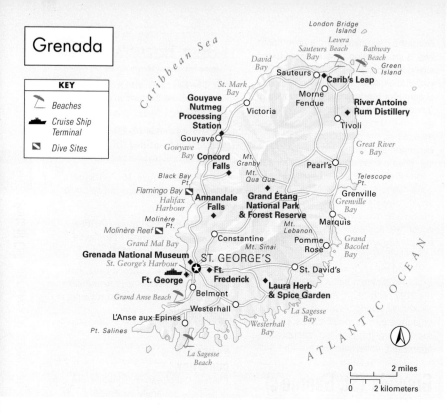

Grenada

KEY

- Beaches
- Cruise Ship Terminal
- Dive Sites

London Bridge Island

Caribbean Sea

David Bay

St. Mark Bay

Gouyave Nutmeg Processing Station

Gouyave
Gouyave Bay

Black Bay Pt.

Flamingo Bay

Halifax Harbour

Molinère Pt.

Molinère Reef

Grand Mal Bay

Grenada National Museum
St. George's Harbour

Ft. George

Grand Anse Beach

L'Anse aux Epines

Pt. Salines

La Sagesse Beach

Levera

Sauteurs Beach
Bathway Beach

Sauteurs

Green Island

Carib's Leap

Morne Fendue

Victoria

River Antoine Rum Distillery

Tivoli

Concord Falls

Mt. Granby

Mt. Qua Qua

Pearl's

Great River Bay

Telescope Pt.

Annandale Falls

Grand Étang National Park & Forest Reserve

Grenville
Grenville Bay

Mt. Lebanon

Marquis

Constantine
Mt. Sinai

Pomme Rose

Grand Bacolet Bay

ST. GEORGE'S

Ft. Frederick

St. David's

Belmont

Laura Herb & Spice Garden

Westerhall

La Sagesse Bay

Westerhall Bay

ATLANTIC OCEAN

CARIBBEAN SEA

0 — 2 miles
0 — 2 kilometers

guided tour is more sensible than renting a car. Taxis are plentiful, and fixed rates to popular island destinations are posted at the terminal's welcome center.

A taxi ride from the terminal to Grand Anse Beach will cost $20, but water taxis are a less expensive and more picturesque way to get there; the one-way fare is about $8 per person, depending on the number of passengers. Minibuses are the least expensive way to travel between St. George's and Grand Anse; pay EC$1.50 ($0.55) and hold on to your hat. They're crowded with local people getting from here to there and often make quick stops and take turns at quite a clip. Still, it's an inexpensive, fun, and safe way to travel around the island. If you want to rent a car and explore on your own, be prepared to pay $12 for a temporary driving permit (arranged by the car-rental agency) and about $75 to $85 for a day's car rental.

◉ Sights

ST. GEORGE'S

Grenada's capital is a bustling West Indian city, much of which remains unchanged from colonial days. Narrow streets lined with shops wind up, down, and across steep hills. Brick warehouses cling to the waterfront, and pastel-painted homes disappear into steep green hills.

Horseshoe-shape **St. George's Harbour,** a submerged volcanic crater, is arguably the prettiest harbor in the Caribbean. Schooners, ferries, and tour boats tie up along the seawall or at the small dinghy dock. **The Carenage** (pronounced car-a-NAHZH), which surrounds the harbor, is the capital's center. Warehouses, shops, and restaurants line the waterfront. The *Christ of the Deep* statue sits on the pedestrian plaza at the center of the Carenage; it was presented to Grenada by Costa Cruise Line in remembrance of its ship, *Bianca C,* that burned and sank in the harbor in 1961. *Bianca C* is now a popular dive site.

An engineering feat for its time, the 340-foot-long **Sendall Tunnel** was built in 1895 and named for Walter Sendall, an early governor. The narrow tunnel, used by both pedestrians and vehicles, separates the harbor side of St. George's from the Esplanade on the bay side of town, where you will find the markets (produce, meat, and fish), the Cruise Ship Terminal, the Esplanade Mall, and the public bus station.

Ft. Frederick

HISTORIC SITE | Overlooking the city of St. George's and the picturesque harbor, historic Ft. Frederick provides a panoramic view of about one-fourth of Grenada. The French began construction of the fort; the British completed it in 1791. Fort Frederick was the headquarters of the People's Revolutionary Government before and during the 1983 coup. Today, it's simply a peaceful spot with a bird's-eye view of much of Grenada. ■**TIP**➔ **Visit in the morning for the best photos of the harbor.** ✉ *Richmond Hill.*

★ Ft. George

HISTORIC SITE | **FAMILY** | Ft. George is perched high on the hill at the entrance to St. George's Harbour. Grenada's oldest fort was built by the French in 1705 to protect the harbor, yet no shots were ever fired here until October 1983, when Prime Minister Maurice Bishop and several of his followers were assassinated in the courtyard. The fort now houses police headquarters but is open to the public daily. The 360-degree view of the capital city, St. George's Harbour, and the open sea is spectacular. ■**TIP**➔ **Visit in the afternoon for the best photos of the**

harbor. ✉ *Grand Étang Rd., St. George's* ☎ *473/417–2761* ⛴ *$2.*

Grenada National Museum

HISTORIC SITE | **FAMILY** | A block from The Carenage, the Grenada National Museum is built on the foundation of a French army barracks and, later, British prison (for female inmates) that was originally built in 1704. The small museum has exhibitions of news items, photos, and proclamations relating to the 1983 intervention, along with fragments of Amerindian pottery, the childhood bathtub of Empress Joséphine (who was born on Martinique), and other memorabilia. ✉ *Young and Monckton Sts., St. George's* ☎ *473/440–3725* ⊕ *www.grenadamuseum.gd* ⛴ *$2.50* ⊙ *Closed Sun.*

ELSEWHERE ON GRENADA

Annandale Falls

BODY OF WATER | This is a lovely, cool spot for swimming and picnicking. A mountain stream cascades 40 feet into a natural pool surrounded by exotic vines. A paved path leads to the bottom of the falls, and a trail leads to the top. You'll often find local boys diving from the top of the falls—and hoping for a small tip. ✉ *Main interior rd., 15 mins northeast of St. George's, Annandale Estate* ☎ *473/440–2452* ⛴ *$2.*

Caribs' Leap

LOCAL INTEREST | At Sauteurs (the French word for "jumpers" or "leapers") on the island's northernmost tip, Caribs' Leap (or Leapers Hill) is the 100-foot vertical cliff from which the last of the indigenous Carib Indians flung themselves into the sea in 1651. After losing several bloody battles with European colonists, they chose suicide over surrender to the French. ✉ *Sauteurs.*

★ Concord Falls

BODY OF WATER | About 8 miles (13 km) north of St. George's, a turnoff from the West Coast Road leads to Concord Falls—actually three separate waterfalls. The first is at the end of the road; when the currents aren't too strong, you can take a dip under the 35-foot cascade. Reaching the two other waterfalls requires a hike into the forest reserve. The hike to the second falls (Au Coin) takes about 30 minutes. The third and most spectacular waterfall (Fontaineb-leau) thunders 65 feet over huge boul-ders and creates a small pool. It's smart to hire a guide for that trek, which can take an hour or more. The path is clear, but slippery boulders toward the end can be treacherous without assistance. ■TIP→ It can be dangerous to swim direct-ly under the cascade due to swift currents, an undertow, and falling rocks. ⊠ Concord Valley, off West Coast Rd., Gouyave ☎ 473/440–2279 🎫 Changing room $2.

★ **Gouyave Nutmeg Processing Station**
FACTORY | FAMILY | Touring the nutmeg-pro-cessing co-op, right in the center of the west-coast fishing village of Gouyave (pronounced GWAHV), is a fragrant, fas-cinating way to spend a half hour. You can learn all about nutmeg and its uses; see the nutmegs laid out in bins; and watch the workers sort them by hand, grade them, and pack them into burlap bags for shipping worldwide. The three-story plant is one of the largest nutmeg process-ing factories on the island. ⊠ Central Depradine St., Gouyave ☎ 473/444–8337 ⊕ www.grenadanutmeg.com 🎫 $1.

★ **Grand Étang National Park & Forest Reserve**
BODY OF WATER | FAMILY | A rain forest and wildlife sanctuary deep in the mountain-ous interior of Grenada, Grand Étang has miles of hiking trails for all levels of abili-ty. There are also lookouts to observe the lush flora and many species of birds and other fauna (including the Mona monkey) and a number of streams for fishing.
Grand Étang Lake is a 36-acre expanse of cobalt-blue water—1,740 feet above sea level—that fills the crater of an extinct volcano. Although legend has it that the lake is bottomless, maximum soundings have been recorded at just 18 feet. The

informative **Grand Étang Forest Center** has displays on the local wildlife and vegeta-tion. A forest ranger is on hand to answer questions; a small snack bar and souvenir stands are nearby. ⊠ Main interior rd. between Grenville and St. George's ☎ 473/440–6160 🎫 $2.

Laura Herb & Spice Garden
GARDEN | FAMILY | The 6½ acres of gar-dens here are part of an old plantation at Laura, near the village of Perdmontemps in St. David Parish and about 6 miles (10 km) east of Grand Anse. On the 20-min-ute tour, you will learn all about spices and herbs grown in Grenada—includ-ing cocoa, clove, nutmeg, pimiento, cinnamon, turmeric, and tonka beans (sometimes used in vanilla substitutes)—and how they're used for flavoring and for medicinal purposes. ⊠ Laura Rd., Perdmontemps ☎ 473/443–2604 🎫 $2 ⊘ Closed weekends.

★ **River Antoine Rum Distillery**
HISTORIC SITE | At this rustic operation, kept open primarily as a museum, a limited quantity of rum is produced by the same methods used since the distillery opened in 1785. River Antoine (pronounced an-TWYNE) is the oldest functioning water-propelled distillery in the Caribbean. The process begins with the crushing of sugarcane from adjacent fields; the discarded canes are then used as fuel to fire the boilers. The end result is a potent overproof rum, sold only in Grenada, that will knock your socks off. (A less strong version is also available.) ⊠ River Antoine Estate ☎ 473/442–7109 🎫 Guided tour $2.

🏖 Beaches

Bathway Beach
BEACH—SIGHT | This broad strip of white sand on the northeastern tip of Gre-nada is part of Levera National Park. A natural coral reef protects swimmers and snorkelers from the rough Atlantic surf; swimming beyond the reef is dangerous.

St. George's is the bustling capital of Grenada.

A magnet for local folks on national holidays, the beach is almost deserted at other times. Changing rooms are located at the park headquarters. A vendor or two sometimes sets up shop near the beach, but you're smart to bring your own refreshments. **Amenities:** parking (no fee); toilets. **Best for:** snorkeling; solitude; swimming; walking. ⊠ *Levera National Park, Levera.*

★ Grand Anse Beach

BEACH—SIGHT | FAMILY | Grenada's loveliest and most popular beach is Grand Anse, a gleaming 2-mile (3-km) semicircle of white sand lapped by gentle surf and punctuated by seagrapes and coconut palms that provide shady escapes from the sun. Several resorts face the beach and have dive shops where you can arrange trips and rent snorkeling equipment. A water-taxi dock is at the midpoint of the beach, along with the Grand Anse Craft and Spice Market, where vendors also rent beach chairs and umbrellas. Restrooms and changing facilities are available at Camerhogne

Park, which is the public entrance and parking lot. **Amenities:** food and drink; parking (no fee); toilets; water sports. **Best for:** sunset; swimming; walking. ⊠ *3 miles (5 km) south of St. George's, Grand Anse.*

🍴 Restaurants

The Nutmeg Bar & Restaurant

$$ | CARIBBEAN | FAMILY | West Indian specialties, fresh seafood, hamburgers, and a waterfront view make the Nutmeg a favorite with locals and visitors alike. It's upstairs along the Carenage, with large, open windows from which you can view the harbor activity and catch a cool breeze as you eat. **Known for:** harbor view; delicious rotis; good choice for in-town lunch. ⑤ *Average main: $18* ⊠ *The Carenage, St. George's* ☎ *473/440–3654.*

Victory Bar & Restaurant

$$$ | INTERNATIONAL | Boaters, businesspeople, vacationers, and anyone else looking for good food in a waterfront atmosphere close to town keep the

Victory busy. Overlooking the docks at Port Louis Marina, with views of the lagoon and masts swaying in the breeze, the restaurant is open every day for all-day dining, starting with breakfast and ending with a lively bar. **Known for:** outdoor dining with a view; best thin-crust pizza on the island; good selection of beer and wine. $ *Average main: $22* ✉ *Port Louis Marina, Kirani James Blvd. (Lagoon Rd.), St. George's* ☎ *473/435–7263* ⊕ *victorybargrenada.com.*

🧳 Shopping

Grenada is truly a nation of entrepreneurs, from retail businesses and processing operations, both with employees, to vendors (about one-third of the population) who personally sell their handicrafts in the markets. Note that bargaining isn't customary either in shops or markets.

Stores in Grenada are generally open weekdays from 8 to 4 or 4:30 and Saturday from 8 to 1; some close from noon to 1 during the week. Most are closed Sunday, although tourist shops usually open if a cruise ship is in port, and some mall stores, particularly supermarkets, are open for longer hours on weekends.

Some unique, locally made goods to look for in gift shops and supermarkets are locally made chocolate bars, nutmeg jam and syrup, spice-scented soaps and body oils, and (no kidding) Nut-Med Pain Relief Spray. Grenada's best souvenirs or gifts for friends back home, though, are spice baskets in a variety of shapes and sizes that are filled with cinnamon, nutmeg, mace, bay leaves, cloves, turmeric, and ginger. You can buy them for as little as $5 to $10 in practically every shop, at the open-air produce market at **Market Square** in St. George's, at vendor stalls along the Esplanade near the port, and at the Vendor's Craft & Spice Market on Grand Anse Beach. Vendors also sell handmade fabric dolls, coral jewelry, seashells, spice necklaces, and hats and baskets handwoven from green palm fronds.

Here's some local terminology you should know. If someone asks if you'd like a "sweetie," you're being offered a candy. When you buy spices, you may be offered "saffron" and "vanilla." The "saffron" is really turmeric, a ground yellow root, rather than the (much more expensive) fragile pistils of crocus flowers; the "vanilla" is extracted from locally grown tonka beans rather than from actual (also much more expensive) vanilla beans. No one is trying to pull the wool over your eyes; these are common local terms. That said, the U.S. Food and Drug Administration warns that "vanilla" extracts made from tonka beans can have toxic effects and may pose a significant health risk for individuals taking certain medications.

🏃 Activities

DIVING AND SNORKELING

You can see hundreds of varieties of fish and some 40 species of coral at more than a dozen sites off Grenada's southwestern coast (only 15 to 20 minutes away by boat) and another couple of dozen sites around Carriacou's reefs and neighboring islets. Depths vary from 20 to 120 feet, and visibility varies from 30 to 100 feet.

For a spectacular dive, visit the ruins of *Bianca C*, a 600-foot cruise ship that caught fire in 1961, sank to 100 feet, and is now a coral-encrusted habitat for giant turtles, spotted eagle rays, barracuda, and jacks. **Boss Reef** extends 5 miles (8 km) from St. George's Harbour to Point Salines, with a depth ranging from 20 to 90 feet. **Flamingo Bay** has a wall that drops to 90 feet. It teems with fish, sponges, sea horses, sea fans, and coral. **Molinère Reef** slopes from about 20 feet below the surface to a wall that drops to 65 feet. Molinère is also the location of the **Underwater Sculpture Park,** a rather odd artificial reef consisting of more than 55 life-size figures that were sculpted by artist and scuba instructor Jason Taylor and placed on the sea floor. An underwater bench gives divers a good view of the art gallery. Its most recent addition is a replica of *Christ of the Deep,* the statue that's on the promenade along the Carenage in St. George's. Molinère is a good dive for beginners; advanced divers can continue farther out to view the wreck of the *Buccaneer,* a 42-foot sloop.

Aquanauts Grenada

SCUBA DIVING | Every morning Aquanauts Grenada heads out on two-tank dive trips, each accommodating no more than eight divers, to both the Caribbean and Atlantic sides of Grenada. Also available: guided snorkel trips; beach snorkeling; and special activities, courses, and equipment for children. ⊠ *True Blue Bay Resort, True Blue* ☎ *473/444–1126, 850/303–0330 in U.S.* ⊕ *www.aquanauts-grenada.com.*

EcoDive

SCUBA DIVING | This full-service PADI dive shop offers two trips daily for both drift and wreck dives, as well as weekly trips to dive Isle de Ronde and a full range of diving courses. EcoDive employs two full-time marine biologists who run Grenada's marine-conservation and education center and conduct coral-reef monitoring and restoration efforts. ⊠ *Coyaba Beach Resort, Grand Anse Beach, Grand Anse* ☎ *473/444–7777* ⊕ *www. ecodiveandtrek.com.*

FISHING

Deep-sea fishing around Grenada is excellent. The list of likely catches includes marlin, sailfish, yellowfin tuna, and dorado (also known as mahimahi or dolphinfish). You can arrange sport fishing trips that accommodate up to six people starting at $500 for a half day and $750 for a full day.

True Blue Sportfishing

FISHING | British-born Captain Gary Clifford, who has been fishing since the age of six, has run True Blue Sportfishing since 1998. He offers big-game charters for up to six passengers on the 31-foot *Yes Aye.* The boat has an enclosed cabin, a fighting chair, and professional tackle. Refreshments and transportation to the marina are included. ⊠ *Port Louis Marina, Kirani James Blvd., St. George's* ☎ *173/107–4688* ⊕ *www.ycsayc.com.*

Guadeloupe (Pointe-à-Pitre)

On a map, Guadeloupe looks like a giant butterfly resting on the sea between Antigua and Dominica. Its two wings—Basse-Terre and Grande-Terre—are the two largest islands in the 659-square-mile (1,054-square-km) Guadeloupe archipelago. The Rivière Salée, a 4-mile (6-km) channel between the Caribbean and the Atlantic, forms the "spine" of the butterfly. A drawbridge near the main city, connects the two islands. Gorgeous scenery awaits, as Guadeloupe is one of the most physically attractive islands in the Caribbean. If you're seeking a resort atmosphere, casinos, and nearly white sandy beaches, your target is Grande-Terre. On the other hand, Basse-Terre's Parc National de la Guadeloupe, laced with trails and washed by waterfalls and rivers, is a 74,100-acre haven for hikers, nature lovers, and anyone brave enough to peer into the steaming crater of an active volcano. The tropical beauty suggests the mythical Garden of Eden.

ESSENTIALS
CURRENCY

The euro. You must exchange currency at a *bureau de change,* but ATMs are your best bet if you need euros.

TELEPHONE

The country code is 0590 and also the country's single area code for landlines. To call Guadeloupe from the United States, dial 00–590–590, then the local number; for mobile phone numbers, dial 00–590–690, then the local number. If you're on one of the other islands in the French West Indies, dial 0590 and then the local number. Digicel and Orange are the major mobile providers using GSM (900 and 1800 bands).

COMING ASHORE

Ships now dock at a cruise terminal in downtown Pointe-à-Pitre, at Pier 5/6. It houses an Internet café, a duty-free shop, and the colorful Karuland Village, where cruisers can browse and buy spices, pareos, and souvenirs, or just sit and listen to the local music while having coconut ice cream. It's about a five-minute walk from the shopping district. Passengers are greeted by local musicians and hostesses, usually dressed in the traditional madras costumes—often dispensing samplings of local rum and creole specialties. These multilingual staffers operate the information booth and can pair you up with an English-speaking taxi driver for a customized island tour. To get to the main tourist office, walk along the quay to the Place de la Victoire and look for a large white Victorian building with wraparound verandah.

Taxis are metered and expensive; during rush hour, they can be *very* expensive. Renting a car is a good way to see Guadeloupe, but it, too, is expensive and best booked in advance. Be aware that traffic around Pointe-à-Pitre can be horrible during rush hour, so allow plenty of time to drop off your rental car and get back to the ship. There are many rental agencies at the airport, but it will be at least a €35 taxi ride from the city each way, so if you can't find a rental closer to town, it's certainly not worth it.

Best Bets

- **Beaches.** The southern coast of Grand-Terre has stretches of soft, nearly white sand.

- **Diving.** Jacques Cousteau called the reef off Pigeon Island one of the world's top dive sites.

- **Hiking.** The Parc National de la Guadeloupe is one of the Caribbean's most spectacular scenic destinations.

- **Shopping.** Though Pointe-à-Pitre itself can be frenetic, it does have a good choice of French goods.

Sights

POINTE-À-PITRE

Although not the capital, this is the island's largest city, a commercial and industrial hub in the southwest of Grande-Terre. The Isles of Guadeloupe have 450,000 inhabitants, most of whom live in the cities. Pointe-à-Pitre is bustling, noisy, and hot—a place of honking horns and traffic jams and cars on sidewalks for want of a parking place. By day its pulse is fast, but at night, when its streets are almost deserted, you may not want to be there.

The heart of the old city is Place de la Victoire; surrounded by wooden buildings with balconies and shutters (including the tourism office) and by sidewalk cafés, it was named in honor of Victor Hugues's 1794 victory over the British. During the French Revolution Hugues ordered the guillotine set up here so that the public could witness the bloody end of 300 recalcitrant royalists, mainly the prosperous plantation owners.

Even more colorful is the bustling marketplace, between rues St-John Perse, Frébault, Schoelcher, and Peynier. It's

Guadeloupe

KEY
- Beaches
- Cruise Ship Terminal
- Dive Sites
- Ferry

La Pointe de la Grande Vigie

Guadeloupe Passage

Anse Bertrand
Campêche
Port Louis
Gros-Cap

ATLANTIC OCEAN

Pte. Allègre
Plage de la Grande-Anse
Petit-Canal
Vieux-Bourg
GRANDE
Ste-Rose
Morne-à-l'Eau
Le Moule
Anse de la Gourde
Deshaies
Pointe-à-Pitre
TERRE
La Désirade
Pointe-Noire BASSE
Abymes
St-
Pointe Tarare
Grande-Anse
Lamentin
Ft. Fleur
François
Destrelan
d'Épée
Mahaut
Gosier
Ste-
Anne
Plage du
Helleux
TO LA DÉSIRADE
Ilet de Pigeon
Pigeon Island
Cascade aux
Ecrevisses
Plage
Caravelle
Iles de la
Petite Terre
Malendure
Petit-
Bourg
Ilet du
Gosier
Bouillante
Parc National
de la Guadeloupe
Ste-Marie
Aquarium de la
Guadeloupe
TERRE
Vieux-
Habitants
La Soufrière
Capesterre-
Belle-Eau
BASSE-TERRE
Trois-Rivières
Saint Louis
Marie-Galante
Vieux
Fort
Caribbean
Sea
Grand-Bourg
Petite-Anse
Terre-de-Bas
Iles des Saintes
(Les Saintes)

0 ——— 10 miles
0 ——— 10 kilometers

a cacophonous place where shoppers bargain for spices, herbs (and herbal remedies), and a bright assortment of papayas, breadfruits, christophenes, and tomatoes.

Cathédrale de St-Pierre et St-Paul

RELIGIOUS SITE | If you like churches, then make a pilgrimage to the imposing Cathédrale de St-Pierre et St-Paul, built in 1807. Although it has been battered by hurricanes over the years, it has fine stained-glass windows and Creole-style balconies. ⊠ *Rue Alexandre Isaac at Rue de l'Eglise.*

Musée St-John Perse

MUSEUM | Those with a strong interest in French literature and culture (not your average sightseer) will want to see the Musée St-John Perse, which is dedicated to the poet Alexis Léger, Guadeloupe's most famous son. Better known as

Saint-John Perse, he was the winner of the Nobel Prize for literature in 1960. Some of his finest poems are inspired by the history and landscape—particularly the sea—of his beloved Guadeloupe. This literary museum, in a restored colonial house, contains a collection of his poetry and some of his personal belongings. Before you go, look for his birthplace at 54 rue Achille René-Boisneuf. ⊠ *9 rue Nozières, Pointe-à-Pitre* ☎ *0590/90–01– 92* ≊ *€2.50* ⊗ *Closed weekends.*

ELSEWHERE ON GRANDE-TERRE
Aquarium de la Guadeloupe

ZOO | FAMILY | Unique in the Antilles, this aquarium in the marina near Pointe-à-Pitre (totally renovated in 2018) is a good place to spend time. Its motto is "Visit the sea." The well-planned facility has an assortment of tropical fish, crabs, lobsters, moray eels, cofferfish, and some live coral. It's also a turtle rescue center, and the shark tank is spectacular. A restaurant serves kid-friendly fare, snacks, salads, pastas, etc. A small shop stocks marine toys and souvenirs. ⊠ *Pl. Créole, off Rte. N4, Le Gosier* ☎ *0590/90–92–38, 0690/90–92–38, 0690/57–60–69 Seatours* ⊕ *www.aquariumdelaguadeloupe. com* ☎ *€14 aquarium, €27 aquarium and zoo.*

Cascade aux Ecrevisses

BODY OF WATER | Within the Parc National de la Guadeloupe, Crayfish Falls is one of the island's loveliest (and most popular) spots. There's a marked trail (walk carefully, the rocks can be slippery) leading to this splendid waterfall, which dashes down into the Corossol River—a good place for a dip. Come early, though; otherwise you definitely won't have it to yourself. ⊠ *St-Claude* ⊕ *www.guadeloupe-parcnational.com.*

Ft. Fleur d'Épée

MUSEUM | The main attraction in Bas-du-Fort is this fortress, built between 1759 and 1763. It hunkers down on a hillside behind a deep moat. The fort was the scene of hard-fought battles between the French and the English in 1794. You can explore its well-preserved dungeons and battlements and take in a sweeping view of Îles des Saintes and Marie-Galante. The free guided tour here explores the fort's history and architecture and helps explain the living conditions of the soldiers who lived here. Included on the tour is an exploration of its underground galleries, now decorated with graffiti. The fort sometimes has art exhibits. If a bilingual person is on duty, she will explain it all in English. Call ahead, and make certain of that day's hours. You will only need 30 minutes on your own. Registered as a historic monument since 1979, the fort also provides superb bay views for walkers. ⊠ *Bas du Fort* ☎ *0590/90–94–61* ☎ *Free.*

Parc National de la Guadeloupe

NATIONAL/STATE PARK | This 74,100-acre park has been recognized by UNESCO as a Biosphere Reserve. Before going, pick up a *Guide to the National Park* from the tourist office; it rates the hiking trails according to difficulty, and most are quite difficult indeed. Most mountain trails are in the southern half. The park is bisected by the route de la Traversée, a 16-mile (26-km) paved road lined with masses of tree ferns, shrubs, flowers, tall trees, and green plantains. It's the ideal point of entry. Wear rubber-soled shoes and take along a swimsuit, a sweater, water, and perhaps food for a picnic. Cruise passengers tend ot arrive in the late morning or early afternoon. Check on the weather; if Basse-Terre has had a lot of rain, give it up. In the past, after intense rainfall, rock slides have closed the road for months. ⊠ *Habitation Beausoleil-Montéran, BP-93, St-Claude* ☎ *0590/80–86–00* ⊕ *www. guadeloupe-parcnational.com* ☎ *Free.*

🏖 Beaches

Plage Caravelle

BEACH—SIGHT | Just southwest of Ste-Anne is one of Grande-Terre's longest and prettiest stretches of sand, the occasional dilapidated shack notwithstanding. Protected by reefs, it's also a fine snorkeling spot. Club Med occupies one end of this beach, and nonguests can enjoy its beach and water sports, as well as lunch and drinks, by buying a day pass. You can also have lunch on the terrace of La Toubana Hotel & Spa, then descend the stairs to the beach or enjoy lunch at its beach restaurant, wildly popular on Sunday. **Amenities:** food and drink; parking (no fee); toilets; water sports. **Best for:** partiers; snorkeling; sunset; swimming; walking; windsurfing. ⊠ *Rte. N4, southwest of Ste-Anne, Ste-Anne.*

Plage de la Grande-Anse

BEACH—SIGHT | One of Guadeloupe's widest beaches has soft beige sand sheltered by palms. To the west is a round

verdant mountain. It has a large parking area and some food stands, but no other facilities. The beach can be overrun on Sunday, not to mention littered, due to the food carts. Right after the parking lot, you can see signage for the Creole restaurant Le Karacoli; if you have lunch there (it's not cheap), you can *sieste* on the chaise longues. At the far end of the beach, which is more virgin territory, is Tainos Cottages, which has a restaurant. **Amenities:** food and drink; parking (no fee). **Best for:** partiers; solitude; swimming; walking. ⊠ *Rte. N6, north of Deshaies, Deshaies.*

Plage de Malendure

BEACH—SIGHT | Across from Pigeon Island and the Jacques Cousteau Underwater Park, this long, gray, volcanic beach on the Caribbean's calm waters has restrooms, a few beach shacks offering cold drinks and snacks, and a huge parking lot. There might be some litter, but the beach is cleaned regularly. Don't come here for solitude, as the beach is a launch point for many dive boats. The snorkeling's good. Le Rocher de Malendure, a fine seafood restaurant, is perched on a cliff over the bay. Food carts work the parking lot. **Amenities:** food and drink; parking (no fee); toilets. **Best for:** partiers; snorkeling; swimming. ⊠ *Rte. N6, Bouillante.*

Restaurants

Caraïbes Café

$$ | **CAFÉ** | This sidewalk café straight out of Paris is an "in" place for lunch and also a spot for a quick breakfast. During the afternoon, order a pastis while you people-watch and listen to French crooners. **Known for:** cappuccino; sundaes; fresh tropical juices. ⑤ *Average main: €15* ⊠ *Pl. de la Victoire, Pointe-à-Pitre* ☎ *0590/82–92–23* ⊗ *Closed Sun. No dinner.*

Café Wango

$$$ | **ECLECTIC** | At this alfresco hot spot, Asian wok dishes, sushi, skewers, fish carpaccios, and tartares dominate the menu, and there are no fewer than five better-than-average salads. The chef, who devotees will know from his previous stint at Iguane Café, is known for his original Asian-, Indian-, Creole-, and African-influenced dishes. **Known for:** lobster medallions with shrimp, avocado, and citrus chili sauce; ice cream; French expat crowd. ⑤ *Average main: €21* ⊠ *Marina St-François, Marines 1, St-François* ☎ *0590/83–50–41* ⊕ *www.cafewango. com* ⊗ *Closed June 17–July 6.*

🛍 Shopping

The island has a lot of desirable French products, from designer fashions for women and men and sensual lingerie to French china and liqueurs. As for local handicrafts, you can find attractive wood carvings, madras table linens, island dolls dressed in madras, woven straw baskets and hats, and *salakos*—fishermen's hats made of split bamboo, some covered in madras—which make great wall decorations. Of course, the favorite Guadeloupean souvenir is rum. Look for *rhum vieux,* the top of the line. Be aware that the only liquor bottles allowed on planes have to be bought in the duty-free shops at the airport. Usually the shops have to deliver purchases to the aircraft. For foodies, the market ladies sell aromatic fresh spices, crisscrossed with cinnamon sticks, in little baskets lined with madras.

AREAS AND MALLS

Bas-du-Fort's two shopping areas are the Cora Shopping Center and the marina, where there are 20 or so shops and some restaurants, many right on the water. This marina has an active social scene.

Bustling Point-à-Pitre has obtained the prestigious French label of "Ville d'Art et d'Histoire" (Town of Art and History). You can browse in the street stalls around the harbor quay and at the two markets (the best is the Marché de Frébault). The town's main shopping streets with lots of French merchandise, from pâté to sexy lingerie, are rue Schoelcher, rue de Nozières, and the busy rue Frébault. At the St-John Perse Cruise Terminal, there's an attractive mall with about two dozen shops.

In St-François there are more than a dozen shops surrounding the marina, some selling French lingerie, swimsuits, and fashions. The supermarket has particularly good prices on French wines and cheeses, and if you pick up a fresh baguette, you'll have a picnic. (Then you can go get lost at a secluded beach.) Don't forget some island chocolates or individual fruit and custard tarts.

Activities

DIVING
The main diving area at the **Cousteau Underwater Park,** just off Basse-Terre near Pigeon Island, offers routine dives to 60 feet. The numerous glass-bottom boats and other craft make the site feel like a marine parking lot; however, the underwater sights are spectacular. Guides and instructors are certified under the French CMAS (some also have PADI, but none have NAUI). Most operators offer two-hour dives three times per day for about €50 to €55 per dive; three-dive packages are €120 to €145. Hotels and dive operators usually rent snorkeling gear.

Les Heures Saines
SCUBA DIVING | FAMILY | Les Heures Saines is the premier operator for dives in the Cousteau Underwater Park. Trips to Les Saintes offer one or two dives for average and advanced divers, with plenty of time for lunch and sightseeing. Wreck, night, and nitrox diving are also available. Despite this operator's popularity, it has kept its prices moderate, with many packages available. The instructors, young and fun types from the metropole—many of them English speakers—are excellent with children. The company also offers

winter whale- and dolphin-watching trips with marine biologists as guides aboard a 60-foot catamaran. Inquire also about going canyoning and/or hiking with Les Heures Saines. ⊠ *Le Rocher de Malendure, Plage de Malendure, Bouillante* ☎ *0590/98–86–63* ⊕ *www.heures-saines. gp* ⊠ *From €50.*

HIKING
With hundreds of trails and countless rivers and waterfalls, the **Parc National de la Guadeloupe** on Basse-Terre is the main draw for hikers. Some of the trails should be attempted only with an experienced guide. All tend to be muddy, so wear a good pair of boots. Know that even the young and fit can find these outings arduous; the unfit may find them painful. Start off slowly, with a shorter hike, and then go for the gusto. All water sports—even canoeing and kayaking—are forbidden in the center of the park. Scientists are studying the impact of these activities on the park's ecosystem.

Vert Intense
HIKING/WALKING | Vert Intense organizes hikes in the national park and to the volcano. You move from steaming hot springs to an icy waterfall in the same hike. Guides are patient and safety-conscious, and can bring you to heights that you never thought you could reach, including the top of La Soufrière. The volcano hike, the cheapest excursion, must be booked four days in advance. When you are under the fumaroles you can smell the sulfur (like rotten eggs) and you will smell like sulfur until you take a shower (as will your clothes until you launder them). A mixed-adventure package spanning three days costs considerably more. The two-day bivouac and other adventures can be extreme, so before you decide to play Indiana Jones, know what is expected. The French-speaking guides, who also know some English and Spanish, can take you to other tropical forests and rivers for canyoning (climbing and scrambling on outcrops, usually

along and above the water). If you are just one or two people, the company can team you up with a group. Vert Intense now has a guesthouse, Les Bananes Vertes (The Green Bananas), where you can combine a stay with trekking and other activities. ⊠ *Rte. de la Soufrière, St-Claude* ☎ *0590/99–34–73, 0690/55–40–47* ⊕ *www.vert-intense.com* 🛥 *From €50.*

Half Moon Cay, Bahamas

Little San Salvador, one of the Bahamian Out Islands, was renamed Half Moon Cay by Holland America to honor Henry Hudson's ship (depicted on the cruise line's logo) as well as to reflect the beach's crescent shape (the island is also used by Holland America's sister company Carnival Cruise Lines) Even after development, the island is still so unspoiled that it has been named a Wild Bird Preserve by the Bahamas National Trust. Passengers, who are welcomed ashore at a West Indies Village complete with shops and straw market, find Half Moon Cay easily accessible—all facilities are connected by hard-surfaced and packed-sand pathways and meet or exceed ADA requirements. An accessible tram also connects the welcome center with the food pavilion and bars; wheelchairs with balloon tires are available. However, the island is only accessible by tender, which makes it harder to get ashore. In addition to the beach area for lazing in the sun or in the shade of a rented clamshell (from $20), the island has a post office, Bahamian-style chapel, a lagoon where you can interact with stingrays (for an extra charge), and the Captain Morgan on the Rocks Island Bar in a "beached" pirate ship. For family fun, you'll find a beachfront water park with waterslides and fanciful sea creatures tethered to the sandy bottom of the shallow water. Massage services are available, as are fitness activities.

Air-conditioned Cabanas (starting at $280), two-story Beach Villas with hot tubs on the second floor (starting at $500), and a Grand Cabana that features an eight-person hot tub and a slide from the cabana deck straight into the ocean can be rented for the day (starting at $1,000), with or without the services of your own butler (extra charge on top of the cabana cost). **Available Activities:** Aqua Bikes, basketball, bicycles, fishing, hiking, horseback riding, jet-skiing, kayaking, massages, parasailing, sailing, scuba diving, shopping, shuffleboard, snorkeling, volleyball, windsurfing.

Harvest Caye, Belize

Off the coast of southern Belize, Norwegian has developed the very elaborate Harvest Caye. The resort-style island stop features a pier and a large marina, which serves as a gateway for excursions to explore the mainland, including trips to Maya ruins, river rafting, and nature tours. The heart of Harvest Caye is a 7-acre beach where 11 enclosed beach villas with concierge service, air-conditioning, and exclusive dining and beverage services are available to rent (from $599). A resort-style pool has a swim-up bar, lounge chairs and umbrellas, and 15 cabanas for rent. A 130-foot "Flighthouse" offers a variety of extra-charge aerial activities including a zip line (from $29), suspension bridges, free-fall jumps, a tandem "superman" style zip line, and a fun ropes course (from $19) located on a platform in the saltwater lagoon. The shopping village mixes popular name-brand retailers with local Belizean craftspeople. The island also has dining and bar options, including the indoor-outdoor Landshark Bar & Grill (an expansion of Norwegian's partnership with Jimmy Buffett's Margaritaville); street vendors, and grills at the beach and in the marina. (All bars and restaurants cost extra: to the dismay of many passengers, there is no food or drink offered for free on the island, nor can purchases be charged to your ship account.) **Available Activities:** bird-watching; kayaking, stand-up paddleboarding, motor-boating, and canoeing in the lagoon area; shopping; snorkeling; and zip-lining.

Key West, Florida

Along with the rest of Florida, Key West—the southernmost city in the continental United States—became part of American territory in 1821. In the late 19th century it was Florida's wealthiest city per capita. The locals made their fortunes from "wrecking"—rescuing people and salvaging cargo from ships that foundered on nearby reefs. Cigar making, fishing, shrimping, and sponge gathering also became important industries. Locally dubbed the "Conch Republic," Key West today makes for a unique port of call. A genuinely American town, it nevertheless exudes the relaxed atmosphere and pace of a typical Caribbean island. Major attractions include the home of the Conch Republic's most famous residents, Ernest Hemingway and Harry Truman; the imposing Key West Museum of Art and History (situated within a former U.S. Customs House) and site of the military inquest of the USS *Maine*; and the island's renowned sunset celebrations.

ESSENTIALS
CURRENCY
The U.S. dollar.

TELEPHONE
You'll be able to find plenty of public phones around Mallory Square. They're also along the major tourist thoroughfares.

COMING ASHORE
Cruise ships dock at three different locations in Key West. Mallory Square and Pier B are within walking distance of Duval and Whitehead Streets, the two main tourist thoroughfares. Passengers

Best Bets

■ **Boat Cruise.** Being out on the water is what Key West is all about.

■ **Conch Train.** Hop aboard for a narrated tour of the town's tawdry past and rare architectural treasures.

■ **Hemingway.** Visit Ernest Hemingway's historic home for a literary treat.

■ **Duval Crawl.** Shop, eat, drink, repeat.

■ **Sunset in Mallory Square.** The nightly street party is the quintessential Key West experience.

on ships that dock at Outer Mole Pier (aka Navy Mole) are shuttled via Conch Train or Old Town Trolley to Mallory Square. Because Key West is so easily explored on foot, there's rarely a need to hire a taxi. If you plan to venture beyond the main tourist district, a fun way to get around is by bicycle or scooter (bike rentals begin at about $12 per day). Key West is a cycling town. In fact, there are so many bikes around that cyclists must watch out for one another as much as for cars. You can get tourist information from the Greater Key West Chamber of Commerce, which is located one block off Duval Street, at 510 Greene Street, in the old "city hall."

The Conch Tour Train can be boarded at Mallory Square or Flagler Station every half-hour; it costs $30.45 per adult for the 90-minute tour. The Old Town Trolley operates trolley-style buses starting from Mallory Square every 30 minutes for the same price, and these smaller trolleys go places the train won't fit. The Old Town Trolley also has pick up and drop off locations at numerous points around the island.

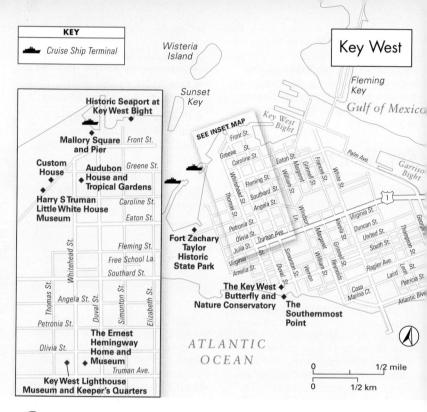

Map Labels

KEY

 Cruise Ship Terminal

Key West

Wisteria Island

Fleming Key

Sunset Key

Gulf of Mexico

Historic Seaport at Key West Bight

Key West Bight

SEE INSET MAP

Mallory Square and Pier

Front St.

Front St.

Greene St.

Caroline St.

Custom House

Audubon House and Tropical Gardens

Greene St.

Eaton St.

Grinnell St.

Frances St.

Palm Ave.

White St.

Garriso Bight

Harry S Truman Little White House Museum

Caroline St.

Whitehead St.

Fleming St.

William St.

Margaret St.

Thomas St.

Southard St.

Angela St.

Eaton St.

Windsor Ln.

Virginia St.

1

Petronia St.

Olivia St.

Truman Ave.

Duncan St.

Fleming St.

Fort Zachary Taylor Historic State Park

Julia St.

United St.

Varela St.

Margaret St.

Grinnell St.

Reynolds St.

Thompson St.

George

Free School La.

Southard St.

Virginia St.

St.

South St.

Whitehead St.

Amelia St.

Simonton St.

Vernon

William St.

Flagler Ave.

Laird

Patricia St.

Angela St.

Thomas St.

Duval St.

Simonton St.

Elizabeth St.

The Key West Butterfly and Nature Conservatory

The Southernmost Point

Casa Marina Ct.

Leon St.

Atlantic Blvd

Petronia St.

The Ernest Hemingway Home and Museum

ATLANTIC OCEAN

Olivia St.

Truman Ave.

Key West Lighthouse Museum and Keeper's Quarters

0   1/2 mile

0   1/2 km

👁 Sights

Audubon House and Tropical Gardens

GARDEN | If you've ever seen an engraving by ornithologist John James Audubon, you'll understand why his name is synonymous with birds. See his works in this three-story house, which was built in the 1840s for Captain John Geiger and filled with period furniture. It now commemorates Audubon's 1832 stop in Key West while he was traveling through Florida to study birds. After an introduction by a docent, you can do a self-guided tour of the house and gardens. An art gallery sells lithographs of the artist's famed portraits. ✉ 205 Whitehead St., Key West 📞 305/294–2116, 877/294–2470 ⊕ www.audubonhouse.com 💲 $14.

★ Custom House

HISTORIC SITE | When Key West was designated a U.S. port of entry in the early 1820s, a customhouse was established. Salvaged cargoes from ships wrecked on the reefs were brought here, setting the stage for Key West to become—for a time—the richest city in Florida. The imposing redbrick-and-terra-cotta Richardsonian Romanesque–style building reopened as a museum and art gallery in 1999. Smaller galleries have long-term and changing exhibits about the history of Key West, including a Hemingway room and a permanent Henry Flagler exhibit that commemorates the arrival of Flagler's railroad to Key West in 1912. ✉ 281 Front St., Key West 📞 305/295–6616 ⊕ www.kwahs.com 💲 $10.

★ The Ernest Hemingway Home and Museum

HOUSE | Amusing anecdotes spice up the guided tours of Ernest Hemingway's home, built in 1801 by the town's most successful wrecker. While living here between 1931 and 1942, Hemingway wrote about 70% of his life's work, including classics like *For Whom the Bell Tolls.* Few of his belongings remain aside from some books, and there's little about his actual work, but photographs help you visualize his day-to-day life. The famous six-toed descendants of Hemingway's cats—many named for actors, artists, authors, and even a hurricane—have free rein of the property. Tours begin every 10 minutes and take 30 minutes; then you're free to explore on your own. Be sure to find out why there is a urinal in the garden! ✉ *907 Whitehead St., Key West* ☎ *305/294–1136* ⊕ *www.hemingwayhome.com* 🖭 *$14.*

Fort Zachary Taylor Historic State Park

BEACH—SIGHT | Construction of the fort began in 1845 but was halted during the Civil War. Even though Florida seceded from the Union, Yankee forces used the fort as a base to block Confederate shipping. More than 1,500 Confederate vessels were detained in Key West's harbor. The fort, finally completed in 1866, was also used in the Spanish-American War. Take a 30-minute guided walking tour of the redbrick fort, a National Historic Landmark, at noon and 2, or self-guided tour anytime between 8 and 5. In February a celebration called Civil War Heritage Days includes costumed reenactments and demonstrations. From mid-January to mid-April the park serves as an open-air gallery for pieces created for Sculpture Key West. One of its most popular features is its man-made beach, a rest stop for migrating birds in the spring and fall; there are also picnic areas, hiking and biking trails, and a kayak launch. ✉ *End of Southard St., through Truman Annex, Key West* ☎ *305/292–6713* ⊕ *www.floridastateparks.org/park/Fort-Taylor*

🖭 *$4 for single-occupant vehicles, $6 for 2–8 people in a vehicle, plus $0.50 per person county surcharge.*

Harry S Truman Little White House Museum

HOUSE | Renovations to this circa-1890 landmark have restored the home and gardens to the Truman era, down to the wallpaper pattern. A free photographic review of visiting dignitaries and presidents—John F. Kennedy, Jimmy Carter, and Bill Clinton are among the chief executives who passed through here—is on display in the back of the gift shop. Engaging 45-minute tours begin every 20 minutes until 4:30. They start with an excellent 10-minute video on the history of the property and Truman's visits. On the grounds of **Truman Annex,** a 103-acre former military parade grounds and barracks, the home served as a "winter White House" for presidents Truman, Eisenhower, and Kennedy. Entry is cheaper when purchased in advance online; tickets bought on-site add sales tax. ■**TIP**➜ **The house tour does require climbing steps. Visitors can do a free self-guided botanical tour of the grounds with a brochure from the museum store.** ✉ *111 Front St., Key West* ☎ *305/294–9911* ⊕ *www.trumanlittlewhitehouse.com* 🖭 *$21.45.*

Historic Seaport at Key West Bight

HISTORIC SITE | What was once a funky—in some places even seedy—part of town is a 20-acre historic restoration of businesses, including waterfront restaurants, open-air bars, museums, clothing stores, and water-sports concessions. It's all linked by the 2-mile waterfront **Harborwalk,** which runs between Front and Grinnell Streets, passing big ships, schooners, sunset cruises, fishing charters, and glass-bottom boats. This is where the locals go for great music and good drinks. ✉ *100 Grinnell St., Key West* ⊕ *www.keywesthistoricseaport.com.*

The Key West Butterfly Garden an Nature Conservatory has a large collection of both butterflies and birds, including flamingoes.

The Key West Butterfly and Nature Conservatory

GARDEN | FAMILY | This air-conditioned refuge for butterflies, birds, and the human spirit gladdens the soul with hundreds of colorful wings—more than 45 species of butterflies alone—in a lovely glass-encased bubble. Waterfalls, artistic benches, paved pathways, birds, and lush, flowering vegetation elevate this above most butterfly attractions. The gift shop and gallery are worth a visit on their own. ⊠ *1316 Duval St., Key West* ☎ *305/296–2988, 800/839–4647* ⊕ *www. keywestbutterfly.com* ⊠ *$12.*

Key West Lighthouse Museum and Keeper's Quarters

LIGHTHOUSE | For the best view in town, climb the 88 steps to the top of this 1847 lighthouse. The 92-foot structure has a Fresnel lens, which was installed in the 1860s at a cost of $1 million. The keeper lived in the adjacent 1887 clapboard house, which now exhibits vintage photographs, ship models, nautical charts, and artifacts from all along Key West's

reefs. A kids' room is stocked with books and toys. ⊠ *938 Whitehead St., Key West* ☎ *305/294–0012* ⊕ *www.kwahs.com* ⊠ *$10.*

Mallory Square and Pier

LOCAL INTEREST | For cruise-ship passengers, this is the disembarkation point for an attack on Key West. For practically every visitor, it's the requisite venue for a nightly sunset celebration that includes street performers—human statues, sword swallowers, tightrope walkers, musicians, and more—plus craft vendors, conch-fritter fryers, and other regulars who defy classification. With all the activity, don't forget to watch the main show: a dazzling tropical sunset. ⊠ *Mallory Sq., Key West.*

The Southernmost Point

HISTORIC SITE | Possibly the most photographed site in Key West (even though the actual geographic southernmost point in the continental United States lies across the bay on a naval base, where you see a satellite dish), this is a mustsee. Have your picture taken next to the big striped buoy that's been marking the southernmost point in the continental United States since 1983. A plaque next to it honors Cubans who lost their lives trying to escape to America, and other signs tell Key West history. ⊠ *Whitehead and South Sts., Key West.*

🏖 Beaches

Fort Zachary Taylor Beach

BEACH—SIGHT | FAMILY | The park's beach is the best and safest place to swim in Key West. There's an adjoining picnic area with barbecue grills and shade trees, a snack bar, and rental equipment, including snorkeling gear. A café serves sandwiches and other munchies. Water shoes are recommended since the bottom is rocky here. **Amenities:** food and drink; showers; toilets; water sports. **Best for:** snorkeling; swimming. ⊠ *End of Southard St., through Truman Annex, Key West* ☎ *305/292–6713* ⊕ *www.fortzacharytaylor.com* 🖝 *$4 for single-occupant vehicles, $6 for 2–8 people, plus $0.50 per person county surcharge.*

🍴 Restaurants

★ B.O.'s Fish Wagon

$$ | SEAFOOD | What started out as a fish house on wheels appears to have broken down on the corner of Caroline and William Streets and is today the cornerstone for one of Key West's junkyard-chic dining institutions. Step up to the window and order a grouper sandwich fried or grilled and topped with key lime sauce. **Known for:** lots of Key West charm; Friday-night jam sessions; all seating on picnic tables in the yard. ⑤ *Average main: $18* ⊠ *801 Caroline St., Key West* ☎ *305/294–9272* ⊕ *bosfishwagon.com.*

El Meson de Pepe

$$ | CUBAN | If you want a taste of the island's Cuban heritage, this is the place to dine alfresco or in the dining room on refined Cuban classics. Begin with a megasize mojito while you browse the expansive menu offering *tostones rellenos* (green plantains with different traditional fillings), ceviche, and more. **Known for:** authentic plantain chips; Latin band during the nightly sunset celebration; touristy atmosphere. ⑤ *Average main: $19* ⊠ *Mallory Sq., 410 Wall St., Key West* ☎ *305/295–2620* ⊕ *www.elmesondepepe.com.*

🍸 Nightlife

Three spots stand out for first-timers among the saloons frequented by Key West denizens. All are within easy walking distance of the cruise-ship piers.

Capt. Tony's Saloon

BARS/PUBS | When it was the original Sloppy Joe's in the mid-1930s, Hemingway was a regular. Later, a young Jimmy Buffett sang here and made this watering hole famous in his song "Last Mango in Paris." Captain Tony was even voted mayor of Key West. Yes, this place is a beloved landmark. Stop in and take a look at the "hanging tree" that grows through the roof, listen to live music seven nights a week, and play some pool. ⊠ *428 Greene St., Key West* ☎ *305/294–1838* ⊕ *www.capttonyssaloon.com.*

Schooner Wharf Bar

BARS/PUBS | This open-air waterfront bar and grill in the historic seaport district retains its funky Key West charm and hosts live entertainment daily. Its margaritas rank among Key West's best, as does the bar itself, voted Best Local's Bar six years in a row. For great views, head up to the second floor and be sure to order up some fresh seafood and fritters and Dark and Stormy cocktails. ⊠ *202 William St., Key West* ☎ *305/292–3302* ⊕ *www.schoonerwharf.com.*

Sloppy Joe's

BARS/PUBS | There's history and good times at the successor to a famous 1937 speakeasy named for its founder, Captain Joe Russell. Decorated with Hemingway memorabilia and marine flags, the bar is popular with travelers and is full and noisy all the time. A Sloppy Joe's T-shirt is a de rigueur Key West souvenir, and the gift shop sells them like crazy. Grab a seat (if you can) and be entertained by the bands and by the parade of people in constant motion. ⌧ *201 Duval St., Key West* ☎ *305/294–5717* ⊕ *www.sloppy-joes.com.*

🛍 Shopping

On these streets you'll find colorful local art of widely varying quality, key limes made into everything imaginable, and the raunchiest T-shirts in the civilized world. Browsing the boutiques—with frequent pub stops along the way—makes for an entertaining stroll down Duval Street. Key West is filled with art galleries, and the variety is truly amazing. Much is locally produced by the town's large artist community, but many galleries carry international artists from as close as Haiti and as far away as France. Local artists do a great job of preserving the island's architecture and spirit.

Bahama Village
SHOPPING CENTERS/MALLS | Where to start your shopping adventure? This cluster of spruced-up shops, restaurants, and vendors is responsible for the restoration of the colorful historic district where Bahamians settled in the 19th century. The village lies roughly between Whitehead and Fort Streets and Angela and Catherine Streets. Hemingway frequented the bars, restaurants, and boxing rings in this part of town. ⌧ *Between Whitehead and Fort Sts. and Angela and Catherine Sts., Key West.*

🎿 Activities

BOAT TOURS
Dancing Dolphin Spirit Charters
BOATING | FAMILY | Victoria Impallomeni-Spencer, a wilderness guide and environmental marine science walking encyclopedia, invites up to six nature

lovers—especially children—aboard the *Imp II,* a 25-foot Aquasport, for four- and seven-hour ecotours that frequently include encounters with wild dolphins. While island-hopping, you visit underwater gardens and reefs, natural shoreline, and mangrove habitats. For the Dolphin Day for Humans tour, you'll be pulled through the water, equipped with mask and snorkel, on a specially designed "dolphin water massage board" that simulates dolphin swimming motions. All equipment is supplied. Captain Victoria is known around these parts as the dolphin whisperer, as she's been guiding for over 40 years. ⌧ *Murray's Marina, 5710 Overseas Hwy. (MM 5 OS), Key West* ☎ *305/304–7562, 305/745–9901* ⊕ *www.dancingdolphinspirits.com* 🖃 *From $600.*

Lazy Dog
KAYAKING | Take a two-hour backcountry mangrove ecotour or a four-hour guided sea kayak–snorkel tour around the mangrove islands just east of Key West. Costs include transportation, bottled water, a snack, and supplies, including snorkeling gear. Paddleboard tours, PaddleYoga, and PaddleFit classes are also available, as are maps and rentals for self-touring. ⌧ *5114 Overseas Hwy., Key West* ☎ *305/295–9898* ⊕ *www.lazydog.com* 🖃 *From $50.*

DIVING AND SNORKELLING
The Florida Keys National Marine Sanctuary extends along Key West and beyond to the Dry Tortugas. Key West National Wildlife Refuge further protects the pristine waters. Most divers don't make it this far out in the Keys, but if you're looking for a day of diving as a break from the nonstop party in Old Town, expect to pay about $65 and upward for a two-tank dive. Serious divers can book dive trips to the Dry Tortugas.

Captain's Corner
SCUBA DIVING | This PADI-certified dive shop has classes in several languages and twice-daily snorkel and dive trips to reefs and wrecks aboard a 60-foot dive

boat, the *Sea Eagle*. Use of weights, belts, masks, and fins is included. ☒ *125 Ann St., Key West* ☎ *305/296–8865* ⊕ *www.captainscorner.com* ☎ *From $45.*

Snuba of Key West

SCUBA DIVING | FAMILY | If you've always wanted to dive but never found the time to get certified, Snuba is for you. You can dive safely using a regulator tethered to a floating air tank with a simple orientation. Ride out to the reef on a catamaran, then follow your guide underwater for a one-hour tour of the coral reefs. It's easy and fun. No prior diving or snorkeling experience is necessary, but you must know how to swim and be at least eight years old. The price includes beverages. ☒ *Garrison Bight Marina, Palm Ave. between Eaton St. and N. Roosevelt Blvd., Key West* ☎ *305/292–4616* ⊕ *www.snubakeywest.com* ☎ *From $109.*

FISHING

Any number of local fishing guides can take you to where the big ones are biting, either in the backcountry for snapper and snook or to the deep water for the marlins and shark that brought Hemingway here in the first place.

Key West Bait & Tackle

FISHING | Prepare to catch a big one with the live bait, frozen bait, and fishing equipment provided here. They even offer rod and reel rentals (starting at $15 for one day, $5 each additional day). Stop by their on-site Live Bait Lounge where you can sip $3.25 ice-cold beer while telling fish tales. ☒ *241 Margaret St., Key West* ☎ *305/292–1961* ⊕ *www.keywestbaitandtackle.com.*

Key West Pro Guides

FISHING | This outfitter offers private charters, and you can choose four-, five-, six-, or eight-hour trips. Choose from flats, backcountry, reef, offshore fishing, and even specialty trips to the Dry Tortugas. Whatever your fishing (even spearfishing) pleasure, their captains will hook you up. ☒ *G–31 Miriam St., Key West* ☎ *866/259–4205* ⊕ *www.keywestproguides.com* ☎ *From $450.*

Labadee, Haiti

Labadee is a 260-acre peninsula approximately 6 miles (10 km) from Cap Haitien on the secluded north coast of Haiti (the port of call is still occasionally called "Hispaniola") that is used by Royal Caribbean, Celebrity, and Azamara Club Cruises ships. Passengers can step ashore on the dock (no tenders here), from which water taxis and five different walking paths, trails, and avenues lead to many areas throughout the peninsula, including the Labadee Town Square and Dragon's Plaza, where a welcome center and central tram station are located. In addition to swimming, water sports, an Aqua Park with floating trampolines and waterslides, and nature trails to explore, bonuses on Labadee include an authentic folkloric show presented by island performers and a market featuring work of local artists and crafters, where you might find an interesting painting or unique wood carving. Only cash is accepted, and bargaining is expected in the market. More adventurous activities include an Alpine Coaster, a thrilling roller-coaster experience, and one of the most exciting—and at 2,600 feet in length the longest—zip-line experiences in the Caribbean, 500 feet above the beaches of Labadee, where riders can reach speeds of 40 to 50 mph over the water (extra charge). There's also an alpine-style (gravity-driven) roller coaster (extra charge). The use of beach chairs is complimentary; however, tipping the beach attendants for their service is always appreciated. The Arawak Aqua Park has an extra charge. The Barefoot Beach Club & Cabanas is reserved for top suite guests and those who rent one of the 20 cabanas, which can accommodate four to five guests. Only the nine Palm Cabanas are wheelchair-accessible, but even they have two steps to climb. **Available Activities:** hiking, jet-skiing, kayaking, organized games, parasailing, shopping, snorkeling, volleyball, zip-lining.

La Romana, Dominican Republic

The Dominican Republic is a beautiful island nation bathed by the Atlantic Ocean to the north and the Caribbean Sea to the south, and some of its most beautiful beaches are in the area surrounding La Romana, notably Bayahibe Bay. The famed Casa de Campo resort and Marina will be the destination for most cruise passengers who land at La Romana's International Tourist Pier. A port call here will allow you to explore the immediate region—even take a day-trip into Santo Domingo—or simply stay and enjoy some nice (but expensive) restaurants and shops. There is also a host of activities cruise passengers can take part in on organized shore excursions.

ESSENTIALS
CURRENCY
The Dominican peso, but you can almost always use U.S. dollars.

TELEPHONE
Country codes are 1 809, 1 829, and 1 849, and depend on the type of phone you are calling. Claro, Orange, Tricom, and Viva are the major mobile providers, using GSM (850, 900, 1800 and 1900 bands).

COMING ASHORE
Ships enter the Casa de Campo International Tourist Port (Muelle Turístico Internacional Casa de Campo). A group of folkloric dancers and local musicians, playing merengue, greets passengers as they come down the gangway. An information booth with English-speaking staffers is there to assist cruise-ship passengers; the desk is open the entire time the ship is in port.

Best Bets

- **Altos de Chavón.** You'll find shopping and dining as well as great views.

- **Golf.** The Teeth of the Dog is one of the Caribbean's best courses, despite the cost.

- **Horseback Riding.** Casa de Campo has an excellent equestrian center.

- **Isla Saona.** The powder-soft beach and beautiful water are excellent.

- **Kandela.** The tropical, Las Vegas-style review is a highlight if your ship stays late on a night it is performed.

It is a 15-minute walk into the town of La Romana, or you can jump into a waiting taxi. It's safe to stroll around town, but it's not particularly beautiful, quaint, or even historic; however, it is a real slice of Dominican life. Most people just board the complimentary shuttle and head for the Casa de Campo Marina and/or Altos de Chavón, both of which are within the Casa de Campo resort. Shuttles run all day long.

Taxis line up at the port's docks, and some, but not all, drivers speak English. Staff members from the information kiosk will help to make taxi arrangements. Most rates are fixed and spelled out on a board: $15 to Casa de Campo Marina, $20 to Altos de Chavón. You may be able to negotiate a somewhat lower rate if a group books a taxi for a tour. You can also rent a car at Casa de Campo from National Car Rental; rates are expensive, usually more than $70 per day. Driving into Santo Domingo can be a hair-raising experience and isn't for the faint of heart, so we don't recommend it.

La Romana

👁 Sights

★ Altos de Chavón

STORE/MALL | This replica 16th-century Mediterranean village sits on a bluff overlooking the Río Chavón, on the grounds of Casa de Campo but about 3 miles (5 km) east of the main facilities. There are cobblestone streets lined with lanterns, wrought-iron balconies, wooden shutters, courtyards swathed with bougainvillea, and **Iglesia St. Stanislaus,** the romantic setting for many a Casa de Campo wedding. More than a museum piece, this village is a place where artists live, work, and play. Emilio Robba, a famous European designer, is now directing the art studios. You can visit the ateliers and see the talented artisans making pottery, tapestry, and serigraphic art. The artists sell their finished wares at the Art Studios Boutique. The village also has an amber museum, an archaeological museum, a handful of restaurants, and a number of unique shops. Strolling musicians enliven the rustic ambience of ceramic tiles and cobblestone terrace, but there are now more bars and nightclubs geared to Casa de Campo's guests. Big names, including Elton John, perform at the amphitheater. Christmastime is sheer magic, with lights, music concerts, a giant Christmas tree, and a cameo appearance by Santa. ⊠ *Casa de Campo, La Romana* ⊕ *www. casadecampo.com.do.*

Isla Catalina

BEACH—SIGHT | This diminutive, picture-postcard Caribbean island lies off the coast of the mainland. Catalina is about a half hour away from Bayahibe by catamaran, and most excursions offer the use of snorkeling equipment as well as a beach barbecue. Some cruise lines also

The architecture in the town of Altos de Chavón re-creates a 16th-century Mediterranean village.

use it as a "private island" experience. ⊠ *Isla Catalina* ⟊ *30 mins from Bayahibe Bay by boat.*

Isla Saona

BEACH—SIGHT | Off the east coast of Hispaniola and part of Parque Nacional del Este lies this island, inhabited by sea turtles, pigeons, and other wildlife. Indigenous people once used the caves here. The beaches are beautiful, and legend has it that Columbus once stopped over. However, the island is not nearly as pristine as one might expect for a national park. Getting here, on catamarans and other excursion boats, is half the fun, but it can be a crowded scene once you arrive. Vendors are allowed to sell to visitors, and there are a number of beach shacks serving lunch and drinks. Most boats traveling here leave out of the beach at Bayahibe Village. Most tourists book through their hotel. ⚠ **Please note that there is little to no refrigeration on the island and the sun is strong, so take caution when dining.** ⊠ *Bayahibe* ⟊ *20 mins from Bayahibe Bay by boat.*

Santo Domingo

NEIGHBORHOOD | Spanish civilization in the New World began in the 12-block Zona Colonial of Santo Domingo. Strolling its narrow streets, it's easy to imagine this old city as it was when the likes of Columbus, Cortés, and Ponce de León walked the cobblestones, pirates sailed in and out, and colonists were settling themselves. Tourist brochures tout that "history comes alive here"—a surprisingly truthful statement. A fun horse-and-carriage ride around the Zona costs $25 for an hour; the steeds are no thoroughbreds but they move at a good clip, though any commentary will be in Spanish. The drivers usually hang out in front of the Hodelpa Nicolás de Ovando. History buffs will want to spend a day exploring the many "firsts" of this continent, which will be included in any cruise-ship excursion. Do wear comfortable shoes.

Beaches

Cruise passengers can buy a day pass to use the beach and facilities at Casa de Campo ($75), which gets them a place in the sun at Minitas Beach, towels, access to nonmotorized water sports, lunch in the Beach Club, and admission to Altos de Chavón. Otherwise, excursions (sometimes cheaper) are available to several area beaches, including trips to Isla Catalina and Isla Saona.

Playa Bayahibe

BEACH—SIGHT | Playa Bayahibe, where several seafood restaurants are situated, is somewhat thin, with hard-packed taupe sand and no lounge chairs. However, as you move away from the village, a 10-minute walk along the shoreline, you'll reach the glorious, half-moon cove. Although you'll be able to get to the cove and the soft sand, bring a towel (resort security won't let you use the facilities). At night, when no one is on the playa and the silver moon illuminates the phosphorescence, it's the stuff that Caribbean dreams are made of. **Amenities:** food and drink; toilets. **Best for:** partiers; sunset; swimming; walking; windsurfing. ⊠ Near the Dreams resort, Bayahibe ⊹ Starts in the center of town.

Restaurants

La Casita

$$$ | MEDITERRANEAN | On the waterfront, La Casita (a spin-off of the original in La Romana's downtown) has a contemporary feel; at night dramatic lighting positioned over waterfront tables casts a beautifying glow. Professional waiters guide you through the menu of pastas, risottos, shellfish stew, and paella, which reflects the Spanish owner's heritage. **Known for:** romantic marina front restaurant; fideuà (a variation of paella made with pasta); professional waiters can handle large parties. ⑤ Average main: $26 ⊠ Casa de Campo Marina, La Romana ☎ 809/523–2529, 809/523–3333 ☯ Closed Sun. No lunch.

Peperoni

$$$ | ECLECTIC | Although the name may sound as Italian as amore, this restaurant's menu is more eclectic than Italian. It has a classy, contemporary white-dominated decor in a dreamy marina setting. **Known for:** international menu; goat cheese salad; beef carpacchio is a staple. ⑤ Average main: $21 ⊠ Casa de Campo Marina, Plaza Portofino 16, La Romana ☎ 809/523–2227, 809/523–3333.

Shopping

Altos de Chavón

SHOPPING CENTERS/MALLS | Altos de Chavón is a re-creation of a 16th-century Mediterranean village on the grounds of the Casa de Campo resort, where you can find a church, art galleries, boutiques, restaurants, nightspots, and souvenir shops, and a 5,000-seat amphitheater for concerts grouped around a cobbled square. At the Altos de Chavón Art Studios you can find ceramics, weaving, and screen prints made by local and resident artists. Extra special is the Jenny Polanco Project. A top Dominican fashion designer, she has made an outlet for Dominican, Haitian, and Caribbean craftsmen to sell their wares, from Carnival masks to baskets and carved plates. Tienda Batey sells fine linens handcrafted by women from the sugar plantation bateys (poor villages). ⊠ Casa de Campo, La Romana ⊕ www.casadecampo.com.do.

Casa de Campo Marina

SHOPPING NEIGHBORHOODS | Casa de Campo's top-ranked marina is home to shops and international boutiques, galleries, and jewelers scattered amid restaurants, banks, and other services. The chic shopping scene includes Luxury Shops Carmen Sol and Kiwi St. Tropez for French bathing suits. Polanco-Leon with Dominican designer Jenny Polanco's has resort wear, purses, and jewelry as well as Bibi Leon's tropical-themed home accessories. There's also a marvelous Italian antiques shop, Nuovo Rinascimento, and Club Del Cigarro (Fumo). The *supermercado* Nacional has not only groceries but sundries, postcards, and snacks. ✉ *Casa de Campo Marina, Calle Barlovento, La Romana* ⊕ *www.marinacasadecampo.com.do.*

🏃 Activities

Most activities available at Casa de Campo are open to cruise-ship passengers. You'll need to make reservations on the ship, particularly for golf.

FISHING

Casa de Campo Marina

FISHING | Casa de Campo Marina is the best charter option in the La Romana area. Yachts (22- to 60-footers) are available for deep-sea fishing charters for half or full days. Prices go from $824 for a half day on *Scorpio* to $3,555 for a full day on *Gabriella*. They can come equipped with rods, bait, dinghies, drinks, and experienced guides. Going out for the big billfish that swim the depths of the Caribbean is a major adrenaline rush. The marina hosts the annual Casa de Campo International Blue Marlin Classic Tournament in late March, which is celebrated with a round of parties. ✉ *Casa de Campo, Calle Barlovento 3, La Romana* ☎ *809/523–3333, 809/523–3333* ⊕ *www.marinacasadecampo.com.do* 🔁 *Charters from $824.*

GOLF

⭐ Casa de Campo Resort

GOLF | The Resort is considered by most to be the premier multiple golf resort in the Caribbean. The famed 18-hole Teeth of the Dog course at Casa de Campo, with seven holes on the sea, is usually ranked as the number-one course in the Caribbean and is among the top courses in the world. Pete Dye regards Teeth of the Dog as one of his

best designs and has long enjoyed living at Casa part-time. The Teeth of the Dog requires a caddy for each round (for an additional fee). Pete Dye has designed this and two other globally acclaimed courses here. Dye Fore, now with a total of 27 holes, is close to Altos de Chavón, hugging a cliff that features commanding vistas of the sea, a river, Dominican mountains, and the marina. The Links is a gamey 18-hole inland course. Resort guests must reserve tee times for all courses at least one day in advance; nonguests should make reservations earlier. ✉ *Casa de Campo, La Romana* ☎ *809/523–3333 resort, 809/523–8115 golf director* ⊕ *www.casadecampo.com.do* 🔁 *Teeth of the Dog: $395 per round per golfer for nonguests; Dye Fore: $295 for nonguests; The Links: $175 for nonguests* 🏌 *. Teeth of the Dog: 18 holes, 6989 yards, par 72; Dye Fore: 18 holes, 7740 yards, par 72; The Links: 18 holes, 6664 yards, par 71.*

HORSEBACK RIDING

Equestrian Center at Casa de Campo

HORSEBACK RIDING | The 250-acre Equestrian Center at Casa de Campo has something for both Western and English riders—a dude ranch, a rodeo arena (where Casa's trademark "Donkey Polo" is played), three polo fields, guided trail rides, riding, jumping, and polo lessons. There are early-morning and sunset trail rides, too. Unlimited horseback riding is included in some Casa de Campo packages. Trail rides are offered through the property's private cattle ranch, which houses a herd of water buffalo and lakes populated with ducks as well as the resort's on-site horse-breeding operation. Unlimited horseback riding is included in Casa's all-inclusive experience. Three ponies are now available to kids for trail ride. ✉ *Casa de Campo, La Romana* ☎ *809/523–3333* ⊕ *www.casadecampo.com.do* 🔁 *From $57.*

Martinique (Fort-de-France)

The largest of the Windward Islands, Martinique is 4,261 miles (6,817 km) from Paris, but its spirit and language are decidedly French, despite more than a soupçon of West Indian spice. Tangible, edible evidence of the fact is the island's cuisine, a superb blend of French and Creole. Martinique is lushly landscaped with tropical flowers. Trees bend under the weight of fruits such as mangoes, papayas, lemons, limes, and bright-red West Indian cherries. Acres of banana plantations, pineapple fields, and waving sugarcane stretch to the horizon. The towering mountains and verdant rain forest in the north lure hikers, while underwater sights and sunken treasures attract snorkelers and scuba divers. Martinique is also wonderful if your idea of exercise is turning over every 10 minutes to get an even tan and your taste in adventure runs to duty-free shopping. One popular excursion goes to St-Pierre, which was buried by ash when Mount Pelée erupted in 1902.

ESSENTIALS
CURRENCY
The euro. Change currency at a bureau de change, but you'll get the best rate from any ATM.

TELEPHONE
The country code is 596. Digicel and Orange are the primary mobile providers, using GSM (900 and 1800 bands).

COMING ASHORE
Most cruise ships call either at Tourelles (in the old port, about 1½ miles [2 km] from Fort-de-France) or at Pointe Simon, right in downtown Fort-de-France. (It is rare to have a ship anchor in the Baie des Flamands and tender passengers ashore.) Tourist information offices are at each cruise terminal. Uniformed dispatchers assist passengers in finding English-speaking taxi drivers. Passengers who do not wish to walk 20 minutes into Fort-de-France from Tourelles can take a taxi (set rate of €8 for up to four passengers in a van, or €2 for each additional passenger). Expect to pay about €50 per hour for touring; in larger vans the price is usually €10 per person per hour. Independent cruisers can explore the capital and the nearby open-air market on their own. Beaming and knowledgeable hostesses in creole dress greet cruise passengers. Civilian auxiliary police (in blue-and-orange uniforms) supplement the regular police.

Know that traffic in Fort-de-France can be nightmarish. If you want to go to the beach, a much cheaper option is to take a ferry from Fort-de-France. *Vedettes* (ferries) operate daily between the waterfront pier next to the public land-transport terminal and the marina in Pointe du Bout, Anse Mitan, and Anse à l'Ane. Any of the three trips takes about 15 minutes, and the ferries operate about every 30 minutes on weekdays. Renting a car in Fort-de-France is possible, but the heavy traffic can be forbidding. Rates are about €80 per day (high season) for a car with manual transmission; automatics are substantially more expensive and seldom available without reservations.

◉ Sights

If you want to see the lush island interior and St-Pierre on your own, take the N3, which snakes through dense rain forests, north through the mountains to Le Morne Rouge, then take the coastal N2 back to Fort-de-France via St-Pierre. You can do the 40-mile (64-km) round trip in half a day, but your best option is to hire an English-speaking driver.

FORT-DE-FRANCE
With its historic fort and superb location beneath the towering Pitons du Carbet on the Baie des Flamands, Martinique's capital—home to about one-quarter of

the island's 400,000 inhabitants—should be a grand place. It hasn't been for decades but it's now coming up fast. An ambitious redevelopment project, still under way, hopes to make it one of the most attractive cities in the Caribbean. The most pleasant districts—such as Didier, Bellevue, and Schoelcher—are on the hillside, reachable only by car or taxi; there are some good shops with Parisian wares and lively street markets. Near the harbor is a marketplace where local crafts and souvenirs are sold. The urban beach between the waterfront and the fort, La Française, has been cleaned up; white sand was brought in, and many cruise-ship passengers frequent it. The new Stewards Urbaine, easily recognized by their red caps and uniforms, are able to answer most visitor questions and give directions.

Fort St. Louis

HISTORIC SITE | Fort Saint Louis (pronounced *lou-EE*), an imposing stone fortress that has guarded the island's principal port city for some 375 years, offers panoramic views of the surrounding seaside urban landscape. Guided tours are available, but visitors must first check in at tourist information kiosk 1, at the northwest corner of La Savane—at the intersection of rue de la Liberté and boulevard Alfassa. ⊠ *Bd. Chevalier, Sainte-Marthe, Fort-de-France* ☎ *0596/75–41–44* ⊕ *www.tourismefdf. com* 🎫 *€8* ⊘ *Fort closed for tours Sun.–Mon.*

La Savane

CITY PARK | The heart of Fort-de-France, La Savane is a 12½-acre park filled with trees, fountains, and benches. A massive revitalization made it the focal point of the city again, with entertainment, shopping, and a pedestrian mall. Attractive wooden stands have been constructed along the edge of the park that house public restrooms, arts-and-crafts vendors, a crepe stand, an ice-cream stand, and numerous other eateries. Although

Best Bets 👁

■ **Beaches.** If you want to relax or party, one of the most beautiful beaches is Les Salines.

■ **French food and music.** A *paradis* for Francophiles.

■ **La Route des Rhums.** Visit several distilleries and become a rum connoisseur. (Visit ⊕ *www. martinique.org* for a good map.)

■ **Shopping.** Browse Fort-de-France's many upscale boutiques and department stores for French wares.

■ **St-Pierre.** Wander the narrow, winding streets of this hill town.

homeless people frequent the park, they generally do not bother anyone.

Diagonally across from La Savane, you can catch the ferries for the 20-minute run across the bay to Pointe du Bout and the beaches at Anse-Mitan and Anse-à-l'Ane. It's relatively cheap as well as stress-free—much safer, more pleasant, and faster than by car. ⊠ *Fort-de-France.*

Musée d'Histoire et d'Ethnographie

MUSEUM | This museum is best undertaken at the beginning of your vacation, so you can better understand the history, background, and people of the island. Housed in an elaborate former military residence (circa 1888) with balconies and fretwork, the museum displays some of the garish gold jewelry that prostitutes wore after emancipation as well as the sorts of rooms that a proper middle-class Martinican would have lived in. Oil paintings, engravings, and old historical documents also help sketch out the island's culture. ⊠ *10 bd. Général de Gaulle, Fort-de-France* ☎ *0596/72–81–87* 🎫 *€3.*

Martinique

Martinique Passage

ATLANTIC OCEAN

Grand-Rivière
Basse-Pointe
Anse-Ceron
Mont Pelée
Le Prêcheur
D21
N1
Le Lorrain
Marigot
N3
Morne Jakob
N1
Havre de la Trinité
Ste-Marie
N2
Depaz Distillery
Caravelle Peninsula
Rade de St-Pierre
La Trinité
Tartane
St-Pierre
D1
D2
N4
Baie du Galion
Carbet
Morne Vert
Gros-Morne
Pitons du Carbet
Balata
Havre du Robert
N2
Le Robert
Bellefontaine
N3
N4
Pte. Larose
Case-Pilote
Fort-de-France
N1
Le François
Schoelcher
Lamentin International Airport
Mt. Vauclin
Baie de Fort-de-France
N6
Anse-Mitan
N5
Le Vauclin
Pointe du Bout
Les Trois-Ilets
D7
N5
Rivière-Salée
Rivière-Pilote
D7
Mt. Bigot
D7
D17
N6
Anse-d'Arlets
D37
Le Diamant
Ste-Luce
N5
Cul-de-Sac du Marin
D9
Les Salines

Caribbean Sea

St. Lucia Channel

KEY
Beach
Ferry Lines
Cruise Ship Terminal

Rue Victor Schoelcher

NEIGHBORHOOD | Stores sell Paris fashions and French perfume, china, crystal, and liqueurs, as well as local handicrafts along this street running through the center of the capital's primary shopping district, a six-block area bounded by rue de la République, rue de la Liberté, rue Victor Sévère, and rue Victor Hugo. ⊠ *Fort-de-France.*

St-Louis Cathedral

RELIGIOUS SITE | This Romanesque cathedral with lovely stained-glass windows was built in 1878, the sixth church on this site (the others were destroyed by fires, hurricanes, and earthquakes). Classified as a historical monument, it has a marble altar, an impressive organ, and carved wooden pulpits. ⊠ *Rue Victor Schoelcher, Schoelcher* ☎ *0596/60–59–00.*

ELSEWHERE ON MARTINIQUE
BALATA

This quiet little town has two sights worth visiting. Built in 1923 to commemorate those Martinicans who fought and died in World War I, **Balata Church** is an exact replica of Paris's Sacré-Coeur Basilica. The gardens, **Jardin de Balata,** are lovely.

Jardin de Balata (*Balata Gardens*)

GARDEN | The Jardin de Balata has thousands of varieties of tropical flowers and plants; its owner is a dedicated horticulturist. There are shaded benches from which to take in the mountain views and a plantation-style house furnished with period furniture. An aerial path gives visitors an astounding, bird's-eye view of the gardens and surrounding hills, from wooden walkways suspended 50 feet in the air. There is no restaurant, though

The town of St-Pierre is beneath the 4,600-foot Mont Pelée.

beverages are for sale. This worthy site shows why Martinique is called "the Island of Flowers." It's 15 minutes from Fort-de-France, in the direction of St-Pierre. You can order anthuriums and other tropical flowers to be delivered to the airport from the mesmerizing flower boutique here. ■TIP→ **The gardens close at 6, but the ticket office will not admit anyone after 4:30. Children get a discount.** ⊠ *Km. 10, rte. de Balata, Balata* ☎ *0596/64–48–73* ⊕ *www.jardindebalata. fr* 🖭 *€14.*

ST-PIERRE

The rise and fall of St-Pierre is one of the most remarkable stories in the Caribbean and one of its worst disasters. Martinique's modern history began here in 1635. By the turn of the 20th century St-Pierre was a flourishing city of 30,000, known as the Paris of the West Indies. As many as 30 ships at a time stood at anchor. By 1902 it was the most modern town in the Caribbean, with electricity, phones, and a tram. On May 8, 1902, two thunderous explosions rent the air. As the nearby

volcano erupted, Mount Pelée split in half, belching forth a cloud of burning ash, poisonous gas, and lava that raced down the mountain at 250 mph. At 3,600°F, it instantly vaporized everything in its path; 30,000 people were killed in two minutes.

The **Cyparis Express,** a small tourist train, will take you on an hour-long tour (€12) of the main sights, with running narrative (in French), Monday through Saturday at 11 am, with reservations (☎ *0596/55–50–92, 0696/81–88–70*).

An Office du Tourisme is on the *moderne* seafront promenade. Stroll the main streets and check the blackboards at the sidewalk cafés before deciding where to lunch. At night some places have live music. Like stage sets for a dramatic opera, there are the ruins of the island's first church (built in 1640), the imposing theater, and the toppled statues. This city, situated on its naturally beautiful harbor and with its narrow, winding streets, has the feel of a European seaside hill town. With every footstep, you touch a page of history. Although many of the historic buildings need work, stark modernism has not invaded this burg.

★ Depaz Distillery

WINERY/DISTILLERY | An excursion to Depaz Distillery is one of the best things to do on the island. Established in 1651, it sits at the foot of the volcano. After a devastating eruption in 1902, the fields of blue cane were replanted, and in time, the rum-making began all over again. A self-guided tour includes the workers' gingerbread cottages. The tasting room sells Depaz rum, including its golden and aged rums, as well as liqueurs made from orange, ginger, and basil (among other flavors) that can enhance your cooking. Unfortunately, the plantation's greathouse, or château, is unlikely to be open. Allow time and make a reservation for Depaz's restaurant, **Le Moulin a Canne** (☎ *0596/69–80–44*). Open only for lunch (even on Sunday when the distillery is closed), it has the views, the service, and flavorful creole specialties as well as some French classics on the menu, plus—you guessed it—Depaz rum to wash it down. It's "on the house." ■**TIP**➜ **Shutters are drawn at the tasting room and the staff leave at exactly 5 pm (4 on Saturday), so plan to be there at least an hour before.** ⊠ *Mount Pelée Plantation, St-Pierre* ☎ *0596/78–13–14* ⊕ *www. depaz.fr/en* 🎫 *Distillery free.*

Musée Volcanologique Franck Perret

MUSEUM | FAMILY | For those interested in Mount Pelée's eruption of 1902, the Musée Vulcanologique Franck Perret is a must. It was established in 1933 by Franck Perret, a noted American volcanologist. Small but fascinating and insightful, the museum houses photographs of the old town before and after the eruption, documents, and a number of relics—some gruesome—excavated from the ashy ruins, including molten glass, melted iron, the church bell, and contorted clocks stopped at 8 am. The 30-minute film is a good way to begin. An English-speaking guide is often available and may tell you that the next lava flow is expected within 50 years. (No wonder the price of real estate in St-Pierre is among the lowest on the island.) The museum requires a renovation, and some signs have become difficult to read. ⊠ *Rue Victor Hugo (D10) at rue du Theatre, St-Pierre* ☎ *0596/78–15–16* 🎫 *€5.*

Le Centre de Découverte des Sciences de la Terre

MUSEUM | If you want to know more about volcanoes, earthquakes, and hurricanes, check out Le Centre de Découverte des Sciences de la Terre. Housed in a sleek building that looks like a dramatic white box, this earth-science museum has high-tech exhibits and interesting films. Watch the documentary on the volcanoes in the Antilles, highlighting the eruption of the nearby Mount Pelée. Le Centre has fascinating Wednesday summer programs on dance, food, and ecotourism. ■**TIP**➜ **The Depaz Distillery is nearby, and it's easy to visit both on the same day.** ⊠ *Habitation Perinelle, Quartier la Galere, St-Pierre* ☎ *0596/52–82–42* ⊕ *cdst.e-monsite.com* 🎫 *€5.*

🏖 Beaches

Anse-Mitan

BEACH—SIGHT | There are often yachts moored offshore in these calm waters. This long stretch of beach can be particularly fun on Sunday. Small, family-owned seaside restaurants are half-hidden among palm trees and are footsteps from the lapping waves. Nearly all offer grilled lobster and some form of music on weekends, perhaps a zouk band. Inexpensive waterfront hotels line the clean, golden beach, which has excellent snorkeling just offshore. Chaise longues are available for rent from hotels, and there are also usually vendors on weekends. The abandoned public housing visible from the beach has finally been razed. When you get to Pointe du Bout, take a left at the yellow office of Budget Rent a Car, then the next left up a hill, and park near the little white church. **Amenities:** food and drink. **Best for:** partiers; snorkeling; swimming; walking. ⊠ *Pointe du Bout, Les Trois-Îlets.*

Les Salines

BEACH—SIGHT | FAMILY | A short drive south of Ste-Anne brings you to a mile-long (1½-km-long) cove lined with soft white sand and coconut palms. The beach is awash with families and children during holidays and on weekends, but quiet during the week. The far end—away from the makeshift souvenir shops—is most appealing. The calm waters are safe for swimming, even for the kids. You can snorkel, but it's not that memorable. Food vendors roam the sand, and there are also pizza stands and simple seafood restaurants. From Le Marin, take the coastal road toward Ste-Anne. You will see signs for Les Salines. If you see the sign for Pointe du Marin, you have gone too far. **Amenities:** food and drink; parking; showers; toilets. **Best for:** partiers; swimming; walking. ⊠ *Ste-Anne.*

Pointe du Bout

BEACH—SIGHT | FAMILY | The beaches here are small, man-made, and lined with resorts. Each little strip is associated with its resident hotel, and security guards and closed gates make access difficult. However, if you take a left across from the main pedestrian entrance to the marina, after the taxi stand, then go left again, you will reach the beach for Hotel Bakoua, which has especially nice facilities and several options for lunch and drinks. If things are quiet (particularly during the week) one of the beach boys may rent you a chaise; otherwise, just plop your beach towel down, face forward, and enjoy the delightful view of the Fort-de-France skyline. The water is dead calm and quite shallow, but it eventually drops off if you swim out a bit. **Amenities:** food and drink; showers. **Best for:**

snorkeling; sunset; swimming. ⊠ *Pointe du Bout, Les Trois-Îlets.*

🍴 Restaurants

Le Bistrot des Flamands

$$ | FRENCH | Located within the new Simon Hotel and more casual than its sister restaurant (La Table de Marcel), Le Bistrot des Flamands is also under the direction of Michelin-starred Chef Marcel Ravin, known for his contemporary innovations. Patrons often order off the Bistrot menu and dine in the adjacent Bolibar lounge, with its convivial barmen and view of the Fort-de-France harbor. **Known for:** stunning black and white decor; social scene; breakfast buffet. $ *Average main: €15* ⊠ *1 rue Loulou Boislaville, Fort-de-France* ☎ 596/50–22–22.

🛍 Shopping

French fragrances; leather goods; liquor; wine (inexpensive at supermarkets); fine china and crystal; and designer clothes, scarves, and sunglasses are all good buys in duty-free Fort-de-France. Purchases are further sweetened by the 20% discount on luxury items when paid for with certain credit cards. Among the items produced on the island, look for *bijoux creole* (local jewelry, such as hoop earrings and heavy bead necklaces); white, dark, and aged rums; and handcrafted straw goods, pottery, and tapestries.

The striking 215,000-square-foot Cour Perrinon Mall in Fort-de-France, bordered by rue Perrinon, houses a Carrefour supermarket, a bookstore, perfume shops, designer boutiques, a French bakery, and a café-brasserie. The area around the cathedral in Fort-de-France has a number of small shops that carry luxury goods. Of particular note are the shops on rue Victor Hugo, rue Moreau de Jones, rue Antoine Siger, and rue Lamartine. Ongoing efforts to be more inviting to the North American market—with particular emphasis on offering English-language classes to staff—have dozens of shops participating. The **Galeries Lafayette** department store on rue Schoelcher in downtown Fort-de-France sells everything from perfume to pâté. On the outskirts of Fort-de-France, the **Centre Commercial de Cluny, Centre Commercial de Dillon, Centre Commercial de Bellevue,** and **Centre Commercial Le Rond Point** are among the major shopping malls.

⚡ Activities

GOLF

Golf de l'Impératrice Josephine (*Martinique Golf and Country Club*)
GOLF | Although it's named in honor of Empress Joséphine Napoléon, this Robert Trent Jones Sr. course is completely American in design, with an English-speaking pro, a pro shop, a bar, and an especially good restaurant. The best hole on the course may just be the par-5 15th. Sandwiched between two good par-3s, the 15th plays to an island fairway and then to a green situated by the shore. Try not to be mesmerized by the turquoise waters. (You can finish your visit here with foie gras torchon or a full meal at Restaurant Le Golf.) The club offers special greens fees to cruise-ship passengers. Club trolleys (called "chariots") are €6 for 18 holes, €4 for 9. There are no caddies. ⊠ *Quartier la Pagerie, Les Trois-Îlets* ☎ *0596/61–05–24* ✉ *€32 for 9 holes, €46 for 18; carts €25 for 9 holes, €40 for 18* ⚡. *18 holes, 6640 yards, par 71.*

HIKING

Parc Naturel Régional de la Martinique
HIKING/WALKING | Two-thirds of Martinique is designated as protected land, and trails—all 31 of them—are well marked and maintained. At the beginning of each, a notice is posted advising on the level of difficulty, the duration of a hike, and any interesting facts. The Parc Naturel Régional de la Martinique organizes

inexpensive guided excursions year-round. If there have been heavy rains, though, give it up. The tangle of ferns, bamboo trees, and vines is dramatic, but during the rainy season, the wet, muddy trails will temper your enthusiasm. ⊠ *9 bd. Général de Gaulle, Fort-de-France* ☎ *0596/64–45–64.*

HORSEBACK RIDING

Horseback-riding excursions can traverse scenic beaches, palm-shaded forests, sugarcane fields, and a variety of other tropical landscapes. Trained guides often include running commentaries on the history, flora, and fauna of the island.

Ranch Jack
HORSEBACK RIDING | FAMILY | Equipped with a large stable of some 30 horses, Ranch Jack's (English-style) trail rides cross some beautiful country for 90 minutes to two hours. Half-day excursions (inquire about transfers from nearby hotels) go through the fields and forests to the beach. Short rides ranging from an hour are also available. The company has a wonderful program to introduce kids ages three to seven to horses. Online comments reflect riders' satisfaction with the professionalism of the stable and the beautiful acreage they traverse. Their mounts are Creole horses, descended from Spanish horses that have adapted to the tropical climate. ⊠ *Morne habitué, Les Trois-Îlets* ☎ *0596/68–37–69, 0696/92–26–58* ✉ *ranch.jack@wanadoo.fr* ⚡ *From €31.*

Montego Bay, Jamaica

Today many explorations of MoBay are conducted from a reclining chair, frothy drink in hand, on Doctor's Cave Beach. As home of Jamaica's busiest cruise pier and the north-shore airport, Montego Bay—or MoBay—is the first taste most visitors have of the island. Travelers from around the world come and go in this bustling community, which ranks as Jamaica's second-largest city. The Spanish first named this port city Bahía de Manteca, or "Lard Bay," because they once shipped hogs from here. This is where Jamaican tourism began, in 1924, when the first resort opened at Doctor's Cave Beach so that health-seekers could "take the waters." If you can pull yourself away from the water's edge and brush the sand off your toes, you'll find some very interesting colonial sights in the surrounding area.

ESSENTIALS
CURRENCY
The Jamaican dollar, but U.S. dollars are widely accepted.

TELEPHONE
The country code for Jamaica is 1 876. Digicel and Flow are the major mobile phone providers, using GSM (850, 900, 1800, and 1900 bands).

COMING ASHORE
Ships dock at the Montego Cruise Terminal, operated by the Port Authority of Jamaica. Located west of Montego Bay, the cruise terminal has five berths and accommodates both cruise and cargo shipping. There are shops, a communications center, a visitor information booth, and a taxi stand supervised by the Port Authority of Jamaica. The cruise port in Montego Bay is not within walking distance of the heart of town; however, there's one shopping center (the Freeport Shopping Centre) within walking distance of the docks, though it has relatively little to offer. If you just want to visit a beach, then Doctor's Cave or the Cornwall Bathing Beach—both public beaches—are very good nearby options, and they are right in town.

From the Montego Cruise Terminal both taxis and shuttle buses take passengers downtown. Taxi service is about $7 each way to downtown. Expect to pay $5 per person each way by shuttle bus to the two crafts markets, the City Centre Shopping Mall, Margaritaville, or Doctor's Cave

Best Bets

- **Doctor's Cave Beach.** This public beach club is in the heart of Montego Bay.

- **Dunn's River Falls.** A visit to the falls is touristy but exhilarating.

- **Martha Brae Rafting.** A slow rafting trip is relaxing and very enjoyable.

- **Shopping.** MoBay has several good shopping centers and craft markets.

- **Rose Hall.** Peek back into the days of the plantation and its owner, the "white witch" Annie Palmer.

Beach. A day pass for the shuttle bus is $17 and allows passengers to get on and off as they wish. Jamaica is one place in the Caribbean where it's usually to your advantage to take an organized shore excursion offered by your ship, unless you just want to do a bit of shopping in town. Private taxis and other transportation providers aren't particularly cheap, and a full-day tour for a small group will run $150 to $180; however, road conditions and travel time have improved significantly with the completion of the North Coast Highway.

If you take a private taxi, you should know that rates are per car, not per passenger. All licensed and properly insured taxis display red Public Passenger Vehicle (PPV) license plates. Licensed minivans also bear the red PPV plates. If you hire a taxi driver as a tour guide, be sure to agree on a price before the vehicle is put into gear. Car-rental fees in Jamaica include the cost of insurance. It is not difficult to rent a car, but driving in Jamaica is done on the left side of the road, and it can take a little getting used to.

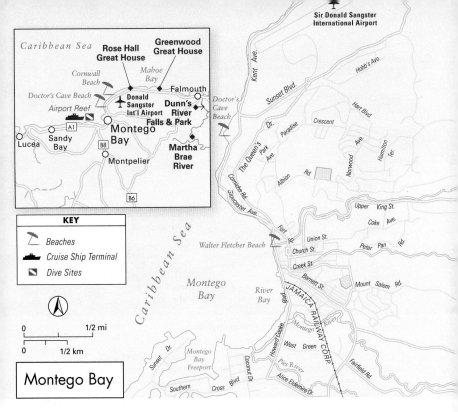

Montego Bay

KEY

🛠 Beaches
🚢 Cruise Ship Terminal
🥽 Dive Sites

0 _____ 1/2 mi
0 _____ 1/2 km

Sights

★ Dunn's River Falls & Park

BODY OF WATER | A popular natural attraction that is an eye-catching sight: 600 feet of cold, clear mountain water splashing over a series of stone steps to the Caribbean Sea. The best way to enjoy the falls is to climb the slippery steps in a swimsuit (there are changing rooms at the entrance), as you take the hand of the person ahead of you. After the climb, you exit through a crowded market, another reminder that this is one of Jamaica's top tourist attractions. ■**TIP➔ Always climb with a licensed guide at Dunn's River Falls, who can be hired inside the gates, not outside (ask at the ticket window). Freelance guides might be a little cheaper, but the experienced guides can tell you just where to plant each footstep—helping you prevent a fall.** ⊠ *Ocho Rios* ✛ *Off Hwy.*

A1, between St. Ann's Bay and Ocho Rios ☎ *876/974–4767* ⊕ *www.dunnsriver-fallsja.com* ✉ *$25.*

Greenwood Great House

HOUSE | This historic greathouse may not have a spooky legend to titillate, like Rose Hall, but it's much better at evoking life on a sugar plantation. The Barrett family, from whom the English poet Elizabeth Barrett Browning descended, once owned all the land from Rose Hall to Falmouth; on their vast holdings they built this and several other greathouses. (The poet's father, Edward Moulton Barrett, "the Tyrant of Wimpole Street," was born at nearby Cinnamon Hill, later the estate of country singer Johnny Cash.) Highlights of Greenwood include oil paintings of the Barretts, china made for the family by Wedgwood, a library filled with rare books from as early as 1697,

Dunn's River Falls is one of Jamaica's top tourist attractions.

fine antique furniture, and a collection of exotic musical instruments. There's a pub on-site as well. It's 15 miles (24 km) east of Montego Bay. ⊠ *435 Belgrade Ave., Montego Bay* ☎ *876/631–4701* ⊕ *www.greenwoodgreathouse.com* ☜ *$20.*

★ Martha Brae River
BODY OF WATER | This gentle waterway takes its name from an Arawak woman who drowned herself because she refused to reveal the whereabouts of a local gold mine. According to legend, she agreed to take her Spanish inquisitors there and, on reaching the river, used magic to change its course, drowning herself and the greedy Spaniards with her. Her *duppy* (ghost) is said to guard the mine's entrance. Rafting on this river is a very popular activity—many operators are on hand to take you for a glide downstream. ⊠ *Trelawny* ✛ *4½ miles (7 km) southeast of Falmouth* ☎ *876/952–0889* ⊕ *www.jamaicarafting.com* ☜ *From $65.*

★ Rose Hall Great House
HISTORIC SITE | In the 1700s it may well have been one of the greatest greathouses in the West Indies. Today it's popular less for its architecture than for the legend surrounding its second mistress, Annie Palmer. As the story goes, she was born in 1802 in England, but when she was 10, her family moved to Haiti. Soon after, her parents died of yellow fever. Adopted by a Haitian voodoo priestess, Annie became skilled in the practice of witchcraft. She moved to Jamaica, married, and became mistress of Rose Hall, an enormous plantation spanning 6,600 acres with more than 2,000 slaves. ■**TIP**➜ **A spooky nighttime tour of the property—recommended if you're up for a scare—is offered every evening. After the tour, have a drink at the White Witch pub, in the greathouse's cellar.** ⊠ *North Coast Hwy., St. James* ✛ *15 miles (24 km) east of Montego Bay* ☎ *876/953–2323* ⊕ *www.rosehall.com* ☜ *$25.*

🏖 Beaches

Doctor's Cave Bathing Club

BEACH—SIGHT | FAMILY | Located along Montego Bay's touristy Hip Strip, this famous beach first gained notoriety for its waters, said to have healing powers. It's a popular beach with a perpetual spring-break feel. The clubhouse has changing rooms, showers, a gift shop, and restaurant. You can rent beach chairs, pool floats, and umbrellas. Its location within the Montego Bay Marine Park—with protected coral reefs and plenty of marine life—makes it good for snorkeling and glass-bottom boat rides. Chairs, umbrellas, and pool floats are available to rent for $6 per item for the day. **Amenities:** food and drink; lifeguards; parking (fee); showers; toilets; water sports. **Best for:** partiers; snorkeling; sunset; swimming. ⊠ *Jimmy Cliff Blvd., Montego Bay* ☎ *876/952–2566* ⊕ *www.doctorscave-bathingclub.com* 🎫 *$6.*

Walter Fletcher Beach

BEACH—SIGHT | FAMILY | Renovated in 2018, the Walter Fletcher Beach is home to Aquasol Theme Park, which offers a large beach (with lifeguards and security personnel) and for an additional cost, glass-bottom boats, snorkeling, go-kart racing, a skating rink at night, and a bar and restaurant. Near the center of town, the beach has unusually fine swimming, and fun waterslides for children. **Amenities:** food and drink; lifeguards; parking (no fee); showers; toilets; water sports. **Best for:** partiers; snorkeling; sunset; swimming. ⊠ *Jimmy Cliff Blvd., Montego Bay* ☎ *876/979–9447* 🎫 *J$500* ⊗ *Closed Mon.–Tues.*

🍴 Restaurants

The Pork Pit

$ | JAMAICAN | A no-frills eatery favored by locals, Pork Pit is an authentic, open-air Jamaican restaurant that serves the best of Jamaican jerk meats and seafood dishes. The restaurant is close to Doctor's Cave Beach and is surrounded by all the attractions of MoBay's Hip Strip. **Known for:** cheap meals to go; jerk pork; jerk chicken. ⑤ *Average main: $12* ⊠ *27 Jimmy Cliff Blvd., Montego Bay* ☎ *876/940–3008.*

Scotchies Montego Bay

$ | JAMAICAN | Portland may be the birthplace of jerk cooking, but Scotchies is one of Jamaica's premier jerk eateries. It serves genuine jerk—chicken, pork, fish, sausage, and more—with fiery sauce and delectable side dishes including festival (bread similar to a hush puppy) and rice and peas. **Known for:** jerk chicken; lively domino games; local side dishes like festival, bammy (a flatbread made from cassava), and rice and peas. ⑤ *Average main: J$1000* ⊠ *North Coast Hwy., across from Holiday Inn Montego Bay, Montego Bay* ⊹ *10 miles (16 km) east of Montego Bay* ☎ *876/953–8043.*

🛍 Shopping

Jamaican artisans express themselves in silk-screening, wood carvings, resort wear, hand-loomed fabrics, and paintings. Jamaican rum makes a great gift, as does Tia Maria (the famous coffee liqueur) and Blue Mountain coffee. Wood carvings are one of the top purchases; the finest carvings are made from the Jamaican national tree, lignum vitae, or "tree of life," a dense wood that talented carvers transform into dolphins, heads, or fish. Bargaining is expected with crafts vendors.

Half Moon Shopping Village

SHOPPING CENTERS/MALLS | The bright yellow buildings at Half Moon hotel contain some of the finest and most expensive wares money can buy, as well as more affordable boutiques, a post office, bank, a medical center, and restaurants. The shopping village is also home to the "Bob Marley Experience," an exhibition featuring a 68-seat theater showing a daily film of the life and times of Bob Marley, and a Bob Marley gift shop. ⊠ *Half Moon, North Coast Hwy., Montego Bay* ⊹ *7 miles (11 km) east of Montego Bay* ☎ *876/953–2211* ⊕ *www. halfmoon.com.*

 ## Activities

GOLF

Golfers appreciate both the beauty and the challenges offered by Jamaica's courses. Caddies are almost always mandatory throughout the island and are paid by the round, the rate varying by the course. Cart rentals are available at most courses. Some of the best courses in the country are found near MoBay.

Half Moon Golf Course

GOLF | Swaying palms, abundant bunkering, and large greens greet you on this flat Robert Trent Jones Sr.–designed course, home of the Jamaica Open. The course was renovated in 2005 by Jones protégé Roger Rulewich to better position the hazards for today's longer hitters. The Half Moon Golf Academy offers one-day sessions, multiday retreats, and hour-long private sessions. ⊠ *Half Moon, North Coast Hwy., Montego Bay* ⊹ *7 miles (11 km) east of Montego Bay* ☎ *876/953–2560* ⊕ *www.halfmoon.com/ golf* ⊠ *Nonguests: $275 for 18 holes, $150 for 9 holes* ⅂ *18 holes, 7141 yards, par 72.*

White Witch Golf Course

GOLF | One of the nicest courses in Montego Bay, if not Jamaica, is the White Witch course, named for Annie Palmer, the wicked 19th-century plantation mistress, whose greathouse looms above the course. The course was designed by Robert von Hagge and Rick Baril. Annie's Revenge is one of five tournaments hosted at the course that occupies mountainous terrain high above the sea and features bold, attractive bunkering and panoramic views. Legend has it that Annie still haunts the area, but not your golf game. Rental clubs are available

for $55. Prebooking is recommended. ⊠ *Rose Hall Main Rd., Rose Hall, St. James* ☎ *876/632–7444, 876/632–7445* ⊕ *www.whitewitchgolf.com* ⊠ *$179 in winter, $139 in summer, $49 replay* ⅂ *18 holes, 6758 yards, par 71.*

RIVER RAFTING

Jamaica's many rivers mean a multitude of freshwater experiences, from mild to wild. The island's first tourist activity off the beaches was a relaxing trip aboard bamboo rafts, which was poled by local boatmen and originated on the **Rio Grande.** Jamaicans had long used rafts to transport bananas downriver. Decades ago actor and local resident Errol Flynn saw the rafts and thought they'd make a good tourist attraction. Today the slow rides are a favorite with romantic travelers and anyone looking to get off the beach for a few hours. The popularity of the Rio Grande's trips spawned similar trips down the **Martha Brae River,** about 25 miles (38 km) from MoBay. Near Ocho Rios, the **Great River** has lazy river rafting as well as energetic kayaking.

Jamaica Tours Limited

WHITE-WATER RAFTING | This big tour company offers various tour packages that include raft trips down the Martha Brae and Great Rivers. Price depends on number of people and pickup location. Hotel tour desks can book it. ⊠ *Providence Dr., Montego Bay* ☎ *876/953–3700* ⊕ *www. jamaicatoursltd.com.*

River Raft Ltd.

WHITE-WATER RAFTING | This company leads 1½-hour trips down the Martha Brae River, about 25 miles (38 km) from most MoBay hotels. ☎ *876/940–7018, 876/952–0889, 876/940–6398* ⊕ *www. jamaicarafting.com* ⊠ *$65.*

Nassau, Bahamas

Nassau, the capital of the Bahamas, has witnessed Spanish invasions and hosted pirates, who made it their headquarters for raids along the Spanish Main. The heritage of old Nassau blends the Southern charm of British loyalists from the Carolinas, the African tribal traditions of freed slaves, and a bawdy history of blockade-running during the Civil War and rum-running in the Roaring Twenties. The sheltered harbor bustles with cruise-ship hubbub, while a block away, broad, shop-lined Bay Street is alive with commercial activity. Over it all is a subtle layer of civility and sophistication, derived from three centuries of British rule. Nassau's charm, however, is often lost in its commercialism. There's excellent shopping, but if you look past the duty-free shops you'll also find sights of historical significance that are worth seeing.

ESSENTIALS
CURRENCY
The Bahamian dollar, which is on par with U.S. dollar, but U.S. dollars are widely accepted.

TELEPHONE
The country code in the Bahamas is 1 242. BTC and Aliv are the major mobile phone providers, using GSM (850 and 1900 bands).

COMING ASHORE
Cruise ships dock at one of three piers on Prince George Wharf. Taxi drivers who meet the ships may offer you a $2 "ride into town," but the historic government buildings and duty-free shops lie just steps from the dock area. As you leave the pier, look for a tall pink tower—diagonally across from here is the tourist information office. Stop in for maps of the island and downtown Nassau. On most days you can join a one-hour walking tour ($10 per person) conducted by a well-trained guide. Tours generally start every hour on the hour from 10 am to 4 pm; confirm the day's schedule in the office. Just outside, an ATM dispenses U.S. dollars.

As you disembark from your ship, you will find a row of taxis and air-conditioned

Best Bets

- **Ardastra Gardens.** Flocks of flamingos, the country's national bird, "march" in three shows daily (you can mingle with the flamboyant pink stars afterward).

- **Aquaventure.** Though very costly, the Atlantis water park is a must for families.

- **Shopping.** To many, shopping is one of Nassau's great delights.

- **Junkanoo Beach.** Head to this beach (aka Long Wharf Beach) and sit in the shade of a coconut palm (it's a 10-minute walk from the duty-free shops on Bay Street).

4

Ports of Call NASSAU, BAHAMAS

limousines. Fares are fixed by the government by zones. Unless you plan to jump all over the island, taxis are the most convenient way to get around. The fare is $9 plus $2 bridge toll between downtown Nassau and Paradise Island, $20 from Cable Beach to Paradise Island (plus $1 toll), and $18 from Cable Beach to Nassau. Fares are for two passengers; each additional passenger is $3. It's customary to tip taxi drivers 15%.

Water taxis travel between Prince George Wharf and Paradise Island during daylight hours at half-hour intervals. The one-way cost is $3 per person, and the trip takes 12 minutes.

Sights

Shops angle for tourist dollars with fine imported goods at duty-free prices, yet you will find a handful of stores overflowing with authentic Bahamian crafts, foods, and other delights. Most of Nassau's historic sites are centered on downtown.

With its thoroughly revitalized downtown—the revamped British Colonial

Hilton led the way—Nassau is recapturing some of its glamour. Nevertheless, modern influence is apparent: fancy restaurants, suave clubs, and trendy coffeehouses have popped up everywhere. This trend comes partly in response to the burgeoning upper-crust crowds that now supplement the spring-breakers and cruise passengers who have traditionally flocked to Nassau.

Today the seedy air of the town's not-so-distant past is almost unrecognizable. Petty crime is no greater than in other towns of this size, and the streets not only look cleaner but feel safer. You can still find a wild club or a rowdy bar, but you can also sip a cappuccino while viewing contemporary Bahamian art or dine by candlelight beneath prints of old Nassau, serenaded by soft, island-inspired calypso music.

Arawak Cay

RESTAURANT—SIGHT | Known to Nassau residents as "the Fish Fry," Arawak Cay is one of the best places to knock back a Kalik beer, chat with locals, watch or join in a fast-paced game of dominoes, or sample traditional Bahamian fare. The two-story Twin Brothers and Goldie's Enterprises are two of the most popular places. Local fairs and craft shows are often held in the adjacent field. ⊠ *W. Bay St. and Chippingham Rd., Nassau* ✆ *Free.*

Ardastra Gardens, Zoo, and Conservation Centre

GARDEN | **FAMILY** | Marching flamingos give a parading performance at Ardastra daily at 10:30, 2:15, and 4. Children can walk among the brilliant pink birds after the show. The zoo, with more than 5 acres of tropical greenery and ponds, also has an aviary of rare tropical birds including the bright-green Bahama parrot, native Bahamian creatures such as rock iguanas, the little (harmless) Bahamian boa constrictors, and a global collection of small animals. ⊠ *Chippingham Rd. south of W. Bay St., Nassau*

☎ *242/323–5806* ⊕ *www.ardastra.com* ✆ *$18.*

Fort Charlotte

HISTORIC SITE | **FAMILY** | Built in 1788, this imposing fort features a waterless moat, drawbridge, ramparts, and a dungeon with a torture device. Local guides bring the fort to life (tips are expected), and tours are suitable for children. Fort Charlotte was built by Lord Dunmore, who named the massive structure after George III's wife. The fort and its surrounding 100 acres offer a wonderful view of the cricket grounds, the beach, and the ocean beyond. On Wednesday and Friday enjoy fully regaled actors reenacting life as it was in the Bahamas in the 18th and 19th centuries. An historic military parade and canon firing takes place daily at noon. ⊠ *W. Bay St. at Chippingham Rd., Nassau* ✛ *Opposite Arawak Cay* ✆ *Nonresidents $5.*

★ National Art Gallery of the Bahamas

MUSEUM | Opened in 2003, the museum houses the works of esteemed Bahamian artists such as Max Taylor, Amos Ferguson, Brent Malone, John Cox, and Antonius Roberts. The glorious Italianate colonial mansion, built in 1860 and restored in the 1990s, has double-tiered verandas with elegant columns. It was the residence of Sir William Doyle, the first chief justice of the Bahamas. Don't miss the museum's gift shop, where you'll find books about the Bahamas as well as Bahamian quilts, prints, ceramics, jewelry, and crafts. ⊠ *West and W. Hill Sts., across from St. Francis Xavier Cathedral, Nassau* ☎ *242/328–5800* ⊕ *www.nagb.org.bs* ✆ *$10* ☾ *Closed Mon.*

Parliament Square

GOVERNMENT BUILDING | Nassau is the seat of the national government. The Bahamian Parliament comprises two houses—a 16-member Senate (Upper House) and a 39-member House of Assembly (Lower House). If the House is in session, sit in to watch lawmakers debate. Parliament

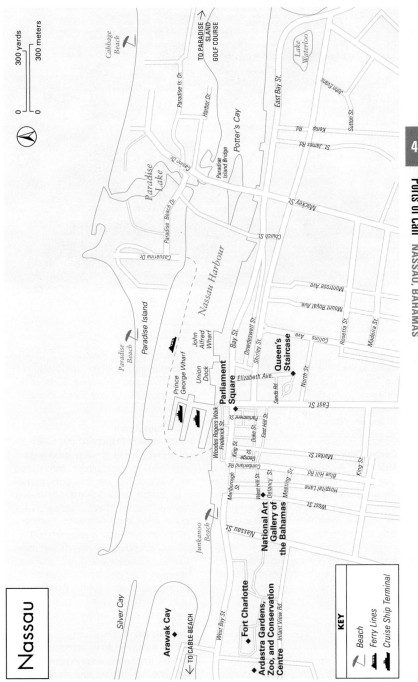

Nassau

300 yards

300 meters

Cabbage Beach

TO PARADISE ISLAND GOLF COURSE

Paradise Is. Dr.

Harbor Dr.

Potter's Cay

Lake Waterloo

East Bay St.

John Evans

Kemp Rd.

Sutton St.

St. James Rd.

Casino Dr.

Paradise Island Bridge

Paradise Lake

Mackey St.

Paradise Beach Dr.

Church St.

Casuarina Dr.

Montrose Ave.

Nassau Harbour

Mount Royal Ave.

Collins Ave.

Rosetta St.

Madeira St.

Paradise Island

Paradise Beach

John Alfred Wharf

Bay St.

Dowdeswell St.

Shirley St.

Queen's Staircase

North St.

Prince George Wharf

Union Dock

Parliament Square

Elizabeth Ave.

Sands Rd.

East St.

Woodes Rogers Walk

Frederick St.

Parliament St.

Duke St.

East Hill St.

King St.

George St.

Market St.

Cumberland Rd.

Blue Hill Rd.

King St.

Silver Cay

Junkanoo Beach

Nassau St.

Marlborough St.

West Hill St.

Delancy St.

National Art Gallery of the Bahamas

Hospital Lane

Meeting St.

West St.

Arawak Cay

TO CABLE BEACH

West Bay St.

Fort Charlotte

Ardastra Gardens, Zoo, and Conservation Centre

Infant View Rd.

KEY

Beach

Ferry Lines

Cruise Ship Terminal

You can see flamingoes at Ardastra Gardens, Zoo, and Conservation Centre.

Square's pink, colonnaded government buildings were constructed in the late 1700s and early 1800s by Loyalists who came to the Bahamas from North Carolina. The square is dominated by a statue of a slim young Queen Victoria that was erected on her birthday, May 24, in 1905. ⊠ *Bay St., Nassau* ☎ *242/322–2041* ⊡ *Free* ☉ *Closed weekends.*

Queen's Staircase

MEMORIAL | A popular early-morning exercise regime for locals, "the 66 Steps" (as Bahamians call them) are thought to have been carved out of a solid limestone cliff by slaves in the 1790s. The staircase was later named to honor Queen Victoria's reign. Pick up some souvenirs at the ad hoc straw market along the narrow road that leads to the site. ⊠ *Top of Elizabeth Ave. hill, south of Shirley St., Nassau* ⊡ *Free.*

🏖 Beaches

The island of New Providence is blessed with stretches of white sand studded with palms and seagrapes. Some of the beaches are small and crescent-shape; others stretch for miles.

★ Cabbage Beach

BEACH—SIGHT | FAMILY | At this beach you'll find 3 miles of white sand lined with shady casuarina trees, sand dunes, and sun worshippers. This is the place to go to rent Jet Skis or get a bird's-eye view of Paradise Island while parasailing. Hair braiders and T-shirt vendors stroll the beach, and hotel guests crowd the areas surrounding the resorts, including Atlantis. For peace and quiet, stroll east. **Amenities:** food and drink; lifeguards; parking (fee); water sports. **Best for:** partiers; solitude; swimming; walking. ⊠ *Paradise Island* ⊡ *Free.*

Junkanoo Beach

BEACH—SIGHT | Right in downtown Nassau, this beach is spring-break central from late February through April. The man-made beach isn't the prettiest on the island, but it's conveniently located if you only have a few quick hours to catch a tan. Music is provided by bands, DJs, and boom boxes; a growing number of bars keep the drinks flowing. **Amenities:** food and drink; parking (no fee); toilets; water sports. **Best for:** partiers; swimming. ⊠ *Immediately west of British Colonial Hilton, Nassau* 🖾 *Free.*

 ## Restaurants

The Green Parrot

$$ | **AMERICAN** | Two locations, at Harbourfront and Hurricane Hole, mean you get incomparable views of Nassau Harbour and a fresh breeze, whichever way the wind is blowing. The large burgers are a favorite at these casual, all-outdoor restaurants and bars. **Known for:** harbor views; simple but tasty American fare; large, lively bars. $ *Average main: $28* ⊠ *E. Bay St. west of bridges to Paradise Island, Nassau* 🕾 *242/322–9248, 242/328–8382* ⊕ *greenparrotbar.com.*

★ Lukka Kairi

$$ | **BAHAMIAN** | Lukka Kairi means "people of the Islands," and at this hot spot you can experience the food, live music, and hospitality Bahamian people are known for. The tapas-style menu lets you sample a variety of traditional Bahamian dishes with a twist. **Known for:** some of the best conch fritters around; live Bahamian music on stage; great harbor views. $ *Average main: $22* ⊠ *Woodes Rodgers Walk, Nassau* 🕾 *242/326–5254* ⊕ *www. lukkakairi.com.*

The Poop Deck

$$ | **BAHAMIAN** | Just east of the bridges from Paradise Island and a quick cab ride from the center of town is this favorite local haunt that is always busy. Start with the conch fritters, then move on to the fish. (it's usually served head-to-tail, so if you're squeamish, ask your waiter to have the head cut off before it comes out on your plate). **Known for:** pick your

own fish; calypso coffee spiked with secret ingredients; marina and harbor views. $ *Average main: $30* ⊠ *E. Bay St. at Nassau Yacht Haven Marina, Nassau* ✛ *East of bridges from Paradise Island* 🕾 *242/393–8175* ⊕ *www.thepoopdeck. com.*

🛍 Shopping

Most of Nassau's shops are on Bay Street between Rawson Square and the British Colonial Hotel, and on the side streets leading off Bay Street. Some stores are popping up on the main shopping thoroughfare's eastern end and just west of the Cable Beach strip. Bargains abound between Bay Street and the waterfront. Upscale stores can also be found in Marina Village and the Crystal Court at Atlantis. You'll find duty-free prices—generally 25%–50% less than U.S. prices—on imported items such as crystal, linens, watches, cameras, jewelry, leather goods, and perfumes.

The Craft Cottage

GIFTS/SOUVENIRS | This small shop situated in a traditional wooden structure is a great place to buy locally made souvenirs and gifts including soaps and oils, hand-painted glassware, jewelry, straw bags, and textiles. The artists and artisans are often on-site. ⊠ *20 Village Rd., Nassau* 🕾 *242/446–7373* ⊕ *www. craftcottagebahamas.com.*

🏃 Activities

FISHING

The waters here are generally smooth and alive with many species of game fish, which is one of the reasons why the Bahamas has more than 20 fishing tournaments open to visitors every year. A favorite spot just west of Nassau is the Tongue of the Ocean, so called because it looks like that part of the body when viewed from the air. The channel stretches for 100 miles. For boat rental, parties of two to six will pay $600 or so for a half-day, $1,600 for a full day.

Charter Boat Association

FISHING | The Charter Boat Association has 15 boats available for fishing charters. Pickup is from Paradise Island Ferry Terminal or Nassau Harbour in front of the Straw Market. ☎ *242/393–3739.*

Chubasco Charters

FISHING | This charter company has four boats for deep-sea and light tackle sportfishing. Half- and full-day charters are available. Pickup is from Paradise Island Ferry Terminal or Nassau Harbour in front of the Straw Market. ☎ *242/324–3474* ⊕ *www.chubascocharters.com.*

GOLF
Ocean Club Golf Course

GOLF | Designed by Tom Weiskopf, the Ocean Club Golf Course is a championship course surrounded by the ocean on three sides, which means that the views are incredible but the winds can get stiff. Call to check on current availability and up-to-date prices. (Those not staying at Atlantis or the One&Only Ocean Club can play at management's discretion— and at a higher rate.) The course is open daily from 6 am to sunset. ⊠ *One&Only Ocean Club, Paradise Island Dr., Paradise Island* ☎ *242/363–6682* ⊕ *www. oceanclub.oneandonlyresorts.com* ⚐ *$225–$295 for 18 holes (discounted after 1 pm); club rentals $70* ⚐ *18 holes, 6805 yards, par 72.*

Nevis (Charlestown)

In 1493, when Columbus spied a cloud-crowned volcanic isle during his second voyage to the New World, he named it Nieves (the Spanish word for "snows") because it reminded him of the peaks of the Pyrenees. Nevis rises from the water in an almost perfect cone, the tip of its 3,232-foot central mountain hidden by clouds. Even less developed than sister island St. Kitts—2 miles (3 km) away

at their closest point—Nevis is known for its long beaches with white and black sand, its lush greenery, mountain hikes, the charming if slightly dilapidated Georgian capital of Charlestown, and its restored sugar plantations that now house quaint inns. Even on a day trip Nevis feels relaxed and quietly upscale. You might run into celebrities at the Four Seasons or lunching at the beach bars on Pinney's, the showcase strand. Yet Nevisians (not to mention the significant expat American and British presence) never put on airs, offering warm hospitality to all visitors. These days, given the popularity of a Broadway musical devoted to a certain founding father (who was born on Nevis), Alexander Hamilton has become the star of the Nevis show as well.

ESSENTIALS
CURRENCY

The Eastern Caribbean dollar (EC$), but U.S. dollars are readily accepted.

TELEPHONE

The country code is 1 869. Digicel, LIME, and Orange are the major mobile phone companies, using GSM (850, 900, 1800 and 1900 bands).

Nevis

The Narrows

Newcastle Airport
Newcastle Beach
Mosquito Bay
Newcastle
Long Haul Bay

Oualie Beach
Jones Bay
Cades Bay

TO ST. KITTS

Brick Kiln

ATLANTIC OCEAN

Cotton Ground

ST. JAMES WINDWARD

Caribbean Sea

Pinney's Beach
ST. THOMAS LOWLAND
Nevis Peak
Jamestown

Huggins Bay

Charlestown see inset map

ST. PAUL CHARLESTOWN

Zion

Museum of Nevis History
Fig Tree
Bath Springs

ST. GEORGE GINGERLAND

White Bay

ST. JOHN FIG TREE
Botanical Gardens of Nevis
Saddle Hill

Red Cliff

Long Pt.

Charlestown
Alexander Hamilton Birthplace
Low St.
Chapel St.
Main St.

KEY
- Beaches
- Dive Sites
- Ferry

Dogwood Pt.
The Devil's Caves

0   3 miles
0   3 km

Saba
St. Eustatius
St. Kitts
Nevis

COMING ASHORE

Cruise ships dock in Charlestown harbor; all but the smallest ships bring passengers in by tender to the central downtown ferry dock. The pier leads smack onto Main Street, with shops and restaurants steps away. Taxi drivers often greet tenders, and there's also a stand a block away. Fares are fairly expensive, but a three-hour driving tour of Nevis costs about $80 for up to four people. Several restored greathouse plantation inns are known for their lunches; your driver can provide information and arrange drop-off and pickup. Before setting off in a taxi, be sure to clarify whether the rate quoted is in Eastern Caribbean or U.S. dollars. Because you must visit the police station to get a local driving permit, renting a car for the day is not practical.

If your ship docks in St. Kitts, Nevis is a 30- to 45-minute ferry ride from Basseterre. You can tour Charlestown, the capital, in a half hour or so, but you'll need three to four hours to explore the entire island. Most cruise ships arrive in port around 8 am, and the ferry schedule (figure $18 round-trip) can be irregular, so many passengers sign up for a cruise-line-run shore excursion. If you travel independently, confirm departure times with the tourist office to be sure you'll make it back to your ship on time.

⊙ Sights

CHARLESTOWN

About 1,200 of Nevis's 10,000 inhabitants live in the capital. If you arrive by ferry, as most people do, you'll walk smack onto Main Street from the pier. It's easy to imagine how tiny Charlestown, founded in 1660, must have looked in its heyday. The weathered buildings still have fanciful galleries, elaborate gingerbread fretwork, wooden shutters, and hanging plants. The stone building with the clock tower (circa 1825, but mostly rebuilt after a devastating 1873 fire) houses the courthouse and second-floor library (a cool respite on sultry days). The little park next to the library is Memorial Square, dedicated to the fallen of World Wars I and II. Down the street from the square, archaeologists have discovered the remains of a Jewish cemetery and synagogue (Nevis reputedly had the Caribbean's second-oldest congregation), but there's little to see.

Alexander Hamilton Birthplace

HISTORIC SITE | The Alexander Hamilton Birthplace, which contains the Hamilton Museum, sits on the waterfront. This bougainvillea-draped Georgian-style house is a reconstruction of what is believed to have been the American patriot's original home, built in 1680 and likely destroyed during a mid-19th-century earthquake. Born here in 1755, Hamilton moved to St. Croix when he was about 12. He moved to the American colonies to continue his education at 17; he became George Washington's Secretary of the Treasury and died in a duel with political rival Aaron Burr in 1804. The Nevis House of Assembly occupies the second floor; the museum (newly installed across the courtyard) contains Hamilton memorabilia, documents pertaining to the island's history, and displays on island geology, politics, architecture, culture, and cuisine. The gift shop is a wonderful source for historic maps, crafts, and books on Nevis. ⊠ *Low St., Charlestown* ☎ *869/469–5786* ⊕ *www. nevisheritage.org* ✉ *$5; combination ticket $7, includes Museum of Nevis History.*

ELSEWHERE ON NEVIS

Bath Springs

HOT SPRINGS | The Caribbean's first hotel, the Bath Hotel, built by businessman John Huggins in 1778, was so popular in the 19th century that visitors, who included Samuel Taylor Coleridge, traveled months by ship to "take the waters" in the property's hot springs. It suffered extensive hurricane and earthquake damage over the years and long languished in disrepair. Local volunteers have cleaned up the spring and built stone pools and steps to enter the waters, though signs still caution that you bathe at your own risk, especially if you have heart problems. The development houses the Nevis Island Administration offices; there's still talk of adding massage huts, changing rooms, a restaurant, and a culture and history center on the original hotel property. ⊠ *Charlestown* ⊕ *Follow Main St. south from Charlestown.*

★ Botanical Gardens of Nevis

GARDEN | In addition to terraced gardens and arbors, this remarkable 7.8-acre site in the glowering shadow of Mt. Nevis has natural lagoons, streams, and waterfalls, superlative bronze mermaids, Buddhas, egrets and herons, and extravagant fountains. You can find a proper rose garden, sections devoted to orchids and bromeliads, cacti, and flowering trees and shrubs—even a bamboo garden. The entrance to the Rain Forest Conservatory, which attempts to include every conceivable Caribbean ecosystem and then some, duplicates an imposing Mayan temple. A splendid re-creation of a plantation-style greathouse contains the appealing Oasis Thai restaurant with sweeping sea views (and wonderfully inventive variations on classic cocktails utilizing local ingredients), and the Galleria Gift Shop selling art, textiles, glass items, and jewelry. ⊠ *Montpelier Estate* ☎ *869/469–3509* ⊕ *www.botanicalgardennevis.com* ✉ *$13.*

Museum of Nevis History

HISTORIC SITE | Purportedly this is the Western Hemisphere's largest collection of Lord Horatio Nelson memorabilia, including letters, documents, paintings,

Mt. Nevis rising behind the Botanical Gardens of Nevis.

and even furniture from his flagship. Nelson was based in Antigua but came on military patrol to Nevis, where he met and eventually married Frances Nisbet, who lived on a 64-acre plantation here. Half the space is devoted to often-provocative displays on island life, from leading families to vernacular architecture to the adaptation of traditional African customs, from cuisine to Carnival. The shop is an excellent source for gifts, from homemade soaps to historical guides. ⊠ *Bath Rd., Charlestown* 🕾 *869/469–0408* ⊕ *www.nevisheritage.org* 🕾 *$5; combination ticket $7, includes Alexander Hamilton Birthplace* ☉ *Closed Sun.*

🌀 Beaches

All beaches on Nevis are free to the public (the plantation inns cordon off "private" areas on Pinney's Beach for guests), but there are no changing facilities, so wear a swimsuit under your clothes.

Oualie Beach

BEACH—SIGHT | South of Mosquito Bay and north of Cades and Jones Bays, this beige-sand beach lined with palms and seagrapes is where the folks at Oualie Beach Hotel can mix you a drink and fix you up with water-sports equipment. There's excellent snorkeling amid calm water and fantastic sunset views with St. Kitts silhouetted in the background. Several beach chairs and hammocks (free with lunch, $3 rental without) line the sand and the grassy "lawn" behind it. Oualie is at the island's northwest tip, approximately 3 miles (5 km) west of the airport. **Amenities:** food and drink; water sports. **Best for:** snorkeling; sunset. ⊠ *Oualie Beach.*

Pinney's Beach

BEACH—SIGHT | The island's showpiece has soft golden sand on the calm Caribbean, lined with a magnificent grove of palm trees. The Four Seasons Resort is here, as are the plantation inns' beach clubs and casual beach bars such as Sunshine's, Chevy's, and the Lime (which morphs into the island's disco on Friday night). Beach chairs are gratis when you purchase a drink or lunch. Regrettably, the waters can be murky and filled with kelp if the weather has been inclement anywhere within a hundred miles, depending on the currents. **Amenities:** food and drink; water sports. **Best for:** swimming; walking. ⊠ *Pinney's Beach.*

🍴 Restaurants

Double Deuce

$$ | **SEAFOOD** | **FAMILY** | Mark Roberts, the former chef at Montpelier, chucked the "five-star lifestyle" and now co-owns this bar, which jams with locals and is jam-packed with everything from license plates and pennants to fishnets and Balinese masks. Behind the cool mauve bar is a gleaming modern kitchen where Mark and Lyndeta, his fun-loving partner, prepare sublime seafood (try the ginger garlic shrimp), organic beef burgers, inventive pastas, lip-smacking ribs, and a few British pub standards. **Known for:** creative cocktails and fine, fairly priced fare; free Wi-Fi and proper espresso; fun events. ⑤ *Average main: US$18* ⊠ *Pinney's Beach* ☎ *869/469–2222* ⊕ *www.doubledeucenevis.com* ➡ *No credit cards* ⊗ *Closed Mon.*

Sunshine's

$$ | **CARIBBEAN** | Everything about this beach shack is larger than life, from the Rasta man Llewellyn "Sunshine" Caines himself to the walls plastered with flags and license plates that reflect a very international clientele, to the picnic tables and palm trees splashed with bright sunrise-to-sunset color. With the restaurant's addition of VIP cabanas, locals say "it gone upscaled," but fishermen still cruise up with their catch, keeping things real and ensuring that the lobster rolls and snapper creole are truly fresh. **Known for:** Killer Bee rum punch ("One and you're stung; two, you're stunned; three, it's a knockout"); boisterous crowd; occasional celebrity sightings.

⑤ *Average main: US$19* ⊠ *Pinney's Beach* ☎ *869/469–5817.*

🛍 Shopping

Nevis is certainly not the place for a shopping spree, but there are some unusual and wonderful surprises, notably the island's pottery, hand-embroidered clothing, and dolls by Jeannie Rigby. Honey is another buzzing biz: Quentin Henderson, the amiable former head of the **Nevis Beekeeping Cooperative,** will even arrange trips by appointment to various hives for demonstrations of beekeeping procedures. Other than a few hotel boutiques and isolated galleries, virtually all shopping is concentrated on or just off Main Street in Charlestown. The lovely old stonework and wood floors of the waterfront Cotton Ginnery Complex make an appropriate setting for stalls of local artisans.

CraftHouse

CRAFTS | This marvelous source for local specialties, from vetiver mats to leather moccasins, also has a smaller branch in the Cotton Ginnery. ⊠ *Pinney's Rd., Charlestown* ☎ *869/469–5505.*

Nevis Handicraft Co-op Society

CRAFTS | This shop across from the tourist office offers works by local artisans (clothing, ceramic ware, woven goods) and locally produced honey, hot sauces, and jellies (try the guava and soursop). ⊠ *Main St., Charlestown* ☎ *869/469–1746* ⊗ *Closed Sun.*

Philatelic Bureau

CRAFTS | St. Kitts and Nevis are famous for their decorative, and sometimes valuable, stamps. Collectors will find real beauties here, including the butterfly, hummingbird, and marine-life series. ⊠ *Cotton Ginnery, opposite the tourist office, Charlestown* ☎ *869/469–0617.*

⚡ Activities

GOLF

⭐ Four Seasons Golf Course

GOLF | The Robert Trent Jones Jr.–designed Four Seasons Golf Course is beautiful and impeccably maintained. The front 9 holes are fairly flat until hole 8, which climbs uphill after your tee shot. Most of the truly stunning views are along the back 9. The signature hole is the 15th, a 660-yard monster that encompasses a deep ravine; other holes include bridges, steep drops, rolling pitches, extremely tight and unforgiving fairways, sugar-mill ruins, and fierce doglegs. Attentive attendants canvass the course in beverage buggies, handing out chilled, peppermint-scented towels and preordered Cubanos to help test the wind. There are kids', twilight, and off-season discounts. ✉ *Four Seasons Resort Nevis, Pinney's Beach* ☎ *869/469–1111* ⊕ *www.fourseasons.com/nevis* 💲 *$230; rental clubs $85* ⛳ *18 holes, 6766 yards, par 72.*

HIKING

The center of the island is Nevis Peak (aka Mt. Nevis), which soars 3,232 feet and is flanked by Hurricane Hill on the north and Saddle Hill on the south. If you plan to scale Nevis Peak, a daylong affair, it's highly recommended that you go with a guide. Your hotel can arrange it (and a picnic lunch) for you. The 9-mile (15-km) **Upper Round Road Trail** was constructed in the late 1600s and cleared and restored by the Nevis Historical and Conservation Society. It connects the Golden Rock Plantation Inn, on the east side of the island, with Nisbet Plantation Beach Club, on the northern tip. The trail encompasses numerous vegetation zones, including pristine rain forest, and impressive plantation ruins. The original cobblestones, walls, and ruins are still evident in many places.

Sunrise Tours

HIKING/WALKING | Run by Lynell and Earla Liburd (and their son Kervin), Sunrise Tours offers a range of hiking trips, but their most popular is Devil's Copper, a rock configuration full of ghostly legends. Local people gave it its name because at one time the water was hot—a volcanic thermal stream. The area features pristine waterfalls and splendid bird-watching. They also do a Nevis village walk, a Hamilton Estate Walk, a Charlestown tour, an Amerindian walk along the wild southeast Atlantic coast, and trips to the rain forest and Nevis Peak. They love highlighting Nevisian heritage, explaining time-honored cooking techniques, the many uses of dried grasses, and medicinal plants. Hikes range from $25 to $40 per person, and you receive a certificate of achievement. ☎ *869/469–2758* ⊕ *www.nevisnaturetours.com.*

Ocho Rios, Jamaica

About 90 minutes east of Montego Bay lies Ocho Rios (often just "Ochi"), a lush destination that's favored by honeymooners for its tropical beauty. Often called the garden center of Jamaica, this community is perfumed by flowering hibiscus, bird of paradise, bougainvillea, and other tropical blooms year-round. Ocho Rios is a popular cruise port, and the destination where you'll find one of the island's most recognizable attractions: Dunn's River Falls, which invites travelers to climb in daisy-chain fashion, hand-in-hand behind a sure-footed guide. This spectacular waterfall is actually a series of falls that cascades from the mountains to the sea. That combination of hills, rivers, and sea also means many activities in the area, from seaside horseback rides to mountain biking and lazy river rafting.

ESSENTIALS

CURRENCY

The Jamaican dollar, but the U.S. dollar is widely accepted.

TELEPHONE

The country code for Jamaica is 1 876. Digicel and Flow are the major mobile phone providers, using GSM (850, 900, 1800, and 1900 bands).

COMING ASHORE

Most cruise ships are able to dock at this port on Jamaica's North Coast, near Dunn's River Falls (a $10 taxi ride from the pier). Also less than 1 mile (2 km) from the Ocho Rios pier are Island Village (within walking distance), Taj Mahal Duty-Free Shopping Center, and the Ocean Village Shopping Center. If you're going anywhere else beyond Island Village, a taxi is recommended; expect to pay $10 for a taxi ride downtown. The pier, which includes a cruise terminal with the basic services and transportation, is also within easy walking distance of Turtle Beach.

Licensed taxis are available at the pier; expect to pay about $35 per hour for a guided taxi tour. Jamaica is one place in the Caribbean where it's usually to your advantage to take an organized shore excursion offered by your ship unless you just want to go to the beach or do a bit of shopping in town. Car rental isn't recommended off the main highways in Jamaica because of high prices, bad roads, and aggressive drivers.

⊙ Sights

★ Dunn's River Falls & Park

BODY OF WATER | A popular natural attraction that is an eye-catching sight: 600 feet of cold, clear mountain water splashing over a series of stone steps to the Caribbean Sea. The best way to enjoy the falls is to climb the slippery steps in a swimsuit (there are changing rooms at the entrance), as you take the hand of the person ahead of you. After the climb, you exit through a crowded market, another reminder that this is one of Jamaica's top tourist attractions. ■TIP➜ Always **climb with a licensed guide at Dunn's River Falls, who can be hired inside the gates,**

Best Bets ⊙

■ **Chukka Caribbean.** Any of the great adventure tours here are sure to please.

■ **Dunn's River Falls.** A visit to the falls is touristy, but it's still exhilarating.

■ **Mystic Mountain.** Live out your *Cool Runnings* fantasies on the bobsled ride.

■ **Dolphin Cove at Treasure Reef.** Swim with a dolphin, stingray, or shark at this popular stop.

■ **Firefly.** The former home of playwright Noël Coward can be seen on a guided tour.

not outside (ask at the ticket window). Freelance guides might be a little cheaper, but the experienced guides can tell you just where to plant each footstep—helping you prevent a fall. ⊠ *Ocho Rios* ✛ *Off Hwy. A1, between St. Ann's Bay and Ocho Rios* ☎ *876/974–4767* ⊕ *www.dunnsriverfallsja.com* ☞ *$25.*

Fern Gully

NATURE PRESERVE | Don't miss this natural canopy of vegetation, which sunlight barely penetrates. (Jamaica has the world's largest number of fern species—more than 570.) The winding road through the gully has been resurfaced, making for a smoother drive, and most tours of the area include a drive through this natural wonder. But to really experience it, stop and take a walk. The 3-mile (5-km) stretch of damp, fern-shaded forest includes many walking paths as well as numerous crafts vendors. ✛ *Hwy. A3, 2 miles (3 km) south of Ocho Rios.*

Firefly Estate

HOUSE | Noël Coward's vacation home is now a national monument managed by Chris Blackwell's Island Outpost

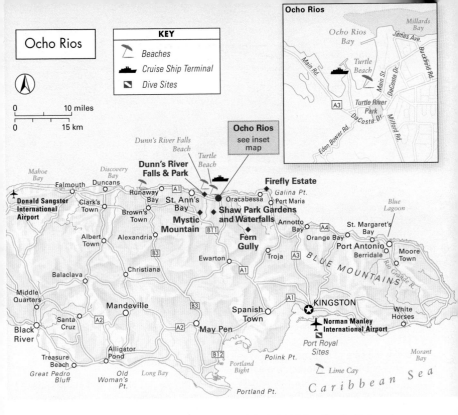

company. Although the setting is Edenic, the house is surprisingly spartan. Coward decamped uphill from his original home at Blue Harbour to escape the jet-setters who came to visit. He wrote *High Spirits, Quadrille,* and other plays here, and his simple grave is next to a small stage where his works are occasionally performed. Recordings of Coward singing about "mad dogs and Englishmen" echo over the lawns. Tours include a walk through the house and grounds. The view from the house's hilltop perch, which was a lookout for Captain Morgan, is one of the best on the North Coast. Firefly is also a perfect place to host weddings, picnics, photo shoots, stage shows, retreats, full-moon parties, and sunset cocktails. Contact Island Outpost (⊕ *www.islandoutpost.com*) for more information. ⊠ *St. Mary* ⊕ *About 20 miles (32 km) east of Ocho Rios*

☎ *876/420–5544* ⊕ *www.firefly-jamaica. com* ✉ *$20.*

★ **Mystic Mountain**

AMUSEMENT PARK/WATER PARK | This attraction covers 100 acres of mountainside rain forest near Dunn's River Falls. Visitors board the Rainforest Sky Explorer, a chairlift that soars through and over the pristine rain forest to the apex of Mystic Mountain. On top, there is a restaurant with spectacular views of Ocho Rios, arts-and-crafts shops, and the attraction's signature tours, the Rainforest Bobsled Jamaica ride and the Rainforest Zipline Canopy ride. Custom-designed bobsleds, inspired by Jamaica's Olympic bobsled team, run downhill on steel rails with speed controlled by the driver, using simple push-pull levers. Couples can run their bobsleds in tandem. The zip-line tours streak through lush rain forest

Climbing the 600-foot-tall Dunn's River Falls is a popular sunny day activity.

under the care of an expert guide who points out items of interest. The entire facility was built using environmentally friendly techniques and materials in order to leave the native rain forest undisturbed. ⊠ *North Coast Hwy., Ocho Rios* ☎ *876/618–1553* ⊕ *www.mysticmountain.com* ⊠ *$38–$120.*

Shaw Park Gardens and Waterfalls
BODY OF WATER | Perched above Ocho Rios and originally used for growing sugarcane and later oranges, this estate became the original site of the exclusive Shaw Park Hotel (today relocated to the beach). The owner's daughter, appropriately named Flora, worked to create the lush gardens, which now fill the 25-acre site with flame flowers, birds of paradise, and orchids. There is also a waterfall on the property that is worth seeing. ⊠ *Shaw Park Rd., Ocho Rios* ☎ *876/429–3424* ⊠ *$10.*

🏖 Beaches

There's a small beach right at the cruise port in Ocho Rios, with sand accessible directly from Margaritaville. Many passengers who don't want to travel are satisfied to stop here for a dip.

★ Dunn's River Falls Beach
BEACH—SIGHT | You'll find a crowd (especially if there's a cruise ship in town) at the small beach at the foot of the falls, one of Jamaica's most-visited landmarks. Although tiny—considering the crowds—the beach has a great view. Look up for a spectacular vista of the cascading water, the roar from which drowns out the sea as you approach. All-day access to the beach is included in the falls' entrance fee. **Amenities:** lifeguards; parking (no fee); toilets. **Best for:** swimming. ⊠ *Ocho Rios* ✛ *Off Hwy. A1, between St. Ann's Bay and Ocho Rios* ☎ *876/974–4767* ⊕ *www.dunnsriverfallsja.com* ⊠ *$20.*

🍴 Restaurants

Island Village has a popular Margaritaville restaurant if you don't want to venture far from the cruise port.

Island Grill

$ | JAMAICAN | With 18 locations across the island, this eat-in or take-out restaurant about a block from the main tourist area serves a Jamaican version of fast food. Jerk chicken, sandwiches, soups, and Jamaican dinner combo meals (called *yabbas,* an African-Jamaican term for bowl) are all on the menu. Many meals are served with festival (sweet, fried dumpling) and are spiced for the local palate. **Known for:** jerk chicken; natural juices made from local vegetables and fruits; yaad-style sandwich (lettuce, tomatoes, grilled chicken, and fried plantains). ⑤ *Average main: $7* ✉ *59 Main St., Ocho Rios* ☎ *876/974–3160* ⊕ *www. islandgrillja.com.*

Ocho Rios Jerk Centre

$ | JAMAICAN | This canopied, open-air eatery is a great place for island fare like fiery jerk meals or seafood such as fish and conch, which are perfectly complemented by frosty Red Stripe beers and signature cocktails. Milder barbecued meats—also sold by weight (a quarter- or half-pound makes a good serving)—turn up on the daily chalkboard menu posted on the wall. **Known for:** jerk pork; specialty cocktails; curry goat served with rice and peas. ⑤ *Average main: $12* ✉ *14 DaCosta Dr., Ocho Rios* ☎ *876/974–2549.*

👜 Shopping

Ocho Rios has several malls that draw day-trippers from the cruise ships. The best are **Soni's Plaza** and the **Taj Mahal,** two malls on the main street with stores selling jewelry, cigars, and clothing. Another popular mall on the main street is **Ocean Village.** On the North Coast Highway slightly east of Ochos Rios are **Pineapple Place** and **Coconut Grove.**

🏃 Activities

GUIDED TOURS

Half- and full-day tours can be arranged with many taxi drivers. Be sure to agree on a price before heading out on the tour.

Chukka Caribbean Zion Bus Tour

TOUR—SPORTS | A country-style bus painted in bright colors travels inland to the village of Nine Mile and the simple house where Bob Marley was born and is now buried. The six-hour tour ($114, including lunch at a jerk stand) is for those ages 16 and older. ✉ *Chukka Cove, Llandovery, Ocho Rios* ☎ *876/619–1441, 876/619–1382, 877/424–8552 in U.S.* ⊕ *chukka. com* 🎟 *$114.*

Jamaica Tours Limited

TOUR—SPORTS | This operator offers several tours with stops that include gardens and Dunn's River Falls. ☎ *876/953–3700* ⊕ *www.jamaicatoursltd.com.*

HORSEBACK RIDING

With its combination of hills and beaches, Ocho Rios is a natural for horseback excursions. Most are guided tours taken at a slow pace and perfect for those with no previous equestrian experience. Many travelers opt to wear long pants for horseback rides, especially those away from the beach.

★ Chukka Caribbean Adventures

HORSEBACK RIDING | The two-hour ride-and-swim tour ($89) travels along Papillon Cove (where the 1973 movie *Papillon* was filmed) as well as to locations used in *Return to Treasure Island* (1985) and *Passion and Paradise* (1988). The trail continues along the coastline to Chukka Beach and a bareback ride in the sea. Chukka has a location west of Montego Bay and handles other activities and tours, too. ✉ *Chukka Cove, Ocho Rios* ☎ *876/619–1441, 876/619–1382, 877/424–8552 in U.S.* ⊕ *chukka.com* 🎟 *$89.*

Hooves Jamaica

HORSEBACK RIDING | This stable offers several guided tours, including a popular 2½-hour beach ride (heritage rides $85, private rides $95, and honeymoon rides $105 per person—including transportation) suitable for adults and children taller than 3 feet. The trip begins with a visit to the Seville Great House estate before making its way to the beach for a ride. Hooves is home to many rescue horses that have been rehabilitated. ⊠ *61 Windsor Rd., St. Ann's Bay* ☎ *876/972–0905* ⊕ *www.hooves-jamaica.com.*

RAFTING

Chukka Caribbean Adventures

WHITE-WATER RAFTING | The big activity outfitter offers the Chukka River Tubing Safari on the White River, an easy trip that doesn't require previous tubing experience. The three-hour tour lets you travel in your very own tube through gentle rapids. ⊠ *Chukka White River Valley, Ocho Rios* ☎ *876/619–1441, 876/619–1382, 877/424–8552 in U.S.* ⊕ *chukka.com* 💬 *$69.*

Princess Cays, Bahamas

Princess Cays is a 40-acre haven on the southern tip of Eleuthera Island in the Bahamas. Not quite an uninhabited island, it nevertheless offers a wide ribbon of beach—long enough for passengers to splash in the surf, relax in a hammock, or limbo to the beat of local music and never feel crowded. In a similar fashion to booking shore excursions, snorkeling equipment, sea boards, floats, kayaks, paddleboats, banana boat rides, aqua chairs, beach clamshells, and bungalows can be reserved on Princess Cruises' website. All other equipment and activities must be booked onboard. Nestled in a picturesque palm grove, private bungalows with air-conditioning and ceiling fans and decks for lounging can be rented for parties of up to six (from $199.95). The Sanctuary at Princess Cays, complete with bungalows for parties of four (two additional guests may be added at an additional charge), is an adults-only haven (from $249.95). A pirate-themed play area for children is supervised. In addition to three tropical bars and the area where a Bahamian barbecue is served, permanent facilities include small shops that sell island crafts and trinkets; but if you head around the back and through the fence, independent vendors sell similar goods at lower prices. **Available Activities:** Aqua Bikes, banana boat rides, deep-sea fishing, hiking, kayaking, organized games, paddleboats, sailing, shopping, snorkeling, surf fishing, windsurfing.

Progreso, Mexico

The waterfront town closest to Mérida, Progreso is not particularly historic—nor is it terribly picturesque. Still, it provokes a certain sentimental fondness for those who know it well. On weekdays during most of the year the beaches are deserted, but when school is out (Easter week and July through August) and on summer weekends, it's bustling with families from Mérida.

Progreso's charm (or lack thereof) seems to hinge on the weather: When the sun is shining, the water looks translucent green and feels bathtub-warm, and the fine sand makes for lovely long walks. When the wind blows during one of Yucatán's winter *nortes,* the water churns with whitecaps and looks gray and unappealing. Whether the weather is good or bad, however, everyone ends up eventually at one of the restaurants lining the main street, Calle 19. Across the street from the oceanfront *malecón,* restaurants serve cold beer, seafood cocktails, and freshly grilled fish. Most cruise passengers head immediately for Mérida or for one of the nearby archaeological sites.

ESSENTIALS
CURRENCY
The Mexican peso, but U.S. dollars are widely accepted in the area.

TELEPHONE
Most pay phones accept prepaid Ladatel cards, sold in 30-, 50-, or 100-peso denominations. To use the card, insert it in the pay phone's slot, dial 001 (for calls to the United States) or 01 (for calls within Mexico), followed by the area code and number. Credit is subtracted from the card as you use it, and the balance is displayed on the small screen on the phone. Most triband mobile phones from the U.S. work in Mexico, though you must pay roaming charges.

COMING ASHORE
The pier in Progreso is an astounding 5 miles long—it's billed as the world's longest—and cruise ships dock at its end, so passengers are shuttled to the foot of the pier. Visitors' first stop is the Progreso Cruise Terminal, which houses small restaurants and shops selling locally produced crafts. These are some of the best shops in sleepy Progreso (a much wider selection is available in nearby Mérida). The beach lies just east of the pier and can easily be reached on foot. If you want to a peaceful afternoon in the sun, grabbing a drink at one of the small palapa restaurants that line the beach is a good option.

If you are looking to explore, there are plenty of taxis around the pier. A trip around town should not cost more than $5, but ask the taxi driver to quote you a price. If you want to see more of Progreso, a cab can also take you to the local sightseeing tour bus. These bright-blue, open-air double-decker buses depart every 10 minutes or so from the Casa de Cultura and costs only $2. A taxi ride from Progreso to Mérida runs about $30, and most drivers charge around $15 per hour to show you around. If you plan on renting the cab for a good part of the day, talk about the number of hours and the

Best Bets

- **Chichén Itzá.** The famous Maya city is an easy day trip from Progreso and is home to the enormous and oft-photographed pyramid El Castillo.

- **Mérida.** This delightful, though busy, colonial town is full of life as people take to the streets for music, dance, food, and culture.

- **Uxmal.** One of the most beautiful Maya cities is reachable on a day trip from Progreso. If you've seen Chichén Itzá already, go here.

cost with the driver before you take off. It's difficult to rent a car, so most people just band together in a taxi.

Sights

MÉRIDA
Just south of Progreso (about 20 or 30 minutes by taxi), Mérida, the cultural and intellectual hub of the Yucatán, offers a great deal to explore. Mérida is rich in art, history, and tradition. Most streets are numbered, not named, and most run one-way. North–south streets have even numbers, which descend from west to east; east–west streets have odd numbers, which ascend from north to south. One of the best ways to see the city is to hire a calesa, a horse-drawn carriage. They congregate on the main square or at the Palacio Cantón, near the anthropology museum. Drivers charge about $25 for an hour-long circuit around downtown and up Paseo de Montejo, pointing out notable buildings and providing a little historic background along the way. An extended tour costs $35 to $50.

Casa de Montejo
BUILDING | Three Franciscos de Montejo—father, son, and nephew—conquered the peninsula and founded Mérida in

4

Ports of Call PROGRESO, MEXICO

January of 1542, and they completed construction of this stately home on the south side of the central plaza in 1549. It's the city's oldest and finest example of colonial plateresque architecture, a Spanish architectural style popular in the 16th century and typified by the kind of elaborate ornamentation you'll see here. A bas-relief on the doorway—the facade is all that remains of the original house—depicts Francisco de Montejo the younger, his wife, and daughter, as well as Spanish soldiers standing on the heads of the vanquished Maya. The building now houses a branch of the Banamex bank and the Museo del Sitio, with interesting exhibits of Meridano life in the 19th century. ⊠ Calle 63, No. 506, Centro ☎ 999/923–0633 ⊕ www.casasdecultura-banamex.com ⊠ Free ⊙ Closed Mon.

★ **Catedral de Mérida**

RELIGIOUS SITE | Begun in 1561, Mérida's archdiocesan seat is the oldest cathedral on the North American mainland (an older one can be found in the Dominican Republic). It took several hundred Maya laborers, working with stones from the pyramids of the ravaged Maya city, 37 years to complete it. Designed in the somber Renaissance style by an architect who had worked on El Escorial in Madrid, its facade is stark and unadorned, with gunnery slits instead of windows and faintly Moorish spires. Inside, the black Cristo de las Ampollas (Christ of the Blisters) occupies a side chapel to the left of the main altar. At 23 feet tall, it's the tallest Christ figure inside a Mexican church. The statue is a replica of the original, which was destroyed during the revolution in 1910 (also when the gold that typically decorated Mexican cathedrals was carried off). According to one of many legends, the Christ figure burned all night and appeared the next morning unscathed—except for its namesake blisters. You can hear the pipe organ play at the 11 am Sunday Mass. ⊠ Calles 60 and 61, Centro ☎ 999/924–7777 ⊕ www.arquidiocesisdeyucatan.com.mx ⊠ Free.

Paseo de Montejo

NEIGHBORHOOD | North of downtown, this 10-block-long street was *the* place to reside in the late 19th century, when wealthy plantation owners sought to outdo each other with the opulence of their elegant mansions. They typically opted for the decorative styles popular in New Orleans, Cuba, and Paris (imported Carrara marble, European antiques) rather than any style from Mexico. The broad boulevard, lined with tamarind and laurel trees, has lost much of its former panache—many mansions are now used as office buildings, while others have been or are being restored as part of a privately funded citywide beautification program—but the street is still a lovely place to explore on foot or in a horse-drawn carriage. ⊠ Mérida.

Plaza Grande

PLAZA | Mérida's main square is a Wi-Fi hot spot, but don't be so glued to your smartphone that you fail to take in the parade of activity in one of Mexico's loveliest town centers. Locals refer to it as the Plaza Grande or Plaza de la Independencia, and you'll also hear it called "the *zócalo* " (primarily by foreigners). Whichever name you prefer, it's a good place to start a city tour, watch dance performances, listen to music, or chill in the shade of a laurel tree. You'll find a few vendors here, but they're all low-key. Plaza Grande was laid out in 1542 on the ruins of T'Hó, the Maya city demolished to make way for Mérida, and it's still the focal point around which the most important public buildings cluster. *Confidenciales* (S-shape benches) invite intimate tête-à-têtes, and lampposts keep the park beautifully illuminated at night. ⊠ Bordered by Calles 60, 62, 61, and 63, Centro.

Teatro Peón Contreras

ARTS VENUE | This 1908 Italianate theater was built along the same lines as grand turn-of-the-20th-century European theaters and opera houses. Its

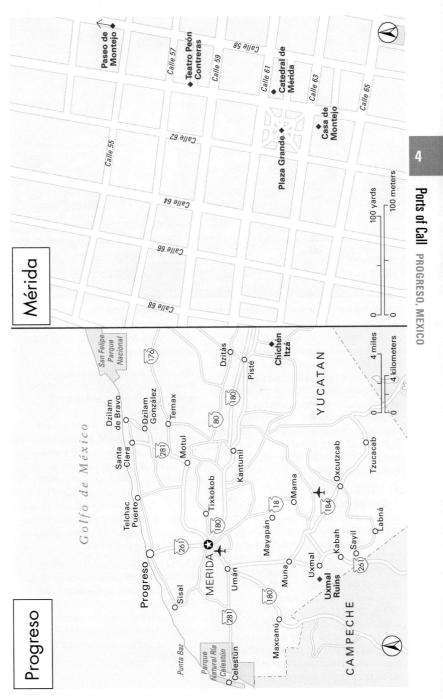

Mérida

Progreso

Paseo de Montejo

Teatro Peón Contreras

Calle 57

Calle 58

Calle 59

Calle 61

Catedral de Mérida

Calle 63

Calle 55

Calle 62

Plaza Grande

Casa de Montejo

Calle 65

Calle 64

Calle 66

Calle 68

100 yards

100 meters

San Felipe Parque Nacional

Dzitás

Pisté

Chichén Itzá

176

180

Temax

80

YUCATAN

4 miles

4 kilometers

Dzilam de Bravo

Dzilam González

Motul

Kantunil

Santa Clara

281

Tixkokob

Oxcutzcab

Tzucacab

Golfo de México

Telchac Puerto

180

18

Mama

184

Labná

Progreso

261

MERIDA

Mayapán

Kabah

Sayil

Sisal

Umán

Muna

Uxmal

261

180

Uxmal Ruins

Punta Baz

281

Maxcanú

CAMPECHE

Parque Natural Ría Celestún

Celestún

Chichén Itzá is one of the best-preserved Maya sites in all of Mexico and Central America.

marble staircase, dome, and frescoes were restored in the early 1980s, and today, in addition to being a performing arts venue, it houses a branch of the tourist information office for the state of Yucatán. The theater's most popular attraction, however, is the café-bar spilling out into the street facing Parque de la Madre. ⊠ *Calle 60 between Calles 57 and 59, Centro* ☎ *999/924–3954* ⊕ *www. culturayucatan.com.*

BEYOND MÉRIDA
★ Chichén Itzá

ARCHAEOLOGICAL SITE | One of the most dramatically beautiful ancient Maya cities, Chichén Itzá (pronounced *chee-CHEN eet-ZAH*) draws over 1 million visitors annually. Since the remains of this once-thriving kingdom were rediscovered by Europeans in the mid-1800s, many of the travelers making the pilgrimage here have been archaeologists and scholars, who study the structures and glyphs and try to piece together the mysteries surrounding them. While the artifacts here give fascinating insight into Maya civilization, they also raise many unanswered questions.

The name of this ancient city, which means "the mouth of the well of the Itzá," is a mystery in and of itself. Although it likely refers to the valuable water sources at the site (there are several cenotes here), experts have little information about who might have actually founded the city; some structures, likely built in the 5th century, predate the arrival of the Itzá, who occupied the city starting around the late 8th and early 9th centuries. Why the Itzá abandoned the city in the early 1200s is also unknown, as is its subsequent role.

Most of the visitors who converge on Chichén Itzá come to marvel at its beauty. Even among laypeople, this ancient metropolis, which encompasses 6 square km (2¼ square miles), is known around the world as one of the most stunning and well-preserved Maya sites in existence.

You've likely seen photos of the immense pyramid **El Castillo,** but they can't capture the moment you first gaze in person upon the structure rising imposingly yet gracefully from the surrounding plain. El Castillo (the Castle) dominates the site both in size and in the symmetry of its perfect proportions. Open-jawed serpent statues adorn the corners of each of the pyramid's four stairways, honoring the legendary priest-king Kukulcán (also known as Quetzalcóatl), an incarnation of the feathered serpent god. More serpents appear at the top of the building as sculpted columns. At the spring and fall equinoxes, the afternoon light strikes the trapezoidal structure so that the shadow of the snake god appears to undulate down the side of the pyramid to bless the fertile earth.

The question on everybody's lips is: "May I climb the pyramid?" The answer is a resounding "No." Disappointing though that response may be, wear and tear on the staircases and numerous injuries to visitors have necessitated an end to the climbing.

On the **Anexo del Templo de los Jaguares** (Annex to the Temple of the Jaguars), just west of El Castillo, bas-relief carvings represent more important deities. On the bottom of the columns is the rain god Tlaloc. It's no surprise that his tears represent rain—but why is the Toltec god Tlaloc honored here, instead of the Maya rain god, Chaac?

Just west of the jaguar annex, another puzzle presents itself: the auditory marvel of Chichén Itzá's main ball court. At 490 feet, this **Juego de Pelota** is the largest in Mesoamerica. Yet if you stand at one end of the playing field and whisper something to a friend at the other end, incredibly, you'll be heard. The game played on this ball court was apparently something like soccer (no hands were used), but it likely had some sort of ritualistic significance.

On the other side of El Castillo, just before a small temple dedicated to the planet Venus, a ruined *sacbé,* or raised white road, leads to the **Cenote Sagrado** (Holy Well, or Sinkhole), also probably used for ritualistic purposes.

Older Maya structures at Chichén Itzá lie south and west of Cenote Xtaloc. Archaeologists have been restoring several buildings in this area, including the **Templo del Osario** (Ossuary Temple), which, as its name implies, concealed several tombs with skeletons and offerings. Behind the smaller **Casa Roja** (Red House) and **Casa del Venado** (House of the Deer) are the site's oldest structures, including **El Caracol** (the Snail), one of the few round buildings built by the Maya, with a spiral staircase within. Clearly built as a celestial observatory, it has eight tiny windows precisely aligned with the points of the compass rose. ✉ *Chichén-Itzá ⊹ Off Carretera 180, 2 km (1½ miles) east of Pisté ☎ 985/851–0137 ⊕ www.inah.gob.mx; www.noches-dekukulkan.com for sound and light show ☞ MX$475, sound and light show MX$510.*

★ Uxmal

ARCHAEOLOGICAL SITE | At 125 feet high, the **Pirámide del Adivino** is the tallest and most prominent structure at the site. Unlike most other Maya pyramids, which are stepped and angular, the "Pyramid of the Magician" has a softer, more refined round-corner design. The pyramid has a stairway on its western side that leads through a giant open-mouth mask to two temples at the summit. During restoration work in 2002 the grave of a high-ranking Maya official, a ceramic mask, and a jade necklace were discovered within the pyramid. Ongoing excavations continue to reveal exciting new finds, still under study. Climbing is prohibited.

West of the pyramid lies the **Cuadrángulo de las Monjas,** often considered to be the finest part of Uxmal. It reminded the conquistadores of typical convent buildings in Spain (*monjas* are nuns). You may enter the four buildings, each comprising a series of low, gracefully repetitive chambers that look onto a central patio.

Covering 5 acres and rising over an immense acropolis, the **Palacio del Gobernador** lies at the heart of what may have been the city's administrative center. It faces east while the rest of Uxmal faces west, and archaeologists suggest this allowed the structure to serve as an observatory for the planet Venus. ⚠ **In the summer months, tarantulas are a common sight on the grounds at Uxmal.** ✉ *Uxmal* ✛ *Carretera 261, 78 km (48 miles) south of Mérida* ☎ *997/976–2064* ⊕ *www.inah. gob.mx* ✏ *MX$413, sound and light show MX$100.*

🏖 Beaches

Progreso Beach
BEACHES | If you want a pristine Caribbean-style strand, you'd better look elsewhere. The primary draw of Progreso's main beach is the distinctive little beach town and its proximity to Mérida, which often leaves the sand packed with tourists and locals alike during summer weekends and holidays. Water shoes are recommended since sharp, slippery rocks lurk below the surface, making this a poor spot for diving or snorkeling. The beach is void of shade, so your best bet is to find refuge in one of the eateries lining the long *malecón* (boardwalk) that runs along the shore. Several restaurant owners rent beach chairs by the hour, but beware: Progreso's peddlers are relentless and leave only once they receive a small tip. Despite its drawbacks, the water here offers a refreshing escape from the bustling city. **Amenities:** food and drink; toilets (restaurant patrons only). **Best for:** partiers; walking. ✉ *Av. Malecón at Calle 28, Progreso.*

🍴 Restaurants

Eladio's
$ | **MEXICAN** | An outpost of lively Eladio's in Mérida, this bar and restaurant is extremely popular with cruise-ship passengers who disembark in Progreso. You can sample typical Yucatecan dishes like *longaniza asada* (baked sausage) and *pollo pibil* (citrus-pickled chicken) while seated beneath a tall palapa on the beach. **Known for:** yummy free appetizers; ocean breezes; fresh seafood. ⑤ *Average main: 175 MP* ✉ *Av. Malecón at Calle 80, Centro* ☎ *969/935–5670* ⊕ *www.eladios. com.mx.*

Flamingo's
$$ | **SEAFOOD** | Facing Progreso's long cement promenade, this restaurant is a cut above its neighbors. Service is professional and attentive; soon after arriving, you'll get at least one free appetizer—maybe black beans with corn tortillas or a plate of shredded shark meat stewed with tomatoes. **Known for:** fried fish fillets; good breakfast spot; great water views. ⑤ *Average main: 200 MP* ✉ *Calle 19, No. 144D, at Calle 72, Progreso* ☎ *969/935–2122.*

🛍 Shopping

In Progreso between Calle 80 and Calle 81, there is also a small downtown area that is a better place to walk than to shop. There you will find banks, supermarkets, and shops with everyday goods for locals as well as several restaurants that serve simple Mexican fare like tortas and tacos.

Mérida offers more places to shop, including colorful Mexican markets selling local goods.

Mercado Lucas de Gálvez
OUTDOOR/FLEA/GREEN MARKETS | Sellers of chiles, herbs, seafood, and fruit fill this pungent and labyrinthine municipal market. In the early morning the first floor is jammed with housewives and

restaurateurs shopping for the freshest fish and produce. The stairs at Calles 56 and 57 lead to the second-floor Bazar de Artesanías Municipales, where you'll find local pottery, embroidered clothes, guayabera shirts, hammocks, straw bags, sturdy leather huaraches, and piñatas in every imaginable shape and color. Note that most prices are inflated, and vendors expect you'll bargain—one way to begin is to politely request a discount. ⚠ **Be wary of pickpockets within the market.** ✉ *Calles 56 and 67, Centro.*

Puerto Limón, Costa Rica

Christopher Columbus became Costa Rica's first tourist when he landed on this stretch of coast in 1502 during his fourth and final voyage to the New World. Expecting to find vast mineral wealth, he named the region "Costa Rica" (rich coast). Imagine the Spaniards' surprise eventually to find there was none. Save for a brief skirmish some six decades ago, the country did prove itself rich in a long tradition of peace and democracy. No other country in Latin America can make that claim. Costa Rica is also abundantly rich in natural beauty, managing to pack beaches, volcanoes, rain forests, and diverse animal life into an area the size of Vermont and New Hampshire combined. It has successfully parlayed those qualities into its role as one the world's great ecotourism destinations. One day is a short visit but time enough for a quick sample.

ESSENTIALS

CURRENCY
The colón, but U.S. dollars are widely accepted.

TELEPHONE
Telephone numbers have eight digits. Merely dial the number. There are no area codes. You'll find ample phones for use in the cruise terminal. Public phones accept locally purchased calling cards.

Best Bets ◉

■ **Veragua Rainforest Eco-Adventure.** Think of it as a nature-themed amusement park.

■ **Sloth Sanctuary.** The good folks here have devoted their lives to the rescue of sloths.

■ **Jaguar Rescue Center.** The center works toward integrating abandoned animals back into the wild.

■ **Rainforest Adventures.** You'll float through the rain forest canopy with the greatest of ease.

■ **Tortuguero Canals.** Play Indiana Jones for the day.

COMING ASHORE
Ships dock at Limón's spacious, spiffy Terminal de Cruceros (cruise terminal), one block south of the city's downtown. You'll find telephones, Internet computers, a craft market, tourist information, and tour operators' desks inside the terminal, as well as a small army of manicurists who do a brisk business. Step outside and walk straight ahead one block to reach Limón's downtown.

A fleet of red taxis waits on the street in front of the terminal. Drivers are happy to help you put together a do-it-yourself tour. Most charge $100 to $150 per carload for a day of touring. There is no place to rent a car at the terminal, but you're better off leaving the driving to someone else anyway. Cruise lines offer dozens of shore excursions in Costa Rica, and if you want to go any farther afield than Limón or the coast south, we suggest you take an organized tour. The country looks disarmingly small on a map—it is—but hills give rise to mountains the farther inland you go, and road conditions range from "okay" to "abysmal." Distances are short

BARRA DEL COLORADO
NATIONAL WILDLIFE
REFUGE

Tortuguero

La Pavona

TORTUGUERO
NATIONAL PARK

Tortuguero
Canals

BRAULIO
CARRILLO
NATIONAL
PARK
Santa
Clara

Cariari

Parismina

**Rainforest
Adventures** ◆

Costa
Flores

Guácimo

San Rafael

Cordillera Central

Sacramento

◆ Zorqui

32

Matina

Stratford

Heredia

Pacayas

Bristol

Liverpool

Isla
Uvita

Caribbean

SAN JOSÉ

Cartago

Juan
Viñas

Tres Equis

**Veragua
Rainforest
Eco-Adventure**

Sea

Paraíso

Turrialba

36

TAPANTÍ
NATIONAL WILDLIFE
REFUGE

**Sloth Sanctuary
of Costa Rica** ◆

Penshurt

Playa Blanca

San
Marcos

Cahuita

Playa Cocles

Playa
Grande

Santa
Maria

CA
2

HITOY
CERERE
BIOLOGICAL
RESERVE

**Jaguar Rescue
Center** ◆

Bribri

Manzanillo

Gandoca

Sixaola

Daytonia

Guabito

PANAMÁ

0   20 miles

0   20 kilometers

KEY

🚢 Cruise Ship Terminal

Limón

Caribbean
Sea

Calle 4   Calle 2

Avenida 3

Avenida 2

**Parque
Vargas**

Limón
see inset
map

as the toucan flies, but travel times are longer than you'd expect.

Sights

If you arrive in Limón on a cruise ship, a day in the Caribbean is yours for the taking. The Tortuguero canals, the beaches at Puerto Viejo de Talamanca, the rescue center at the Sloth Sanctuary of Costa Rica near Cahuita, or the Veragua Rainforest Eco-Adventure park, just a few miles away, are four popular excursions. A few hardy souls venture as far away as the Rainforest Adventures complex north of Braulio Carrillo National Park, or even San José. (That last one makes for a *very* tiring day.) A legion of taxi drivers waits at the terminal exit if you have not organized a shore excursion through your cruise line.

LIMÓN
Parque Vargas

CITY PARK | The aquamarine wooden port building faces the cruise terminal, and just to the east lies the city's palm-lined seaside park, Parque Vargas. From the promenade facing the ocean you can see the raised dead coral left stranded by the 1991 earthquake. Ten or so Hoffman's two-toed sloths live in the trees of Parque Vargas; ask a passerby to point them out, as spotting them requires a trained eye. ✉ *Limón*.

TORTUGUERO

The stretch of beach between the Colorado and Matina rivers was first mentioned as a nesting ground for sea turtles in a 1592 Dutch chronicle. Nearly a century earlier, Christopher Columbus compared traversing the north Caribbean coast and its swimming turtles to navigating through rocks. Because the area is so isolated—there's no road here to this day—the turtles nested undisturbed for centuries. By the mid-1900s, however, the harvesting of eggs and poaching of turtles had reached such a level that these creatures faced extinction. In 1963 an executive decree regulated the hunting of turtles and the gathering of eggs, and in 1970 the government established Tortuguero National Park; modern Tortuguero bases its economy on tourism.

In 1970 a system of canals running parallel to the shoreline was constructed to provide safer access to the region than the dangerous journey up the seacoast. You can continue up the canals (natural and man-made) that begin in Moín, near Limón, and run all the way to Tortuguero. Or you can embark at various points north of Guápiles and Siquirres, as do public transportation and most package tours.

ELSEWHERE IN THE REGION

★ **Jaguar Rescue Center** (Centro de Rescate Jaguar)

NATURE PRESERVE | FAMILY | Many regard a visit to the Jaguar Rescue Center as the highlight of their trip to Puerto Viejo de Talamanca. The name is a bit misleading. The original rescued animal here was an orphaned, injured jaguar cub that ultimately did not survive. His memory lives on in the facility's name, even if there are no other jaguars on-site. Primarily howler monkeys, sloths, and lots of snakes make up the charges of the capable staff here. The goal, of course, is to return the animals to the wild, but those that are too frail are assured a permanent home here. Your admission fee for the 90-minute tour (English or Spanish) helps fund the rescue work. (Tours in French, German, or Dutch can be arranged with advance notice.) A two-hour tour, morning or evening, at Punta Uva lets you participate in the release of rehabilitated animals. ⊠ 3 km (2 miles) southeast of Puerto Viejo, between Playa Cocles and Playa Chiquita, Puerto Viejo de Talamanca ☎ 2750–0710 ⊕ www.jaguarrescue.foundation ⊠ From $20 ⊙ Closed Sun.

★ **Rainforest Adventures**

NATURE PRESERVE | Just beyond the northeastern boundary of Braulio Carrillo National Park, about 15 km (9 miles) before the Caribbean-slope town of Guápiles, a 1,200-acre reserve houses a privately owned and operated engineering marvel: a series of gondolas strung together in a modified ski-lift pulley system. Each of the 21 gondolas holds five people plus a bilingual biologist-guide equipped with a walkie-talkie to request brief stops for snapping pictures. The ride covers 2½ km (1½ miles) in 80 minutes. The price includes a biologist-guided walk through the area for ground-level orientation before or after the tram ride. Several add-ons are possible, too, with frog and butterfly exhibits, a medicinal-plant garden, and a zip-line canopy tour on-site, as well as a half-day birding tour. There is also on-site lodging. You can arrange a personal pickup in San José for a fee, or there are public buses (on the Guápiles line) every half hour from the Gran Terminal del Caribe in San José. Drivers know the tram as the teleférico. Many San José tour operators offer a day tour that combines the tram with another half-day option; combos with the Britt Coffee Tour, near Heredia, are especially popular. These folks operate a similar facility near the Central Pacific town of Jacó as well as in Panama and the Caribbean islands of Jamaica, Saint Lucia, and St. Maarten. ⊠ Hwy. 32, 10 km (6 miles) northeast of Braulio Carrillo National Park, Braulio Carrillo National Park ☎ 2257–5961 ⊕ www.rainforestadventure.com ⊠ Tram $65, multiactivity packages $99.

★ **Sloth Sanctuary of Costa Rica**

NATURE PRESERVE | FAMILY | This full-fledged nature center a few miles northwest of Cahuita is well worth a stop. Many of the sloths that live on the premises are here because of illness or injury and are not

You can see sloths both in the wild and in the Sloth Sanctuary of Costa Rica.

on display to the public, but Buttercup, the very first of their charges, holds court in the nature-focused gift shop. She has been joined by Leno, a Bradypus male—that's one of the two sloth species found in Costa Rica—who can be found in the aquarium. A visit is a good way to learn about these little-known animals. (Numerous requests from visitors to hold or pet the sloths have to be turned down.) Your admission includes a two-hour tour (no reservations are needed) and contributes to further care and research by the good-hearted folks who operate the facility. Reservations are required for a special insider's tour that takes you behind the scenes into the sloth clinic and nursery. ⊠ *Cahuita* ✛ *9 km (5 miles) northwest of Cahuita; follow signs on Río Estrella delta* ☎ *2750–0775* ⊕ *www.slothsanctuary.com* ✉ *From $30* ⊙ *Closed Mon.*

★ Veragua Rainforest Eco-Adventure

NATURE PRESERVE | FAMILY | Limón's hottest attraction is a 4,000-acre nature theme park, about 30 minutes west of the city.

It's popular with cruise-ship passengers in port for the day and is well worth a stop if you're in the area. Veragua's great strength is its small army of enthusiastic, super-informed guides who take you through a network of nature trails and exhibits of hummingbirds, snakes, frogs, butterflies, and other insects. A gondola ride overlooks the complex and transports you through the rain-forest canopy. A branch of the Original Canopy Tour, with nine platforms rising 150 feet above the forest floor, is here. The zip-line tour is not included in the basic admission to the park. ⊠ *Veragua de Liverpool, 15 km (9 miles) west of Limón, Limón* ☎ *4000–0949* ⊕ *www.veraguarainforest. com* ✉ *From $69* ⊙ *Closed Mon. unless a cruise ship is in port in Limón.*

🏖 Beaches

The dark-sand beaches on this sector of the coast are pleasant enough, but won't dazzle you if you've made previous stops at Caribbean islands with their white-sand strands. Nicer beaches than

Limón's Playa Bonita lie farther south along the coast and can be reached by taxi or organized shore excursion. Strong undertows make for ideal surfing conditions on these shores, but risky swimming. Exercise caution.

Playa Blanca (*White Beach*)

BEACH—SIGHT | Costa Rica's Caribbean coast has no true white-sand beaches, but Cahuita's in-town beach is as close as it gets (*blanca* means "white" in Spanish). Right at the town entrance to the national park, you're a few steps from local eateries. The park's jungle comes right up to the beach's edge, creating one of those postcard-perfect views. The undertow can be strong here; swimmers are more likely to venture out near the center of the beach. Use caution in any case. **Amenities:** food and drink. **Best for:** sunrise; walking. ⊠ *Town center, Cahuita.*

Playa Cocles

BEACH—SIGHT | The sand gets a bit lighter and the crowd slightly more upscale—it is still Puerto Viejo, though—a couple of kilometers outside of town. Fewer vendors will pester you here than in the town itself, and it'll be mostly you and other travelers. (If there's nobody around, don't linger. There's always safety in numbers.) As with all Puerto Viejo area beaches, the undertow can be strong on Cocles. Never venture out too far. **Amenities:** food and drink. **Best for:** partiers; sunrise; surfing, walking. ⊠ *Puerto Viejo de Talamanca* ✢ *2 km (1 mile) southeast of Puerto Viejo de Talamanca.*

Playa Grande

BEACH—SIGHT | Beyond the Atlántida Lodge, Playa Negra's black sand lightens to a dark brown. Whether this constitutes a separate beach or not is open for debate, but the lodgings out here distinguish their stretch of sand as "Playa Grande." You're much farther from town here; the beach feels even more isolated. Do be careful. As with all beaches on this coast, the undertow makes swimming

risky. **Amenities:** none. **Best for:** sunrise; walking. ⊠ *Cahuita.*

🍴 Restaurants

If you are looking for a bite to eat while off the ship, your best bet is one of the simple "sodas," small restaurants serving local food. There are several in the vicinity of the Mercado Municipal, but Limón isn't a particularly pleasant place to stroll around, so if you aren't on a more far-flung tour you may be happier returning to your ship for lunch. Most tours will include lunch.

🛍 Shopping

The cruise-ship terminal contains an orderly maze of souvenir stands. Vendors are friendly; there's no pressure to buy. Many shops populate the restored port building across the street as well.

Puerto Plata, Dominican Republic

Although it has been sleeping for decades, this was a dynamic city in its heyday. You can get a feeling for this past in the magnificent Victorian gazebo in the central **Parque Independencia.** Painted a crisp white, the park looks postcard pretty, with gleaming statuary. On the Malecón, which had had a multimillion-dollar refurbishment, the **Fortaleza de San Felipe** protected the city from many a pirate attack and was later used as a political prison. Nearby, a new amphitheater is in the planning stages. The nearby **lighthouse** has been restored. Much is happening in Puerto Plata and its original hotel zone, Playa Dorada. The Amber Cove Cruise Center, which opened in 2016, was part of this revitalization effort.

ESSENTIALS

CURRENCY

The Dominican peso, but you can almost always use U.S. dollars.

TELEPHONE

Country codes are 1 809, 1 829, and 1 849 (depending on the type of phone you are calling). Claro, Orange, Tricom, and Viva are the major mobile providers, using GSM (850, 900, 1800 and 1900 bands).

COMING ASHORE

At the Port of Puerto Plata, Carnival's 30-acre Amber Cove Cruise Center enjoyed its inaugural season in 2016, hosting the first cruise ships to dock here since the 1980s. It's located west of the heart of Puerto Plata, about midway between Playa Grande and Cofresí. You'll find restaurants, bars, retail shops, and an elaborate pool complex with waterslides. Several ships stop here each week, but there's never more than one ship here in any given day. A host of shore excursions are offered along the north coast, but if you aren't feeling energetic, you can rent a cabana for the day right at the port (from $295), which has its own zip line (extra charge). The port also offers water-sports rentals and umbrellas (and Wi-Fi).

◉ Sights

Casa Museo General Gregorio Luperón

HOUSE | A long time in the making, this modest wood-frame house is where Puerto Plata's famous son, General Gregorio Luperón, spent his last years. Known for his courage and patriotic love of his homeland, he led the Dominican revolution against Spain, ending the island's foreign occupation in 1865. The museum's mission is to expose the life and ideals of this national hero to visitors both foreign and domestic. It has been accomplished with quality cultural displays depicting the various stages of Luperón's life, enhanced with signposting

Best Bets ◉

■ **Hanging in Port.** If you aren't feeling energetic, Amber Cove has a nice pool with cabanas and food service.

■ **Ocean World.** The nearby aquatic park has myriad activities and opportunities to see wildlife.

■ **Hit the Beach.** Nearby Playa Grande is one of the Caribbean's best beaches.

■ **Adventure Tours.** Well-regarded operator Iguana Mama will pick you up at the port for some active fun.

in both Spanish and English. The home is a slice of 19th-century life and an emblem of the city's rich history. ⊠ *Calle 12 de Julio 54, Puerto Plata* ☎ *809/261–8661, 809/261–9028* ✉ *$5.*

Museo de Ámbar Dominicano

HISTORIC SITE | In an opulent, galleried mansion, restored to its former Victorian glamour, the museum displays and sells the Dominican Republic's national stone: semiprecious, translucent amber. Amber is essentially prehistoric hardened tree sap, and Dominican amber is considered the best in the world. Many pieces are fascinating for what they have trapped inside, and the small second-floor museum contains a piece with a lizard reported to be 50 million years old, give or take a few millennia. The museum's English text is informative. Shops on the museum's first floor sell authentic, albeit rather expensive, amber, souvenirs, and ceramics. ⊠ *Calle Duarte 61, Puerto Plata* ☎ *809/586–2848 museum, 809/320–2215 gift shop* ⊕ *www.ambermuseum.com* ✉ *RD$50.*

Ocean World Adventure Park

AMUSEMENT PARK/WATER PARK | FAMILY | This multimillion-dollar aquatic park in Cofresí has marine and wildlife

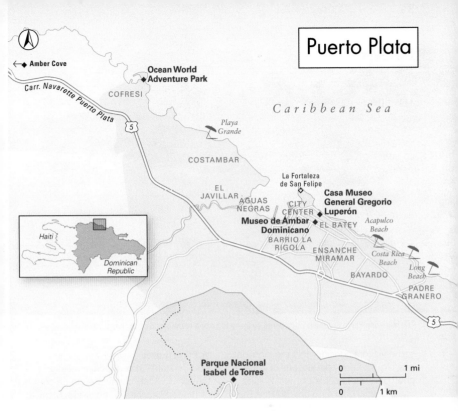

Amber Cove

Carr. Navarette Puerto Plata

COFRESI

Ocean World Adventure Park

Caribbean Sea

5

Playa Grande

COSTAMBAR

La Fortaleza de San Felipe

EL JAVILLAR

AGUAS NEGRAS

CITY CENTER

Casa Museo General Gregorio Luperón

Museo de Ámbar Dominicano

EL BATEY

Acapulco Beach

BARRIO LA RIGOLA

ENSANCHE MIRAMAR

Costa Rica Beach

BAYARDO

Long Beach

PADRE GRANERO

5

Haiti

Dominican Republic

Parque Nacional Isabel de Torres

0   1 mi

0   1 km

---

interactive programs, including dolphin and sea lion shows and encounters, a double-dolphin swim, a tropical reef aquarium, stingrays, shark tanks, an aviary, a rain forest, and a new pirates pool for kids. You must make advance reservations if you want to participate in one of the swims or encounters; children must be at least six years old and accompanied by an adult. The exhilarating (though expensive) double-dolphin swim will produce lifelong memories. If you are brave enough for the (nurse) shark encounter, you will feed them and touch them in the shark cove; the stingray encounter is also included. A photo lab and video service can capture the moment, but there is an extra charge. If you're staying at nearby Lifestyle resorts, or hotels in Puerto Plata, transfers are free. If in Sosúa or Cabarete, transfers are $5 per person; hotels should have the

tour schedules. ■TIP➜ **There's a private beach, showers, and a locker room on-site.** ✉ *Calle Principal 3, 3 miles (5 km) west of Puerto Plata, Cofresi* ☎ *809/291–1000* ⊕ *www.oceanworld.net* ✈ *From $69.*

Parque Nacional Isabel de Torres

MOUNTAIN—SIGHT | Southwest of Puerto Plata, Mount Isabel de Torres soars 2,600 feet above sea level and is notable for its huge statue of Christ. Up there also are botanical gardens that, despite efforts, still are not memorable. If you go independently, you can choose to hire a knowledgeable English-speaking guide. A cable car takes you to the top for a spectacular view. The cars usually wait until filled to capacity before going up—which can make them crowded. You should visit in the morning, preferably by 9 am; by afternoon, the cloud cover rolls in, and you can see practically nothing. That said,

The mile-long Playa Grande is considered by many to be one of the world's best beaches.

some visitors consider this the highlight of a city tour and take dozens of aerial photos from the cable car, which runs continuously until 4:45 pm. ■**TIP→ The vendors are particularly tenacious here.** ⊠ *Av. Manolo Tavárez Justo, off Autopista Duarte (Hwy. 1), follow signs, Puerto Plata* 🕾 *809/970–0501* ⊕ *telefericopuerto-plata.com* 🖃 *Cable car RD$350.*

😎 Beaches

Cofresí Beach

BEACH—SIGHT | This long stretch of golden sand is good for swimming, and a bit of wave action provides an opportunity for surfing. Locals mainly use the public area, particularly on Sunday. To the immediate north are Ocean World and its marina. To the south, a five-minute walk in the sand, is a semiprivate beach for the Cofresí Palm Beach resort. **Amenities:** food and drink. **Best for:** surfing; swimming; walking. ⊠ *Calle Principal, 4½ miles (7 km) west of Puerto Plata town center, just south of Ocean World, Cofresi.*

★ Playa Grande

BEACH—SIGHT | This dramatic mile-long stretch is widely considered to be one of the top beaches in the world. Many a photo shoot has been staged at this picture-perfect beach with off-white sands and turquoise water. Just east of the famous golf course of the same name, Playa Grande's drama comes from craggy cliffs dropping into the crystalline sea. Shade can be found in the palm trees that thicken into Parque Nacional Cabo Francés Viejo, a jungle preserve south of the beach.

Food shacks and cheapie souvenir stands once marred the beauty of this simply gorgeous stretch of sand, but vendors now have cutesy, brightly painted Victorian-style huts and have relocated to one end of the beach, where a large parking area was constructed. Security is present, and there are clean restrooms. Surfboards, paddleboards, and boogie boards are for rent—although the surf can swell, it can also be smooth. Two luxury resorts can be found nearby: the

Playa Grande Beach Club, just behind the beach and screened by a palm-frond fence, as well as the newer Amanera. **Amenities:** food and drink; toilets. **Best for:** surfing; swimming; walking. ⊠ *Carretera Río San Juan–Cabrera, Km 12, Río San Juan* ⊕ *www.playagrande.com* ⊠ *Free.*

🍴 Restaurants

You can eat at Coco Caña Lounge right in the port, drink at the rooftop Sky Bar, or you can go into Puerto Plata and eat at one of the many restaurants along the Malecón. The area's hotels also have restaurants, and if you are spending the day at one of them, that might be an attractive option, but they are typically more expensive.

🏃 Activities

A wide variety of organized shore excursions, which explore the nearby city of Puerto Plata or the countryside, are offered from the port and can be arranged through your ship. Some of these excursions include time at one of the nearby spectacular beaches. You can also arrange deep sea fishing, ATV tours, adventure tours, sailing excursions, horseback riding, a day at Ocean World (though you can easily get here or to one of the area's beaches yourself by taxi), or just a relaxing beach day. It is generally easier to arrange tours through your ship. Some of the options also include volunteering opportunities that were established by Carnival's now-defunct Fathom brand. Some of the best tours are offered by Cabarete-based Iguana Mama.

ADVENTURE TOURS
⭐ Iguana Mama
BICYCLING | **FAMILY** | This well-established, safety-oriented company's offerings include mountain bike tours that will take you along the coastal flats or test your mettle on steeper climbs in the national parks. Downhill rides (half- or full-day) include a taxi up to 3,000 feet, as well

as breakfast and lunch. Advanced rides on- and off-road are also offered, as are guided day hikes. Other half- and full-day trips include swimming, climbing up and jumping off various waterfalls, rappelling, and natural waterslides, white-water rafting, horseback riding, ecotours, and other adventure sports. The company also organizes longer, multiday excursions that include outdoor activities. ⊠ *Calle Principal 74, across from Scotia Bank, Cabarete* ☎ *809/571–0908, 809/571–0734, 809/654–2325* ⊕ *www.iguanamama.com* ⊠ *From $55.*

Roatán, Honduras

You'll swear you hear Jimmy Buffett singing as you step off the ship onto Roatán. The flavor is decidedly "Margaritaville," but with all there is to do on this island off the north coast of Honduras, you'll never waste away here. Roatán is the largest and most important of the Bay Islands—though at a mere 40 miles (65 km) from tip to tip and no more than 3 miles (5 km) at its widest, "large" is a relative term here. As happened elsewhere on Central America's Caribbean coast, the British got here first—the Bay Islands didn't become part of Honduras until the mid-1800s—and left an indelible imprint in the form of place names such as Coxen Hole, French Harbour, and West End, as well as, of course, their language (albeit a Caribbean-accented English). The eyes of underwater enthusiasts mist over at the mention of Roatán, one of the world's premier diving destinations, but plenty of topside activity will keep you busy, too.

ESSENTIALS
CURRENCY
The Honduran lempira.

TELEPHONE
All phone numbers in Honduras have eight digits. There are no area codes, so just dial the number. Public phones

are hard to find, but some hotels and businesses will offer phone services to walk-up users for a small fee.

COMING ASHORE

Roatán has two cruise terminals. Carnival and its affiliates own and operate an $80-million installation called Mahogany Bay, at Dixon Cove, halfway between the towns of Coxen Hole and French Harbour. The facility is designed to be entirely self-contained, with shops, restaurants, and attractions; a chairlift ($12 for a day pass) transports you to a private beach. You can also partake of an entire slate of shore excursions, if you wish to see more of the island. Other lines use the original Terminal de Cruceros (cruise terminal) in the village of Coxen Hole, the island's administrative center. You'll find telephones, Internet computers, and stands with tour information inside the terminal, as well as a flea market of crafts just outside the gate. Not to be outdone, Coxen Hole's facility is undergoing a major facelift at this writing. Periodically, schedules and weather mean cruise lines use the opposite terminal.

Taxis are readily available outside the cruise-ship docks, but be prepared to pay a premium for services there. Trips to the major tourism centers like West End and West Bay beach will cost around $20 per person round-trip. (Negotiate the price before you go, and be sure to clarify that the fare is indeed per person and round-trip.) If you would like to save money on your taxi fares, you can walk to the main highway (or into the town of Coxen Hole, if you dock near there) and look for taxis marked "Colectivo." These taxis charge a flat rate of L20–L150 ($1–$6), depending on the distance. They also pick up as many passengers as they can hold, so plan on riding with other locals or tourists. The local public-transport system consists of blue minivans that leave from Main Street in Coxen Hole to various points on the island until 6 pm. Simply wave if you want a minivan to stop.

Best Bets

- **Diving and Snorkeling.** Roatán is one of the world's great diving destinations. There's snorkeling, too, and most of it easily accessible from shore.

- **Explore Garífuna Culture.** You'd never know it while wandering West End, but the island has an original culture that predates the arrival of tourism and still dominates Roatán's eastern half.

- **Hands-On Animal Adventures.** Macaws and monkeys scurry around you at the Gumbalimba Nature Park; dolphin encounters are available at Anthony's Key Resort.

Expect to pay L30 to French Harbour and L50 to Sandy Bay or West End.

Look for the cadre of tourist police if you need help with anything. They wear tan shirts and dark-green trousers and are evident on cruise days. You certainly can rent a car here, but the island's compact size makes it unnecessary. Taxis will happily take you anywhere; expect to pay $80 to $120 for a day's private tour, depending on how far you wish to travel.

Sights

Carambola Botanical Gardens

GARDEN | FAMILY | With one of the country's most extensive orchid collections, the Carambola Botanical Gardens are home to many different varieties of tropical plant. It is also a breeding area for iguanas. There are several trails to follow, and many of the trees and plants are identified by small signs. The longest trail leads up to the top of the hill, where you find an amazing view of the West End of the island. Guides can be hired at the visitor center. ⊠ *Across from Anthony's*

Map Labels

Half Moon Bay

West End

West Bay

◆ Carambola Botanical Gardens
◆ Roatán Institute for Marine Sciences

Sandy Bay

Caribbean Sea

◆ Gumbalimba Park

Flower Bay

Roatán Airport

Crawfish Rock

Maya Key ◆

Coxen Hole

Brick Bay

French Harbour

Politilli Bight

Punta Gorda

Paya Bay

Oak Ridge

Bahía de Honduras

Camp Bay

Port Royal

Helene Island

0   6 mi

0   6 km

KEY

☂ Beaches

🚢 Cruise Ship Terminal

Key Resort, Sandy Bay ☏ 9961–3074 ⊕ www.carambolagardens.com ✉ L245, guided tour L370.

Gumbalimba Park

NATURE PRESERVE | FAMILY | This park is part nature reserve, part tourism fun. Macaws, parrots, and monkeys will land on your shoulders as iguanas scuttle around more than 200 tropical tree and plant species. Paved paths lined with boulders lead to a 91-meter (300-foot) suspension bridge that crosses a lagoon. The park's zip-line tour is its main attraction, with 13 lines traversing the rain forest canopy. There is also snorkeling, Snuba (a form of surface-supplied diving), horseback riding, kayaking, and a white sandy beach. Coxen's Cave is reminiscent of a theme park ride: recreated cave drawings line the walls; and dotting the interior are life-size pirate statues and

replicas of maps, weapons, and treasure. Grab a bite at the poolside grill and take a refreshing shower in the outdoor stalls. Park admission includes the pirate cave, animal preserve, botanical gardens, and the pool. All other activities cost extra. ✉ West Bay ☏ 2445–1033 ⊕ www.gumbalimbapark.com ✉ From L600.

Maya Key

ISLAND | FAMILY | One of the premier day excursions—and a great place for children—for cruisers visiting Roatán is this small, private island near Coxen Hole. The park offers a wide variety of amenities and activities, including sandy beaches, tropical gardens, a museum with cultural displays, and an animal rescue center, where you can meet the animals. The 10-acre island also has spectacular snorkeling. Most cruise lines offer the island as a shore excursion, and that's the only

Maya Key, a private island near Coxen Hole, is a popular day-trip in Roatán.

way it can be visited—the park takes no independent bookings. It's a 3-minute water shuttle from the pier 50 yards east of the Terminal de Cruceros in Coxen Hole. ✉ *Maya Cay, Coxen Hole* ☎ *9995–9589* ⊕ *www.mayakeyroatan.com.*

Roatán Institute for Marine Sciences

COLLEGE | FAMILY | One of the attractions at Anthony's Key Resort, the Roatán Institute for Marine Sciences is an educational center that researches bottlenose dolphins and other marine animals. A dolphin show takes place every day at 4 pm. For an additional fee, you can participate in a Dolphin Encounter, which allows you to interact with the dolphins while either swimming or snorkeling. There are also programs for children ages 5 to 14, including snorkeling experiences, as well as a Dolphin Trainer for a Day program. ■TIP→ **Cruise-ship passengers must make reservations for dolphin encounters through their ship's excursion desk.** ✉ *Anthony's Key Resort, Sandy Bay* ☎ *9556–0212* ⊕ *www.roatanims.org* ✉ *L125, Dolphin Enounter L2200, Dolphin Trainer for a Day L5600.*

🅰 Beaches

You really can't go wrong with any of Roatán's white-sand beaches. Even those adjacent to populated areas manage to stay clean and uncluttered, thanks to efforts of residents. Water is rougher for swimming on the less-protected north side of the island.

Half Moon Bay

BEACH—SIGHT | Roatán's most popular beach is also one of its prettiest. Coconut palms and foliage come up to the crescent shoreline. The beach lies just outside the tourist-friendly West End. Crystal-clear waters offer abundant visibility for snorkeling. ✉ *West End.*

West Bay Beach

BEACH—SIGHT | Roatán is famous for the picturesque West Bay Beach. It's a de rigueur listing on every shore-excursions list. Once there, you can lounge on the beach or snorkel. ✉ *West Bay.*

🍴 Restaurants

Anthony's Chicken

$ | **CARIBBEAN** | A West End staple with plenty of local flavor, Anthony's Chicken is famous for the best chicken *baleadas* (grilled tortillas stuffed with refried beans and white cheese, with your choice of toppings) in town. Take a seat inside surrounded by the bright aqua walls and benches, and right across from the turquoise water outside. **Known for:** extensive menu; very casual setting with picnic tables; delicious jerk chicken. ⑤ *Average main: L130* ⊠ *Near Booty Bar, West End* ☎ *9839–7851* ▭ *No credit cards.*

Por Qué No?

$$ | **IRISH** | **FAMILY** | Serving up traditional Mediterranean fare, Por Qué No? is a hidden gem tucked away off the main road. Assemble a mix-and-match meal of appetizers: couscous, hummus, and the best potato salad on the island will do well. **Known for:** everything from hummus to pizza; good breakfast option; great water views. ⑤ *Average main: L200* ⊠ *Next to Chocolate Factory, West End* ☎ *9628–6994* ⊕ *www.porquenoroatan. com* ⊗ *Closed Mon.*

🛍 Shopping

At the cruise ship dock in Coxen Hole you can find craft vendors, who set up shop outside the cruise-terminal gates; a small number of souvenir shops are scattered around the center of Coxen Hole, a short walk from the docks. Few of the souvenirs for sale here—or anywhere else on the island for that matter—were actually made in Roatán; most come from mainland Honduras. The terminal at Mahogany Bay has 22 shops as well. If you get as far as West End, there are a variety of souvenir and craft sellers in small shops lining the main sand road that runs parallel to the beach.

🏃 Activities

DIVING AND SNORKELING

Most of the activity on Roatán centers on scuba diving and snorkeling, as well as the newest sensation—Snuba, a cross between the two whereby your mask is connected by a hose to an air source that remains above the water, allowing you to dive for several feet without carrying an air tank on your back. Warm water, great visibility, and thousands of colorful fish make the island a popular destination. Add to this a good chance of seeing a whale shark, and you'll realize why so many people head here each year. Dive sites cluster off the island's western and southern coasts.

One of the most popular destinations—particularly for budget travelers—is West End, offering idyllic beaches stretching as far as the eye can see. One of the loveliest spots is Half Moon Bay, a crescent of brilliant white sand. A huge number of dive shops offer incredibly low-price diving courses. Competition among dive shops is fierce in West End, so check out a few. West Bay has great dive sites, but few actual centers. When shopping around, ask about class size (eight is the maximum), the condition of the diving equipment, and the safety equipment on the dive boat.

Native Sons

SCUBA DIVING | **FAMILY** | One of the first dive shops in West End, Native Sons was started by a local diving legend, Alvin Jackson, who also helped form Roatán Marine Park. It's now a bustling shop with beautiful dive boats, as well as an on-site hostel that attracts backpackers. ⊠ *West End* ☎ *9670–6530* ⊕ *www. roatandivingnativesons.com.*

Quality Time Divers

SCUBA DIVING | If you want the best gear, boats, and service on the island—and you're willing to pay for it—head to Quality Time Divers. They will craft custom dive trips for you and your entire group, including dock pickup and drop-off for those staying outside of West End. The boat captain usually fishes while heading back, and if he catches something, you'll likely be having a barbecue on the deck after you arrive back at the dock. ✉ *Behind Roatán Rentals, West End* ☎ *2445–4182* ⊕ *www.qualitytimedivers.com.*

Roatán Divers

SCUBA DIVING | FAMILY | One of the most organized dive operations on the island, this boutique-style shop delivers great service at affordable prices. The owners are dive instructors themselves, and it shows in their appreciation for safety, quality, and fun. ✉ *West End* ☎ *9949–3781, 315/507–8656 in U.S.* ⊕ *www. roatandivers.com.*

West End Divers

SCUBA DIVING | FAMILY | This shop has a fun, youthful vibe and always seems to see the best underwater animals—check out their recent sightings board for proof. They are also the only shop in the area offering blackwater dives, which are specialized late-night dives done two miles off the reef over hundreds of feet of open ocean. Cafe Escondido, located directly upstairs, is a great place to grab a quick lunch between dives. ✉ *West End* ☎ *9565–4465, 786/623–5627 in U.S.* ⊕ *www.westenddivers.info.*

FISHING

★ Wahoo Slayer Fishing Charters

FISHING | FAMILY | If you're more interested in catching fish than hanging out with them underwater, get yourself a spot on the *Wahoo Slayer*. Captain Enrick Bush was raised on these waters and knows them accordingly, making sure to take you to the best places to get a good catch. Wahoo, mahimahi, and barracuda are all possibilities. Day trips to Pigeon Cay, Utila, and Cayos Cochinos are also available. ✉ *Across from Woody's Supermarket, West End* ☎ *9883–3346* ⊕ *www. wahooslayer.com* ✉ *From L11000.*

Samaná (Cayo Levantado), Dominican Republic

Samaná, the name of both a peninsula in the Dominican Republic as well as the largest town on Samaná Bay, is one of the least-known regions of the country. That perception is changing quickly, however, with help from a nearby international airport, which opened in El Catey in 2006, and a highway from Santo Domingo, which has cut drive time to two hours. Much development has just been completed or is nearing completion, so now is a good time to visit, before it attracts a great deal of mainstream tourism. That, too, is changing rapidly, as some megaships make use of the port. Samaná is one of the Dominican Republic's newest cruise-ship destinations, with one of the island's greatest varieties of shore excursions. You can explore caves and see an amazing waterfall. And since many humpback whales come here each year to mate and give birth, it's a top whale-watching destination from January through March. While some cruise lines still use Cayo Levantado as a private island–type experience, for other lines it is just one of several options.

ESSENTIALS

CURRENCY

The Dominican peso, but you can almost always use U.S. dollars.

TELEPHONE

Country codes are 1 809, 1 829, and 1 849 (depending on the type of phone you are calling). Claro, Orange, Tricom, and Viva are the major mobile providers, using GSM (850, 900, 1800 and 1900 bands).

COMING ASHORE

Cruise ships can dock at Embarcadero (name of dock) in Santa Bárbara de Samaná. If you come aboard on a tender, they will take you to one of three docks on the Malecón, referred to as the Samaná Bay Piers. The farthest is a five-minute walk from the town center.

Renting a car, although possible, isn't a good option. Driving in the Dominican Republic can be a hectic and even harrowing experience; if you are in port one only day, don't risk it. You'll do better if you pool your resources with friends from the ship and share a taxi to do some independent exploring. Negotiate and settle on a price before getting in the taxi. To give you an idea of what to expect, a minivan that can take eight people will normally charge $90 for the round trip to Las Terrenas, including a two-hour wait while you explore or enjoy the beach. Similarly, you'll pay $80 to travel round-trip to Las Galeras. Many drivers speak some English. Within Samaná, rickshaws are far less costly and are also fun. Called *motoconchos de carretas,* they are not unlike larger versions of the Thai tuk-tuk, but can hold up to six people. The least you will pay is RD$10. They're fine for getting around town, but don't even think about going long distance with them.

⊙ Sights

SANTA BÁRBARA DE SAMANÁ
Dominican Evangelical Church
RELIGIOUS SITE | The historic Dominican Evangelical Church is the oldest original building left in Samaná. Back in 1824, a sailing vessel called the *Turtle Dove,* carrying several hundred slaves who had escaped from Philadelphia, was blown ashore in Samaná. The structure actually came across the ocean from England in 1881 in a hundred pieces and was reassembled here, serving the spiritual needs of the African-American freedmen. In 1946 a citywide fire wiped out most of Samaná's wooden buildings and Victorian architecture; this church was miraculously saved. ⊠ *Calle Theodore Chaseurox, Samaná ✝ In front of Catholic church, 2 blocks north of the cruise*

Best Bets ⊙

■ **Cayo Levantado.** This resort island puts on an excellent show for day-trippers.

■ **El Limón Waterfall.** The dazzling falls are reached by horseback.

■ **Los Haitises National Park.** The caves are filled with Taíno drawings; the mangroves are magnificent.

■ **Playa Rincón.** The perfect, quiet beach offers a river, unspoiled mountain scenery, and privacy.

■ **Whale-watching.** In season, this is the top activity in the area.

ship pier ☎ *809/538–2579* ✉ *Donations appreciated.*

Whale Museum & Nature Center (*Centro de Naturaleza*)
MUSEUM | This tiny museum is dedicated to the mighty mammals of the sea. Samaná Bay is part of one of the largest marine mammal sanctuaries in the world and is a center for whale-watching during the winter migration of humpback whales. The Center for Conservation and Ecodevelopment of Samaná Bay and its Environment (CEBSE) manages this facility, which features a 40-foot female humpback skeleton. Information in English is available at the entrance. ⊠ *Av. La Marina, Tiro al Blanco, Samaná ✝ Turn left from the main section of the Malecón, en route to the hotel Bahía Príncipe Cayacoa, to find the tiny Centro de Naturaleza* ☎ *809/538–2042* ✉ *RD$100.*

ELSEWHERE IN THE SAMANÁ PENINSULA
★ **Los Haitises National Park**
ARCHAEOLOGICAL SITE | A highlight of any visit to the Samaná Peninsula is Los Haitises National Park (pronounced *high-TEE-sis*), which is across Samaná Bay.

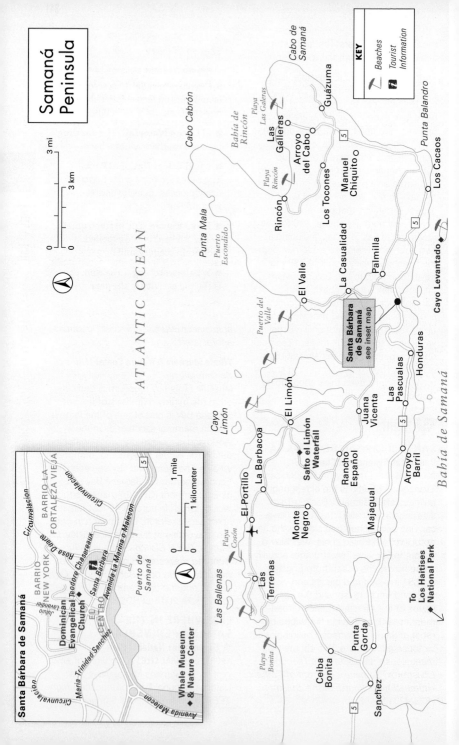

The park is famous for its karst limestone formations, caves, and grottoes filled with pictographs and petroglyphs left by the indigenous Taínos. The park is accessible only by boat, and a professionally guided kayak tour is highly recommended (a licensed guide from a tour company or the government is mandatory for any visitor). You'll paddle around dozens of dramatic rock islands and spectacular cliff faces, while beautiful coastal birds—magnificent frigate birds, brown pelicans, brown booby, egrets, and herons—swirl around overhead. A good tour will also include the caverns, where your flashlight will illuminate Taíno petroglyphs. It's a continual sensory experience, and you'll feel tiny, like a human speck surrounded by geological grandeur. Dominican Shuttles (⊕ *DominicanShuttles.com*) can arrange a park tour and a stay at the adjacent and rustic Paraíso Caño Hondo Ecolodge, which has authentic Creole cuisine and multiple waterfalls. ⊠ *Samaná Bay, Samaná* ☎ *809/472–4204* 🗺 *$4, not including mandatory use of licensed guide.*

Salto el Limón Waterfall

BODY OF WATER | Provided that you're fit and willing to deal with a long and slippery path, an adventurous guided trip (three hours) to the spectacular Salto el Limón Waterfall is a delight. It's mostly on horseback, but includes walking down rocky, sometimes muddy trails. Horse paths are slippery, and the trek is strenuous. The well-mannered horses take you across two rivers and up mountains to El Limón, the 165-foot waterfall amid luxuriant vegetation. Some snacks and drinks are usually included, but a grilled chicken lunch is only a few more pesos. The outpost for the trek, a local guide service called Santi Rancho, is difficult to find; it's best to arrange a tour from a professional operator like **Flora Tours** (☎ *809/240–5482* ⊕ *flora-tours.net*) in Las Terrenas. However, in times of drought, the waterfall is not as interesting. ⊠ *Santi Rancho, El Limón* ☎ *829/923–2792 Santi Rancho.*

🌀 Beaches

There are no recommendable beaches in Santa Bárbara de Samaná itself. You will have to travel to one of the beautiful ones elsewhere on the peninsula, another reason why the Cayo Levantado excursion is popular on most ships.

Cayo Levantado

BEACH—SIGHT | There are no public beaches in Samaná town, but you can hire a boat to take you to Cayo Levantado, which has a wonderful white-sand beach on an island in Samaná Bay. Today the small island has largely been turned into a commercial enterprise to accommodate the 1,500 cruise-ship passengers who anchor here; it has dining facilities, bars, restrooms, and lounge chairs. It can be extremely crowded and boisterous when there's a ship in port. The beach, however, is undeniably beautiful. The Bahía Príncipe Cayo Levantado (☎ *809/538–3131*), an upscale, all-inclusive resort with its own launch, sells day passes (adults only) for about $3. ⊠ *Samaná Bay, Samaná* 🗺 *Public beach free.*

★ Playa Cosón

BEACH—SIGHT | This is a long, wonderful stretch of nearly white sand and the best beach close to the town of Las Terrenas. Previously undeveloped, it's now reachable by a new highway, Carretera Cosón, and there are a number of condo developments under construction (so the current sense of solitude probably won't last). One excellent restaurant, called The Beach, serves the entire 15-mile (24-km) shore, and there's the European-owned boutique hotel Casa Cosón and its restaurant and bar. If beachgoers buy lunch and/or drinks at either, then they can use the restrooms. **Amenities:** food and drink; parking; toilets. **Best for:** sunset; swimming; walking; windsurfing. ⊠ *Las Terrenas.*

🍴 Restaurants

Café del Mar

$$$ | SEAFOOD | As the name suggests, seafood is the headliner at this sophisticated marina-side restaurant serving Caribbean-influenced Mediterranean cuisine. By day, have lunch outdoors while dipping in and out of the infinity pool. **Known for:** fine dining for lunch and dinner; never overcrowded; can hear the wind in the riggings. $ *Average main: $23* ✉ *Puerto Bahía Marina, Carretera Sánchez–Samaná, Samaná* ☎ *809/503–6363* ⊕ *www.puertobahiasamana.com.*

La Mata Rosada

$$ | SEAFOOD | This Malecón landmark has been luring local expats and foodies since the late 1990s. Ceiling fans keep you cool as sea breezes waft in from the bay across the street while you dine on mahimahi, shrimp, or a mix of grilled lobster and other shellfish. **Known for:** an oldie but goodie; unsophisticated table arrangement; begin with ceviche, a specialty of this port town. $ *Average main: $16* ✉ *Av. Malecón 5B, Samaná* ☎ *809/538–2388* ⊗ *Closed Wed., and June–Oct.*

🛍 Shopping

Rum, coffee, and cigars are popular local products. You may also find good coconut handicrafts, including coconut-shell candles. Whale-oriented gift items are particularly popular. Most souvenir shops are on the Malecón or in the market plaza; you will find more on the major downtown streets, all within easy walking distance of the tender piers.

🏃 Activities

DIVING AND SNORKELING

In 1979 three atolls disappeared after a seaquake off Las Terrenas, providing an opportunity for truly memorable dives. Also just offshore from Las Terrenas are the Islas Las Ballenas (Whale Islands), a cluster of four little islands with good snorkeling. A coral reef is off Playa Jackson, a beach accessible only by boat.

Las Galeras Divers

SCUBA DIVING | This is a professional, safety-conscious operation. Owner Serge is a PADI, OWSI, and nitrox instructor, and every level of PADI course is offered. Diving lessons and trips are offered in English, French, and Spanish, and diving equipment rentals are also available. Discounts are given to groups, families, and divers who want a package deal. ✉ *Calle Principal, Las Galeras* ☎ *809/538–0220, 809/715–4111* ⊕ *www.las-galeras-divers. com* ⌾ *From $50.*

WHALE-WATCHING

Humpback whales come to Samaná Bay to mate and give birth each year for a relatively limited period, from approximately January 15 through March 30. Samaná Bay is considered one of the top 10 destinations in the world to watch humpbacks. If you're here during the brief season, this can be the experience of a lifetime. You can listen to the male humpback's solitary courting song and witness incredible displays as the whales flip their tails and breach (humpbacks are the most active species of whales in the Atlantic).

★ Whale Samaná

WHALE-WATCHING | Owned by Kim Beddall, a Canadian who is incredibly knowledgeable about whales and Samaná in general, having lived here for decades, this operation is far and away the region's best, both professional and environmentally sensitive. On board *Pura Mia,* a 55-foot motor vessel, a marine mammal specialist narrates and answers questions in several languages. Kim herself conducts almost all the English-language tours. Normal departure times are 9 for the morning trip and 1:30 for the afternoon trip; she is flexible whenever possible for cruise-ship passengers but does require advance reservations. ✉ *Calle Sra. Morellia Kelly, Samaná*

✢ *Across street from town dock, beside park* ☎ *809/538–2494* ⊕ *www.whalesamana.com* ✉ *From $59, plus $5 entrance to Marine Mammal Sanctuary.*

San Juan, Puerto Rico

Although Puerto Rico is a commonwealth of the United States, few cities in the Caribbean are as steeped in Spanish tradition as San Juan. Within a seven square-block area in Old San Juan you'll find restored 16th-century buildings, museums, art galleries, bookstores, and 200-year-old houses with balustraded balconies overlooking narrow cobblestone streets. In contrast, San Juan's sophisticated Condado and Isla Verde areas have glittering hotels, fancy boutiques, casinos, and discos. Out in the countryside is 28,000-acre El Yunque National Forest, a rain forest with more than 240 species of trees growing at least 100 feet high. You can stretch your sea legs on dramatic mountain ranges, numerous trails, in vast caves, at coffee plantations, old sugar mills, and hundreds of beaches. No wonder San Juan is one of the busiest ports of call in the Caribbean.

ESSENTIALS
CURRENCY
The U.S. dollar.

TELEPHONE
Calling the United States from Puerto Rico is the same as calling within the United States (you just dial "1"), and virtually all U.S. mobile phone plans work here just as they do at home. You can use the long-distance telephone service office in the cruise-ship terminal, or you can use your calling card by dialing the toll-free access number of your long-distance provider from any pay phone. You'll find a phone center by the Paseo de la Princesa.

Best Bets ◉

■ **El Morro.** Explore the giant labyrinthine fort.

■ **El Yunque National Forest.** This rain forest east of San Juan is a great half-day excursion.

■ **Casa Bacardí.** Rum lovers can jump on the public ferry and then taxi over to the factory.

■ **Old San Juan.** Walk the cobblestone streets of Old San Juan.

■ **Shopping.** Within a few blocks of the port there are plenty of factory outlets and boutiques.

COMING ASHORE
Most cruise ships dock within a couple of blocks of Old San Juan; however, the Pan American terminal is across the bay, and if your ship docks there you'll need to take a taxi to get anywhere on the island. The Paseo de la Princesa, a tree-lined promenade beneath the city wall, is a nice place for a stroll—you can admire the local crafts and stop at the refreshment kiosks. Major sights in the Old San Juan area are mere blocks from the piers, but be aware that the streets are narrow and steeply inclined in places. Like any other big city, San Juan has its share of petty crime, so guard your wallet or purse, especially in crowded markets and squares.

It's particularly easy to get to Cataño and the Bacardí rum distillery on your own; take the ferry that leaves from the cruise piers every half hour, then a taxi on the other side. Taxis, which line up to meet ships, are the best option if you want to explore beyond Old San Juan. White taxis labeled "Taxi Turístico" charge set fares of $10 to $24. Less common are metered cabs authorized by the Public Service Commission that charge an

Old San Juan

0 — 1/4 mile

0 — 400 meters

ATLANTIC OCEAN

Castillo San ◆
Felipe del Morro

El Campo
del Morro

Calle del Morro

City Wall

Bajada
Matadero
San Miguel

San Juan Blvd.

Norzagaray

City Wall

Museo de las
Américas ◆

Cristo

San Sebastián

Tanca

Sol

Luna

O'Donnell

Castillo ◆
San Cristóbal

San José

Casa Alcaldía
de San Juan

San Francisco

El Convento

Las Monjas

Cruz

San Justo

Fortaleza

Paseo de Covadonga

Catedral de
San Juan Bautista
La Fortaleza ◆

Plaza
de Armas

Tetuán

Recinto Sur

Comercio

Paseo de La Princesa

Bahía de San Juan

Paseo Gilberto Concepción de Gracia

Pier
3

Pier
2

Pier 4

La Casita
(Tourist
Information
Center)

Pier
1

Cruise Ship Piers

Museo de Arte ◆
de Puerto Rico

Puntilla

Presidio

Casa Bacardí
Visitor Center

KEY

🚢 Cruise Ship Terminal

⛴ Ferry

🛈 Tourist Information

initial $1; after that, it's about $0.10 for each additional 1/13 mile. If you take a metered taxi, insist that the meter be turned on, and pay only what is shown, plus a tip of 15% to 20%. You can negotiate with taxi drivers for specific trips, and you can hire a taxi for as little as $36 per hour for sightseeing tours. If you want to see more of the island but don't want to drive, you may want to consider a shore excursion, though almost all trips can be booked more cheaply with local tour operators.

If you are embarking or disembarking in San Juan, the ride to or from the Luis Muñoz Marín International Airport, east of downtown San Juan, to the docks in Old San Juan takes about 20 minutes, depending on traffic. White Taxi Turístico cabs have a fixed rate of $19 to and from the cruise-ship piers; there is a $1 charge

for each piece of luggage. Other taxi companies charge by the mile, which can cost a little more. Be sure the driver starts the meter, or agree on a fare beforehand.

◉ Sights

OLD SAN JUAN

Old San Juan, the original city founded in 1521, contains carefully preserved examples of 16th- and 17th-century Spanish colonial architecture. More than 400 buildings have been beautifully restored. Graceful wrought-iron and wooden balconies with lush hanging plants extend over narrow streets paved with *adoquines* (blue-gray stones originally used as ballast on Spanish ships). The Old City is partially enclosed by walls that date from 1633 and once completely surrounded it. Designated a U.S. National Historic Site in 1949, Old San Juan is chockablock with shops, open-air cafés, homes, tree-shaded squares, monuments, and people. You can get an overview on a morning's stroll, which includes some steep climbs. However, if you plan to immerse yourself in history or to shop, you'll need a couple of days.

Casa Alcaldía de San Juan (*San Juan City Hall*)

GOVERNMENT BUILDING | San Juan's city hall was built between 1602 and 1789. In 1841, extensive alterations made it resemble Madrid's city hall, with arcades, towers, balconies, and an inner courtyard. Renovations have refreshed the facade and some interior rooms, but the architecture remains true to its colonial style. Only the patios are open to public viewings. A municipal tourist information center and an art gallery with rotating exhibits are in the lobby. Call ahead to schedule a free tour. ⊠ *153 Calle San Francisco, Plaza de Armas, Old San Juan* ☏ *787/480–2910* ⊕ *www.sanjuanciudad-patria.com* ⊠ *Free* ⊘ *Closed weekends.*

★ Castillo San Cristóbal

MILITARY SITE | FAMILY | This huge stone fortress, built between 1634 and 1783, guarded the city from land attacks from the east. The largest Spanish fortification in the New World, San Cristóbal was known in the 17th and 18th centuries as "the Gibraltar of the West Indies." Five freestanding structures divided by dry moats are connected by tunnels. You're free to explore the gun turrets (with cannon in situ), officers' quarters, re-created 18th-century barracks, and gloomy passageways. Along with El Morro, San Cristóbal is a National Historic Site administered by the U.S. National Park Service; it's a UNESCO World Heritage Site as well. Rangers conduct tours in Spanish and English. ⊠ *Calle Norzagaray at Av. Muñoz Rivera, Old San Juan* ☏ *787/729–6777* ⊕ *www.nps.gov/*

saju ⊠ *$7, includes Castillo San Felipe del Morro.*

★ Castillo San Felipe del Morro (*El Morro*)

HISTORIC SITE | FAMILY | At the northwestern tip of Old San Juan, El Morro (the promontory) was built by the Spaniards between 1539 and 1790. Rising 140 feet above the sea, the massive six-level fortress was built to protect the port and has a commanding view of the harbor. It is a labyrinth of cannon batteries, ramps, barracks, turrets, towers, and tunnels, through which you're free to wander. The cannon emplacement walls and the dank secret passageways are a wonder of engineering. A small but enlightening museum displays ancient Spanish guns and other armaments, military uniforms, and blueprints for Spanish forts in the Americas, although Castillo San Cristóbal has more extensive and impressive exhibits. There's also a gift shop. The fort is a National Historic Site administered by the U.S. National Park Service, and a UNESCO World Heritage Site as well. Various tours and a video are available in English. ⊠ *Calle del Morro, Old San Juan* ☏ *787/729–6960* ⊕ *www.nps.gov/saju* ⊠ *$7, includes Castillo San Cristóbal.*

Catedral de San Juan Bautista

RELIGIOUS SITE | The Catholic shrine of Puerto Rico had humble beginnings in the early 1520s as a thatch-roofed wooden structure. After a hurricane destroyed the church, it was rebuilt in 1540, when it was given a graceful circular staircase and vaulted Gothic ceilings. Most of the work on the present cathedral, however, was done in the 19th century. The remains of Ponce de León are behind a marble tomb in the wall near the transept, on the north side. The trompe-l'oeil work on the inside of the dome is breathtaking. Unfortunately, many of the other frescoes have suffered water damage. ⊠ *151 Calle Cristo, Old San Juan* ☏ *787/722–0861* ⊠ *$1 suggested donation.*

La Fortaleza

GOVERNMENT BUILDING | Sitting atop the fortified city walls overlooking the harbor, La Fortaleza was built between 1533 and 1540 as a fortress, but it proved insufficient, mainly because it was built inside the bay. It was attacked numerous times and occupied twice, by the British in 1598 and the Dutch in 1625. When the city's other fortifications were finished, this became the governor's palace. Changes made over the past four centuries have resulted in the current eclectic yet eye-pleasing collection of marble and mahogany, medieval towers, and stained-glass galleries. Still the official residence of the island's governor, it is the Western Hemisphere's oldest executive mansion in continual use. Guided tours of the gardens and exterior are conducted several times a day in English and Spanish; call ahead, as the schedule changes daily. Proper attire is required: no sleeveless shirts or very short shorts. Tours begin near the main gate in a yellow building called the Real Audiencia, housing the Oficina Estatal de Conservación Histórica (State Historic Preservation Office). ⊠ *West end of Calle Fortaleza, Old San Juan* 🕾 *787/721–7000* ⊕ *www.fortaleza. pr.gov* 🖅 *Free* ☉ *Closed weekends.*

Museo de las Américas

MUSEUM | On the second floor of the imposing former military barracks, Cuartel de Ballajá, this museum houses four permanent exhibits: Folk Arts, African Heritage, the Indian in America, and Conquest and Colonization. You'll also find a number of temporary exhibitions of works by regional and international artists. A wide range of handicrafts is available in the gift shop. ⊠ *Calle Norzagaray and Calle del Morro, Old San Juan* 🕾 *787/724–5052* ⊕ *www.museolasamericas.org* 🖅 *$6* ☉ *Closed Mon.*

ELSEWHERE IN SAN JUAN

Casa Bacardí Visitor Center

INFO CENTER | Exiled from Cuba, the Bacardí family built a small rum distillery here in the 1950s. Today it's the world's largest, able to produce 100,000 gallons of spirits a day and 21 million cases a year. A basic tour of the visitor center includes one free drink, or you can opt for a mixology class or rum tasting. If you don't want to drive, you can take a ferry from Pier 2 for $0.50 and then a *público* (public van service) from the ferry pier to the factory for about $3 per person. ⊠ *Bay View Industrial Park, Rte. 165, Km 2.6, at Rte. 888, Cataño* 🕾 *787/788–8400* ⊕ *www.visitcasabacardi.com* 🖅 *Tour $15, mixology class or rum tasting $50.*

★ Museo de Arte de Puerto Rico

MUSEUM | One of the Caribbean's biggest museums, this beautiful Neoclassical building was once the San Juan Municipal Hospital. The collection of Puerto Rican art starts with the colonial era, when most art was commissioned for churches. Works by José Campeche, the island's first great painter, include his masterpiece, *Immaculate Conception,* finished in 1794. Also well represented is Francisco Oller, who was the first to move beyond religious subjects to paint local scenes; another room has works by artists inspired by him. The original building, built in the 1920s, proved too small to house the collection; a newer east wing is dominated by a five-story stained-glass window by local artist Eric Tabales. The museum also has a beautiful garden with native flora and a 400-seat theater with a remarkable hand-crocheted lace curtain. ⊠ *299 Av. José de Diego, Santurce* 🕾 *787/977–6277* ⊕ *www. mapr.org* 🖅 *$6 (free Wed. 2–8)* ☉ *Closed Mon.–Tues.*

🅐 Beaches

The city's beaches can get crowded, especially on weekends. There's free access to all of them, but parking can be an issue in the peak sun hours—arriving early or in the late afternoon is a safer bet.

Hear your footsteps echo throughout Castillo San Felipe's vast network of tunnels, designed to amplify the sounds of approaching enemies.

★ Balneario de Carolina

BEACH—SIGHT | FAMILY | When people talk about a "beautiful Isla Verde beach," this Blue Flag beach is the one, located so close to the airport that leaves rustle when planes take off. Thanks to an offshore reef, the surf here is not as strong as at other nearby beaches, so it's good for families. There's plenty of room to spread out underneath the palm and almond trees, and there are picnic tables and grills. Although there's a charge for parking, there's not always someone to take the money. On weekends, the beach is crowded; get here early to nab parking. The newly opened Vivo Beach Club offers lounge chairs and beautiful facilities for food and drink. **Amenities:** lifeguards; parking (fee); showers; toilets. **Best for:** swimming; walking. ⊠ *Av. Los Gobernadores, Carolina* 🚗 *Parking $4.*

🍴 Restaurants

Cafetería Mallorca

$ | CAFÉ | The specialty at this old-fashioned, 1950s-style diner is the *mallorca*, a sweet pastry that's buttered, grilled, and then sprinkled with powdered sugar. Wash one down with a cup of café con leche. **Known for:** old-school diner feel; mallorcas; café con leche. ⑤ *Average main: $10* ⊠ *300 Calle San Francisco, Old San Juan* ☎ *787/724–4607* ⊘ *No dinner.*

El Jibarito

$$ | PUERTO RICAN | The menus are handwritten and the tables wobble, but locals in the know have favored this no-frills, family-run restaurant—tucked away on a quiet cobblestone street—for years. The *bistec encebollado*, goat fricassee, and shredded beef stew stand out on the comida criolla menu. **Known for:** traditional Puerto Rican comfort food; casual atmosphere; gentle prices. ⑤ *Average main: $14* ⊠ *280 Calle Sol, Old San Juan* ☎ *787/725–8375.*

ⓨ Nightlife

Almost every ship stays in San Juan late or even overnight to give passengers an opportunity to revel in the nightlife—the most sophisticated in the Caribbean.

BARS AND MUSIC CLUBS

★ La Factoría

BARS/PUBS | La Factoría, the former Hijos de Borinquen, is hands-down the best cocktail bar in San Juan. Here, artisanal drinks are crafted with the highest-quality ingredients. Many bitters are homemade, as is the ginger beer, which is used in their popular Lavender Mule. Whether it's sweet, spicy, bitter, or something completely out of the box, these drinks will blow your mind. Behind the bar, there is a secret wooden door that leads to Vino Wine Bar, which has a great speakeasy feel. Tasty tapas are available and can be enjoyed in the adjacent room. These bars stay open till sunup, and a DJ spins in the back room on weekends. Salsa is played on Sunday and Monday. There's no sign on the door, so just look for the terra-cotta building at the corner of San Sebastián and San José. ⊠ *148 Calle San Sebastián, Old San Juan* ☏ *787/594–5698.*

The Mezzanine

BARS/PUBS | In the former headquarters of the Nationalist Party, The Mezzanine is a contemporary take on the 1920s speakeasy. The chic space is conducive to sipping a creative cocktail and very refreshing after walking the hills of Old San Juan. Tapas are served all day. The Mezzanine also hosts one of the best happy hours in town (Tuesday–Friday 4–8); enjoy select tapas and cocktails for half off. You can't beat that in San Juan! Their brunch is very popular on weekends. It's typically closed on Monday. ⊠ *St. Germain Bistro & Café, 156 Calle Sol, 2nd fl., Old San Juan* ☏ *787/724–4657.*

CASINOS

All casinos must operate in hotels by law, and most are in San Juan, where the government keeps a close eye on them.

The dress code for larger casinos is on the formal side, and the atmosphere is refined, particularly in the Isla Verde resorts. In addition to slot machines, typical games include blackjack, roulette, craps, Caribbean stud (a five-card poker game), and *pai gow* poker (a combination of American poker and Chinese dominoes). Hotels with casinos have live entertainment most weekends, as well as restaurants and bars. The minimum age to gamble (and to drink) is 18. Casinos set their own hours, which change seasonally but generally run from noon to 4 am, although the casino in the Condado Plaza Hilton is open 24 hours. Other hotels with casinos include the InterContinental San Juan, the Ritz-Carlton San Juan, and the Sheraton Old San Juan.

🛍 Shopping

San Juan has the island's best range of stores (many closed on Sunday) but it isn't a free port, so you won't find bargains on electronics and perfumes. You can, however, find excellent prices on china, crystal, clothing, and jewelry. When shopping for local crafts, you'll find tacky along with treasures; in many cases you can watch the artisans at work. Popular items include *santos* (small carved figures of saints or religious scenes), hand-rolled cigars, handmade *mundillo* lace from Moca, *vejigantes* (colorful masks used during Carnival and local festivals) from Loíza and Ponce, and fancy men's shirts called *guayaberas*.

Old San Juan—especially Calles Fortaleza and Cristo—has T-shirt emporiums, crafts stores, bookshops, art galleries, jewelry boutiques, and even shops that specialize in made-to-order Panama hats. Calle Cristo has factory outlets, including Coach and Dooney & Bourke.

With many stores selling luxury items and designer fashions, the shopping spirit in the San Juan neighborhood of Condado is reminiscent of Miami.

Avenida Ashford, the heart of San Juan's fashion district, has plenty of high-end clothing stores.

🏃 Activities

GOLF

TPC Dorado Beach

GOLF | Three 18-hole regulation courses blend Caribbean luxury and great golf at this iconic property with a storied tradition. Designed by Robert Trent Jones Sr. and renovated by his son in 2011, the famous **East** course lies in seaside seclusion along 3 km (2 miles) of northeasterly shore within the former Rockefeller estate. Two Plantation Courses—the **Sugarcane** (more challenging) and **Pineapple** (easier)—complete the offerings. All three were purchased by the Tournament Players Club (TPC) in 2015. ⊠ *5000 Plantation Dr., Dorado* ☎ *787/262–1010* ⊕ *www.tpc.com* ✉ *East Course $282, Plantation Courses $170* ⚲ *East Course: 18 holes, 7200 yards, par 72; Sugarcane: 18 holes, 7119 yards, par 72; Pineapple: 18 holes, 6196 yards, par 72.*

Santo Domingo, Dominican Republic

Spanish civilization in the New World began in Santo Domingo's 12-block Zona Colonial (Colonial Zone). As you stroll its narrow streets, it's easy to imagine this old city as it was when the likes of Columbus, Cortés, and Ponce de León walked the cobblestones, when pirates sailed in and out of the harbor and when colonists first started building the New World's largest city. Tourist brochures tout that "history comes alive here," a surprisingly truthful statement. However, many tourists bypass the large, sprawling, and noisy city—and it's their loss. Despite such detractions as poverty and sprawl (not to mention a population of some 2 million people) the Dominican

Best Bets 👁

■ **Zona Colonial.** Santo Domingo's Zona Colonial is a UNESCO World Heritage Site and a great place to stroll; a real trip to Old World, it is Spain in the 16th century.

■ **Dining.** Some of the best restaurants in the Dominican Republic can be found in the capital. Take advantage of them if you have any extra time to spend here.

■ **Shopping.** The country's best shopping can be found in Santo Domingo. You can go souvenir shopping right on Calle Conde, a pedestrian street that is the main drag of the Zona Colonial.

Republic's seaside capital has some of the country's best hotels, restaurants, and nightlife, as well as some great casinos. Many of these are right on or near the Malecón and within the historic Zona Colonial area, which is separated from the rest of the city by Parque Independencia. If your ship calls or even embarks here, you'll be treated to a vibrant Latin cultural center unlike any other in the Caribbean.

ESSENTIALS

CURRENCY

The Dominican peso, but you can almost always use U.S. dollars.

TELEPHONE

Country codes are 1 809, 1 829, and 1 849 (depending on the type of phone you are calling). Claro, Orange, Tricom, and Viva are the major mobile providers, using GSM (850, 900, 1800 and 1900 bands).

COMING ASHORE

Santo Domingo has two stellar cruise-ship terminals, and has become a growing port for cruise passengers, despite the sluggish economy.

The **Don Diego Terminal** is on the Ozuma River, facing the Avenida del Puerto, and across the street are steps that lead up to the main pedestrian shopping street of the Zona Colonial, Calle El Conde. A lovely yellow and white building with stained-glass windows and faux gaslights, it has a small cafeteria, and potted palms soften the cordoned-off lines where passengers wait to have their tickets checked and go through immigration. The reception area has telephones, Internet access, and a currency exchange. Just down the dock is an ATM; in front of that is a counter where you can get cold drinks and snacks.

The **Sans Souci Terminal** complex, diagonally across the Ozama River from Don Diego Terminal, on Avenida España, has been operational since 2010, but this long-term redevelopment project is still a work in progress. Its mezzanine level accommodates immigration and customs, duty-free shops, and both Internet and information centers. Like the Port of Don Diego, it has stunning lighting systems that cover the exterior and perimeter areas for greater security and visibility for visitors. When completed, the complex will have finished its marina, and have a full complement of stores, a 122-acre real-estate development, a new sports arena, and more. This major project is aimed at integrating the port area and the Zona Colonial to create an appealing destination for cruisers, yachtsmen, and high-end tourists.

AIRPORT TRANSFERS

If you are embarking in Santo Domingo, you should fly into Las Américas International Airport (SDQ), about 15 miles (24 km) east of downtown. On arrival you will have to pay $10 in cash for a tourist tax. Transportation into the city is usually by taxi; figure on $40 to or from hotels on the Malecón or in the Zona Colonial. You'll be greeted by a melee of hawking taxi drivers and sometimes their English-speaking solicitors (who expect to be tipped, as do the freelance porters who will undoubtedly scoop up your luggage). If you're spending a night or two in Santo Domingo before a cruise, you can arrange a driver through ⊕ *www.dominicanshuttles.com* or possibly through your hotel, so that you'll be met with someone holding a sign with your name. (It's worth the extra $10 or so to avoid the hassle.) If you're going straight to your cruise ship, do consider taking the cruise line's prearranged transfer. When you disembark from your ship, expect long lines at check-in, and be sure to give yourself a full two hours for check-in and security. The government departure tax should be included in your airline ticket.

◉ Sights

History buffs will want to spend a day exploring the many "firsts" of our continent. A horse-and-carriage ride throughout the Zona Colonial costs $25 per hour. A fun horse-and-carriage ride around the Zona costs $25 for an hour; the steeds are no thoroughbreds but they move at a good clip, though any commentary will be in Spanish. You can also negotiate to use them as a taxi, say, down to the Malecón. The drivers usually hang out in front of the Hodelpa Nicolás de Ovando.

Alcázar de Colón

HOUSE | The castle of Don Diego Colón, built in 1517, was the home to generations of the Christopher Columbus family. The Renaissance-style structure, with its balustrade and double row of arches, has strong Moorish, Gothic, and Isabelline influences. The 22 rooms are furnished in a style to which the viceroy of the island would have been accustomed—right down to the dishes and the viceregal shaving mug. The mansion's 40-inch-thick coral-limestone walls make air-conditioning impossible. Bilingual guides are on hand for tours peppered with fascinating anecdotes, like once-upon-a-time weddings. Audio tours (about 25 minutes) are available in English. ⊠ *Plaza de España,*

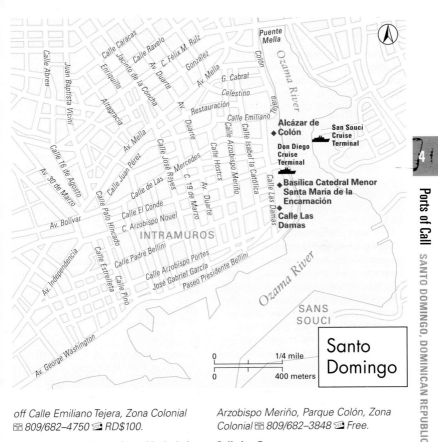

Santo
Domingo

off *Calle Emiliano Tejera, Zona Colonial* ☎ *809/682–4750* ✉ *RD$100.*

Basílica Catedral Menor Santa María de la Encarnación

RELIGIOUS SITE | The coral-limestone facade of the first cathedral in the New World (Catedral Primada de América) towers over the south side of the Parque Colón. Spanish workmen began building the cathedral in 1514, but left to search for gold in Mexico. The church was finally finished in 1540. Its facade is composed of architectural elements from the late Gothic to the lavish Plateresque style. Inside, the high altar is made of hammered silver. A museum houses the cathedral's treasures; it's in the former jail, a yellow building just across the street. Mass times vary, so check before going there the day before. ✉ *Calle*

Arzobispo Meriño, Parque Colón, Zona Colonial ☎ *809/682–3848* ✉ *Free.*

Calle Las Damas

NEIGHBORHOOD | "Ladies Street" was named after the elegant ladies of the court: in the Spanish tradition, they promenaded in the evening. Here you can see a sundial dating from 1753 and the Casa de los Jesuitas, which houses a fine research library for colonial history as well as the **Institute for Hispanic Culture**; admission is free, and it's open weekdays from 8 to 4:30. The boutique Hodelpa Nicolás de Ovando is on this street, across from the French Embassy. If you follow the street going toward the Malecón, you will pass a picturesque alley, fronted by a wrought-iron gate, where there are perfectly maintained colonial structures owned by the Catholic Church. ✉ *Calle Las Damas, Zona Colonial.*

⓵ Beaches

If you are in port for just a day, you'll have a better time if you skip the beach and spend some time in the Zona Colonial and on the Malecón.

Playa Boca Chica

BEACH—SIGHT | FAMILY | You can walk far out into warm, calm, clear waters protected by coral reefs here. On weekends, the strip with the mid-rise resorts is busy, drawing mainly Dominican families and some Europeans. But midweek is better, when the beaches are less crowded. Sadly, on the public beach you will be pestered and hounded by a parade of roving vendors of cheap jewelry, sunglasses, hair braiders, seafood cookers, ice-cream men, and masseuses (who are usually peddling more than a simple beach massage). Young male prostitutes also roam the beach and often hook up with older European and Cuban men. The best section of the public beach is in front of Don Emilio's (the blue hotel), which has a restaurant, bar, decent bathrooms, and parking. Better, go to one of the nicer waterfront restaurants—Boca Marina Restaurant & Lounge, El Pelicano, Neptuno's Club—and skip the public beach altogether. **Amenities:** food and drink; parking; toilets. **Best for:** partiers; sunset; swimming; walking. ✉ *Autopista Las Américas, Boca Chica* ✚ *21 miles (34 km) east of Santo Domingo.*

⓫ Restaurants

Mesón De Bari

$$ | CARIBBEAN | For some 30 years, this popular restaurant, where baseball is invariably on the TV at the bar, has been feeding the local Zoners what their grandmothers used to make. It's still a hangout for artists, baseball players, politicians, businessmen, tourists, and even unaccompanied gringas, who feel comfortable here. **Known for:** authentic Dominican specialties; old-timey local ambience; stewed, sweet orange peels.

⑤ *Average main: $16* ✉ *Calle Hostos 302, corner of Calle Salomé Ureña, Zona Colonial* ☎ *809/687–4091.*

Pat'e Palo European Brasserie

$$$ | INTERNATIONAL | Ideally located on Plaza de España across from the Alcázar de Colón, this restaurant has a good claim to being the first tavern in the New World (the building itself is 500 years old) and capitalizes on its historic heritage. The terrace makes is perfect for watching free cultural performances across from the plaza while dining alfresco from the contemporary, gastro-fusion menu. **Known for:** the salmon purple passion; shrimp in coconut curry sauce; goat osso buco with pumpkin risotto. ⑤ *Average main: $26* ✉ *Calle Atarazana 25, Plaza de España, Zona Colonial* ☎ *809/687–8089* ⊕ *www.patepalo.com.*

🛏 Hotels

If you are embarking in Santo Domingo, it makes sense to arrive the day before your cruise, if only to make sure you don't have any issues with flights. Luckily, the city offers a wide range of reasonably priced hotels at all levels, some in the historic colonial zone.

★ Hodelpa Nicolás de Ovando

$ | HOTEL | This historic boutique hotel now owned by Hodelpa Hotels was sculpted from the residence of the first governor of the Americas, and it just might be the best thing to happen in the Zona Colonial since Diego Columbus's palace was finished in 1517. **Pros:** lavish breakfast buffet; beautifully restored historic section; a safe haven with tight security. **Cons:** breakfast is no longer included in rates; some rooms could be larger; no happy hour scene. ⑤ *Rooms from: $138* ✉ *Calle Las Damas, Zona Colonial* ✚ *Across the street from the French Embassy* ☎ *809/685–9955, 800/763–4835, 809/685–9955 reservations* ⊕ *www.hodelpa.com* ⇄ *101 rooms* ⫟❍⫟ *No meals.*

Renaissance Santo Domingo Jaragua Hotel & Casino

$ | **HOTEL** | It's remarkable what a major renovation can do to revive an iconic (albeit tired) landmark; the newly transformed Jaragua is jaw-dropping. **Pros:** security is tight and solo female travelers feel safe; large, well-appointed fitness center and spa; room service is surprisingly good. **Cons:** can be a bit noisy at times, with conventions and large meetings; service in restaurants can be slow, especially with a language barrier; more of a business hotel than a leisure hotel. $ *Rooms from: $162 ⊠ Av. George Washington 367, Gazcue ☎ 809/221–2222 ⊕ www.marriott.com ⤻ 300 rooms ⦿ No meals.*

▼ Nightlife

Santo Domingo's nightlife is vast and ever changing. Check with the concierges and hip capitaleños. Clubs and bars must close at midnight during the week, and at 2 am on Friday and Saturday nights. There are some exceptions to the latter, primarily those clubs and casinos in hotels. Sadly, the curfew has put some clubs out of business, but it has cut down on the crime and late-night noise, particularly in the Zona Colonial. Some clubs are now pushing the envelope and staying open until 3, but they do get in trouble with authorities when caught, and you probably don't want to be there then.

⬤ Shopping

Exquisitely hand-wrapped cigars continue to be the hottest commodity coming out of the D.R. Only reputable cigar shops sell the real thing. Dominican rum and coffee are also good buys. Mamajuana, an herbal liqueur, is said to be the Dominican answer to Viagra. Look also for the delicate, faceless ceramic figurines that symbolize Dominican culture. Though locally crafted products are often affordable, expect to pay for designer jewelry made of amber and larimar, an indigenous semiprecious stone the color of the Caribbean. Amber, a fossilization of resin from a prehistoric pine tree, often encasing ancient animal and plant life, from leaves to spiders to tiny lizards, is mined extensively. (Beware of fakes, which are especially prevalent in street stalls.)

Acropolis Mall, between Avenida Winston Churchill and Calle Rafael Augusto Sánchez, has become a favorite shopping arena for the young and/or hip capitaleños. Stores like Zara and Mango (both from Spain) have today's look without breaking your budget.

One of the main shopping streets in the Zona is **Calle El Conde,** a pedestrian thoroughfare. With the advent of so many restorations, the dull and dusty stores with dated merchandise are giving way to some hip new shops. However, many of the offerings, including local designer shops, are still of a caliber and cost that the Dominicans can afford. Some of the best shops are on **Calle Duarte,** north of the Zona Colonial, between Calle Mella and Avenida Las Américas. **El Mercado Modelo,** a covered market, borders Calle Mella in the Zona Colonial; vendors here sell a dizzying selection of Dominican crafts.

Piantini is a swanky residential neighborhood that has an increasing number of fashionable shops and clothing boutiques, often housed in contemporary shopping malls. Its borders run from Avenida Winston Churchill to Avenida Lope de Vega and from Calle José Amado Soler to Avenida 27 de Febrero.

Santo Tomás de Castilla, Guatemala

Guatemala's short Caribbean shoreline doesn't generate the buzz of those of neighboring Belize and Mexico. The coast weighs in at a scant 74 miles (123 km), and this mostly highland country wears its indigenous culture on its sleeve and has historically looked inland rather than to the sea. You'll be drawn inland, too, with a variety of shore excursions—this is the land of the Maya, after all. But there's plenty to keep you occupied here in the lowlands. Tourist brochures tout the Caribbean coast as "the Other Guatemala." The predominantly indigenous and Spanish cultures of the highlands give way to an Afro-Caribbean tradition that listens more closely to the rhythms of far-off Jamaica rather than taking its cue from Guatemala City. Think of it as mixing a little reggae with your salsa.

ESSENTIALS

CURRENCY

The Guatemalan quetzal. Make sure you get money from the ATM in the cruise terminal in Santo Tomás de Castilla. Outside the terminal, few businesses accept U.S. dollars. Honduras's currency is the lempira for shore excursions to Copán, but U.S. dollars will suffice on an organized trip through your cruise line.

TELEPHONE

Guatemalan phone numbers have eight digits. There are no city or area codes. Simply dial the number for any in-country call. Most towns have offices of Telgua, the national telephone company, where you can place both national and international calls. Avoid the ubiquitous public phones with signs promising "Free calls to the USA." The number back home being called gets socked with a hefty bill.

COMING ASHORE

Cruise ships dock at the modern, spacious Terminal de Cruceros, where you'll find a bank, a post office, money exchange, telephones, Internet access, a lively craft market, and an office of INGUAT, Guatemala's national tourist office. A marimba band serenades you with its clinking xylophone-like music; a Caribbean ensemble dances for you (and may even pull you in to take part).

Best Bets ⊙

■ **Quiriguá.** If you want to see Maya ruins but don't want to spend an entire day on the bus, nearby Quiriguá can be impressive.

■ **Copán.** In neighboring Honduras, this Maya site is a worthwhile day trip from Santo Tomás.

■ **Riding on the Río Dulce.** A ride on this river is one of Guatemala's most beautiful boat trips.

Taxis take you to various destinations in the area by land or sea. Plan on paying $3 to Santo Tomás de Castilla proper, and $5 to Puerto Barrios. Boats transport cruise visitors to Livingston, charging about $6 for the 20-minute trip. The Amatique Bay Resort provides water taxis from port to resort of $10 per person; by land, taxis charge $35 per head.

⊙ Sights

SANTO TOMÁS DE CASTILLA

Belgian immigrants settled Santo Tomás in the 19th century, but little remains of their heritage today, save for the preponderance of French and Flemish names in the local cemetery. The city has experienced a small renaissance as the country's most important port, receiving growing numbers of cruise and cargo ships, and serving as the headquarters of the Guatemalan navy. Most visitors move on, however.

PUERTO BARRIOS

3 miles (5 km) north of Santo Tomás de Castilla.

Puerto Barrios maintains the atmosphere of an old banana town—humid and a tad down at the heels, perhaps longing for better days. Santo Tomás has replaced it as the country's largest port, and you'll likely zip through the Caribbean coast's

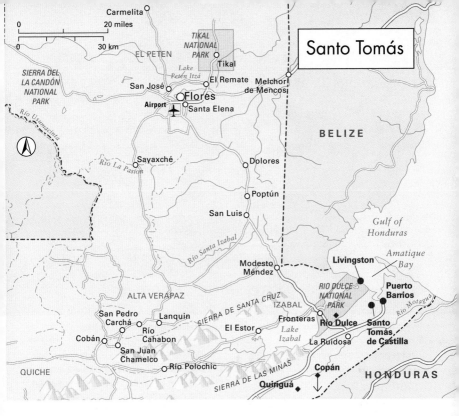

biggest city on your way to somewhere else, but the cathedral and municipal market are worth a look if you find yourself here. Water taxis depart from the municipal docks for Livingston, across the bay, where you start your trip up the Río Dulce.

"Bahía de Amatique" refers to the large bay that washes the Caribbean coast of Guatemala and southern Belize just north of Puerto Barrios, but for most travelers the name is inexorably linked with the **Amatique Bay Resort and Marina,** the region's only five-star hotel. The 61-room resort opens itself up for day visitors, and many cruise passengers stop by for a drink, a meal, or an entire day of swimming, watersliding, kayaking, horseback riding, or bicycling. ⊠ *6 miles (10 km) north of Santo Tomás; 14 Calle Final, Finca Pichilingo, Puerto Barrios* ☎ *7931–0000.*

LIVINGSTON

15 miles (25 km) by water northwest of Santo Tomás.

Visitors compare Livingston with Puerto Barrios across the bay, and the former wins hands down, for its sultry, seductive Caribbean flavor. Wooden houses, some on stilts, congregate in this old fishing town—once an important railroad hub, but today inaccessible by land from the outside world. Livingston proudly trumpets its Garífuna heritage. This culture is descended from the intermarriage of African slaves with Caribbean indigenous people, and it's unique to Central America's eastern coast. Music and dance traditions and a Caribbean-accented English remain, even if old-timers lament

Much of Río Dulce is protected in a national park, which includes Guatamala's largest lake.

creeping outside influences, namely Spanish rap and reggae.

RÍO DULCE
30 miles (48 km) southwest of Santo Tomás.

The natural crown jewel of this region is the 13,000-hectare (32,000-acre) national park that protects the river leading inland from Livingston to Lago de Izabal, Guatemala's largest lake. Pelicans, herons, egrets, and terns nest and fly along the Río Dulce, which cuts through a heavily forested limestone canyon. Excursions often approach the park by land, but we recommend making the trip upriver from Livingston to immerse yourself in the entire "Indiana Jones" experience. Some cruise ships offer day trips to Hacienda Tijax for their activities; these trips usually include lunch.

Castillo de San Felipe de Lara
MILITARY SITE | Once an important Maya trade route, the Río Dulce later became the route over which the conquistadores sent the gold and silver they plundered back to Spain. All this wealth attracted Dutch and English pirates, who attacked both the ships and the warehouses on shore. Spanish colonists constructed this fortress in 1595 to guard the inland waterway from pirate incursions. A 1999 earthquake in this region destroyed the river pier and damaged portions of the fort. If you wish to visit, rather than simply see the structure from the water, you'll need to approach the park overland (not upriver)—all best accomplished on an organized shore excursion. ⊠ *Southwest of Fronteras, Río Dulce* ☎ *7947–0661* 🖃 *$3 or Q25.*

QUIRIGUÁ
60 miles (96 km) southwest of Puerto Barrios.

Quiriguá Archaeological Park and Ruins
ARCHAEOLOGICAL SITE | Quiriguá, a Maya city that dates from the Classic period, is famous for the amazingly well-preserved stelae, or carved pillars—the largest yet discovered, they dwarf those of Copán, Honduras, some 50 km (30 miles) south. The stelae depict Quiriguá's

ruling dynasty, especially the powerful Cauac Chan (Jade Sky), whose visage appears on nine of the structures circling the Great Plaza. Stela E, the largest of these, towers 10 meters (33 feet) high and weighs 65 tons. Several monuments, covered with interesting zoomorphic figures, still stand. The most interesting of these depicts Cauac Chan's conquest of Copán and the subsequent beheading of its then-ruler, 18 Rabbit. The remains of an acropolis and other structures have been partially restored. The ruins are surrounded by a strand of rain forest—an untouched wilderness in the heart of banana country. A small museum here gives insight into Quiriguá's history. ✉ *Los Amates* ✛ *54 miles (90 km) southwest of Santo Tomás de Castilla* ✆ *$4 or Q30.*

COPÁN
122 miles (203 km) southeast of Santo Tomás.

Although Copán is not in Guatemala, it's very close to Guatemala's border with Honduras.

Copán
ARCHAEOLOGICAL SITE | Just across the border in Honduras lie the famed ruins of Copán, the center of a kingdom that rose to prominence in the Classic period (5th to 9th centuries AD).

As you stroll past towering cieba trees on your way in from the gate, you'll find the Great Plaza to your left. The ornate stelae standing around the plaza were monuments erected to glorify rulers. The most impressive (located in the middle of the plaza) depict King 18 Rabbit.

The city's most important ball court lies south of the Great Plaza. The game was more spiritual than sportslike in nature: the losers—or the winners in some cases—were killed as a sacrifice to Maya gods.

Near the ball court lies the Hieroglyphic Stairway, containing the largest single collection of hieroglyphs in the world. The 63 steps immortalize the battles won by Copán's kings, especially those of the much revered King Smoke Jaguar.

Below the Acropolis here wind tunnels leading to some of the most fascinating discoveries at Copán. Underneath Structure 16 are the near-perfect remains of an older structure, called the Rosalila Temple, dating from AD 571. Uncovered in 1989, the Rosalila was notable in part because of the paint remains on its surface—rose and lilac—for which it was named. Another tunnel called Los Jaguares takes you past tombs, a system of aqueducts, and even an ancient bathroom.

East of the main entrance to Copán, the marvelous Museo de Escultura Maya provides a closer look at the best of Maya artistry. ✉ *1 km (½ mile) east of Copán Ruinas, Copán Ruinas* ☏ *2651–4018* ✆ *Ruins $15 or L360, museum $7 or L170, tunnels $15 or L360.*

🛍 Shopping

The rest of Guatemala overflows with indigenous crafts and art, but the famous market towns of the highlands are nowhere to be found in Caribbean region. Quite honestly, your best bet for shopping is the Terminal de Cruceros at Santo Tomás de Castilla, and you'll have plenty of opportunity to buy before you board your ship. What you'll find here comes from Guatemala's highlands—the coast does not have a strong artisan tradition—with a good selection of fabrics, weavings, woodwork, and basketry.

🏃 Activities

PUERTO BARRIOS
Amatique Bay Resort & Marina
BEACHES | The only real beach in the region lies within the confines of the Amatique Bay Resort & Marina, which is the only place here that has a resort

atmosphere to it. Day visitors partake in swimming, waterslides, and kayaking. The resort's launch will bring you over from the cruise-ship terminal in Santo Tomás de Castilla. **Amenities:** food and drink; showers; toilets. **Best for:** swimming; walking. ⊠ *14 Calle Final, Puerto Barrios ⊹ 10 km (6 miles) north of Santo Tomás de Castilla* ☎ *7931–0000* ⊕ *www. amatiquebay.net.*

LIVINGSTON

Hacienda Tijax

KAYAKING | The unusual-looking name of this eco-lodge is pronounced *tee-HAHSH*. It lies inland, near the point where the Río Dulce meets the vast Lake Izabal. The staff oversee kayaking, hiking, horseback riding, and zip-lining for day visitors. ⊠ *Río Dulce ⊹ Northeast of Fronteras, near bridge that crosses over Río Dulce* ☎ *7930–5505* ⊕ *www.tijax.com.*

St. Barthélemy (Gustavia)

Hilly St. Barthélemy, popularly known as St. Barth (or St. Barts) is just 8 square miles (21 square km), but the island has at least 20 good beaches. What draws visitors is its sophisticated but unstudied approach to relaxation: the finest food, excellent wine, high-end shopping, and lack of large-scale commercial development. A favorite among upscale cruise-ship passengers, who also appreciate the shopping opportunities and fine dining, St. Barth isn't really equipped for megaship visits, which is why most ships calling here are from smaller premium lines. This is one place where you don't need to take the ship's shore excursions to have a good time. Just hail a cab or rent a car and go to one of the many wonderful beaches, where you will find some of the best lunchtime restaurants, or wander around Gustavia, shopping and eating. It's the best way to relax on this most relaxing of islands.

Best Bets

- **Soaking up the Atmosphere.** It's the French Riviera transported to the Caribbean.

- **Beautiful Beaches.** Pick any of the lovely, uncrowded beaches.

- **French Food.** St. Barth has some of the best restaurants in the Caribbean.

- **Shopping.** There is no better fashion shopping in the Caribbean, especially if you are young and slim.

ESSENTIALS

CURRENCY

The euro. However, U.S. dollars are accepted in almost all shops and in many restaurants.

TELEPHONE

The country code is 590. Digicel, Orange, CHIPPIE, and Dauphin Telecom are the major mobile providers, using GSM (900 and 1800 bands).

COMING ASHORE

Even medium-size ships must anchor in Gustavia Harbor and bring passengers ashore on tenders. The tiny harbor area is right in Gustavia, which is easily explored on foot. Shell Beach is accessible by a 10-minute walk, so you can take a swim during your explorations. Taxis, which meet all cruise ships, can be expensive. Technically, there's a flat rate for rides up to five minutes long and an additional amount for every three minutes thereafter. In reality, however, cabbies usually name a fixed rate—and will not budge. Fares are 50% higher on Sunday and holidays. St. Barth is one port where it's really worth it to arrange a car or moped rental for a full-day exploration of the island, including the island's out-of-the-way beaches. But be aware that during high season there is often a three-day

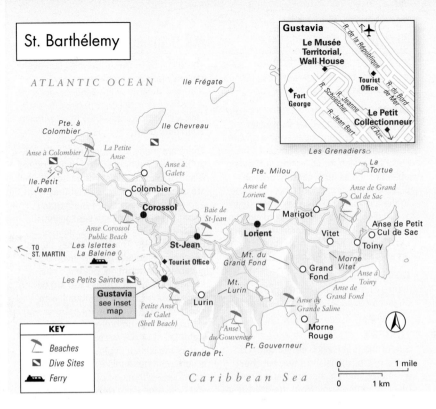

St. Barthélemy

ATLANTIC OCEAN

Ile Frégate

Pte. à Colombier

Ile Chevreau

Anse à Colombier

La Petite Anse

Ile. Petit Jean

Anse à Galets

Pte. Milou

La Tortue

Colombier

Anse de Lorient

Anse de Grand Cul de Sac

Corossol

Baie de St-Jean

Marigot

Anse Corossol Public Beach

Lorient

Vitet

Anse de Petit Cul de Sac

Les Islettes
La Baleine

St-Jean

Toiny

TO ST. MARTIN

Tourist Office

Mt. du Grand Fond

Morne Vitet

Les Petits Saintes

Grand Fond

Anse à Toiny

Gustavia
see inset map

Mt. Lurin

Anse de Grand Fond

Petite Anse de Galet (Shell Beach)

Lurin

Anse de Grande Saline

Anse du Gouverneur

Morne Rouge

Grande Pt.

Pt. Gouverneur

Caribbean Sea

Les Grenadiers

Gustavia

Le Musée Territorial, Wall House

Tourist Office

Fort George

Le Petit Collectionneur

KEY

Beaches

Dive Sites

Ferry

0 — 1 mile

0 — 1 km

minimum, so this may not be possible except through your ship (and then you'll pay premium rates indeed). Most car-rental firms operate at the airport; however, renting on your own is usually cheaper than what you'll get if you go with one of the ship's car rentals (you may be able to find a car for $55 per day).

◉ Sights

With practice, negotiating St. Barth's narrow, steep roads soon becomes fun. Infrastructure upgrades and small, responsive rental cars have improved driving. Free maps are everywhere, and roads are smooth and well marked. The tourist office has annotated maps with walking tours that highlight sights of interest.

GUSTAVIA

You can easily explore all of Gustavia during a two-hour stroll. Some shops close from noon to 3 or 4—so plan lunch accordingly—and then stay open past 7 in the evening. Parking in Gustavia is a challenge, especially during vacation times. A good spot to park is rue de la République, alongside the catamarans, yachts, and sailboats.

★ Le Musée Territorial, Wall House

MUSEUM | FAMILY | On the far side of the harbor known as La Pointe, the charming Municipal Museum on the first floor of the restored Wall House has watercolors, portraits, photographs, traditional costumes, and historic documents detailing the island's history over many hundreds of years, as well as displays of the island's flowers, plants, and marine life. There are also changing contemporary art exhibitions. It's a must-stop on your St. Barth visit, and it's free. ✉ *La Pointe, Gustavia* ☎ *0590/29–71–55* ⊕ *visitersaint-barthelemy.com/musee-territorial-de-gustavia* ✉ *Free.*

Le Petit Collectionneur

MUSEUM | Encouraged by family and friends, André Berry opened this private museum in his home to showcase his lifelong passion for collecting fascinating objects such as 18th-century English pipes and the first phonograph to come to the island. Today there are more than 1,000 pieces here, ranging from cannon balls to coins that are hundreds of years old. Berry will happily show you his treasures. ✉ *La Pointe, Gustavia* ✉ *€2.*

COROSSOL

Traces of the island's French provincial origins are evident in this two-street fishing village with a little rocky beach.

LORIENT

Site of the first French settlement, Lorient is one of the island's two parishes; a restored church, a school, and a post office mark the spot. Note the gaily decorated graves in the cemetery.

ST-JEAN

There is a monument at the crest of the hill that divides St-Jean from Gustavia. Called *The Arawak,* it symbolizes the soul of St. Barth. A warrior, one of the earliest inhabitants of the area, holds a lance in his right hand and stands on a rock shaped like the island; in his left hand he holds a conch shell, which sounds the cry of nature; perched beside him are a pelican (which symbolizes the air and survival by fishing) and an iguana (which represents the earth). The half-mile-long crescent of sand at St-Jean is the island's favorite beach. A popular activity is watching and photographing the hair-raising airplane landings (but it is extremely dangerous to stand at the beach end of the runway). Some of the best shopping on the island is here, as are several restaurants.

☺ Beaches

There is a beach in St. Barth to suit every taste. Wild surf, complete privacy in nature, a dreamy white-sand strand, and a spot at a chic beach club close to shopping and restaurants—they're all within a 20-minute drive.

There are many *anses* (coves) and nearly 20 *plages* (beaches) scattered around the island, each with a distinct personality; all are open to the public, even if they front a tony resort. Because of the number of beaches, even in high season you can find a nearly empty one, despite St. Barth's tiny size. That's not to say that all beaches are equally good or even equally suitable for swimming, but each has something to offer. Unless you are having lunch at a beachfront restaurant with lounging areas set aside for patrons, you should bring an umbrella, beach mat, and water (all of which are easily obtainable across the island). Topless sunbathing is common, but nudism is supposedly forbidden—although both Grande Saline and Gouverneur are de facto nude beaches, albeit less than in the past. Shade is scarce.

Anse de Grand Cul de Sac

BEACH—SIGHT | FAMILY | The shallow, reef-protected beach is nice for small children, fly-fishermen, kayakers, and windsurfers—and for the amusing frigate birds that dive-bomb the water fishing for their lunch. You needn't do your own fishing; you can have a wonderful lunch at one of the excellent restaurants nearby and use their lounge chairs for the afternoon. You may see some turtles in the shallow water. After storms the water may be a bit murky. **Amenities:** food and drink; parking (no fee); toilets; water sports. **Best for:** swimming; walking. ✉ *Grand Cul de Sac.*

★ Anse de Grande Saline

BEACH—SIGHT | With its peaceful seclusion and sandy ocean bottom, this is just about everyone's favorite beach and is great for swimming, too. Without any major development, it's an ideal Caribbean strand, though there can be a bit of wind at times. In spite of the prohibition, young and old alike go nude. The beach is a 10-minute walk up a rocky dune trail, so wear sneakers or water shoes, and bring a blanket, umbrella, and beach towels. There are several good lunch restaurants near the parking area, but the beach itself is just sand, sea, and sky. The big salt ponds here are no longer in use, and the place looks a little desolate on approach, but don't despair. **Amenities:** parking (no fee). **Best for:** nudists; swimming; walking. ⊠ *Grande Saline.*

Baie de St-Jean

BEACH—SIGHT | FAMILY | Like a mini Côte d'Azur—beachside bistros, terrific shopping, bungalow hotels, bronzed bodies, windsurfing, and day-trippers who tend to arrive on *big* yachts—the reef-protected strip is divided by the Eden Rock promontory. Except when the hotels are filled, you can rent chaises and umbrellas at the Pearl Beach restaurant or Eden Rock (reopened 2019), where you can lounge for hours over lunch. **Amenities:** food and drink; toilets. **Best for:** partiers; walking. ⊠ *St-Jean.*

🍽 Restaurants

A service charge is always added by law, but you should leave the server 5% to 10% extra in cash. It is generally advisable to charge restaurant meals to a credit card, as the issuer will offer a better exchange rate than the restaurant.

Le Repaire

$$ | BRASSERIE | FAMILY | Overlooking the harbor, this friendly classic French brasserie is busy from its 7 am opening to its late-night closing. The flexible hours are great if you arrive on the island midafternoon and need a substantial snack. **Known for:** St. Barth's only early breakfast restaurant; reliable any time of day; well-prepared, simple food. ⑤ *Average*

main: €19 ⊠ *Rue de la République, Gustavia* ☎ 0590/27–72–48 ⊙ *Closed Sun.*

L'Isoletta

$$$ | PIZZA | This casual Roman-style pizzeria run by the popular L'Isola restaurant is a lively, chic lounge-style gastropub serving delicious thin-crust pizzas by the slice or the meter. There are even dessert pizzas, and excellent tiramisu. **Known for:** meter-long pizzas; lively atmosphere; wait times at peak hours. ⑤ *Average main: €30 ⊠ Rue du Roi Oscar II, Gustavia* ☎ 0590/52–02–02.

🛍 Shopping

St. Barth is a duty-free port, and its sophisticated visitors find shopping in its 200-plus boutiques a delight, especially for beachwear, accessories, jewelry, and casual wear. It's no overstatement to say that shopping for fashionable clothing, jewels, and designer accessories is better in St. Barth than anywhere else in the Caribbean. New shops open all the time, so there's always something to discover. Some stores close from noon to 3, but they are open until 7 pm. Many are closed on Sunday. A popular afternoon pastime is strolling the two major shopping areas in Gustavia and St-Jean. While high fashion is as pricey here as everywhere, French brands sell for up to 30% less than in the U.S.

In Gustavia, boutiques pack the three major shopping streets. Quai de la République, which is right on the harbor, rivals New York's Madison Avenue or Paris's avenue Montaigne for high-end designer retail, including shops for **Louis Vuitton, Bulgari, Cartier, Chopard, Erès,** and **Hermès.** These shops often carry items that are not available in the United States. The elegant **Carré d'Or plaza** and the adjacent **Coeur Vendome** are great fun to explore. Shops are also clustered in **La Savane Commercial Center** (across from the airport), **La Villa Créole** (in St-Jean), and **Espace Neptune** (on the road to Lorient). It's worth working your way from one end to the other at these shopping complexes—just to see or, perhaps, be seen. Boutiques in all three areas carry the latest in French and Italian sportswear, charming children's togs, and some haute couture. Bargains may be tough to come by, but you might be able to snag that Birkin that has a long waiting list stateside, and in any case, you'll have a lot of fun hunting around.

For locally made art and handicrafts, the tourist office can provide information and arrange visits to studios of island artists, including Christian Bretoneiche, Robert Danet, Nathalie Daniel, Patricia Guyot, Rose Lemen, Aline de Lurin, and Marion Vinot. Gustavia, La Villa Créole, and the larger hotels have a few good galleries–craft boutiques.

🏃 Activities

BOATING AND SAILING

St. Barth is a popular yachting and sailing center, thanks to its location midway between Antigua and St. Thomas.

Gustavia's harbor, 13 to 16 feet deep, has mooring and docking facilities for 40 yachts. There are also good anchorages at Public, Corossol, and Colombier. You can charter sailing and motorboats in Gustavia Harbor for as little as a half day, staffed or bareboat. Ask at the Gustavia tourist office or your hotel for a list of recommended charter companies.

Jicky Marine Service

BOATING | This company offers private full-day outings on motorboats, Zodiacs, and 42- or 46-foot catamarans to the uninhabited Île Fourchue for swimming, snorkeling, cocktails, or lunch, as well as scheduled cruises including weekly half- and full-day group cruises and twice-weekly group sunset catamaran cruises. Private fishing charters are also offered, as is private transport from St. Martin. Skippered motorboat rentals run about €1,400 per day. A one-hour

group Jet Ski tour of the island is also offered, as are private tours. ✉ 26 rue Jeanne D'Arc, Gustavia ☎ 0590/27–70–34 ⊕ www.jickymarine.com.

DIVING AND SNORKELING

Several dive shops arrange scuba excursions. Depending on weather conditions, you may dive at **Pain de Sucre, Coco Island,** or toward nearby **Saba.** There's also an underwater shipwreck, plus sharks, rays, sea tortoises, coral, and the usual varieties of colorful fish. The waters on the island's leeward side are the calmest. For the uncertified, there's a shallow reef right off the beach at Anse de Cayes, which you can explore with mask and fins, and a hike down to the beach at Corossol brings you to a very popular snorkeling spot.

Plongée Caraïbes

DIVING/SNORKELING | FAMILY | This company is recommended for its up-to-the-minute equipment, dive boat, and scuba discovery program. They offer nitrox diving and certification, and they also run two-hour group snorkeling trips on the Blue Cat Catamaran (€60 per person), or you can enjoy a private charter from €690. ✉ Quai de la République, Gustavia ☎ 0590/27–55–94 ⊕ www.plongee-caraibes.com.

St. Croix (Frederiksted)

St. Croix is the largest of the three U.S. Virgin Islands (USVI) that form the northern hook of the Lesser Antilles; it's 40 miles (64 km) south of its sister islands, St. Thomas and St. John. Christopher Columbus landed here in 1493, skirmishing briefly with the native Carib Indians. Since then, the USVI have played a colorful, if painful, role as pawns in the game of European colonialism. Theirs is a history of pirates and privateers, sugar plantations, slave trading, and slave revolt and liberation. Through it all, Denmark had staying power. From the 17th to the 19th century, Danes oversaw a plantation slave economy that produced molasses, rum, cotton, and tobacco. Many of the stones you tread on in the streets were once used as ballast on sailing ships, and the yellow fort of Christiansted is a reminder of the value once placed on this island treasure. Never a major cruise destination, it is still a stop for several ships each year.

ESSENTIALS
CURRENCY
The U.S. dollar.

TELEPHONE
Calling to or from the U.S. Virgin Islands works the same as any domestic call; dial 1 and the area code 340. Most U.S. cell phone plans include the Virgin Islands for no additional cost. The major mobile phone providers are AT&T, Choice Wireless, Sprint, and T-Mobile US, using GSM (850 and 1900 bands).

COMING ASHORE
All cruise ships dock in Frederiksted, on the island's West End. You'll find an information center at the pier, and the town is easy to explore on foot. Beaches are nearby. The only difficulty is that you are far from the island's main town, Christiansted. Some cruise lines offer bus transportation there; otherwise, you are probably better off renting a car to explore the island, since both car-rental rates and gasoline prices are reasonable—just remember to drive on the left.

Taxis of all shapes and sizes are available at the cruise-ship pier and at various shopping and resort areas. Remember, too, that you can hail a taxi that's already occupied. Drivers take multiple fares and sometimes even trade passengers at midpoints. Taxis don't have meters, but there is a list of official per-person rates for most trips (available at the visitor centers or from drivers); still, agree on a fare before you start. A taxi to Christiansted will cost about $25 for two people for transportation only; an island tour

Best Bets ⊙

■ **Buck Island.** The snorkeling trail here is fun, but go by catamaran.

■ **Christiansted.** The best shopping on the island, as well as interesting historical sights.

■ **Cruzan Rum Distillery.** This West End rum distillery gives you a tour and samples.

■ **Kayaking.** The Salt River, with few currents, is a great place to take a guided kayak trip.

■ **West End Beaches.** The island's best beaches are on the West End, just a short hop from the cruise pier.

including Christiansted will cost $110 for four people.

⊙ Sights

CHRISTIANSTED
In the 1700s and 1800s Christiansted was a trading center for sugar, rum, and molasses. Today law offices, tourist shops, and restaurants occupy many of the same buildings, which start at the harbor and go up the gently sloped hillsides. Your best bet to see the historic sights in this Danish-style town is in the morning, when it's still cool. Break for lunch at an open-air restaurant before spending as much time as you like exploring the shopping opportunities. You can't get lost, since all streets lead back downhill to the water.

★ Fort Christiansvaern
HISTORIC SITE | FAMILY | The large yellow fortress dominates the waterfront. Because it's so easy to spot, it makes a good place to begin a walking tour. In 1749 the Danish built the fort to protect the harbor, but the structure was repeatedly damaged by hurricane-force winds and had to be partially rebuilt in 1771. It's

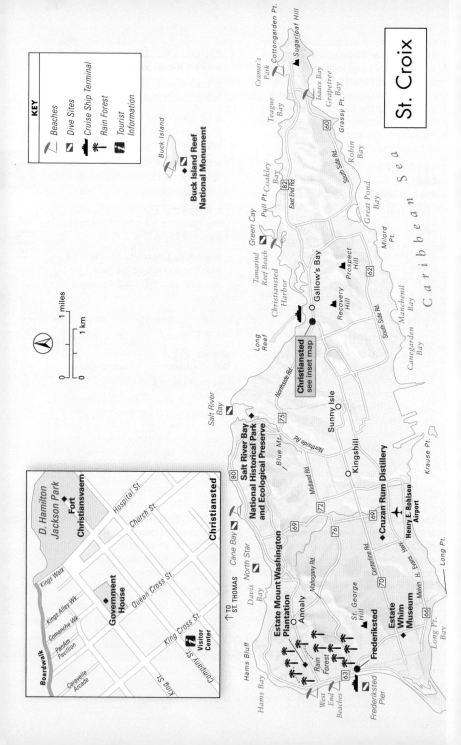

St. Croix

KEY

⟋	Beaches
🤿	Dive Sites
⚓	Cruise Ship Terminal
✳	Rain Forest
ℹ	Tourist Information

Buck Island

◆ **Buck Island Reef National Monument**

Christiansted

Boardwalk

D. Hamilton Jackson Park

Fort Christiansvaern

Hospital St.

Church St.

Kings Walk

Kings Alley Wk.

Comanche Wk.

PanAm Pavilion

Caravelle Arcade

◆ **Government House**

Queen Cross St.

King Cross St.

ℹ **Visitor Center**

Company St.

King St.

↑ TO ST. THOMAS

0 ——— 1 miles

0 ——— 1 km

N

Salt River Bay

◆ **Salt River Bay National Historical Park and Ecological Preserve**

Cane Bay

North Star

Davis Bay

Hams Bluff

Hams Bay

West End Beaches

Estate Mount Washington Plantation

Annaly

Rain Forest

Frederiksted

Frederiksted Pier

63

Blue Mt.

Northside Rd.

80

75

Mahogany Rd.

69

St. George Hill

Estate Whim Museum

70

Centerline Rd.

Melvin H. Evans Hwy.

66

Long Pt. Bay

Long Pt.

Krause Pt.

Midland Rd.

Kingshill

72

76

69

◆ **Cruzan Rum Distillery**

✈ **Henry E. Rohlsen Airport**

Sunny Isle

Christiansted see inset map

Long Reef

Christiansted Harbor

⚓

Tamarind Reef Beach

Green Cay

Pull Pt.

Coakley Bay

82

East End Rd.

Gallow's Bay

◆

Recovery Hill ▲

Prospect Hill ▲

62

South Side Rd.

Robin Bay

Great Pond Bay

Milord Pt.

Manchenil Bay

Canegarden Bay

South Side Rd.

Cramer's Park

Cottongarden Pt.

Sugarloaf Hill ▲

Isaacs Bay

Grapetree Bay

Grassy Pt. Bay

60

Teague Bay

Caribbean Sea

now a national historic site, the best pre-served of the few remaining Danish-built forts in the Virgin Islands. The park's visitor center is here. Rangers are on hand to answer questions. ■ TIP→ **Your paid admission also includes the Steeple Building.** ☒ *Hospital St., Christiansted* ☎ *340/773–1460* ⊕ *www.nps.gov/chri* ☜ *$7.*

Government House

HISTORIC SITE | One of the town's most elegant structures was built as a home for a Danish merchant in 1747. Today it houses offices and serves as the residence of the governor of the Virgin Islands. A sweeping staircase leads to a second-story ballroom, still used for official government functions. Out front, the traditional red guard booth with its pointed top is a popular photo op. ☒ *105 King St., Christiansted* ☎ *340/773–1404.*

EAST END

★ Buck Island Reef National Monument

BEACH—SIGHT | Buck Island has pristine beaches that are just right for sunbath-ing, but there's also some shade for those who don't want to fry. The snorke-ling trail set in the reef allows close-up study of coral formations and tropical fish. Overly warm seawater tempera-tures have led to a condition called coral bleaching that has killed some of the coral. The reefs are starting to recover, but how long it will take is anyone's guess. There's an easy hiking trail to the island's highest point, where you are rewarded for your efforts by spectacular views of St. John. Charter-boat trips leave daily from the Christiansted waterfront or from Green Cay Marina, about 2 miles (3 km) east of Christiansted. Check with your hotel for recommendations. ☒ *Off North Shore of St. Croix* ☎ *340/773–1460* ⊕ *www.nps.gov/buis.*

MID ISLAND

★ Cruzan Rum Distillery

STORE/MALL | A tour of this distillery, established in 1760, culminates in a rum tasting, all of which are sold here at good prices—including more than a dozen fla-vored rums you'll find in popular St. Croix cocktails like the Cruzan Confusion. The distillery is also the best place to pick up a bottle or two of Cruzan's premium single-barrel and Estate Diamond rums. It's worth a stop to look at the charm-ing old buildings and learn about the distillation process, even if you're not a rum connoisseur. ☒ *3A Estate Diamond, Frederiksted* ☎ *340/692–2280* ⊕ *www. cruzanrum.com* ☜ *$8.*

Estate Whim Museum

HISTORIC SITE | FAMILY | The restored estate, with a windmill, cookhouse, and other buildings, gives a sense of what life was like on St. Croix's sugar plantations in the 1800s. The oval-shape greathouse has high ceilings and antique furniture and utensils. Notice its fresh, airy atmos-phere—the waterless stone moat around the greathouse was used not for defense but for gathering cooling air. The estate produced sugar and molasses from 1767 to 1934, first with animal power, then wind, and finally with a steam engine to crush the cane. If you have kids, the grounds are the perfect place for them to run around, perhaps while you browse in the museum gift shop or attend a food demonstration using the still function-ing ovens in the cookhouse. It's just outside of Frederiksted. ☒ *Rte. 70, Whim* ☎ *340/772–0598* ⊕ *www.stcroixland-marks.com* ☜ *$10.*

FREDERIKSTED AND ENVIRONS

St. Croix's second-largest town, Fred-eriksted, was founded in 1751. Just as Christiansted is famed for its Danish buildings, Frederiksted is known for its Victorian architecture. A stroll around its historic sights will take you no more than an hour. Allow a little more time if you want to duck into the few small shops. One long cruise-ship pier juts into the sparkling sea. It's the perfect place to start a tour of this quaint city.

Caribbean Museum Center for the Arts

MUSEUM | Sitting across from the waterfront in a historic building, this small museum hosts an always-changing roster of exhibits and also houses a bookstore and a gift shop. Some works are cutting-edge multimedia efforts that you might be surprised to find in such an out-of-the-way location. Openings are popular events, as are the occasional jazz concerts presented in the upstairs galleries. The back courtyard is a peaceful space, where sculptures and statues are on display; free Wi-Fi is an added inducement to linger. ⊠ *10 Strand St., Frederiksted* ☎ *340/772–2622* ⊕ *www.cmcarts. org* ✉ *Free* ⊘ *Closed Sun.–Mon.*

Estate Mount Washington Plantation

ARCHAEOLOGICAL SITE | Several years ago, while surveying the property, its owners discovered the ruins of a sugar plantation beneath the rain forest brush. The grounds have since been cleared and opened to the public. The estate is private property, but the owners allow visitors to take a self-guided walking tour of the mill, the rum distillery, and other ruins. A oversize wind chime ringing softly in the breeze and a stone-lined labyrinth create a sense of serenity. ⊠ *Rte. 63, Estate Mount Washington and Washington Hill* ⊕ *www.estatemtwashington.com.*

Fort Frederik

HISTORIC SITE | **FAMILY** | On July 3, 1848, some 8,000 slaves marched on this fort to demand their freedom. Danish governor Peter von Scholten, fearing they would burn the town to the ground, stood up in his carriage parked in front of the fort and granted their wish. The fort, completed in 1760, houses an art gallery and a number of interesting exhibits, including a collection of mahogany furniture. The walls, constructed of coral and rubble bound together with molasses, are a testament to the ingenuity and durability of 18th-century engineering. Climb the battlements for great views of the cruise dock and the Caribbean Sea. ⊠ *Waterfront, Frederiksted* ☎ *340/772–2021* ✉ *$5* ⊘ *Closed weekends.*

NORTH SHORE

Salt River Bay National Historical Park and Ecological Preserve

BEACH—SIGHT | This joint national and local park commemorates the area where Christopher Columbus's men skirmished with the Carib Indians in 1493, on his second visit to the New World. The peninsula on the bay's east side is named for the event: Cabo de las Flechas (Cape of the Arrows). Although the park is still developing, it has several sights of cultural significance. A ball court, used by the Caribs in religious ceremonies, was discovered at the spot where the taxis park. Take a short hike up the dirt road to the ruins of an old earthen fort for great views of Salt River Bay. The area also encompasses a coastal estuary with the region's largest remaining mangrove forest, a submarine canyon, and several endangered species, including the hawksbill turtle and the roseate tern. The visitor center was badly damaged by Hurricane Maria in 2017 and remains closed. The water at the beach can be on the rough side, but it's a nice place for sunning. Local tour companies offer tours by kayak and pontoon boat. ⊠ *Rte. 75 to Rte. 80, Estate Salt River* ☎ *340/773–1460* ⊕ *www.nps.gov/sari.*

Beaches

West End beaches

BEACH—SIGHT | There are several unnamed beaches along the coast road north of Frederiksted, but it's best if you don't stray too far from civilization. Most vacationers plop down their towel near one of the casual restaurants spread out along Route 63. The beach at the Rainbow Beach Club, a five-minute drive outside Frederiksted, has the lively Rhythms beach bar, a casual restaurant decorated with license plates from around the world, and West End Watersports, which rents Jet Skis, Flyboards, and stand-up paddleboards by the half hour and beach chairs and umbrellas by the day. The beach is broad and sandy, the waters clear and calm. If you want to be close to the cruise-ship pier, just stroll on over to the adjacent sandy beach in front of Fort Frederik. On the way south out of Frederiksted, the stretch near Sandcastle on the Beach hotel is also lovely. **Amenities:** food and drink; water sports. **Best for:** snorkeling; swimming; walking. ⊠ *Rte. 63, north and south of Frederiksted, Frederiksted.*

🍴 Restaurants

Polly's at the Pier

$$ | ECLECTIC | With an emphasis on fresh ingredients, this casual spot right on the waterfront serves delicious fare. For breakfast, the BELT (bacon, egg, lettuce, and tomato) sandwich is the go-to, and at lunch, the gourmet grilled-cheese sandwich comes with your choice of three cheeses as well as delicious additions like basil, fresh Bosc pears, and avocado. **Known for:** local ingredients; waterfront location; neighborhood eatery. ⑤ *Average main: $13 ⊠ 3 Strand St., Frederiksted ☎ 340/719–9434 ⊕ pollysatthepierstcroix. com.*

★ Rum Runners

$$$ | ECLECTIC | FAMILY | Sitting right on the Christiansted boardwalk, Rum Runners serves a little bit of everything, including a to-die-for tropical salad topped with fresh local mango (in season) or pineapple. Heartier fare includes chili and lime shrimp and spaghetti tossed with crab and bacon. **Known for:** stellar views; local hangout; boardwalk location. ⑤ *Average main: $30 ⊠ Hotel Caravelle, 44A Queen Cross St., Christiansted ☎ 340/773–6585 ⊕ www.rumrunnersstcroix.com ⊗ Closed Tues.*

🛍 Shopping

Although the shopping on St. Croix isn't as varied or extensive as that on St. Thomas, the island does have several small stores with unusual merchandise. St. Croix shop hours are usually Monday through Saturday 9 to 5, but there are some shops in Christiansted open in the evening. Stores are often closed on Sunday.

The best shopping in Frederiksted is along **Strand Street** and in the side streets and alleyways that connect it with **King Street.** Most stores close on Sunday, except when a cruise ship is in port. Keep in mind that Frederiksted has a reputation for muggings, so it's best to stick to populated areas of Strand and King Streets, where there are few (if any) problems.

In Christiansted the best shopping areas are the **Pan Am Pavilion** and **Caravelle Arcade,** off Strand Street, and along **King** and **Company Streets,** which give way to arcades filled with boutiques. **Gallows Bay** has a blossoming shopping area in a quiet neighborhood.

🏃 Activities

BOAT TOURS

Almost everyone takes a day trip to Buck Island aboard a charter boat. Most leave from the Christiansted waterfront or from Green Cay Marina and stop for a snorkel at the island's eastern end before dropping anchor off a gorgeous sandy beach for a swim, a hike, and lunch. Sailboats can often stop right at the beach; a larger boat might have to anchor a bit farther offshore. A full-day sail runs about $100, with lunch included on most trips; a half-day sail costs about $68.

Big Beard's Adventure Tours

SAILING | From catamarans that depart from the Christiansted waterfront, you can head to Buck Island for half- and full-day snorkeling tours. The 42-foot

Adventure has a glass-viewing platform for those who want to see the fish but don't want to get in the water. The full-day tour on the Renegade concludes with dropping anchor at a private beach for an all-you-can-eat-and-drink barbecue. Sunset sails and tours of Salt River Bay also are offered. ⊠ *Queen Cross St. Waterfront, Christiansted* ☎ *340/773–4482* ⊕ *www.bigbeards.com.*

DIVING AND SNORKELING
N2 the Blue

SCUBA DIVING | N2 takes divers right off the beach near the Frederiksted Pier to see seahorses on night dives off the pier, or on boat trips to the Salt River Wall. Half-day intro-to-diving courses also are offered. The shop is a short walk from the cruise pier, making it easy to work a dive into a shore visit. ⊠ *202 Custom House St., Frederiksted* ☎ *340/772–3483* ⊕ *www.n2theblue.com.*

HORSEBACK RIDING
Paul and Jill's Equestrian Stables

HORSEBACK RIDING | From Sprat Hall, just north of Frederiksted, co-owner Jill Hurd will take you through the rain forest, across the pastures, along the beaches, and through valleys—explaining the flora, fauna, and ruins on the way. A 1½-hour group ride costs $100. ⊠ *Sprat Hall, Rte. 58, Frederiksted* ☎ *340/772–2880, 340/332–0417* ⊕ *www.paulandjills.com.*

KAYAKING
Caribbean Adventure Tours

KAYAKING | These kayak tours take you on trips through Salt River Bay National Historical Park and Ecological Preserve, one of the island's most pristine areas, including night paddles through the park's bioluminescent bay. All tours cost $50. ⊠ *Salt River Marina, Rte. 80, Estate Salt River* ☎ *340/778–1522, 800/532–3483* ⊕ *www.stcroixkayak.com.*

St. John (Cruz Bay)

St. John's heart is Virgin Islands National Park, a treasure that takes up a full two-thirds of St. John's 20 square miles (53 square km). The park helps keep the island's interior in its pristine and undisturbed state, but if you go at midday you'll probably have to share your stretch of beach with others, particularly at Trunk Bay. The island is booming, and while it can get a tad crowded at the ever-popular Trunk Bay Beach during the busy winter season, you won't find traffic jams or pollution. It's easy to escape from the fray, however: just head off on a hike. St. John doesn't have a grand major agrarian past like her sister island, St. Croix, but if you're hiking in the dry season, you can probably stumble upon the stone ruins of old plantations. The less adventuresome can visit the repaired ruins at the park's Annaberg Plantation and Caneel Bay resort. Of the three U.S. Virgin Islands, St. John, which has 5,000 residents, has the strongest sense of community, which is primarily rooted in a desire to protect the island's natural beauty.

ESSENTIALS
CURRENCY
U.S. dollar.

TELEPHONE
Calling to or from the U.S. Virgin Islands works the same as any domestic call; dial 1 and the area code 340. Most U.S. cell phone plans include the Virgin Islands for no additional cost. The major mobile phone providers are AT&T, Choice Wireless, Sprint, and T-Mobile US, using GSM (850 and 1900 bands).

COMING ASHORE
Although a few smaller ships drop anchor at St. John, most people taking a cruise aboard a larger ship visit St. Thomas's sister island on a shore excursion or on an independent day trip from St. Thomas. If you prefer to not take a tour, ferries leave St. Thomas from the Charlotte Amalie

Cruz Bay, St. John's main town, is filled with restaurants, bars, shopping opportunities, and dive centers.

waterfront and Red Hook. You'll have to take a taxi to reach the ferry dock.

If you're aboard a smaller ship that calls in St. John, your ship may simply pause outside Cruz Bay Harbor to drop you off or drop anchor if it's spending the day. You'll be tendered to shore at the main town of Cruz Bay. The shopping district starts just across the street from the tender landing. You'll find an eclectic collection of shops, cozy restaurants, and places where you can just sit and take it all in. The island has few sights to see. Your best bet is to take a tour of the Virgin Islands National Park. (If your ship doesn't offer such a tour, arrange one with one of the taxi drivers who meet your tender.) The drive takes you past luscious beaches to a restored sugar plantation. With only a single day in port, you're better off just using the island's shared taxi vans rather than renting a car (they offer set rates per passenger for major destinations); but if you want to do some independent exploring, you can rent a car in Cruz Bay. If you do rent a car,

remember that driving in the U.S. Virgin Islands is on the left.

◉ Sights

CRUZ BAY

St. John's main town may be compact (it consists of only several blocks), but it's definitely a hub: the ferries from St. Thomas and the British Virgin Islands pull in here, and it's where you can get a taxi or rent a car to travel around the island. There are plenty of shops, a number of watering holes and restaurants, and a grassy square with benches where you can sit back and take everything in. Look for the current edition of the handy, amusing "St. John Map," featuring Max the Mongoose.

★ Virgin Islands National Park

NATIONAL/STATE PARK | If you're interested in bird-watching, snorkeling, camping, history, or just strolling in beautiful environs, then Virgin Islands National Park is the place for you. At Francis Bay there's a boardwalk through the mangroves, where birds may be plentiful; Salt Pond Bay offers pleasant snorkeling; and plantation history can be explored at Annaberg Sugar Mill ruins. There are more than 20 trails on the north and south shores, with guided hikes along the most popular routes. To pick up a useful guide to St. John's hiking trails, see various large maps of the island, and find out about current Park Service programs—including guided walks and cultural demonstrations—stop by the park visitor center at the western tip of the park in Cruz Bay on North Shore Road. ⊠ *North Shore Rd., near creek, Cruz Bay* ☎ *340/776–6201* ⊕ *www.nps. gov/viis.*

NORTH SHORE
★ Annaberg Plantation
HISTORIC SITE | In the 18th century, sugar plantations dotted the steep hills of this island. Slaves and free Danes and Dutchmen toiled to harvest the cane that was used to create sugar, molasses, and rum for export. Built in the 1780s, the partially restored plantation at Leinster Bay was once an important sugar mill. Although there are no official visiting hours, the National Park Service has regular tours, and some well-informed taxi drivers will show you around. Occasionally you may see a living-history demonstration— someone making johnnycakes or weaving baskets. For information on tours and cultural events, contact the Virgin Islands National Park Visitors Center. ⊠ *Leinster Bay Rd., Annaberg* ☎ *340/776–6201* ⊕ *www.nps.gov/viis* 🎫 *Free.*

 Beaches

Cinnamon Bay Beach
BEACH—SIGHT | This long, sandy beach faces beautiful cays. There's excellent snorkeling off the point to the right; look for the big angelfish and large schools of purple triggerfish. Afternoons on Cinnamon Bay can be windy—a boon for windsurfers but an annoyance for sunbathers—so arrive early to beat the

gusts. The Cinnamon Bay hiking trail begins across the road from the beach parking lot; ruins mark the trailhead. There are actually two paths here: a level nature trail (with signs to identify flora) that loops through the woods and passes an old Danish cemetery, and a steep trail that starts where the road bends past the ruins and heads straight up to Route 10. **Amenities:** parking; toilets. **Best for:** snorkeling; swimming; walking; windsurfing. ⊠ *North Shore Rd., Rte. 20, Cinnamon Bay* ✛ *About 4 miles (6 km) east of Cruz Bay* ⊕ *www.nps.gov/viis.*

★ Trunk Bay Beach
BEACH—SIGHT | St. John's most photographed beach is also the preferred spot for beginning snorkelers because of its underwater trail. (Cruise-ship passengers interested in snorkeling for a day flock here, so if you're looking for seclusion, arrive early or later in the day.) Crowded or not, this stunning beach is one of the island's most beautiful. There are changing rooms with showers, bathrooms, a food truck, picnic tables, a gift shop, phones, lockers, and snorkeling-equipment rentals. The parking lot often overflows, but you can park along the road as long as the tires are off the pavement. **Amenities:** lifeguards; parking; toilets. **Best for:** snorkeling; swimming; windsurfing. ⊠ *North Shore Rd., Rte. 20, Estate Trunk*

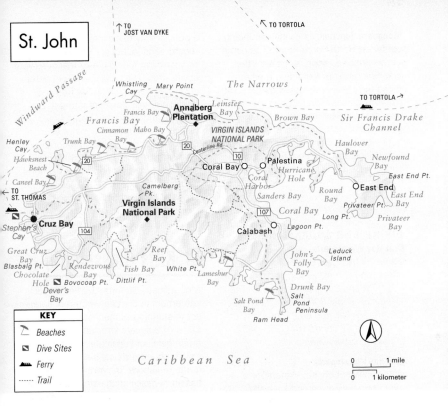

Bay ✛ About 2½ miles (4 km) east of Cruz Bay ⊕ www.nps.gov/viis ☞ Free.

🍴 Restaurants

Lime Inn

$$$ | ECLECTIC | The vacationers and mainland transplants who call St. John home like to flock to this alfresco spot for the congenial hospitality and good food, including all-you-can-eat shrimp on Wednesday night. Fresh lobster is the specialty, and the menu also includes shrimp-and-steak dishes and rotating chicken and pasta specials. **Known for:** fresh lobster; local hangout; kids' menu. ⑤ *Average main: $30 ⊠ Lemon Tree Mall, King St., Cruz Bay ☎ 340/776–6425 ⊕ thelimeinn.com ☉ No lunch weekends.*

★ Sam and Jack's Deli

$$ | DELI | The sandwiches are scrumptious, but this deli also dishes up wonderful meals to-go that just need heating. There are a few seats inside, but most folks opt to eat at the tables in front of the deli. **Known for:** picnic-ready meals; truffle-and-wild-mushroom ravioli; villa and yacht provisioning available. ⑤ *Average main: $14 ⊠ Marketplace Shopping Center, 3rd fl., Rte. 104, Cruz Bay ☎ 340/714–3354 ⊕ www.samand-jacksdeli.com.*

🛍 Shopping

Luxury goods and handicrafts can be found on St. John. Most shops carry a little of this and a bit of that, so it pays to poke around. The Cruz Bay shopping district runs from **Wharfside Village,** just around the corner from the ferry dock, to

Mongoose Junction, an inviting shopping center on North Shore Road. (The name of this upscale shopping mall, by the way, is a holdover from a time when those furry island creatures gathered at a nearby garbage bin.) Out on Route 104, stop in at the **Marketplace** to explore its gift and crafts shops. On St. John, store hours run from 9 or 10 to 5 or 6. Wharfside Village and Mongoose Junction shops in Cruz Bay are often open into the evening.

🏃 Activities

DIVING AND SNORKELING
Cruz Bay Watersports

SCUBA DIVING | Cruz Bay Watersports offers regular reef, wreck, and night dives and USVI and BVI snorkel tours. ⊠ *The Westin St. John, 300 Chocolate Hole, Cruz Bay* ⚓ *Located on the property of the Westin St. John* ☎ *844/359–5457* ⊕ *www.cruzbaywatersports.com.*

Low Key Watersports

SCUBA DIVING | Low Key Watersports offers two-tank dives and specialty courses. It's a PADI 5 Star training facility. ⊠ *1 Bay St., Cruz Bay* ☎ *340/693–8999* ⊕ *www.divelowkey.com.*

FISHING
Offshore Adventures

FISHING | FAMILY | An excellent choice for fishing charters, Captain Rob Richards is patient with beginners—especially kids—but also enjoys going out with more experienced anglers. He runs the 33-foot inboard tuna-tower-topped *Mixed Bag I* and 32-foot center-console *Mixed Bag II.* Although he's based in St. John, he will pick up parties in St. Thomas. ⊠ *The Westin St. John, 300A Chocolate Hole Rd., Estate Chocolate Hole and Great Cruz Bay* ☎ *340/513–0389* ⊕ *www. sportfishingstjohn.com.*

HIKING

Virgin Islands National Park has more than 20 trails from which to choose. Guided trips with the park service are a popular way to explore and are highly recommended, but you can also set out on your own. To find a hike that suits your ability, stop by the park's visitor center in Cruz Bay and pick up the free trail guide; it details points of interest, trail lengths, and estimated hiking times, as well as any dangers you might encounter. Although the park staff recommend long pants to protect against thorns and insects, most people hike in shorts because it can get very hot. Wear sturdy shoes or hiking boots even if you're hiking to the beach. Don't forget to bring water and insect repellent.

St. Kitts (Basseterre)

Mountainous St. Kitts, the first English settlement in the Leeward Islands, crams some stunning scenery into its 65 square miles (168 square km). Vast, brilliant green fields of sugarcane (the former cash crop, now slowly being replanted) run to the shore. The fertile, lush island has some fascinating natural and historical attractions: a rain forest replete with waterfalls, thick vines, and secret trails; a central mountain range dominated by the 3,792-foot Mt. Liamuiga, whose crater has long been dormant; and Brimstone Hill, known in the 18th century as the Gibraltar of the West Indies. St. Kitts and Nevis, along with Anguilla, achieved self-government as an associated state of Great Britain in 1967. In 1983 St. Kitts and Nevis became an independent nation. English with a strong West Indian lilt is spoken here. People are friendly but can be shy; always ask before you take photographs. Also, be sure to wear wraps or shorts over beach attire when you're in public places.

ESSENTIALS
CURRENCY
Eastern Caribbean (EC) dollar, but U.S. dollars are widely accepted.

TELEPHONE

The country code is 1 869. Digicel, LIME, and Orange are the major mobile phone companies, using GSM (850, 900, 1800 and 1900 bands).

COMING ASHORE

Cruise ships calling at St. Kitts dock at Port Zante, which is a deepwater port directly in Basseterre, the capital of St. Kitts. The cruise-ship terminal is right in the downtown area, two minutes' walk from sights and shops. Taxi rates on St. Kitts are fixed and should be posted right at the dock. If you'd like to go to Nevis, several daily ferries (30 to 45 minutes, $8 to $10 one-way) can take you to Charlestown in Nevis; the Byzantine schedule is subject to change, so double-check times.

Taxi rates on St. Kitts are fairly expensive, and you may have to pay $32 for a ride to Brimstone Hill (for one to four passengers). A four-hour tour of St. Kitts runs about $100. It's often cheaper to arrange an island tour with one of the local companies than to hire a taxi driver to take your group around. Several restored plantation greathouses are known for their lunches; your driver can provide information and arrange drop-off and pickup. Before setting off in a cab, be sure to clarify whether the rate quoted is in EC or U.S. dollars.

⊙ Sights

BASSETERRE

On the south coast, St. Kitts's walkable capital is graced with tall palms and flagstone sidewalks; although many of the buildings appear run-down, there are interesting shops, excellent art galleries, and some beautifully maintained houses. Duty-free shops and boutiques line the streets and courtyards radiating from the octagonal **Circus,** built in the style of London's famous Piccadilly Circus.

Best Bets ⊙

■ **Brimstone Hill Fortress.** Stop here for some of the best views on St. Kitts and historic ambience.

■ **Nevis.** A trip to Nevis is a worthwhile way to spend the day.

■ **Plantation Greathouses.** Stop for a lunch at Ottley's.

■ **Rain-forest Hikes.** Several operators on the island lead daylong hikes through the rain forest.

■ **Romney Manor.** This partially restored manor house is enhanced by the chance to shop at Caribelle Batik and watch the elaborate wax-and-dye process.

Independence Square

PLAZA | There are lovely gardens and a fountain on this site of a former slave market at Independence Square. The square is surrounded on three sides by 18th-century Georgian buildings. ⊠ *Off Bank St., Basseterre.*

National Museum

MUSEUM | In the restored former treasury building, the National Museum presents an eclectic collection of artifacts reflecting the history and culture of the island. ⊠ *Bay Rd., Basseterre* ☎ *869/465–5584* ⊠ *$5.*

Port Zante

MARINA | Port Zante is an ambitious, ever-growing 27-acre cruise-ship pier and marina in an area that has been reclaimed from the sea. The domed welcome center is an imposing neoclassical hodgepodge, with columns and stone arches, shops, walkways, fountains, and West Indian–style buildings housing both cheap souvenir and luxury shops, galleries, restaurants, and a small casino. The crafts and T-shirt booths of the Amina Marketplace sit at the entrance beyond

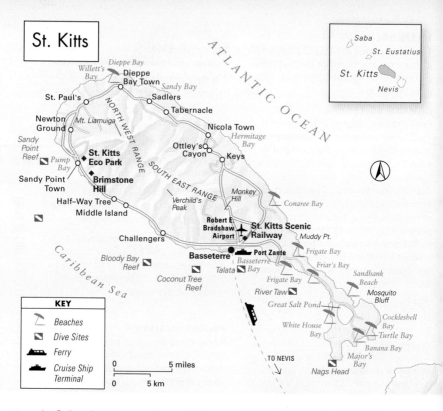

St. Kitts

Saba
St. Eustatius
St. Kitts
Nevis

ATLANTIC OCEAN

Willett's Bay
Dieppe Bay
Dieppe Bay Town
Sandy Bay
St. Paul's
Sadlers
Tabernacle
Newton Ground
Mt. Liamuiga
NORTH WEST RANGE
Nicola Town
Hermitage Bay
Sandy Point Reef
Pump Bay
St. Kitts Eco Park
Ottley's
Cayon
Keys
SOUTH EAST RANGE
Sandy Point Town
Brimstone Hill
Half-Way Tree
Verchild's Peak
Middle Island
Monkey Hill
Conaree Bay
Challengers
Robert E Bradshaw Airport
St. Kitts Scenic Railway
Muddy Pt.
Caribbean Sea
Bloody Bay Reef
Basseterre
Port Zante
Frigate Bay
Talata
Basseterre Bay
Friar's Bay
Coconut Tree Reef
Frigate Bay
Sandbank Beach
River Taw
Mosquito Bluff
Great Salt Pond
Cockleshell Bay
White House Bay
Turtle Bay
Banana Bay
TO NEVIS
Major's Bay
Nags Head

KEY
- Beaches
- Dive Sites
- Ferry
- Cruise Ship Terminal

0   5 miles
0   5 km

---

the Pelican Mall. A second pier, 1,434 feet long, has a draft that accommodates even leviathan cruise ships. The selection of shops and restaurants (Twist serves global fusion cuisine and rocks with DJs several nights of the week) is expanding as well. ⊠ *Waterfront, behind Circus, Basseterre* ⊕ *www.portzante.com; www. portzantemarina.com.*

St. George's Anglican Church

RELIGIOUS SITE | This handsome stone building has a crenellated tower originally built by the French in 1670 that is called Nôtre-Dame. The British burned it down in 1706 and rebuilt it four years later, naming it after the patron saint of England. Since then it has suffered a fire, an earthquake, and hurricanes, and was once again rebuilt in 1869. ⊠ *Cayon St., Basseterre.*

ELSEWHERE ON ST. KITTS

Brimstone Hill

HISTORIC SITE | After routing the French in 1690, the English erected a battery here; by 1736 the fortress held 49 guns, earning it the moniker "Gibraltar of the West Indies." A hurricane severely damaged the fortress in 1834, and in 1852 it was evacuated and dismantled. The beautiful stones were carted away to build houses. The citadel has been partially reconstructed and its guns remounted. It's a steep walk up the hill from the parking lot. A seven-minute orientation film recounts the fort's history and restoration. You can see remains of the officers' quarters, redoubts, barracks, ordnance store, and cemetery. Its museum collections were depleted by hurricanes, but it still has a few interesting exhibits. The spectacular view includes Montserrat and Nevis to the southeast; Saba and St.

Eustatius to the northwest; and St. Barth and St. Maarten to the north. ⊠ *Main Rd., Brimstone Hill* ☎ *869/465–2609* ⊕ *www. brimstonehillfortress.org* ⊠ *$10.*

St. Kitts Eco Park

GARDEN | FAMILY | Created in collaboration with the Taiwanese government (and now under sole Kittitian ownership), St. Kitts Eco Park essentially functions as an agritourism demonstration farm, with soaring, light-filled glass and fiber-reinforced concrete structures that are powered by state-of-the-art solar trackers. Antique cannons and old-fashioned gas lamps lead to the handsome Victorian plantation-style visitors center, divided into Kittitian and Taiwanese sections, each selling local foodstuffs and specialty items (ceramics for St. Kitts, tea and technology for Taiwan). You can stroll through the greenhouse, viewing orchids in the working nursery, then scale the watchtower for scintillating views of the farm and the Caribbean, with Saba and Statia in the distance. Kids will love challenging the map mazes (plantings shaped like the partner nations), while parents can wander the orchards and desert garden or savor bush tea in the herb gazebo. The property provides environmental edutainment while delivering on its so-called 4G promise: greenhouse, green beauty, green energy, green landscape. ⊠ *Sir Gillies Estate, Sandy Point* ☎ *869/465–8755* ⊕ *www.ecopark.kn; www.stkittstourism.kn/activities/excursions/st-kitts-eco-park* ⊠ *$5.*

St. Kitts Scenic Railway

TOUR—SIGHT | FAMILY | The old narrow-gauge train that had transported sugarcane to the central sugar factory since 1912 is all that remains of the island's once-thriving sugar industry. Two-story cars bedecked in bright Kittitian colors circle much of the island (the final segment is aboard a bus) in just under three hours (a Rail and Sail option takes guests going or returning via catamaran). Each passenger gets a comfortable, downstairs air-conditioned seat fronting vaulted picture windows and an upstairs open-air observation spot. The conductor's running narration encompasses not only the history of sugar cultivation but also the railway's construction, local folklore, island geography, even other agricultural mainstays from papayas to pigs. You can drink in complimentary tropical beverages (including luscious guava daiquiris) along with the sweeping rain-forest and ocean vistas, accompanied by an a cappella choir's renditions of hymns, spirituals, and predictable standards like "I've Been Workin' on the Railroad." ⊠ *Needsmust Estate* ☎ *869/465–7263* ⊕ *www.stkittsscenicrailway.com* ⊠ *$99.*

☺ Beaches

Beaches on St. Kitts are free and open to the public (even those occupied by hotels). The best beaches, with powdery white sand, are in the Frigate Bay area or on the lower peninsula. The Atlantic waters are rougher, and many black-sand beaches northwest of Frigate Bay double as garbage dumps.

Banana/Cockleshell Bays

BEACH—SIGHT | These twin connected eyebrows of glittering champagne-color sand—stretching nearly 2 miles (3 km) total at the southeastern tip of the island—feature majestic views of Nevis and are backed by lush vegetation and coconut palms. The first-rate restaurant-bar Spice Mill (next to Rasta-hued Lion Rock Beach Bar—order the knockout Lion Punch) and Reggae Beach Bar & Grill bracket either end of Cockleshell. A 125-room Park Hyatt, which will eventually have additional residential condos and villas, debuted in late 2017. The water is generally placid, ideal for swimming. The downside is irregular maintenance, with seaweed (particularly after rough weather) and occasional litter. Follow Simmonds Highway to the end and bear right, ignoring the turnoff for Turtle Beach. **Amenities:** food and drink; parking.

Best for: partiers; snorkeling; swimming; walking. ⊠ *Banana Bay.*

Friar's Bay

BEACH—SIGHT | Locals consider Friar's Bay, on the Caribbean (southern) side, the island's finest beach. It's a long, tawny scimitar, where the water always seems warmer and clearer. The upscale Carambola Beach Club, which has co-opted roughly one third of the strand, is popular with cruise ship passengers at lunch. Still, several happening bars—including Jam Rock (great grouper and jerk), ShipWreck, and Sunset—serve terrific, inexpensive local food and cheap, frosty drinks. Chair rentals cost around $3, though if you order lunch, you can negotiate a freebie. Friar's is the first major beach along Southeast Peninsula Drive (aka Simmonds Highway), approximately a mile (1½ km) southeast of Frigate Bay. **Amenities:** food and drink. **Best for:** snorkeling; swimming; walking. ⊠ *South Friar's Bay.*

Frigate Bay

BEACH—SIGHT | The Caribbean side offers talcum-powder-fine beige sand framed by coconut palms and seagrapes, and the Atlantic side (a 15-minute stroll)—sometimes called North Frigate Bay—is a favorite with horseback riders. South Frigate Bay is bookended by the Timothy Beach Club's Sunset Café and the popular, pulsating Buddies Beach Hut. In between are several other lively beach spots, including Cathy's (fabulous jerk ribs), Chinchilla's, Vibes, and Mr. X Shiggidy Shack. Most charge $3 to $5 to rent a chair, though they'll often waive the fee if you ask politely and buy lunch. Locals barhop late into Friday and Saturday nights. Waters are generally calm for swimming; the rockier eastern end offers fine snorkeling. The incomparably scenic Atlantic side is—regrettably—dominated by the Marriott (plentiful dining options), attracting occasional pesky vendors. The surf is choppier and the undertow stronger here. On cruise-ship days,

groups stampede both sides. **Amenities:** food and drink; water sports. **Best for:** partiers; snorkeling; swimming; walking. ⊠ *Frigate Bay* ⊹ *Less than 3 miles (5 km) from downtown Basseterre.*

🍴 Restaurants

El Fredo's

$$ | **CARIBBEAN** | The decor is basic at this humble wooden shack across from the waterfront, but locals swear that the bounteous dishes, some of the best local fare on St. Kitts, will cure—or at least absorb—any hangover. It's also a terrific place to eavesdrop on local gossip, with politicians and expats grabbing a quick lunch alongside local workers, who shyly banter with the waitresses. **Known for:** traditional fare (swordfish creole, curry goat, garlic conch, dumplings); heaping helpings; authentic island ambience. ⑤ *Average main: US$14* ⊠ *Newtown Bay Rd. at Sanddown Rd., Basseterre* ☎ *869/764–9228* ▭ *No credit cards* ⊗ *Closed Sun.–Mon. No dinner.*

Reggae Beach Bar & Grill

$$$ | **ECLECTIC** | Treats at this popular daytime watering hole include honey-mustard ribs, coconut shrimp, grilled lobster, banana bread pudding with rum sauce, and lots of tempting tropical libations. Business cards and pennants plaster the bar, and the open-air space is decorated with fishnets, turtle shells, and other nautical accoutrements. **Known for:** chill vibe with free beach chairs and Wi-Fi; live music on Sunday and bonfire-dinner on Friday; host of aquatic activities on tap. ⑤ *Average main: US$21* ⊠ *S.E. Peninsula Rd., Cockleshell Beach* ☎ *869/762–5050* ⊕ *www.reggaebeachbar.com* ⊗ *No dinner.*

🛍 Shopping

St. Kitts has limited shopping, but several duty-free shops offer good deals on jewelry, perfume, china, and crystal. Numerous galleries sell excellent paintings and sculptures. The batik fabrics, scarves, caftans, and wall hangings of Caribelle Batik are well known. British expat Kate Spencer is an artist who has lived on the island for years, reproducing its vibrant colors on everything from silk pareus (beach wraps) and scarves to note cards. Other good island buys include crafts, jams, and herbal teas. Don't forget to pick up some CSR (Cane Spirit Rothschild), which is distilled from fresh wild sugarcane right on St. Kitts. The Brinley Gold Company has made a splash among spirits connoisseurs with its coffee, mango, coconut, lime, and vanilla rums (there is a tasting room at Port Zante).

⚡ Activities

DIVING AND SNORKELING
Though unheralded as a dive destination, St. Kitts has more than a dozen excellent sites, protected by several new marine parks. The surrounding waters feature shoals, hot vents, shallows, canyons, steep walls, and caverns at depths from 40 to nearly 200 feet.

Dive St. Kitts
SCUBA DIVING | This PADI–NAUI facility offers competitive rates (including a price-matching guarantee), computers to maximize time below, a wide range of courses from refresher to rescue, and friendly, laid-back dive masters. The Bird Rock location features superb shore diving (unlimited when you book packages): common sightings 20 to 30 feet out include octopuses, nurse sharks, manta and spotted eagle rays, seahorses, even barracudas George and Georgianna. It also offers kayak and snorkeling tours. ✉ 2 miles (3 km) east of Basseterre, Frigate Bay ☎ 800/403–5966, 869/465–8914 ⊕ www.divestkitts.com.

GOLF
Royal St. Kitts Golf Club
GOLF | This 18-hole links-style championship course underwent a complete redesign by Thomas McBroom to

maximize Caribbean and Atlantic views and increase the challenge (there are 12 lakes and 83 bunkers). Holes 15 through 17 (the latter patterned after Pebble Beach No. 18) skirt the Atlantic in their entirety, lending new meaning to the term sand trap. The sudden gusts, wide but twisting fairways, and extremely hilly terrain demand pinpoint accuracy and finesse, yet holes such as 18 require pure power. The development includes practice bunkers, a putting green, a short-game chipping area, and the fairly high-tech Royal Golf Academy. Twilight and super-twilight discounts are offered. ✉ St. Kitts Marriott Resort, 858 Zenway Blvd., Frigate Bay ☎ 869/466–2700, 866/785–4653 ⊕ www.royalstkittsgolf-club.com 🏌 $150 for Marriott guests in high season, $165 for nonguests ⅃. 18 holes, 6900 yards, par 71.

HIKING
Trails in the central mountains vary from easy to don't-try-it-by-yourself. Monkey Hill and Verchild's Peak aren't difficult, although the Verchild's climb will take the better part of a day. Don't attempt Mt. Liamuiga without a guide. You'll start at Belmont Estate—at the west end of the island—on horseback, and then proceed on foot to the lip of the crater, at 2,600 feet. You can go down into the crater—1,000 feet deep and 1 mile (1½ km) wide, with a small freshwater lake—clinging to vines and roots and scaling rocks, even trees. Expect to get muddy. There are several fine operators (each hotel recommends its favorite); tour rates generally range from $50 for a rain-forest walk to $95 for a volcano expedition and usually include round-trip transportation from your hotel and picnic lunch.

Greg's Safaris
HIKING/WALKING | Greg Pereira, whose family has lived on St. Kitts since the early 19th century, takes groups on half-day trips ($65 and up) into the rain forest and on full-day hikes up the volcano and through the grounds of a private

18th-century greathouse. The rain forest trips include visits to sacred Carib sites, abandoned sugar mills, and an excursion down a 100-foot coastal canyon containing a wealth of Amerindian petroglyphs. The Off the Beaten Track 4X4 Plantation Tour provides a thorough explanation of the role sugar and rum played in the Caribbean economy and colonial wars. He and his staff relate fascinating historical, folkloric, and botanical information. ☎ 869/465–4121 ⊕ www.gregsafaris. com.

HORSEBACK RIDING
Trinity Stables
HORSEBACK RIDING | Guides from Trinity Stables offer beach rides ($60) and trips into the rain forest ($70), both including hotel pickup. The latter is intriguing, as guides discuss plants' medicinal properties along the way (such as sugarcane to stanch bleeding) and pick oranges right off a tree to squeeze fresh juice. The staffers are cordial but shy; this isn't a place for beginners' instruction. ✉ Palmetto Point ☎ 869/465–3226, 869/726–3098.

St. Lucia (Castries)

Magnificent St. Lucia—with its towering mountains, dense rain forest, fertile green valleys, and acres of banana plantations—lies in the middle of the Windward Islands. Nicknamed "Helen of the West Indies" because of its natural beauty, St. Lucia is distinguished from its neighbors by its unusual geological landmarks, the Pitons—the twin peaks on the southwestern coast that soar nearly ½ mile (1 km) above the ocean floor. Named a World Heritage Site by UNESCO in 2004, the Pitons are the symbol of this island. Nearby, in the former French colonial capital of Soufrière, you'll find a "drive-in" volcano, its neighboring sulfur springs that have rejuvenated bathers for nearly three centuries, and one of the most beautiful botanical gardens in the

Best Bets

- **The Pitons.** You must see the Pitons, St. Lucia's unique twin peaks.

- **The Rain Forest.** St. Lucia's rain forest is truly a natural wonder.

- **Diamond Botanical Garden.** Stroll through this tropical paradise to Diamond Waterfall.

- **Reduit Beach.** St. Lucia's broadest, most popular beach is at Rodney Bay, north of Castries.

- **Pigeon Island National Landmark.** This national park is both a historic site and a playground.

Caribbean. A century and a half of battles between the French and English resulted in St. Lucia's changing hands 14 times before 1814, when England secured possession. In 1979, the island became an independent state within the British Commonwealth of Nations. The official language is English, although most people also speak a French Creole patois.

ESSENTIALS
CURRENCY
Eastern Caribbean (EC) dollar, but U.S. dollars are widely accepted.

TELEPHONE
The country code for St. Lucia is 1 758. Digicel and Flow are the primary mobile providers, using GSM (850, 900, 1800 and 1900 bands).

COMING ASHORE
Most cruise ships dock at the capital city of Castries, on the island's northwestern coast, at either of two docking areas: Pointe Seraphine, a port of entry and duty-free shopping complex, or Port Castries (Place Carenage), a commercial wharf across the harbor. A water taxi ($3 each way) connects the two piers.

Smaller vessels occasionally call at Soufrière, on the island's southwestern coast. Ships calling at Soufrière must anchor offshore and bring passengers ashore via tender. Tourist information booths are at Pointe Seraphine, at Place Carenage, and along the waterfront on Bay Street in Soufrière. Downtown Castries is within walking distance of the pier, and the produce market and adjacent crafts and vendors' markets are the main attractions. Soufrière is a sleepy West Indian town, but it's worth a short walk around the central square to view the French colonial architecture; many of the island's interesting natural sights are in or near Soufrière.

Taxis are available at the docks in Castries. Although they are unmetered, the standard fares are posted at the entrance to Pointe Seraphine. Taxi drivers are well informed and can give you a full tour—often an excellent one—thanks to government-sponsored training programs. From the Castries area, full-day island tours for up to four people cost $40 to $75 per person, depending on the route and whether entrance fees and lunch are included; a private sightseeing trip, including lunch, costs around $190 for two people. If you plan your own day, expect to pay the driver at least $40 per hour plus a 10% tip. Whatever your destination, negotiate the price with the driver before you depart—and be sure that you both understand whether the rate is quoted in EC or U.S. dollars.

◉ Sights

CASTRIES AND THE NORTH

Castries, the capital and a busy commercial city of about 65,000 people (one-third of the island's population), wraps around sheltered Castries Bay. The charm of Castries lies in its liveliness rather than its architecture, since four fires between 1796 and 1948 destroyed most colonial buildings. Freighters (exporting bananas, coconut, cocoa, mace, nutmeg, and

citrus fruits) and cruise ships come and go frequently, making Castries Harbour one of the Caribbean's busiest ports.

Castries, and the area north and just south of it, are the island's most developed areas. The roads are mostly flat, straight, and easy to navigate. The beaches are among the island's best. Rodney Bay Village, Rodney Bay Marina, and many resorts, restaurants, and nightspots are north of Castries. Morne Fortune rises sharply to the south, creating a dramatic green backdrop. Pigeon Island, one of the important historical sites, is at the island's northwestern tip.

★ Castries Central Market
MARKET | FAMILY | Under a brilliant orange roof, this bustling market is at its liveliest on Saturday morning, when farmers bring their produce and spices to town, as they have for more than a century. (It's closed Sunday.) Next door to the produce market is the **Craft Market,** where you can buy pottery, wood carvings, handwoven straw articles, and innumerable souvenirs, trinkets, and gewgaws. At the **Vendors' Arcade,** across Peynier Street from the Craft Market, you'll find still more handicrafts and souvenirs. ⊠ *55 John Compton Hwy., Castries.*

Fort Charlotte
CEMETERY | Begun in 1764 by the French as the Citadelle du Morne Fortune, Fort Charlotte was completed after 20 years of battling and changing hands. Its old barracks and batteries are now government buildings and local educational facilities, but you can drive around and look at the remains of redoubts, a guardroom, stables, and cells. You can also walk up to the Inniskilling Monument, a tribute to the 1796 battle in which the 27th (Inniskilling) Regiment of Foot wrested the Morne from the French. At the military cemetery, first used in 1782, faint inscriptions on the tombstones tell the tales of French and English soldiers who died in Saint Lucia. Six former governors of the island are also buried here.

From this point atop Morne Fortune, you have a beautiful view of Castries Harbour, Martinique farther north, and the Pitons to the south. ⊠ *Morne Fortune.*

Pigeon Island National Landmark

BEACH—SIGHT | FAMILY | Jutting out from the northwest coast, Pigeon Island connects to the mainland via a causeway. Tales are told of the pirate Jambe de Bois (Wooden Leg), who once hid out on this 44-acre hilltop islet—a strategic point during the French and British struggles for control of Saint Lucia. Now Pigeon Island is a national park and a venue for concerts, festivals, and family gatherings. There are two small beaches with calm waters for swimming and snorkeling, a restaurant, and picnic areas. Scattered around the grounds are ruins of barracks, batteries, and garrisons that date from 18th-century French and English battles. In the Museum and Interpretative Centre, housed in the restored British officers' mess, a multimedia display explains the island's ecological and historical significance. The site is administered by the Saint Lucia National Trust. ⊠ *Pigeon Island* ☎ 758/452–5005 ⊕ *www.slunatrust.org* 🖃 *$8.*

Rainforest Adventures

AMUSEMENT PARK/WATER PARK | FAMILY | Ever wish you could get a bird's-eye view of the rain forest? Or at least experience it without hiking up and down miles of mountain trails? Here's your chance. Depending on your athleticism and spirit of adventure, choose a two-hour aerial tram ride, a zip-line experience, or both. Either activity guarantees a magnificent view as you peacefully ride above or actively zip through the canopy of the 3,442-acre Castries Waterworks Rain Forest in Babonneau, 30 minutes east of Rodney Bay. On the tram ride, eight-passenger gondolas glide slowly among the giant trees, twisting vines, and dense thickets of vegetation accented by colorful flowers, as a tour guide explains and shares anecdotes about the various trees, plants, birds, and other wonders of nature found in the area. The zip line, on the other hand, is a thrilling experience in which you're rigged with a harness, helmet, and clamps that attach to cables strategically strung through the forest. Short trails connect 18 platforms, so riders come down to earth briefly and hike to the next station before speeding through the forest canopy to the next stop. There's even a nighttime zip-line tour. ■TIP→ **Bring binoculars and a camera.** ⊠ *Chassin, Babonneau* ☎ 758/458–5151 ⊕ *www.rainforestadventure.com* 🖃 *Tram $80, zip line $80; combo $95.*

★ Splash Island Water Park

AMUSEMENT PARK/WATER PARK | FAMILY | The Eastern Caribbean's first open-water-sports park, installed just off Reduit Beach a dozen or so yards from the sand in front of Bay Gardens Beach Resort, thrills kids and adults alike—but mostly kids. They spend hours on the colorful, inflatable, modular features, which include a trampoline, climbing wall, monkey bars, swing, slide, hurdles, double rocker, and water volleyball net. Children must be at least six, and everyone must wear a life vest. A team of lifeguards is on duty when the park is open. ⊠ *Reduit Beach, Reduit Beach Rd., Rodney Bay* ⊹ *Facing Bay Gardens Beach Resort* ☎ 758/457–8532 ⊕ *www.saintluciawaterpark.com* 🖃 *$13 per hr, $34.50 half-day pass, $57.50 full-day pass.*

SOUFRIÈRE AND THE WEST COAST

The oldest town in St. Lucia and the island's former colonial capital, Soufrière was founded by the French in 1746 and named for its proximity to the volcano of the same name. The wharf is the center of activity in this sleepy town (population: 9,000), particularly when a cruise ship anchors in pretty Soufrière Bay. French colonial influences are evident in the second-story verandahs, gingerbread trim, and other appointments of the wooden buildings that surround the

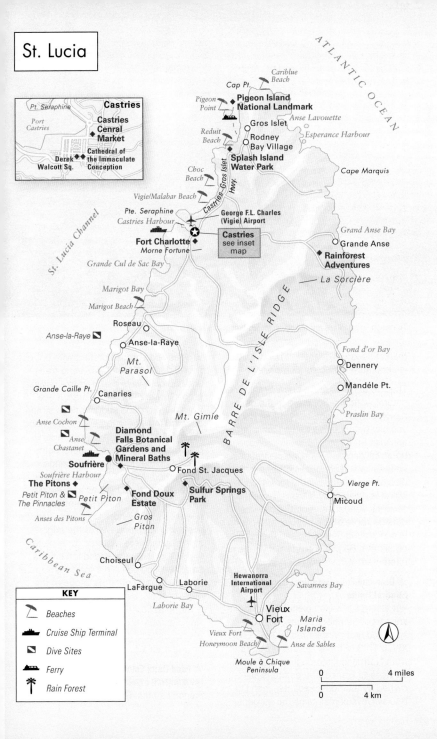

The magnificent Pitons are the most famous landmarks in St. Lucia.

market square. The market building itself is decorated with colorful murals.

The site of much of St. Lucia's renowned natural wonders, Soufrière is the destination of most sightseeing trips. Here you can get up close to the iconic Pitons and visit St. Lucia's "drive-in" volcano, botanical gardens, working plantations, waterfalls, and countless other examples of the natural beauty for which the island is deservedly famous. Note that souvenir vendors station themselves outside some of the popular attractions in and around Soufrière, and they can be persistent. Be polite but firm if you're not interested.

★ Diamond Falls Botanical Gardens and Mineral Baths

HOT SPRINGS | These splendid gardens are part of Soufrière Estate, a 2,000-acre land grant presented by King Louis XIV in 1713 to three Devaux brothers from Normandy in recognition of their services to France. The estate is still owned by their descendants; Joan Du Boulay Devaux maintains the gardens.

Bushes and shrubs bursting with brilliant flowers grow beneath towering trees and line pathways that lead to a natural gorge. Water bubbling to the surface from underground sulfur springs streams downhill in rivulets to become Diamond Waterfall, deep within the botanical gardens. Near the falls, mineral baths are fed by the underground springs. It's claimed that the future Joséphine Bonaparte bathed here as a young girl while visiting her father's plantation nearby. In 1930 André Du Boulay had the site excavated, and two of the original stone baths were restored for his use. Outside baths were added later. For a small fee, you can slip into your swimsuit and soak for 30 minutes in one of the outside pools; a private bath costs slightly more. ✉ *Soufrière Estate, Diamond Rd., Soufrière* ☎ *758/459–7155* ⊕ *www. diamondstlucia.com* 🎫 *$7, public bath $6, private bath $7.*

★ Fond Doux Estate

FARM/RANCH | **FAMILY** | One of the earliest French estates established by land grants (1745 and 1764), this plantation still produces cocoa, citrus, bananas, coconuts, and vegetables on 135 hilly acres. The restored 1864 plantation house is still in use, as well. A 90-minute guided walking tour begins at the cocoa fermentary, where you can see the drying process. You then follow a trail through the cultivated area, where a guide points out various fruit- or spice-bearing trees, tropical flowers, and indigenous birds (and their unique songs). Additional trails lead to old military ruins, a religious shrine, and a vantage point for viewing the spectacular Pitons. Cool drinks and a Creole buffet lunch are served at the Cocoa Pod restaurant. Souvenirs, including just-made chocolate sticks, are sold at the boutique. ⊠ *Vieux Fort Rd., Château Belair* ☎ *758/459–7545* ⊕ *www. fonddouxestate.com* ☟ *$20 with snacks, $40 with lunch.*

★ The Pitons

HISTORIC SITE | Rising precipitously from the cobalt-blue Caribbean just south of Soufrière Bay, these two unusual mountains—named a UNESCO World Heritage Site in 2004—have become the iconic symbol of Saint Lucia. Covered with thick tropical vegetation, the massive outcroppings were formed by a volcanic eruption 30 to 40 million years ago. They are not identical twins, since 2,619-foot Gros Piton is taller and 2,461-foot Petit Piton is broader. It's possible to climb the Pitons, but it's a strenuous trek. Gros Piton is the easier climb and takes about four hours round-trip. Either climb requires permission and a guide; register at the base of Gros Piton. ⊠ *Soufrière.*

★ Sulphur Springs Park

HOT SPRINGS | **FAMILY** | As you approach Sulphur Springs Park and the crater of the "drive-in volcano," your nose will pick up a strong scent emanating from more than 20 belching pools of murky water, crusty sulfur deposits, and other multicolor minerals baking and steaming on the surface. You don't actually drive all the way in. Rather, you drive within a few hundred feet of the gurgling, steaming mass and then walk behind your guide (whose service is included in the admission price) around a fault in the substratum rock. Following the fascinating, educational half-hour tour, you're welcome to take a quick dip in the nearby hot, mineral-rich bathing pools—they can also be pretty stinky on a hot day, but your skin (and joints) will thank you! ⊠ *Malgretoute, Soufrière* ⊕ *Off West Coast Rd., south of town* ☎ *758/459–7686* ⊕ *www.sulphurspringssaintlucia. com* ☟ *$9 tour, $5 bath; $13 combo.*

🜨 Beaches

★ Reduit Beach

BEACH—SIGHT | **FAMILY** | Many feel that Reduit (pronounced *red-WEE*) is the island's finest beach. The long stretch of golden sand that frames Rodney Bay is within walking distance of many hotels and restaurants in Rodney Bay Village. Bay Gardens Beach Resort and Mystique Royal St. Lucia face the beachfront; Blu St. Lucia, Harmony Suites, and Ginger Lily hotels are across the road. At the Royal's water-sports center, you can rent sports equipment and beach chairs and take windsurfing or waterskiing lessons. Kids (and adults alike) love Splash Island Water Park, an open-water inflatable playground near Bay Gardens Beach Resort with a trampoline, climbing wall, monkey bars, swing, slide, and more. **Amenities:** food and drink; toilets; water sports. **Best for:** snorkeling; sunset; swimming; walking; windsurfing. ⊠ *Rodney Bay.*

Vigie/Malabar Beach

BEACH—SIGHT | This 2-mile (3-km) stretch of lovely white sand runs parallel to the George F. L. Charles Airport runway in Castries and continues on past the Rendezvous resort, where it becomes Malabar Beach. In the area opposite the airport departure lounge, a few vendors sell refreshments. **Amenities:** food and drink. **Best for:** swimming. ⊠ *Castries*

⟴ *Adjacent to George F. L. Charles Airport runway.*

🍴 Restaurants

Lifeline Bar and Restaurant

$$$ | CARIBBEAN | The cheerful restaurant-bar in the Hummingbird Beach Resort specializes in French creole cuisine. Try fresh seafood or chicken seasoned with local herbs and accompanied by fresh-picked vegetables from the Hummingbird's garden. **Known for:** authentic Caribbean food; great in-town, on-the-beach location; a favorite for three decades. $ *Average main: US$25* ✉ *Hummingbird Beach Resort, Anse Chastanet Rd., Soufrière* ☎ *758/459–7232* ⊕ *www.istlucia.co.uk.*

★ Jacques Waterfront Dining

$$$$ | FRENCH | Chef-owner Jacky Rioux creates magical dishes in his waterfront restaurant set within the gardens of Harmony Suites Hotel in Rodney Bay. The cooking is decidedly French, as is Rioux, but fresh produce and local spices create a memorable fusion cuisine. **Known for:** long-standing reputation for quality cuisine; waterfront location; jazz brunch on Sunday. $ *Average main: US$34* ✉ *Harmony Suites Hotel, Reduit Beach Ave., Rodney Bay* ☎ *758/458–1900* ⊕ *www.jacquesrestaurant.com* ⊗ *No dinner Sun.*

🛍 Shopping

The island's best-known products are artwork and wood carvings, straw mats, clay pottery, and clothing and household articles made from batik and silk-screened fabrics that are designed and produced in island workshops. You can also take home straw hats and baskets and locally grown cocoa, coffee, spices, sauces, and flavorings. The Castries **Craft Market** has aisles and aisles of baskets and other handmade straw work, rustic brooms made from palm fronds, wood carvings, leather work, clay pottery, and souvenirs—all at affordable prices. The

Vendors' Arcade, across the street from the Craft Market, is a maze of stalls and booths where you can find handicrafts among the T-shirts and costume jewelry. Duty-free shopping areas are at **Pointe Seraphine,** an attractive Spanish-motif complex on Castries Harbour with a dozen shops that are open mainly when a cruise ship is in port, and **La Place Carenage,** an inviting three-story complex on the opposite side of the harbor. You can also find duty-free items at stores in **Baywalk Mall** and **J. Q.'s Rodney Bay Mall** in Rodney Bay.

🏃 Activities

DIVING AND SNORKELING

The coral reefs at Anse Cochon and Anse Chastanet, on the southwest coast, are popular beach-entry dive sites. In the north, Pigeon Island is the most convenient site.

Scuba St. Lucia

SCUBA DIVING | Daily (and nightly) beach and boat dives and resort and certification courses are available from this PADI 5 Star facility located on Anse Chastanet, and so is underwater photography and snorkeling equipment. Transportation from the north of the island can be arranged. ✉ *Anse Chastanet Resort, Anse Chastanet Rd., Soufrière* ☎ *758/459–7755, 800/223–1108 in U.S.* ⊕ *www.scubastlucia.com.*

FISHING

Sportfishing is generally done on a catch-and-release basis, but the captain may permit you to take a fish back to your hotel to be prepared for your dinner. Neither spearfishing nor collecting live fish in coastal waters is permitted. Half- and full-day deep-sea fishing excursions can be arranged at Vigie Marina. A half day of fishing on a scheduled trip runs about $85 to $90 per person; a private charter costs $500 to $1,200 for up to six or eight people, depending on the size of the boat and the length of time. Beginners are welcome.

Captain Mike's

FISHING | Named for Captain Mike Hackshaw and run by his family, Bruce and Andrew, this operation has a fleet of Bertram powerboats (31 to 46 feet) that accommodate up to eight passengers for half- or full-day sportfishing charters (tackle and cold drinks are supplied). Customized sightseeing or whale/dolphin-watching trips ($55 per person) can also be arranged for four to six people. ✉ *Vigie Marina, Vigie* ☎ *758/452–7044* ⊕ *www.captmikes.com.*

HIKING

St. Lucia Forestry Department

HIKING/WALKING | Trails under this department's jurisdiction include the Barre de L'Isle Trail (just off the highway, halfway between Castries and Dennery), the Forestiere Trail (20 minutes east of Castries), the Des Cartiers Rain Forest Trail (west of Micoud), the Edmund Rain Forest Trail and Enbas Saut Waterfalls (east of Soufrière), the Millet Bird Sanctuary Trail (east of Marigot Bay), and the Union Nature Trail (north of Castries). Most are two-hour hikes on 2-mile (3-km) loop trails; the bird-watching tour lasts four hours. The Forestry Department charges $25 for access to the hiking trails ($10 for nature trails), and provides guides ($20 to $30, depending on the hike) who explain the plants and trees that you'll encounter and keep you on the right track. Seasoned hikers climb the Pitons, the two volcanic cones rising 2,461 feet and 2,619 feet from the ocean floor just south of Soufrière. Hiking is recommended only on Gros Piton, which offers a steep but safe trail to the top. The first half of the hike is moderately difficult; reaching the summit is challenging and should be attempted only by those who are physically fit. The view from the top is spectacular. Tourists are also permitted to hike Petit Piton, but the second half of the hike requires a good deal of rock climbing, and you'll

need to provide your own safety equipment. Hiking either Piton requires permission from the Forestry Department and a knowledgeable guide. ✉ *Gabriel Charles Forestry Complex, Union, Castries* ☎ *758/468–5645, 758/489–0136 for Pitons permission.*

St. Maarten (Phillipsburg)

St. Martin/St. Maarten: one tiny island, just 37 square miles (59 square km), with two different vibes ruled by two sovereign nations. Here French and Dutch have lived side by side for hundreds of years, and when you cross from one country to the next there are no border patrols, no customs agents. In fact, the only indication that you have crossed a border at all is a small sign and a change in road surface. It is really fun to cross from side to side experiencing all the interesting variations on tropical fun and food, especially when currently favorable exchange rates brings prices near par. St. Martin/St. Maarten epitomizes tourist islands in the sun, where services are well developed but there's still some Caribbean flavor. The Dutch side is ideal for people who like plenty to do. The French side has a more genteel ambience, and a Continental flair. The combination makes an almost ideal port. On the negative side, the island has been completely developed. It can be fun to shop, and you'll find an occasional bargain, but many goods are cheaper in the United States.

ESSENTIALS
CURRENCY
On the Dutch side, the NAf guilder. On the French side, the euro. However, U.S. currency is accepted almost everywhere on the island.

TELEPHONE

The country codes for St. Maarten/St. Martin are 1 721 (Dutch side) and 1 590 (French side). It's an international call to call French St. Martin from Dutch St. Maarten, and vice versa. Most U.S. multi-band GSM mobile phones will work on either side of the island. Digicel, Orange, CHIPPIE, and Dauphin Telecom are the major mobile phone providers, using GSM (850, 900, 1800 and 1900 bands).

COMING ASHORE

Most cruise ships drop anchor off the Dutch capital of Philipsburg or dock in the marina at the southern tip of the Philipsburg harbor; a very few small or medium-size ships drop anchor in Marigot Bay and tender passengers ashore in the French capital. If your ship anchors, tenders will ferry you to the town pier in the middle of town, where taxis await passengers. If your ship docks at the marina, downtown is a 15-minute taxi ride away. The walk is not recommended. The island is small, and most spots aren't more than a 30-minute drive from Marigot or Philipsburg.

Doing your own thing will be much less expensive here than a ship-sponsored tour, and since rental cars are cheap (starting at $35 per day for a local car rental), you can easily strike out as soon as your ship docks. This is the best thing to do if you just want to see the island and spend a little time at a beach. Compare costs of ship excursions and activities to prices offered directly by the operators on their websites to make sure you're saving money. Taxis are government-regulated and fairly costly, so they aren't really an option if you want to do much exploring, but if you just want to go to a beach for the day, there are taxis at the dock. Authorized taxis display stickers of the St. Maarten Taxi Association. Taxis are also available at Marigot. You may be able to negotiate a favorable deal with a taxi driver for a two- to three-hour island tour for as little as $70 for two

Best Bets ⊙

- **Beaches.** The island has 37 beautiful beaches, all open to the public, most with chairs to rent and beach bars and barbecues or restaurants.

- **Butterfly Farm.** The terrarium-like Butterfly Farm is a treat for all ages.

- **The 12-Metre Challenge.** Help sail an America's Cup yacht.

- **Loterie Farm.** On the slopes of Pic du Paradis, an amazing eco-friendly preserve with fun activities, and great food.

- **Shopping.** Both sides of the island are a shopper's paradise.

passengers or $30 per person for more than two. Minibuses run between major areas; destinations are posted on the front. The fare is $2, payable in cash to the driver.

⊙ Sights

PHILIPSBURG

The capital of Dutch St. Maarten stretches about a mile (1½ km) along an isthmus between Great Bay and the Salt Pond and has five parallel streets. Most of the village's dozens of shops and restaurants are on narrow, cobblestone Front Street, closest to Great Bay. It's generally congested when cruise ships are in port because of its many duty-free shops and several casinos. Little lanes called *steegjes* connect Front Street with Back Street. Along the beach is a ½-mile-long (1-km-long) boardwalk with restaurants, souvenir shops, and beach concessions where you can rent chairs and umbrellas for about $15, cold drinks included. There are many Wi-Fi hot spots.

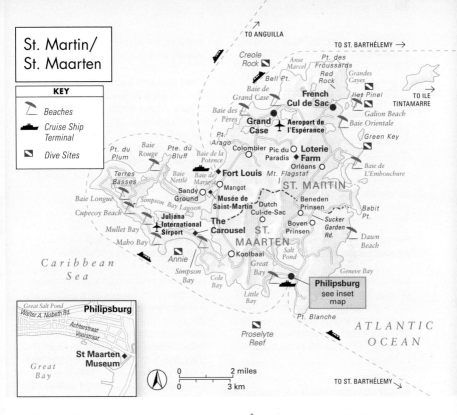

St. Maarten Museum

MUSEUM | Hosting rotating cultural exhibits that address the history, industry, geology, and archaeology of the island, the museum contains artifacts ranging from Arawak pottery shards to objects salvaged from the wreck of HMS *Proselyte*. An interesting exhibit about hurricanes focuses on Hurricane Luis, which devastated the island in 1995. There is a good reference and video library as well. ✉ *7 Front St., Philipsburg* ☎ *721/542–4917* ✉ *Free.*

FRENCH CUL DE SAC

North of Orient Bay Beach, the French colonial mansion of St. Martin's mayor is nestled in the hills. Little red-roof houses look like open umbrellas tumbling down the green hillside. The area is peaceful and good for hiking. From the beach here, shuttle boats make the five-minute trip to Îlet Pinel, an uninhabited island that's fine for picnicking, snorkeling, sunning, and swimming. There are full-service beach clubs there, so just pack the sunscreen and head over.

GRAND CASE

The Caribbean's own Restaurant Row is the heart of this French-side town, a 10-minute drive from either Orient Bay or Marigot, stretching along a narrow beach overlooking Anguilla. You'll find a first-rate restaurant for every palate, mood, and wallet. At lunchtime, or with kids, head to the casual *lolos* (open-air barbecue stands) and feet-in-the-sand beach bars. Twilight drinks and tapas are fun. At night, stroll the strip and preview the sophisticated offerings on the menus posted outside before you settle in for a long and sumptuous meal (reservations are required for some of the top restaurants). If you still have the energy, there are lounges with music (usually a DJ) that get going after 10 pm.

ELSEWHERE IN ST. MAARTEN/ST. MARTIN

★ The Carousel

CAROUSEL | FAMILY | After riding this beautiful restored Italian carousel in the heart of Simpson Bay, kids of all ages can enjoy dozens of flavors of homemade gelato, an engaging photo exhibit of famous people eating ice cream, and a carousel museum with great souvenirs. ⊠ *60 Welfare Rd., Cole Bay* ☎ *721/544–3112* ⌸ *$2.*

Fort Louis

ARCHAEOLOGICAL SITE | Though not much remains of the structure itself, Fort Louis, completed by the French in 1789, is great fun if you want to climb the 92 steps to the top for the wonderful views of the island and neighboring Anguilla. On Wednesday and Saturday there is a market in the square at the bottom. ⊠ *Marigot.*

★ Loterie Farm

NATURE PRESERVE | FAMILY | Almost halfway up the road to Pic Paradis is a peaceful 150-acre private nature preserve, opened to the public in 1999 by American expat B. J. Welch. There are trail maps, so you can hike on your own or hire a guide. Marked trails traverse native forest with tamarind, gum, mango, and mahogany trees—the same as it was hundreds of years ago. You might well see some wild vervet monkeys, now rather common here. L'Eau Lounge is a lovely tropical garden with a chain of spring-fed pools and Jacuzzi area plus pool with lounge chairs, great music, roaming iguanas, and chic tented cabanas with a St. Barth–meets–Wet 'n' Wild atmosphere. A delicious, healthy lunch or dinner can be had at NuitLeau, and if you are brave—and over 4 feet 5 inches tall—you can try soaring over trees on one of the longest ziplines in the western hemisphere. (There is a milder version, but people love the more extreme one.) "Treehab," a wild party

at the end of every month, brings the island's best DJs; and the Garden Groove Party enlivens every Saturday night in June, July, and August. It features barbecue, drinks, DJs, live music, and entertainers. A new 9-hole golf course added in 2019 promises to give the course on the Dutch side in Mullet Bay some competition. ⊠ *103 rte. de Pic du Paradis, Rambaud* ☎ *0590/87–86–16* ⊕ *www. loteriefarm.com* ⌸ *Hiking €5, guide €26, zipline €40–€60.*

Ⓢ Beaches

Baie des Pères (*Friar's Bay*)

BEACH—SIGHT | FAMILY | This quiet, occasionally rocky cove close to Marigot has beach grills and bars, with chaises and umbrellas, usually calm waters, and a lovely view of Anguilla. Kali's Beach Bar, open daily for lunch and (weather permitting) dinner, has a Rasta vibe and color scheme. It's the best place to be on the full moon, with music, dancing, and a huge bonfire, but you can get lunch, beach chairs, and umbrellas anytime. Friar's Bay Beach Café is a French bistro on the sand, open from breakfast to sunset. To get to the beach, take National Road 7 from Marigot, go toward Grand Case to the Morne Valois hill, and turn left on the dead-end road at the sign. Note the last 200 yards of road to the beach is dirt and quite bumpy. **Amenities:** food and drink; toilets. **Best for:** partiers; swimming; walking. ⊠ *Anse des Pères.*

★ Baie Orientale (*Orient Bay*)

BEACH—SIGHT | FAMILY | Even though Hurricane Irma destroyed nearly every business on Orient Beach in 2017, they're practically all back now, and the beach is as vibrant as ever (wider even, with more sand to enjoy now than in years). Many consider this the island's most beautiful beach, with 2 miles (3 km) of champagne sand, underwater marine reserve, a variety of water sports, and re-emerging beach clubs and hotels. At its southern end, "naturists" enjoy the Club Orient

Get the best sunset view over Marigot from Fort Louis.

area's clothing-optional policy, limited by regulation to that portion of the beach only. (Topless sunbathing is allowed on the entire beach.) Naturally, cameras are forbidden and may be confiscated. Plan to spend the day at one of the clubs; each bar has different color umbrellas, and most boast excellent restaurants and lively bars. You can have an open-air massage, try any sea toy you fancy, and stay until late afternoon, though the beach starts to empty like clockwork daily around 4 p.m. To get here from Marigot, take the main road north past Grand Case, past the French side Aéroport de L'Espérance, and watch for the left turn. **Amenities:** food and drink; parking; toilets; water sports. **Best for:** nudists; partiers; swimming; walking; windsurfing. ⊠ *Baie Orientale.*

★ Îlet Pinel

BEACH—SIGHT | FAMILY | A protected nature reserve, this kid-friendly island is a five-minute ferry ride from French Cul de Sac (about $12 per person round-trip). The ferry runs every half hour from midmorning until 4 pm. The water is clear and shallow, and the shore is sheltered. Snorkelers can swim a trail between both coasts of this pencil-shape speck in the ocean. You can rent equipment on the island or in the parking lot before you board the ferry. Yellow Beach has more of a party vibe with cocktail tables in the water. Chairs and umbrellas can be rented for about $25 for two. **Amenities:** food and drink; parking. **Best for:** snorkeling; sunning; swimming. ⊠ *Îlet Pinel.*

★ Mullet Bay Beach

BEACH—SIGHT | FAMILY | Many believe that this mile-long, powdery white-sand beach behind the Mullet Bay Golf Course is the island's best. You can rent umbrellas and chairs here. Swimmers like it because the water is usually calm, but when the swell is up, surfers take over. Be cautious here; undertow can be challenging. Always swim with others nearby, since there are no lifeguards. The comparatively calm cove at the south end is good for kids. Listen for the "whis-pering pebbles" as the waves wash up. Beach bars serve lunch and cold drinks. **Amenities:** food and drink. **Best for:** families; snorkeling; surfing; swimming. ⊠ *South of Cupecoy and Northwest of the Maho area, Mullet Bay.*

🍴 Restaurants

★ Cynthia's Talk of the Town
$$ | **CARIBBEAN** | **FAMILY** | One of the half-dozen lolos in the middle of town on the water side, Cynthia's (better known simply as "Talk of the Town") is a fun, relatively cheap, and iconic St. Martin meal. With plastic utensils and paper plates, it couldn't be more informal, and the menu includes everything from succulent grilled ribs to stewed conch, fresh snapper, and grilled lobster. **Known for:** lobster; succulent ribs; low pricing and big portions. ⑤ *Average main: €14* ⊠ *Bd. de Grand Case, Grand Case* ☎ *0590/35–67–84* ▭ *No credit cards.*

Taloula's Blue Bitch Bar
$$ | **ECLECTIC** | **FAMILY** | Ribs and burgers are the specialty at this casual beach-front restaurant, but the jerk chicken and thin-crust pizza, not to mention a few vegetarian items, are not to be ignored. Lunch is accompanied by (warning: loud) live music; every Friday a DJ spins tunes. **Known for:** location on the Philipsburg boardwalk; delicious tapas; entertainment night and day. ⑤ *Average main: $19* ⊠ *Sint Rose Arcade, Philipsburg* ⊹ *Off Front St. on the boardwalk* ☎ *721/542–1645* ⊕ *www.bluebitchbar.com.*

🛍 Shopping

Shopaholics are drawn to the array of stores, and jewelry in particular is big business on both sides of the island. Duty-free shops can offer substantial savings (about 15% to 30% below U.S. prices) on cameras, expensive jewelry, watches, liquor, cigars, and designer clothing—but not always, so make sure you're familiar with U.S. prices to know if you're getting a deal (and be prepared to bargain hard). Stick with the big vendors that advertise in the tourist press, and you will be more likely to avoid today's ubiquitous fakes and replicas. On both sides of the island, be alert for idlers; they can snatch unwatched purses.

Prices are in dollars on the Dutch side, in euros on the French side. As for bargains, there are more to be had on the Dutch side; prices on the French side may be higher than those back home, and being in euros doesn't help. Merchandise may not be from the newest collections, especially with regard to clothing; there are items available on the French side that are not available on the Dutch side.

PHILIPSBURG
Philipsburg's **Front Street** has reinvented itself. Now it's mall-like, with a redbrick walk and streets, palm trees lining the sleek boutiques, jewelry stores, souvenir shops, outdoor restaurants, and the old reliables, such as McDonald's and Burger King. Here and there a school or a church appears to remind visitors there's more to the island than shopping. On Back Street, the **Philipsburg Market Place** is a daily open-air market where you can haggle on handicrafts, souvenirs, and beachwear. **Old Street,** near the end of Front Street, has stores, boutiques, and open-air cafés offering French crepes, rich chocolates, and island mementos.

🏃 Activities

DIVING AND SNORKELING
Diving in St. Maarten/St. Martin is mediocre at best, but those who want to dive will find a few positives. The water temperature here is rarely below 70°F (21°C) and visibility is often 60 to 100 feet. The island has more than 30 dive sites, from wrecks to rocky labyrinths. Right outside Philipsburg, 55 feet under the water, is the HMS *Proselyte,* once explored by Jacques Cousteau. Although it sank in

1801, the boat's cannons and coral-encrusted anchors are still visible. Off the north coast, in the protected and mostly current-free Grand Case Bay, is **Creole Rock.** The water here ranges in depth from 10 feet to 25 feet. Other sites off the north coast include **Îlet Pinel,** with its good shallow diving; **Green Key,** with its vibrant barrier reef; and **Tintamarre,** with its sheltered coves and geologic faults. On average, one-tank dives start at $58; two-tank dives are about $100. Certification courses start at about $450.

Dive Safaris
SCUBA DIVING | Certified divers who have dived within the last two years can watch professional feeders give reef sharks a little nosh in a half-hour shark-awareness dive. The company also offers a full PADI training program and can tailor dive excursions and sophisticated, sensitive instruction to any level. ⊠ *16 Airport Rd., Simpson Bay* ☏ *721/545–2401* ⊕ *www. divesafarisstmaarten.com.*

FISHING
You can angle for yellowtail snapper, grouper, marlin, tuna, and wahoo on deep-sea excursions. Costs range from $150 per person for a half day to $250 for a full day. Prices usually include bait and tackle, instruction for novices, and refreshments. Ask about licensing and insurance.

★ Rudy's Deep Sea Fishing
FISHING | One of the more experienced sport-angling outfits runs private charter trips. Half-day excursions for up to four people start at $595. Rudy is reasonable; you can have the fillets you need and he keeps the rest. ■TIP→ **Check the website for great tips on fishing around St. Maarten.** ⊠ *14 Airport Rd., Simpson Bay* ☏ *721/545–2177* ⊕ *www.rudysdeepseafishing.com.*

St. Thomas (Charlotte Amalie)

St. Thomas is the busiest cruise port of call in the Caribbean. Up to eight megaships may visit in a single day. Don't expect an exotic island experience: St. Thomas is as American as any place on the mainland, complete with McDonald's and HBO. The positive side of all this development is that there are more tours here than anywhere else in the Caribbean, and every year the excursions get better. Of course, shopping is the big draw in Charlotte Amalie, but experienced travelers remember the days of "real" bargains—today, passengers fill the stores and it's a seller's market. On some days there are so many cruise passengers on St. Thomas that you must book a ship-sponsored shore excursion if you want to do more than just take a taxi to the beach or stroll around Charlotte Amalie.

ESSENTIALS
CURRENCY
U.S. dollar.

TELEPHONE
Calling to or from the U.S. Virgin Islands works the same as any domestic call; dial 1 and the area code 340. Most U.S. mobile phone plans include the Virgin Islands for no additional cost. The major service providers are AT&T, Choice Wireless, Sprint, and T-Mobile US, using GSM (850 and 1900 bands).

COMING ASHORE
Depending on how many ships are in port, cruise ships drop anchor in the harbor at Charlotte Amalie and tender passengers directly to the waterfront duty-free shops, dock at the Havensight Mall at the eastern end of the crescent bay, or dock at Crown Bay Marina a few miles west of town (Holland America almost always docks at Crown Bay).

The distance from Havensight to the duty-free shops is 1½ miles (3 km), which can be walked in less than half an hour; a shared-van taxi ride there costs $6 per person. Tourist information offices are at the Havensight Mall (across from Building No. 1) for docking passengers and downtown near Fort Christian (at the eastern end of the waterfront shopping area) for those coming ashore by tender. Both offices distribute free maps. From Crown Bay it's a half-hour walk or a $5-per-person shared-van taxi ride. Virgin Islands Taxi Association drivers offer a basic two-hour island tour for $29 per person for two or more people. You can rent a car in St. Thomas (where you drive on the left), but with all the tour options it's often easier and cheaper to take an organized excursion or just hop in a cab.

◉ Sights

CHARLOTTE AMALIE

St. Thomas's major burg is a hilly shopping town. There are also plenty of interesting historic sights—so take the time to see at least a few.

Fort Christian

MILITARY SITE | FAMILY | St. Thomas's oldest standing structure, this remarkable building was built between 1672 and 1680 and now has U.S. National Historic Landmark status. Over the years, it was used as a jail, governor's residence, town hall, courthouse, and church. In 2005, a multimillion-dollar renovation project started to stabilize the structure and halt centuries of deterioration. This project was completed in 2017 in time to commemorate the territory's centennial, or 100 years after the U.S. purchased the islands from Denmark in 1917. Outside, look for historic features, like the four renovated faces of the famous 19th-century clock tower. ⊠ *Waterfront Hwy., east of shopping district, Charlotte Amalie* ☎ *340/774–5541* ⊕ *stthomashistorical-trust.org* ⊠ *$10* ⊗ *Closed weekends.*

Best Bets ◉

■ **Coral World Ocean Park.** This aquarium attraction is a great bet for families, and it's on one of the best snorkeling beaches.

■ **Magens Bay Beach.** St. Thomas has one of the most picture-perfect beaches you'll ever see. It's great for swimming.

■ **St. John.** It's easy to hop on the ferry to St. John for a day of hiking, then relax for an hour or two on the beach afterward.

■ **Shopping.** Charlotte Amalie is one of the best places in the Caribbean to shop.

Gallery Camille Pissarro

BUILDING | Housing an antiques shop and an art gallery, this was the birthplace and childhood home of the acclaimed 19th-century impressionist painter Camille Pissarro, who lived for most of his adult life in France. The art gallery on the second floor contains three original pages from Pissarro's sketchbook and two pastels by Pissarro's grandson, Claude. ⊠ *14 Dronningens Gade (Main St.), between Raadets Gade and Trompeter Gade, Charlotte Amalie.*

Hassel Island

ARCHAEOLOGICAL SITE | East of Water Island in Charlotte Amalie harbor, Hassel Island is part of the Virgin Islands National Park. On it are the ruins of a British military garrison (built during a brief British occupation of the USVI during the 1800s) and the remains of a marine railway (where ships were hoisted into dry dock for repairs). Daily guided kayak tours to the island are available from VI Ecotours. The St. Thomas Historical Trust leads three-hour walking tours throughout the year. ⊠ *Charlotte Amalie harbor, Charlotte Amalie* ☎ *340/776–6201 Virgin Islands*

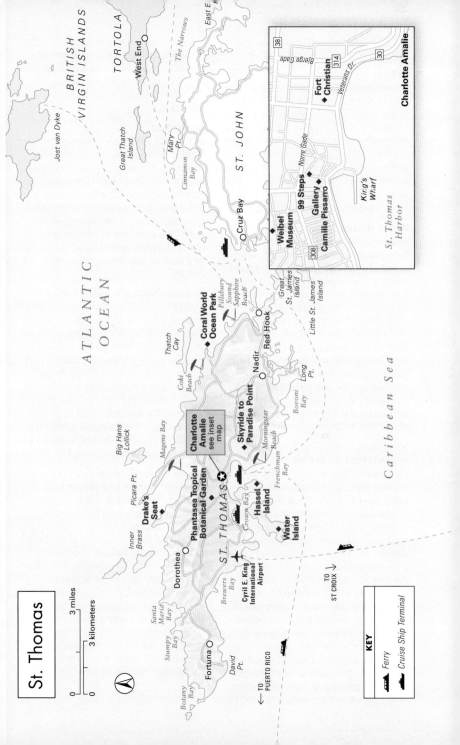

National Park main office ⊕ www.nps.gov/viis.

99 Steps

NEIGHBORHOOD | This staircase "street," built by the Danes in the 1700s, leads to the residential area above Charlotte Amalie and to Blackbeard's Castle, a U.S. National Historic Landmark. If you count the stairs as you go up, you'll discover, as thousands have before you, that there are more than the name implies. ⊠ Charlotte Amalie ✦ Look for steps heading north from Government Hill.

Weibel Museum

MUSEUM | This museum next to the Synagogue of Beracha Veshalom show-cases 300 years of Jewish history on St. Thomas. The small gift shop sells a commemorative silver coin celebrating the anniversary of the Hebrew congregation's establishment on the island in 1796. There are also tropically inspired items, such as menorahs painted to resemble palm trees. ⊠ Synagogue Hill, 15 Crystal Gade, Charlotte Amalie ✦ From Main St., walk up Raadets Gade (H. Stern is on the corner) to the top of the hill; turn left and it's the 2nd building on the right ☎ 340/774–4312 ⊕ synagogue.vi ☒ Free.

ELSEWHERE ON ST. THOMAS
★ Coral World Ocean Park

ZOO | FAMILY | This interactive aquarium and water-sports center lets you experience a variety of sea life and other animals. A new 2-acre dolphin habitat opened in 2019. There's also several outdoor pools where you can pet baby sharks, feed stingrays, touch starfish, and view endangered sea turtles. During the Sea Trek Helmet Dive, you walk along an underwater trail wearing a helmet that provides a continuous supply of air. You can also try Snuba, a cross between snorkeling and scuba diving. Swim with a sea lion for the chance to play ball or get a big, wet, whiskered kiss. The park also has an offshore underwater observatory, an 80,000-gallon coral reef exhibit (one of the largest in the world), and a nature

trail with native ducks and tortoises. Daily feedings take place at most exhibits. ⊠ 6450 Estate Smith Bay, Estate Smith Bay ✦ Coki Point Rd. north of Rte. 38 ☎ 340/775–1555 ⊕ www.coralworldvi.com ☒ $15.

Drake's Seat

VIEWPOINT | Sir Francis Drake was supposed to have kept watch over his fleet from this vantage point, looking for enemy ships. The panorama is especially breathtaking (and romantic) at dusk, and if you plan to arrive late in the day, you'll miss the hordes of day-trippers on taxi tours who stop here to take pictures. ⊠ Rte. 40, Mafolie ✦ Located ¼ mile (½ km) west of the intersection of Rtes. 40 and 35.

Phantasea Tropical Botanical Garden

GARDEN | Orchids, palms, cactus, and bromeliads are a few of the stunning plants that bloom along the self-guided hiking trails. These gardens are the essence of peace and quiet; they are located high on the island's lush north side. There's critters here too: peacocks, hummingbirds, and hermit crabs, to name a few. ⊠ Bishop Dr. (intersection of Rtes. 334 and 33) ✦ On the road to Mountain Top ☎ 340/774–2916 ⊕ www.stthomasbotanicalgarden.com ☒ Admission $10.

Skyride to Paradise Point

VIEWPOINT | FAMILY | Fly skyward in a seven-minute gondola ride to Paradise Point, an overlook with breathtaking views of Charlotte Amalie, the harbor, and the neighboring islands of St. Croix to the south and Vieques and Culebra to the west. You'll find several shops, a bar (the specialty here is the Bushwacker, a creamy frozen alcoholic libation), and a restaurant. You can also skip the $21 gondola ride and take a taxi to the top for $7 per person from the Havensight Dock. ⊠ Rte. 30, across from Havensight Mall, Havensight ☎ 340/774–9809 ⊕ www.paradisepointvi.com ☒ $21.

★ Water Island

ISLAND | FAMILY | This island, the fourth largest of the U.S. Virgin Islands, floats about a ¼ mile (½ km) out in Charlotte Amalie harbor. A ferry between Crown Bay Marina and the island ($10 round-trip) operates several times daily, Monday through Saturday from 7 to 6 and Sunday and holidays 8 to 6. From the ferry dock, it's a hike of less than half a mile to Honeymoon Beach (though you have to go up a big hill), where Brad Pitt and Cate Blanchett filmed a scene of the movie *The Curious Case of Benjamin Button.* Get lunch from a food truck, which pulls up daily. Monday night is Movie Night at Honeymoon Beach, a fun activity for the whole family after a day on the beach. The Water Island Music Festival, which features some of the world's best classical performers, takes place here each January. ⊠ *Charlotte Amalie harbor, Water Island* ☎ *340/690–4159 for ferry info.*

🏖 Beaches

★ Coki Beach

BEACH—SIGHT | FAMILY | Funky beach huts selling local foods such as pâtés (fried turnovers with a spicy ground-beef filling), quaint vendor kiosks, and a brigade of hair braiders and taxi men make this beach overlooking picturesque Thatch Cay feel like a carnival. But this is the best place on the island to snorkel and scuba dive. Fish—including grunts, snappers, and wrasses—are like an effervescent cloud you can wave your hand through. **Amenities:** food and drink; lifeguards; parking; showers; toilets; water sports. **Best for:** partiers; snorkeling. ⊠ *Rte. 388, Estate Smith Bay* ✛ *Next to Coral World Ocean Park.*

★ Magens Bay

BEACH—SIGHT | FAMILY | Deeded to the island as a public park, this heart-shape stretch of white sand is considered one of the most beautiful in the world. The bottom of the bay is flat and sandy, so this is a place for sunning and swimming rather than snorkeling. On weekends and holidays the sounds of music from groups partying under the sheds fill the air. There's a bar, snack shack, and beachwear boutique; bathhouses with restrooms, changing rooms, and saltwater showers are close by. Sunfish, kayaks, and paddleboards are the most popular rentals at the water-sports kiosk. **Amenities:** food and drink; lifeguards; parking (fee); showers; toilets; water sports. **Best for:** partiers; swimming; walking. ⊠ *Magens Bay, Rte. 35, at end of road on north side of island* ☎ *340/777–6300* ⊕ *www.magensbayauthority.com* 🎟 *Adults $5, kids under 12 free, parking $2.*

🍴 Restaurants

★ Gladys' Cafe

$$ | CARIBBEAN | This cozy alleyway restaurant is rich in atmosphere, with its mahogany bar and native stone walls, making dining a double delight. Try the local specialties like conch in butter sauce, jerk pork, or panfried yellowtail snapper. **Known for:** service with a smile; homemade hot sauce; great places to sample local West Indian cuisine. 💲 *Average main: $15* ⊠ *Waterfront, 28A Dronningens Gade, Charlotte Amalie* ✛ *West side of Royal Dane Mall* ☎ *340/774–6604* ⊕ *www.gladyscafe.com* ⊗ *No dinner* ☞ *Only Amex credit cards accepted.*

Greenhouse Bar and Restaurant

$$ | AMERICAN | FAMILY | Fun-lovers come to this waterfront restaurant to eat, listen to music, and play games. Even the most finicky eater should find something to please on the eight-page menu that offers burgers, salads, and pizza all day long, along with peel-and-eat shrimp, Caribbean lobster tail, Alaskan king crab, and Black Angus filet mignon for dinner. **Known for:** family-friendly vibe; live music; eight-page menu with huge selection of American-style fare. 💲 *Average main: $18* ⊠ *Waterfront Hwy. at Store Tvaer*

Charlotte Amalie's historic center and shopping district are great places to explore.

Gade, Charlotte Amalie ☎ *340/774–7998*
⊕ *www.thegreenhouserestaurant.com.*

🧳 Shopping

St. Thomas lives up to its billing as a duty-free shopping destination. Even if shopping isn't your idea of how to spend a vacation, you still may want to browse (Monday and Sunday are usually the least crowded). Among the best buys are liquor, linens, china, crystal (most stores will ship), and jewelry. The amount of jewelry available makes this one of the few items for which comparison shopping is worth the effort. Local crafts include shell jewelry, carved calabash bowls, straw brooms, woven baskets, and dolls. Spice mixes, hot sauces, and tropical jams and jellies are other native products.

On St. Thomas stores on Main Street in Charlotte Amalie are open weekdays and Saturday 9 to 5. The hours of the shops in the Havensight Mall (next to the cruise-ship dock) and the Crown Bay Commercial Center (next to the Crown Bay cruise-ship dock) are the same, though occasionally some stay open until 9 on Friday, depending on how many cruise ships are anchored nearby. You may also find some shops open on Sunday if cruise ships are in port. Hotel shops are usually open evenings as well.

The prime shopping area in **Charlotte Amalie** is between Post Office and Market squares; it consists of two parallel streets that run east–west (Waterfront Highway and Main Street) and the alleyways that connect them. Particularly attractive are the historic **A. H. Riise Alley, Drake's Passage, Royal Dane Mall, Palm Passage,** and pastel-painted **International Plaza.**

Vendors Plaza, on the waterfront side of Emancipation Gardens in Charlotte Amalie, is a central location for vendors selling handmade earrings, necklaces, and bracelets; straw baskets and handbags; T-shirts; fabrics; African artifacts; and local fruits. Look for the many brightly colored umbrellas.

There's no sales tax in the USVI, and you can take advantage of the $1,600 duty-free allowance per family member (remember to save your receipts). Although you can find the occasional salesclerk who will make a deal, bartering isn't the norm.

🏃 Activities

DIVING AND SNORKELING
Coki Dive Center
SCUBA DIVING | FAMILY | Snorkeling and dive tours in the fish-filled reefs off Coki Beach are available from this PADI 5 Star outfit, as are classes, including one on underwater photography. It's run by the avid diver Peter Jackson. ✉ *Rte. 388 at Coki Point, Frydendal* 📞 *340/775–4220* 🌐 *www.cokidive.com.*

Snuba of St. Thomas
SCUBA DIVING | FAMILY | In Snuba, a snorkeling and scuba-diving hybrid, a 20-foot air hose connects you to the surface. The cost is $78. Children must be age eight or older to participate. ✉ *Rte. 388 at Coki Point, Estate Smith Bay* 📞 *340/693–8063* 🌐 *www.visnuba.com.*

FISHING
⭐ **Double Header Sportfishing**
FISHING | FAMILY | This company offers trips out to the North Drop on its 40-foot sportfisher and half-day reef and bay trips aboard its two speedy 37-foot center consoles. ✉ *Sapphire Bay Marina, Rte. 38, Sapphire Bay* 📞 *340/777–7317* 🌐 *www.doubleheadersportfishing.net.*

St. Vincent (Kingstown)

You won't find glitzy resorts or flashy discos in St. Vincent. Rather, you'll be fascinated by its busy capital, mountainous beauty, and fine sailing waters. St. Vincent is the largest and northernmost island in the Grenadines archipelago; Kingstown, the capital city of St. Vincent & the Grenadines, is the government

Best Bets 👁

- **Island Tour.** Tour the greater Kingstown area, then travel up the leeward coast to Wallilabou.

- **Falls of Baleine.** A boat trip to the 60-foot falls is a beautiful way to spend the day.

- **Ferry to Bequia.** Laid-back Bequia is one hour by ferry from St. Vincent.

- **Hiking.** Whether you hike in the rain forest or take on the greater challenge of La Soufrière, it's worth exploring some of the island's rugged terrain.

and business center and major port. Except for one barren area on the island's northeast coast—remnants of the 1979 eruption of La Soufrière, one of the last active volcanoes in the Caribbean—the countryside is mountainous, lush, and green. St. Vincent's topography thwarted European settlement for many years. As colonization advanced elsewhere in the Caribbean, in fact, the island became a refuge for Carib Indians, descendants of whom still live in northeastern St. Vincent. After years of fighting and back-and-forth territorial claims, British troops prevailed by overpowering the French and banishing Carib warriors to Central America. Independent since 1979, St. Vincent & the Grenadines remains a member of the British Commonwealth.

ESSENTIALS
CURRENCY
Eastern Caribbean (EC) dollar, but U.S. dollars are widely accepted.

TELEPHONE
The country code for St. Vincent & the Grenadines is 1 784. Digicel and Flow are the major service providers, using GSM (850, 900, and 1800 bands).

COMING ASHORE

The Cruise Ship Complex at Kingstown, St. Vincent's capital city, accommodates two cruise ships; additional vessels anchor offshore and transport passengers to the jetty by launch. The facility has about two dozen shops that sell duty-free items and handicrafts. There's a communications center, post office, tourist information desk, restaurant, and food court.

Buses and taxis are available at the wharf. Taxi drivers are well equipped to take you on an island tour; expect to pay $30 per hour for up to four passengers. The ferry to Bequia (one hour each way, with frequent daily service) is at the adjacent pier. Renting a car for just one day isn't advisable, since car rentals are expensive (at least $55 per day) and require a $38 temporary driving permit on top of that. It's almost always a better deal to take a tour, though you don't have to limit yourself to excursions offered by your ship.

◉ Sights

You can explore Kingstown's shopping and business district, historic churches and cathedrals, and other points of interest in a half day, with another couple of hours spent in the Botanical Gardens. The coastal roads of St. Vincent offer spectacular panoramas and scenes of island life. The Leeward Highway follows the scenic Caribbean coastline; the Windward Highway follows the more dramatic Atlantic coast. A drive along the the latter requires a full day. Exploring La Soufrière or the Vermont Nature Trails is also a major undertaking, requiring a very early start and a full day of strenuous hiking.

★ Botanical Gardens

GARDEN | FAMILY | One of the oldest botanical gardens in the Western Hemisphere is just north of downtown Kingstown, a few minutes by taxi. The garden was created in 1765 by General Robert Melville, governor of the British Caribbean islands, after Captain Bligh—of HMS *Bounty* fame—brought the first breadfruit tree to this island for landowners to propagate. The prolific bounty of the breadfruit trees was used to feed the slaves. You can see a direct descendant of the original tree among the specimens of mahogany, rubber, teak, and other tropical trees and shrubs across 20 acres of gardens. Two dozen rare St. Vincent parrots (*Amazona guildingii*), confiscated from illegal collections, live in the small aviary. Guides explain all the medicinal and ornamental trees and shrubs. A gift shop (open weekdays) has local crafts, artwork, books, confections, and a traditional creole lunch menu. ⊠ *Off Leeward Hwy., northeast of town, Montrose* ☎ *784/493–5824* ⊕ *botanicalgarden.gov. vc* ⊠ *$2, guided tour $4.*

Falls of Baleine

BODY OF WATER | The falls are impossible to reach by car, so book an all-day escorted boat trip from Villa Beach. The boat ride along the coast offers scenic island views. When you arrive, you have to wade through shallow water to get to the beach. Then local guides help you make the easy 10-minute trek to the 60-foot falls and their rock-enclosed freshwater pool. Wear a bathing suit. ■**TIP→ Avoid visiting after heavy rainfall, when the area is prone to swift water flow and falling rocks.** ⊠ *Baleine Bay, at the northern tip of the island* ⊕ *nationalparks.gov.vc.*

★ Ft. Charlotte

HISTORIC SITE | FAMILY | Started by the French in 1786 and completed by the British in 1806, the fort was ultimately named for Britain's Queen Charlotte, wife of King George III. It sits on Berkshire Hill, a dramatic promontory 2 miles (3 km) north of Kingstown and 636 feet above sea level, affording a stunning view of the capital city and the Grenadines. Interestingly, its cannons face inland, as the fear of attack—by the French and their Carib allies—from the ridges above

Kingstown was far greater than any threat approaching from the sea. In any case, the fort saw no action. Nowadays, it serves as a signal station for ships; the ancient cells house historical paintings of the island by Lindsay Prescott. ⊠ *Berkshire Hill, off Edinboro Rd., Kingstown* ✛ *2 miles (3 km) north of town.*

Kingstown

COMMERCIAL CENTER | The capital of St. Vincent & the Grenadines, a city of 16,500 residents, wraps around Kingstown Bay on the island's southwestern coast; a ring of green hills and ridges studded with homes forms a backdrop for the city. This is very much a working city, with a busy harbor and few concessions to tourists. Kingstown Harbour is the only deepwater port on the island.

A few gift shops can be found on and around **Bay Street,** near the harbor. Upper Bay Street, which stretches along the bayfront, bustles with daytime activity—workers going about their business and housewives doing their shopping. Many of Kingstown's downtown buildings are built of stone or brick brought to the island as ballast in the holds of 18th-century ships (and replaced with sugar and spices for the return trip to Europe). The Georgian-style stone arches and second-floor overhangs on former warehouses—which provide shelter from midday sun and the brief, cooling showers common to the tropics—have earned Kingstown the nickname "City of Arches."

Grenadines Wharf, at the south end of Bay Street, is busy with ships loading supplies and ferries loading people bound for the Grenadines. The **Cruise-Ship Complex,** adjacent to the commercial wharf, has a mall with a dozen or more shops, plus restaurants, communications facilities, and a taxi stand.

A huge selection of produce fills the noisy, colorful **Kingstown Market,** a three-story building that takes up a whole city block on Upper Bay, Hillsboro, and Bedford Streets in the center of town. The market is open Monday through Saturday, but the busiest times (and the best times to go) are Friday and Saturday mornings. In the courtyard, vendors sell local arts and crafts. On the upper floors, merchants sell clothing, household items, gifts, and other products.

St. George's Cathedral, on Grenville Street, is a pristine, creamy yellow Anglican church built in 1820. The dignified Georgian architecture includes simple wooden pews, an ornate chandelier, and beautiful stained-glass windows; one was a gift from Queen Victoria, who actually commissioned it for London's St. Paul's Cathedral in honor of her first grandson. When the artist created an angel with a red robe, she was horrified by the color and sent the window abroad. The markers in the cathedral's graveyard recount the history of the island. Across the street is **St. Mary's Roman Catholic Cathedral of the Assumption,** built in stages beginning in 1823. The strangely appealing design is a blend of Moorish, Georgian, and Romanesque styles applied to black brick. Nearby, freed slaves built the **Kingstown Methodist Church** in 1841. The exterior is brick, simply decorated with quoins (solid blocks that form the corners), and the roof is held together by metal straps, bolts, and wooden pins. **Scots Kirk** was built from 1839 to 1880 by and for Scottish settlers but became a Seventh-Day Adventist church in 1952. ⊠ *Kingstown.*

La Soufrière

MOUNTAIN—SIGHT | This towering volcano, which last erupted in 1979, is 4,048 feet high and so huge in area that its surrounding mountainside covers virtually the entire northern third of the island. The eastern trail to the rim of the crater, a two-hour ascent, begins at Rabacca Dry River. ⊠ *Rabacca Dry River, Rabacca.*

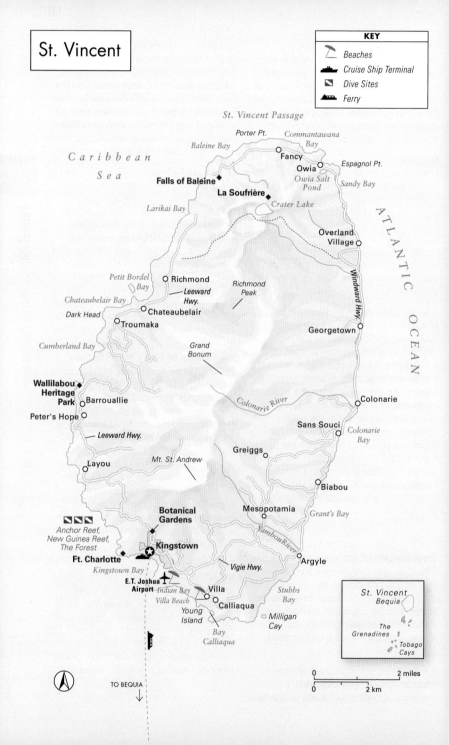

St. Vincent

KEY
- Beaches
- Cruise Ship Terminal
- Dive Sites
- Ferry

St. Vincent Passage

Caribbean Sea

Porter Pt.
Baleine Bay
Fancy
Owia
Commantawana Bay
Espagnol Pt.
Falls of Baleine
Owia Salt Pond
Sandy Bay
La Soufrière
Larikai Bay
Crater Lake

ATLANTIC OCEAN

Overland Village
Richmond
Petit Bordel Bay
Leeward Hwy.
Richmond Peak
Chateaubelair Bay
Chateaubelair
Dark Head
Troumaka
Windward Hwy.
Georgetown
Cumberland Bay
Grand Bonum
Wallilabou Heritage Park
Barrouallie
Colonarie River
Colonarie
Peter's Hope
Sans Souci
Colonarie Bay
Leeward Hwy.
Greiggs
Layou
Mt. St. Andrew
Biabou
Mesopotamia
Grant's Bay
Botanical Gardens
Yambou River
Anchor Reef, New Guinea Reef, The Forest
Kingstown
Argyle
Ft. Charlotte
Vigie Hwy.
Kingstown Bay
Stubbs Bay
E.T. Joshua Airport
Indian Bay
Villa
Villa Beach
Calliaqua
Milligan Cay
Young Island
Bay Calliaqua

TO BEQUIA

St. Vincent
Bequia
The Grenadines
Tobago Cays

0   2 miles
0   2 km

Wallilabou Heritage Park

LOCAL INTEREST | **FAMILY** | The Wallilabou Estate, halfway up the island's leeward coast, once produced cocoa, cotton, and arrowroot. Today, it is Wallilabou Heritage Park, a recreational site with a river and small waterfall, which creates a small pool where you can take a freshwater plunge. You can also sunbathe, swim, picnic, or buy your lunch at Wallilabou Anchorage—a favorite stop for boaters staying overnight. The *Pirates of the Caribbean* movies left their mark on Wallilabou (pronounced *wally-la-BOO*), a location used for filming the opening scenes of *The Curse of the Black Pearl* in 2003. Many of the buildings and docks built as stage sets remain, giving Wallilabou Bay (a port of entry for visiting yachts) an intriguingly historical (if ersatz) appearance. ⊠ *Wallilabou Bay* 🖃 *$2.*

🏖 Beaches

St. Vincent's origin is volcanic, so its beaches range in color from golden-brown to black. Swimming is recommended only in the lagoons and bays along the leeward coast. By contrast, beaches on Bequia and the rest of the Grenadines have pure white sand, palm trees, and crystal-clear aquamarine water; some are even within walking distance of the jetty.

Indian Bay Beach

BEACH—SIGHT | South of Kingstown and separated from Villa Beach by a rocky promontory, Indian Bay has golden sand but is slightly rocky in some places; it's very good for snorkeling. Grand View Hotel, high on a cliff overlooking Indian Bay Beach, operates a beach bar and grill. **Amenities:** food and drink. **Best for:** snorkeling; swimming. ⊠ *Windward Hwy., Villa* ✛ *3½ miles (5.5 km) south of Kingstown* 🖃 *$2 restroom and showers.*

Villa Beach

BEACH—SIGHT | The long stretch of sand in front of the row of hotels facing the Young Island Channel (Mariners, Paradise Beach, Sunset Shores, and Beachcombers on the "mainland" and Young Island Resort across the channel) varies from 20 to 25 feet wide to practically nonexistent. The broadest, sandiest part is in front of Beachcombers Hotel, which is also the perfect spot for sunbathers to get lunch and liquid refreshments. Villa Beach is a popular beach destination for cruise-ship passengers when a ship is in port. **Amenities:** food and drink; water sports. **Best for:** swimming. ⊠ *Villa.*

🍴 Restaurants

Basil's Bar and Restaurant

$$$ | **CARIBBEAN** | It's not just the air-conditioning that makes this restaurant cool. Basil's, at street level in the Cobblestone Inn, is the Kingstown power-lunch venue. **Known for:** convenient downtown location close to wharf; buffet lunch; tasty West Indian curry. Ⓢ *Average main: $24* ⊠ *The Cobblestone Inn, Upper Bay St., Kingstown* ☎ *784/457–2713* ⊘ *Closed Sun.*

Cobblestone Rooftop Bar & Restaurant

$$ | **CARIBBEAN** | To reach what is perhaps the most pleasant, the breeziest, and the most satisfying breakfast and lunch spot in downtown Kingstown, diners must climb the equivalent of three flights of interior stone steps within the historic Cobblestone Inn. But getting to the open-air rooftop restaurant is half the fun, as diners get an up-close view of a 19th-century Georgian sugar (and later arrowroot) warehouse that's now a very appealing boutique inn. **Known for:** good food in an interesting location; daily lunch special and delicious desserts; a favorite of locals and tourists alike. Ⓢ *Average main: $15* ⊠ *The Cobblestone Inn, Upper Bay St., Kingstown* ☎ *784/456–1937* ⊕ *www.thecobblestoneinn.com* ⊘ *No dinner.*

🛍 Shopping

The 12 small blocks that hug the waterfront in **downtown Kingstown** make up St. Vincent's main shopping district. Among the shops that sell household necessities are a few that sell local crafts, gifts, and souvenirs. Bargaining is neither expected nor appreciated. The **Cruise-Ship Complex,** on the waterfront in Kingstown, has a collection of a dozen or so boutiques, shops, and restaurants that cater primarily to cruise-ship passengers but welcome all shoppers. The best souvenirs of St. Vincent are intricately woven straw items, such as handbags, hats, slippers, baskets, and grass mats that range in size from place mats to room-size floor mats. If you're inclined to bring home a floor mat, they aren't heavy and roll or fold rather neatly; wrapped tightly and packed in an extra (soft-sided) suitcase or tote, it can be checked as luggage for the flight home. Local artwork and carvings are available in galleries, from street vendors, and in shops at the Cruise-Ship Complex. Hot sauce and other condiments, often produced in St. Vincent and sold in markets and gift shops, make tasty souvenirs to bring back home.

🏃 Activities

DIVING AND SNORKELING

Novices and advanced divers alike will be impressed by the marine life in the waters around St. Vincent—brilliant sponges, huge deepwater coral trees, and shallow reefs teeming with colorful fish. Many sites in the Grenadines are still virtually unexplored. It can't be emphasized enough, however, that the coral reef is extremely fragile; you must only look and never touch.

A day-trip to the pristine waters surrounding the **Tobago Cays,** in the southern Grenadines, provides a spectacular diving or snorkeling experience.

Dive St. Vincent

SCUBA DIVING | Two PADI-certified dive masters offer beginner and certification courses for ages eight and up, an introductory scuba course for novices, and advanced water excursions along the St. Vincent coast and to the southern Grenadines for diving connoisseurs. ✉ *Windward Hwy., Young Island Dock, Villa* ☎ *784/457–4714* ⊕ *www.divestvincent.com.*

GUIDED TOURS

Several operators on St. Vincent offer sightseeing tours on land or by sea. You can also arrange for informal land tours through taxi drivers, who double as knowledgeable guides. Expect to pay $30 per hour for up to four people.

★ Fantasea Tours

TOUR—SPORTS | A fleet of four powerboats, ranging from a 28-foot Bowen to a 60-foot party catamaran, is ready to take you on any of a number of cruises—along the St. Vincent coast, to Bequia and Mustique, snorkeling in the Tobago Cays and Mayreau, or whale- or dolphin-watching. Fantasea also offers land tours along the windward coast to Owia Salt Pond, along the leeward coast to Dark View Falls, or hikes either along the Vermont Nature Trail or up La Soufrière volcano. ✉ *Paradise Beach Hotel, Windward Hwy., Villa* ☎ *784/457–4477* ⊕ *www.fantaseatours.com.*

★ Sailor's Wilderness Tours

TOUR—SPORTS | Options from this company include a comfortable sightseeing drive (by day or by moonlight), mountain biking on remote trails, or a strenuous hike up La Soufrière volcano. The tours are usually conducted under the expert guidance of Trevor "Sailor" Bailey himself. ✉ *Upper Middle St., Kingstown* ☎ *784/457–1712* ⊕ *www.sailorswildernesstours.com.*

Sam's Taxi Tours

TOUR—SPORTS | In addition to half- and full-day tours in Kingstown and around

St. Vincent, Sam's also offers hiking tours to La Soufrière and scenic walks along the Vermont Nature Trail. Also available is a tour on Bequia that includes the Old Hegg Turtle Sanctuary. ⊠ *London Rd., Cane Garden, Kingstown* ☎ *784/456–4338, 703/738–6461 in U.S.* ⊕ *samtaxitours.com.*

Tobago (Scarborough)

The smaller and quieter of the sister islands that make up Trinidad and Tobago offers pristine beaches and friendly people. Tobago has long been a favorite of European visitors, who enjoy the rustic feel of the island and the laid-back pace. There are numerous fine restaurants—though not many in Scarborough, where cruise ships dock. The culinary thrill here is exploring the local cuisine that can be found at food stalls across the island, and you could easily make eating the focus of your shore excursion and be all the happier for it. No trip here is complete without trying the quintessential Tobago dish: curry crab and dumplings. It can be a slow (and messy) experience, but it fits in perfectly with the pace of life on the island.

ESSENTIALS

CURRENCY

The Trinidad and Tobago dollar (TT$). Most places catering to tourists will accept U.S. currency, but the exchange rate may vary wildly from place to place.

TELEPHONE

The country code for Trinidad & Tobago is 1 868. The major mobile providers are BMobile and Digicel, using GSM (850, 1800 and 1900 bands).

COMING ASHORE

Scarborough, Tobago's lazy and hilly capital, is where all cruise ships dock. The cruise terminal is at the base of the city, near the market, fast-food restaurants, and many colorful shops. There are shops selling goods specifically marketed to

Best Bets

- **Bird-Watching.** For such a small island, the diversity of bird life is fascinating.

- **Buccoo Reef.** The reef at the southwestern tip of the island teems with life.

- **Beaches.** If you're craving an excellent Caribbean beach, this is one place where you can take your pick of them, each lovelier than the last.

- **Golf.** The island has one excellent and one very good golf course.

tourists right at the port, but a short stroll around the streets of downtown can yield considerably more interesting treasures.

Although you can easily walk into town, the island's best beaches and restaurants are in Crown Point. Because of the narrow roads and hilly terrain—not to mention aggressive drivers —it's a bad idea to rent a car. If you do choose to drive yourself, remember that driving is on the left, British-style. Taxis flock to the port whenever a cruise ship arrives. Authorized taxis always have a license plate starting with the letter *H* (for "hire"). Although rates are technically fixed, it's still worth negotiating with the driver.

◉ Sights

★ Ft. King George

HISTORIC SITE | On Mount St. George, a short drive up the hill from Scarborough, Tobago's best-preserved historic monument clings to a cliff high above the ocean. Ft. King George was built in the 1770s and operated until 1854. It's hard to imagine that this lovely, tranquil spot commanding sweeping views of the bay and landscaped with lush tropical foliage was ever the site of any

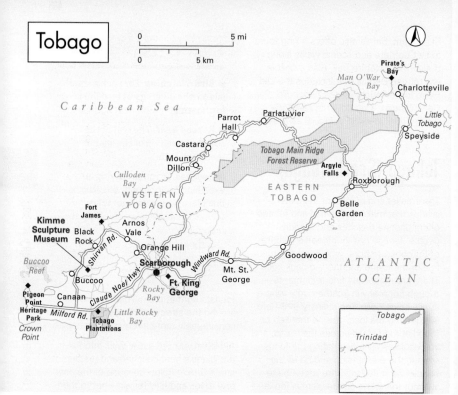

Tobago

0   5 mi

0   5 km

Caribbean Sea

Pirate's Bay
Man O'War Bay
Charlotteville
Parrot Hall
Parlatuvier
Little Tobago
Castara
Speyside
Mount Dillon
Tobago Main Ridge Forest Reserve
Argyle Falls
Culloden Bay
EASTERN TOBAGO
Roxborough
WESTERN TOBAGO
Fort James
Belle Garden
Kimme Sculpture Museum
Arnos Vale
Black Rock
Orange Hill
Windward Rd.
Goodwood
ATLANTIC OCEAN
Buccoo Reef
Scarborough
Mt. St. George
Buccoo
Pigeon Point
Canaan
Rocky Bay
Ft. King George
Heritage Park
Milford Rd.
Little Rocky Bay
Crown Point
Tobago Plantations
Shirvan Rd.
Claude Noel Hwy.

Tobago
Trinidad

---

military action, but the prison, officers' mess, and several stabilized cannons attest otherwise. Just to the left of the tall wooden figures dancing a traditional Tobagonian jig is the former barracks guardhouse, now housing the small **Tobago Museum.** Exhibits include weapons and other pre-Columbian artifacts found in the area; the fertility figures are especially interesting. Upstairs are maps and photographs of Tobago's past. Be sure to check out the gift display cases for the perversely fascinating jewelry made from embalmed and painted lizards and sea creatures; you might find it hard to resist a pair of bright-yellow shrimp earrings. The Fine Arts Centre at the foot of the Ft. King George complex shows the work of local artists. ⊠ *84 Fort St., Scarborough* 🕾 *868/639–3970 for museum* 🖃 *Fort free, museum $2.*

Kimme Sculpture Museum

BUILDING | The diminutive and eccentric German-born sculptress Luise Kimme fell in love with the form of Tobagonians and devoted her life to capturing them in her sculptures. Her pieces can exceed 12 feet in height and are often wonderfully whimsical. Much of her work is done in wood (none of it local), but there are many bronze pieces as well. Ms. Kimme passed away in 2013, but her work remains on permanent display at her former home. The museum itself is a turreted structure with a commanding view of the countryside. Most locals refer to it as "the Castle." There are numerous signs in Mt. Irvine directing visitors to the museum. ⊠ *Mt. Irvine Bay* 🕾 *868/639–0257* ⊕ *www.luisekimme.com* 🖃 *TT$20.*

Scarborough

MARKET | Around Rockley Bay on the island's leeward hilly side, this town is both the capital of Tobago and a popular cruise-ship port, but it feels as if not much has changed since the area was settled two centuries ago. It may not be one of the delightful pastel-color cities of the Caribbean, but Scarborough does have its charms, including several interesting little shops. Whatever you do, be sure to check out the busy Scarborough Market, an indoor and outdoor affair with fresh vegetables, live chickens, and clothing. Note the red-and-yellow Methodist church on the hill, one of Tobago's oldest churches.

☺ Beaches

Tobago has many beautiful beaches, ranging from the popular to the completely isolated. Store Bay, near the airport, is also a popular area for local food and entertainment. The beach most associated with Tobago—and certainly the most photographed—is Pigeon Point Beach, which is a beautiful stretch of white sand lined with palm trees and perfect for swimming. Because of the crime levels on both islands, exercise caution if planning to explore some of the more remote beaches.

Bacolet Beach

BEACH—SIGHT | This dark-sand beach was the setting for the films *Swiss Family Robinson* and *Heaven Knows, Mr. Allison*. If you are not a guest at the Blue Haven Hotel, access is down a track next door to the hotel. The bathroom and changing facilities are for hotel guests only. **Amenities:** food and drink. **Best for:** swimming; walking. ⊠ *Windward Rd., east of Scarborough.*

Great Courland Bay

BEACH—SIGHT | This bay near Ft. Bennett has clear, tranquil waters. Along the sandy beach—one of Tobago's longest—you can find several hotels. A marina attracts the yachting crowd. **Amenities:** none. **Best for:** swimming; walking. ⊠ *Leeward Rd., northeast of Black Rock, Courland.*

King's Bay

BEACH—SIGHT | Surrounded by steep green hills, this is the prettiest swimming site off the road from Scarborough to Speyside. The crescent beach is marked by a sign about halfway between the two towns. Just before you reach the bay, there's a bridge with an unmarked turnoff that leads to a parking lot; beyond that, a landscaped path leads to a waterfall with a rocky pool. Locals will likely offer to guide you to the top of the falls; however, you may find the climb not worth the effort. **Amenities:** food and drink; lifeguards; parking; showers. **Best for:** swimming; walking. ⊠ *Winward Rd., Delaford.*

Pigeon Point Beach

BEACH—SIGHT | This stunning locale is often displayed on Tobago travel brochures. The white-sand beach is lined with swaying coconut trees, and there are changing facilities and food stalls nearby. The beach is public, but there is an admission fee. **Amenities:** food and drink; showers; toilets. **Best for:** partiers; swimming; tanning. ⊠ *Pigeon Point* ⊕ *www.pigeonpoint.tt* ⊞ *TT$20.*

Store Bay

BEACH—SIGHT | This beach, where boats depart for Buccoo Reef, is little more than a small sandy cove between two rocky breakwaters, but the food stands here are amazing. The tourist board has licensed several huts to local ladies, who sell roti, pelau, curry crab, and dumplings. There are also souvenirs ranging from carvings to soap as well as local sweets. It's near the airport; just walk around the Crown Point Hotel to the beach entrance. There's also free parking just off Milford Rd. **Amenities:** food and drink; showers; toilets. **Best for:** partiers; swimming. ⊠ *Crown Point.*

🍴 Restaurants

★ Blue Crab Restaurant

$$$ | CARIBBEAN | The Sardinha family has been serving the best local lunches at their home since the 1980s. The ebullient Alison entertains and hugs diners while her husband, Ken, does the cooking. **Known for:** hearty, filling meals; creole seasoning; Friday night dinner (by reservation). *Average main: $23* ✉ *Robinson and Main Sts., Scarborough* ☎ *868/639–2737* ⊕ *www.tobagobluecrab.com* ☽ *Closed weekends. No dinner Mon.–Thurs.*

★ Shore Things Café & Craft

$ | CAFÉ | With a dramatic setting over the ocean on the Milford Road between Crown Point and Scarborough, this is a good spot to stop for lunch or a coffee break. Survey the view from the deck tables while sipping a variety of freshly prepared juices (the tamarind is particularly refreshing) or nibbling on excellent sandwiches or enjoying a hearty callaloo soup. **Known for:** outstanding ocean views; homemade local coffee and cocoa; delightful desserts. *Average main: $9* ✉ *25 Old Milford Rd., Lambeau* ☎ *868/635–1072* ☽ *Closed Sun. No dinner.*

🛍 Shopping

Souvenir seekers will do better on Trinidad than on Tobago, but determined shoppers ought to be able to find a few things to take home. Scarborough has the largest collection of shops, and Burnett Street, which climbs sharply from the port to St. James Park, is a good place to browse.

Forro's Homemade Delicacies

FOOD/CANDY | Eileen Forrester, wife of the Anglican archdeacon of Trinidad and Tobago, supervises a kitchen full of good cooks who boil and bottle the condiments sold here and pack them in little straw baskets—or even in bamboo. Most of the jars of tamarind chutney, lemon and lime marmalade, hot sauce, and guava and golden-apple jelly are small, easy to carry, and inexpensive. ✉ *St. Andrew's Rectory, Bacolet St., opposite the fire station, Scarborough* ☎ *868/639–2485.*

★ Shore Things Café & Crafts

CRAFTS | Masks and music are just two of the many kinds of souvenirs you can pick up at Shore Things Café & Crafts. ✉ *25 Old Milford Rd., Lambeau* ☎ *868/635–1072* ☽ *Closed Sun.*

🏃 Activities

BIRD-WATCHING

Some 200 varieties of bird have been documented on Tobago: look for the yellow oriole, scarlet ibis, and the comical motmot—the male of the species clears sticks and stones from an area and then does a dance complete with snapping sounds to attract a mate. The flora is as vivid as the birds. Purple-and-yellow *poui* trees and spectacular orange immortelles splash color over the countryside, and something is blooming virtually every season.

NG & Company Nature Tours

BIRD WATCHING | Newton George spent 23 years with the Forestry Division and knows the island intimately. He offers a variety of tours that even include bird-watching in Trinidad. He also has a delightful hummingbird gallery at his home. ✉ *3 Top Hill St., Speyside* ☎ *868/660–5463* ⊕ *www.newtongeorge. com.*

Pioneer Journeys

BIRD WATCHING | Pat Turpin and Renson Jack at Pioneer Journeys can give you information about their bird-watching tours of the Bloody Bay rain forest and the Louis d'Or River valley wetlands. ☎ *868/660–4327* ✍ *patricia@cel2015. com.*

DIVING AND SNORKELING

Tobago is considered a prime diving destination, as the clear waters provide maximum visibility. Every species of hard coral and most soft corals can be found in the waters around the island. Tobago is also home to the largest-known brain coral. Generally, the best diving is around the Speyside area. Many hotels and guesthouses in this area cater to the diving crowd, with basic accommodations and easy access to the water. You can usually get the best deals with these "dive-and-stay" packages.

An abundance of fish and coral thrives on the nutrients of Venezuela's Orinoco River, which are brought to Tobago by the Guyana current. Off the west coast is **Arnos Vale Reef,** with a depth of 40 feet and several reefs that run parallel to the shore. Here you can spot French and queen angelfish, moray eels, southern stingrays, and even the Atlantic torpedo ray. Much of the diving is drift diving in the mostly gentle current. **Crown Point,** on the island's southwest tip, is a good place for exploring the Shallows—a plateau at 50 to 100 feet that's favored by turtles, dolphins, angelfish, and nurse sharks. North of Pigeon Point, long, sandy beaches line the calm western coast; it has a gradual offshore slope and the popular **Mt. Irvine Wall,** which goes down to about 60 feet.

Although the reefs around Speyside in the northeast are becoming better known, **Buccoo Reef,** off the island's southwest coast, is still the most popular snorkeling spot. There's also good snorkeling near the former Arnos Vale Hotel and the Mt. Irvine Bay Hotel.

Blue Waters Dive'n

SCUBA DIVING | On the northeast coast, Dive'n is friendly, laid-back, and caters to divers of all levels. ⊠ *Blue Waters Inn, Batteaux Bay, Speyside* ☎ *868/660–5445* ⊕ *www.bluewatersinn.com.*

GOLF

★ **Tobago Plantations Golf & Country Club**
GOLF | This popular, well-maintained course (managed, together with the clubhouse, by the Magdalena Grand resort) is set on rolling greens, offers amazing ocean views, and contains mangrove and forest areas that are home to many bird species. ⊠ *Lowlands* ☎ *868/387–0287* ⊕ *magdalenagrand.com/activities/golf* ⊲ *$48 for 9 holes, $72 for 18 holes* ⅃. *18 holes, 7036 yards, Par 72.*

Tortola (Road Town)

Once a sleepy backwater, Tortola is definitely busy these days, particularly when several cruise ships tie up at the Road Town dock. Passengers crowd the streets and shops, and open-air jitneys filled with cruise-ship passengers create bottlenecks on the island's byways. That said, most folks visit Tortola to relax on its deserted sands or linger over lunch at one of its many delightful restaurants. Beaches are never more than a few miles away, and the steep green hills that form Tortola's spine are fanned by gentle trade winds. The neighboring islands glimmer like emeralds in a sea of sapphire. Tortola doesn't have many historic sights, but it does have abundant natural beauty. Beware of the roads, which are extraordinarily steep and twisting, making driving demanding. The best beaches are on the north shore.

ESSENTIALS
CURRENCY
U.S. dollar.

TELEPHONE
The country code for the British Virgin Islands is 1 284. Digicel, LIME, and CCT are the major service providers, using GSM (850, 900, 1800, and 1900 bands).

AT&T has service in nearby St. John, USVI, so it's possible to get service from there in some spots in Road Town and along the waterfront highway that leads

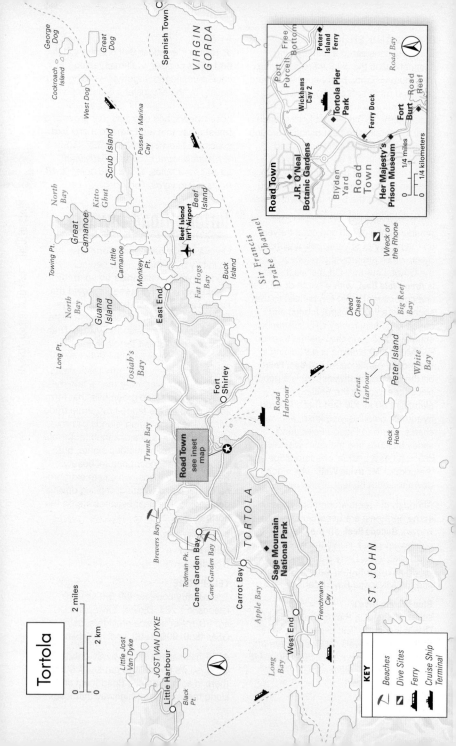

to the West End. You may not have to pay international roaming charges on some U.S. mobile phone plans if you can connect with this network.

COMING ASHORE

Large cruise ships either anchor in Road Town Harbor and bring passengers ashore by tender or tie up at Tortola Pier Park, which opened in 2016. Either way, it's a short stroll to Road Town. If your ship isn't going to Virgin Gorda, you can make the 12-mile (19-km) trip by ferry from the dock in Road Town in about 30 minutes for about $30 round-trip, but you'll still have to take a taxi to get to The Baths for swimming and snorkeling, so it's not necessarily a bad deal to go on your ship's shore excursion.

There are taxi stands at Wickham's Cay and in Road Town. Taxis are unmetered, and there are minimums for travel throughout the island, so it's usually cheaper to travel in groups. Negotiate to get the best fares, as there is no set fee schedule. If you are in the islands for just a day, it's usually more cost-effective to share a taxi with a small group than to rent a car, since you'd have to pay an agency at Wickham's Cay or in Road Town car-rental charges of at least $50 per day. You must be at least age 25 to rent a car.

◉ Sights

AROUND ROAD TOWN

The bustling capital of the BVI looks out over Road Harbour. It takes only an hour or so to stroll down Main Street and along the waterfront, checking out the traditional West Indian buildings painted in pastel colors, with corrugated-tin roofs, bright shutters, and delicate fretwork trim. For sightseeing brochures and the latest information on everything from taxi rates to ferry schedules, stop in at the BVI Tourist Board office. Or just choose a seat on one of the benches in Sir Olva Georges Square, on Waterfront Drive,

Best Bets ◉

■ **The *Rhone*.** For certified divers, this is one of the best wrecks in the Caribbean.

■ **Sage Mountain.** The highest peak in the Virgin Islands is a great hiking destination with breathtaking views.

■ **Sailing Trips.** Because of its proximity to small islets and good snorkeling sights, Tortola is the sailing capital of the Caribbean.

■ **Virgin Gorda.** Ferries link Tortola and Virgin Gorda, making a half-day trip to The Baths quite possible (just be sure to check the ferry schedules before heading out).

and watch the people come and go from the ferry dock and customs office across the street.

Fort Burt

HISTORIC SITE | The most intact historic ruin on Tortola was built by the Dutch in the early 17th century to safeguard Road Harbour. It sits on a hill at the western edge of Road Town and is now the site of a small hotel and restaurant. The foundations and magazine remain, and the structure offers a commanding view of the harbor. ⊠ *Waterfront Dr., Road Town* ☎ *284/494–2587* ⊕ *www.fortburt. com* ⊿ *Free.*

Her Majesty's Prison Museum

JAIL | Road Town's formidable prison was constructed in the mid-19th century and went on to hold prisoners in relatively primitive conditions for more than a century before closing in 2007. The prisoners confined to the humid barred cells were lucky compared to those who were hung in a creepy chamber, where the gallows claimed its last victim in the 1970s. Informative, docent-led tours offer insights into island history and the administration of justice from the colonial period into the early 21st century. ⊠ *Main St., Road Town* 🕾 *$5* ⊙ *Closed weekends.*

J. R. O'Neal Botanic Gardens

GARDEN | Stripped of nearly all its greenery during the 2017 hurricane season, this 4-acre showcase of once-lush plant life is slowly recovering. There are sections devoted to prickly cacti and succulents, hothouses for ferns and orchids, gardens of medicinal herbs, and plants and trees indigenous to the seashore. From the tourist office in Road Town, cross Waterfront Drive and walk one block over to Main Street and turn right. Keep walking until you see the high school. The gardens are on your left. ⊠ *Botanic Station, Road Town* 🕾 *284/494–2069* ⊕ *www.bvitourism.com* 🕾 *$3.*

Tortola Pier Park

PEDESTRIAN MALL | Tortola's Pier Park is the point of disembarkation for cruise ship passengers visiting the island. This Road Town development contains a dozen restaurants, including a cigar bar, pizza joint, vetetarian eatery, Caribbean fusion restaurant, and ice cream parlor. Diverse shopping options include jewelry stores, art galleries, and clothing boutiques. You can rent a car here or join in one of the frequent festivals and special events held at the complex. 🕾 *284/494–8775* ⊕ *www.tortolapier.com.*

Sage Mountain National Park

NATIONAL/STATE PARK | At 1,716 feet, Sage Mountain is the highest peak in the BVI. From the parking area, a trail leads you in a loop not only to the peak itself (and extraordinary views) but also to a small rain forest that is sometimes shrouded in mist. Most of the forest was cut down over the centuries for timber, to create pastureland, or for growing sugarcane, cotton, and other crops. In 1964 this 127-acre park was established to preserve what remained. Up here you can see mahogany trees, white cedars, mountain guavas, elephant-ear vines, mamey trees, and giant bullet woods, plus birds like mountain doves and thrushes. Take a taxi from Road Town or drive up Joe's Hill Road and make a left onto Ridge Road toward Chalwell and Doty villages. The road dead-ends at the park. ⊠ *Ridge Rd., Sage Mountain* 🕾 *284/852–3650* ⊕ *www.bvitourism.com* 🕾 *$3.*

⊙ Beaches

Brewers Bay Beach

BEACH—SIGHT | This beach is easy to find, but the steep, twisting paved roads leading down to it can be a bit daunting. An old sugar mill and the ruins of a rum distillery are off the beach along the road. Nicole's Beach Bar provides Painkiller cocktails to thirsty sunbathers. You can actually reach the beach from either Brewers Bay Road East or Brewers Bay Road West. **Amenities:** food and drink. **Best for:** snorkeling; swimming. ⊠ *Brewers Bay Rd. E, off Cane Garden Bay Rd., Brewers Bay.*

★ Cane Garden Bay Beach

BEACH—SIGHT | This silky stretch of sand boasts exceptionally calm crystalline waters—except when storms at sea turn the water murky. Snorkeling is good along the edges. Casual guesthouses, restaurants, bars, and shops are steps from the beach in the village of the same name. The beach is a laid-back, even somewhat funky place to put down your towel. It's the closest beach to Road Town (one steep uphill and downhill drive) and one of the BVI's best-known anchorages. Unfortunately, it can be very crowded with day-trippers when cruise ships dock in Road Town. Water-sports shops rent equipment. **Amenities:** food and drink; toilets; water sports. **Best for:** snorkeling; swimming; partiers. ⊠ *Cane Garden Bay Rd., off Ridge Rd., Cane Garden Bay.*

🍽 Restaurants

Island Roots Cafe on Main

$$ | **AMERICAN** | Located in the historic Customs House, Island Roots is part café and part art gallery. You can order sandwiches, salads, espresso, or smoothies from the counter and browse unique artwork and historic prints while waiting for your meal. **Known for:** coffee; light fare; evening cocktails. *$ Average main: $12* ⊠ *Main St., Road Town* ☎ *284/313–8985* ⊗ *Closed Sun.*

Pusser's Road Town Pub

$$ | **ECLECTIC** | **FAMILY** | Almost everyone who visits Tortola stops here at least once to have a bite and to sample the famous Pusser's Rum Painkiller (fruit juice and rum). The nonthreatening menu includes cheesy pizza, shepherd's pie, fish and chips, and hamburgers. (The "potato chip tree" may threaten your beach body, however.) Dine inside in air-conditioned comfort or outside on the verandah, which looks out on the harbor. **Known for:** maritime decor; Pusser's Rum; pub fare. *$ Average main: $15* ⊠ *Waterfront Dr., Road Town* ☎ *284/494–2467* ⊕ *www.pussers.com.*

🛍 Shopping

Many shops and boutiques are clustered along and just off Road Town's **Main Street.** You can shop in Road Town's **Wickham's Cay** adjacent to the marina. The **Crafts Alive Market** on the Road Town waterfront is a collection of colorful West Indian–style buildings with shops that carry items made in the BVI. You might find pretty baskets or interesting pottery or perhaps a bottle of home-brewed hot sauce. A growing number of art and clothing stores are opening at **Soper's Hole** in West End. A new cruise ship pier, the **Tortola Pier Park,** provides another shopping option.

🏃 Activities

DIVING AND SNORKELING

Clear waters and numerous reefs afford some wonderful opportunities for underwater exploration. In some spots visibility reaches 100 feet, but colorful reefs teeming with fish are often just a few feet below the sea surface. The BVI's system of marine parks means the underwater life visible through your mask will stay protected.

The *Chikuzen,* sunk northwest of Brewers Bay in 1981, is a 246-foot vessel in 75 feet of water; it's home to thousands of fish, colorful corals, and big rays. In 1867 the **RMS *Rhone,*** a 310-foot royal mail steamer, split in two when it sank in a devastating hurricane. It's so well preserved that it was used as an underwater prop in the 1977 movie *The Deep.* You can see the crow's nest and bowsprit, the cargo hold in the bow, and the engine and enormous propeller shaft in the stern. Its four parts are at various depths, from 30 to 80 feet. Get yourself some snorkeling gear and hop aboard a dive boat to this wreck near Salt Island (across the channel from Road Town). Every dive outfit in the BVI runs scuba and snorkel tours to this part of the BVI National Parks Trust; if you have time for only one trip, make it this one. Rates start at around $85 for a one-tank dive and $130 for a two-tank dive.

Blue Water Divers

SCUBA DIVING | If you're chartering a sailboat, Blue Waters Divers will meet yours at Peter, Salt, Norman, or Cooper Island for a rendezvous dive. The company teaches resort, open-water, rescue, and advanced diving courses, and also makes daily dive trips. Rates include all equipment as well as instruction. Reserve two days in advance. ⊠ *Nanny Cay Marina, Nanny Cay* ☎ *284/340–4311* ⊕ *www.bluewaterdiversbvi.com.*

FISHING

Most of the boats that take you deep-sea fishing for blue marlin, white marlin, wahoo, tuna, and dolphinfish (mahimahi) leave from nearby St. Thomas, but local anglers like to fish the shallower water for bonefish. A half day for two people runs about $480, a full day around $890. Wading trips are $345.

Caribbean Fly Fishing

FISHING | Wade into the waters of Tortola in pursuit of fierce bonefish. ⊠ *Nanny Cay Marina, Nanny Cay* ☎ *284/494–4797, 284/499–1590* ⊕ *www.caribflyfishing. com.*

SAILING

If a day sail to some secluded anchorage is more your cup of tea, the BVI have numerous boats of various sizes and styles that leave from many points around Tortola. Prices start at around $90 per person for a full-day sail, including lunch and snorkeling equipment.

Aristocat Charters

SAILING | This company's 45-foot catamaran, *Sugar Rush*, sets sail daily to Jost Van Dyke, Norman Island, Cooper Island, and other small islands. Charters run from Soper's Hole (Frenchman's Cay), West End, and the Village Cay Marina in Road Town. ☎ *284/499–1249* ⊕ *www. aristocatcharters.com.*

Trinidad (Port of Spain)

Trinidad, the big sister in the twin-island republic of Trinidad and Tobago, is the most southerly in the Caribbean and a melting pot of African, Indian, European, and South American cultures. Unlike most Caribbean islands, it's energy production rather than tourism that accounts for most of its income. But Trinidadians do know how to party, and the island's population is always celebrating or preparing for some sort of festival, the biggest of which is undoubtedly Carnival, which takes over much of Port of Spain every year for two days of bacchanalian excess. Those expecting pristine white beaches may find the island disappointing, but lovers of the rain forest and wildlife will be in their element.

ESSENTIALS

CURRENCY

The Trinidad and Tobago dollar (TT$). Most places catering to tourists will accept U.S. currency, but the exchange rate may vary wildly from place to place.

TELEPHONE

The country code for Trinidad & Tobago is 1 868. The major service providers are BMobile and Digicel, using GSM (850, 1800 and 1900 bands).

COMING ASHORE

Port of Spain is a bustling and sprawling metropolis with seemingly endless traffic jams. The capital of the twin-island republic is a work in progress, with government investing billions of dollars into upgrading the port area and many other parts of the city. The scale of this project means that the port will be a construction zone for some time to come, but the result is expected to be a mile-long facility designed to offer a range of facilities and services to visitors.

Because of the driving habits of Trinidadians, the often-confusing signposting, and narrow roads, it's not a good idea to rent a car. Taxis flock to the port whenever a cruise ship arrives. Authorized taxis always have a license plate starting with the letter *H* (for "hire"). Although rates are technically fixed, it is never a bad idea to negotiate with the driver.

◉ Sights

The intensely urban atmosphere of Port of Spain belies the tropical beauty of the countryside surrounding it. You'll need a car and three to eight hours to see all there is to see. Begin by circling the Queen's Park Savannah to Saddle Road, in the residential district of Maraval. After a few miles the road begins to narrow and curve sharply as it climbs into the Northern Range and its undulating hills of dense foliage. Stop at the lookout on North Coast Road; a camera is a must-have here, and be sure to try some of the sweet or savory snacks sold under the tents. You pass a series of lovely beaches, starting with Maracas. From the town of Blanchisseuse there's a winding route to the Asa Wright Nature Centre that takes you through canyons of towering palms, mossy grottoes, and imposing bamboo. In this rain forest keep an eye out for vultures, parakeets, hummingbirds, toucans, and (if you're lucky) red-bellied yellow-and-blue macaws. Trinidad also has more than 600 native species of butterfly and far more than 1,000 varieties of orchid.

PORT OF SPAIN

Most organized tours begin at the port. If you're planning to explore on foot, which will take two to four hours, start early in the day; by midday the port area can get very hot and crowded. It's best to end your tour on a bench in the Queen's Park Savannah, sipping a cool coconut water bought from one of the vendors operating out of flatbed trucks. For about $2 he'll lop the top off a green coconut with a deft swing of the machete and, when you've finished drinking, lop again, making a bowl and spoon of coconut shell for you to eat the young pulp. Take extra care at night; women should not walk alone. Local police advise tourists and locals to avoid the neighborhoods just east of Port of Spain.

The town's main dock, King's Wharf, entertains a steady parade of cruise and cargo ships, a reminder that the city started from this strategic harbor. When hurricanes threaten other islands, it's not unusual to see as many as five large cruise ships taking advantage of the safety of the harbor. It's on Wrightson Road, the main street along the water on the southwest side of town. The government

Best Bets

- **Maracas Beach.** Trinidad's most popular beach has some of the island's best food huts.

- **Caroni Bird Sanctuary.** This maze of swamps is one of the island's top birding spots.

- **National Museum & Art Gallery.** A fascinating look into the island's history and culture.

- **Port of Spain.** Madly busy and hectic, this is an entertaining place if you can stand the crowds.

embarked on a massive development plan to turn the area into a vibrant and attractive commercial and tourism zone. Many new high-rises have already been built, and others are in various stages of completion.

Emperor Valley Zoo & Botanical Gardens

GARDEN | FAMILY | The cultivated expanse of parkland north of the Savannah is the site of the president's and prime minister's official residences and also the Emperor Valley Zoo & Botanical Gardens. A meticulous lattice of walkways and local flora, the parkland was first laid out in 1820 for Governor Ralph Woodford. In the midst of the serene wonderland is the 8-acre zoo, which exhibits mostly birds and animals of the region—including the brilliantly plumed scarlet ibis as well as slithering anacondas and pythons; you can also see (and hear) the wild parrots that breed in the surrounding foliage. Two African giraffes and several big cats were added to the collection in 2013 and have proven to be a huge draw for locals. The zoo, which is undergoing a major renovation and expansion to make it more of a naturalistic setting, draws a quarter of a million visitors a year. Tours are free. ⊠ *Northern side of Queen's Park Savannah, Port of Spain* ☎ *868/622–3530,*

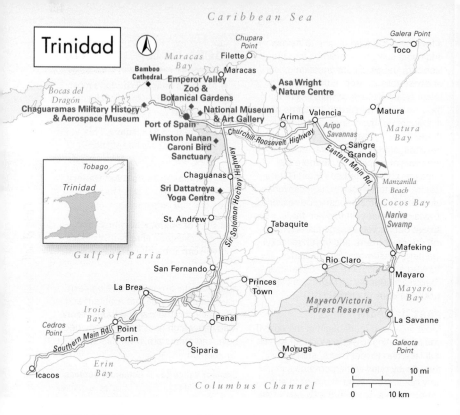

Trinidad

Caribbean Sea

Galera Point
Toco

Chupara Point
Filette
Maracas
Maracas Bay
Bamboo Cathedral
Emperor Valley Zoo & Botanical Gardens
Asa Wright Nature Centre

Bocas del Dragón

Chaguaramas Military History & Aerospace Museum
Port of Spain
National Museum & Art Gallery
Arima Valencia
Aripo Savannas
Matura
Matura Bay

Winston Nanan Caroni Bird Sanctuary
Churchill-Roosevelt Highway
Sangre Grande
Eastern Main Rd.

Tobago

Trinidad

Chaguanas
Sri Dattatreya Yoga Centre
Sir Solomon Hochoy Highway
Manzanilla Beach
Cocos Bay
Nariva Swamp

St. Andrew
Tabaquite
Mafeking

Gulf of Paria

San Fernando
Rio Claro
Mayaro
Mayaro Bay

La Brea
Princes Town
Mayaro/Victoria Forest Reserve

Irois Bay
Penal
La Savanne

Cedros Point
Point Fortin
Southern Main Rd.
Siparia
Moruga
Galeota Point

Erin Bay
Icacos

Columbus Channel

0 ___ 10 mi
0 ___ 10 km

868/622–5343 ⊕ www.zstt.org ✉ Zoo TT$30, gardens free.

National Museum & Art Gallery

MUSEUM | FAMILY | Be sure to see the National Museum & Art Gallery, especially its Carnival exhibitions, the Amerindian collection and historical re-creations, and the fine 19th-century paintings of Trinidadian artist Michel-Jean Cazabon. Tours are free. ✉ 117 Upper Frederick St., Port of Spain ☎ 868/623–0339 ⊕ www.nmag.gov.tt ✉ Free.

BEYOND PORT OF SPAIN
★ Asa Wright Nature Centre

FOREST | Nearly 200 acres are covered with plants, trees, and colorful flowers, and the surroundings are atwitter with more than 200 species of bird—including the gorgeous blue-crowned motmot and the rare (and protected) nocturnal oilbird. If you stay at the center's inn

for two nights or more, take one of the guided hikes (included in your room rate or daily admission) to the oilbirds' breeding grounds in Dunston Cave (reservations for hikes are essential). Those who don't want to hike can relax on the inn's veranda and watch birds swoop about the porch feeders. You are also more than likely to see a variety of other animal species, including agoutis (similar to large guinea pigs) and alarmingly large golden tegu lizards. This stunning plantation house looks out onto the lush, untouched Arima Valley. Even if you're not staying over, book ahead for lunch, offered Monday through Saturday, or for the noontime Sunday buffet. The center is an hour outside Blanchisseuse. ✉ Arima Blanchisseuse Rd., Arima Valley ☎ 868/667–4655 ⊕ www.asawright.org ✉ TT$70.

Chaguaramas Military History & Aerospace Museum

MUSEUM | Although this museum covers everything from Amerindian history to the Cold War, the emphasis is on the two World Wars, and it's a must-see for history buffs. The exhibits, housed on a former U.S. military base, are in a large hangarlike shed without air-conditioning, so dress appropriately. There's a decidedly charming and homemade feel to the place; in fact, most exhibits were made by the curator and founder, Commander Gaylord Kelshall of the Trinidad & Tobago Coast Guard. The museum is set a bit off the main road but is easily spotted by the turquoise British West Indian Airways (BWIA) L-1011 jet parked out front (from Trinidad & Tobago's former national airline). ⊠ *Western Main Rd., Chaguaramas* ☎ *868/634–4391* ⊕ *roamtt.com/chaguaramas-museum* ⊠ *TT$30.*

Sri Dattatreya Yoga Centre

PUBLIC ART | FAMILY | This impressive temple site was constructed by artisans brought in from India. It is well worth a visit to admire the intricate architectural details of the main temple, learn about Trinidad Hinduism, and marvel at the towering 85-foot statue of the monkey deity Hanuman. Krishna Ramsaran, the compound manager, is extremely helpful and proud to explain the history of the center and the significance of the various *murtis* (sacred statues). Kids are welcome, so this makes for a pleasant and educational family outing (kids seem especially interested in the giant elephant statues that guard the temple doors). This is a religious site, so appropriate clothing is required (no shorts), and shoes must be left outside the temple door. It's fine to take pictures of the statue and the temple exterior and grounds, but permission is required to take pictures inside, as it's an active place of worship. The temple is half an hour from Port of Spain; take Churchill Roosevelt Highway east to Uriah Butler south; turn off at the Freeport flyover (overpass); then turn right and follow the signs east to Waterloo; then follow signs to the temple. ⊠ *Datta Dr. at Orangefield Rd., Carapichaima* ☎ *868/673–5328* ⊕ *sridattatreyayogacentrett.com* ⊠ *Free.*

★ Winston Nanan Caroni Bird Sanctuary Tours

BODY OF WATER | FAMILY | This large swamp with mazelike waterways is bordered by mangrove trees, some plumed with huge termite nests. If you're lucky, you may see lazy caimans idling in the water and large snakes hanging from branches on the banks, taking in the sun. In the middle of the sanctuary are several islets that are home to Trinidad's national bird, the scarlet ibis. Just before sunset the ibis arrive by the thousands, their richly colored feathers brilliant in the gathering dusk, and as more flocks alight, they turn the mangrove foliage a brilliant scarlet. Bring a sweater and insect repellent. The sanctuary was renamed in 2015 following the death of its founder, Winston Nanan. He was also the owner of the only official tour operator, and his family continues to operate tours. ⊠ *Port of Spain* ⊹ *½ hr from Port of Spain; take Churchill Roosevelt Hwy. east to Uriah Butler south; turn right and in about 2 mins, after passing Caroni River Bridge, follow sign for sanctuary* ☎ *868/645–1305* ⊕ *www.nananecotours.com* ⊠ *TT$70.*

🌀 Beaches

Trinidad has some good beaches for swimming and sunning, particularly on the north coast, though none as picture perfect as those on Tobago. Although popular with some locals, the beaches of the western peninsula (such as Maqueripe) are not particularly attractive. All beaches on Trinidad are free and open to the public. Many locals are fond of playing loud music wherever they go, and even the most serene beach may suddenly turn into a seaside party.

★ Maracas Bay

BEACH—SIGHT | This stretch of peach-color sand has a cove and a fishing village at one end. It's the local favorite, so it can get crowded on weekends. The government is constantly trying to upgrade the facilities (with limited success), so the areas around the beach are less than pristine. Lifeguards will guide you away from strong currents. Parking sites are ample, and there are snack bars selling the famous bake and shark, a must-try. Take the winding North Coast Road from Maraval (it intersects with Long Circular Road right next to KFC Maraval) over the Northern Range; the beach is about 7 miles (11 km) from Maraval. **Amenities:** food and drink; lifeguards; parking; toilets. **Best for:** partiers; swimming; walking. ⊠ *North Coast Rd.*

Salybia Bay

BEACH—SIGHT | This gentle beach has shallows and plenty of shade—perfect for swimming. Snack vendors abound in the vicinity. Like many of the beaches on the northeast coast, this one is packed with people and music trucks blaring soca and reggae on weekends. It's off the Toco Main Road, just after the town of Matura. **Amenities:** food and drink; parking; toilets. **Best for:** partiers; swimming; walking. ⊠ *Off Toco Main Rd., south of Toco.*

 Restaurants

★ Veni Mangé

$$ | CARIBBEAN | FAMILY | Set in a traditional West Indian house filled to the brim with Caribbean art, this restaurant is the creation of Rosemary (Roses) Hezekiah and her late sister, Allyson Hennessy, a Cordon Bleu–trained chef who was a local television celebrity. The creative creole menu changes regularly, but there's always an unusual vegetarian entrée; the callaloo is considered one of the island's best; and the chip chip cocktail, a restaurant rarity, is deliciously piquant. **Known for:** authentic "Trini" dining experience;

enthusiastic hostess; chatty bar patrons, including artists and sports celebrities. ⑤ *Average main: $20* ⊠ *67A Ariapita Ave., Woodbrook* ☎ *868/624–4597* ⊘ *Closed weekends. No dinner Mon.– Tues. and Thurs.*

Wings Restaurant & Bar

$ | CARIBBEAN | Rum shops and good food are an intrinsic part of Trinidad life, and both are combined in this colorful eatery, which is open from 10 to 6. Regulars from the nearby university and industrial park flock here at lunchtime to enjoy a wide selection of local Indian food. **Known for:** authentic Trinidad curries; lively local ambience; cheap and cheerful food and drinks. ⑤ *Average main: $7* ⊠ *16 Mohammed Terr., Tunapuna* ☎ *868/645– 6607* ▭ *No credit cards* ⊘ *Closed Sun. No dinner.*

🛍 Shopping

Good buys in Trinidad include Angostura bitters, Old Oak or Vat 19 rum, and leather goods, all widely available throughout the country. Thanks in large part to the costumes needed for Carnival, there's no shortage of fabric shops. The best bargains for Asian and East Indian silks and cottons can be found in downtown Port of Spain, on Frederick Street and around Independence Square. The tourism office can provide a list of local artisans who sell straw and cane work, miniature steel pans, and other crafts. Recordings of local calypsonians and steel-pan performances as well as *chutney* (local East Indian music) are available throughout the islands and make great gifts. Note that duty-free goods are available only at the airport upon departure or arrival.

Downtown Port of Spain—specifically the area encompassing **Frederick, Queen,** and **Henry Streets**—is full of fabrics and shoes. **Ellerslie Plaza** is an attractive outdoor mall well worth a browse. **Excellent City Centre** is set in an old-style oasis under the lantern roofs of three of downtown's oldest commercial buildings. Look for cleverly designed keepsakes, trendy cotton clothes, and original artwork. The upstairs food court overlooks bustling Frederick Street. The **Falls at West Mall,** just west of Port of Spain, is a dazzling temple to upscale shopping that could hold its own anywhere in the world. **Long Circular Mall** has upscale boutiques that are great for window-shopping. **Trincity Mall,** near the airport, is the largest mall on the island and has everything from souvenirs to high-end fashion. The **Market at the Normandie Hotel** is a small collection of shops that specialize in indigenous fashions, crafts, jewelry, basketwork, and ceramics. You can also have afternoon tea in the elegant little café.

Cocoyea

CRAFTS | For painted plates, ceramics, aromatic candles, wind chimes, and carved-wood pieces and instruments, check out Cocoyea. ✉ *Level 3, Long Circular Mall, Long Circular Rd., St. James* 🕾 *868/628–6546* ⊘ *Closed Sun.*

★ **Meiling**

CLOTHING | Acclaimed local designer Meiling Esau showcases her classically detailed Caribbean resort clothing here. ✉ *6 Carlos St., Woodbrook* 🕾 *868/627–6975* ⊕ *www.meilinginc.com.*

★ **101 Art Gallery at Holder's Studio**

ART GALLERIES | Trinidad's foremost gallery showcases Jackie Hinkson (figurative watercolors), Peter Sheppard (stylized realist local landscapes in acrylic), Sundiata (semiabstract watercolors), and other local artists. Openings are usually held on Tuesday evening. ✉ *84 Woodford St., Newtown* 🕾 *868/628–4081* ⊘ *Closed Sun.–Mon.*

Radical

CLOTHING | Radical is a good spot for T-shirts and original men's and women's casual clothing. ✉ *The Falls at West Mall, Western Main Rd., Bayshore* 🕾 *868/632–5800* ⊕ *radicaldesignstt.com.*

Rainy Days Gift Shop

CRAFTS | Stylish handmade batik items, Ajoupa (an attractive, local terra-cotta pottery), CDs, local art, T-shirts, and many other gift items are available here. ✉ *Ellerslie Plaza, Long Circular Rd., Maraval* 🕾 *868/622–5597* ⊘ *Closed Sun.*

Activities

BIRD-WATCHING

Trinidad and Tobago are among the top 10 spots in the world in terms of the number of species of bird per square mile—more than 430, many living within pristine rain forests, lowlands and savannas, and fresh- and saltwater swamps. If you're lucky, you might spot the collared trogon, Trinidad piping guan (known locally as the common pawi), or rare white-tailed sabrewing hummingbird. Restaurants often hang feeders outside on their porches, as much to keep the birds away from your food as to provide a chance to see them. Both the Asa Wright Nature Centre and Caroni Bird Sanctuary are major destinations.

★ **Nanan Ecotours**

BIRD WATCHING | Although Winston Nanan, a self-taught ornithologist, passed away in 2015, his company still operates tours in the Winston Nanan Caroni Bird Sanctuary. The two-hour boat tours depart every day at 4 pm from the sanctuary dock. His family, which continues the tour operation, also offers tours elsewhere on Trinidad & Tobago. 🕾 *868/645–1305.*

GOLF

St. Andrew's Golf Club

GOLF | The best course in Trinidad is just outside Port of Spain. Picture a valley setting adorned with beautiful mature tropical trees and you get an idea of St. Andrews. Established in 1892, it qualifies as one of the region's oldest layouts. As one might expect, this vintage course is not particularly long at 6,555 yards, but narrow tree-lined fairways and contoured putting surfaces place a premium upon accuracy and make it a sporting challenge. The most convenient tee times are available on weekdays. Golf shoes with soft spikes are required. ⊠ *Moka, Saddle Rd., Maraval* ☎ *868/629–0066* ⊕ *golftrinidad.com* ✉ *$55 for 9 holes, $95 for 18 holes* 🏌 *18 holes, 6555 yards, par 72.*

Virgin Gorda (The Valley)

Virgin Gorda, or "Fat Virgin," received its name from Christopher Columbus. The explorer envisioned the island as a pregnant woman in a languid recline with Gorda Peak being her big belly and the boulders of The Baths her toes. Different in topography from Tortola, with its arid landscape covered with scrub brush and cactus, Virgin Gorda has a slower pace of life, too. Goats and cattle have right-of-way, and the unpretentious friendliness of the people is winning. The top sight (and beach for that matter) is The Baths, which draws scores of cruise-ship passengers and day-trippers to its giant boulders and grottoes that form a perfect snorkeling environment. While ships used to stop only in Tortola, saving Virgin Gorda for shore excursions, smaller ships are coming increasingly to Virgin Gorda directly.

ESSENTIALS
CURRENCY
U.S. dollar.

TELEPHONE
The country code for the British Virgin Islands is 1 284. Digicel, LIME, and CCT are the major service providers, using GSM (850, 900, 1800, and 1900 bands).

COMING ASHORE
Ships often dock off Spanish Town, Leverick Bay, or in North Sound and tender passengers to the ferry dock. A few taxis will be available at Leverick Bay and at Gun Creek in North Sound—you can set up an island tour for about $45 for two people—but those landings are far away from The Baths, the island's must-see

beach, so a shore excursion is often the best choice. If you are tendered to Spanish Town, then it's possible to take a shuttle taxi to The Baths for as little as $4 per person each way. If you are on Virgin Gorda for just a day, it's usually more cost-effective to share a taxi with a small group than to rent a car, since you'd have to pay car-rental charges of at least $50 per day. You must be at least age 25 to rent a car.

◉ Sights

One of the most efficient ways to see Virgin Gorda is by sailboat. The craggy coast, cut through with grottoes and fringed by palms and boulders, has a primitive beauty. There are few roads, and most byways don't follow the scalloped shoreline. The main route sticks resolutely to the center of the island, linking The Baths on the southern tip with Gun Creek and Leverick Bay at North Sound. If you drive, you can hit all the sights in one day. Explore Spanish Town or North Sound first, then take a day to drive to the other end. Stop to climb Virgin Gorda Peak, which is at the island's center. There are few signs, so come prepared with a map.

★ The Baths National Park
BEACH—SIGHT | FAMILY | At Virgin Gorda's most celebrated sight, giant boulders are scattered about the beach and in the water. Some are almost as large as houses and form remarkable grottoes. Climb between these rocks to swim in the many placid pools. Early morning and late afternoon are the best times to visit if you want to avoid crowds. If it's privacy you crave, follow the shore northward to quieter bays—Spring Bay, the Crawl, Little Trunk, and Valley Trunk—or head south to Devil's Bay. ⊠ *Off Tower Rd., Spanish Town* ☎ *284/852–3650* ⊕ *www.bvitourism.com* ✉ *$3.*

Copper Mine National Park

HISTORIC SITE | A tall stone shaft silhouetted against the sky, a small stone structure that overlooks the sea, and a deep cistern are part of what was once a copper mine, now in ruins. Established 400 years ago, it was worked first by the Spanish, then by the English, until the early 20th century. ⊠ *Copper Mine Rd., Spanish Town* ⚐ *Free.*

Spanish Town

TOWN | Virgin Gorda's peaceful main settlement, on the island's southern wing, is so tiny that it barely qualifies as a town at all. Also known as "the Valley," Spanish Town has a marina, some shops, a few restaurants and bars, and a couple of car-rental agencies. Just north of town is the ferry slip. At the Virgin Gorda Yacht Harbour you can stroll along the dock, but the hotel and other facilities were badly damaged in the 2017 hurricane and are still under repair. ⊠ *Spanish Town.*

Virgin Gorda Peak National Park

MOUNTAIN—SIGHT | There are two trails at this 265-acre park, which contains the island's highest point, at 1,359 feet. Signs on North Sound Road mark both entrances. It's a short but steep 30- to 45-minute hike (depending on which trail you take) to a small clearing, where you can enjoy some high-level views that will be better if and when the observation tower knocked down by Hurricane Irma gets rebuilt. ⊠ *North Sound Rd., Gorda Peak* ⊕ *www.bvitourism.com* ⚐ *Free.*

Beaches

The Baths Beach

BEACH—SIGHT | The most popular tourist destination in the BVI, this stunning maze of huge granite boulders extending into the sea is usually crowded midday with day-trippers, especially when cruise ships are in port (come early in the morning or toward evening for more solitude). The snorkeling is good, and you're likely to see a wide variety of fish. Public bathrooms and a handful of bars and shops are close to the water and at the start of the path that leads to the beach. Lockers are available to keep belongings safe. **Amenities:** food and drink; parking; toilets. **Best for:** snorkeling; swimming. ⊠ *Tower Rd., about 1 mile (1½ km) west of Spanish Town ferry dock, Spanish Town* ☎ *284/852–3650* ⊕ *www.bvitourism.com* ⚐ *$3.*

Savannah Bay Beach

BEACH—SIGHT | This is a wonderfully private beach close to Spanish Town. It may not always be completely deserted, but you can find a spot to yourself on this long stretch of soft white sand. Bring your own mask, fins, and snorkel, as there are no facilities. Villas are available through rental property agencies. The view from above is a photographer's delight. **Amenities:** none. **Best for:** solitude; snorkeling; swimming. ⊠ *Off N. Sound Rd., ¾ mile (1¼ km) east of Spanish Town ferry dock, Savannah Bay* ⚐ *Free.*

Spring Bay Beach

BEACH—SIGHT | This national park beach gets much less traffic than the nearby Baths, and has similarly large, imposing boulders that create interesting grottoes for swimming. Plus, there's the added benefit of no admission fee. The snorkeling is excellent, and the grounds include

Best Bets ◉

■ **The Baths.** This unique beach strewn with giant boulders and grottos is a favorite snorkeling destination.

■ **Virgin Gorda Peak.** This lofty peak is a great hiking destination with excellent views.

■ **Sailing Trips.** Like Tortola, Virgin Gorda is within easy reach of many small islets and good snorkeling sights.

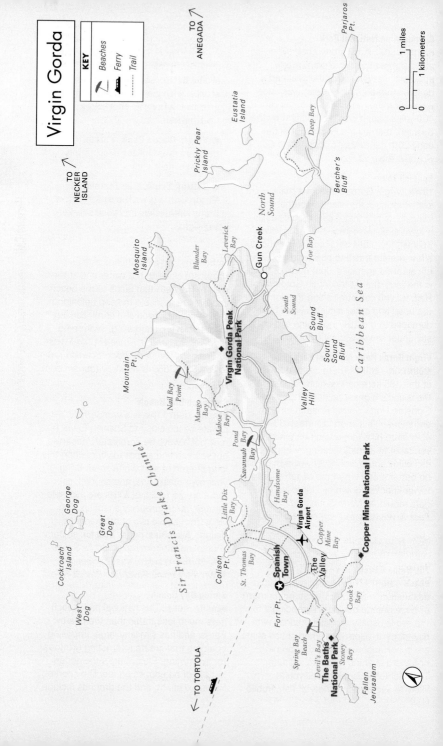

swings and picnic tables. Guavaberry Spring Bay Vacation has villas and cottages right near the beach. **Amenities:** none. **Best for:** snorkeling; swimming. ⊠ *Spanish Town* ☎ *284/852–3650* ⊕ *www.bvitourism.com* ⌫ *Free.*

🍴 Restaurants

Bath and Turtle

$$ | **ECLECTIC** | Sit back and relax at this informal tavern with a friendly staff, co-located with the more upscale Chez Bamboo. Well-stuffed sandwiches, homemade pizzas, pasta dishes, and daily specials such as conch soup round out the casual menu. **Known for:** live music; bar scene; pizza. $ *Average main: $19* ⊠ *Spanish Town* ☎ *284/545–1861* ⊕ *www.bathandturtle.com.*

Top of the Baths

$$$ | **ECLECTIC** | **FAMILY** | At the entrance to The Baths, this popular restaurant has tables on an outdoor terrace or in an open-air pavilion; all have stunning views of the Sir Francis Drake Channel. The restaurant starts serving at 8 am for breakfast; for lunch, hamburgers, coconut chicken sandwiches, and fish and chips are among the offerings. **Known for:** great location with stunning views; fire dancer performances; Sunday barbecue. $ *Average main: $23* ⊠ *Spanish Town* ☎ *284/495–5497* ⊕ *www.topofthebaths.com.*

🛍 Shopping

Most boutiques are within hotel complexes or at the **Virgin Gorda Yacht Harbour**. One of the best is at **Little Dix Bay**. Other properties—the Bitter End and Leverick Bay—have small but equally good boutiques.

🏃 Activities

DIVING AND SNORKELING

Dive companies on Virgin Gorda are all certified by PADI. Costs vary, but count on paying about $85 for a one-tank dive

and $130 for a two-tank dive. All dive operators offer introductory courses as well as certification and advanced courses. There are some terrific snorkel and dive sites off Virgin Gorda, including areas around The Baths, the North Sound, and the Dogs. The Chimney at Great Dog Island has a coral archway and canyon covered with a wide variety of sponges. At Joe's Cave, an underwater cavern on West Dog Island, huge groupers, eagle rays, and other colorful fish accompany divers as they swim. At some sites, you can see 100 feet down, but snorkelers and divers who don't want to go that deep will find plenty to look at just below the surface.

Dive BVI

SCUBA DIVING | In addition to day trips, Dive BVI also offers expert instruction and certification. The Yacht Harbour location is closed on Sunday. ⊠ *Virgin Gorda Yacht Harbour, Lee Rd., Spanish Town* ☎ *284/541–9818* ⊕ *www.divebvi.com.*

Sunchaser Scuba

SCUBA DIVING | Resort, advanced, and rescue courses are all available here along with dive charters to northern BVI sites, the Dog Islands, and other destinations—all 15 to 45 minutes away. ⊠ *North Sound* ☎ *284/344–2766* ⊕ *www.sunchaserscuba.com.*

SAILING AND BOATING

The BVI waters are calm and terrific places to learn to sail. You can also rent sea kayaks, waterskiing equipment, dinghies, and powerboats, or take a parasailing trip.

Double "D" Charters

BOATING | If you just want to sit back, relax, and let the captain take the helm, choose a sailing or power yacht from Double "D" Charters. Rates run from $300 for a day trip. Private full-day cruises or sails for up to eight people run from $1,100. ⊠ *Virgin Gorda Yacht Harbour, Lee Rd., Spanish Town* ☎ *284/499–2479* ⊕ *www.doubledbvi.com.*

Index

Photo Credits

Fodor's CARIBBEAN CRUISE PORTS OF CALL

Publisher: Stephen Horowitz, *General Manager*

Editorial: Douglas Stallings, *Editorial Director;* Jacinta O'Halloran, Amanda Sadlowski, *Senior Editors;* Kayla Becker, Alexis Kelly, Teddy Minford, Rachael Roth, *Editors*

Design: Tina Malaney, *Director of Design and Production;* Jessica Gonzalez, *Graphic Designer;* Mariana Tabares, *Design & Production Intern*

Production: Jennifer DePrima, *Editorial Production Manager;* Carrie Parker, *Senior Production Editor;* Elyse Rozelle, *Production Editor;* Jackson Pranica, *Editorial Production Assistant*

Maps: Rebecca Baer, *Senior Map Editor;* David Lindroth, Mark Stroud (Moon Street Cartography), *Cartographers*

Photography: Viviane Teles, *Senior Photo Editor;* Namrata Aggarwal, Ashok Kumar, Carl Yu, *Photo Editors;* Rebecca Rimmer, *Photo Intern*

Business & Operations: Chuck Hoover, *Chief Marketing Officer;* Robert Ames, *Group General Manager;* Tara McCrillis, *Director of Publishing Operations;* Victor Bernal, *Business Analyst*

Public Relations and Marketing: Joe Ewaskiw, *Senior Director Communications & Public Relations;* Esther Su, *Senior Marketing Manager*

Fodors.com: Jeremy Tarr, *Editorial Director;* Rachael Levitt, *Managing Editor*

Technology: Jon Atkinson, *Director of Technology;* Rudresh Teotia, *Lead Developer;* Jacob Ashpis, *Content Operations Manager*

Writers: Laura Adzich-Brander, Carol M. Bareuther, Carol Buchanan, Susan Campbell, Linda Coffman, Greg Devilliers, Lynda Lohr, Elise Meyer, Amy Peniston, Ann L. Phelan, Rika Purdy, Jessica Robertson, Laura Rodini, Paul Rubio, Paulina Salach, Julie Schwietert Collazo, Jordan Simon, Richard Sitler, Eileen Robinson Smith, Roberta Sotonoff, Robin Sussman, Jeffrey Van Fleet, Jane E. Zarem.

Editor: Douglas Stallings

Production Editor: Carrie Parker

18th Edition

ISBN 978-1-64097-230-8

ISSN 2331–9275

Library of Congress Control Number 2019952361

All details in this book are based on information supplied to us at press time. Always confirm information when it matters, especially if you're making a detour to visit a specific place. Fodor's expressly disclaims any liability, loss, or risk, personal or otherwise, that is incurred as a consequence of the use of any of the contents of this book.

SPECIAL SALES

This book is available at special discounts for bulk purchases for sales promotions or premiums. For more information, e-mail SpecialMarkets@fodors.com.

About Our Writers

A veteran travel journalist, media and content consultant, **Brian Major** is Executive Editor, Caribbean and Latin America, for New Jersey-based travAlliancemedia LLC, w hich offers several publications for travel agents. Brian also has an extensive background in cruise journalism and public relations, having served as Director of Public Relations for the Cruise Lines International Association (CLIA). Brian's articles and travel photography have appeared on the Afar.com, Fodors.com, Forbes.com, and USAToday.com; in 2015 he was named the Caribbean Tourism Organization's 2015 "Inner Circle King" Award winner for trade journalism feature writing. He has is also a 2017 recipient of the Martha Vickery-Wallace Memorial Award for Excellence in Travel Journalism. Brian updated "Planning Your Caribbean Cruise" as well as the coverage of cruise line private islands.

Many other writers updated content that appears in this book, including the following.

Antigua (St. John's): Alicia Simon

Aruba (Oranjestad): Sue Campbell

Bahamas (Nassau): Jessica Robertson

Baltimore, Maryland: Laura Rodini

Barbados (Bridgetown): Jane E. Zarem

Belize (Belize City): Jeffrey Van Fleet

Bequia, St. Vincent & the Grenadines: Jane E. Zarem

Bermuda: Robyn Bardgett

Bonaire (Kralendijk): Sue Campbell

Cayman Islands (Grand Cayman): Jordan Simon

Charleston, South Carolina: Stratton Lawrence

Colombia (Cartagena): Jeffrey Van Fleet

Costa Rica (Puerto Limón): Jeffrey Van Fleet

Curaçao (Willemstad): Sue Campbell

Dominica (Roseau): Roberta Sotonoff

Dominican Republic (La Romana, Puerto Plata, Samana, Santo Domingo): Eileen Robinson Smith

Fort Lauderdale, Florida: Galena Mosovich

Galveston, Texas: Robin Sussman

Grenada: St. George's: Jane E. Zarem

Guadeloupe (Point-à-Pitre): Eileen Robinson Smith

Guatemala (Santo Tomás de Castillo): Jeffrey Van Fleet

Honduras (Roatán Island): Jeffrey Van Fleet

Jacksonville, Florida: Jennifer Greenhill-Taylor

Jamaica: Falmouth, Montego Bay, Ocho Rios): Sheri-Kae McLeod

Key West, Florida: Jill Martin

Martinique (Fort-de-France): Eileen Robinson Smith

Mexico (Calica, Costa Maya-Mahahual, Cozumel, Progreso): Jeffrey Van Fleet

Miami, Florida: Paul Rubio

Mobile, Alabama: Robin Sussman

New Orleans, Louisiana: Robin Sussman

New York, New York: Kelsy Chauvin, Joshua Rogol, Caroline Trefler

Norfolk, Virginia: Amber Stitt

Panama (Colón): Jeffrey Van Fleet

Port Canaveral, Florida: Jennifer Greenhill-Taylor

Puerto Rico (San Juan): Paulina Salach

St-Barthélemy (Gustavia): Jeff Berger

St. Croix, U.S. Virgin Islands: Robert Curley

St. John, U.S. Virgin Islands (Cruz Bay): Carol Bareuther

St. Kitts & Nevis (Basseterre and Charlestown): Jordan Simon

St. Lucia (Castries): Jane E. Zarem

St. Maarten (Phillipsburg): Jeff Berger

St. Thomas, U.S. Virgin Islands (Charlotte Amalie): Carol Bareuther

St. Vincent, St. Vincent & the Grenadines (Kingstown): Jane E. Zarem

Tampa, Florida: Tiffany Razzano

Tobago, Trinidad & Tobago (Scarborough): Vernon O'Reilly-Ramesar

Tortola, British Virgin Islands (Road Town): Robert Curley

Trinidad, Trinidad & Tobago (Port of Spain): Vernon O'Reilly-Ramesar

Turks and Caicos Islands (Grand Turke): Jessica Robertson

Virgin Gorda, British Virgin Islands (The Valley): Robert Curley